Landscape Ecology *and* Resource Management

LINKING THEORY WITH PRACTICE

Edited by
John A. Bissonette *and* Ilse Storch

ISLAND PRESS
Washington • Covelo • London

Library of Congress Cataloging-in-Publication Data
Landscape ecology and resource management : linking theory with practice
/ edited by John A. Bissonette and Ilse Storch.
        p.   cm.
Includes bibliographical references (p.   ).
ISBN 1-55963-972-5 (hardcover : alk. paper) —
ISBN 1-55963-973-3 (pbk. : alk. paper)
1. Landscape ecology. 2. Conservation of natural resources.
I. Bissonette, John A. II. Storch, Ilse.
QH541.15.L35 L3455 2002
333.7—dc21   2002009835

British Cataloguing-in-Publication Data available.

Printed on recycled, acid-free paper ✪

Manufactured in the United States of America
02 03 04 05 06 07 08 09   8 7 6 5 4 3 2 1

ABOUT ISLAND PRESS

Island Press is the only nonprofit organization in the United States whose principal purpose is the publication of books on environmental issues and natural resource management. We provide solutions-oriented information to professionals, public officials, business and community leaders, and concerned citizens who are shaping responses to environmental problems.

In 2002, Island Press celebrates its eighteenth anniversary as the leading provider of timely and practical books that take a multidisciplinary approach to critical environmental concerns. Our growing list of titles reflects our commitment to bringing the best of an expanding body of literature to the environmental community throughout North America and the world.

Support for Island Press is provided by The Nathan Cummings Foundation, Geraldine R. Dodge Foundation, Doris Duke Charitable Foundation, Educational Foundation of America, The Charles Engelhard Foundation, The Ford Foundation, The George Gund Foundation, The Vira I. Heinz Endowment, The William and Flora Hewlett Foundation, Henry Luce Foundation, The John D. and Catherine T. MacArthur Foundation, The Andrew W. Mellon Foundation, The Moriah Fund, The Curtis and Edith Munson Foundation, National Fish and Wildlife Foundation, The New-Land Foundation, Oak Foundation, The Overbrook Foundation, The David and Lucile Packard Foundation, The Pew Charitable Trusts, The Rockefeller Foundation, The Winslow Foundation, and other generous donors.

The opinions expressed in this book are those of the author(s) and do not necessarily reflect the views of these foundations.

Landscape
Ecology *and*
Resource
Management

Contents

   Disturbance Regimes to Maintain Forest Biodiversity in Europe   193
   Per Angelstam

10. Landscape Ecology, Wildlife Management, and Conservation in
    Northern Australia: Linking Policy, Practice, and Capability in
    Regional Planning   227
    *Peter J. Whitehead, John C. Z. Woinarski, Donald Franklin, and
    Owen Price*

11. Habitat Models to Link Situation Evaluation and Planning
    Support in Agricultural Landscapes   261
    *Alfred Schultz, Reinhard Klenke, Gerd Lutze, Marion Voss,
    Ralf Wieland, and Bettina Wilkening*

12. A Park Is Not an Island: Linking Different Wildlife Management
    Strategies in the Area of Lake Mburo National Park, Uganda   283
    Christiane Averbeck

Part 3: Linking Theory and Application: Case Studies

13. Linking a Multiscale Habitat Concept to Species Conservation   303
    Ilse Storch

14. Landscape History: Linking Conservation Approaches for
    Large Mammals   321
    David S. Maehr, John J. Cox, and Jeffery L. Larkin

15. Giant Otters in the Peruvian Rainforest: Linking Protected Area
    Conditions to Species Needs   341
    *Christof Schenck, Jessica Groenendijk, Frank Hajek, Elke Staib,
    and Karin Frank*

16. Linking Landscape Management with the Conservation of
    Grassland Birds in Wisconsin   359
    David W. Sample, Christine A. Ribic, and Rosalind B. Renfrew

17. Foraging by Herbivores: Linking the Biochemical Diversity of
    Plants to Herbivore Culture and Landscape Diversity   387
    Frederick D. Provenza, Juan J. Villalba, and John P. Bryant

    Conclusion   423
    About the Contributors   437
    Index   451

Preface

Landscape ecology as a discipline is growing rapidly; however, its incorporation into practice is proceeding more slowly. It was a well-established discipline in Europe by the time of its first recognition in North America in the early 1980s, and by 2001 the number of journal articles that mentioned landscapes, scale, and fragmentation had grown exponentially (Schneider 2001). Agencies and organizations worldwide have embraced large-scale ideas such as ecosystem management, gap analysis, and metapopulation conservation and have tried to put some of these concepts into practice. What practitioners have lacked is a conceptual foundation of applicable and operational theory, with examples of successful case studies to guide their efforts. As is the case in many developing disciplines, theory has been borrowed and cobbled together from related fields and provides an incomplete framework for application. Eventually, the conceptual basis increasingly appears to be inadequately confirmed by data. Use of the framework in management further exposes the problem of inadequate theory. What often is missing in developing disciplines is the linkage between theory and practice. This drives the need to devise a more realistic and relevant conceptual basis for guiding management. We believe this is the current state of landscape ecology and its application by wildlife and fishery biologists and resource managers. A cohesive theory of landscape ecology is not yet possible. Rather, several developments have begun to provide elements of a framework. This book was developed specifically to provide insights into some of the applicable theory that underlies resource management and to provide examples of successful case studies to help guide future efforts.

This book began as an idea after the publication of *Wildlife and Landscape Ecology: Effects of Pattern and Scale* (1997), edited by John Bissonette. After its appearance, we discussed the observation that much of the effort in landscape ecology was on theory development, with not enough attention to application, at least in North America. In Europe, and North America, and other parts of the world, we observed that despite obvious progress in landscape ecological awareness among scientists, little of that appeared to enter practitioners' discussions or actions. We asked, "How can the manager or biologist working for a resource agency or conservation organization put the powerful ideas and concepts that stem from landscape ecology into practice?" The field is expanding so rapidly that it is difficult to keep up with new developments, to say nothing of synthesizing the ideas into a workable framework. We decided to address this concern directly. In 1999 we organized a plenary session at the Second International Wildlife Management Congress held in Gödöllõ, Hungary, titled "Landscape Linkages: Ecosystem Science and Management" and a symposium titled "Scaling in Conservation Biology: Is There a Mismatch between Theory and Practice?" where we began to address this idea. This edited volume was envisioned to help further link landscape theory and resource management practice in the field. Because the application of science to management tasks is always influenced by the nature of the problem and therefore by its cultural and sociopolitical settings, we made an effort to assemble authors and studies from different parts of the world to provide examples from a wide range of problems, approaches, and biogeographic regions.

We organized the resulting 17 chapters into three sections. Part 1, "Conceptual and Quantitative Linkages," contains seven chapters intended to address fundamental aspects of landscape ecology. Part 2, "Linking People, Land Use, and Landscape Values," contains five chapters that address the links between people and the landscape. Part 3, "Linking Theory and Application: Case Studies," includes five chapters that present case studies to make the links between theory and management real.

We are especially grateful to Barbara Dean, Barbara Youngblood, Laura Carrithers, Donica Collier, Chace Caven, Carol Peschke, and all at Island Press for their continuing support and help in putting this book together. We are also grateful to the authors for promptly responding to our many requests and to all colleagues who read parts of the manuscript. Each chapter in this volume was peer reviewed by at least two scientists, and the final form of each chapter was influenced by reviewer and editor comments, and changes suggested by the authors themselves. We are thankful for a grant from the Deutsche Forschungsgemeinschaft to Ilse Storch and for a distinguished lectureship sponsored by DAAK (Stiftung Deutsch-Amerikanisches Konzil), the University of Munich, and the Munich Wildlife Society to John Bissonette that allowed us to develop our ideas further.

This book is meant to be heuristic and to provide ideas that may advance landscape ecology as a science. It is also intended to provide links between theory and practice. It is evident that there is a significant gap between current scientific understanding and its application. We hope that this book will help bridge that gap. We encourage those who develop the science to think about and try to elucidate how the ideas may be used in practice. We ask those who are charged with resource management and conservation practice to try to incorporate relevant landscape ecological ideas into their efforts. If this happens, then theory and practice can effectively be linked.

LITERATURE CITED

Schneider, D. C. 2001. The rise of the concept of scale in ecology. BioScience 51(7):545–553.

Landscape
Ecology *and*
Resource
Management

Introduction

The great obstacle to discovering the shape of the earth, the continents,
and the oceans was not ignorance, but the illusion of knowledge.

The Discoverers, Daniel J. Boorstin, 1983

The greatest obstacle in conducting effective conservation is not ignorance;
we now know a great deal about the scope and extent of conservation
problems around the world. Rather, there are two obstacles: the purview
of science and human will. We have had the illusion that large landscapes
could be restored and managed without grounding in adequate theory to
guide efforts. Absolute habitat loss, coupled with fragmentation, has
resulted in a pattern of ever smaller and more isolated parcels of intact
habitat that are becoming increasingly inadequate to support viable populations of species and intact communities across the world. Anthropogenic influences are largely responsible. Another part of our illusion has
been the tacit assumption that understanding the science alone would
result in successful conservation efforts, without considering that the priorities of society must be modified if we are to maintain biodiversity. We
now know differently. We no longer believe that complex conservation
problems and conflicts can be solved quickly or without significant cross-
disciplinary efforts. We also know that it will take great effort to raise conservation issues to a level where they are considered of primary importance. We are fortunate to have a developing foundation of landscape
ecology and wildlife and conservation biology that can provide the scientific basis for guiding natural resource management and correcting land
abuse. Modification of human behavior will remain a challenge, given the
influence of culture, economics, and politics.

Land Use and Land Abuse

With the disappearance of the forest, all is changed. . . . The earth, stripped of its vegetable glebe, grows less and less productive, and, consequently, less able to protect itself . . . and thus the earth is rendered no longer fit for the habitation of man.

Man and Nature, George Perkins Marsh, 1864

Man and Nature, written at a time when forest cutting had radically changed the face of New England and especially Vermont, was recognized internationally within a decade of its publication (Meyer and Turner 1992). As Americans moved west, similar scenarios were played out as uncontrolled wood harvesting changed forest cover, structure, and composition; unsustainable overgrazing by domestic livestock and the historic loss of native herbivores in grasslands and arid rangelands resulted in desertification and permanent changes in grass, brush, and succulent (cacti) vegetation (Dyer et al. 1982; McNaughton 1985; Janzen 1986); and uncontrolled draining and development drastically reduced wetlands (Noss and Cooperrider 1994), changing the face of the landscape. In the first three decades of the twentieth century, *Man and Nature* was all but forgotten, but it gained a new following in the 1930s as Americans became aware of growing and persistent environmental problems. From 1900 to 1930, the political cartoons of J. Ding Darling (Lendt 1979) did much to raise environmental consciousness. During this period, Aldo Leopold (1933) put forth principles of management that would provide a conceptual foundation for the restoration of wildlife species. Although his focus was on vertebrate biota, Leopold recognized that habitat was the key to abundant and viable wildlife populations.

Squandered Resources

Before the industrial revolution and the subsequent explosion in human population density, the limitations of natural resources and wildlife habitats across the world were not a concern. Although much of Europe and Asia had been depleted of forest by the end of the Middle Ages, few were concerned about wildlife habitat in the early years of settlement in the United States. Resources were abundant, and little thought was given to conservation. However, things were to change. Between the mid-1600s and about 1920, almost one third of U.S. forests were cut. By 1920, a large percentage of land once forested in the United States was covered by second-growth forest (Miller and

Tangley 1991). Currently, about 33 percent or 302.3 million ha (about 747 million acres) of the United States is forested (Forestinformation.com 2002). Logging continued throughout the twentieth century and was accompanied by the construction of many thousands of miles of roads to provide access to the wood supply. In recent years, recreational use of forests and wildlands has increased greatly, and roads that once had only limited use have been rediscovered, further fragmenting the landscape. Although gaining an exact value is difficult, best estimates suggest that there are more than 600,300 km (about 373,000 miles) of roads in U.S. national forests alone (Williams 1998; The Lands Council 1998), and an additional 96,560 km (about 60,000 miles) of ghost roads not included in the government's inventory. For perspective, the entire U.S. interstate highway system includes 73,230 km (~45,500 miles) of roads, or about 10.5 percent of the length of all forest roads (Forman et al. 2002). If placed end to end, U.S. forest roads would circle the equator about 17 times. Increasingly recognized as a major threat to biodiversity and the integrity of forest, grassland, and desert ecosystems, concern for roads prompted 10 scientists to petition the U.S. president to support a strong roadless area conservation rule (Gould et al. 2001).

Concern for the effects of forest harvesting has not been limited to the North American continent. Although published figures vary widely, about 30 percent of the terrestrial surface of the earth (roughly 3.9 billion ha or about 9.8 billion acres; Forestinformation.com 2002; Coble et al. 1987) is covered by forest, and half of these are tropical forests (Miller and Tangley 1991). Much has been written about the destruction of tropical rainforests. Meyers (1986) reported that approximately 19 million ha (about 46.9 million acres) of tropical rainforests were destroyed annually. That harvest may have increased in the past decade and a half. Concerns about species extinctions (Meyers 1986) and climate change (Wolf 1987) have driven part of the concern about forest loss (Vaughan 1990). More than 50 percent of the earth's species live in tropical forests (World Resources Institute 1998), and tropical forests contain about 70 percent of the world's vascular plants, about 30 percent of all bird species, and about 90 percent of all invertebrates (Canadian International Development Agency 1998).

Assessing the bottom line for forest biodiversity globally is difficult at best. The World Resources Institute (2001, p. 99) wrote, "Forests have the highest species diversity and endemism of any ecosystem. Pressure on this diversity is immense, as judged from forest loss and fragmentation, but direct information about conditions is more limited. What evidence exists suggests that the number of threatened forest species is significant and growing. . . .

The capacity of remaining forests to maintain biodiversity appears to be significantly diminished."

Forest ecosystems are not the only landscapes that have been affected. Grasslands and savannas are among the most endangered terrestrial ecosystems in the world. In the United States, overgrazing, invasion of exotic species, large-scale agricultural activities, and fire suppression have been documented as major causes for their decline (Noss and Cooperrider 1994). For example, sagebrush steppe is a major vegetation type in Utah and the intermountain West and once covered more than 51.8 million ha (about 128 million acres; Rickard et al. 1988). Almost all (99 percent) of the sagebrush steppe type has been grazed by livestock, and the structure and composition of about 30 percent have been changed significantly by heavy grazing (Noss et al. 1995; West 1993, 1999). Similarly, at one time tallgrass prairie covered about 101.2 million ha (about 250 million acres) of mid–North America; today only scattered remnants of intact prairie exist.

Perhaps most affected ecosystems are wetlands. Dahl (1990) reported that over a period of 200 years, from the 1780s to the 1980s, an estimated 53 percent of all wetlands, which in the United States originally totaled 85.3 to 87.8 million ha (about 211–217 million acres) not including Hawaii or Alaska, were lost to draining and development. Significantly, a large proportion of the loss has been attributed to agriculture. A 1997 survey by the U.S. Fish and Wildlife Service (Dahl 1997) estimated that more than 23,470 ha (about 58,000 acres) of wetlands continue to be destroyed annually in the United States. At least one half of all animal species and about one third of all plant species listed under the Endangered Species Act depend on wetlands (Noss and Cooperrider 1994). Additionally, Dahl (1990) argued that so much wetland habitat had been lost that ground water supply, water quality, shoreline erosion, floodwater storage, trapping of sediments, and climatic changes were seriously threatened.

Clearly, use and abuse of land has had profound effects on the biota, but other parts of the world have been affected as profoundly. For example, "nowhere else is forest loss occurring faster in absolute terms" than in the Brazilian Amazon, which contains 40 percent of the remaining tropical forests in the world (Peres 2001). In the late 1990s, deforestation rates averaged 1.9 million ha (about 4.7 million acres) per year (Peres 2001, p. 217). This is especially troublesome because biological diversity was initially so rich. Of the 3,507 vertebrate species in the world listed as critically endangered, endangered, or vulnerable, 236 are in Brazil, 315 are in North America, and 648 are in Europe (IUCN 2000). Of the 3,331 plants so listed, Brazil accounts for 338 endangered plants, and North America and Europe have 310 and 88, respectively (IUCN 2000).

It is clear that conservation problems span the world and are large in scale. Therefore, they necessitate the linking of small- and larger-scale science to understand context, constraint, and causality and thereby inform management. Linking theory, data collection and interpretation, and application to management objectives in meaningful ways remains the challenge for conservationists and resource managers.

Linking Theory, Data, and Practice in Conservation

Although the cumulative effects of widespread, unsustainable resource use were recognized more than 150 years ago, the rudiments of a large-scale science on which to base consistent and effective management did not exist. Until recently, we assumed that smaller-scale studies, using small sampling units, could be scaled to provide answers. In the past two decades we have realized that scaling across hierarchical levels and landscape extents often results in qualitatively different patterns, making meaningful interpretation of data difficult or impossible (O'Neill et al. 1985). Even at smaller scales, a close matching of theory with data is difficult. Fagerström (1987) and Haila (1988) argued that even the simplest ecological statements include more than can be concluded by observation alone. Additionally, indirect effects, such as the presence of trophic cascades (Wootton 1994; but see Strong 1992 and Chase 2000 for counterarguments), and pulsed resources (Ostfeld and Keesing 2000), that is, the availability of much higher than normal resources for short periods of time (mast crops), seriously complicate our understanding of species interactions, even when larger-scale environmental constraints (the spatial explicitness of landscape pattern) and extreme stochastic weather events and other natural and anthropogenic disturbances are not considered. An exact match between theory and practice at any scale may be impossible, but an effective linking of relevant theory with management practice is not only possible but essential if management is to be based on sound ecological principles. However, both philosophical and technical problems must be addressed.

Technical Difficulties and Normative Paradigms

Linking theory to management at the landscape level is a worthy goal but one not easily achieved. There are at least two main difficulties. One rests with the nature of what conservation (the practice) means, what it includes, and how its concepts are interpreted; the other rests with the complex nature of larger-scale ecology (the science).

Difficulties with Normative Paradigms

The conservation literature is rife with multimeaning concepts that are used to guide conservation efforts. For example, the normative concept of ecosystem management; that is, managing for "ecosystem health with commodity extraction as an ancillary goal" (Callicott et al. 1999, p. 28; Grumbine 1997), was institutionalized by the U.S. Forest Service in 1992 (Forest Ecosystem Management Assessment Team 1993), but there has been controversy over its definition (Stanley 1995; Grumbine 1994, 1997). To provide clarification, Callicott et al. (1999) organized "normative" or "umbrella" (Noss 1995) conservation concepts into two philosophical camps based on whether *Homo sapiens* was included as part of nature (functionalism) or not (compositionalism). They argued that compositionalism included the conservation concepts of biological diversity (Wilson 1992), biological integrity (Angermeier and Karr 1994), and ecological restoration (Society for Ecological Restoration 1997), clearly concepts in which *Homo sapiens* is not considered a part of nature but rather an intrusion. Functionalism included normative concepts such as ecological services (Constanza 1991; Daily et al. 2000), ecological rehabilitation (Meffe 1995), ecological sustainability (Callicott and Mumford 1997), ecosystem health (Constanza et al. 1992), ecosystem management (Grumbine 1994, 1997), and adaptive management (Walters 1986), concepts that attempt to harmonize anthropogenic influence and disturbance with the natural world. Callicott et al. (1999) emphasized that these were extremes on a continuum and were presented for the sake of clarification. Willers (2000) and Hunter (2000) criticized aspects of the dichotomy that Callicott et al. (1999) presented, but it seems apparent that precise, clear, and standardized definitions of conservation concepts are helpful. When concepts are used loosely, much of their power is lost. Unless clear definitions are developed and used, conservation concepts become pseudocognates; that is, each person who uses the term feels that everyone else shares her or his definition (Bissonette 1997), when upon closer evaluation it is evident that is not the case. A finer grasp of meaning and context is imperative. Furthermore, a closer examination suggests that some concepts, as currently defined, cannot be made operational. For example, effective monitoring of biological diversity over space and time entails attention to the "what," "why," and "how" of data collection (Yoccoz et al. 2001). Therefore, measurable state variables are needed. Nonquantitative state variables, such as "ecosystem health" (Yoccoz et al. 2001) are difficult or impossible to measure and hence monitor. Callicott et al. (1999) have provided context and a framework that places anthropogenic disturbances and influences as the defining distinction between the two philosophical camps. This appears to be useful when addressing conservation conflicts and problems.

Difficulties with the Science

There has been much development in landscape theory in the past two decades and much discussion about how to deal with scale problems. We know what most of the relevant problems with the science are; we are only now learning how to solve them. Briefly, the science is multicausal (Bissonette 1997), nonlinear dynamics predominate (Kawata 1995), thresholds seem to exist everywhere (Levin 1992, 1999), and scaling from one hierarchical level to another often leads to qualitatively different results (O'Neill et al. 1985). These characteristics result in such complexity of causal influences and constraints at multiple hierarchical levels and with contingent feedbacks that many consider ecological systems to behave as complex adaptive systems (Levin 1999). Understanding ecological complexity and applying that knowledge to solve pressing problems in conservation is the challenge. We have had limited success. Much remains to be done. A quest for understanding complexity remains the focus of much of the discipline of landscape ecology. The attempt to link knowledge gained from research to its management application is the reason the chapters in this book have been written.

Goal

In this volume, we have assembled 17 chapters that address some of the relevant underlying theory and how landscape ecologists have tried to deal with the links to effective practice. We think that many of the approaches illustrated by these chapters are innovative and provide solid advances on which to base resource management. The coverage is by no means complete; no book of this size could provide complete coverage of the emerging field of landscape ecology or its application. However, we hope that there is sufficient heuristic content to stimulate fertile minds to strive to improve our understanding of large-scale ecology put to practice. It will be the work of others to put theory and data-based management on the ground.

LITERATURE CITED

Angermeier, P. L., and J. R. Karr. 1994. Biological integrity versus biological diversity as policy directives. BioScience 44:690–697.

Bissonette, J. A. 1997. Scale-sensitive ecological properties: historical context, current meaning. Pages 3–15 in J. A. Bissonette (ed.), Wildlife and landscape ecology: effects of pattern and scale. Springer-Verlag, New York.

Boorstin, D. J. 1983. The discoverers. Random House, New York.

Callicott, J. B., and K. G. Mumford. 1997. Sustainability as a conservation concept. Conservation Biology 11:32–40.

Callicott, J. B., L. B. Crowder, and K. G. Mumford. 1999. Current normative concepts in conservation. Conservation Biology 13:22–35.

Canadian International Development Agency. 1998. Deforestation: tropical forests in decline. www.rcfa-cfan.org/English/issues.12. html.

Chase, J. M. 2000. Are there real differences among aquatic and terrestrial food webs? Trends in Ecology and Evolution 15:408–412.

Coble, C. R., E. G. Murray, and D. R. Rice. 1987. Earth science. Prentice Hall, Englewood Cliffs, NJ.

Constanza, R. (ed.). 1991. Ecological economics: the science and management of sustainability. Columbia University Press, New York.

Constanza, R., B. G. Norton, and B. D. Haskell (eds.). 1992. Ecosystem health: new goals for environmental management. Island Press, Washington, DC.

Dahl, T. E. 1990. Wetlands losses in the United States 1780s to 1980s. U.S. Department of the Interior, Fish and Wildlife Service, Washington, DC.

Dahl, T. E. 1997. Status and trends of wetlands in the conterminous United States 1986 to 1997. U.S. Department of the Interior, Fish and Wildlife Service, Washington, DC.

Daily, G. C., T. Söderqvist, S. Aniyar, K. Arrow, P. Dasgupta, P. R. Ehrlich, C. Folke, A. Jansson, B.-O. Jansson, N. Kautsky, S. Levin, J. Lubchenco, K.-G. Mäler, D. Simpson, D. Starrett, D. Tilman, and B. Walker. 2000. The value of nature and the nature of value. Science 289:395–396.

Dyer, M. I., J. K. Detling, D. C. Coleman, and D. W. Hilbert. 1982. The role of herbivores in grasslands. Pages 255–295 in J. R. Estes, R. J. Tyrl, and J. N. Brunken (eds.), Grasses and grasslands. University of Oklahoma Press, Norman.

Fagerström, T. 1987. On theory, data and mathematics in ecology. Oikos 50:258–261.

Forest Ecosystem Management Assessment Team. 1993. Forest ecosystem management: an ecological, economic, and social assessment. U. S. Government Printing Office, Washington, DC.

Forestinformation.com. 2002. http://www.forestinformation.com/Forest_Statistics.asp.

Forman, R. T. T., D. Sperling, J. A. Bissonette, A. P. Clevenger, C. D. Cutshall, V. H. Dale, L. Fahrig, R. France, C. R. Goldman, K. Heanue, J. A. Jones, F. J. Swanson, T. Turrentine, and T. C. Winter. 2002. Road ecology: science and solutions. Island Press, Washington, DC.

Gould, S. J., T. E. Lovejoy, R. Noss, S. Pimm, M. Soulé, G. S. Hartshorn, G. Maser, E. P. Odum, D. Simberloff, and R. E. Train. 2001. Letter to the president of the United States regarding support for the Roadless Area Conservation Rule. September 6, 2001. http://www.worldwildlife.org/forests/attachments/roadless_letter.pdf.

Grumbine, R. E. 1994. What is ecosystem management? Conservation Biology 8:27–38.

Grumbine, R. E. 1997. Reflections on "What is ecosystem management?" Conservation Biology 11:41–47.

Haila, Y. 1988. The multiple faces of ecological theory and data. Oikos 53:408–411.

Hunter, M. L., Jr. 2000. Refining normative concepts in conservation. Conservation Biology 14:573–574.

IUCN. 2000. The 2000 IUCN Red List of Threatened Species. www.redlist.org.

Janzen, D. H. 1986. Chihuahuan desert nopaleras: defaunated big mammal vegetation. Annual Review of Ecology and Systematics 17:595–636.

Kawata, M. 1995. Emergent and effective properties in ecology and evolution. Researches in Population Ecology 37:93–96.

The Lands Council. 1998. Saving tax dollars to save forests. Transitions 11(1):1–31.

Lendt, D. L. 1979. Ding: the life of Jay Norwood Darling. Iowa State University Press, Ames.

Leopold, A. 1933. Game management. Charles Scribner's Sons, New York.

Levin, S. A. 1992. The problem of pattern and scale in ecology. Ecology 73:1943–1967.

Levin, S. A. 1999. Fragile dominion: complexity and the commons. Perseus Books, Reading, MA.

Marsh, G. P. 1864/1998. Man and nature, or physical geography as modified by human action. Belknap Press of Harvard University Press, Cambridge, MA.

McNaughton, S. J. 1985. Ecology of a grazing ecosystem: the Serengeti. Ecological Monographs 55:259–294.

Meffe, G. K. 1995. Genetic and ecological guidelines for species reintroduction programs: applications to Great Lakes fishes. Journal of Great Lakes Research 21 (Supplement 1):3–9.

Meyer, W. B., and B. L. Turner II. 1992. Human population growth and global land-use/cover change. Annual Review of Ecology and Systematics 23:39–61.

Meyers, N. 1986. Tropical deforestation and mega-extinction spasm. Pages 394–409 in M. Soulé (ed.), Conservation biology: the science of scarcity and diversity. Sinauer Press, Sunderland, MA.

Miller, K., and L. Tangley. 1991. Trees of life: saving tropical forests and their biological wealth. Beacon Press, Boston, MA.

Noss, R. F. 1995. Ecological integrity and sustainability: buzzwords in conflict. Pages 60–76 in L. Westra and J. Lemons (eds.), Perspectives on ecological integrity. Kluwer Academic Publishers, Dordrecht, The Netherlands.

Noss, R. F., and A. Y. Cooperrider. 1994. Saving nature's legacy: protecting and restoring biodiversity. Island Press, Washington, DC.

Noss, R. F., E. T. LaRoe, and J. M. Scott. 1995. Endangered ecosystems of the United States: a preliminary assessment of loss and degradation. U.S. Geological Survey, Washington, DC.

O'Neill, R. V., D. L. DeAngelis, J. B. Waide, and T. F. H. Allen. 1985. A hierarchical concept of ecosystems. Monographs in Population Biology #23. Princeton University Press, Princeton, NJ.

Ostfeld, R. S., and F. Keesing. 2000. Pulsed resources and community dynamics in terrestrial ecosystems. Trends in Ecology and Evolution 15:232–237.

Peres, C. A. 2001. Paving the way to the future of Amazonia. Trends in Ecology and Evolution 15:217–219.

Rickard, W. H., L. E. Rogers, B. E. Vaughan, and S. F. Liebetrau. 1988. Shrub-steppe: balance and change in a semi-arid terrestrial ecosystem. Elsevier, New York.

Society for Ecological Restoration. 1997. Strategic plan for the Society for Ecological Restoration. Society for Ecological Restoration, Tucson, AZ.

Stanley, T. R. 1995. Ecosystem management and the arrogance of humanism. Conservation Biology 9:255–262.

Strong, D. R. 1992. Are trophic cascades all wet? Differentiation and donor-control in speciose ecosystems. Ecology 73:747–754.

Vaughan, C. 1990. Patterns in natural resource destruction and conservation in Central America: a case for optimism? Transactions of the 55th North American Wildlife and Natural Resources Conference. Wildlife Management Institute, Washington, DC.

Walters, C. J. 1986. Adaptive management of renewable resources. Macmillan, New York.

West, N. E. 1993. Biodiversity of rangelands. Journal of Range Management 46:2–13.

West, N. E. 1999. Managing for biodiversity of rangelands. Pages 101–126 in W. A. Collins and C. O. Qualset (eds.), The importance of biodiversity in agroecosystems. CRC Press, Boca Raton, FL.

Willers, B. 2000. A response to "Current Normative Concepts in Conservation" by Callicott et al. Conservation Biology 14:570–572.

Williams, T. 1998. The unkindest cuts. Audubon (Jan/Feb)100:24–31.

Wilson, E. O. 1992. Biodiversity. National Academy Press, Washington, DC.

Wolf, E. C. 1987. On the brink of extinction: conserving the diversity of life. Worldwatch Paper No. 78. Worldwatch Institute, Washington, DC.

Wootton, J. T. 1994. The nature and consequences of indirect effects in ecological communities. Annual Review of Ecology and Systematics 25:443–466.

World Resources Institute. 1998. World resources 1998–99: a guide to the global environment. Oxford University Press, Oxford, UK.

World Resources Institute. 2001. World resources 2000–2001: people and ecosystems: the fraying web of life. World Resources Institute, Washington, DC.

Yoccoz, N. G., J. D. Nichols, and T. Boulinier. 2001. Monitoring of biological diversity in space and time. Trends in Ecology and Evolution 16:448–452.

PART ONE

CONCEPTUAL AND QUANTITATIVE LINKAGES

I f linking pattern to process in landscape ecology is not a growth industry, it should be. With the recognition that pattern exists at every scale
resolution and extent, understanding how populations are influenced by
landscape patterns and, conversely, how animals may influence landscape
pattern and processes is crucial if species management or conservation efforts
are to be informed. At the same time, elaboration of landscape theory has
seldom, if ever, been focused so as to provide specific recommendations to
fishery and wildlife biologists or resource managers. Chapters 1–7 focus on
conceptual and quantitative links that are intended to provide a framework
and are written in a style and manner so that practitioners who may not be
familiar with the material can understand it in context.

The recognition that pattern is ubiquitous in landscapes and ecosystems
is certainly important and not a novel idea; however, practitioners charged
with solving everyday land use and species management problems may not
have considered the idea explicitly. In Chapter 1, John Bissonette argues that
thinking about the putative relevance of pattern forces one to focus more
closely on the problem. The recognition that multiple spatial and temporal
scales usually are operating when one deals with natural resource problems
affects the necessary management decisions.

As managers and practitioners strive to develop management plans for
species harvest, maintenance, or control, an understanding of how the
amount and the spatial and temporal distribution of individual vegetation
types might affect population response seems necessary for any habitat

manipulation contemplated. However, our understanding of the effect of variations in landscape pattern on wildlife populations is still in its infancy. Furthermore, the impact of fragmented or patchy landscapes on the movement of animals is poorly understood. Prerequisites for effective movement across a landscape include perception and tracking of suitable habitat. In Chapter 2, Therese Donovan and Allan Strong argue that habitat patchiness and movement dynamics have subtle but certain effects on future population size and genetic composition. Landscape theory predicts that as habitat is lost to development or disturbance, abrupt thresholds in connectivity occur. What this means to wildlife populations and species biodiversity is largely unknown. One of the lessons learned over the last decade is that studies conducted over large spatial scales tended to find thresholds in population parameters; more local studies often did not. The prediction that small incremental losses of habitat may lead to large changes in mortality rates or population viability has important conservation implications.

In Chapter 3, James Sanderson and Larry Harris make the distinction between landscape ecology and ecosystem science. Landscape ecology explicitly recognizes temporal and spatial heterogeneity; nothing either explicit or implicit in the definition of *ecosystem* implies spatial heterogeneity. Landscape studies necessarily take place in three dimensions and across several hierarchical levels and over many scale resolutions and extents. This is an important distinction because simple concepts that appear to have relevance have been used indiscriminately in conservation efforts. For example, the use of indicator species as a way to assist biodiversity conservation is used widely and is likely to grow.

However, in Chapter 4, Ilse Storch and John Bissonette suggest that it is important to understand the limitations of the concept in order to assess its usefulness. The idea behind the use of indicator species is a simple one; their well-being may reflect the well-being of other species that putatively have the same habitat needs. Accordingly, measures designed to maintain or enhance the population viability of indicator species may favor larger segments of the wildlife community. However, the question of how scale-related species–habitat associations influence the applicability of the indicator species concept warrants attention. Indicator species may not sufficiently represent habitat suitability, richness, or diversity of other species at small scales, much less at larger scales. The scale sensitivity of species–habitat relationships represents a significant limitation to the applicability of the indicator concept in wildlife management and conservation.

There are at least two different ways to define *habitat*. The most common method is typological and classes the independently distributed components of habitat into abstracted discrete habitat classes. In Chapter 5, Michael Mitchell and Roger Powell develop another approach and argue for a different visualization of habitat. If habitat can be envisioned as a continuous fitness surface, the assumptions of homogeneity within habitat patches and hence the problems of defining boundaries between patches can be avoided. Behavior in accordance with predictions gives us confidence that bolsters the more traditional approach of inductively derived, a posteriori correlations. If the biological meaning of habitat is itself scale dependent, developing workable conceptual and technical approaches will continue to be difficult. If habitat can be depicted as a fitness surface, it may offer a biologically robust tool for understanding animal–habitat relationships across multiple spatial scale extents and resolutions.

In Chapter 6, Jan Sendzimir, Craig Allen, Lance Gunderson, and Craig Stow look at system organization as a way to address the problem of species protection. There is evidence that ecosystems are organized and function as complex adaptive systems. Landscape patterns that are different at different scales and that change abruptly as scale breaks are encountered entrain morphologic and behavioral characteristics of species. That entrainment is reflected in discontinuous animal body mass patterns (lumps and gaps in body mass distributions). These clusters of process–landscape–species may prove more practical to detect and manage species than efforts that marshal data on dozens of species and landscape characteristics. This approach also provides a more informed context for asking specific questions about the habitat needs of individual species. One striking example to date is the capacity of lump pattern analysis to predict species characteristics (nomadism, invasiveness, and vulnerability). This has significant conservation implications.

In general, ecologists have been unsuccessful in attempting to link information collected at multiple scales to explore landscape theory. Often data have different resolutions and thematic content, making it difficult to scale measured responses of ecological systems upward or downward. In Chapter 7, Thomas Edwards, Gretchen Moisen, Tracey Frescino, and Joshua Lawler explain how it is possible to focus first on approaches to modeling habitat that provide fine-grained estimations of landscape patterns at large spatial extents and then, using these representations of landscapes, to explore habitat use by terrestrial vertebrates at multiple scales. Flexible regression techniques, such as generalized additive models, can be linked with spatially explicit environmental information to map forest structure, for example, and to develop spatially explicit probability maps for the presence of other forest attributes. The spatially explicit maps of forest or, more generally, habitat structure that are produced can be used to model and predict suitable habitat. In Part 1 these issues are addressed and provide an introduction to some of the underlying theory and quantitative approaches that will be useful for resource managers.

CHAPTER ONE

Linking Landscape Patterns to Biological Reality

JOHN A. BISSONETTE

In landscapes, pattern is ubiquitous and emerges at every scale of resolution. However, seldom is the specific resolution or extent of the scale used in wildlife and ecological studies explicitly scaled to the process being studied. When scale is addressed, statistics at two to four different spatial extents are used to discern the association of pattern with the dynamics or processes of interest. The assumption is that whatever association emerges is real. This assumption has seldom been challenged or evaluated overtly (but see Mitchell et al. 2001), yet it is the basis for one of the most interesting questions landscape ecologists can pose: When are landscape patterns biologically relevant? Landscape patterns have properties that may or may not affect ecological systems and animal population dynamics. Whether this happens is related to whether the patterns are "effective" or "noneffective." Not all patterns are effective. Only some are relevant. In this chapter, I address the issues of the ubiquity of landscape pattern and the reality of pattern at multiple scale resolutions and extents, and I ask, "When are landscape patterns relevant?" I delve into the idea of effective and noneffective properties associated with patterns and argue that in some cases, pattern may have no biological relevance for the question at hand; in most studies, there is no independent corroboration for the pattern effect presented; and we currently have no cohesive and widely accepted theory to guide biologically relevant scale selection.

The Ubiquity of Pattern

Forman (1995) and Turner et al. (2001) described landscapes as areas that are heterogeneous in at least one factor of interest. Indeed, few landscapes are not heterogeneous or patchy in some factor of interest at some scale. When we look across any landscape from a hill, mountain, or airplane, we are struck by its patchiness. In recent flights over the island of Cyprus, the Tuscan hill country, the Kansas plains, the Vermont countryside, and the intermountain region of Utah, it was apparent to me that although essential differences between these landscapes (topography, vegetation type, and size and spatial configuration of the landscape elements) existed, the defining characteristic was heterogeneity. All landscapes showed obvious pattern; none were homogeneous. Even the continental shelf waters showed differences in color that reflect heterogeneity in habitat pattern and process (Brock et al. 1988).

The emergence of pattern in the landscape has been addressed by Levin (1976), who listed three causes: local uniqueness, which was held to be the result of both temporal and spatial variation in microhabitat variables (Whittaker 1974) and chance events; phase differences, which refer to the patterns caused primarily by the dynamics of succession in different phases of development and driven by disturbance regimes; and "fugitive" dispersal strategies by plants in time and space, as well as time-independent spatial strategies characterized by differential dispersal abilities of species, that result in the maintenance of certain species within the system and that contribute to pattern. Turner et al. (2001, p. 72) provide a nice explanation of these causes. Other, more general causes of landscape pattern include both anthropogenic (human land use [Meyer and Turner 1994; Meyer 1995; Ahern 1999; Pan et al. 2001; Chapter 8, this volume]) and naturally driven (e.g., fire [Swain 1973, Bartuska 1999; Wall et al. 2001], severe wind events [Boose et al. 2001; Dale et al. 2001], and floods [Xue et al. 2001]) disturbance regimes and their associated patch dynamics (Pickett and White 1985). Other causes include biotic interactions (Fowler and Smith 1981), for example, from keystone species (Paine 1974; Dyer et al. 1986; Johnston and Naiman 1990a, 1990b; Johnston 1995) and from what Jones et al. (1994) call ecosystem engineers (see Chapter 3, this volume). Farnsworth and Anderson (2001) coupled herbivore grazing intensity with a plant competition model to demonstrate how simple grazing rules resulted in stable edge boundaries in landscapes.

For ecologists, the question is not whether there is landscape pattern. Rather, our interest is in what effect or constraint landscape pattern has on faunal and floral associations and dynamics and on system processes of interest. The very foundation of landscape ecology as a discipline was aptly described by Wiens (1995) and Turner et al. (2001, p. 4), who addressed this same issue: "The underlying premise of landscape ecology is that the explicit composition and spatial form of a landscape mosaic affect ecological systems in ways that would be different if the mosaic composition or arrangement were different." An important question to ask is whether all landscape patterns have biological relevance. I doubt that is the case.

A Clarification of Terminology

In ecology, different meanings and terms often are used to convey similar concepts (MacArthur and Levins 1964; Forman and Godron 1986; Wiens 1989, 1990; Norton and Lord 1990). Specifically, the term *scale* has many technical meanings in science (Schneider 2001), but its use by population ecologists has often been to denote either resolution or extent, either as perceived by the animal (MacArthur and Levins 1964; Levins 1968; Ritchie 1997) or as defined by the study method (Wiens 1989). In the recent past, the meaning has seldom been defined explicitly; however, the meaning usually becomes clear upon reading the text. Furthermore, both spatial and time components are involved, so one can speak of spatial resolution or extent and temporal resolution or extent (horizon). In this chapter, I use the convention of not using the word *scale* without adding *resolution* or *extent,* its two components (Wiens 1989), unless I am specifically referring to both. Because changes in either study component influence the resulting pattern, it seems sensible to maintain the distinction. Additionally, when I refer to *pattern,* I am referring collectively to both the amount or density (Ritchie 1997) of habitat and its spatial arrangement taken together. If my intention is to highlight either aspect, I will refer to it specifically. Finally, I distinguish between the terms *hierarchical constraint* and *hierarchical causation.* Williams (1997, p. 1007) argued, "Causation can be described in terms of antecedent conditions, consequent effects, and a rule of correspondence for their conjoint occurrence." Defined in this manner, no distinction is made between bottom-up and top-down effects. However, *causation* implies that a specific event has a primary position among the many events that may precede a consequent effect. Furthermore, the meaning is clear: Without the preceding event, the consequent result would not have happened. I focus on this distinction because works on landscape ecology issues have implied top-down causality by landscape pattern when the term *constraint* may have been more appropriate. For

example, certain attributes of landscape pattern may constrain animal movement and dispersal between habitat patches (indeed, constraint of movement
is one of the fundamental characteristics that define metapopulation dynamics). However, selection pressure from predation or some other mechanism,
such as pollination (Groom 1998), may be the causal mechanism that changes
an animal's behavioral response, ultimately altering its movement. Hierarchically, landscape pattern may more accurately be thought of as constraint.
This appears to force a recognition that ecological problems are most often
multiscalar, multicausal, complex adaptive systems (Levin 1999) that beg for
"consilient" (sensu Ruse 1979; Wilson 1998, p. 8) explanation.

There Is Pattern at All Scale Resolutions

It is perhaps trivial to say that there is pattern in the landscape at all practical scale resolutions. Whether we use aerial photos, forest type maps, or geographic information system (GIS) data to analyze satellite imagery, the
method used will produce maps with a specific resolution and the extent.
Some pattern of heterogeneity will emerge. In fact, both the resolution and
extent of the landscape portrayed will influence not only the pattern that
emerges but also our interpretation (Schneider 1994; Wiens 1996b). Resolution (pixel size) for satellite data ranges from 1 km to 80 m for multispectral scanner (MSS) advanced very high resolution radiometer (AVHRR)
data, to 30 m for Landsat thematic mapper (TM), to 5 and 10 m for Spo-
tImage (SPOT) sensors (Wadsworth and Treweek 1999). A new approach,
called light detecting and ranging (LIDAR), uses aircraft-mounted scanning
lasers to detect elevation data to the nearest millimeter (Wadsworth and Treweek 1999), well beyond the minimum resolution that might be needed by
landscape ecologists.

Similarly, landscape extent has consequences that affect our interpretation of ecological phenomena. For example, many studies in wildlife have
reported species' habitat use. Just about every metric dealing either with
determination of home range or with habitat use in home ranges uses some
measure of "availability" (see Hall et al. 1997 for a discussion of the con-
fusion that exists in habitat terminology, e.g., *availability*) against which animal use is compared, such as minimum convex polygon (Mohr 1947), kernel estimator (Worton 1987, 1989), and compositional analysis (Aebischer
et al. 1993). Used this way, habitat availability is made exactly equivalent to
landscape extent for the species of interest; occasional travels outside the

area of availability are not accounted for. Differences in spatial extent encompass different levels of heterogeneity; that is, different proportions of habitat types and the possibility of adding or removing types as extent increases or decreases (Wiens 1989), potentially biasing the habitat index used. It may not seem that the "availability problem" would be acute for third-order selection (Johnson 1980), that is, use of habitats within the home range, because the extent of the home range has already been determined. However, definition of an animal's home range (second-order selection) is inextricably linked to the methods we use. The minimum convex polygon and the kernel methods rely on relocation points to determine extent. Typically, some percentage of the total number of relocation points is used (e.g., 90 percent), and we draw a polygon around the outermost points to create the home range. Regardless of the proportion of points used to create home range extent, that area remains an abstraction of the real area used because seldom if ever is every part of the home range used. Given abrupt topographic features, for example, some parts may be inaccessible.

As prevalent as habitat preference studies are in wildlife biology, it is remarkable that there is no dependable way to select habitat extent (i.e., availability) to understand habitat use, although some attempts have been made (Worton 1989). For example, Pearson et al. (1995) evaluated the influence of spatial environmental characteristics on the minimum cumulative grazing intensity (habitat use) at four spatial extents for ungulates in Yellowstone National Park. Milne (1997), Ritchie (1997), and Ritchie and Olff (1999) have used power scaling functions to link species to resources. They used fractal geometry to incorporate the central features of landscape pattern (habitat density, spatial arrangement) into models of source–sink and metapopulation dynamics and demonstrated that conceptually one can separate the effects of habitat density from spatial arrangement. Morrison (2001) proposed a different research emphasis that focused on mechanisms to overcome some of the limits of wildlife–habitat relationships and that should help address the fundamental problems inherent in current approaches; however, the determination of habitat extent, or availability, remains a persistent problem. My colleague, M. Mitchell (U.S. Geological Survey Alabama Cooperative Fish and Wildlife Research Unit, Auburn University) suggests that we have two problems: an uncritical acceptance of arbitrary choices by many practitioners of use and availability analyses and a lack of biologically meaningful alternatives. This leaves us with little more than arbitrary choices.

Hierarchical Structuring: A Starting Point for Considering Scale Issues

Having only arbitrary choices is not sufficient if we are to make progress in scaling organisms to landscape pattern. Clearly some conceptual framework is needed. Allen and Starr (1982) and O'Neill et al. (1986) argued that the nature of nature is hierarchical. Although we realize that whatever construct we devise to explain nature is, in some sense, artificial, putting natural science problems into a hierarchical framework appears a closer fit than most; indeed, it is part of the conceptual foundation of landscape ecology (Urban et al. 1987; King 1997). King (1997) provides a lucid description of hierarchical system structuring, and I will not repeat it here. In brief, a triadic approach, with L as the focal level of concern from which all other levels are referenced, $L - 1$ as the next lower level providing mechanistic explanation, and the next higher level $L + 1$ providing context and constraint, is the simplified essence of hierarchical structuring. The organization and separation of the different levels is achieved by "differences in rate structure: frequency of behavior, frequency of interaction, and interaction strength" (King 1997, p. 189). To add reality, it is necessary to realize that subsystems (sometimes called "holons"; Koestler 1967; O'Neill et al. 1986; Allen and Starr 1982; King 1997) exist within any system level. Each subsystem is at the same time a whole, and part of a whole at the next higher level. Koestler (1967) called this characteristic "Janus-faced," referring to its dual nature. It seems that if progress is to be made in finding the right scale, a good starting point would be to put the problem into an overtly hierarchical framework, with some exploration of the different rate structures involved. Is it possible to develop a theory that allows us to conceptualize and measure how the differences in interaction rates at different hierarchical levels structure the links between species behavioral responses and specific attributes of landscape pattern? Or would our time and energy be better spent exploring how scaling functions change with changes in pattern and then attempting to understand the biological reasons for the power law (Schneider 2001)?

Finding the Right Scale

Clearly, because there is pattern at every scale resolution and extent, it is necessary to link the organism or species, or the problem or process under consideration, to the appropriate scale and hence to the appropriate pattern. Early investigations (e.g., Kotlier and Wiens 1990; O'Neill et al. 1991) explored multiple scales with a focus on hierarchical structuring. However, the process for finding the relevant scales for the problem at hand is not yet well understood. Turner et al. (2001, p. 39) identified several different approaches that ecologists have used to detect or discover the right scales. Perhaps the most common approach might be called extent aggregation. It involves analyzing data at multiple scale extents to find some concordance with the response variables (e.g., Pearson 1993; Pearson et al. 1995; Obeysekera and Rutchey 1997; Pedlar et al. 1997; Gergel et al. 1999). In almost all cases, innovative analyses were used to detect relationships that involved spatial statistics of one form or another, combined with other more familiar approaches, such as correlation and multiple regression (Pearson 1993; Pearson et al. 1995; Pedlar et al. 1997). O'Neill et al. (1991) used Hill analysis (Hill 1973), as well as correlation (Carlile et al. 1989), ratio (Carlile et al. 1989), and spectral (Ripley 1978) analyses in their detection of landscape pattern. Turner et al. (1991), Baker and Cai (1992), McGarigal and Marks (1995), and Gustafson (1998) presented different analysis techniques used by landscape ecologists to quantify landscape pattern. However, given the number of different analyses and spatial techniques that exist in the literature, we are still faced with difficult problems. We can choose the wrong scale and still produce statistically significant results. How would we know? Alternatively, we may see nonsignificant results that actually may have biological meaning. How would we know? One has to question the meaning of spatial statistics that are not rigorously tied to biological phenomena conceptually. Understanding the natural history of the species in question certainly seems to be a prerequisite. Mitchell et al. (2001) explored scale dependencies and found that to explain and predict accurately the distribution of songbirds on two managed forests, the appropriate scale appeared to be very much a function of the unique natural history of a species. They found that no single scale was universally appropriate to any grouping of birds. These studies have profound implications for our elusive search for the appropriate scale. Although it is difficult to disagree with Pearson et al. (1996, p. 78) when they say that selection of "landscape scale should depend on the relevant organisms and ecological processes," the devil is in the details. From the preceding discussion, it is clear that there is no uniquely correct scale extent or resolution that can be universally used, there is no single method that one can use to find the "correct" scale, and any landscape problem may warrant investigation at multiple scales to elucidate the dynamics. It is just as evident that a conceptual basis for understanding biologically relevant spatial dependency is absolutely necessary if landscape metrics are to have meaning.

Scale Dependencies

When we investigate processes or dynamics in patchy landscapes, we have to deal with possible scale dependency issues such as changes in pattern, process, or phenomena that change with both scale resolution and extent (Turner 1989) or, as defined by Schneider (1994), interactions or phenomena in which the rate of one process as compared with a second changes as the resolution or extent of the landscape (or the measurement used) changes (Turner et al. 2001). O'Neill et al. (1996) showed that landscape indices at regional scales were sensitive to both scale resolution and extent and provided a guideline for deciding what scale parameters to use (i.e., resolution two to five times finer and extent two to five times larger than the feature of interest) to avoid biases in the calculated indices. Gao et al. (2001) and Tischendorf (2001) addressed similar difficulties with simulation studies. Additionally, Jelinski and Wu (1996) showed that the modifiable areal unit problem (MAUP) has at least two serious consequences for spatial analysis. The pertinent one here concerns the situation in which one basic set of areal data at some specified resolution and extent is aggregated into several sets with different resolutions, with each combination resulting in different spatial values and interpretations. The main problem appears to be that spatial autocorrelation is not uniform across the landscapes that are created by aggregation, and it changes with scale extent. Jelinski and Wu (1996) suggested that MAUP may affect the results of spatial simulation models when aggregation is used. This is called aggregation error. Given these results from a wide array of different types of landscape studies, it is clear that scale dependency has everything to do with the question, When are landscape patterns biologically relevant?

When Are Landscape Patterns Relevant?

Even though the process of matching scale to problem is not easy, it involves the assumption that some scale resolutions and extents exist that, if we were able to identify them, would help explain the relevant dynamics of the questions of interest. However, this appears to skip a necessary step in logic and method. I have seldom seen a work that challenges the relevancy of a specific pattern. We have come to accept as dogma, even if tacitly, that pattern is always relevant. We proceed with our science as if it is, even though we recognize that not every pattern at every scale resolution and extent has an impact on the problem of interest. Our attempts to find the right scale imply that some patterns are irrelevant. Yet we appear not to have addressed that problem directly, suggesting a clear asymmetry in our collective approaches. I argue that landscape ecologists often work backward in the sense that GIS satellite data, often used in landscape ecological studies, have a fixed resolution and arbitrary extent and dictate the minimum resolution available. These concerns suggest that it is reasonable to question the relevance of pattern generated by analysis of satellite imagery by GIS analysis, or by any other source or method, and ask whether it is biologically real or relevant to the question at hand. Schneider (2001, p. 548) suggested a useful approach. He used space–time graphs, defining the term *scope* as the ratio of extent to resolution. He demonstrated that power scaling laws "coordinate the scope of one measured quantity to another"; in other words, over some extent, pattern changed with scale as a power law. If one can understand the biological basis for power scaling, there is hope in applying this approach to practical problems (Schneider 2001 and personal communication, 2001).

Certainly, many have argued for higher-level, hierarchically structured, top-down constraints or causality (most of the chapters in this volume, Allen and Starr 1982; O'Neill et al. 1988; May 1994; Brown 1995). However, I argue that every investigator of landscape phenomena must ask the necessary and intervening questions: Does the landscape pattern generated in my study indeed have an impact? Is it real? Or are the results spurious? Would the relationships hold if tested on another similar landscape? Mitchell et al. (2001) did conduct tests of their model on an independent forest landscape and assessed model fit. Their approach is a good one and suggests that we should treat every landscape pattern effect as a null hypothesis and attempt to disprove it rather than tacitly accepting the relationship as relevant. This would place the science in a more self-critical context, something that Wiens (1996a, p. 1) suggested when he said, "The second challenge for landscape ecology . . . is to advance . . . [it] as a science. If we expect to have credibility in applying landscape ecology . . . we must be certain that our conclusions have a firm scientific basis, founded on solid empirical information and sound practices." It seems to me this critical step is missing in many articles.

How can we approach this question conceptually? We can start by asking, Is there downward causation or constraint operating for the problem under consideration? Kawata (1995) "recognized the distinction between observed higher level patterns unrelated to unique properties and patterns characterized by properties that affect and cause change in ecological and evolutionary processes" (Bissonette 1997, p. 18). Kawata (1995) called these noneffective and effective, respectively. Here, property is defined as "an essential or distinctive attribute or quality of a thing" (Dictionary of the English Language 1971). In other words, landscape pattern, as measured at a specific scale resolution and extent, may be effective or noneffective. Given a mismatch of pattern to problem, a pattern may have no biological reality for the problem of interest.

To be useful to ecologists, properties must be operational (i.e., measurable). Certainly, higher-level patterns, such as the amount and spatial configurations of landscape elements, have unique properties or attributes. They include differences in isolation and distance effects, differences in the spatial distribution of patch sizes, differences in connectivity, differences in patch edge contrast, variation in the number and sizes of core areas, and differences in the proportion of the landscape occupied by a patch type. In short, landscape properties can be measured but may involve one or a suite of measurements. Given the number of landscape metrics available, the theoretical number of potential properties is combinatorial and very large. Selecting the correct mix of variables from among those available takes not only exploration to ascertain relevant relationships but also knowledge of underlying species life history needs to help direct the selection of the putative explanatory (or constraint) variables; a priori thinking is needed.

The determination of the type of dynamics (e.g., simple or spatially complicated) that might characterize an animal population should help illustrate my point of whether landscape pattern has downward causation or constraint. Ritchie (1997) distinguished between three scenarios that might characterize wildlife populations. The first is how ecologists until recently have typically treated populations (i.e., as a single cluster of individuals using an arbitrarily defined area). The second scenario recognizes that there is spatial heterogeneity in the landscape. The third scenario recognizes not only that spatial heterogeneity exists but also that it introduces spatial complexity into the dynamics of populations on the landscape. The first two scenarios assume that we have properly assessed the appropriate operational demographic unit (Merriam 1998). The first scenario assumes panmictic breeding and something close to an ideal free distribution (Fretwell 1972); that is, averaging dynamics can legitimately be used (Ritchie 1997). Under the second and much more interesting case, even though spatial complexity characterizes the habitat (i.e., it is spatially structured), the assumption of a panmictic or mixed population may still hold if a species population continues to distribute itself proportionally across the landscape according to the relative quality of the habitat patches, even after changes in population size over time occur. Under this scenario, even though the landscape is spatially structured, averaging dynamics can still be used; the conclusion is that the pattern (i.e., habitat amount and arrangement) is noneffective. It does not affect species population dynamics. Landscape pattern per se has little or no influence on species movement, and species responses can be interpreted as related to resource distribution alone. In other words, if animals can move freely throughout the landscape, there is no effective property (i.e., no constraint imposed by the spatial arrangement and amount of habitat). Here I assume that the resources available are sufficient for the putative species in question to meet its needs.

The early concept of grain (MacArthur and Levins 1964; Levin 1976), which was used to describe the manner in which different species visualized and used their environment, is useful, although the critique by Peters (1991, p. 48); that is, the criticism of using binary distinctions to represent a gradient of responses, is appropriate. Needless dichotomy is not helpful. Accordingly, a finer-grained species uses its resources more in the proportion they occur than does a coarser-grained species. The ability to be fine-grained is enabled by landscapes whose pattern is noneffective for the species in question. The interesting problem here is how a species that uses the landscape in a coarser-grained manner can become finer-grained or, differently put, under what circumstances the effects of landscape pattern are minimized and have lesser effect on species dynamics. One line of argument links smaller-scale mechanisms, such as predation, to animal habitat use and movement patterns. Connectivity is achieved by the ability or willingness of species to move between habitat patches. If constraints to movement other than landscape pattern can be reduced or eliminated, it is probable that resources would be used more in proportion to their availability. Under this scenario, species response is increasingly dependent on the distribution of resources and less dependent on landscape pattern. In other words, a change in the constraints to animal movement may enable a species to perceive and use the landscape as more fine-grained.

Most species are subject to predation (Dawkins and Krebs 1979), including predators themselves (Arjo and Pletscher 1999; Crabtree and Sheldon 1999). Predation often results in vigilance behavior in both prey species and predators that are preyed upon (e.g., African ungulates [Hunter and Skinner 1998], meerkats [*Suricata suricatta;* Moran 1984], cheetahs [*Acinonyx jubatus;* Caro 1987) and may be the predominant form of mortality for some species (Palomares and Caro 1999). Vigilant behavior (response to predation) has been proposed as one of the reasons why some species (e.g., martens [*Martes americana*] in Newfoundland; Bissonette 1996; Bissonette et al. 1997) limit their movements both temporally and spatially to habitats with cover (Drew 1995). To the extent that predation limits animal movement to habitats with cover, so also is the effect of landscape pattern, with its accompanying differences in cover, more of a constraint. Landscapes with highly isolated habitat patches tend to constrain animal movement strongly, and constraint may change with differences in patch size, edge gradients (Lidicker and Koenig 1996), and contrast with the matrix vegetation. Given the increasing recognition that many predators perform keystone functions (Berger et al. 2001), as keystone predator populations are reduced or lost, one can expect cascading effects on species in the assemblage. For example, white-tailed deer in the northeastern United States, who themselves are having increasing effects on vegetation (Stromayer and Warren 1997) and have consequently been called keystone herbivores (Waller and Alverson 1997) have increased dramatically in urban and suburban areas where mortality by hunting has been reduced to low or nonexistent levels. As effective predation is removed, species populations whose movement patterns and choice of habitat were influenced by predation are "released." This may have the effect of allowing a species whose coarser-grained use of patchy landscapes was previously largely determined by predation, and not the pattern of the habitat per se, to become effectively more fine-grained.

The third scenario, a spatially structured landscape with spatial complications in population dynamics, such as metapopulation or source sink dynamics, appears to be the default assumption for many landscape studies. Pattern is assumed to be effective.

Implications

At least two general conclusions follow from the preceding discussion. First, landscape patterns may be effective or noneffective; the presumptive approach appears to be that patterns are effective and influence population dynamics or other processes. Little thought has been given to the alternative. I argue that we should consider that assumption overtly when we conduct landscape studies. Second, the difficulty in selecting the correct scales notwithstanding, correlations that link landscape pattern to population dynamics or other system processes are simply associations and do not necessarily imply cause and effect or, in a hierarchical sense, constraint. Verification of the effective nature of landscape pattern appears to be the province of additional studies that support and help confirm the relationship (e.g., repeatability) along with a more robust approach that takes the relationship as a working hypothesis and tests its ability to predict accurately on independent landscapes (Mitchell, personal communication, 2001).

Summary

Landscape pattern is ubiquitous. All landscapes exhibit pattern at some scale resolution and extent. Progress in understanding the effects of pattern may entail a change of focus. Schneider (personal communication, 2001) asks, "Could we not understand pattern as a function of scale" rather than pursuing the notion of a "correct" scale? These concerns suggest that it is reasonable to question the relevance of pattern obtained from any source or method, ask whether it is biologically real or relevant to the question at hand, and, perhaps most importantly, question whether our search for the "right" scale is even the most appropriate approach. Even if there is congruence or correspondence with landscape pattern to population dynamics or other system processes, the putative relationship remains only an association until further work suggests a causal or hierarchical constraint relationship. The advancement of understanding of interesting ecological problems within a spatial context appears to entail the collection of data at multiple scale resolutions and extents appropriate to the question of interest. A reasonable first step might begin simply with a multiscalar triadic approach (O'Neill et al. 1986), where if L is the hierarchical level of interest, level $L + 1$ provides context; that is, higher-level explanation of the possible constraints in the dynamics (e.g., differences in foraging opportunities), and elucidating the interactions at smaller spatial resolutions and extents ($L - 1$) will help explain causal mechanisms (e.g., vigilance when foraging). Understanding that within-level (L) feedbacks are what make ecological complex adaptive systems complex may eventually lead us to better explanations for the landscape phenomena we try to understand. Recent work suggests that exploring scaling functions in which pattern and process are quantified as functions of resolution and extent (Schneider 2001) may be most fruitful. Uncrippling the hierarchy (i.e., attempting to understand top-down, bottom-up, and within-level constraint and causality) will further our understanding of spatial phenomena.

Once we reach the point where the effects of landscape pattern can be rigorously confirmed by reliable measures, one of the next challenges in landscape ecology will involve investigation into the compositional contribution of different habitat elements in the landscape to population persistence or other processes (see Chapter 15, this volume). Sisk et al. (1997) generally, and Wagner and Edwards (2001) specifically, addressed the effects of the surrounding matrix on species assemblages and the contribution of individual patches to species richness, respectively. Given the multiscale nature of these approaches, progress may be made in verifying and elucidating the effects of landscape pattern.

Acknowledgments

I thank D. Maehr, M. Mitchell, I. Storch, and D. Schneider for their helpful comments on earlier drafts of this chapter. I especially thank my colleague I. Storch for her invaluable help in detecting numerous errors. All reviewers helped to clarify my thinking about these matters but are not responsible for whatever errors I have made in logic or explanation. The USGS Utah Cooperative Fish and Wildlife Research Unit is jointly supported by the USGS, the Utah Division of Wildlife Resources, Utah State University, the Wildlife Management Institute, and the U.S. Fish and Wildlife Service.

LITERATURE CITED

Aebischer, N. J., P. A. Robertson, and R. E. Kenward. 1993. Compositional analysis of habitat use from animal radio-tracking data. Ecology 74:1313–1325.

Ahern, J. 1999. Spatial concepts, planning strategies, and future scenarios: a framework method for integrating landscape ecology and landscape planning. Pages 175–201 in J. M. Klopatek and R. H. Gardner (eds.), Landscape ecological analysis: issues and applications. Springer-Verlag, New York.

Allen, T. F. H., and T. B. Starr. 1982. Hierarchy: perspectives for ecological complexity. University of Chicago Press, Chicago.

Arjo, W. M., and D. H. Pletscher . 1999. Behavioral responses of coyotes to wolf recolonization in northwestern Montana. Canadian Journal of Zoology 77:1919–1927.

Baker, W. L., and Y. Cai. 1992. The rule programs for multiscale analysis of landscape structure using the GRASS geographical information system. Landscape Ecology 7:291–302.

Bartuska, A. M. 1999. Cross-boundary issues to manage for healthy forest ecosystems. Pages 24–34 in J. M. Klopatek and R. H. Gardner (eds.), Landscape ecological analysis: issues and applications. Springer-Verlag, New York.

Berger, J., P. B. Stacey, L. Bellis, and M. P. Johnson. 2001. A mammalian predator–prey imbalance: grizzly bear and wolf extinction affect avian neotropical migrants. Ecological Applications 11:947–960.

Bissonette, J. A. 1996. Linking temporal with spatial scales in wildlife research. Transactions of the 61st North American Wildlife and Natural Resources Conference 61:161–168.

Bissonette, J. A. 1997. Scale-sensitive properties: historical context, current meaning. Pages 3–31 in J. A. Bissonette (ed.), Wildlife and landscape ecology: effects of pattern and scale. Springer-Verlag, New York.

Bissonette, J. A., D. J. Harrison, C. D. Hargis, and T. G. Chapin. 1997. Scale-sensitive properties influence marten demographics. Pages 368–385 in J. A. Bissonette (ed.), Wildlife and landscape ecology: effects of pattern and scale. Springer-Verlag, New York.

Boose, E. R., K. E. Chamberlin, and D. R. Foster. 2001. Landscape and regional impacts of hurricanes in New England. Ecological Monographs 71:27–48.

Brock, J. C., S. Sathyendranath, and T. Platt. 1988. Biohydro-optical classification of the northwestern Indian Ocean. Marine Ecology Progress Series 165:1–15.

Brown, J. H. 1995. Macroecology. University of Chicago Press, Chicago.

Carlile, D. W., J. R. Skalski, J. E. Batker, J. M. Thomas, and V. I. Cullinan. 1989. Determination of ecological scale. Landscape Ecology 2:203–213.

Caro, T. M. 1987. Cheetah mothers' vigilance: looking out for prey or for predators. Behavioral Ecology and Sociobiology 20:351–361.

Crabtree, R. L., and J. W. Sheldon. 1999. Coyotes and canid coexistence in Yellowstone. Pages 127–163 in T. W. Clark, A. P. Curlee, S. C. Minta, and P. M. Kareiva (eds.), Carnivores in ecosystems: the Yellowstone experience. Yale University Press, New Haven, CT.

Dale, V. H., L. A. Joyce, S. McNulty, R. P. Neilson, M. P. Ayres, M. D. Flannigan, P. J. Hanson, L. C. Irland, A. E. Lugo, C. J. Peterson, D. Simberloff, F. J. Swanson, B. J. Stocks, and B. M. Wotton. 2001. Climate change and forest disturbances. BioScience 51:723–734.

Dawkins, R., and J. R. Krebs. 1979. Arms races between and within species. Proceedings of the Royal Society of London, B 205:489–511.

Dictionary of the English Language (unabridged). 1971. Random House, New York.

Drew, G. S. 1995. Winter habitat selection by American marten (*Martes americana*) in Newfoundland: why old growth? Ph.D. dissertation, Utah State University, Logan.

Dyer, M. I., D. L. DeAngelis, and W. M. Post. 1986. A model of herbivore feedback on plant productivity. Mathematical Biosciences 79:171–184.

Farnsworth, K. D., and A. R. A. Anderson. 2001. How simple grazing rules can lead to persistent boundaries in vegetation communities. Oikos 95:15–24.

Forman, R. T. T. 1995. Land mosaics. Cambridge University Press, Cambridge, UK.

Forman, R. T. T., and M. Godron. 1986. Landscape ecology. Wiley, New York.

Fowler, C. F., and T. D. Smith (eds.). 1981. Dynamics of large mammal populations. Wiley, New York.

Fretwell, S. D. 1972. Populations in a seasonal environment. Princeton University Press, Princeton, NJ.

Gao, Q., M. Yu, X. Yang, and J. Wu. 2001. Scaling simulation models for spatially heterogeneous ecosystems with diffusive transportation. Landscape Ecology 16:289–300.

Gergel, S. E., M. G. Turner, and T. K. Kratz. 1999. Dissolved organic carbon as an indicator of the scale of watershed influence of lakes and rivers. Ecological Applications 9:1377–1390.

Groom, M. J. 1998. Allee effects limit population viability of an annual plant. American Naturalist 151:487–496.

Gustafson, E. J. 1998. Quantifying landscape spatial pattern: what is the state of the art? Ecosystems 1:143–156.

Hall, L. S., P. R. Krausman, and M. L. Morrison. 1997. The habitat concept and a plea for standard terminology. Wildlife Society Bulletin 25:173–182.

Hill, M. O. 1973. The intensity of spatial pattern in plant communities. Journal of Ecology 61:225–235.

Hunter, L. T. B., and J. D. Skinner. 1998. Vigilance behaviour in African ungulates: the role of predation pressure. Behaviour 135:195–211.

Jelinski, D. E., and J. Wu. 1996. The modifiable areal unit problem and implications for landscape ecology. Landscape Ecology 11:129–140.

Johnson, D. H. 1980. The comparison of usage and availability measurements for evaluating resource preference. Ecology 61:65–71.

Johnston, C. A. 1995. Effects of animals on landscape pattern. Pages 57–80 in L. Hansson, L. Fahrig, and G. Merriam (eds.), Mosaic landscapes and ecological processes. Chapman and Hall, London.

Johnston, C. A., and R. J. Naiman 1990a. Aquatic patch creation in relation to beaver population trends. Ecology 71:1617–1621.

Johnston, C. A., and R. J. Naiman 1990b. The use of a geographic information system to analyze landscape alteration by beaver. Landscape Ecology 4:5–19.

Jones, C. G., J. H. Lawton, and M. Shachak. 1994. Organisms as ecosystem engineers. Oikos 69:373–386.

Kawata, M. 1995. Emergent and effective properties in ecology and evolution. Researches in Population Ecology 37:93–96.

King, A. W. 1997. Hierarchy theory: a guide to system structure for wildlife biologists. Pages 185–212 in J. A. Bissonette (ed.), Wildlife and landscape ecology: effects of pattern and scale. Springer-Verlag, New York.

Koestler, A. 1967. The ghost in the machine. Macmillan, New York.

Kotlier, N. B., and J. A. Wiens. 1990. Multiple scales of patchiness and patch structure: a hierarchical framework for the study of heterogeneity. Oikos 59:253–260.

Levin, S. A. 1976. Spatial patterning and the structure of ecological communities. Lectures on Mathematics in the Life Sciences (Some Mathematical Questions in Biology) 8:1–35.

Levin, S. A. 1999. Fragile dominion: complexity and the commons. Helix Books, Perseus Publishing, Cambridge, MA.

Levins, R. 1968. Evolution in changing environments. Princeton University Press, Princeton, NJ.

Lidicker, W. Z., Jr., and W. D. Koenig. 1996. Responses of terrestrial vertebrates to habitat edges and corridors. Pages 85–109 in D. R. McCullough (ed.), Metapopulations and wildlife conservation. Island Press, Washington, DC.

MacArthur, R., and R. Levins. 1964. Competition, habitat selection, and character displacement in a patchy environment. Proceedings of the National Academy of Science 51:1207–1210.

May, R. M. 1994. The effects of spatial scale on ecological questions and answers. Pages 1–17 in P. J. Edwards, R. M. May, and N. R. Webb (eds.), Large-scale ecology and conservation biology (35th symposium of the British Ecological Society, with the Society for Conservation Biology). Blackwell Scientific Publications, London.

McGarigal, K., and B. J. Marks. 1995. FRAGSTATS: spatial pattern analysis program for quantifying landscape pattern. USDA Forest Service, Pacific Northwest Research Station, General Technical Report PNW-GTR-351, Portland, OR.

Merriam, G. 1998. Important concepts from landscape ecology for game biologists. Pages 525–531 in P. Havet, E. Taran, and J. C. Berthos (eds.), Proceedings of the International Union of Game Biologists 23rd Congress: Game Management and Land Use in Open Landscapes. Gibier Faune Sauvage 15, Paris.

Meyer, W. B. 1995. Past and present land use and land cover in the USA. Consequences 1995:25–33.

Meyer, W. B., and B. L. Turner II (eds.). 1994. Changes in land use and land cover: a global perspective. Cambridge University Press, Cambridge, UK.

Milne, B. T. 1997. Applications of fractal geometry in wildlife biology. Pages 32–69 in J. A. Bissonette (ed.), Landscape and wildlife ecology: effects of pattern and scale. Springer-Verlag, New York.

Mitchell, M. S., R. A. Lancia, and J. A. Gerwin. 2001. Using landscape data to predict the distribution of birds on a managed forest: effects of scale. Ecological Applications 11:1692–1708.

Mohr, C. O. 1947. Table of equivalent populations of North American small mammals. American Midland Naturalist 37:223–249.

Moran, G. 1984. Vigilance behavior and alarm calls in a captive group of meerkats, *Suricata suricatta*. Zeitschrift Tierpsychologie 65:228–240.

Morrison, M. L. 2001. A proposed research emphasis to overcome the limits of wildlife–habitat relationships studies. Journal of Wildlife Management 65:613–623.

Norton, D. A., and J. M. Lord. 1990. On the use of "grain size" in ecology. Functional Ecology 4:719–720.

Obeysekera, J., and K. Rutchey. 1997. Selection of scale for Everglades landscape models. Landscape Ecology 12:7–18.

O'Neill, R. V., D. L. DeAngelis, J. B. Waide, and T. F. H. Allen. 1986. A hierarchical concept of ecosystems. Monographs in Population Biology, no. 23, Princeton University Press, Princeton, NJ.

O'Neill, R. V., B. T. Milne, M. G. Turner, and R. H. Gardner. 1988. Resource utilization scales and landscape pattern. Landscape Ecology 2:63–69.

O'Neill, R. V., S. J. Turner, V. I. Cullinan, D. P. Coffin, T. Cook, W. Conley, J. Brunt, J. M. Thomas, M. R. Conley, and J. Gosz. 1991. Multiple landscape scales: an intersite comparison. Landscape Ecology 5:137–144.

O'Neill, R. V., C. T. Hunsaker, S. P. Timmons, B. L. Jackson, K. B. Jones, K. H. Ritters, and J. D. Wickkam. 1996. Scale problems in reporting landscape pattern at the regional scale. Landscape Ecology 3:169–180.

Paine, R. T. 1974. Intertidal community structure: experimental studies on the relationship between a dominant competitor and its principal predator. Oecologia 15:93–120.

Palomares, F., and T. M. Caro. 1999. Interspecific killing among mammalian carnivores. American Naturalist 153:492–508.

Pan, D., G. Domond, D. Marceau, and A. Bouchard. 2001 Spatial pattern of coniferous and deciduous forest patches in an eastern North American agricultural landscape: the influence of land use and physical attributes. Landscape Ecology 16:99–110.

Pearson, S. M. 1993. The spatial extent and relative influence of landscape-level factors on wintering bird populations. Landscape Ecology 8:3–18.

Pearson, S. M., M. G. Turner, L. L. Wallace, and W. H. Romme. 1995. Winter habitat use by large ungulates following fires in northern Yellowstone National Park. Ecological Applications 5:744–755.

Pearson, S. M., M. G. Turner, R. H. Gardner, and R. V. O'Neill. 1996. An organism-based perspective of habitat fragmentation. Pages 77–95 in R. C. Szaro and D. W. Johnston (eds.), Biodiversity in managed landscapes. Oxford University Press, New York.

Pedlar, J. H., L. Fahrig, and H. G. Merriam. 1997. Raccoon habitat use at two spatial scales. Journal of Wildlife Management 61:102–112.

Peters, R. H. 1991. A critique for ecology. Cambridge University Press, Cambridge, UK.

Pickett, S. T. A., and P. S. White. 1985. The ecology of natural disturbance and patch dynamics. Academic Press, San Diego, CA.

Ripley, B. D. 1978. Spectral analysis and the analysis of pattern in plant communities. Journal of Ecology 66:965–981.

Ritchie, M. E. 1997. Populations in a landscape context: sources, sinks, and metapopulations. Pages 160–184 in J. A. Bissonette (ed.), Landscape and wildlife ecology: effects of pattern and scale. Springer-Verlag, New York.

Ritchie, M. E., and H. Olff. 1999. Spatial scaling laws yield a synthetic theory of biodiversity. Nature 400:557–560.

Ruse, M. 1979. Falsifiability, consilience, and synthesis. Systematic Zoology 28:530–536.

Schneider, D. C. 1994. Quantitative ecology: spatial and temporal scaling. Academic Press, San Diego, CA.

Schneider, D. C. 2001. The rise of the concept of scale in ecology. BioScience 51:545–553.

Sisk, T. D., N. M. Haddad, and P. R. Ehrlich. 1997. Bird assemblages in patchy woodlands: modeling the effects of edge and matrix habitats. Ecological Applications 7:1170–1179.

Stromayer, K. A. K., and R. J. Warren. 1997. Are overabundant deer herds in the eastern United States creating alternate stable states in forest plant communities? Wildlife Society Bulletin 25:227–234.

Swain, A. M. 1973. A history of fire and vegetation in northwestern Minnesota as recorded in lake sediments. Quaternary Research (New York) 3:383–396.

Tischendorf, L. 2001. Can landscape indices predict ecological processes consistently? Landscape Ecology 16:235–254.

Turner, M. G. 1989. Landscape ecology: the effect of pattern on process. Annual Review of Ecology and Systematics 20:171–197.

Turner, S. J., R. V. O'Neill, W. Conley, M. R. Conley, and H. Humphries. 1991. Pattern and scale: statistics for landscape ecology. Pages 17–49 in M. G. Turner and R. H. Gardner (eds.), Quantitative methods in landscape ecology. Springer-Verlag, New York.

Turner, M. G., R. H. Gardner, and R. V. O'Neill. 2001. Landscape ecology in theory and practice. Springer, New York.

Urban, D. L., R. V. O'Neill, and H. H. Shugart, Jr. 1987. Landscape ecology. BioScience 37:119–127.

Wadsworth, R., and J. Treweek. 1999. Geographical information systems for ecology. Addison-Wesley-Longman, Essex, UK.

Wagner, H. H., and P. J. Edwards. 2001. Quantifying habitat specificity to assess the contribution of a patch to species richness at the landscape scale. Landscape Ecology 16:121–131.

Wall, T. G., R. F. Miller, and T. J. Svejcar. 2001. Juniper encroachment into aspen in the Northwest Great Basin. Journal of Range Management 54:691–698.

Waller, D. M., and W. S. Alverson. 1997. The white-tailed deer: a keystone herbivore. Wildlife Society Bulletin 25:217–226.

Whittaker, R. H. 1974. Climax concepts and recognition. Pages 139–356 in R. Knapp (ed.), Handbook of vegetation science, Part VIII, Vegetation dynamics. W. Junk B. V., The Hague, Netherlands.

Wiens, J. A. 1989. Spatial scaling in ecology. Functional Ecology 3:385–397.

Wiens, J. A. 1990. On the use of "grain" and "grain size" in ecology. Functional Ecology 4:720.

Wiens, J. A. 1995. Landscape mosaics and ecological theory. Pages 1–26 in L. Hansson, L. Fahrig, and G. Merriam (eds.), Mosaic landscapes and ecological processes. Chapman & Hall, London.

Wiens, J. A. 1996a. Comments. International Association for Landscape Ecology Bulletin 14:1.

Wiens, J. A. 1996b. Wildlife in patchy environments: metapopulations, mosaics, and management. Pages 53–84 in D. R. McCullough (ed.), Metapopulations and wildlife conservation. Island Press, Washington, DC.

Williams, B. K. 1997. Logic and science in wildlife biology. Journal of Wildlife Management 61:1007–1015.

Wilson, E. O. 1998. Consilience: the unity of knowledge. Random House, New York.

Worton, B. J. 1987. A review of models of home range for animal movement. Ecological Modelling 38:277–298.

Worton, B. J. 1989. Kernel methods for estimating the utilizations distribution in home range studies. Ecology 70:164–168.

Xue, Y., F. J. Zeng, K. E. Mitchell, Z. Janjic, and E. Rogers. 2001. The impact of land surface processes on simulations of the US hydrological cycle: a case study of the 1993 flood using the SSiB land surface model in the NCEP Eta regional model. Monthly Weather Review 129:2833–2860.

CHAPTER TWO

Linkages between Landscape Theory and Population Dynamics

A Review of Empirical Evidence

THERESE M. DONOVAN AND ALLAN M. STRONG

The study of population dynamics has been and continues to be a fundamental building block in ecological studies. A population is a group of individual organisms belonging to the same species living in the same area at the same time. They are considered to be actually or potentially interbreeding or exchanging genes at least at some scale. The term *population dynamics* refers to change in population size (number of individuals) or population density (number of individuals per unit area) over time. Four fundamental demographic processes influence population dynamics: birth, death, immigration (individuals moving into the population), and emigration (individuals moving out of the population). The dynamics of change in numbers over time can be written as

$$N_{t+1} = N_t + B - D + I - E$$

where the number of individuals present in the population at time step $t + 1$ is equal to the numbers of individuals in the population in the previous time step, plus the new individuals that enter the population through birth or immigration, minus individuals that leave the population through emigration or death. The *BIDE* parameters (birth, immigration, death, and emigration rates) not only determine how population numbers will change over time but also shape the population's structure. For example, if $I = 0$ and $E = 0$, then the population is closed, and any changes in numbers are strictly a function of B and D. If $I \gg 0$ and $E \gg 0$, then the population is likely to be part of a larger, freely mixing (panmictic) population. If $I > 0$ and $E > 0$ but I and E are low, then multiple subpopulations interact through dispersal, and the population is said to be structured (Pulliam 1988; Hanski and Gilpin 1991, 1997).

The *BIDE* parameters also shape the genetic structure of a population (Wright 1931; Fisher 1930), or how genes are partitioned within and between both individuals and local subpopulations. Gene flow (through I and E) is a major component of population structure because it determines the extent to which each local population or subpopulation is an independent evolutionary unit. If I and E are low, or if dispersing individuals fail to breed successfully, populations are essentially closed and different populations evolve almost independently. If gene flow is substantial (I and E are high), then the collection of subpopulations evolves together (Slatkin 1985).

Landscape Ecology and Population Dynamics

Landscape ecology is the study of how the composition and spatial structure of habitats affect ecological patterns and processes (Forman and Godron 1986; Urban et al. 1987; Turner 1989; Pickett and Cadenasso 1995). From a population perspective, the spatial pattern of a landscape can affect all four *BIDE* parameters as well as genetic structure and rates of genetic change. Spatial pattern can also affect extinction probabilities, which can be defined as the probability that $N_{t+1} = 0$. The underlying premise of landscape ecology is that the explicit composition and spatial form of a landscape mosaic directly affect ecological systems (Chapter 1, this volume; Wiens 1992, 1997).

Landscape pattern has long been known to affect *BIDE* parameters, but only recently have the implications been placed into a conservation context (McCullough 1996; Young and Clarke 2000). For instance, metapopulation dynamics (Hanski and Gilpin 1997) and source–sink dynamics (Pulliam 1988) both implicitly assume that populations occur in discrete habitat patches and that landscape pattern affects dispersal rates (I and E) between patches. As a discipline, landscape ecology has progressed dramatically from purely descriptive and nonquantitative studies (Wiens 1992) to a greater emphasis on modeling and use of statistics in more recent years (Hobbs

1996, 1999). But how strong is the evidence to date that landscape pattern directly affects the *BIDE* parameters in naturally occurring populations?

Two theoretical models have been fundamental in guiding landscape research on population dynamics. The first is the MacArthur and Wilson (1967) model of island biogeography, and the second is neutral landscape theory (Gardner et al. 1987). Our goal in this chapter is to briefly review elements of these theories, describe the predictions they make about land-scape effects on *BIDE,* and briefly review empirical studies that specifically test these predictions. Because the literature on these topics is enormous and growing rapidly, and because of space limitations in this chapter, we focus on field studies that clearly illustrate a specific point rather than providing a complete literature review.

The Theory of Island Biogeography

The equilibrium theory of island biogeography, developed by MacArthur and Wilson (1967), modeled species richness (number of species) on an island as the result of two processes: immigration and extinction. Although their model was intended as an explanation for species–area relationships on true islands, they noted that similar relationships might exist on habitat islands in a landscape context. In their model, species immigrate to an island randomly from a mainland pool. The rate at which new species immigrate to an island is determined by three factors: the distance from the island to the mainland, the number of species left in the mainland pool that have not already established themselves on the island, and the probability that any species will disperse from the mainland to the island. The rate at which species on the island go extinct is determined by three different factors: the area of the island, the number of species present, and the probability that any species on the island will go extinct.

This model suggests several predictions that can be tested on habitat patches in a landscape context, including the following: Immigration (I) is affected by habitat isolation and the permeability of the matrix surrounding the habitat island, and extinction probability ($N_{t+1} = 0$) is a function of patch size. In closed populations, extinction occurs when $B < D$, so birth and death rates are expected to vary as a function of patch size. In open populations, extinction occurs when $B < D$ and $I < E$ (Pulliam 1988). In this case, small patches may be rescued from extinction if they can receive enough immi-grants (I) from other populations, which is a function of the degree of iso-lation (Brown and Kodric-Brown 1977).

Neutral Landscape Models

Neutral landscape models (also called null models or random models) are a more recent theoretical development in the field of landscape ecology (Gardner et al. 1987). Neutral models are process-free and can modify the predictions made by island biogeography theory in several ways. Neutral models generate habitat patterns randomly and thereby remove the effects of land use or other nonrandom properties that might affect landscape pattern. In other words, these models can be used to answer the question, What would a landscape look like if no processes affected the distribution of a particular habitat type on the land? Such null models are common in ecology (Gotelli and Graves 1996) and provide the necessary reference point against which alternatives may be compared. Figure 2.1 shows an example of two neutral landscapes, or grid-based random maps. These maps were generated by assigning a random number between 0 and 1 to each cell and then assigning a habitat type (suitable or nonsuitable habitat) to the random numbers according to some arbitrary value, p. Thus, p gives the approximate proportion of suitable habitat in the landscape, and $1 - p$ is the proportion of unsuitable habitat in the landscape. In the top map, p was set to 0.3 so that approximately 30 percent of the landscape consists of suitable habitat, and 70 percent consists of nonsuitable habitat. Random numbers less than $p = 0.3$ are shaded gray (suitable habitat for a hypothetical species), and numbers greater than 0.3 appear white (unsuitable habitat). The bottom landscape was also generated with random numbers, except that random numbers less than $p = 0.7$ are shaded gray and those above 0.7 are white so that the landscape consists of approximately 70 percent suitable habitat.

Randomly generated landscapes have several properties that are of interest to landscape ecologists. First, neutral landscape models have been used to determine the extent to which structural properties of real landscapes (e.g., patch size) deviate from some theoretical spatial distribution. Second, neutral models allow prediction of how ecological processes, such as *BIDE*, are affected by landscape pattern (With and King 1997). As the proportion of habitat to nonhabitat is increased (e.g., increase p from 0 to 1 in increments of 0.1), nearly all of the standard metrics used to describe landscapes (such as average patch size, amount of edge, and average distance between patches) change. However, the metrics do not change in a linear fashion. For example, the number of suitable habitat patches in neutral landscapes abruptly changes around $p = 0.4$ as suitable habitat is added to the landscape (Fig. 2.2). This occurs because the number of possible arrangements of the

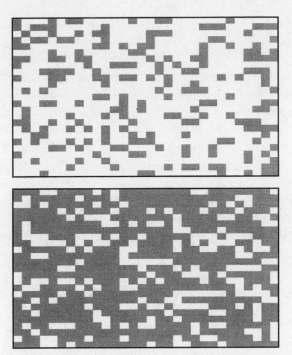

Figure 2.1 Neutral, random landscapes with 30 percent habitat cover *(top)* and 70 percent habitat cover
(bottom), indicated by gray pixels. See text for
description.

suitable habitat decreases as p increases, and new habitat parcels adjoin
existing patches. Such an abrupt, nonlinear change is called a threshold, and
such thresholds, if they exist in real landscapes, can have a profound effect
on *BIDE* and population persistence.

Percolation thresholds are an example of a threshold derived from neutral
landscape theory. The word *percolate* means "to trickle or filter through a
permeable substance." A landscape composed of two habitat types, suitable
and unsuitable, is said to percolate if an organism can successfully navigate
from its current location to a preferred destination point by traversing suitable habitat patches. Thus, if a hypothetical organism can navigate across the
heterogeneous landscape by moving only to adjacent, suitable patches, the
landscape percolates. In random landscapes, percolation theory suggests that
landscapes should percolate as long as there is about 58 percent cover (Gardner et al. 1987). This point is called a percolation threshold because the landscape is on the brink of being either connected or disconnected at this point.

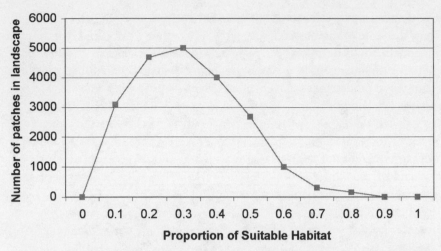

Figure 2.2 Number of patches in a landscape as a function of proportion of habitat available on the landscape. Note that the number of patches peaks when the landscape is composed of less than 40 percent habitat and that the function is nonlinear.

The percolation threshold varies depending on the landscape mosaic, the "permeability" of the matrix, and the dispersal ability of the species of interest (With et al. 1997).

Several predictions of landscape effects on $N_{t+1} = N_t + B + I - D - E$ can be made from integrating neutral landscape models with island biogeography models. These include the predictions that organisms can percolate (I and E) through suitable habitat and that thresholds in actual landscape metrics exist. If thresholds exist, island biogeography predictions about $BIDE$ should vary depending on whether the amount is above or below the threshold. Next, we will briefly review the empirical evidence that tests these predictions.

Empirical Evidence of Percolation

Because landscapes can be defined at any spatial scale, the study of percolation (or the movement of individuals from point A to destination point B) must be centered on the biology of the species of interest. For example, amphibians that breed in aquatic habitats but live most of their lives in terrestrial habitats must disperse from one habitat to another to carry out their life cycle (Dodd and Cade 1998). If amphibians do not cross unsuitable habitats, they must percolate across suitable habitats to carry out their life cycle. Thus, the scale of investigation depends on whether we are studying plants or animals, adults or immatures, males or females, or beetles or cougars. The ability of organisms to move across a landscape has been studied in three major ways: modeling (e.g., Tischendorf and Wissel 1997; With et al. 1999), experimental studies, and observations of the movement of organisms through critical habitat junctions called corridors (generally narrow patches of vegetation that differ from the surrounding vegetation matrix and connect larger patches of habitat) or across landscapes in general (reviewed in Tischendorf and Fahrig 2000). We will focus on the experimental and observational studies in the field.

For effective percolation to occur, organisms must be able to perceive the presence of suitable habitat and follow or track their preferred habitat type across the landscape. Such movements probably will affect N_{t+1} demographically or genetically, including the probability of extinction. On all counts, the literature suggests that these conditions are sometimes but not always supported.

First, with respect to the perception of suitable habitat, Zollner and Lima (1997) captured forest-dwelling mice (*Peromyscus leucopus*) and released them into an unfamiliar habitat in the surrounding matrix. They found that mice failed to orient toward forest habitat located within 10 m of the release point, emphasizing that perceptual abilities can dramatically affect the movements across a landscape. In contrast, during postfledging dispersal, white-crowned pigeons (*Columba leucocephala*) moved from offshore mangrove islands to the largest available patches of tropical forest without any previous experience with these feeding sites (Strong and Bancroft 1994). Thus the scale of habitat fragmentation, coupled with the scale at which an organism is able to perceive the distribution of resources, can dramatically affect how individuals move across landscapes (Bissonette et al. 1997; Wiens et al. 1997).

Second, many species do not track a preferred habitat type in their movements, affecting the threshold responses of organisms to landscape pattern. Experimental tests of percolation by necessity have focused on the dispersal of insects or small mammal across experimentally manipulated landscapes. For example, Wiens et al. (1997) experimentally studied the movements of tenebrionid beetles (*Eleodes obsolete*) in random landscapes (5 m²) consisting of grass (suitable) and bare ground (unsuitable) habitat. In each trial they released a beetle on bare ground near the center of the plot and then documented its movement pathway. They found that beetles moved through both grass and nongrass habitat in roughly the same way in all landscapes where a mix of habitat was present. Similarly, With et al. (1999) examined the movement behavior of crickets (*Acheta domestica*) in experimental neutral fractal landscapes consisting of grass and sand. Movement in general was not affected by the amount of habitat in the landscape; crickets tended to use grass for cover and, when in sand habitat, tended to move. However, arrangement of habitat was important; crickets in small isolated patches of grass were reluctant to move, suggesting that they not only preferred grass habitat but also perceived their isolation.

As with the experimental beetle and cricket studies, many observational studies focus on movement and orientation of individuals through heterogeneous landscapes. For example, Dodd and Cade (1998) found that striped newts (*Notophthalmus perstriatus*) and narrow-mouthed toads (*Gastrophryne carolinensis*) used only wider corridors to reach breeding pond sites and oriented their movements nonrandomly. In agricultural or heavily disturbed landscapes, corridors have been shown to be preferred for dispersal by birds (Haas 1995; Machtans et al. 1996) and mammals (Beier 1995). Schultz (1998) observed Fender's blue butterfly (*Icaricia icarioides fenderi*) flight patterns and documented butterfly use of both lupine (preferred habitat) and nonlupine habitat, although butterflies dispersed across nonlupine habitat much more rapidly than in lupine habitat. However, corridor use by butterflies appears to be species-specific and depends on the degree of habitat specialization and nature of the matrix habitat (Haddad 1999). Thus, it is clear from both experimental and observational studies that definitions of landscape connectivity depend on both the spatial pattern of the landscape and habitat use by individuals within and between patches, which in turn can determine the rate of movement through the mosaic as well as the residency time of the individuals within patches (see also Gustafson and Gardner 1996; Keitt et al. 1997).

Animals use patches and corridors to percolate across a landscape. From a conservation or management perspective, such movements are thought to affect population viability ($N_{t+1} > 0$) and population structure (Young and Clarke 2000). However, the majority of studies to date do not explicitly assess population viability but simply examine use of corridors at snapshot time intervals to answer questions such as Which species occur in corridors? What is the species richness? Does corridor width affect abundance and distribution? For example, Corbit et al. (1999) sampled richness and abundance of forest herbs in regenerated and remnant hedgerows, and Laurance and Laurance (1999) and Perault and Lomolino (2000) surveyed organisms in corridors that varied in width, height, isolation, elevation, and floristic composition. Such studies are important because they reveal clear patterns of occupancy, but usually they do not reveal the *BIDE* mechanisms that produced the patterns or show how the presence of corridors affects population persistence (Noss 1987; Simberloff and Cox 1987; Beier and Noss 1998).

The importance of connectivity in terms of *BIDE* and N_{t+1} has been poorly studied, perhaps because of the scale of landscape studies and the time needed to track individuals and populations over time. A few model studies are exemplary (e.g., Aars and Ims 1999; Ims and Andreassen 1999). For example, Ims's studies on root voles (*Microtus oeconomus*) demonstrate that connectivity is critical to maintaining population processes (*BIDE*) as well as the genetic structure in an experimentally fragmented ecosystem. Boudjemadi et al. (1999) also found that connectivity between patches affects dispersal patterns and has cascading effects on the reproductive rate, *B*. Thus, where experimental studies have been able to directly determine the effects of *I* and *E* on population dynamics, connectivity has been largely beneficial in promoting gene flow and enhancing persistence.

In summary, species use a variety of habitats. The ability of organisms to perceive preferred habitat and move through it depends on both the nature of the habitat matrix and the properties of the corridor itself. However, connectivity of a landscape does not necessarily mean that the landscape supports viable populations ($N_{t+1} > 0$; Boswell et al. 1998; With and King 1999a, 1999b), so the demographic and genetic population consequences of movements in landscapes must be emphasized in future research.

Evidence of Thresholds in Landscape Pattern and Threshold Effects on BIDE Population Parameters

A second major prediction from neutral landscape models is that real landscapes should exhibit thresholds in common metrics used to describe landscape composition (features associated with the presence and amount of each habitat patch type within the landscape, but without being spatially explicit) and structure (the physical distribution or spatial character of habitat patches and matrix within the landscape). Gardner et al. (1992) compared actual landscapes with real landscapes in Georgia and showed that although real landscapes deviate from random, very small shifts in disturbance regimes or changes in land use led to critical thresholds in landscape metrics and sudden changes in landscape pattern. As With and King (1997) pointed out, it is no surprise that real landscapes are not random aggregates of habitats. What is surprising is that they exhibit thresholds in metrics as predicted by neutral landscape theory.

If we can extrapolate from this result, the effects of landscape pattern on population processes (*BIDE*) should depend on whether the amount of total habitat in the landscape is above or below some threshold. Recall that island biogeography theory predicts that immigration (*I*) is a function of distance to mainland (source population), and that extinction (*B* < *D*) is a function of patch area. As the proportion of suitable habitat in a landscape decreases, habitat loss often is accompanied by fragmentation of the remaining habitat parcels. Thus, landscapes below the threshold habitat amount have smaller, more isolated patches than landscapes above the habitat threshold. Therefore, Andren (1994) hypothesized that there may be thresholds at which the effects of habitat isolation become more important than total habitat amount to local population dynamics. In the next section, we briefly review empirical studies that tested the hypothesis that thresholds of suitable habitat in the landscape affect distribution patterns, movements, and *BIDE* in organisms.

Threshold Effects on Abundance and Distribution Patterns

Studies of threshold effects on the distribution of organisms have been rapidly accumulating and generally examine how the configuration of habitats on the landscape under varying levels of total habitat affects animal distribution and abundance (e.g., Debinski et al. 2001). The work to date has focused on observational studies across landscapes that vary in several landscape metrics, and statistical methods are used to evaluate whether "amount" metrics such as percentage of cover explain distribution patterns better than "arrangement" metrics such as isolation. For example, McGarigal and McComb (1995) sampled birds in 30 landscapes in Oregon and developed measures of forest configuration (fragmentation) and forest amount that were statistically independent. They found that bird abundance among landscapes was related more strongly to changes in habitat area and that configuration was secondary. They found no evidence of threshold effects on vagile bird species (see also Bender et al. 1998). Villard et al. (1999) asked similar questions but specifically looked for thresholds in abundance and distribution in response to forest cover. They examined the distribution of forest birds in 33 landscapes in eastern Ontario that varied between 3.4 and 66.8 percent forest cover. After statistically controlling for the effects of total habitat amount, they found that both amount and configuration were important predictors of species occurrence. They did not find evidence of thresholds either.

Evidence of threshold effects on distribution come largely from large-scale studies or meta-analyses where regional differences in habitat cover vary widely. For instance, Rosenberg et al. (1999) studied the occurrence of scarlet tanagers (*Piranga olivacea*) across North America and found that sensitivity to fragmentation varied geographically and may be lower in regions with greater overall forest cover. Andren (1995) reviewed studies on birds and mammals in habitat patches in landscapes with different proportions of suitable habitat. He concluded that patch size and isolation are not important when landscapes consist of more than 30 percent habitat and that in landscapes with less than 30 percent habitat, patch size and isolation complement the effect of habitat loss so that the effect is greater than that of habitat loss alone. Therefore, the relative importance of pure habitat loss, patch size, and isolation is expected to differ at different degrees of habitat fragmentation (see also Schmiegelow et al. 1997; Drapeau et al. 2000).

Threshold Effects on Movements

Percolation theory suggests sharp thresholds in movement patterns as the amount of total habitat in the landscape changes. Experimental tests on random landscapes to date either do not provide evidence of thresholds (With et al. 1999) or show that thresholds occur at much lower amounts of total habitat than predicted by theory (Wiens et al. 1997). However, experimental landscapes that specifically examine how habitat amount and fragmentation affect movements reveal that the amount of habitat present exerts a greater influence on movement behaviors than did configuration and that habitat quantity exerted its strongest influence on movement behaviors when the habitat was sparse, regardless of the configuration (McIntyre and Wiens 1999). However (although not specifically testing for a threshold effect), Dunning et al. (1995) found that colonization of newly available habitat patches by Bachman's sparrows (*Aimophila aestivalis*) was more rapid in a landscape in which suitable habitat showed greater connectivity.

Threshold Effects on BIDE

Estimating the *BIDE* parameters for a population is tremendously labor intensive, and this effort is magnified when these parameters must be estimated across a variety of landscape types. Again, meta-analyses of the landscape context of locally conducted studies have been illuminating. For instance, predation rates on bird nests (sometimes considered a measure of B because they target the production of independent young) in habitat edges have been a topic of great interest from a management and conservation perspective (Paton 1994), but results of locally conducted studies have been mixed; some studies demonstrate an edge effect, but others do not. Donovan et al. (1997) tested the hypothesis that the effect of edge on nesting success depends on the landscape context in which the edge is embedded. They monitored predation rates on artificial nests in edge and core habitat in 36 randomly selected landscapes throughout the midwestern United States and documented that edge effects were present in landscapes with low and moderate amounts of forest cover but absent in forested landscapes. This experimental result was confirmed by meta-analyses of edge effect studies in North America (Hartley and Hunter 1998) and in Europe (Andren 1995). It is clear that a threshold in edge effects on nest success (a measure of B) exists between 50 and 70 percent forest cover.

Studies on B for individual species across different landscape patterns also suggest that thresholds exist. For instance, Driscoll (2001) studied the nest success of wood thrushes in edge and interior habitat across landscape types and generally concluded that edge effects depended on the amount of forest cover at the landscape scale. However, only two landscapes were evaluated (low and high forest coverage), and the nature of how predation rates on edge change in landscapes with intermediate forest coverage is still unclear.

Assessments of how dispersal rates (I and E) affect population dynamics also suggest that thresholds exist. In studies in which dispersal rates (I and E) were measured and the consequences of such movements were known, arrangement of patches appeared to be critical below a threshold amount of habitat in the landscape. For instance, interpatch movements in root voles decreased when patches were highly isolated (Andreassen and Ims 1998), subsequently affecting the demographic and genetic structure of the population. The investigators suggested that patch isolation may be the most influential aspect of habitat fragmentation on demography because of high predation suffered when dispersing between highly isolated patches.

Several models have predicted threshold effects on extinction risk in species ($N_{t+1} = 0$). For instance, Lande's (1987) classic model showed that habitat loss on the landscape may precipitate extinction thresholds in which the equilibrium fraction of suitable habitat occupied by the population crashes abruptly once the total habitat amount is reduced below some threshold level (see also Bascompte and Sole 1998). Other models illustrate that the amount of habitat in a landscape affects population distribution and persistence more than fragmentation and that fragmentation may be important only when the total habitat is reduced below some threshold value (Lande 1987; Hanski et al. 1996; Fahrig 1997; With and King 1999b).

Empirical evidence of the consequences of threshold effects on population persistence is beginning to accumulate. For instance, Groom (1998) documented that small patches of pink ribbons (*Clarkia concinna*) suffered reproductive failure caused by lack of effective pollination when critical thresholds of patch isolation were exceeded; large patches attracted pollinators regardless of their isolation. This study is perhaps the first documentation of a mechanism (lack of pollination) that promotes extinction on small and isolated patches. Burkey (1997) examined small-scale communities of bacteria and protozoa to quantify population viability in response to habitat loss and habitat fragmentation. Habitat loss reduced the time to extinction in isolated populations. Fragmented systems went extinct sooner than corresponding continuous systems of the same total habitat amount, regardless of the connectivity between fragments.

Threshold Effects on Community and Ecosystem Processes

The empirical data generally show that percolation thresholds have significant effects on demographic parameters. However, should we expect to see similar thresholds involving community interactions or ecological processes? Certainly, where tightly evolved mutualisms occur, thresholds in community interactions would be expected and have been supported through modeling studies (Anstett et al. 1997). In other instances, the loss of a keystone species may have significant effects on interactions across multiple trophic levels. In southern California, loss of coyotes (*Canis latrans*) from forest fragments has led to an increase in mesopredators (e.g., fox [*Vulpes vulpes*] and opossum [*Didelphis virginiana*]), which in turn negatively affect songbird diversity (Crooks and Soulé 1999). Although critical thresholds were not explicitly analyzed, coyote abundance was significantly correlated with fragment area. The army ant (*Eciton burchelli*) is also considered to be a keystone species as a result of its foraging habits and the myriad bird species that are obligate ant-followers. Boswell et al. (1998) used a parameterized patch occupancy model to show a critical percolation threshold at 45 percent habitat loss, with habitat amounts less than the critical threshold leading to extinction of the army ant. Consequently, bird communities that depend on this species for food probably would experience similar thresholds because their primary prey base would no longer be present.

Disturbance of ecosystem function may also show similar thresholds. Human access to forest fragments may show a nonlinear relationship with forest size, negatively affecting species persistence. In Amazon forests, for example, subsistence hunting exacerbates recolonization rates of midsized to large-bodied bird and mammal species in forest fragments such that species richness shows a significant threshold at fragment sizes between 5,000 and 10,000 ha, sizes much greater than these species' minimum area needs (Peres 2001). An additional concern is that the anthropogenic disturbances that affect threshold responses may not necessarily occur on site. Recent work in the Amazon basin suggests positive feedbacks between forest loss and regional rainfall, leading to increased fire frequency (Laurance and Williamson 2001). The drier microclimate of the fragmented landscape results in a nonlinear relationship between forest fragmentation and fire frequency, such that a critical threshold may exist below which rainforests cannot be maintained in areas with seasonal rainfall. Such thresholds may occur across a variety of ecosystems, such that small perturbations may lead to irreversible changes in ecosystem function (Scheffer et al. 2001).

Implications for Conservation

What implications can be drawn from the studies discussed? In 1997, With and King suggested that neutral landscape theory should shift from development to application and model testing. This has occurred, but experimental manipulations of landscapes have tended to focus on small organisms (beetles, ants, crickets, or voles) whose habitats (grass and sand) can be manipulated in a field or laboratory experiment. How likely is it that the rules generated from these studies can be applied to other taxa? It is apparent that the relationship $N_{t+1} = N_t + B + I - D - E$ has been assessed directly in relation to landscape structure for only a handful of species, often with mixed results, and that a guideline that can be used for management purposes has yet to emerge. Much exciting but difficult work remains to be done in the field.

As far as we know, the only application to date of percolation theory in a management context is the inclusion of a percolation-based analysis of habitat connectivity in the recovery plan for the Mexican spotted owl (U.S. Fish and Wildlife Service 1995). However, ecosystem- or landscape-scale management, by definition, means managing for a variety of species with unique habitat needs (see Chapter 4, this volume). Providing connectivity in one habitat type for a given species by definition will limit the connectivity for species that use different habitat types. Vos et al. (2001) recognized this problem and proposed a framework of ecologically scaled landscape indices. They developed ecological species profiles to group species according to characteristics that are important for persistence: minimum area needs and dispersal abilities. Average patch carrying capacity and average patch connectivity were then modeled to derive an overall viability threshold that can be used in landscape planning and nature conservation. Such approaches hold promise for implementing conservation plans on the ground but clearly depend on knowledge of how landscape patterns directly affect *BIDE* and persistence.

Thus, although predictions from island biogeography and neutral landscape theories provide a useful conceptual framework to address the effects of landscape fragmentation on *BIDE* parameters and population viability, how specific management or development actions will affect any species' population is a growing field of inquiry. However, the empirical studies that have documented threshold effects in landscape metrics and population parameters should serve as a red flag for both conservation biologists and regional planners. For example, large developments or road projects may not in themselves create extreme risks to population persistence(but see Forman et al. 2002). However, these disturbances often bring the necessary infrastructure for housing, agriculture, or other businesses. These associated losses of natural habitat will be less severe, but over time they may have cumulative effects that could lead to abrupt changes in the viability of wildlife populations. Consequently, fragmentation, isolation, and habitat loss should be addressed in long-term development plans that enable managers, planners, and biologists to consider wildlife populations in a comprehensive manner rather than guessing which new home might be the straw that breaks the camel's back.

Summary

Landscape ecology has emerged as a powerful conceptual framework that allows assessment of how the composition and spatial structure of a landscape mosaic affect ecological systems. However, our understanding of the effect of variations in landscape pattern on the dynamics of wildlife populations is still in its infancy. We generated a series of predictions using the MacArthur–Wilson equilibrium theory of island biogeography and neutral landscape and percolation theory to evaluate the ability of landscape ecology to address variation in birth, death, immigration, and emigration rates, as well as population persistence, and tested these predictions using published literature. Prerequisites for animals to effectively percolate across a landscape include perception and tracking of suitable habitat. Such movements are thought to affect the future size or genetic makeup of a population. Although these conditions were often met, we found surprisingly few tests of whether dispersal directly affects population genetics or viability. Neutral landscape theory predicts that as habitat is lost to development or disturbance, changes in landscape metrics will not be linear but will show abrupt thresholds. Do similar thresholds occur in wildlife population parameters as landscapes become more fragmented? Again, few studies have explicitly tested this prediction, although the literature is growing. In general, meta-analyses or studies conducted over large spatial scales tended to find thresholds in population parameters; more local studies often did not. The prediction that small incremental losses of habitat may lead to large changes in mortality rates or population viability has important conservation implications because habitat loss in more developed areas often proceeds by the hectare rather than by the square kilometer.

Acknowledgments

We thank Peter Jones and John Bissonette for their critical reviews of the manuscript. The Vermont Cooperative Fish and Wildlife Research Unit is jointly supported by the U.S. Geological Survey, the Vermont Department of Fish and Wildlife, the University of Vermont, and the Wildlife Management Institute.

LITERATURE CITED

Aars, J., and R. A. Ims. 1999. The effect of habitat corridors on rates of transfer and interbreeding between vole demes. Ecology 80:1648–1655.

Andreassen, H. P., and R. A. Ims. 1998. The effects of experimental habitat destruction and patch isolation on space use and fitness parameters in female root *Microtus oeconomus*. Journal of Animal Ecology 67:941–952.

Andren, H. 1994. Effects of habitat fragmentation on birds and mammals in landscapes with different proportions of suitable habitat: a review. Oikos 71:355–366.

Andren, H. 1995. Effects of landscape composition on predation rates at habitat edges. Pages 225–255 in L. Hansson, L. Fahrig, and G. Merriam (eds.), Mosaic landscapes and ecological processes. Chapman & Hall, London.

Anstett, M.-C., M. Hossaert-McKey, and D. McKey. 1997. Modeling the persistence of small populations of strongly interdependent species: figs and fig wasps. Conservation Biology 11:204–213.

Bascompte, J., and R. V. Sole. 1998. Spatiotemporal patterns in nature. Trends in Ecology and Evolution 13:173–174.

Beier, P. 1995. Dispersal of juvenile cougars in fragmented habitat. Journal of Wildlife Management 59:228–237.

Beier, P., and R. F. Noss. 1998. Do habitat corridors provide connectivity? Conservation Biology 12:1241–1252.

Bender, D. J., T. A. Contreras, and L. Fahrig. 1998. Habitat loss and population decline: a meta-analysis of the patch size effect. Ecology 79:517–533.

Bissonette, J. A., D. J. Harrison, C. D. Hargis, and T. G. Chapin. 1997. The influence of spatial scale and scale-sensitive properties on habitat selection by American marten. Pages 368–385 in J. A. Bissonette (ed.), Wildlife and landscape ecology. Springer-Verlag, New York.

Boswell, G. P., N. F. Britton, and N. R. Franks. 1998. Habitat fragmentation, percolation theory and the conservation of a keystone species. Proceedings of the Royal Society of London Series B, Biological Sciences 26:1921–1925.

Boudjemadi, K, J. Lecomte, and J. Clobert. 1999. Influence of connectivity on demography and dispersal in two contrasting habitats: an experimental approach. Journal of Animal Ecology 68:1207–1224.

Brown, J. H., and A. Kodric-Brown. 1977. Turnover rates in insular biogeography: effect of immigration on extinction. Ecology 58:445–449.

Burkey, T. V. 1997. Metapopulation extinction in fragmented landscapes: using bacteria and protozoa communities as model ecosystems. American Naturalist 150:568–591.

Corbit, M., P. L. Marks, and S. Gardescu. 1999. Hedgerows as habitat corridors for forest herbs in central New York, USA. Journal of Ecology 87:220–232.

Crooks, K. R., and M. E. Soulé. 1999. Mesopredator release and avifaunal extinctions in a fragmented system. Nature 400:563–566.

Debinski, D. M., C. Ray, and E. H. Saveraid. 2001. Species diversity and the scale of the landscape mosaic: do scales of movement and patch size affect diversity? Biological Conservation 98:179–190.

Dodd, K. C., and B. S. Cade. 1998. Movement patterns and the conservation of amphibians breeding in small, temporary wetlands. Conservation Biology 12:331–339.

Donovan, T. M., P. W. Jones, E. M. Annand, and F. R. Thompson, III. 1997. Variation in local-scale edge effects: mechanisms and landscape context. Ecology 78:2064–2075.

Drapeau, P., A. Leduc, J.-G. Giroux, L. Savard, Y. Bergeron, and W. L. Vickery. 2000. Landscape-scale disturbances and changes in bird communities of boreal mixed-wood forests. Ecological Monographs 70:423–444.

Driscoll, M. L. 2001. Nesting success of wood thrushes in edge in various landscapes. M.S. thesis, State University of New York, Syracuse.

Dunning, J. B., Jr., R. Borgella, Jr., K. Clements, and G. K. Meffe. 1995. Patch isolation, corridor effects, and colonization by a resident sparrow in a managed pine woodland. Conservation Biology 9:542–550.

Fahrig, L. 1997. Relative effects of habitat loss and fragmentation on population extinction. Journal of Wildlife Management 61:603–610.

Fisher, R. A. 1930. The genetical theory of natural selection. Clarendon Press, Oxford, UK.

Forman, R. T. T., and M. Godron. 1986. Landscape ecology. Wiley, New York.

Forman, R. T. T., D. Sperling, J. A. Bissonette, A. P. Clevenger, C. D. Cutshall, V. H. Dale, L. Fahrig, R. France, C. R. Goldman, K. Heanue, J. A. Jones, F. J. Swanson, T. Turrentine, and T. C. Winter. 2002. Road ecology: science and solutions. Island Press, Washington, DC.

Gardner, R. H., B. T. Milne, M. G. Turner, and R. V. O'Neill. 1987. Neutral models for the analysis of broad-scale landscape pattern. Landscape Ecology 1:5–18.

Gardner, R. H., M. G. Turner, R. V. O'Neill, and S. Lavorel. 1992. Simulation of the scale-dependent effects of landscape boundaries on species persistence and dispersal. Pages 76–89 in M. M. Holland, P. G. Risser, and R. J. Naiman (eds.), The role of landscape boundaries in the management and restoration of changing environments. Chapman & Hall, New York.

Gotelli, N. J., and G. R. Graves. 1996. Null models in ecology. Smithsonian Institution Press, Washington, DC.

Groom, M. J. 1998. Allee effects limit population viability of an annual plant. American Naturalist 151:487–496.

Gustafson, E. J., and R. H. Gardner. 1996. The effect of landscape heterogeneity on the probability of patch colonization. Ecology 77:94–107.

Haas, C. A. 1995. Dispersal and use of corridors by birds in wooded patches on an agricultural landscape. Conservation Biology 9:845–854.

Haddad, N. M. 1999. Corridor use predicted from behaviors at habitat boundaries. American Naturalist 153:215–227.

Hanski, I., and M. Gilpin. 1991. Metapopulation dynamics: brief history and conceptual domain. Biological Journal of the Linnaean Society 42:3–16.

Hanski, I., and M. Gilpin. 1997. Metapopulation biology. Academic Press, New York.

Hanski, I., A. Moilanen, and M. Gyllenberg. 1996. Minimum viable metapopulation size. American Naturalist 147:527–541.

Hartley, M. J., and M. L. Hunter. 1998. A meta-analysis of forest cover, edge effects, and artificial nest predation rates. Conservation Biology 12:465–469.

Hobbs, R. J. 1996. Future landscapes and the future of landscape ecology. Landscape and Urban Planning 37:1–9.

Hobbs, R. J. 1999. Clark Kent or Superman? Where is the phone booth for landscape ecology? Pages 11–23 in J. M. Klopatek and R. H. Gardener (eds.), Landscape ecological analysis. Springer-Verlag, New York.

Ims, R. A., and H. P. Andreassen. 1999. Effects of experimental habitat fragmentation and connectivity on root vole demography. Journal of Animal Ecology 68:839–852.

Keitt, T. H., D. L. Urban, and B. T. Milne. 1997. Detecting critical scales in fragmented landscapes. Conservation Ecology 1:4 (online at http://ns2.resalliance. org/pub/www/Journal/vol1/iss1/art4/).

Lande, R. 1987. Extinction thresholds in demographic models of territorial populations. American Naturalist 130:624–635.

Laurance, S. G., and W. F. Laurance. 1999. Tropical wildlife corridors: use of linear rainforest remnants by arboreal mammals. Biological Conservation 91:231–239.

Laurance, W. F., and G. B. Williamson. 2001. Positive feedbacks among forest fragmentation, drought, and climate change in the Amazon. Conservation Biology 15:1529–1535.

MacArthur, R. H., and E. O. Wilson. 1967. The theory of island biogeography. Princeton University Press, Princeton, NJ.

Machtans, C. S., M.-A. Villard, and S. J. Hannon. 1996. Use of riparian buffer strips as movement corridors by forest birds. Conservation Biology 10:1366–1379.

McCullough, D. R. 1996. Metapopulations and wildlife conservation. Island Press, Washington, DC.

McGarigal, K., and W. C. McComb. 1995. Relationships between landscape structure and breeding birds in the Oregon Coast Range. Ecological Monographs 65:235–260.

McIntyre, N. E., and J. A. Wiens. 1999. Interactions between habitat abundance and configuration: experimental validation of some predictions from percolation theory. Oikos 86:129–137.

Noss, R. F. 1987. Corridors in real landscapes: a reply to Simberloff and Cox. Conservation Biology 1:159–164.

Paton, P. 1994. The effect of edge on avian nest success: how strong is the evidence? Conservation Biology 8:17–26.

Perault, D. R., and M. V. Lomolino. 2000. Corridors and mammal community structure across a fragmented, old-growth forest landscape. Ecological Monographs 70:401–422.

Peres, C. A. 2001. Synergistic effects of subsistence hunting and habitat fragmentation on Amazonian forest vertebrates. Conservation Biology 15:1490–1505.

Pickett, S. T. A., and M. L. Cadenasso. 1995. Landscape ecology: spatial heterogeneity in ecological systems. Science 269:331–334.

Pulliam, H. R. 1988. Sources, sinks, and population regulation. American Naturalist 132:652–661.

Rosenberg, K. V., J. D. Lowe, A. A. Dhondt. 1999. Effects of forest fragmentation on breeding tanagers: a continental perspective. Conservation Biology 13:568–583.

Scheffer, M., S. Carpenter, J. A. Foley, C. Folke, and B. Walker. 2001. Catastrophic shifts in ecosystems. Nature 413:591–596.

Schmiegelow, F. K., C. S. Machtans, and S. J. Hannon. 1997. Are boreal birds resilient to forest fragmentation? An experimental study of short-term community responses. Ecology 78:1914–1932.

Schultz, C. B. 1998. Dispersal behavior and its implications for reserve design in a rare Oregon butterfly. Conservation Biology 12:284–292.

Simberloff, D., and J. Cox. 1987. Consequences and costs of conservation corridors. Conservation Biology 1:62–71.

Slatkin, M. 1985. Gene flow in natural populations. Annual Review of Ecology and Systematics 16:393–430.

Strong, A. M., and G. T. Bancroft. 1994. Postfledgling dispersal of white-crowned pigeons: implications for conservation of deciduous seasonal forests in the Florida Keys. Conservation Biology 8:770–779.

Tischendorf, L., and L. Fahrig. 2000. On the usage and measurement of landscape connectivity. Oikos 90:7–19.

Tischendorf, L., and C. Wissel. 1997. Corridors as conduits for small animals: attainable distances depending on movement pattern, boundary reaction and corridor width. Oikos 79:603–611.

Turner, M .G. 1989. Landscape ecology: the effect of pattern on process. Annual Review of Ecology and Systematics 20:171–197.

Urban, D. L., R. V. O'Neill, and H. H. Shugart. 1987. Landscape ecology. BioScience 37:119–127.

U.S. Fish and Wildlife Service. 1995. Recovery plan for the Mexican spotted owl, Vol. 1. USFWS, Albuquerque, NM.

Villard, M. A., M. K. Trzcinski, and G. Merriam. 1999. Fragmentation effects on forest birds: relative influence of woodland cover and configuration on landscape occupancy. Conservation Biology 13:774–783.

Vos, C. C., J. Verboom, P. F. Opdam, and C. J. F. ter Braak. 2001. Toward ecologically scaled landscape indices. American Naturalist 157:24–41.

Wiens, J. A. 1992. What is landscape ecology, really? Landscape Ecology 7:149–150.

Wiens, J. A. 1997. Metapopulation dynamics and landscape ecology. Pages 43–62 in I. Hanski and M. E. Gilpin (eds.), Metapopulation biology: ecology, genetics, and evolution. Academic Press, New York.

Wiens, J. A., R. L. Schooley, and R. D. Weeks, Jr. 1997. Patchy landscapes and animal movements: do beetles percolate? Oikos 78:257–264.

With, K. A., and A. W. King. 1997. The use and misuse of neutral landscape models in ecology. Oikos 97:219–229.

With, K. A., and A. W. King. 1999a. Dispersal success on fractal landscapes: a consequence of lacunarity thresholds. Landscape Ecology 14:73–82.

With, K. A., and A. W. King. 1999b. Extinction thresholds for species in fractal landscapes. Conservation Biology 13:314–326.

With, K. A., R. H. Gardner, and M. G. Turner. 1997. Landscape connectivity and population distributions in heterogeneous environments. Oikos 78:151–169.

With, K. A., S. J. Cadaret, and C. Davis. 1999. Movement responses to patch structure in experimental fractal landscapes. Ecology 14:73–82.

Wright, S. 1931. Evolution of Mendelian populations. Genetics 16:97–159.

Young, A. G., and G. M. Clarke. 2000. Genetics, demography and viability of fragmented populations. Cambridge University Press, Cambridge, UK.

Zollner, P. A., and S. L. Lima. 1997. Landscape-level perceptual abilities in white-footed mice: perceptual range and the detection of forested habitat. Oikos 80:51–60.

CHAPTER THREE

The Rest of the Story

Linking Top-Down Effects to Organisms

JAMES G. SANDERSON AND LARRY D. HARRIS

We suggest that scientists study ecosystem and landscape processes in fundamentally different ways. Others have agreed (Naiman 1988; Naiman et al. 1988; Hansson and Angelstam 1991; Harris 1992; Golley 1993; Jones et al. 1994; Johnston 1995; Harris et al. 1996; Sanderson and Harris 1999). Discussions of *ecosystem* studies often involve phrases such as "ion flows in watersheds" or "plant sequestration of carbon." The study of ecosystem processes such as those that move nutrients from soil to roots to leaves can, in principle, take place on areas no bigger than a pinhead. Time and space are rarely independent variables in ecosystem studies, even in watersheds. In contrast, a *landscape* generally has a large areal extent, so processes acting on landscapes are studied on three-dimensional surfaces and therefore clearly depend on time, which is nearly always an independent variable. Anyone who has visited a national park would agree that although a rotting log might be an ecosystem, it hardly qualifies as a landscape. Moreover, results obtained from studying organisms navigating 1 m^2 plots cannot be scaled to predict the effects of the once great herds of bison on the shortgrass prairies. Indeed, the study of the effects of bison, beavers, and many other ecosystem engineers on landscapes should fall under the science of landscape ecology. Therefore, we want to remove the burden of understanding nature across space and through time by scaling up ecosystem results and instead place such studies under the purview of the science of landscape ecology. Each discipline has made important contributions and is supported by fundamentally different theory.

Traditional Ecosystem Studies: The Story We Know

Theories developed to support studies of ecosystems are different from those that form a basis for studies of the ecology of landscapes. For instance, Lindeman (1942), after his fieldwork on small Cedar Bog Lake near the University of Minnesota, deduced that the lake was an entity called an ecosystem that could be described as a network of processes or interactions within groups of subentities called organisms, linked by the process of feeding and contained within the ecosystem. Lindeman described the interaction between the biotic and abiotic entities of the lake envisioned earlier by Forbes (1887) and others. The lake ecosystem through its constituent subentities took in energy from the sun and nutrients and recycled them into insects and food for terrestrial animals.

Lindeman's theory asserted that nature was organized into ecological systems that were recognizable objects (e.g., lakes) that had an origin and development leading to a steady state or dynamic equilibrium. Lindeman asserted that these systems had a structure defined as a network of feeding relationships between their species' populations that could be simplified by grouping the populations into food chains or trophic levels. An ecosystem process, beyond development through time, was that energy received from the sun went into heat and work to process chemical elements. Lindeman expressed the structure and function of the ecosystem mathematically as a series of equations describing the interactions between system components. For instance, Lindeman claimed that the ratio of transfer up the food pyramid varied from 10 to 22.3 percent depending on the trophic level. Seven years after Tansley's (1935) definition of an ecosystem, Lindeman provided an example and stated a theory that enabled testing of hypotheses and thereby defined a program that occupied ecologists for the next 40 years (Golley 1993). Such was the power of Lindeman's trophic dynamic theory.

Lindeman's trophic dynamic theory addressed trophic interactions within a bog lake ecosystem that was at equilibrium, a steady state system (thus eliminating the time variable), and spatially homogeneous (thus eliminating the space variable). The lake was necessarily an open system connected to the landscape by natural atmospheric processes and mammals, birds, insects, and other organisms that used the lake, but this did not concern Lindeman. Suppose for the moment that we could change the context of the lake from an open system to a partially closed system. That is, suppose we could build a wall around the lake and put a net over the lake to prevent living organisms and detritus from either entering or leaving the system. Sunlight, precipitation, and respiration would be unaffected. This would be equivalent to Lindeman's approach. His ecosystem theory dealt with the *contents* of a lake assumed to be homogeneous and at equilibrium. However, a landscape ecologist must also deal with the *context* of the lake. From a landscape perspective the first fundamental question might be, Is context important? The pertinent question here is that if the bog lake were isolated from its contextual setting, the trophic system would be altered measurably. Clearly the answer is yes; context is important. Herein lies the essence of the difference between ecosystem and landscape ecology. Landscapes evolve in space and time; understanding spatial heterogeneity and changes through time is vital. Ecosystems are homogeneous, and time is often omitted or of short duration.

Landscape Ecological Studies: Effects of Pattern on Process

A landscape, Forman (1982) claimed, consisted of a matrix of patches perhaps linked by corridors. To maintain biological diversity in Forman's landscape, Noss (1983) advocated a regional landscape approach that considered regional biogeography and dynamic landscape patterns. A regional network of preserves, with highly sensitive habitats insulated from human influences, might best preserve landscape processes, Noss suggested. Noss and Harris (1986) urged conservationists to think in terms of preserving ecological phenomena that functioned in space as well as in time. They argued that multiple-use modules (MUMs) integrating areas of high ecological value in human-dominated landscapes were necessary for preserving biological diversity at all scales. For wide-ranging species, MUMs had to be implemented on a landscape incorporating humans to reconcile species management and ecosystem conservation concerns. They proposed that a large tract of land on the Georgia–Florida border connecting Okefenokee Swamp, Georgia, with Osceola National Forest, Florida, be acquired as a demonstration that MUMs actually work on the regional landscape. This tract of land was eventually purchased by the State of Florida and set aside as a state preserve, thus creating a regional network of reserves across state boundaries.

Habitat diversity in space is critical to species with limited ranges. Wilcox and Murphy (1985, p. 884) used the checkerspot butterfly, whose populations were monitored for at least 25 years, to explore the effects of local habitat fragmentation and its conservation consequences for endangered species. Using arguments similar to those made earlier by Birch (1957), Wilcox and Murphy suggested that microhabitat conditions influenced survival and that only heterogeneous microhabitats could sustain the populations in time. Wilcox and Murphy concluded that "habitat fragmentation is the most serious threat to biological diversity and is the primary cause of the present extinction crisis." Habitat fragmentation and destruction are far more insidious than even Wilcox and Murphy suggested. Fragmentation causes insularization and dismemberment of ecosystem processes such as fire. For instance, roads act as barriers to fires. Fragmentation also thwarts dispersal and movement of some species, lessening recolonization possibilities. Some species are reluctant to move from one fragment to another across an inhospitable matrix. Fragmentation also increases the ability of invasive generalist and weedy species to penetrate further into the interior of isolated habitats.

Janzen (1986) reiterated his theme (Chapter 12, this volume) that continental parks and reserves are not islands surrounded by a neutral sea. Reserves suffered cross-boundary subsidies of weedy species, waterways often contained pesticides, natural fire regimes were disrupted, and even the local climate could be modified. He elaborated on negative edge effects but went further, suggesting that exotic seeds transported by vertebrates could take root 5 km or more within a reserve, thus extending edge effects. Janzen concluded that understanding the natural history of the organisms within a protected area was crucial for their perpetuation. Although studies of the natural history of organisms became passé, more than a decade later Paine (2000) recognized the need for such studies.

As the new science of landscape ecology gained acceptance, a working paradigm or conceptual framework was needed. Urban et al. (1987, p. 120) suggested in their classic article that pattern was the hallmark of a landscape. Moreover, "component events and patches occur at characteristic scales that are positively correlated in space and time." That is, events that took place over longer time periods affected greater areas than events that took place over shorter time periods. For instance, landslides occur quickly and have local effects, whereas plate tectonics take place over long time periods and affect organisms on all continents. Such spatial- versus temporal-scale graphs became a mainstay in the ecological literature. The authors offered a hierarchical system to organize the analysis of landscape patterns. Humans were capable of rescaling patterns in time and space by suppressing natural fires or by creating edges, for example. Such activities led to alteration of landscape patterns because they were cumulative. Whereas Forman proposed a patch–matrix–corridor paradigm, the Urban et al. paradigm for landscape ecology, hierarchy theory, decomposed landscape processes operating at different scales and frequencies and organized them according to their functional roles.

That landforms affect ecosystem patterns and processes seems obvious to even the most casual observer. Rain shadow deserts are an example of the effects of landforms on the biota. Ancient peoples probably understood as well as we do that animal migrations over landscapes were tied to temporal resource availability. Nevertheless, for the science of landscape ecology to develop these effects entailed description, classification, and quantification. Swanson et al. (1988) offered such a classification at the scale of the landscape. Landscapes, they suggested, consisted of landforms and their ecological units. Thus the study of the effect of landforms (land shapes) on ecosystem processes was a necessary first step in studying landscape effects on ecosystem processes.

Heterogeneity in Space and Time

After MacArthur and Wilson (1967) proposed the theory of island biogeography, ecologists applied its conclusions to islands as well as fragmented continental habitats. The mid-1970s saw debates on reserve design (single large versus several small, or SLOSS) emerging in biodiversity conservation (Diamond 1975; Simberloff and Abele 1976; Terborgh 1976). The shifting pattern of population changes in 16 species of ciconiiform wading birds in Everglades National Park, Kushlan (1979) argued, indicated that the application of island biogeographic theory to the design and management of continental wildlife reserves warranted more consideration. Isolating a continental reserve could lead to ecosystem degeneration whose extent and rapidity depended on the ecological condition of *adjacent* habitats. Thus Kushlan recognized that the contents of a protected area could be negatively affected by the area's context. Conflicts between species management and ecosystem management illustrated the need for a regional basis for preservation.

Kushlan (1979) realized that size alone was an inadequate measure of the effectiveness of a reserve. Everglades National Park was 5,670 km^2; the park was bounded by Big Cypress National Preserve of 2,370 km^2 and three water conservation areas totaling 3,490 km^2, making the total protected area about 12,000 km^2. The importance of environmental heterogeneity and maintenance of the reserve's functional characteristics (e.g., the timing of changes in water levels beyond the park boundary) were of profound importance. Spatial isolation from the buffering of contiguous habitats resulted in quantitative and qualitative alteration of the functional relations within the reserve that led to environmental degradation and the decline in wading bird populations. Because local extirpations might occur in highly specialized species, Kushlan recommended a regional approach to biodiversity management and perpetuation that would permit recolonization from refugia when conditions changed. Environmental heterogeneity at the landscape scale was critical to maintaining biodiversity, especially in managed landscapes.

Edges and Patches

The line or disjuncture created by convergence of different landforms or landscape subsystems arguably is one of the most important features of any landscape (Harris 1988a). Not only is this the zone where ecological tension (hence ecotone) or interaction is greatest, but in some cases it is so notable as to demand recognition, study, and conservation in its own right (Shelford 1913, 1963; Holland et al. 1991). Indeed, in the North American Southeast, a galaxy of species occurs only along the edge of specific subsystems or in ecotones. Early naturalists in Florida often commented on the sharpness of the edges between naturally occurring vegetation community types despite the fact that it would take decades to determine the causal mechanisms such as interaction effects between processes (e.g., flood, fire, and frost). Although Hansson (1994) was correct in reaffirming that eurytopic species commonly dominate edges in modern landscapes, one cannot overlook the myriad species and processes that occur only at these zones on the landscape (e.g., estuaries). When viewed in their full four-dimensional function these "hard" edges function as faces that capture auxiliary energy such as wind and horizontal radiation as well as transferring information that almost always flows from the less complex system (e.g., an open field) into the more complex system (e.g., a forest) via mechanisms ranging from the foraging of large mammals (elephants) to sallying forager birds such as eastern bluebirds (Margalef 1968).

Woodroffe and Ginsberg (1998) reported that 10 species of wide-ranging carnivores were more likely to disappear from protected areas regardless of their population size because they came into contact with people along reserve edges more frequently. The study of *Oncifelis guigna*, a small forest cat, by Sanderson et al. (2002) suggested that male carnivores were more likely than females to suffer human-caused conflicts. Males traveled between females and therefore invariably came into contact with humans, pets, and domestic fowl. Males more frequently crossed roads, thus risking exposure to domestic dogs. Inevitably, males were more tempted to take domestic free-ranging fowl that females avoided. During the study, local residents killed two adult male guignas for eating chickens.

Edges and patches also affect the quality of movement corridors. Edges invite invasive species, and nearby unfavorable habitats negatively influence corridors. Gascon et al. (2000) showed that processes acting along edges continued to negatively affect forests long after edge creation. Wind speeds and light penetration were greater along edges and caused microclimate changes. Exotic species often found footholds in edge habitats. Management of surrounding areas influenced fire frequency within the forest, thus altering forest composition. Use of agricultural chemicals also negatively affected the remaining forest and its inhabitants (Forman 1995).

Corridors

Fahrig and Merriam (1985) and Merriam (1991) discussed the role of corridors in patchy habitats in the demographics of small rodents and outlined three effects of interpatch dispersal. First, interpatch movement enhanced metapopulation survival. Second, interpatch dispersal supplemented population growth in certain instances. Third, patches where extinction occurred were recolonized. The greater the connectivity between patches, the more likely the metapopulation was to persist. Merriam (1991) concluded that connectivity was critical to species' long-term survival.

But what constitutes connectivity? Species-specific behavior determined whether suitable corridors and landscape connectivity existed. Thus Merriam (1991) noted that the assessment of connectivity must come from species-specific empirical studies. That is, looking at a highly detailed vegetation cover map and quantifying habitat simply was not good enough to determine whether landscape connectivity existed for the mobile species considered. Species-specific movement behavior must be known. Learned behaviors related to food and habitat selection influence species-specific behaviors (Chapter 17, this volume).

External Impacts

A hurricane is a natural process that acts episodically. During hurricane season, the probability of an isolated fragment of beach being visited by a hurricane is near zero. However, given a long enough period of time the isolated beach will eventually be affected. The probability of complete destruction is small, but given enough time, disaster will occur. Hurricanes, acid rain, and meteorite impacts are examples of processes that originate elsewhere and then travel stochastically, affecting landscapes in their path.

Obviously, an isolated coastal habitat will not be sufficient to protect the Florida beach mouse from extinction, no matter how many habitat conservation plans are written. The probability of a catastrophic disturbance over time is too high. Thus many isolated coastal habitat patches are necessary to protect the Florida beach mouse. Similarly, seemingly random events such as floods, earthquakes, or landslides that occur with certainty, given enough time, are considered disasters by humans. Even though we anticipate such events, we apparently are unable to plan for them. Therefore, such events are usually not incorporated into conservation planning.

In our view, by the early 1990s half of the science of landscape ecology, the study of *landscape effects,* was well established and sufficiently differentiated ecosystem science from landscape ecology. However, the top-down effects exerted by mobile organisms and stochastic physical events such as volcanic eruptions on maintaining or creating landscape patterns had attracted little attention. Studies by Naiman (1988) and random eruptions of volcanoes had not yet sparked more investigations.

The Rest of the Story: Top-Down Effects of Organisms and Stochastic Events

That the state of Florida is one of a very few geographic areas from whence the global supply of phosphate mineral is mined and exported is a nontrivial twenty-first-century landscape management issue. This massive phosphate resource represents the composted bodies and lives of terakilos of marine animals that concentrated at this spot on Earth when the present-day peninsula lay beneath the sea. Although the concentration of phosphate occurred through geologic time, it represents an important challenge for landscape managers for the foreseeable future. Guano birds feeding from the Humboldt Current and depositing their daily excrement over several millennia is an equally significant demonstration of the top-down effects that seemingly trivial animals can have on their environment (Coker 1919; Caviedes 2001). But these phenomena are almost as difficult for students to fathom as is the nature of the universe. Perhaps an intermediate example will bring the point closer to home. Nationally renowned ornithologists and conservationists recorded the vast numbers of passenger pigeons, bison, and wading birds of south Florida before settlement by Europeans. A sound and responsible number of 2.5 million wading birds existing in the Everglades region before 1900 was reported by Robertson and deducible from the writings of many others. Nutrient transfer analysis of these birds was analyzed and presented by Harris (1988b). He calculated that 2.5 million wading birds (of a dozen species) scavenged about 400 metric tons of nutrients from the regional land-scape per year and redeposited them beneath roosting and nesting colonies annually. Therefore, fully 40,000 metric tons of nutrients would have been moved and concentrated by the wading birds in the last century had they not been absent. Tree islands that support roosting and nesting bird colonies have higher productivity and regional conservation value than forest islands that do not. The regional forest of south Florida is rapidly disappearing, and most of the tree islands of the Everglades landscape are in serious trouble from regional-level mismanagement. A principal challenge of the present Everglades restoration efforts must certainly focus on the critical roles that wading birds, alligators, and other wildlife unique to the biotic province pre-viously played and should once again play in the twenty-first century.

Important themes in ecological research began to converge in 1994. The recognition that organisms were important contributors to landscape cre-ation and maintenance was gaining appreciation. Furthermore, threatened and endangered species lists were growing in length, demonstrating that whatever conservation biologists were doing wasn't working.

Jones et al. (1994) came right to the point in their opening paragraph:

> Conspicuously lacking from the list of key processes in most text books is the role that many organisms play in the creation, modification and maintenance of habitats. . . . Population and community ecology have neither defined nor systematically identified and studied the role of organisms in the creation and maintenance of habitats.

They coined the term *ecosystem engineers* to describe organisms such as beavers that perform ecosystem engineering. They used the terms *allogenic* and *autogenic engineers,* terms similar to those used by Tansley nearly 50 years previously, and gave examples of each. Weather apparently was not the only factor determining where species could survive. They compared and contrasted keystone species with ecosystem engineers. Moreover, Jones et al. (1994) made clear that many keystone species were also ecosystem engineers even though they might play minor roles in community food webs.

Holling (1992) suggested that all terrestrial ecosystems were structured by a small number of species. Jones et al. concluded that keystone engineers occurred in almost all habitats on Earth, not just terrestrial systems. This bases the case for the preservation of many more species on firm ecological grounds. Furthermore, if the impacts to the environment made by the engineer ultimately affect the engineer's fitness, the evolutionary significance becomes clear.

Animals acting as ecosystem engineers or as keystone species influence ecosystem processes. Elephants push over trees to strip bark and thus convert forest to savanna. Mound-building ants carry subsoil to the surface. Johnston (1995) suggested that most natural history studies of species ignored the consequences (but not the activities) of organisms on the landscape. For instance, wide-ranging carnivores influenced herbivore populations on landscapes. Herbivores influenced vegetation patterns and also soil formation, particularly in North American prairies. Therefore, the top-down effects of organisms on ecosystem processes should be included in any emerging paradigm of landscape ecology. Environmental modification by animals has previously been studied quantitatively, especially by Russian ecologists (Zlotin and Khodashova 1980). The role of heterotrophs in determining ecosystem processes and the functioning of natural systems was the subject of an eight-year (1963–1970) investigation.

Mobile Organisms and Stochastic Events Maintain Biodiversity and Connect Ecosystems

Willson et al. (1998) explained how aquatic and nearby terrestrial systems are intimately connected by resource transport achieved by mobile organisms. They suggested that anadromous and inshore-spawning marine fish that provided a rich, seasonal food resource affected the biology of both aquatic and terrestrial consumers and indirectly affected the entire food web that tied water to land. They called the fish a cornerstone species because of the disproportionate resource they provided to the coastal water–land ecotone. Marine-derived nutrients passed from the fish to birds of prey and terrestrial carnivores such as bears into the soil via invertebrates and then into plants. With the large reduction of many fish species caused by anthropogenic activities, top predators disappeared. Without the transport of seeds and nutrients from dung, reductions in vegetation occurred, in turn providing less insect prey for young fish.

East African elephants can destroy patches of forest in a few hours and so can be classified as ecosystem engineers. When populations are large, habitat damage can be extensive. When large mammalian herbivores were excluded for 24 years from a grassland plot in Uganda, soil nutrients increased dramatically, litter accumulated, and trees regenerated (Hatton and Smart 1984). For two years McNaughton et al. (1997) studied nitrogen (N) and sodium (Na) recycling by nonmigratory grazing herbivores in Serengeti National Park, Tanzania. They concluded that terrestrial grazers modified ecosystem processes in ways that alleviated nutritional deficiencies. This study also showed that accelerated nutrient cycling was an important property of habitats critical to large mammal conservation. Paine (2000) cited these and other examples to support the argument that grazing mammals could dominate the vegetation, change soil nutrients, and change trajectories of grasslands and forests alike. Indeed, Paine suggested that substantial evidence existed for top-down influences and possibly control by mammalian herbivores, thus bringing into agreement a generalized structure of intertrophic level interactions to both aquatic and terrestrial communities. There can be little doubt that predators acting to structure herbivore communities thus influence vegetation communities.

Wolves are an archetypal keystone species that spatially structure herbivore populations and are wide-ranging and hence capable of moving through poor habitat to settle in more favorable habitat. Reserve boundaries will not contain wolves, so human–wolf interactions will occur. Mladenoff et al. (1997) found that wolves exerted top-down control in forest food chains and had to be managed as a part of the regional landscape. Where ungulate prey were adequate and where wolves were not killed, wolves could occupy semiwild lands formerly thought to be unsuitable. Current landscapes in the United States being recolonized by wolves were different from original presettlement conditions where wolves and other carnivores were previously widespread. In the United States deer and elk now occupy human-disturbed landscapes and are the prey base that attracts wolves. This invariably brings wolves into contact with humans.

Naiman (1988) and Naiman et al. (1988) found that herbivores exerted top-down effects that altered ecosystem functioning, changed species composition in communities, modified nutrient cycling and hence productivity, and thereby changed landscape structure. Pastor et al. (1998) studied moose foraging and plant communities on Isle Royale, Michigan. Because moose are large browsers in less diverse forests, their top-down effects were possible to measure. A high density of moose ($3.7/km^2$) occurred in the area. They concluded that there were no differences in nitrogen availability or browse consumption based on slope, aspect, underlying bedrock, fire history, or glacial history. Moose avoided spruce and only lightly browsed balsam fir. Thus, where browsing was intense, spruce and balsam fir dominated aspens and other hardwoods. Because leaves of spruce and fir were high in lignin and resin, they were slow to decay and release nitrogen in the soil.

Pastor et al. (1998) argued that selective foraging by moose caused and maintained local patches of vegetation and nitrogen cycling rates and resulted in the development of higher order patterns across the larger landscape of the boreal forest. Furthermore, because moose and wolf populations oscillate through time, some properties of the boreal forest may exhibit long-term periodicity. As Pastor et al. (1998, p. 422) stated,

> Such population cycles and associated spatial patterns may, therefore, be an intrinsic property of an intact, properly functioning ecosystem or landscape. A characteristic of such oscillating systems is not some particular population level, or rate of ecosystem process, or even a particular static pattern in the landscape, but rather a spatial and temporal variance structure of all components of the landscape.

Keystone species alter and might even control the dynamics of ecosystems. Thus we agree with Paine (2000) and Hansson and Larsson (1997) that understanding the role of keystone and indicator species to elucidate their roles in ecosystem functions and structuring processes is important. Understanding these roles in the context of heterogeneous landscapes is even more important. With the emergence of a new appreciation for keystone species and ecosystem engineers, it may be that all organisms, including those whose functions appear to be redundant, will be found to be important contributors to the ecology of landscapes. Simberloff (1998, p. 247) wrote,

> The recognition that some ecosystems have keystone species whose activities govern the well-being of many other species suggests an approach that may unite the best features of single-species and ecosystem management. If we can identify keystone species and the mechanisms that cause them to have such wide-ranging impacts, we would almost certainly derive information on the functioning of the entire ecosystem that would be useful in its management.

Simberloff offers a valuable approach to the study of the ecology of landscapes, especially when such studies are undertaken as Johnston (1995) suggested. As might be suspected, insights into how organisms, especially top carnivores, influence landscape ecology can be built on the thousands of natural history studies of single organisms already completed. We are not suggesting a new approach to the study of ecology but rather asking researchers to consider the top-down effects of organisms. One way to prevent further degradation of the earth's biological resources is to make the case that each organism, especially those threatened or endangered by extinction, has a measurable impact on the ecology of landscapes. Our challenge is to quantify this impact, which may be measurable only in ecological or evolutionary time.

Considering mobile organisms in a landscape context is a major step in conserving biota. Certainly such research will add impetus and direction to the discipline of landscape ecology and highlight contributions to biological conservation across landscapes. Simberloff (1998) suggested that ecologists identify keystone species and attempt to elucidate the mechanisms that cause them to contribute disproportionately to ecosystem functions. Gaining an understanding of the ecology of landscapes entails consideration of mobile species such as carnivores that need large natural or seminatural areas to survive. These species might use corridors and so would benefit from reconnecting landscapes. We do not expect that the full complexity of nature will be revealed anytime soon, but we must not delay our quest to appreciate these complexities and put what we learn into practice. Landscapes rather than patches or species should be the focus of management (Hansson, 1997).

We disagree with those who suggest that many threatened species, including flagship species such as the spotted owl, red-cockaded woodpecker, and Florida panther, could disappear entirely from an ecosystem without major or even detectable changes in key processes. However, we suspect that our differences have to do with time spans. Certainly we agree that, over the short-term, the disappearance of spotted owls from forests would go unnoticed. However, over ecological time the disappearance of owls would probably lead to changes in ecosystem dynamics, probably indirectly through their prey species, and so produce noticeable, quantifiable changes to the forest but only in the absence of human alterations acting more rapidly in time. We do not believe that evolution produces superfluous organisms, and that is a compelling reason for urging a top-down approach to the study of the ecology of landscapes.

Conclusion

Ecosystem studies are fundamentally different from landscape ecological studies. Just as all the weather stations on the planet cannot predict global warming, ecosystem results can be neither scaled nor repeated over a landscape to study the ecology of landscapes. Much current research by practicing landscape ecologists is devoted to elucidating the *effects* of landscape patterns on ecosystem processes. To complete the circle in landscape ecology, we believe the top-down effects of mobile organisms and stochastic physical events must be moved to the forefront of landscape ecological research. As knowledge has expanded, ecologists have invented terms such as *keystone species, keystone processes, ecosystem engineers,* and most recently *cornerstone species,* which encompass an increasing array of species and processes. Mobile organisms clearly connect and alter landscapes across space and through time. Measurable changes occur when such organisms are absent from their traditional landscapes. Arguably, managing landscapes for highly mobile species such as predators and other wide-ranging species would keep landscapes connected and protect existing biodiversity from further erosion. The creation of wallows by bison, the nutrients transported by wide-ranging wading birds, seed dispersal by mammalian herbivores and frugivorous birds, and numerous other examples support the premise that mobile organisms help create, support, and maintain the environments they inhabit. The explosion of Mount St. Helens makes clear the need to consider stochastic, often cataclysmic, events. Habitat is not a place, it is space, and humans call that space a landscape.

Summary

There is nothing either explicit or implicit in the definition of *ecosystem* that implies spatial heterogeneity or, for that matter, any aspect of two-dimensional space whatsoever. At least in part, for this reason, ecosystem studies usually take place in systems that can be typed specifically by one name or another (e.g., grassland biome, freshwater pond). Historically, these studies have emphasized an implicit homogeneity, and only rarely have they put emphasis on the importance of edges or heterogeneity. The overwhelming predominance of ecological functions traditionally included in ecosystem (and even ecoregion) studies involves material or energy flows or processes (e.g., nutrient cycles or trophic relations) that can, in theory, occur vertically on a tiny study plot. Nothing about nutrient flow studies involving rainfall, root uptake, and transpiration, or anything to do with Lindeman's trophic-dynamic theory, requires any more horizontal space than the size of the largest organism involved in the plot.

Landscape ecology is different because it explicitly recognizes spatial heterogeneity and critical phenomena such as community faces and interfaces, linkages, and horizontal processes such as fire and allelochemy as critical to long-term system dynamics or stability. It is the spatial (and hence temporal) interactions and interactions between landscape subsystems and those of larger scale that occur across many degrees latitude or longitude (e.g., hurricanes) that distinguish landscape studies from ecosystem analyses. Such studies necessarily take place in three dimensions, but unlike ecosystem analyses, the horizontal dimension may be profoundly more interesting and important than the vertical one. Experiments such as those that evaluate the effects of movement-exclusion fences for mobile organisms, the shifts in biodiversity distribution caused by climate change, or the heterogeneity associated with horizontally moving forces such as fires, floods, wind, or herds of grazing herbivores are needed to fully appreciate the distinctiveness of landscape ecology science. Landscape ecology as currently conceived deals with only half of the science of the ecology of landscapes. We contend that the promise of landscape ecology can be met only by elucidating the top-down effects on natural ecological processes caused by wide-ranging mobile organisms, tides, or tsunamis as well as stochastic events such as tornados, hurricanes, and pulse-phasing effects of forest-defoliating or lethal insects.

LITERATURE CITED

Birch, L. C. 1957. The role of weather in determining the distribution and abundance of animals. Pages 203–215 in Population studies: animal ecology and demography. Cold Spring Harbor Vol. 22. The Biological Laboratory, Long Island, NY.

Caviedes, C. N. 2001. El Niño in history, storming through the ages. University Press of Florida, Gainesville.

Coker, R. E. 1919. Habits and economic relations of the guano birds of Peru. Pages 449–511 in Proceedings of the U. S. National Museum, Vol. 56. U.S. Government Printing Office, Washington, DC.

Diamond, J. M. 1975. The island dilemma: lessons of modern biogeographic studies for the design of natural reserves. Biological Conservation 7:129–146.

Fahrig, L., and G. Merriam. 1985. Habitat patch connectivity and population survival. Ecology 66:1762–1768.

Forbes, S. A. 1887. The lake as a microcosm. Bulletin of the Peoria Scientific Association, Illinois Natural History Survey Bulletin 15:537–550.

Forman, R. T. T. 1982. Interaction among landscape elements: a core of landscape ecology. Pages 35–48 in S. P. Tjallingii and A. A. de Veer (eds.), Perspectives in landscape ecology. Centre for Agricultural Publishing and Documentation, Wageningen, The Netherlands.

Forman, R. T. T. 1995. Land mosaics. Cambridge University Press, Cambridge, UK.

Gascon, C., G. B. Williamson, and G. A. B. da Fonseca. 2000. Receding forest edges and vanishing reserves. Science 288:1356–1358.

Golley, F. B. 1993. A history of the ecosystem concept in ecology. Yale University Press, New Haven, CT.

Hansson, L. 1994. Gradients in herbivory of small mammal communities. Mammalia 58:85–92.

Hansson, L. 1997. The relationship between patchiness and biodiversity in terrestrial systems. Pages 146–155 in S. T. A. Pickett, R. S. Ostfeld, M. Shachak, and G. E. Likens (eds.), The ecological basis of conservation. Chapman & Hall, New York.

Hansson, L., and P. Angelstam. 1991. Landscape ecology as a theoretical basis for nature conservation. Landscape Ecology 5:191–201.

Hansson, L., and T. B. Larsson. 1997. Conservation of boreal environments: a completed research program and a new paradigm. Pages 9–15 in L. Hansson (ed.), Ecological Bulletins 46. Munksgaard International Publishers, Copenhagen.

Harris, L. D. 1988a. Edge effects and conservation of biotic diversity. Conservation Biology 2:330–332.

Harris, L. D. 1988b. The nature of cumulative impacts on biotic diversity of wetland vertebrates. Environmental Management 12:675–693.

Harris, L. D. 1992. Some spatial aspects of biodiversity conservation. Pages 97–108 in M. Fenger, E. Miller, J. Johnson, and E. Williams (eds.), Our living legacy. Royal British Columbia Museum, Victoria, BC.

Harris, L. D., T. S. Hoctor, and S. E. Gergel. 1996. Landscape processes and their significance to biodiversity conservation. Pages 319–347 in O. E. Rhodes, Jr., R. K. Chesser, and M. H. Smith (eds.), Population dynamics in ecological space and time. University of Chicago Press, Chicago.

Hatton, J. C., and N. O. E. Smart. 1984. The effect of long-term exclusion of large herbivores on soil nutrient status in Murchison Falls National Park, Uganda. African Journal of Ecology 22:23–30.

Holland, M., P. Risser, and R. Naiman. 1991. Ecotones. Chapman & Hall, New York.

Holling, C. S. 1992. Cross-scale morphology, geometry, and dynamics of ecosystems. Ecological Monographs 62:447–502.

Janzen, D. H. 1986. The eternal external threat. Pages 286–303 in M. E. Soulé (ed.), Conservation biology. Sinauer Associates, Sunderland, MA.

Johnston, C. A. 1995. Effects of animals on landscape pattern. Pages 57–80 in L. Hansson, L. Fahrig, and G. Merriam (eds.), Mosaic landscapes and ecological processes. Chapman & Hall, London.

Jones, C. G., J. H. Lawton, and M. Shachak. 1994. Organisms as ecosystem engineers. Oikos 69:373–386.

Kushlan, J. A. 1979. Design and management of continental wildlife reserves: lessons from the Everglades. Biological Conservation 15:281–290.

Lindeman, R. L. 1942. The trophic-dynamic aspect of ecology. Ecology 23:399–418.

MacArthur, R. H., and E. O. Wilson. 1967. The theory of island biogeography. Princeton University Press, Princeton, NJ.

Margalef, R. 1968. Perspectives in ecological theory. University of Chicago Press, Chicago.

McNaughton, S. J., F. F. Banyikwa, and M. M. McNaughton. 1997. Promotion of the cycling of diet-enhancing nutrients by African grazers. Science 278:1978–1800.

Merriam, G. 1991. Corridors and connectivity: animal populations in heterogeneous environments. Pages 133–142 in D. A. Saunders and R. J. Hobbs (eds.), Nature conservation 2: The role of corridors. Surrey Beatty & Sons, New South Wales, Australia.

Mladenoff, D. J., R. G. Haight, T. A. Sickley, and A. P. Wydeven. 1997. Causes and implications of species restoration in altered ecosystems. BioScience 47:21–31.

Naiman, R. J. 1988. Animal influences on ecosystem dynamics. BioScience 38:750–752.

Naiman, R. J., C. A. Johnston, and J. C. Kelley. 1988. Alteration of North American streams by beaver. BioScience 38:753–762.

Noss, R. F. 1983. A regional landscape approach to maintain diversity. BioScience 33:700–706.

Noss, R. F., and L. D. Harris. 1986. Nodes, networks, and MUMs: preserving diversity at all scales. Environmental Management 10:299–309.

Paine, R. T. 2000. Phycology for the mammalogist: marine rocky shores and mammal-dominated communities—how different are the structuring processes? Journal of Mammalogy 81:637–648.

Pastor, J., B. Dewey, R. Moen, D. J. Mladenoff, M. White, and Y. Cohen. 1998. Spatial patterns in the moose–forest–soil ecosystem on Isle Royale, Michigan, USA. Ecological Applications 8:411–424.

Sanderson, J., and L. D. Harris (eds.). 1999. Landscape ecology: a top-down approach. Lewis Publishers, Boca Raton, FL.

Sanderson, J. G., M. E. Sunquist, and A. W. Iriarte. 2002. Natural history and landscape-use of guignas (*Oncifelis guignä*) on Isla Grande De Chiloé, Chile. Journal of Mammalogy 82:608–613.

Shelford, V. E. 1913. Animal communities in temperate America. Bulletin no. 5. The Geographic Society of Chicago, Chicago (republished in 1937 by University of Chicago Press, Chicago).

Shelford, V. E. 1963. The ecology of North America. University of Illinois Press, Urbana.

Simberloff, D. 1998. Flagships, umbrellas, and keystones: is single-species management passé in the landscape era? Biological Conservation 83:247–257.

Simberloff, D. S., and L. G. Abele. 1976. Island biogeography and conservation practice. Science 191:285–286.

Swanson, F. J., T. K. Kratz, N. Caine, and R. G. Woodmansee. 1988. Landform effects on ecosystem patterns and processes. BioScience 38:92–98.

Tansley, A. G. 1935. The use and abuse of vegetational concepts and terms. Ecology 16:284–307.

Terborgh, J. 1976. Island biogeography and conservation: strategy and limitations. Science 193:1029–1030.

Urban, D. L., R. V. O'Neill, and H. H. Shugart. 1987. Landscape ecology. BioScience 37:119–127.

Wilcox, B. A., and D. D. Murphy. 1985. Conservation strategy: the effects of fragmentation on extinction. American Naturalist 125:879–887.

Willson, M. F., S. M. Gende, and B. H. Marston. 1998. Fishes and the forest. BioScience 48:455–462.

Woodroffe, R., and J. R. Ginsberg. 1998. Edge effects and the extinction of populations inside protected areas. Science 280:2126–2128.

Zlotin, R. I., and K. S. Khodashova. 1980. The role of animals in biological cycling of forest-steppe ecosystems. Dowden, Hutchinson, & Ross, Stroudsburg, PA.

CHAPTER FOUR

The Problem with Linking Scales in the Use of Indicator Species in Conservation Biology

ILSE STORCH AND JOHN A. BISSONETTE

In the last two decades mammals and birds have increasingly been used as indicators of wildlife habitats and communities by land management agencies and conservation organizations (e.g., Bock and Webb 1984; Landres et al. 1988; Hanley 1993, 1996; Bibby 1999; Loh et al. 1999). Particularly with regard to financial and logistic constraints, the indicator species concept appears to offer a practical solution to the problem of meeting the needs of all species in a community without studying each individually.

In forest ecosystems across North America and Europe, wildlife species closely tied to specific habitat types (e.g., old growth or late stages of forest succession) are of particular concern in conservation. Examples of species receiving high attention in coniferous forest systems include spotted owls (*Strix occidentalis*, Forsman 1980), marbled murrelets (*Brachyramphus marmoratum*, Ralph et al. 1995), and martens (*Martes americana*, Thompson 1991) in North America and capercaillie (*Tetrao urogallus*, Rolstad and Wegge 1989; Storch 1997) and white-backed woodpecker (*Dendrocopus Leucotos*, Virkkala et al. 1993; Wesolowski 1995; Mikusinski and Angelstam 1997, 1998) in Europe. As a result of specialized habitat needs, these and other species have been considered indicators of the health of the forest and its fauna (Landres et al. 1988; Caro and O'Doherty 1999). Abundance and population trends of the indicators are believed to reflect the dynamics of other species that use the same habitats, so management measures designed for an indicator supposedly favor larger segments of the associated wildlife community (Murphy and Wilcox 1986; Block et al. 1987; Hanley 1993; Launer and Murphy 1994; Martikainen et al. 1998; Mikusinski and Angelstam 1998). Despite fundamental and valid critiques of its limitations (Landres et al. 1988; Temple and Wiens 1989; Kitching 1994; Lambeck 1997; Niemi et al. 1997) that involve significant conceptual problems (Noss and Harris 1986; Landres et al. 1988; Lambeck 1997; Niemi et al. 1997), including the fact that there are no generally accepted, standardized methods for indicator species selection (Dufrêne and Legendre 1997), the concept is still widely used in conservation practice (Caro and O'Doherty 1999). Despite its pervasiveness as a shortcut to the state of habitats and communities (Landres et al. 1988; Caro and O'Doherty 1999), the indicator species concept has not been rigorously tested. Only a few studies have assessed its suitability for conservation (e.g., Bock and Webb 1984; Block et al. 1987; Strong 1990; Launer and Murphy 1994; Niemi et al. 1997). Studies that contrasted the presence or abundance of an indicator with that of other species found that the indicator function of single species was limited (Block et al. 1987; Plentovich et al. 1998; Fischer and Storch 2001). In one context, the idea is persuasive; when a species declines because of habitat-related changes, it makes sense to infer that habitat quality has declined. But "quality" is largely species specific, and this is the key to understanding why the idea does not work as well as ecologists might like. For example, lack of woody debris on the forest floor may affect martens but may have no impact on associated woodpecker species. Both are old forest specialists, but both have very specific habitat needs at small spatial extents, which influence their response to landscape pattern at larger spatial extents.

The patchy distribution of successional stages is a typical feature of forested landscapes. The size, intensity, and frequency of disturbances (e.g., fire or clear-cutting) influence wildlife–habitat relationships at spatial extents from local vegetation structure to the landscape mosaic (O'Neill et al. 1986; King 1997). At the same time, a species' resilience to fragmentation is related to the graininess of the habitat (MacArthur and Levins 1964; Levins 1968; Wiens 1976, 1990). Many mammal and bird species used as indicators of old forest wildlife habitats are large and mobile species with large spatial needs (Landres et al. 1988). Therefore, they may respond to a certain landscape mosaic in a different way than their smaller or less mobile associates (see Chapter 2, this volume; Vos et al. 2001). Thus, it appears unlikely that the abundances of both indicator and associated species are equally correlated across all scales of observation.

In this chapter, we address the question of how scale-related species–habitat associations may influence the usefulness of the indicator species concept. We reviewed and analyzed literature on vertebrate indicator species in forested habitats, using two older forest habitat specialists: the marten, a carnivorous mammal from North America, and the capercaillie, a herbivorous bird from Europe. We explored the idea that the sensitivity of species–habitat relationships to multiple scale extents represents a significant limitation to the applicability of the indicator concept in wildlife management and conservation.

Methods

We reviewed North American and European literature for consistency of use of the indicator species concept, with particular emphasis on landscape ecological ideas. We considered explicitly only species that were viewed as indicators of habitat, other species, or biodiversity (Landres et al. 1988; Caro and O'Doherty 1999) and restricted our analysis to vertebrates in forest ecosystems, although much of our argument applies to other taxa in other habitats as well. To assess the use of indicator species by North American agencies, we interviewed wildlife conservation and management agency staff and reviewed the land and resource management plans and related documents for three national forests in the greater Yellowstone ecosystem: Bridger-Teton (USDA 1989), Shoshone (USDA 1986), and Targhee (USDA 1997). We summarized spatial and structural habitat needs of the marten and capercaillie based on published work.

We assessed the relationship between capercaillie habitat and montane bird communities in two 20-km² study areas on the mountain ranges Trauchberg (1,589 m elevation) and Teisenberg (1,333 m elevation) in the foothills of the Bavarian Alps, Germany (see Fischer and Storch 2001 for details). We established a grid of evenly spaced sampling points 200 m apart throughout each study area. Per point, we recorded capercaillie habitat suitability within a 20-m radius, based on a habitat suitability index (HSI) model, and capercaillie use within a 5-m radius, based on signs such as feathers and feces (see Storch 2001b for methods). The proportion of points with sign was used as an index of capercaillie abundance in the study areas. HSI scores were grouped in five HSI classes representing excellent, good, fair, moderate, and poor habitat suitability (Storch 2002). In 1998, we resampled a random subset of these points to record woodpecker use based on cavity building and foraging signs (Fischer 1999; see Fischer and Storch 2001 for methods), and presence of bird species, based on early-morning 15-minute point counts (Ebert 2000). For this study, we compared 34 points in habitats with excellent HSI scores (0.8–1) with 40 points in habitats with poor scores (0–0.2); capercaillie sign were found at 14 (41.2 percent) of the excellent points but in none of the poor points.

We tested for possible relationships between capercaillie abundance and the bird community across three scales of observation. At the smallest scale, sampling points with excellent versus poor capercaillie habitat suitability and points with versus without capercaillie sign, respectively, were compared for differences in the bird community. Then, sampling points were aggregated into three 2km × 2km sections on Teisenberg and two sections on Trauchberg. At the largest scale extent, all samples were aggregated to compare the two study areas. We assessed the following characteristics of the bird communities: mean number of species per sampling point (species richness), mean number of woodpecker signs per sampling point, and the Shannon–Wiener diversity index (Krebs 1989; Mühlenberg 1989).

What Is the Response Variable?

The idea of using indicator species to monitor the condition of entire communities or ecosystems is based on the observation that some species are more susceptible to ecological changes than others (Landres et al. 1988). This concept has been used successfully with invertebrates and plants (bioindicators) to monitor water quality, agricultural and range conditions, and environmental stress (Landres et al. 1988; Brown 1991; Pearson and Cassola 1992; Kremen et al. 1993; Oliver and Beattie 1993; Weaver 1995; Favila and Halffter 1997). In this context, the idea of bioindicators has had a reasonably good track record. However, when the response variable is changed from some measure of environmental quality to a species-based response (e.g., the way old forest species are used) difficulties arise as the context of evaluation changes. When using bioindicators, a decline in the well-being of the indicator demonstrates a decline in habitat quality. With indicator species, as they are most generally used in conservation, we take a decline in the well-being of the indicator to infer that other species are in trouble, via a decline in habitat quality. In effect, we are one hierarchical level removed from causality, and seldom do we have the opportunity to demonstrate declining habitat quality for the associated species in the same way we can measure, for example, declining water quality.

The Use of Indicator Species in Conservation

In Europe, indicator species are commonly considered in regional or national conservation programs (e.g., Plachter 1991; Wynne 1994; Walter et al. 1998; Bibby 1999). Often, several surrogate species concepts (Caro and O'Doherty 1999) are combined to select target species (Kratochwil 1989; Mühlenberg 1989; Chapter 9, this volume) for conservation. High-profile vertebrates on the International Union for Conservation of Nature and Natural Resources (IUCN) Red List such as the capercaillie (Suchant 1999), the great bustard (*Otis tarda,* Kaule 1986, p. 22), or the curlew (*Numenius aquata,* Plachter 1991, pp. 221, 351) are used as flagship species (Western 1987), and their presumed indicator functions are addressed to put weight on the importance of the conservation of a certain area or habitat (Mühlenberg 1989; Plachter 1991, pp. 193–197; Vogel et al. 1996). In the United States, each national forest is required to specify management indicator species (MISs; Wilcove 1989), as mandated in regulations pursuant to the National Forest Management Act (NFMA 1976). Among the species designated as ecological MISs in the forest plans we reviewed were marten, beaver (*Castor canadensis*), goshawk (*Accipiter gentilis*), Brewer's sparrow (*Spizella breweri*), hairy woodpecker (*Picoides villosus*), blue grouse (*Dendragapus obscurus*), and ruffed grouse (*Bonasa umbellus*). They were selected by the U.S. Forest Service (USFS) according to their putative association with certain habitat types (e.g., old-growth forest, sagebrush, and aspen), without overt consideration of spatial needs.

Indicators and Scale Dependency of Habitat Relationships

The habitats of wildlife species are typically heterogeneous. In a patchy landscape, a species may be limited by a shortage of critical resources, by its ability to move between suitable habitat patches, and by its area needs. Increasing extent from tree to landscape and level from individual to metapopulation adds further sources of variation. Not only do species–habitat relationships change with changing landscape patterns, but interactions

between species may also change as a result of different species responding in different ways to altered landscape configurations (Lambeck 1997;
Hager 1998). Difficulties in assessing the indicator function arise because
the nature of species interactions with the environment and with each
other are based on competition, niche separation, predation, parasitism,
and other mechanisms as well as the constraints imposed by landscape pattern. Given the complexity of influences, species habitat preferences may
be generally similar at one hierarchical level (e.g., the forest, as in the case
of old forest obligates) but very different from one another at the level of
smaller scale extents (e.g., preference for coarse woody debris on the forest floor rather than standing dead wood). This suggests that species
responses to landscape pattern are likely to be different. In the following,
we summarize spatial and structural habitat needs of the marten and
capercaillie to illustrate scale dependency of their often-assumed indicator
function.

Martens in North America

Martens have been called an old-growth coniferous forest obligate species
(Thompson 1991). Their distribution across the North American continent
is "governed by the distribution of northern evergreen forest" (Hagmeier
1956). The obligate nature of marten habitat needs has long been recognized
(see review by Buskirk and Powell 1994), and perhaps this is why martens
have been considered an indicator for species living in older coniferous
forests. We have not been able to uncover any study that tested their indicator function. However, certain aspects of both small- and large-scale habitat relationships of martens are well known, and we used these studies to
address the question of scale dependency of the indicator concept.

   At smaller scales, martens are closely linked to older coniferous forests for
a variety of reasons. Cover attributes themselves do not constitute a mechanistic explanation for habitat selection (Bissonette et al. 1997), but they act
as a surrogate for a group of mechanisms: thermal advantages (Buskirk 1984;
Buskirk et al. 1988, 1989; Taylor 1993; Harlow 1994; Taylor and Buskirk
1994), predator avoidance and cover (Murie 1961; Thompson 1994; Drew
1995), and prey availability (Bissonette and Sherburne 1993; Buskirk and
Powell 1994; Martin 1994; Sherburne and Bissonette 1993, 1994). In winter, the characteristic coarse woody debris associated with older coniferous
forests provides the forest floor structure that allows martens access to the

subnivean zone, beneath the snow (Bissonette et al. 1989; Thompson and Colgan 1994). Martens have a low critical temperature (Buskirk et al. 1988), and subnivean spaces allow martens to maintain better thermal homeostasis by avoiding extreme cold. Subnivean access point use by martens is associated with high prey biomass (Sherburne and Bissonette 1994), and availability of small mammal species eaten by martens is influenced directly by snow cover (Bissonette and Sherburne 1993; Buskirk and Powell 1994). The unwillingness of martens to cross open areas (Hargis and McCullough 1984) suggests a response to increased risk from predators. In a series of field and enclosure experiments, Drew (1995) found that martens exposed to the threat of predation limited their movements to forested habitats and did not traverse open areas wider than 25 m, even when food was offered. This suggests a predation-mediated risk perception by martens and may help to explain why a carnivore such as this appears restricted to forest cover. These findings may explain why, at the landscape scale, martens are severely affected by forest fragmentation (Thompson 1994; Thompson and Colgan 1994; Thompson and Harestad 1994; Potvin and Breton 1997; Hargis et al. 1999). Hargis (1996) and Bissonette et al. (1997) demonstrated that marten populations are reduced to near zero density when only 25 to 30 percent of the forest is lost (Fig. 4.1). The implication is that, although they may be forest obligates, the response of other organisms to landscape fragmentation is likely to be different from that of martens. Therefore, the indicator function of the marten is called into question.

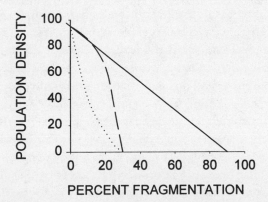

Figure 4.1 The expected response of marten to habitat loss alone. The dashed and dotted lines represent the responses of marten to forest fragmentation in Maine and Utah, respectively. Adapted from Bissonette et al. 1997.

Capercaillie in Central Europe

In central Europe, the capercaillie is limited to a few mountain ranges and is closely associated with older coniferous forest (Klaus et al. 1989; Storch 2001). It is on the Red List in most central European countries (Storch 2000) and is included in Annex I ("species that shall be subject to special habitat conservation measures in order to ensure their survival") of the EU Birds Directive (79/409/EEC). Integrating forestry practices and capercaillie habitat needs is a major conservation challenge (Klaus and Bergmann 1994; Storch 2001). Capercaillie habitat management measures are routinely justified by its role as an indicator of a healthy montane forest community, including other threatened and rare bird species (Scherzinger 1989; Marti 1993; Storch 1994; Suchant 1999). However, the use of the capercaillie as an indicator seems to be based more on intuition and historical precedence than on sound data. Studies that formally assess the suitability of capercaillie habitats for other species and the effects of capercaillie habitat management on biodiversity have long been lacking. Only recently, a localized study in the Swiss Alps showed that montane forests inhabited by capercaillie indeed had a locally greater number of bird species (Graf 1998). Further evidence comes from Finland, where capercaillie abundance turned out as the best predictor of local wildlife species richness (P. Helle, personal communication, 1996) recorded by the nationwide wildlife triangle scheme (Lindén et al. 1996).

As forest obligates with home ranges of several hundred hectares in size (Storch 1995), capercaillie are susceptible to habitat disturbances at various spatial extents: vegetation structure at the forest stand scale, amount and size of old forest stands at the forest mosaic scale, and contiguous forest patch size at the landscape scale (Wegge et al. 1992; Storch 1997). Locally, capercaillie depend on conifer needles for winter food and a well-developed ground vegetation for food and cover in the snow-free seasons. They prefer habitats rich in ericaceous shrubs, particularly bilberry (*Vaccinium myrtillus*). These features are best represented in late successional stages, so capercaillie strongly prefer old forest (see Storch 2001a for a summary of habitat needs). The proportion, size, and distribution of old forest stands influence the size of home ranges (Wegge and Rolstad 1986; Gjerde and Wegge 1989; Storch 1995), the spacing and size of leks (Rolstad and Wegge 1987), and predation risk (Gjerde and Wegge 1989; Wegge et al. 1990). Old forest stands smaller than 50 ha rarely contain leks (Rolstad and Wegge 1987), and in a fine-grained forest, the birds prefer the largest stands (Storch 1997). Populations are likely to decline rapidly when the landscape changes from an old forest matrix to remnant forest patches (Rolstad and Wegge 1987). The minimal area of contiguous montane forest needed for a viable population has been estimated at >10 km^2 (Storch 1995). Variation in capercaillie breeding success is best explained by landscape characteristics within areas of 100 km^2, much larger than individual home ranges (Kurki et al. 2000). Apparently, capercaillie populations are influenced by factors that range across spatial scales from forest stands to landscapes of 10 to 100 km^2 and beyond (see also Chapter 13, this volume).

Capercaillie and Montane Forest Birds: A Case Study

If its presumed indicator function were independent of scale, the presence and abundance of capercaillie should be related to forest bird species composition across all scales of observation. We tested this hypothesis in the Bavarian Alps. In total, 36 bird species were recorded. At the smallest scale, more bird species and also more woodpecker signs were found at sites with capercaillie sign. However, bird species diversity was the same regardless of signs of capercaillie use (Table 4.1). Because absence of capercaillie sign does not necessarily indicate unsuitable habitat, we also compared sample points of different capercaillie habitat suitability (Storch 2002). In excellent capercaillie habitat, more bird species and more woodpecker sign were found than in poor habitat. Bird diversity was not significantly different; however, there was a tendency toward greater diversity in better capercaillie habitat (Table 4.1). Species of older seral stages such as the ring ouzel (*Turdus torquatus*), three-toed woodpecker, crested tit (*Parus cristatus*), nuthatch (*Sitta europaea*), tree-creeper (*Certhia familiaris*), and crossbill (*Loxia curvirostra*) were more common in excellent capercaillie habitats, whereas species of young (e.g., dunnock [*Prunella modularis*]), deciduous (e.g., wood warbler [*Phylloscopus sibilatrix*]), or dense (e.g., firecrest [*Regulus ignicapillus*]) forest were more commonly recorded in plots with poor capercaillie habitats. Aggregating sample points into 4-km^2 sectors and 20-km^2 study areas revealed that at larger spatial extents, both bird species richness and diversity were independent of capercaillie abundance.

Table 4.1. Comparison of bird community variables between 100-m radius plots with regard to (a) capercaillie habitat suitability and (b) presence or absence of indirect capercaillie sign, and (c) between two 20km² study areas. Species richness: species per plot, mean±1SD. Diversity index: Shannon Wiener H±1SD. Woodpecker use: sign/plot, mean±1SD. Capercaillie abundance: % plots with sign, 95% confidence interval (CI). Differences were tested for significance using T-tests (T), Mann-Whitney U tests (U), and Chi²-tests, respectively.

Scale of Observation	Variable	(a) Capercaillie Habitat Suitability (x±1SD)		Difference
		excellent	poor	
Point counts	Species richness	10.0±2.4 (N=34)	8.5±2.3 (N=40)	T=2.70, 72 df, P<0.01
	Diversity index	2.988±0.034	2.911±0.045	T=1.31, 55.8 df, P<0.15
	Woodpecker use	15.8±6.8 (N=40)	3.2±3.9 (N=50)	U=81.0, P<0.001
		(b) Presence of Capercaillie Sign		
		yes	no	
Point counts	Species richness	9.8±2.7 (N=24)	8.7±2.1 (N=134)	T=2.34, 156 df, P<0.05
	Diversity Index	2.991±0.046	2.966±0.025	T=0.48, 43.8 df, n.s.
	Woodpecker use	14.7±7.3 (N=40)	9.4±7.0 (N=332)	U=3896, P<0.001
		(c) Study Areas		
		Teisenberg	Trauchberg	
Study areas 20 km²	Species richness, total	31	33	
	Species richness per plot	9.2±2.2 (N=105)	8.2±2.2 (N=53)	T=2.69, 156 df, P<0.01
	Diversity index	2.939±0.041	2.986±0.024	T=1.00, 53.2 df, n.s.
	Woodpecker use/plot	10.4±7.2 (N=268)	8.8±5.8 (N=104)	U=12526, n.s.
	Capercaillie abundance	9.2 (CI 6.6–12.0; N=467)	1.7 (CI 0.6–3.0; N=448)	Chi²=23.9, P<0.001

Conclusions

Landscapes are heterogeneous. When extent is increased, pattern changes, influencing species interactions that themselves change as a result of the responses of different species complexes to altered landscape configurations (Lambeck 1997). An ideal indicator should be independent of the scale of observation, but this is unlikely. Scale dependency of the indicator function has been shown for arthropods: In some taxa, species composition changed with scale of observation because species were distributed differently across the landscape (Weaver 1995).

Indicator species may not sufficiently represent habitat suitability, richness, or diversity of other species at small scales, much less at larger scales. Larger extents involve additional sources of species-specific variation that make close associations between species unlikely. Both martens (Thompson and Harestad 1994; Bissonette and Hargis 1995; Chapin 1995; Hargis 1996) and capercaillie (Rolstad and Wegge 1989; Storch 1997) are affected by small-scale habitat structure and landscape pattern, suggesting that their effectiveness as indicator species is related to how closely their scale-related responses are approximated by associated species.

The use of vertebrate indicator species in wildlife conservation has become a fact in Europe, North America, and elsewhere. Birds in particular are considered effective indicators of biodiversity trends simply because abundant data are available from all parts of the world (Furness and Greenwood 1993; Tuxill and Bright 1998). National and international biodiversity policy and conservation plans are being developed at a rapid rate (Bibby 1999; Loh et al. 1999). In the context of the global Convention on Biological Diversity, countries have made commitments to developing biodiversity indicators (Bibby 1999). Despite major and significant criticism from ecologists, the indicator species concept will continue to be used; its application is policy driven and not necessarily science driven. In such situations, the challenge for conservationists is to make the concept work despite its many shortcomings. Understanding its limitations may contribute to refining and improving its efficacy in conservation management. We suggest that if the concept is to be used, multispecies indicators (Landres et al. 1988; Noss 1990; Lambeck 1997; see also Chapter 9, this volume) that range across multiple spatial scales from microhabitat to landscapes may be a more fruitful approach.

Summary

Despite major criticism of the concept from ecologists, the use of mammal and bird indicator species as a way to promote biodiversity conservation is likely to grow. However, it is important to understand the limitations of the concept in order to assess its usefulness. The idea behind the use of indicator species is a simple one: Their well-being may reflect the well-being of other species that putatively have the same habitat needs. Accordingly, measures designed to maintain or enhance the population viability of indicator species may favor larger segments of the wildlife community. In this chapter, we address the question of how scale-related species–habitat associations may influence the applicability of the indicator species concept.

Our review of the use of vertebrate indicator species in forested habitats of North America and Europe showed that indicator species were designated based on smaller-scale associations with particular habitat types, whereas larger-scale habitat relationships were typically neglected, even in the face of a growing recognition of the prevalence of scale-dependent effects in natural systems.

To further explore the issue we used two older forest habitat specialists as examples: the marten (*Martes americana*), a carnivorous mammal from North America, and the capercaillie (*Tetrao urogallus*), a herbivorous bird from Europe. We summarized their spatial and structural habitat needs to illustrate scale dependency of their often-assumed indicator function. Both martens and capercaillie are affected by species-specific habitat features ranging from small-scale forest structure to landscape pattern. The implication is that the response of associated species to habitat patterns at various scales is likely to be different from that of martens or capercaillie, so their indicator function is questionable. We supported our argument with a case study from the Bavarian Alps, Germany, in which we tested for associations between capercaillie and bird species richness across three scales of observation. Locally (100-m-radius plots), more bird species and more woodpecker sign were found in excellent than in poor capercaillie habitat. However, at larger spatial extents (4 km^2 and 20 km^2), bird species richness and diversity were independent of capercaillie abundance.

Indicator species may not sufficiently represent habitat suitability, richness, or diversity of other species at small scales, much less at larger scales. Larger extents involve additional sources of species-specific variation that make close associations between species unlikely. We conclude that the scale sensitivity of species–habitat relationships represents a significant limitation to the applicability of the indicator concept in wildlife management and conservation. However, despite justified criticism from ecologists, the indicator species concept will continue to play an important role in conservation policy. The challenge for conservationists is to make the concept work despite its many shortcomings. Understanding its limitations may contribute to refining and improving its efficacy in conservation management. We suggest that if the concept is to be used, multispecies indicators that range across multiple spatial scales from microhabitat to landscapes may be a fruitful approach.

Acknowledgments

The study was supported by a research fellowship to Ilse Storch from the Deutsche Forschungsgemeinschaft (DFG STO-230/3-1). The work on capercaillie and associate species was further supported by the Bavarian State Ministry of Agriculture and Forestry. Irene Fischer and Andreas Ebert conducted the fieldwork on woodpecker use and breeding birds, respectively. The Newfoundland Division of Wildlife and the U.S. Geological Survey Utah Cooperative Fish and Wildlife Research Unit supported the marten work. We thank the following people who provided help and information: S. Cain, W. Brewster, S. Coleman, A. Rodman, S. Consolo Murphy, P. Nordwall, J. Coswell, B. Star, B. Davis, B. Knoblitt, D. Henry, C. McCarthy, M. Cherry, S. Feltis, H. Harlow, W. Paget, B. Rossman, and M. Orme. We thank Christina Hargis and Dan Harrison for use of their original work. We especially thank Hank Harlow for logistic support and housing at the University of Wyoming–National Park Service Research Center. We also thank the anonymous reviewer for many helpful comments. The USGS Utah Cooperative Fish and Wildlife Research Unit is jointly supported by the U.S. Geological Survey, the Utah Division of Wildlife Resources, Utah State University, the Wildlife Management Institute, and the U.S. Fish and Wildlife Service.

LITERATURE CITED

Bibby, C. J. 1999. Making the most of birds as environmental indicators. Ostrich 70:81–88.

Bissonette, J. A., and C. D. Hargis. 1995. Linking landscape and smaller scale responses: a multiscale model. Pages 432–435 in J. A. Bissonette and P. R. Krausman (eds.), Integrating people and wildlife for a sustainable future. Allen Press, Lawrence, KS.

Bissonette, J. A., and S. S. Sherburne. 1993. Subnivean access: the prey connection. Pages 225–228 in I. D. Thompson (ed.), Transactions 21st International Union Game Biologists Congress. Halifax, NS.

Bissonette, J. A., R. J. Fredrickson, and B. J. Tucker. 1989. American marten: a case for landscape management. Transactions North American Wildlife and Natural Resource Conference 54:89–101.

Bissonette, J. A., D. J. Harrison, C. D. Hargis, and T. G. Chapin. 1997. Scale-sensitive properties influence marten demographics. Pages 368–385 in J. A. Bissonette (ed.), Wildlife and landscape ecology: effects of pattern and scale. Springer-Verlag, New York.

Block, W. M., L. A. Brennan, and R. J. Gutiérrez. 1987. The use of guilds and guild-indicator species for assessing habitat suitability. Pages 109–113 in J. Verner, M. L. Morrison, and L. C. Ralph (eds.), Wildlife 2000: modeling habitat relationships of terrestrial vertebrates. University of Wisconsin Press, Madison.

Bock, C. E., and B. Webb. 1984. Birds as grazing indicator species in southeastern Arizona. Journal of Wildlife Management 48:1045–1049.

Brown, K. S. 1991. Conservation of neotropical environments: insects as indicators. Pages 349–404 in N. M. Collins and J. A. Thomas (eds.), The conservation of insects and their habitats. Academic Press, London.

Buskirk, S. W. 1984. Seasonal use of resting sites by marten in south-central Alaska. Journal of Wildlife Management 48:950–953.

Buskirk, S. W., and R. A. Powell. 1994. Habitat ecology of fishers and American martens. Pages 283–296 in S. W. Buskirk, A. S. Harestad, M. G. Raphael, and R. A. Powell (eds.), Martens, sables, and fishers: biology and conservation. Cornell University Press, Ithaca, NY.

Buskirk, S. W., H. J. Harlow, and S. C. Forrest. 1988. Temperature regulation in American marten in winter. National Geographic Research 4:208–218.

Buskirk, S. W., H. J. Harlow, and S. C. Forrest. 1989. Winter resting site ecology of marten in the central Rocky Mountains. Journal of Wildlife Management 53:191–196.

Caro, T. M., and G. O'Doherty. 1999. On the use of surrogate species in conservation biology. Conservation Biology 13:805–814.

Chapin, T. G. 1995. Influence of landscape pattern and forest type on use of habitat by marten in Maine. M.S. thesis, University of Maine, Orono.

Drew, G. S. 1995. Winter habitat selection by American marten (Martes americana) in Newfoundland: why old growth? Ph.D. dissertation, Utah State University, Logan.

Dufrêne, M., and P. Legendre. 1997. Species assemblages and indicator species: the need for a flexible asymmetrical approach. Ecological Monographs 67:345–366.

Ebert, A. 2000. Das Auerhuhn als Leitart im Naturschutz: Ein Vergleich von Auerhuhnhabitaten und Vogelgesellschaften. Diploma thesis, Faculty of Forest Sciences, Technische Universität München, Munich.

Favila, M. E., and G. Halffter. 1997. The use of indicator groups for measuring biodiversity as related to community structure and function. Acta Zoologica Mexico 72:1–25.

Fischer, I. 1999. Das Indikatorartenkonzept am Beispiel von Auerhuhn und Spechten. Diploma thesis, Faculty of Biology, University of Göttingen, Germany. (In German with English summary: Evaluating the indicator species concept: a case study on capercaillie and woodpeckers.)

Fischer, I., and I. Storch. 2001. Capercaillie and woodpeckers in Alpine forests: assessing the indicator species concept. Pages 376–379 in The Wildlife Society. Proceedings of the 2nd International Wildlife Management Congress "Wildlife, land, and people: priorities for the 21st century," Gödöllo, Hungary.

Forsman, E. D. 1980. Habitat utilization by spotted owls in the west-central Cascades of Oregon. Ph.D. dissertation, Oregon State University, Corvallis.

Furness, R. W., and J. J. D. Greenwood (eds.). 1993. Birds as monitors of environmental change. Chapman & Hall, London.

Gjerde, I., and P. Wegge. 1989. Spacing pattern, habitat use, and survival of capercaillie in a fragmented winter habitat. Ornis Scandinavica 20:219–225.

Graf, R. 1998. Bedeutung des Auerhuhns als Indikator für eine hohe Biodiversität. Diploma thesis, Department Umweltnaturwissenschaften, ETH Zürich, Switzerland.

Hager, H. A. 1998. Area-sensitivity of reptiles and amphibians: are there indicator species for habitat fragmentation? Ecoscience 5:139–147.

Hagmeier, E. M. 1956. Distribution of marten and fisher in North America. Canadian Field-Naturalist 70:149–168.

Hanley, T. A. 1993. Balancing economic development, biological conservation, and human culture: the Sitka black-tailed deer as an ecological indicator. Biological Conservation 66:61–67.

Hanley, T. A. 1996. Potential role of deer (Cervidae) as ecological indicators of forest management. Forest Ecology and Management 88:199–204.

Hargis, C. D. 1996. The influence of forest fragmentation and landscape pattern on American martens and their prey. Ph.D. dissertation, Utah State University, Logan.

Hargis, C. D., and D. R. McCullough. 1984. Winter diet and habitat selection of marten in Yosemite National Park. Journal of Wildlife Management 48:140–146.

Hargis, C. D., J. A. Bissonette, and D. L. Turner. 1999. The influence of forest fragmentation and landscape pattern on American marten. Journal of Applied Ecology 36:157–172.

Harlow, H. J. 1994. Trade-offs associated with the size and shape of marten. Pages 391–403 in S. W. Buskirk, A. S. Harestad, M. G. Raphael, and R. A. Powell (eds.), Martens, sables, and fishers: biology and conservation. Cornell University Press, Ithaca, NY.

Kaule, G. 1986. Arten- und Biotopschutz. UTB für Wissenschaft, Verlag Eugen Ulmer, Stuttgart, Germany.

King, A. W. 1997. Hierarchy theory: a guide to system structure for wildlife biologists. Pages 185–212 in J. A. Bissonette (ed.), Wildlife and landscape ecology: effects of pattern and scale. Springer-Verlag, New York.

Kitching, R. L. 1994. Biodiversity: political responsibilities and agendas for research and conservation. Pacific Conservation Biology 1:279–283.

Klaus, S., and H.-H. Bergmann. 1994. Distribution, status and limiting factors of capercaillie in central Europe, particularly in Germany, including an evaluation of reintroductions. Gibier Faune Sauvage 11:57–80.

Klaus, S., A. V. Andreev, H.-H. Bergmann, F. Müller, J. Porkert, and J. Wiesner 1989. Die Auerhühner. Die Neue Brehm-Bücherei, Band 86. Westarp Wissenschaften, Magdeburg, Germany.

Kratochwil, A. 1989. Grundsätzliche Überlegungen zu einer Roten Liste von Biotopen. Schriftenreihe für Landschaftspflege und Naturschutz 29:136–150.

Krebs, C. 1989. Ecological methodology. Harper & Row, New York.

Kremen, C., R. K. Colwell, T. L. Erwin, D. D. Murphy, R. F. Noss, and M. A. Sanjayan. 1993. Terrestrial arthropod assemblages: their use in conservation planning. Conservation Biology 7:796–808.

Kurki, S., A. Nikula, P. Helle, and H. Lindén. 2000. Landscape fragmentation and forest composition effects on grouse breeding success in boreal forests. Ecology 81:1985–1997.

Lambeck, R. J. 1997. Focal species: a multi-species umbrella for nature conservation. Conservation Biology 11:849–856.

Landres, P. B., J. Verner, and J. W. Thomas. 1988. Ecological uses of vertebrate indicator species: a critique. Conservation Biology 2:312–328.

Launer, A. E., and D. D. Murphy. 1994. Umbrella species and the conservation of habitat fragments: a case of a threatened butterfly and a vanishing grassland ecosystem. Biological Conservation 69:145–153.

Levins, R. 1968. Evolution in changing environments. Princeton University Press, Princeton, NJ.

Lindén, H., E. Helle, P. Helle, and M. Wikman. 1996. Wildlife triangle scheme in Finland: methods and aims for monitoring wildlife populations. Finnish Game Research 49:4–11.

Loh, J., J. Randers, A. McGillivray, V. Kapos, M. Jenkins, B. Groombridge, N. Cox, and B. Warren. 1999. Living planet report. WWF International, Gland, Switzerland.

MacArthur, R., and R. Levins. 1964. Competition, habitat selection, and character displacement in a patchy environment. Proceedings of the National Academy of Sciences 51:1207–1210.

Marti, C. 1993. Merkblatt: Waldwirtschaft und Auerhuhn. Bundesamt Umwelt Wald Landschaft (BUWAL) und Schweizerische Vogelwarte Sempach, Switzerland.

Martikainen, P., L. Kaila, and Y. Haila. 1998. Threatened beetles in white-backed woodpecker habitats. Conservation Biology 12:293–301.

Martin, S. K. 1994. Feeding ecology of American martens and fishers. Pages 297–315 in S. W. Buskirk, A. S. Harestad, M. G. Raphael, and R. A. Powell (eds.),

Martens, sables, and fishers: biology and conservation. Cornell University Press, Ithaca, NY.

Mikusinski, G., and P. Angelstam. 1997. European woodpeckers and anthropogenic habitat change: a review. Vogelwelt 118:277–283.

Mikusinski, G., and P. Angelstam. 1998. Economic geography, forest distribution, and woodpecker diversity in central Europe. Conservation Biology 12:200–208.

Mühlenberg, M. 1989. Freilandökologie. UTB für Wissenschaft, Quelle und Meyer Verlag, Heidelberg, Wiesbaden, Germany.

Murie, A. 1961. Some food habits of the marten. Journal of Mammalogy 42:516–521.

Murphy, D. D., and B. A. Wilcox. 1986. Butterfly diversity in natural habitat fragments: a test of the validity of vertebrate-based management. Pages 287–292 in J. Verner, M. L. Morrison, and C. J. Ralph (eds.), Wildlife 2000. Modeling habitat relationships of terrestrial vertebrates. University of Wisconsin Press, Madison.

NFMA. 1976. National Forest Management Act of 1976. 16 U.S.C. 1600. Washington, DC.

Niemi, G. J., J. M. Hanowski, A. R. Lima, T. Nicholls, and N. Weiland. 1997. A critical analysis on the use of indicator species in management. Journal of Wildlife Management 61:1240–1252.

Noss, R. F. 1990. Indicators for monitoring biodiversity: a hierarchical approach. Conservation Biology 4:355–364.

Noss, R. F., and L. D. Harris. 1986. Nodes, networks, and MUMs: preserving diversity at all scales. Environmental Management 10:299–309.

Oliver, I., and A. J. Beattie. 1993. A possible method for rapid assessment of biodiversity. Conservation Biology 7:562–568.

O'Neill, R. V., D. L. DeAngelis, J. B. Waide, and T. F. H. Allen. 1986. A hierarchical concept of ecosystems. Monographs in Population Biology 23. Princeton University Press, Princeton, NJ.

Pearson, D. L., and F. Cassola. 1992. World-wide species richness patterns of tiger beetles: indicator taxa for biodiversity and conservation studies. Conservation Biology 6:376–391.

Plachter, H. 1991. Naturschutz. UTB für Wissenschaft. Gustav Fischer Verlag, Stuttgart, Germany.

Plentovich, S., J. W. Tucker, N. R. Holler, and G. E. Hill. 1998. Enhancing Bachman's sparrow habitat via management of red-cockaded woodpeckers. Journal of Wildlife Management 62:347–354.

Potvin, F., and L. Breton. 1997. Short-term effects of clearcutting on martens and their prey in the boreal forest of western Ontario. Pages 452–474 in G. Proulx, H. N. Bryant, and P. M. Woodard (eds.), Martens: taxonomy, ecology, techniques, and management. Provincial Museum of Alberta, Edmonton.

Ralph, C. J., G. L. Hunt, M. G. Raphael, and J. F. Piatt (eds.). 1995. Ecology and conservation of the marbled murrelet. USDA Forest Service, General Technical Report PSW-GTR-152, Pacific Southwest Research Station, Albany, CA.

Rolstad, J., and P. Wegge. 1987. Distribution and size of capercaillie leks in relation to old forest fragmentation. Oecologia 72:389–394.

Rolstad, J., and P. Wegge. 1989. Capercaillie populations and modern forestry: a case for landscape ecological studies. Finnish Game Research 46:43–52.

Scherzinger, W. 1989. Endangered bird-species of woodland, habitat pretensions and their integration in natural succession. Stapfia 20:81–100.

Sherburne, S. S., and J. A. Bissonette. 1993. Squirrel middens influence marten use of subnivean access points. American Midland Naturalist 129:204–207.

Sherburne, S. S., and J. A. Bissonette. 1994. Marten subnivean access point use: response to subnivean prey levels. Journal of Wildlife Management 58:400–405.

Storch, I. 1994. Auerhuhn-Schutz: aber wie? Ein Leitfaden. Brochure, Munich Wildlife Society, Ettal, Germany.

Storch, I. 1995. Annual home ranges and spacing patterns of capercaillie in central Europe. Journal of Wildlife Management 59:392–400.

Storch, I. 1997. The importance of scale in habitat conservation for an endangered species: the capercaillie in central Europe. Pages 310–330 in J. A. Bissonette (ed.), Wildlife and landscape ecology: effects of pattern and scale. Springer-Verlag, New York.

Storch, I. 2000. Status Survey and Conservation Action Plan 2000–2004 Grouse. WPA/BirdLife/SSC Grouse Specialist Group. IUCN, Gland, Switzerland and World Pheasant Association, Reading, UK.

Storch, I. 2001. Capercaillie. BWP Update. The Journal of Birds of the Western Palearctic 3:1–24.

Storch I. 2002. On spatial resolution in habitat models: can small-scale forest structure explain capercaillie numbers? Conservation Ecology, 6:6 (online at http://www.consecol.org/vol6/iss1/art6).

Strong, P. I. V. 1990. The suitability of the common loon as an indicator species. Wildlife Society Bulletin 18:257–261.

Suchant, R. 1999. Was hat das Auerhuhn mit dem Homo sapiens zu tun? Natur und Mensch, Schweizerische Blätter für Natur und Heimat 41:9–15.

Taylor, S. L. 1993. Thermodynamics and energetics of resting site use by the American marten. M.S. thesis, University of Wyoming, Laramie.

Taylor, S. L., and S. W. Buskirk. 1994. Forest microenvironments and resting energetics of the American marten. Ecography 17:249–256.

Temple, S. A., and J. A. Wiens. 1989. Bird populations and environmental changes: can birds be bio-indicators? American Birds 43:260–270.

Thompson, I. D. 1991. Will the marten become the spotted owl of eastern Canada? Forestry Chronicle 67:136–140.

Thompson, I. D. 1994. Marten populations in uncut and logged boreal forests in Ontario. Journal of Wildlife Management 58:272–280.

Thompson, I. D., and P. W. Colgan. 1994. Marten activity in uncut and logged boreal forests in Ontario. Journal of Wildlife Management 58:280–288.

Thompson, I. D., and A. S. Harestad. 1994. Effects of logging on American martens, and models for habitat management. Pages 355–367 in S. W. Buskirk, A. S. Harestad, M. G. Raphael, and R. A. Powell (eds.), Martens, sables, and fishers: biology and conservation. Cornell University Press, Ithaca, NY.

Tuxill, J., and C. Bright. 1998. Losing strands in the web of life. Pages 41–58 in L. R. Brown, C. Flavin, H. F. French, J. Abramovitz, C. Bright, S. Dunn, G. Gardner, A. McGinn, J. Mitchell, M. Renner, R. Roodman, L. Starke, and J. Tuxill, (eds.), State of the world 1998. A Worldwatch Institute report on progress toward a sustainable society. W.W. Norton, New York.

USDA. 1986. Land and resource management plan. Shoshone National Forest, P.O. Box 2140, 225 West Yellowstone Ave, Cody, Wyoming 82414, USA.

USDA. 1989. National Forest land and resource management plan. Bridger Teton National Forest, Box 1888, Jackson, Wyoming 83001, USA.

USDA. 1997. 1997 revised forest plan. Targhee National Forest, P.O. Box 208, St. Anthony, Idaho 83445, USA.

Virkkala, R., T. Alanko, T. Laine, and J. Tiainen. 1993. Population contraction of the white-backed woodpecker *Dendrocopus leucotos* in Finland as a consequence of habitat alteration. Biological Conservation 66:47–53.

Vogel, K., B. Vogel, G. Rothhaupt, and E. Gottschalk. 1996. Einsatz von Zielarten im Naturschutz. Naturschutz und Landschaftspflege 28:179–184.

Vos, C. C., J. Verboom, P. F. Opdam, and D. J. F. ter Braak. 2001. Towards ecologically scaled landscape indices. American Naturalist 157:24–41.

Walter, R., H. Reck, G. Kaule, M. Lämmle, E. Osinski, and T. Heinl. 1998. Regionalisierte Qualitätsziele, Standards und Indikatoren für die Belange des Arten- und Biotopschutzes in Baden-Württemberg. Das Zielartenkonzept: ein Beitrag zum Landschaftsrahmenprogramm des Landes Baden-Württemberg. Natur und Landschaft 73:9–25.

Weaver, J. C. 1995. Indicator species and scale of observation. Conservation Biology 9:939–942.

Wegge, P., and J. Rolstad. 1986. Size and spacing of capercaillie leks in relation to social behavior and habitat. Behavioural Ecology and Sociobiology 19:401–408.

Wegge, P., I. Gjerde, L. Kastdalen, J. Rolstad, and T. Storaas. 1990. Does forest fragmentation increase the mortality rate of capercaillie? Pages 448–453 in S. Myrberget (ed.), Transactions 19th International Union Game Biologists Congress, Trondheim, Norway.

Wegge, P., J. Rolstad, and I. Gjerde. 1992. Effects of boreal forest fragmentation on capercaillie grouse: empirical evidence and management implications. Pages 738–749 in D. R. McCullough and R. H. Barrett (eds.), Wildlife 2001: populations. Elsevier, Barking, UK.

Wesolowski, T. 1995. Value of Bialowieza forest for the conservation of white-backed woodpecker in Poland. Biological Conservation 71:69–75.

Western, D. 1987. Africa's elephants and rhinos: flagships in crisis. Trends in Ecology and Evolution 2:343–346.

Wiens, J. A. 1976. Population responses to patchy environments. Annual Review of Ecology Systematics 7:81–120.

Wiens, J. A. 1990. On the use of "grain" and "grain size" in ecology. Functional Ecology 4:719.

Wilcove, D. S. 1989. Protecting biodiversity in multiple use lands: lessons from the US Forest Service. Trends in Ecology and Evolution 4:385–388.

Wynne, G. (ed.). 1994. Biodiversity challenge: an agenda for conservation in the UK. Royal Society for the Protection of Birds, Sandy, UK.

CHAPTER FIVE

Linking Fitness Landscapes with the Behavior and Distribution of Animals

MICHAEL S. MITCHELL AND ROGER A. POWELL

Since its beginnings in the 1980s, the discipline of landscape ecology has grown rapidly, concurrent with advances in geographic information system (GIS) technology and increasing availability of georeferenced data. Ecologists and land managers are able to analyze patterns on multiple scales in ways not possible in the past. Indeed, ideas, approaches, and techniques emerge faster than they can be assimilated, resulting in a complex framework of concepts that lacks a unifying structure well supported by empirical data (Wiens 1999). This situation represents a double-edged sword for landscape ecologists. On one hand, the prospects for true paradigm shifts are exciting as we understand better the role of spatial phenomena in the function and management of populations and landscapes. On the other hand, these paradigm shifts will be particularly problematic for resource managers who must deal with promising new concepts of landscape ecology that provide little empirical support or direction for management actions. The risk of failure is high when a management strategy is based on concepts that keep changing.

In a discipline undergoing rapid change and progress, one should reassess regularly the assumptions that underlie dominant concepts so that conceptual grasp does not exceed empirical reach. In this chapter, we evaluate some concepts and assumptions related to interactions across spatial scales between animals and their habitat. We focus on how habitat should be defined in landscape ecology. The ability to portray the distribution and characteristics of habitat in space, and therefore the ability to understand and manage animals that rely on that habitat, is fundamental to what many landscape ecologists do. Whether we want to understand metapopulation dynamics or patch use by individual animals, researchers and managers implicitly or explicitly define habitat as an integral part of their work. Seldom, however, do researchers and managers understand how well these models and maps actually portray the biological meaning of habitat to animals. We contend that models and maps based on rigorous evaluation of biological first principles are the only ones with the potential to provide robust insight into landscape ecology and lead to management actions that will yield desired results. Models adopted because they are convenient to our methods and technology, on the other hand, are very unlikely to do either. In the explosive growth of landscape ecology and in the use of GISs, important biological first principles have been dismissed too easily as fully justified assumptions or ignored completely. Specifically, we consider here how to define habitat biologically, how this definition has and has not been extended to landscape concepts and applications, and how definitions of habitat frequently used in landscape ecology are limiting. We also propose a definition of habitat based on fitness that should be more robust in landscape applications than traditional definitions. We conclude with an example of our concept applied to black bears and their use of habitat on a forested landscape in the southern Appalachians.

Habitat and Fitness

Like many words frequently used within a profession, the term *habitat* has become so widely used in animal and landscape ecology under so many circumstances that its meaning is confused at best. *Habitat* has become jargon, a vague concept that is widely and uncritically used. At the most basic level, the word *habitat* implies that some relationship between animals and their environment is being discussed. The nature of that relationship is rarely defined, however, resulting in ambiguities (at best) or inaccuracies (at worst; Hall et al. 1997).

Garshelis (2000, p. 112) outlined two distinct definitions of *habitat*. The first is "the type of place where an animal normally lives or, more specifically, the collection of resources and conditions necessary for its occupancy."

The second is "a set of specific environmental features that, for terrestrial animals, is often equated to a plant community, vegetative association, or cover type." Garshelis maintained that the prevalence of the second usage confers legitimacy and is consistent with the normally accepted concept of "habitat use." Morrison et al. (1992) acknowledged the frequent use of *habitat* to describe an area with a particular vegetative cover but maintained that a better definition is an area with the resources, environmental conditions, and presence or absence of predators that allows the occupancy, survival, and reproduction of a particular species. Hall et al. (1997) cogently discussed the use and abuse of the term *habitat* in the literature and issued a plea for standardization consistent with Morrison et al.'s (1992) definition. Corsi et al. (2000) added more complexity to the common uses of the term *habitat* by aligning them according to whether they had to do with Cartesian space (where a species is found) or environmental space (under what conditions a species is found), and whether they referred to biota (e.g., deer habitat) or land (e.g., riparian habitat). Corsi et al. (2000) showed that habitat originally was a species-specific property, but with the development of technologies for mapping habitat, land-based definitions became more prevalent because general habitat types easily distinguished by people are easy to map. However, the habitat needs of animals vary across species ranges and with the presence of predators, specific foods, and other resources and therefore cannot be identified as precisely as technologies can map them.

For a habitat model to be useful, it must explain or predict how animals will be associated with the vegetation and physical structure of a particular area. To do this, a model must relate habitat to an animal's fitness or to its correlates. This may not be as obvious as it sounds and is certainly not as simple. Fisher (1930) described fitness for an animal as a relative measure that increases with increasing survival and number of offspring. Stearns (1992) defined fitness more precisely as the expected contribution of an individual to future generations, homologous to the definition of the intrinsic rate of increase, r, for a population. Like habitat, however, *fitness* has also become jargon in animal ecology, and the term is used widely without explicit definition. Although Fisher's and Stearns's definitions of *fitness* are straightforward, fitness is very difficult to measure empirically. Garshelis (2000) provided a detailed presentation of studies that have and have not addressed links between habitat and components of fitness, and he outlined challenges associated with discerning fitness in field studies. Essentially, two approaches exist for discerning the fitness of animals through observation. The most direct approach is to measure vital rates such as survival or reproductive success and infer fitness from them. This approach has appeal because it deals directly with two major components of fitness. Nonetheless, we must emphasize that these are only components of fitness (Caswell 2001, p. 295). Juvenile survival, density dependency, environmental stochasticity, social status, and other factors can also affect fitness. An analysis of survival only will overestimate fitness for long-lived individuals that fail to reproduce, an analysis of reproductive success can misinterpret fitness for fecund individuals that die young, and an analysis of both survival and reproduction can misestimate fitness for individuals whose vital rates are influenced by population density or social status.

A second approach is to infer fitness indirectly from the behavior of animals based on the logic that animals show preferences for environmental characteristics that enhance their fitness. This approach has its theoretical foundations in foraging ecology (optimality) and in research that shows that natural selection has molded foraging decisions, patch selection, and time of patch occupation to maximize fitness or indices of fitness (Stephens and Krebs 1986). This approach has been used extensively in empirical studies of habitat use by animals largely because behavioral data, usually in the form of telemetry locations, are easier to collect than data on vital rates. This approach suffers from significant drawbacks because key assumptions must be made both about the behavior of animals and about what animals select. Behavior is highly plastic for members of most wildlife species, and intraspecific and interspecific interactions affect behaviors (e.g., use of space). Perhaps most problematic in this approach is that it entails a reasonable understanding of what animals select. Most habitat studies that use this approach rely on a posteriori correlations between measures of use by animals and arbitrary classifications of habitat. Not only is this poor science, but it assumes, usually without testing, that the classification schemes developed by the researchers accurately represent the ecological currency used by animals to make decisions. We know of no habitat classification schemes based directly and entirely on factors contributing to reproduction and survival of animals. Some schemes incorporate, to some extent, foods or escape cover potentially available from a particular cover type. However, two patches of the same cover type may have different value to an animal, depending on their sizes and juxtaposition with other resources. The extent to which habitat selection by animals matches human definitions of habitat should be extremely sensitive to the extent to which these definitions abstract important first principles that contribute to the fitness of the animals. Therefore, the ability of a posteriori correlation analyses to reveal relationships between animal behavior and arbitrary habitat definitions becomes more a function of good fortune than of good biology.

Fitness, like the intrinsic rate of increase for a population (r), can almost never be measured directly and therefore must be assessed indirectly with indices. No single index is universally satisfactory or practical for all species. Methods for discerning fitness in the field depend on research techniques available to study a species, its unique life history, and logistic constraints. At least as important, the ability to discern a relationship between fitness and habitat entails not only a reasonable index of an animal's fitness but also a reasonable model of how habitat contributes to that fitness. To fail to do both is to make one of two lamentably common mistakes. A habitat definition based on good estimates of fitness correlated to arbitrary habitat classes is based on inductive, not deductive, reasoning and amounts only to an untested hypothesis. A habitat model with a theoretical basis in fitness that is not tested against actual indices of fitness is also nothing more than an untested hypothesis. In either case, the link between fitness and habitat has not been rigorously established. A manager proposing to manage habitat using either approach has no confidence that management actions will yield desired results.

Calls to understand better the relationship between fitness and habitat are increasing but focus largely on better ways to discern fitness and not on identifying the properties of habitat that contribute to fitness. We suggest that the only definition of habitat with a functional biological basis is one that in some way ties resources contained within an area to the fitness of animals occupying (or potentially occupying) it. Arguments of prevalence aside, the first usage outlined by Garshelis (2000) and the preferred definition of Morrison et al. (1992) are the only definitions that explicitly satisfy this requirement. However, *any* definition of habitat portrays a fitness relationship between an environment and an animal, whether intended or not. Typological approaches to modeling this relationship are simply more abstract and less direct than explicit approaches. Conceivably, either approach has its time and place in landscape ecology and should be a function of where research questions or management objectives fall on two continua: spatial scale (fine scale, such as individual forest stands, to broad scale, such as a forested landscape) and ecological resolution (simple, such as presence of a single species, to complex, such as community structure). However, we see little evidence that managers and landscape ecologists select definitions of habitat based on these continua. Mismatches between the level of abstraction in habitat definitions, spatial scales, and ecological resolution lead not only to poor or misleading insights but also to the propagation of erroneous or vague biological concepts.

Habitat and Landscapes

Biological meaning, scientific predictions, and management utility for any habitat maps depend very much on the definitions used to generate the maps. We are very concerned that definitions of habitat among landscape ecologists are increasingly structured by artifacts of image classification, by an uncritical use of the ubiquitous concept of the habitat patch, and by an excessive reliance on inductive analyses to define habitat.

Classification

Organisms are distributed in a complex manner with respect to the resources that affect fitness. The need to simplify is clear, yet the means for simplifying that are consistent with biology are not always so clear. Distilling ecological patterns into identifiable types has a distinguished history in ecology. Among the earliest debates in ecological literature was whether associations between individual organisms inhabiting a common area were the product of tight interdependence between those organisms, forming an integrated community type distinguishable from others (Clements 1936), or merely a happenstance of the independent distributions of the organisms whereby no typological separation of communities is possible (Gleason 1926). Most ecologists agree now that these two ideas anchor the ends of a continuum. Some typological definitions of communities are justified, many are not, depending largely on scale and spatial heterogeneity. On a continental scale, for example, a community called "boreal forest" includes all species and ecological associations associated with boreal forests. On the scale of 1 m^2, however, numerous community components are absent because they are not uniformly distributed within boreal forests at all scales. The importance of scale in interpreting landscape patterns is well understood in landscape ecology (Wiens 1999), but the use of scale in defining habitat on a landscape is not.

Landscape ecology has an interesting history of its own with regard to defining ecological communities. In one of the earliest textbooks for landscape ecology, Forman and Godron (1986, p. 62) stated that "plant and animal communities are often mapped, and to do this they are named and classified. . . . The primary criteria used in classifications are appearance (physiognomy), species composition, dominant species, and habitat . . . at finer divisions, species composition is almost always used as the classification criterion." Interestingly, we could find no definition of the term *habitat* in the book, yet it is listed as a classification criterion for community types. The vague use of *habitat* and a reliance on typological definitions of communities based on species composition are well rooted within the discipline. Some recent publications acknowledge more explicit definitions of *habitat* based on fitness but continue to rely on the use of habitat types (Kozakiewicz 1995; Morris 1995; Harris and Sanderson 2000). However, the clear majority of publications within landscape ecology either do not define habitat or treat it as a commonly understood entity that need not be discussed. Because the link between animals and where they live is the root of understanding metapopulation dynamics, habitat selection, and the distributions of animals on landscapes, a discipline that addresses these issues must understand what habitat is.

Much of the way landscape ecologists consider (or fail to consider) habitat definitions results from empirical and theoretical stumbling blocks: technological constraints that define the format of the data used in empirical studies and the dominant paradigm of the habitat patch. The first issue is an obvious one. Landscape ecologists and managers often use data derived from remotely sensed satellite imagery, where biological meaning must be inferred from variations in spectral data. Approaches to classifying ecological communities from such images abound and have been widely applied in models of habitat for animals (Scott et al. 1993). Although the confidence with which such definitions may be viewed is questionable (Williams 1996; Morgan and Savitsky 1998), few alternatives exist for converting truly large-scale landscape information into ecologically meaningful data. Nonetheless, landscape classification can generate only typological community definitions. Landscape ecologists who use these data to portray animal habitats must be critical of the assumptions used to define ecological communities from such an extreme, Clementsian perspective. These assumptions may be justified for certain communities or certain scales but by no means for all cases.

Patches

Despite the productive history of research related to habitat patches, we suggest that habitat definitions suffer from the seemingly universal faith landscape ecology has placed on the concept of the patch. Patch theory has its origins in optimal foraging (Charnov 1976) and has been an invaluable tool to pioneers in spatial patterns in ecology. Wiens (1995) explained the predominance in landscape ecology of patch theory over that dealing with spatial heterogeneity by noting that patch theory was familiar and easily adapted and that the concept of heterogeneity is diffuse and does not lend itself well to rigorous theoretical development. Accordingly, patch theory has been integral to developing critical concepts in landscape ecology, particularly for models of metapopulations, biogeography, and ecological flow (Wiens 1995), and has become the analytical foundation for landscape analysis (Turner et al. 1991; McGarigal and Marks 1995). Consequently, the notion of habitat as a spatial array of internally homogeneous patches imbedded in an inert matrix has become fixed in landscape ecology, despite the fact that little empirical evidence exists to suggest that this model is as universal as it is used (Kareiva 1990).

Resources, and therefore individuals, populations, and communities, are patchily distributed in space. However, such patchiness does not mean that organisms are arranged in clearly defined polygons. Patchy distributions are those in which organisms of the same species are clumped in space rather than randomly or evenly distributed. At any scale, clumps of organisms have diffuse edges and heterogeneous densities within those diffuse edges.

Patches, patch characteristics, fragmentation of habitat into patches, and corridors connecting patches are reigning paradigms in landscape ecology that enjoy modest empirical support at best yet are widely and often uncritically applied. Although a powerful conceptual tool, a patch is nothing more than a habitat model, and its application suffers the same limitations as any definition of habitat. At broad spatial scales and coarse ecological resolutions, habitat expressed as homogeneous patches may have explanatory power for understanding the behavior or distribution of animals on a landscape. On fine scales, abstract definitions of habitat explain less and less. Thus, patches may help to explain metapopulation dynamics or behavior of individuals on one scale but not on another.

Inductive Analysis

Inductive reasoning comprises the essential first steps of the scientific method. When researchers collect data, analyze them statistically, and interpret the results without having a priori hypotheses, they use inductive logic to generate hypotheses (i.e., the interpretation of the results) suitable for testing. Only when these hypotheses are tested deductively (the remainder of the scientific method) can strong inferences be made and cause-and-effect relationships be established (Platt 1964). Clearly, robust insights such as these should form the basis for resource management. By contrast, inductively derived insights provide a risky foundation for management of natural systems because such insights are untested and therefore tenuous.

Nonetheless, studies that use a posteriori correlation analysis to associate presence of animals with habitat classifications are very common. Burnham and Anderson (1998) described this method as "data dredging" and argued that inferences drawn from such analyses do not have strong biological, statistical, or logical foundations. Nonetheless, most studies using this approach misrepresent their findings as conclusions rather than identifying them appropriately as hypotheses in need of testing with independent data sets. Granted, one cannot test hypotheses that have not been generated, and inductive analysis is the necessary starting point where no a priori hypotheses can be derived. For most questions relating animals to habitat, however, starting from scratch in this fashion should be uncommon because extensive theory and empirical literature are available to construct hypotheses for nearly all wildlife species. Therefore, the prevalence of habitat definitions based on a posteriori, correlational analysis suggests that landscape ecologists are more often than not in the business of continually generating but not testing new hypotheses of habitat relations. Without identifying which hypotheses are robust and which are not, insights into habitat associations will continue to be ambiguous, to have poor explanatory power, or to lack generality.

Problems with Polygons

Factors that may contribute to the plethora of post hoc analyses of animal habitat relationships include the ready availability of habitat data digitized as polygons and the widespread use of GIS software that depicts landscapes as polygons. Whereas habitat components that contribute to the fitness of animals are commonly modeled on very fine scales (e.g., food-producing plants, extent of escape cover), landscape-scale data simply do not exist for such fine-scale habitat components. Landscape researchers commonly assume a correlation between fine-scale components of habitat and the much coarser landscape data that are available on vegetation associations. When scales differ greatly, such assumptions become dubious.

In fact, reliance on typological definitions of community types for defining habitat, notions of habitat as patches, and the prevalence of inductively derived habitat definitions have created a normative model of habitat among practitioners of landscape ecology that is usually false. The model is simplistic and assumes homogeneity within habitat patches, assumes the existence of distinct boundaries for patches, has no explicit, rigorously established ties (either theoretical or empirical) to the fitness of animals, and is most commonly expressed in GIS applications as a polygon. In the field of landscape ecology, we suggest that the characteristics of polygons have come to shape notions of habitat as much as the biology of the animals being studied. To illustrate our point, we extend the analogy of a human house as habitat that Garshelis (2000) described to illustrate difficulties in evaluating habitat selection. Before doing so we acknowledge that modern human behavior and habitations are limited analogs for wild animals and their habitats, and the parallels we draw here are very general.

Garshelis (2000) presented an imaginary house comprising three areas defined by their uses: the kitchen (meal preparation and eating), the bedroom (sleeping), and other rooms (all other activities, Fig. 5.1A). Note that each of these rooms represents a typological representation of its usefulness, without defining the details within each room that contribute to its use (a table in the kitchen, a bed in the bedroom), and therefore each room can be portrayed as a homogeneous "habitat" patch. Garshelis assigned a percentage of use to each of these rooms and calculated a habitat selection index based on the availability (area) of each room. By making the kitchen larger and the other rooms smaller without changing their percentage of use, he noted that the selectivity index changes, with the presumably improved kitchen counterintuitively becoming less important and the other rooms becoming more important despite being made smaller (Table 5.1). Based on this observation, he concluded that the sensitivity of the selection index to availability of habitat makes use–availability studies fatally flawed. Yet how much of his conclusion is based on use–availability methods and how much on the way he defined habitat?

A graduate student with a small kitchen once noted that increasing the size of her kitchen would do little to increase her use of it until her refrigerator was fixed. Her observation illustrates the point nicely that even though a kitchen contains all the components necessary for eating, more kitchen does not necessarily equate to more opportunities to eat. Therefore, a kitchen is an abstraction of the activities that occur within it. What would change if the value of areas within a house to human activities were portrayed, without regard for the type of the room? In this case we could depict the relative contribution of key resources (e.g., refrigerator, kitchen table, bed, sofa) to the well-being of the house's occupant. To avoid making assumptions of how the resident of this house will use the kitchen in general to maintain her well-being, we can predict how she will use the refrigerator, the stove, the kitchen table, and travel areas, based on what we know about human behavior. From these predictions of the occupant's behavior, we can deduce how the resources

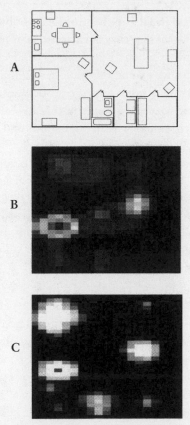

Figure 5.1 Schematic of a house including *(A)* rooms and objects in rooms that are used by the occupant of the house, *(B)* a continuous fitness surface depicting what we might guess the value (ranging from dark hues, low value, to light hues, high value) of each portion of the house is to the occupant based on the objects contained in each room and our knowledge of human behavior, and *(C)* use (ranging from dark hues, low use, to light hues, high use) of the house by the occupant over time, depicted as a utility distribution.

affect the occupant's well-being. These deductions about well-being must be context specific (i.e., the kitchen table will contribute more to the occupant's well-being if the refrigerator works than if it does not, and all resources in the kitchen will have less value if the house has no bed). Where a single location offers more than one resource (say, where standing in front of the stove and sitting at the table coincide in the cramped kitchen), the well-being value reflects the additive effects of multiple resources. The result can be presented

Table 5.1 Changes in how habitat selection is perceived based on whether habitat is modeled as a homogeneous type or as the value of resources to the fitness of the occupant. The analogy of a house and a human occupant is used to differentiate use of rooms defined by their function (kitchen, bedroom, other) based on available area of each room or the availability of resource values (refrigerator, bed, TV, etc.) important to the well-being (loosely analogous to fitness) of the house's occupant. Three different scenarios are presented: an unrenovated house, a renovated house where the kitchen is enlarged but the value of the resources is not increased by the enlargement, and a renovated house with an enlarged kitchen and resource values that are increased 50 percent by the enlargement (adapted from Garshelis 2000).

Rooms	Area			Resources[a]	
	% Used	% Available	Manly–Chesson Standardized Index[b]	% Available	Manly–Chesson Standardized Index
Before renovation					
Kitchen	20	10	.40	30	.20
Bedroom	50	20	.51	25	.60
Others	30	70	.09	45	.20
After renovation (no change in kitchen resources)					
Kitchen	20	20	.25	30	.20
Bedroom	50	20	.63	25	.60
Others	30	60	.12	45	.20
After renovation (kitchen resources increased by 50%)					
Kitchen	20	20	.25	39	.14
Bedroom	50	20	.63	22	.64
Others	30	60	.12	39	.21

[a] Values of room components to the occupant's well-being were assigned on a 0 (no value) to 5 (high value) scale.
[b] Percentage used/percentage available, standardized across rooms to sum to 1.

as a continuous surface representing the potential contribution of each place in the house to the occupant's well-being (Fig. 5.1B).

To construct such a surface, one must know (or be able to hypothesize) in advance how a given resource contributes to the subject's well-being (or fitness) and which resources are ultimately limiting. This approach changes the definition of the "habitat" within the house substantially because rooms are no longer depicted as homogeneous polygons with hard boundaries. The contribution of resources within each room to well-being is no longer abstracted but modeled explicitly based on what is known or hypothesized about the occupant and her needs. In addition, we also no longer have difficulty with artificial polygon boundaries or with the permeability of polygons to movement between rooms. Now, the physical environment (walls) defines the hard boundaries to movement, and the value of explicit travel corridors (via doors) connecting resources can be depicted.

This depiction of habitat changes what we can learn from studying the occupant of the house in at least two ways. First, if we remain interested in the use of specific rooms (habitat types) but define the rooms according to the value of their resources, we can use relative availability of resources between rooms to evaluate use of the rooms by the house's occupant. This approach differs substantially from a typological approach because it does not assume that a given type has uniformly distributed resources or that all patches of a given type are equal. Habitat availability is no longer a simplistic function of the area of the type. Rather, the availability of the resources that contribute to well-being within one room are considered relative to the resources contained in the others. Obviously, when this is done, simply changing the size of the room does not affect an assessment of the value of the room (Table 5.1). The essential resources available within the kitchen (e.g., refrigerator, stove) that contribute to well-being are not changed when the kitchen is enlarged. By eliminating the tenuous assumption that resources are proportional to area that is implicit in a typological definition, we also eliminate the cause for the counterintuitive results of the use–availability analysis performed by Garshelis (2000). The problem was with the way habitat was defined, not the analytical technique used to understand its use. We are not arguing here for the validity of use–availability designs but that a sound biological foundation improves the rigor and performance of any analysis of animal behavior.

Use–availability data can be used to test the accuracy of a fitness surface model. Suppose increasing the size of a really cramped kitchen can make it better able to serve its purpose, as Garshelis (2000) suggested. If our model incorporates comfort for eating areas and multiple uses of comfortable areas (the table can now be used for studying), the area around the kitchen table will gain in value when the kitchen is enlarged. Suppose the remodeling increases the value of resources in the kitchen by 50 percent, but the occupant does not use the larger kitchen more, as was presented by Garshelis. The resulting use–availability analysis indicates a decline in selection for the enlarged kitchen and a counterintuitive increase in preference for the unchanged or smaller other rooms (Table 5.1). What are we to make of this situation, where a predicted increase in resource benefit did not increase its use? Two possible conclusions exist. The value of a resource may be unrelated to the amount of time the occupant uses it. However, people generally do increase use of space when comfort and functionality increase. Alternatively, we modeled the value of the resources incorrectly, and the behavior of the occupant has allowed us to test and reject at least this part of our model. Clearly, this is the value of a priori modeling of fitness value in habitat; we can test our models as hypotheses, modify them accordingly, and then retest the new model with new data. When we predict the values of resources in a house based on what we know of the occupant, we can test our predictions using the occupant's behavior. This important step in modeling habitat is logically impossible and absolutely absent using a posteriori, correlational analyses. The failure of such analyses tells us nothing about why a model failed or how it might be modified or improved.

The second way to understand how habitat as a fitness surface changes our understanding of the house's occupant is to do away with the notion of rooms (habitat types) entirely. Obviously, people characterize rooms by types, but how much these characterizations structure our daily behaviors is not always obvious. Do we go to the kitchen when we are hungry, or do we go to the refrigerator? The answer to both is "yes" as long as we do not also have a refrigerator in the basement where we also keep food. In this latter case, a scientist interested in understanding the foraging behavior of people would be wrong to assume it occurred only in the kitchen (and would be mystified by the unexpected amount of time spent by the occupant in a certain corner of the basement). If a fitness surface can be estimated (Fig. 5.1B) and known locations or a utility distribution derived from known locations of the occupant exist (Fig. 5.1C), by far the most rigorous analysis of predicted habitat associations for an individual is to compare use by the occupant and the distribution of resources directly. In this approach, we can evaluate directly our biological understanding of the critical resources important to the occupant, dispensing with artificial typological abstractions. Because fitness relationships have been modeled a priori, we can have more confidence that behavior consistent with our models reflects true cause-and-effect fitness relationships than if we relied on inductive correlations.

Scaling Up

The biological merits of typological, patch-based definitions of habitats vary with spatial scale and ecological resolution because the assumptions of internal homogeneity and hard boundaries are not universally appropriate. By contrast, habitat defined as a fitness surface has the same biological meaning across all spatial scales and ecological resolutions. Let's extend the house analogy to include houses (habitats) occupied by other people, say, the immediate neighborhood. Assuming all homes are of equal value, we can see the emergence of a more homogeneous resource distribution that begins to approach a polygon depiction (Fig. 5.2). Typological definitions still remain problematic at this spatial resolution, however, because they are limited in what they can tell us about the behaviors or distribution of the people in the neighborhood. They tell us nothing about how people travel between houses, which travel routes are used more often, or whether all living rooms are of equal value within the neighborhood. The simple designation of "living room" fails to explain the distribution of men within the neighborhood on Sunday afternoons during football season when one living room in the neighborhood has a big-screen TV, lots of chairs, a cooler of beer, and a coffee table full of munchies and others do not. Modeling fitness (or well-being) directly allows one to incorporate important differences in the distribution of resources for the entire neighborhood. Approximating this level of information with discrete habitat classes in a way that can explain accurately the behavior and distribution of people within the neighborhood would be very difficult indeed.

Scaling up further, let us consider the neighborhood in the context of the city that contains it. Now we can see a convergence between the city depicted as a homogeneous patch and as a fitness surface (Fig. 5.2), and indeed the patch depiction may be sufficient for modeling some important habitat relationships at this resolution. Some choices for residents at this level are reduced essentially to city or noncity, and the average habitat characteristics within the city may be enough to explain very general population trends for its occupants. Nonetheless, for occupants of the city, it would tell us nothing about good places to live, where shopping is convenient, and so on. The patch model would work best if this were a lone city that filled an isolated island, and distinctions between habitat within (dry land) and without (water) the city are starkest, and justifications for the hard boundary (the shoreline) are strongest. In a more complex environment, questions of clines connecting the city to adjacent rural or suburban habitats, connectivity to other cities, and so on again necessitate simplifying assumptions about how inherently continuous distributions of resources can be modeled as discrete classes. One may argue that at broad scales and coarse ecological resolutions such assumptions are justifiable, but we suggest that this is not always so, and such justifications should be addressed explicitly by those who make

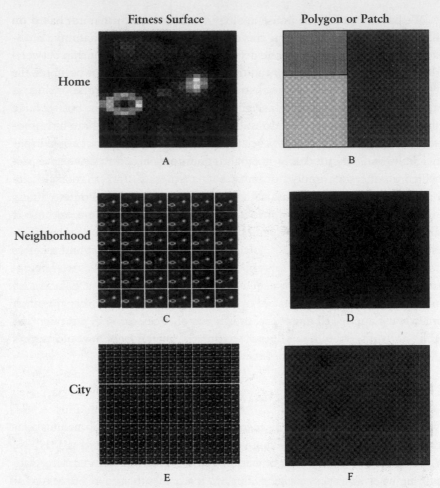

Figure 5.2 Comparison of hypothetical depictions of habitat for humans based on a fitness surface and on habitat types across scales, from house, through neighborhood (a collection of houses), to city (a collection of neighborhoods). A fitness surface depicts the distribution of resources that contribute to the well-being of human occupants within a habitat, whereas a habitat type is portrayed as a homogeneous patch or polygon based on a classification scheme (e.g., room types within a house, a neighborhood, or a city).

them and not established by the form of the data used. As an alternative, scaling up a fitness surface to a broad scale contains in essence the same biological information as a patch depiction but has the added capability of dealing with habitat heterogeneity within the large patch or with complex relationships between the patch, its surroundings, and other patches.

We have stretched the house analogy for definitions of habitat based on fitness quite far. Nonetheless, this analogy has illustrated that any definition of habitat models is, to one degree or another, the relationship between resources within that habitat and the fitness of an animal that occupies. To whatever extent a definition abstracts or generalizes this relationship, it makes simplifying assumptions. Any habitat model simplifies, but we have shown that traditional depictions in landscape ecology of habitat as homogeneous patches of specific types have biological validity only at certain spatial scales and only for certain ecological questions. In contrast, we have presented a conceptual model of habitat as a fitness surface that retains its biological information across all scales and questions. By modeling fitness relationships directly, this approach makes fewer assumptions because it abstracts less. Because of this, and because fitness relationships can be modeled a priori as part of a hypothetico-deductive study design, robust insights can be expected from using this approach to study relationships between animals and their habitats. Although we have focused on behavior (habitat use) as our indicator of fitness in our examples, nothing prevents this approach from being applied to more direct measures of fitness such as reproduction and survival. In the next section, we present a brief overview of insights derived from an application of the fitness surface concept.

Fitness Surfaces and Black Bears

We have modeled habitat as a fitness surface and used it to infer much about the ecology of black bears living in the Pisgah Bear Sanctuary (35°17′ N, 82°47′ W) in the mountains of western North Carolina. Before proceeding further, we wish to acknowledge that when it comes to studying fitness relationships between wild animals and where they live, black bears do not rank high on the list of possible candidate species for study. Bears occur in low densities, they are elusive and live in difficult terrain, and they are long-lived and reproduce slowly. Consequently, detailed information on survival, reproduction, energetics, and behavior is extremely difficult to obtain. However, our understanding of habitat as a fitness surface developed mostly through serendipity as part of our work with bears. One works with the tools one has at hand.

Mitigating the difficulty of obtaining information from bears is the fact that intensive research on bears living in Pisgah has been ongoing since 1981. Over 20 years, approximately 225 bears have been captured nearly 400 times. Many of these bears were fitted with radio collars and tracked under an intensive telemetry protocol that resulted in up to 400 location estimates for individual bears in a given year. Both the frequency and accuracy of locations in the sanctuary were facilitated by the Blue Ridge Parkway, which allowed rapid travel between conveniently located listening points and, because of its elevated location in the sanctuary, minimized the effects of the mountainous terrain on signal bias. Large numbers of accurate locations allow us to estimate the home ranges of bears with a high degree of detail and confidence. Another advantage to studying bears and their habitat is that black bears are predominantly vegetarian, and their diet varies predictably across seasons in the southern Appalachians, with predictable foods making up the bulk of the diet during each season. All food sources can be modeled with reasonable accuracy as fixed in space.

Modeling a Fitness Surface for Pisgah Bears

Zimmerman (1992) and Powell et al. (1997) developed a habitat suitability index (HSI) for black bears living in the southern Appalachians. They developed the index directly from the literature, without using any data collected on bears in the Pisgah Bear Sanctuary, and thus their index represented an a priori hypothesis for the relationship between bears and their habitat. This index was also explicit about how habitat components should contribute to the fitness of bears. The HSI comprises three life requisite variables essential to the fitness of bears: food, den sites, and resources that facilitate escape. Each of these, in turn, is constructed of habitat components (Table 5.2), whose relationship to habitat suitability for black bears is explicitly modeled. The index is spatially explicit, so that relative proximity to food sources and roads and the area of roadless forest are important. Much of the HSI can be modeled using GIS interpretation of U.S. Forest Service inventory data, digital elevation models of terrain, and digital line graphs of linear features such as roads and hydrology. Approximately one third of the HSI components must be estimated from field sampling (Table 5.2). Thus, the HSI consists of layered spatial depictions of the potential contributions of individual habitat components to the fitness of bears, and in its final form it is a continuous map of values that range from 0 (low quality and little potential contribution to fitness) to 1 (high quality and much potential contribution to fitness).

Between 1984 and 1994, we sampled 122 field sites systematically located throughout the sanctuary and used these data, along with data collected from 46 clear-cuts, aerial photographs, and topographic maps, to develop

Table 5.2 Habitat components used to calculate a habitat suitability index for black bears living in the southern Appalachians.

Habitat Component	Relationship to Fitness of Bears	Method of Sampling
Number of fallen logs/ha	Abundance of colonial insects	Field sampling
Anthropogenic food source	Availability of food from human point sources	Aerial or ground survey
Distance to anthropogenic food source	Costs of traveling to human food source	GIS
Distance between anthropogenic food source and escape cover	Risk of acquiring food from human sources	Topographic maps
Distance to perennial water	Abundance of grasses and forbs in spring	GIS
Percentage cover of *Smilax* spp.	Availability of fruit in fall	Field sampling
Percentage cover in berry species	Availability of fruit in summer	Field sampling
Presence of red oak species	Availability of squaw root in summer	Forest inventory data or GIS
Forest cover type	Availability of hard mast in fall	Forest inventory data or GIS
Age of stand	Productivity of hard mast	Forest inventory data or GIS
Number of grape vines/ha	Availability of fruit in fall	Field sampling
Distance to nearest road	Risk of encountering humans	GIS
Area of conterminous forest not bisected by roads	Risk of encountering humans	GIS
Percentage closure of understory	Escape cover	Field sampling
Slope of terrain	Escape cover, availability of caves for denning	GIS
Area in *Rhododendron* spp. or *Kalmia* spp.	Availability of thickets for denning	Aerial photo
Number of trees ≥90 cm DBH*/ha	Availability of large trees for denning	Field sampling

* Diameter breast height (DBH)

an HSI map for the sanctuary. The map shows the predicted quality of habitat (potential contributions to fitness) for each 30- × 30-m pixel in the sanctuary (Fig. 5.3A). We reemphasize that this surface represents an a priori prediction of how each point in space may contribute to the fitness of a bear. It was not derived inductively from correlations between bear locations and arbitrary habitat types, it models first principle relationships between bears and components of their habitat that should be directly related to fitness, and its basis in typological habitat definitions is both minimal and biological (e.g., the use of forest cover type for fall foods reflects the importance of oaks to hard mast production in different forest types and assumes nothing else about contributions of forest types to the fitness of bears). Furthermore, the HSI map for the sanctuary represents a continuous surface that would be difficult to portray as polygons without losing information and even more difficult to develop strictly from polygon-based representations of habitat types such as forest cover (Fig. 5.3B).

Fitness Surfaces and Insights into Bear Biology

The HSI, expressed as a fitness surface, represents a hypothesized relationship between habitat and bears that can be tested as part of a hypothetico-deductive study design. Because the biological meaning of fitness surfaces should be independent of scale, we hypothesized that the HSI should be able to predict behavior of bears on multiple scales, comparable to Johnson's (1980) three orders of habitat selection. This proceeds from a logical extension: If bears prefer habitat that confers high fitness, then on the finest scale they should use areas within their home ranges proportional to the fitness value of those areas (third-order selection), on an intermediate scale they should choose from these landscapes only the best available sites to include within their home ranges (second-order selection), and on a broad scale they ought to choose portions of the landscape that contain high-quality habitat for the general location of their home ranges (first-order selection).

To assess third-order selection of habitat by bears, we evaluated the ability of HSI values to predict habitat preferences of 127 bears (38 adult males, 32 juvenile males, 55 adult females, and 2 juvenile females) within their home ranges and found that preference (estimated as [use – availability]/[use + availability]; Powell et al. 1997) was strongly related to HSI values ($p < .0001$, $r^2 = .45$; Fig. 5.3B). We have not compared values of the HSI with data on survival or reproductive success for individual bears because even after 20 years of work, we do not have enough data to do so.

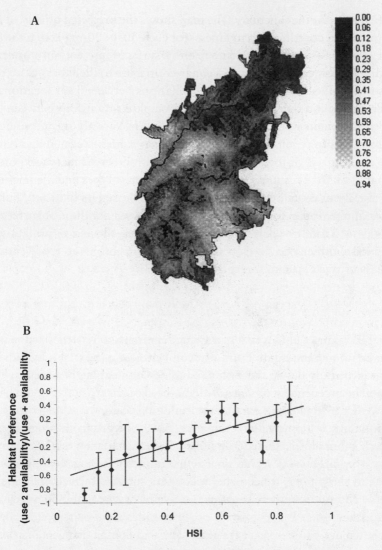

Figure 5.3 A habitat suitability index (HSI) for black bears in the southern Appalachians depicted as *(A)* a fitness surface for the Pisgah Bear Sanctuary in western North Carolina (HSI values range from 0, poor quality, to 1, high quality), and *(B)* the relationship between the HSI and habitat preferences of black bears living in the sanctuary.

Nonetheless, because we modeled the fitness relationship a priori, assumed (with justification) that bears would spend more time in areas that contribute more to their fitness, and found that bears use areas in direct proportion to their HSI value, we have good indirect evidence that the HSI is related to fitness.

Bears respond differently to the distribution of resources on the landscape depending on their age and sex. Adult males range widely (mean home range size of about 45 km^2), and the size of their home ranges appears to be affected primarily by access to females during the breeding season and secondarily by food resources (Powell et al. 1997). Adult females have smaller home ranges (about 16 km^2) whose sizes are affected most by the availability, location, and productivity of food (Powell et al. 1997). Because of this strong tie to food resources, we wanted to test whether the entire HSI or just the food component, F, of the HSI better predicted behavior of adult females. Therefore, we evaluated F against habitat preferences of adult females and found that it had an even stronger relationship ($p < 0.0001$, $r^2 = 0.78$; Mitchell 1997). We can deductively infer from this test that food resources are more important to the fitness of adult females living in the Pisgah Bear Sanctuary than a combination of food, denning, and escape resources. Our tests not only showed that our fitness surface can predict third-order habitat selection by bears, but also gave us biological insights that would be impossible to derive with the same level of rigor from inductive analysis.

To assess second-order habitat selection of bears, we developed a model of optimal selection of sites within that area for inclusion in the home range, based on habitat portrayed as a fitness surface (Mitchell 1997). Because of the particularly strong relationship between the home ranges of adult females and food resources, we depicted the fitness surface for Pisgah as a grid of 250×250-m cells (approximating our telemetry error of ± 260 m), each cell was assigned its own value of F, and we modeled only the home ranges of adult females. For our home range model, we assumed that energy expended for travel diminishes the net value of resources distant from the center point. Because bears have home range cores (Powell et al. 1997), we modeled the fitness value of any given cell as the F value assigned to it (potential contribution of the cell to a bear's fitness) divided by the distance of that cell from the center point or core of the bear's home range (yielding an estimate of the average net contribution of that cell to the bear if it included it in its home range, F). Discounting the value of a distant resource by its distance has a long history in optimal foraging research (Stephens and Krebs 1986). The notion that travel distance should affect whether an animal selects an area for inclusion in its home range strongly argues for a depiction of habitat as a continuous surface, where resource values can be discounted easily by distance between any two points in space. Such an approach would be difficult for landscapes comprising large polygons. For example, in discounting for distance, does one measure distance to the center of the polygon or to the edge? How would the high value of habitat on the near side of a large polygon be distinguished from the lower value on the far side? These are all problematic questions.

Dividing all cells by their distances from the center cell yields a highly kurtotic distribution where F is high near the center but declines exponentially with distance from the center. We modeled second-order habitat selection as the selection of cells in descending order of F until the home range contains fitness resources sufficient to satisfy a hypothesized minimum threshold for survival and reproduction. If all bears used these criteria only to choose home ranges, all would choose the same home range at the single best spot on the landscape. Clearly, bears do not do this. Therefore, we depleted the resources available to other bears after an initial bear selected its home range. Thus, resources on a landscape available to support a bear's home range change as more home ranges are added. Areas with high fitness values can support a high density of bears, but as these areas become depleted, bears will incorporate areas of lesser value into their home ranges, tending toward an ideal free distribution (Fretwell and Lucas 1970).

We used this home range model to generate simulated home ranges based on F for each of 42 home ranges of adult females living in Pisgah from 1981 to 1994. For each home range of a bear, F values were generated by dividing F values by their distance from the center (core) of the bear's true home range. Cells were then selected based on their F values until hypothesized minimum thresholds of accumulated F were reached. We compared the similarity of each of the simulated home ranges with the true home range using an index of spatial similarity, S (Mitchell 1997) that ranges from 0 (no similarity) to 1 (complete similarity). Models predicted the home ranges of bears with reasonable accuracy (Fig. 5.4C). When we considered the simulated home ranges that best fit true home ranges, average S was .80. Our models were able to emulate closely second-order habitat selection by bears using a fitness surface, which would not have been possible had we defined habitat typologically (Fig. 5.4A versus 5.4B).

We did not directly evaluate first-order habitat selection. As an indirect way of assessing how bears placed their home ranges on the landscape, we evaluated the spatial dispersion of their home range centers. At broad scales

A

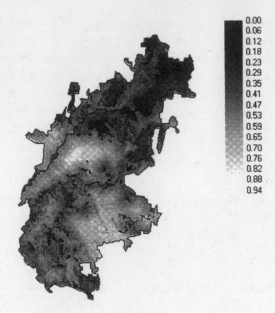

| 0.00 |
| 0.06 |
| 0.12 |
| 0.18 |
| 0.23 |
| 0.29 |
| 0.35 |
| 0.41 |
| 0.47 |
| 0.53 |
| 0.59 |
| 0.65 |
| 0.70 |
| 0.76 |
| 0.82 |
| 0.88 |
| 0.94 |

C

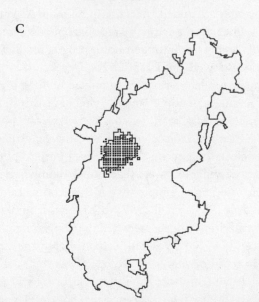

Figure 5.4 Habitat depicted as *(A)* a fitness surface for the Pisgah Bear Sanctuary and *(B)* a function of forest type, presented with the results of home range simulations for female bear 96 in 1984 generated from each of the depictions of habitat (*C* for the fitness surface, *D* for the definition based on forest type). Habitat values range from 0, poor quality, to 1, high quality. The solid outline within

B

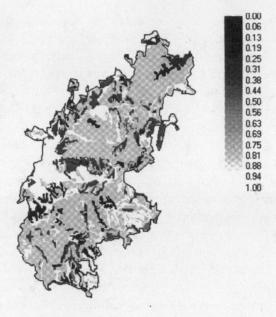

D

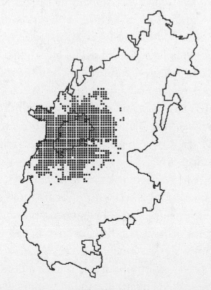

the boundaries of the sanctuary in figures *C* and *D* depicts the true home range of bear 96; the dots depict the simulated home ranges estimated by an optimal home range model. The model selected patches for inclusion in simulated home ranges based on habitat quality and the distance of patches from the center of the home range.

one can expect home ranges of animals to cluster on areas that confer high fitness. We used our home range model to generate 100 simulated home ranges on the fitness surface of F for the sanctuary. Instead of using the center points of observed home ranges as starting points for our models as we did before, we used moving-windows analysis of the fitness surface (Isaaks and Srivastava 1989) to identify the best region of the sanctuary for establishing each home range center. Beginning with windows of large spatial extent, we identified the region within Pisgah with the highest average F value. Within this region we repeated the moving-windows analysis on increasingly finer spatial scales until the single point in space with the highest F value across all grains was identified. Each time a simulated home range was established, resources within that home range were depleted, changing the distribution of F for subsequent home ranges (Mitchell 1997). We then compared the spatial dispersion of simulated home range centers with observed home range centers of adult female bears that lived in Pisgah from 1981 to 1994. Spatial distributions for both simulated and true home ranges were clumped (mean/variance ratio was .37 ± .14 for simulated home ranges and .46 ± .10 for true home ranges) around areas of high F values. The similarity in spatial distribution between simulated and true home ranges suggested that our models mimicked first-order habitat selection by bears. Because of the broad scale of first-order selection, it would be interesting to see whether our results could be duplicated using typological definitions of habitat. The convergence of a fitness surface with a typological definition of habitat at broad scales (Fig. 5.2) suggests that this is a reasonable possibility.

We have demonstrated that a priori modeling of habitat as a fitness surface has allowed us to assess the behavior and distribution of bears across three spatial and behavioral scales: placement of home range locations on a landscape of cells, selection of individual cells for home ranges, and cell use within home ranges. To have such predictive capability, the relationship between our fitness surface and the behavior of bears must capture a biological pattern, a fitness relationship, beyond what a simple correlation between use and habitat types can portray. It is difficult to imagine a typological substitute that would accomplish the same objectives across all three orders of habitat selection. Few of the components of the HSI could be reasonably assigned to a broad habitat type and are for the most part distributed in space independently of each other. For instance, overstory vegetation is commonly used as a habitat class, but maps of the HSI and overstory types for our study area (Figs. 5.4A and 5.4B) are distinctly different. Although overstory may be a good predictor for some elements of bear habitat (e.g., production of hard mast), it clearly captures little of the information that the entire HSI does. Given how closely our home range models were able to approximate the behavior of bears, we doubt that the same or better results could be achieved by defining habitat as polygons depicting overstory vegetation.

Making the Match

Our home range models approximate closely the behavior of bears on multiple scales for several important reasons that illustrate the points we have made in this chapter. First, our definition of habitat was biologically based and modeled directly components of habitat that contribute to the fitness of bears. This differs greatly from a typological definition, which assumes these largely independently distributed components of habitat can be abstracted into discrete habitat classes. Second, we portrayed habitat as a continuous fitness surface, thereby avoiding assumptions of homogeneity within habitat polygons and avoiding the problems of defining boundaries for patches or polygons. Third, our habitat model was developed and tested as an a priori hypothesis about the fitness relationship between bears and where they live. We have more confidence in our understanding of why bears behave in accordance with our predictions than we could were we relying on inductively derived, a posteriori correlations. Importantly, this depiction of habitat, without modification, yielded insights into the biology of bears on three different scales. Much has been written about the role of scale in understanding habitat relationships on landscapes (Wiens 1989), but little has been done to define that role. As long as we use a definition of *habitat* whose biological meaning is itself scale dependent, our conceptual and technical approaches will limit our understanding. Habitat depicted as a fitness surface offers in a single definition a biologically robust tool for understanding animal–habitat relationships across spatial scales and ecological resolutions.

Admittedly, using hypothetico-deductive research to develop a model of habitat as a fitness surface is an intensive, front-loaded process. Management agencies may find the time and effort needed to develop models, to estimate, and then to test fitness surfaces impractical or difficult to justify; inductive use of typological definitions is simpler and less time consuming. Nonetheless, the long-term trade-offs between the two approaches are worth considering. We have demonstrated that the efficacy of a typological definition of habitat as patches depends on a close match between the spatial scale and ecological resolution of the animal–habitat associations being modeled. We have also demonstrated the weaknesses of assuming that a posteriori correlations between animals and abstract habitat classes reflect true fitness relationships. To achieve management objectives based on a single inductive, typological definition of habitat, a manager must be fortunate enough to model the right ecological relationship, at the right scale, using an untested habitat classification scheme that by chance reflects first-order fitness relationships. The likelihood of any of these fortuitous events occurring individually, much less in concert, can never be known under this approach; no assurance can be offered that management practices based on it will achieve their desired ends. Similarly, no assurance exists that they will not result in very unintended and undesirable consequences, either. A trial-and-error approach to evaluating different typological habitat definitions suitable for the scale and ecological relationships of interest, to arrive at one inspiring confidence as a basis for management actions, will easily be more exhaustive than simply modeling fitness and testing the model. Contrast the correlation approach with a fitness surface approach, in which habitat definitions are based on tested biological relationships and can yield robust predictions across spatial scales and ecological resolutions (achieving an economy of scales, so to speak). If one's objective is to obtain models of habitat that in the long term are cost-effective, are biologically robust, and provide sound foundations for successful management across multiple landscape scales, we suggest that adherence to traditional correlational approaches to modeling habitat is the riskier choice. At the very least, we recommend that both researchers and managers step back from the breathtaking pace of developments in landscape ecology and reassess the assumptions that underlie some of our commonly and uncritically accepted paradigms such as how habitat is defined and portrayed on landscape scales. We will have achieved our purpose if this chapter causes landscape ecologists to pause and think every time they see a polygon labeled as animal habitat.

Summary

A dominant paradigm in landscape ecology is depiction of habitat as a patch, with internal homogeneity and a distinct boundary. This definition is based on the ready availability of GIS data on vegetative communities classified from remote sensing, the role of patch theory in laying key foundations of landscape ecology, and the prevalence of a posteriori, correlative approaches to describing habitat of animals. Whereas each of these factors is appropriate or necessary for different management approaches, conceptual pursuits, or research questions, the combination of the three commonly seen for most depictions of habitat within landscape ecology has created a normative model of habitat among landscape ecologists that is usually false. Because any definition of habitat is, directly or indirectly, based on the fitness of animals, we advocate a definition of habitat that proceeds from biological first principles, where the distribution of resources critical to the survival and reproduction of animals is depicted in space, which we call a fitness surface. Habitat modeled and mapped in this way resembles a continuous (as opposed to a classified) surface. Assumptions about relationships between vegetation classes and key resources are minimized, as are the simplifying assumptions of depicting habitat as patches. Furthermore, unlike patch-based definitions of habitat, fitness surfaces are scale-independent and therefore should capture biological meaning at any spatial resolution. We suggest that such models must be developed a priori and tested with data on animals to maximize the scientific rigor of habitat definitions and thereby the confidence that researchers and managers can have in insights derived from them.

In this chapter, we demonstrated the weaknesses of depicting habitat as homogeneous patches that abstract biological reality in ways convenient to our methods and showed that depictions of habitat as a fitness surface are much less susceptible to these problems. We further demonstrated how a fitness surface, developed as an a priori hypothesis, can be used to derive insights on the ecology of black bears, at multiple spatial scales, that could not be achieved using traditional, patch-based definitions of habitat common in landscape ecology. The selection of the best definition to use in any research or management situation should be based on spatial scale and ecological resolution of interest. Because a fitness surface is generally more robust than patch-based definitions for both of these criteria, we recommend modeling habitat as a fitness surface.

Acknowledgments

We thank J. Bissonette, I. Storch, and an anonymous reviewer for their encouragement and helpful comments in developing this chapter. We also thank graduate students Gordon Warburton, John Zimmerman, Peggy Horner, Mike Fritz, Erran Seaman, John Noel, Adrienne Kovach, Vanessa Sorensen, Pete Mooreside, Tim Langer, Melissa Reynolds, Jennifer Sevin, and Jorie Favreau and visiting scientist Francesca Antonelli for their help in collecting data. More than three dozen undergraduate interns, technicians, and volunteers also assisted in data collection, as did personnel from the

North Carolina Wildlife Resources Commission and more than 300 Earth-watch volunteers. We are grateful for their help. Financial and logistic support for our studies came from Bob Bacon and Karen Hailpern, the Bear Fund of the Wyoming Chapter of the Wildlife Society, Joe Busse, Citibank Corp., the Conservation Fund of the Columbus (Ohio) Zoo, the Geraldine R. Dodge Foundation, Earthwatch/The Center for Field Research, Federal Aid in Wildlife Restoration Project W-57 administrated through the North Carolina Wildlife Resources Commission, Grand Valley State University McNair Scholars Program, International Association for Bear Research and Management, Ginger and Dick King, McIntire Stennis funds, the National Geographic Society, the National Park Service, the National Rifle Association, the North Carolina Agricultural Research Service, North Carolina State University, 3M Co., the USDA Forest Service, Wildlands Research Institute, Wil-Burt Corp., and Wildlink, Inc., Port Clyde. Stinson Canning Companies donated sardines for bait. We appreciate all of their support. The USGS Alabama Cooperative Fish and Wildlife Research Unit is jointly supported by the USGS, the Alabama Division of Wildlife and Freshwater Fisheries, Auburn University, the Wildlife Management Institute, and the U.S. Fish and Wildlife Service.

LITERATURE CITED

Burnham K. P., and D. R Anderson. 1998. Model selection and inference: a practical information-theoretic approach. Springer-Verlag, New York.

Caswell, H. 2001. Matrix population models: construction, analysis, and interpretation. Sinauer Associates, Sunderland, MA.

Charnov, E. L. 1976. Optimal foraging, the marginal value theorem. Theoretical Population Biology 9:129–136.

Clements, F. E. 1936. Nature and structure of the climax. Ecology 24:252–284.

Corsi, F., J. De Leeuw, and A. Skidmore. 2000. Modeling species distributions with GIS. Pages 389–434 in L. Boitani and T. K. Fuller (eds.), Research techniques in animal ecology. Columbia University Press, New York.

Fisher, R. A. 1930. The genetical theory of natural selection. Clarendon Press, Oxford, UK.

Forman, R. T. T., and M. Godron. 1986. Landscape ecology. Wiley, New York.

Fretwell, S. D., and H. L. Lucas. 1970. On territorial behavior and other factors influencing habitat distribution in birds. Acta Biotheoretica 19:16–36.

Garshelis, D. L. 2000. Delusions in habitat evaluation: measuring use, selection, and importance. Pages 111–164 in L. Boitani and T. K. Fuller (eds.), Research techniques in animal ecology. Columbia University Press, New York.

Gleason, H. A. 1926. The individualist concept of plant association. Torrey Botanical Club Bulletin 53:7–26.

Hall, L. S., P. R. Krausman, and M. L. Morrison. 1997. The habitat concept and a plea for standard terminology. Wildlife Society Bulletin 25:173–182.

Harris, L. D., and J. Sanderson. 2000. The re-membered landscape. Pages 91–112 in J. Sanderson and L. D. Harris (eds.), Landscape ecology: a top-down approach. Lewis Publishers, New York.

Isaaks, E. H., and R. M. Srivastava. 1989. An introduction to applied geostatistics. Oxford University Press, New York.

Johnson, D. H. 1980. The comparison of usage and availability measurements for evaluating resource preference. Ecology 61:65–71.

Kareiva, P. 1990. Population dynamics in spatially complex environments: theory and data. Philosophical Transactions of the Royal Society of London 330:175–190.

Kozakiewicz, M. 1995. Resource tracking in space and time. Pages 136–148 in L. Hansson, L. Fahrig, and G. Merriam (eds.), Mosaic landscapes and ecological processes. Chapman & Hall, London.

McGarigal, K., and B. J. Marks. 1995. FRAGSTATS: spatial pattern analysis program for quantifying landscape structure. USDA Forest Service, Pacific Northwest Research Station, General Technical Report PNW-GTR-351, Portland, OR.

Mitchell, M. S. 1997. Optimal home ranges: models and application to black bears. Ph.D. thesis, North Carolina State University, Raleigh.

Morgan, J. N., and B. G. Savitsky. 1998. Error and the gap analysis model. Pages 170–178 in B. G. Savitsky and T. E. Lacher (eds.), GIS methodologies for developing conservation strategies: tropical forest recovery and wildlife management in Costa Rica. Columbia University Press, New York.

Morris, D. W. 1995. Habitat selection in mosaic landscapes. Pages 110–135 in L. Hansson, L. Fahrig, and G. Merriam (eds.), Mosaic landscapes and ecological processes. Chapman & Hall, London.

Morrison, M. L., B. G. Marcot, and R. W. Mannan. 1992. Wildlife–habitat relationships: concepts and applications. University of Wisconsin Press, Madison.

Platt, J. R. 1964. Strong inference. Science 146:347–352.

Powell, R. A., J. W. Zimmerman, and D. E. Seaman. 1997. Ecology and behavior of North American black bears: home ranges, habitat and social organization. Chapman & Hall, London.

Scott, J. M., F. Davis, B. Csuti, R. Noss, B. Butterfield, C. Groves, H. Anderson, S. Caicco, F. D'Erchia, T. C. Edwards, Jr., J. Ulliman, and R. G. Wright. 1993. Gap analysis: a geographical approach to protection of biological diversity. Wildlife Monographs 123:1–43.

Stearns, S. C. 1992. The evolution of life histories. Oxford University Press, Oxford, UK.

Stephens, D. W., and J. R. Krebs. 1986. Foraging theory. Princeton University Press, Princeton, NJ.

Turner, S. J., R. V. O'Neill, and H. H. Shugart. 1991. Pattern and scale: statistics for landscape ecology. Pages 17–49 in M. G. Turner and R. H. Gardner (eds.), Quantitative methods in landscape ecology. Springer-Verlag, New York.

Wiens, J. A. 1989. Spatial scaling in ecology. Functional Ecology 3:385–397.

Wiens, J. A. 1995. Landscape mosaics and ecological theory. Pages 1–26 in L. Hansson, L. Fahrig, and G. Merriam (eds.), Mosaic landscapes and ecological processes. Chapman & Hall, London.

Wiens, J. A. 1999. The science and practice of landscape ecology. Pages 371–384 in J. M. Klopatek and R. H. Gardner (eds.), Landscape ecological analysis: issues and applications. Springer-Verlag, New York.

Williams, B. K. 1996. Assessment of accuracy in the mapping of vertebrate biodiversity. Journal of Environmental Management 47:269–282.

Zimmerman, J. W. 1992. A habitat suitability index model for black bears in the southern Appalachian region, evaluated with location error. Ph.D. thesis, North Carolina State University, Raleigh.

CHAPTER SIX

Implications of Body Mass Patterns

Linking Ecological Structure and Process to Wildlife Conservation and Management

JAN P. SENDZIMIR, CRAIG R. ALLEN,
LANCE GUNDERSON, AND CRAIG STOW

The unprecedented scale of problems affecting wildlife ecology today overwhelms many managers. Challenges are no longer local in origin but rather a tangle of local, regional, and even global externalities often interacting in unpredictable ways. Previously isolated ecosystems have become increasingly connected at global, hemispheric, and regional levels, eroding their integrity. Endocrine-disrupting compounds applied in Mexico have changed avian sexual development in the Great Lakes (Colborn et al. 1996). Chamois (*Rupicapra rupicapra*) reproduction in the Carpathian mountains falters when the color of newborns is no longer cryptic because climate change prematurely melts snow cover (K. Perzanowski, Polish Academy of Sciences, personal communication, 1999). Climate change predictions (Houghton et al. 2001) now project sea level rise up to 5 m within the next few centuries, which will displace more than a billion people and inundate coastal plains. The populations of many species have dwindled and disappeared as they have been displaced by invasive and introduced species and as habitat removal and fragmentation change migration patterns and the carrying capacity of landscapes.

These large-scale crises surprise us and force us to look beyond local issues to consider regional influences. This is not the first time that our world views have been challenged to expand. More than a half century ago, collapsing fish and forestry industries forced resource managers to consider regional context when assessing local problems. These reassessments of causes at larger scales provoked a variety of theoretical advances in ecology (see Walters 1986 for forestry and fishery examples). Theories of catastrophe (Casti 1982), complexity (Kauffman 1993; Kay 2000), and hierarchy (Allen and Starr 1982; O'Neill et al. 1986) marked new insights into the structure, function, and dynamics of ecosystems, especially at larger scales. The resulting synthesis of all these initiatives is summed in the descriptive term for ecosystems as "complex, adaptive systems" (Holling 1992; Levin 1992, 1998; Kay 2000). However, whereas these theories increased our understanding of the interactions underlying these resource crises, the science of putting these new insights into practice is in its infancy. What tools do these theories put in the hands of a manager with on-the-ground responsibility to manage and conserve wildlife?

A central question in ecology has been, Is there meaningful, repeatable pattern in ecosystems, or do all apparent patterns and structures arise continuously from chance interactions that are *contingent* (Lawton 1999) on local conditions of species abundance, environment, and the web of species interactions? In the former case, our understanding of ecosystem pattern and structure resulting from the study of one ecosystem can be applied to other systems. On the other hand, if systems are assembled randomly, then each event is unique, and we must learn anew in each ecosystem. Holling (1986, 1992) addressed these questions by asking whether random events could produce the regularity observed in disturbance periodicities (fire, flood, pest outbreaks). Does the regular return (around 8 to 12 years in the absence of intervention) of fire to Florida sand pine forests indicate some deeper, underlying structure that persists despite random variations? Similar clustering of time series data is evident for such processes as insect outbreaks (Clark et al. 1979; McNamee et al. 1981; Holling 1988, 1992), fires (Clark 1990), and floods (Rogers and Fiering 1986), which all cluster into small sets of repetitive cycles. Holling (1992) proposed that ecosystems have structure that emerges from the effects of few processes that operate over distinct scales in space and time. This chapter describes efforts to test how such regularities of pattern in time and space consistently influence (entrain) characteristics of animals, such as body size. In brief, Holling predicted that animal species will cluster in size (lumps) as they interact with the clustering in time (periodicities) and space (landscape structure) of their environment and that those animal size clusters will correspond with the key scales of structure available in a given system.

We first review the findings in support of this proposition and then discuss its management applications for vertebrates in terrestrial ecosystems. In particular, we address four questions directed at wildlife management. What evidence is there that ecosystems operate as complex adaptive systems (CASs)? Are there predictable natural patterns ("Is the world lumpy?"), and does this influence animal behavior, survival, and evolution? How do animals interact with a lumpy world, and what are the consequences for their conservation and management? And finally, does a lumpy framework of analysis help us address at what scales animals respond to pattern in the environment?

The Spoor of Complex Adaptive Systems: Patterns of Ecological Processes, Landscape Structure, and Body Size

Ecological processes such as succession, nutrient cycling, and seed dispersal can sustain and sometimes transform ecosystems over time (Peterson et al. 1998). We can describe an ecosystem as a CAS if complex behavior emerges unpredictably (nonlinearly) without the influence of central control but as a result of adaptive behavior by its component, interacting agents (Holland 1995). Such agents can self-organize (change their rules of interaction as experience accumulates) and act in anticipation such that, under stress, the system coheres or completely changes its composition. If ecosystems operate as CASs, then we predict that they persist or change depending on the functioning of feedback interactions between ecological processes, landscape structure, and biota (Allen and Hoekstra 1992; Levin 1998; Peterson et al. 1998). We emphasize that complex systems, particularly ecosystems, are organized hierarchically because separation into semiautonomous levels is a prerequisite for evolutionary advances to take hold (Simon 1962). Evolution is unlikely in a world without hierarchical levels to isolate organisms from the inordinate distraction possible if all organisms in a system could interact with equal intensity (Allen and Hoekstra 1992). Therefore, the first test is to see whether we detect discontinuities in landscape patterns that suggest hierarchical structure. The second test looks for discontinuities in animal sizes that suggest a hierarchical organization of biota that reflects the discontinuities in the landscape pattern. We describe evidence from these two tests and then consider what interactions might cause them. First, we examine hierarchical landscape pattern more closely.

We refer to landscape structure here as the distribution in space and time of opportunities for animals to eat, compete for mates or territory, find shelter, and nest. Holling (1992) proposed that these opportunities are not spread smoothly across the landscape like continuous gradients running from dry to wet or high to low. Rather, opportunities tend to cluster discontinuously because different sets of opportunities are evident depending on the interaction between discontinuous scales of perception and scales of landscape structure. We use two factors, window (or extent) and grain (resolution), to describe how perception scales with body size. A vole sees very different sets of opportunities than a moose. Both are mutually oblivious to or ignore key landscape features of the other. Grass runway corridors for voles are invisible to or ignored as noise by a moose, and the sizes and distances between alder thickets for moose are ignored as background by voles. How can landscape ecologists begin to imagine the separate perceptive scales of different animals? The book *Powers of Ten* (Morrison and Morrison 1994) illustrates vividly the jerky or discontinuous way in which different landscape features jump out at one as one changes perspective by zooming in or out from any point in space. Starting from a beach blanket and stepping back in stages that differ by an order of magnitude (1 m, 10 m, 100 m, 1 km, and so forth) different patterns of attributes are apparent at different ranges of distance from the origin. After several steps one pattern suddenly disappears, to be replaced by another set previously not evident.

Such jumps between evident sets of pattern are called scale breaks (Allen et al. 1999), which separate the scales at which we can delineate one spatial domain from another. Scale breaks do not necessarily coincide with any measure, such as order of magnitude shifts in distance, and the quantification of scale breaks remains a key future avenue of inquiry. The theories underlying CASs propose that such a discontinuous pattern is fundamental to ecosystems and results when different sets of processes operate over distinct ranges of scale, organizing the landscape into different spatial and temporal domains. If animals perceive and respond to this discontinuous structure (Holling 1992), we may gain insight into the assembly and structure of animal communities. If animals respond to discontinuous scales of landscape structure, the species in an assemblage of animals will cluster at discrete size ranges because specific size ranges will optimally compete for resources in each of these spatiotemporal domains. Briefly, lumpy landscape patterns should be mirrored by lumpy body size patterns, as interactions link animals with the lumpy geometries of structure and the time and space clustering of ecological processes.

The groups of objects that constitute the predominant structure of each level in the landscape hierarchy are intuitive. The fine-scale structure of herbaceous vegetation, the medium-scale mosaic of forest patches, and the grand geological sweep of the landscape have an appealing cohesiveness and fit, nested like Russian dolls. But is there real pattern giving rise to this appealing sense of symmetry, or are these notions just another imposition of human values and scales on the world? And if there is real, discontinuous landscape pattern, what significance does it really have for animals? We discuss efforts to apply objective measures of landscape pattern and then examine evidence of similar patterns in animal assemblages.

Landscape Structure: Multilevel Patterns

Many concepts about hierarchical structure and nonlinear dynamics in ecosystems that suggest a discontinuous or lumpy world were presented decades ago in system science (Simon 1962; von Bertalanffy 1968; Odum 1982). Opportunities to detect pattern and test these ideas at larger scales awaited the advent of satellite sensors and cheap, high-speed computers in the early 1980s. Since then attempts to develop objective means to detect pattern without human bias have created a variety of indices for landscape structure, such as fractal breaks (Mandelbrot 1982; Morse et al. 1985; Milne 1997) and fractal dimensions based on perimeter area and on mass (Hargis et al. 1997).

If key ecological processes interact at characteristic space and time scales to produce discontinuous structures, then data from systems should reflect such a pattern. That is, cross-scale analyses of key spatial variables should reveal discrete changes in pattern as scale changes, and analyses of time series should produce a few dominant frequencies that reflect a clustering of temporal processes. In this chapter we present results that show how such analyses identify key structures and processes from a large freshwater wetland ecosystem, the Florida Everglades, and are indicative of a general pattern for all ecosystem types.

Spatial Attributes of Natural Landscapes

Spatial and temporal data that are thought to represent key variables in the Everglades ecosystem were analyzed for breaks and clusters. Fourier techniques were used to detect dominant frequencies in time series data including rain-fall, water depth, water flow, evaporation, and fire sizes. Spatial data of vegetation and topographic profiles were analyzed using fractal techniques to test for breaks in scaling dimensions.

Three dominant frequencies appear in the time series data. Surface water levels fluctuate on daily, annual, and decadal cycles. The daily and annual fluctuations in stage levels are related to processes that produce convective thunderstorms. The dominant frequencies for water flow, evaporation, and fire frequencies occur at approximately decadal intervals (Gunderson 1992). The longer-term fluctuations appear to coincide with variation patterns in two processes: evapotranspiration rates and, to a less evident degree, decadal fluctuations in rainfall related to the periodicities of El Niño events.

Spatial patterns exhibit scales of self-similarity separated by distinct breaks. The soil surface topography appears to vary at two distinct spatial scales. The broad scale apparently is a result of geologic features, and the small scale appears related to the processes of organic soil accretion and removal. The vegetation patterns exhibit breaks between regions of self-similarity related to the interaction between water levels, water flow, and fire patterns (Gunderson 1992).

Figure 6.1 shows cross-scale ecosystem structure and processes in the Everglades mapped in the form of a Stommel diagram. The primary axes are logarithmic scales over space and time that cover about six orders of magnitude and are matched with their nonlog equivalents. Entities within the diagram are defined by grain and extent. Grain is the smallest resolution needed to identify an entity, as indicated by the lowest margin (time) and the left edge (space) of a polygon in Figure 6.1. These correspond to the minimum time step in sampling to detect an object and the pixel size on a screen at which an object is recognizable. By the same token, the window is the extent of that object, as indicated by the highest margin (time) and the right edge (space) of a polygon in Figure 6.1. These correspond to the lifespan and the window size that can frame the entire object of interest. Breaks in the fractal dimension of spatial patterns can be used to define breaks between entities in the spatial dimension. Similarly, dominant frequencies appear to differentiate temporal entities or levels.

The analysis of the Everglades ecosystem supports the hypothesis that spatial patterns exhibit breaks and that temporal patterns cluster around a few cycles. Spatial patterns exhibit scales of self-similarity separated by distinct breaks. The soil surface topography appears to vary at two distinct spatial

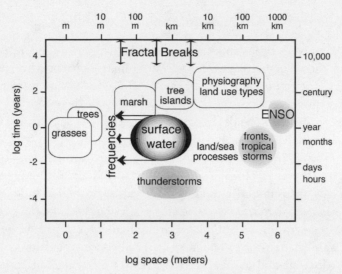

Figure 6.1 Stommel plot of structures and processes in the Everglades ecosystem, along dimensions of space and time. The upper boxes indicate vegetation hierarchy, from individual plants to physiographic groupings. The lower tier represents the scales of meteorological processes that influence the ecosystem. Fractal breaks (scale breaks, as assessed by changes in fractal dimensions) that delimit the domains of landscape features are shown. Dominant frequencies of hydrologic processes in the Everglades are depicted as arrows from the surface water representation.

scales. Breaks in fire size may be related to the approximately decadal time period between large burns. The vegetation patterns exhibit breaks between regions of self-similarity, although the reasons are unclear. Temporal patterns in water stage and flow reflect dominant frequencies in the interplay between the faster dynamics of the atmosphere, the intermediate speeds of the surface water (stage and flow), and the longer-term variations in vegetation, climate, and sea level.

Scale breaks in the time behavior of processes and the spatial distribution of landscape pattern confirm in the Everglades what has seemed apparent in a range of landscapes: The environment is clustered into a small number of groups of objects of similar size. Were variation in object sizes unlimited, then no clustering would be evident. However, size variation is bounded for different types of objects from the smallest to largest scales: vegetation, patches, ecotones, and topography. The conservation implications of hierarchical patterns in landscapes increase if animals respond to it in predictable ways.

Macroecology: Size Attributes of Animal Assemblages

Even if distinctive patterns appear to divide a landscape into separate ranges of scale, is there compelling evidence that animals interact with such discontinuous pattern in ecologically meaningful ways? We now consider evidence from animal assemblages, such as all the animals of one taxon that feed and reproduce on a landscape. A typical example of such an assemblage might be all mammals in the Everglades ecosystem.

Brown (1995) proposed macroecology to explore overarching patterns at larger scales (biome to global scales in space and decadal to millennial in time) to bridge gaps in understanding of processes defined at smaller scales by population and community ecologists. By forging synthetic links between ecology, biogeography, paleobiology, and macroevolution, macroecology aims to establish an informed context for smaller-scale questions of abundance, distribution, and species diversity as affected by interactions between species and their environment. The shapes and bounds of statistical distributions of animal size indices are patterns that reflect either "intrinsic, evolutionary or extrinsic, environmental constraints on variation" (Brown 1995, p. 18). In brief, the echoes of large-scale processes are sought in the size distributions of animal assemblages over wide areas (landscape level and higher). Some general trends do relate animal morphometric patterns to large-scale evolutionary, ecological, and climatic patterns. Mammal body size correlates strongly with seasonality, the amplitude of seasonal climatic variation (Lindstedt and Boyce 1984). For evolutionary lineages, the general trend for body size to increase within a phylogenetic group (Cope's Law) now appears to apply only to the upper size range because many species shrink in size over evolutionary time (LaBarbera 1989).

Macroecology (Brown 1995; Maurer 1999) expands the arena in which we can test ideas about ecological processes from the local to the regional and even continental. However, are these the only scales at which ecological processes operate? Holling (1992) proposed a far wider variety of scales of operation for the ecological processes structuring the boreal forest, dissecting it more finely into eight separate scale ranges. Clearly, the science of defining the scales of operation for ecological processes is in its infancy (Peterson et al. 1998; Peterson 2000). For example, the tension emerging from arbitrary applications of a wide variety of different scales to the term *ecosystem* (Noss and Cooperrider 1994) sparked the struggle to define its true dimensions or abandon it altogether. Examining landscape pattern simultaneously *across scales* will provide a more unifying framework for defining ecologically meaningful scale domains than trying to synthesize analyses done individually at different scales (e.g., mycologists, mammalogists, and forest ecologists).

Lumpy Size Patterns in Animal Assemblages

Intuitive and even objective indications that landscapes are hierarchies do not prove any link with animal behavior or community assembly. Scale breaks are distinct to human eyes, but it is premature to assume what animals perceive (Ims 1995). Even if evidence existed that animals perceive scale breaks, is there evidence that animals respond to scale breaks and clusters of objects within a domain of scale? To test this, Holling (1992) proposed that discontinuities in the landscape would be translated into gaps in the size distributions of the animal assemblages. If a mouse's scale of perception fits only a certain window and reveals only certain objects clearly, then its choices to feed or flee depend on those perceptions. And if the scale of perception is proportional to body size, then for each scale only a certain range of body sizes perceive resources within that scale range. Therefore, animal species should cluster in certain size ranges that compete best over specific scale ranges. Animals would not be competitive if their size fell in the range that perceives resources best within scale breaks or the ranges of scale over which resources were not apparent (or poorly so) or were hypervariable (Allen et al. 1999). In summary, "lumps" of similarly sized animals will be adapted to "lumps" of apparent resources in the landscape.

The methods for finding gaps or discontinuities that separate lumps (modes, aggregations, or clusters) in size distributions are new and nontrivial. We can profile the size distribution of any animal assemblage by lining up, by mean adult body size, all the animals that live in a landscape from the smallest to the largest species. Viewing across the profile we may notice that sections have continuous outlines where the species are quite similar in size. These smooth sections stand out further because they are bounded on either end by jumps in size from one species to the next. This jump in size between two species is the simplest notion of a size gap between the clusters of animals of similar size. We use a cumulative distribution function to illustrate the locations of lumps and gaps in the size distribution of a mammal assemblage (Fig. 6.2).

While a debate continues (Manly 1994; Siemann and Brown 1999) regarding the methods and conceptual justification for identifying lumps, gap pattern analysis (Restrepo et al. 1997) has shown credible consistency

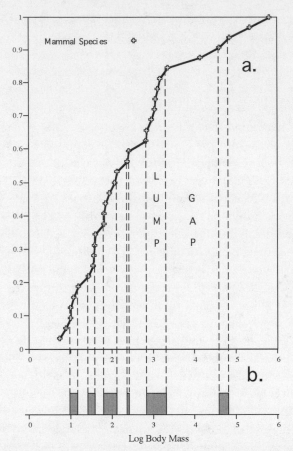

Figure 6.2 Extrapolation of *(A)* cumulative distribution function for log 10 body masses of shortgrass steppe mammals from southwest Kansas to *(B)* an interpretation of lump structure wherein each gray box represents a distance along the size axis occupied by a cluster of species of similar size (body size lump). These lumps are separated by gap zones on the size axis that are occupied by no or very few species.

in supporting visual inference regarding the body mass distributions of a variety of taxa around the world. Discontinuous body mass distributions have been shown for the bird and mammal assemblies of the Canadian boreal forest and prairie (Holling 1992); birds in Colombian montane forests (Restrepo et al. 1997); birds, mammals, and herpetofauna in the south Florida ecoregion (Allen et al. 1999); birds and mammals of Mediterranean-climate Australia (Allen et al. 1999); Mexican cave bats (Allen et al. 1999); Pleistocene mammals in savanna–forests (Lambert and Holling 1998); and birds in North American suburban landscapes and neoboreal and paleoboreal forests (Hostetler 1997). Sendzimir (1998) tested for and confirmed lumpiness in 150 mammal data sets in 18 different biomes from four continents. Lumpy size patterns for animal communities are revealed by size gaps as well as the regularity of size distributions within clusters. Allen and Sendzimir (unpublished data) found that within the clusters the animal sizes are more evenly spaced than expected by chance.

The consistency with which lumpy size distributions are found in terrestrial ecosystems makes them compelling. What processes might cause such ubiquitous lumpiness? Sendzimir (1998) found no evidence that membership in a lump is correlated with membership in a trophic class or taxonomic order. Gaps between lumps are not explained by size differences because of trophic relationships, and lumps are not explained because of limited adaptive radiation from a common ancestor (Holling 1992). The remaining explanation, that animal lumps arise from animal interactions with a lumpy landscape, becomes more compelling when we examine the regularities of lump pattern. If body size distributions reflect animal interactions with landscape structure, then certain lumpy body size patterns should be consistently associated with particular landscape structures. In fact, lumps and gaps in different animal assemblages tend to line up at the same places along the size axis, but only if the two assemblages inhabit similar landscapes, such as in the same biome (Sendzimir, unpublished data). Taxonomic overlap does exist to various extents between such assemblages, but it does not explain these pattern regularities. When comparing different animal assemblages, indices of lump pattern regularity had only a random relationship with indices of species similarity (Sendzimir 1998). Finally, these regularities of lump pattern gained a further degree of credibility when computer simulation showed that their degree of regularity was not the product of chance.

Implications for Conservation and Management

Animals are not merely passive responders to ecological patterns in space and time. They interact by using ecological pattern at certain scales and, in some cases, by reinforcing processes that structure the landscape. Conversely, structure is not simply the end product of processes mediated by animals or abiotic factors. Landscape patterns interact with processes (and therefore animals), often in mutually reinforcing ways that sustain the pathways, cycles, and species of a landscape as a complex, adaptive system.

Exploitation of Ecological Pattern and Architecture

Evidence links certain body sizes to certain landscape features evident within one or a few ranges of scale. Groups of similarly sized animals show regular associations with certain sets of landscape features at different scales. At microscales, arthropod body sizes have been related to various vegetation architectures (Morse et al. 1988; Shorrocks et al. 1991). In the boreal forest, guilds of small birds, such as foliage gleaners, forage for insects among the microarchitecture of tree needles and leaves (Holling 1992). Between microscales and mesoscales, artiodactyl size correlates with the structure of the undergrowth so as to minimize resistance from vegetation (Dubost 1979), and small rodents use overgrown fencelines and hedgerows as corridors (Fahrig and Merriam 1985, 1994). At mesoscales, medium to large animals such as raccoons and white-tailed deer (*Odocoileus virginianus*) interact with larger structures, such as patchy edges and ecotones. Megafauna discriminate and respond to specific macroscale structures. For example, moose (*Alces alces*) interact with large-scale landscape patterns, such as the distribution of marshes within a landscape. Grizzly bears (*Ursus ursus horribilis*) seldom use habitat within 100 m of a highway, whether the road is in use or not (Turner 1989), and European bison (*Bison bonsasus*) often will not cross a road even in total absence of vehicles or people (K. Perzanowski, personal communication, 1999). The link between body size and landscape structure was dramatically demonstrated by Smith et al. (1997) in Cameroon, where subpopulations of the same bird species, the little greenbul (*Andropadus virens*), have significantly different body size and wing size morphometrics that correlate with differences in landscape structure but are not attributable to genetic drift. As Holling predicted, birds in more open habitats (the forest–savanna ecotone) have larger body and wing sizes than birds in the more enclosed habitat (interior forest).

Measuring landscape structure is far easier than quantifying links between structure and animal behavior. From the wider perspective *across* all scales in a landscape, work on quantifying and describing landscape structure (Turner and Gardner 1991; Hargis et al. 1997) dwarfs research on animal responses to spatial patterns, especially landscape mosaics (Ims 1995). A variety of theories (optimal search, optimal foraging, habitat selection and dispersal, source and sink, and metapopulation) provide useful predictive frameworks to test observations of how animals respond to what structures (see Table 6.1 for a small sample). What kind of structure and at what scale an animal responds to it depend on the life process involved. In the Everglades, wading birds make decisions at microscales (food capture in littoral

Table 6.1 Links between landscape patterns and patterns of animal survival, size, and movement as predicted separately by optimal search theory (OST), habitat selection and dispersal theory (HSD), and metapopulation theory (MPT).

Theory	Structure	Observation (O) or Prediction from Theory (P)	Reference[a]
Boundary	Hard edge	O: Species crosses habitat boundary only in extreme circumstances.	2
HSD	Patch size	O: Smaller habitat patches have higher rates of extinction and emigration, lower rates of immigration.	1, 2
OST		P: Foraging movements are scale specific; step length decreases and turning rate increases when entering a smaller patch.	2
		O: Increasing minimum patch size is associated with increasing body size for occupant species.	1
MPT	Patch shape	O: Concave edges act as funnels to channel migration from peninsulas and facilitate boundary crossings by dispersers.	2
		O: Convex edges are crossed more frequently by animals doing daily foraging.	2
		P: Emigration rate increases with edge/area ratio.	2
OST	Interpatch distance	P: Traplining (rotational foraging along a memorized circuit) optimally exploits patchy resources (food or shelter).	2
		O: Increasing interpatch distance is associated with declining patch occupancy.	1
HSD	Fragmentation	P: Hampers migration of "matrix-sensitive" or "interior" species.	2
HSD	Corridors	P: May lower fragmentation's impact, especially as corridor width increases.	2
	Landscape mosaic	O: Fewer large, extinction-resistant patches and many small, extinction-prone patches.	1

[a]References: 1, Ritchie (1997); 2, Ims (1995).

zones), mesoscales (choice of pond in which to forage), and macroscales (migration). Similar hierarchies relate spatial scale to movement response for a variety of taxa (Senft et al. 1987; Kotliar and Wiens 1990; Ims 1995).

What process links hierarchies of landscape structure and scale-dependent animal decision making? Holling (1992) proposed that scale-dependent animal perception is a key link. If animal perception and use of habitat are scale dependent, and perception of landscape structure is allometric with body size, then animals in a lumpy landscape should cluster into sizes that can sense and exploit specific scale domains. As opposed to separate and unique connections between single species and landscape features, lump analysis can help define which animal groups are linked with which sets of habitat features or landscape structures. Sendzimir (1998) used lump analysis to contrast two mammal assemblages in African woodland ecosystems. Despite the lack of species overlap, the lump patterns of the two assemblages were highly similar (Fig. 6.3). Not only do the lumps and gaps occur in very similar locations on the size axis, but the landscape texture used by different species in each ecosystem is best predicted by the lump (size class) they occur in. The discrete jumps in size that separate lumps are associated with qualitative differences in landscape

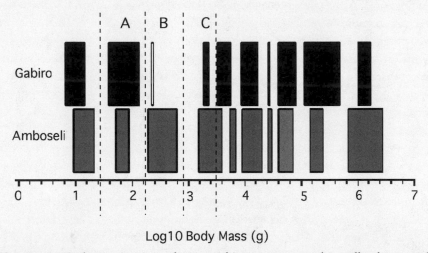

Figure 6.3 Body mass patterns for two African savanna and woodland mammal assemblages with no taxonomic overlap at the species level. Discontinuities in these lump patterns identify the distinctions in the scale and texture of landscape use of the species in the body size zones *A*, *B*, and *C*. With jumps in body size, landscape textural use grades from very fine (*A*, burrows under sandy or wet soil, herbaceous mats), to fine (*B*, extensive ground cover, hollows, holes, crevices), to coarse (*C*, fringes of water, forest, and open areas).

structure used, with larger size classes using coarser and coarser textures in the ecosystem. For example, mammals in the lump containing the smallest species sizes used microscale architectures such as grass runways, and those in the next larger lump exploited cavities between rocks and under logs. Species in the third largest lump associate with mesoscale linear features such as ecotones between wetlands and water bodies or forests and open spaces.

Maintenance of Ecological Pattern and Architecture

Animals within a size class may perceive and use ecological architecture within a range of scale, but how they use it may reinforce and maintain that architecture as well. Landscapes are structured by a variety of processes. Vegetative processes of growth and senescence and disturbance processes of wind throw, flooding, and fire all contribute to the architecture of landscapes. However, certain landscape structures are also sustained over time by animal-mediated processes that reinforce the distribution of structure at several scales (Table 6.2). Note that the structuring effect does not necessarily scale with animal body size. Large animals can affect small-scale patterns (bear browsing and defecation reinforce patch spatial distributions of alpine flowers), and small animals can affect large-scale patterns (defoliating insects can denude vegetation over 100,000 km^2 in the boreal forest over a seven-year outbreak; Ludwig et al. 1978). In the latter case, overdevelopment of biomass during succession can overconnect an ecosystem, making it vulnerable to contagious spread of processes that usually work at small scales. Spruce budworm outbreaks in most years may create patches less than several hectares if there is any outbreak at all.

Resilience of Ecosystems

Lumpy body size patterns may link aggregations of animal species with processes that structure the landscape at specific scales. Understanding the distribution of function both within and across lumps provides a framework for understanding how resilience is generated in ecological systems. Resilience is the capacity of an ecosystem to absorb a shock while retaining the sets of processes that structure and maintain its character (Holling 1973, 1992; Peterson et al. 1998). The resilience of ecosystems depends on the distribution of functional groups within and across scales. If the species that make up a functional group operate at different scales, they provide mutual reinforcement that contributes to the resilience of a function while minimizing competition between species within the functional group. For example, whereas small foliage gleaners such as kinglets and warblers forage for spruce budworm at low larval densities, a larger class of birds, such as

Table 6.2 Fauna-mediated processes that create and maintain patchy landscape patterns (after Johnson 1995).

Patches: Surface, Two-Dimensional

Pattern	*Process*	*Fauna*	*Reference[a]*
Tree stems and crown	Seedling recruitment boosted by mycorrhizae enhanced by defecation	Small rodents	14
Patches of flowers in alpine meadows	Germination enhanced by higher nutrient levels from defecation	Bears	14
Small to medium-sized patches (conspecific tree patch distribution in rainforest mosaic)	Patchy defecation: Seed dispersal, latrines Seed predation	Tapirs Howler monkeys Collared peccaries, agoutis	9, 11, 13 9 10
Medium-sized patches	Selective herbivory: Diffuse effects of single individuals Seed and seedling consumption Intense effect of herd: Digging, wallowing Destructive browsing	Moose White-lipped peccaries Wild boar Elephants	1, 2 9, 10, 12 3 4
Medium to large patches	Selective herbivory: concentrated effects of swarms	Gypsy moth Spruce budworm	5 6

Patch Bodies: Volumetric, Three-Dimensional

Small patches	Soil mixing	Earthworms	5
	Mounds: nutrient and water concentration	Termites, ants	5
	Den burrowing	Pocket gophers Prairie dogs	7 8
Small to large patches (ponds)	Dam construction	Beavers	5

[a]References: 1, Pastor et al. (1988); 2, Bowyer et al. (1997); 3, Holling (1992); 4, Bratton (1975); 5, Laws (1970); 6, Ludwig et al. (1978); 7, Huntley and Inouye (1988); 8, Agnew et al. (1986); 9, Fragoso (1999); 10, Silvius (1999); 11, Julliot (1997); 12, Fragoso (1998); 13, Fragoso and Huffman (2000); 14, Sendzimir (1998).

corvids, converges to forage on budworm when an outbreak aggregates individual budworms so that they constitute a large-scale resource. This cross-scale resilience complements a within-scale resilience that is produced by an overlap of function between species of different functional groups that operate at the same scales (Peterson et al. 1998). Within-scale resilience arises from a "fuzzy" redundancy because each species within a scale has similar but not at all identical effects. They differ in function and in degree of influence and sensitivity to change. We propose that this resilience can be assessed by analyzing the distribution of function within and across lumps in the body mass distribution of an animal assemblage.

Understanding and Predicting Vulnerability

In hierarchical complex systems, breaks between levels indicate the scales at which the processes controlling structure shift from one set to another. Scale breaks in attributes of animal communities such as body masses correlate strongly with a set of poorly understood biological phenomena that mix contrasting attributes. These phenomena include invasion, extinction, high population variability, migration, and nomadism—in other words, high variability at the species, population, and community levels. Recently, Allen et al. (1999) documented that the body masses of endangered and invasive species in a community occur at the edges of body mass aggregations two to four times as often as expected by chance. For example, Fig. 6.4 illustrates the locations of invasive species (arrows) within body mass aggregations (hatched polygons) of a body size distribution for south Florida mammals. That correlation is consistent in all eight data sets examined so far. Those data include four different taxa in two different ecosystems. The strong correspondence between the independent attributes of population status and body mass pattern in three different taxa confirms the existence of discontinuous body mass distributions. It may seem surprising that both invasive and declining species are located at the edge of body mass aggregations. These results suggest that something similar must be shared by the two extreme biological conditions represented by invasive species and declining species. An examination of the phenomena of nomadism in birds in an Australian Mediterranean climate ecosystem (Allen and Saunders 2002) found that nomadic birds also cluster about scale breaks (occur at the edge of body mass aggregations). The clustering of these phenomena at predictable locations—the edge of body mass aggregations—suggests that variability in resource distribution or availability is greatest at scale breaks.

South Florida Mammals

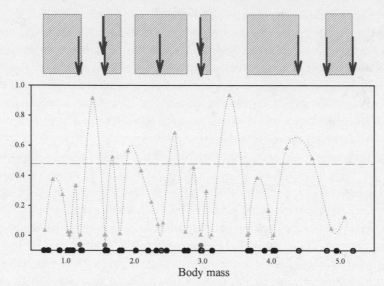

Figure 6.4 Gap statistic *(triangles)*, body mass pattern *(dark circles)*, and occurrence of listed species *(light circles)* for Everglades mammals. All data are presented in the lower graphic; the upper graphic displays a stylized version of the body mass pattern and location of listed species *(arrows)*. Aggregations *(shaded boxes)* were defined as groups of three or more species bordered by significant gaps; this criterion led us to disregard some high values of the gap statistic. Note, however, that these changes in body mass patterns make no difference in the overall patterns detected. (Modified from Allen et al. 1999.)

Rapid anthropogenic disturbance affects the processes that structure ecosystems. If animal body mass aggregations are linked to scale-specific structures, such perturbations should reveal themselves by rate changes in species turnover that affect body mass aggregation patterns or changes in the pattern itself. Feedback from taxa adapted to the altered ecosystem structure (e.g., invasive species) can prevent return to the original system state. As more invasive species become established, they may further alter the environment and promote a new regime of processes that entrench structural change. The lower turbidity induced by zebra mussel invasion of the Great Lakes is one example (MacIsaac 1996; Budd et al. 2001). Even if original key processes are reestablished, the original animal community is not likely to be reassembled (Case 1990; Drake et al. 1996). Understanding the nature, location, and drivers of turnover in complex systems may help us understand how these systems are established and maintained.

There are unusual characteristics associated with scale breaks. The edges of aggregations may be considered zones of crisis or opportunity depending on the way a given species at these scales exploits resources and interacts with its environment. Therefore, scale breaks may be analogous to phase transitions. In perturbed systems, we have documented that biological invasions, extinctions, and nomadism tend to occur at aggregation edges. However, we suspect that variability in species composition and population status is higher at scale breaks (the edge of body mass aggregations), whether or not the system has been perturbed. Human landscape transformations simply heighten the inherent variability. Highly variable behavior such as this has been demonstrated for the area between domains of scale in physical systems (Nittmann et al. 1985; O'Neill et al. 1986; Grebogi et al. 1987) and postulated for biological communities (Wiens 1989). This discontinuous pattern may have predictive power: Invasive species and extinct or declining species tend to be located at the edge of body mass aggregations, which may be transition zones between distinct ranges of scale. Location at scale breaks affords species great opportunity but also potential crisis. Complex behaviors such as migration and rapid adaptation leading to speciation may evolve most efficiently and commonly at scale breaks, where there is the greatest potential reward, though with the highest potential cost.

Wildlife Management and Landscape Pattern

By practical imperative, protocols to manage landscape pattern tend to become diffuse and vague as the scale of the conservation goal increases. Conservation of an individual species mandates identifying, conserving, or creating the specific metrics of patch size, shape, and diversity in the landscape mosaic that favor the species, whereas regional goals broadly aim to preserve diversity at all scales including the processes that create diversity (Arnold 1995). From vegetation distributions to patch metrics to corridor width, the work of identifying landscape pattern types critical to conservation at different scales is young, and developing spatial pattern statistics has only begun (Turner and Gardner 1991). Determining the metrics of critical landscape patterns separately for each species would be an overwhelming task even if landscapes remained stable. In a world of shifting climates, nutrient and material fluxes, and land cover, how can we practically assess and manage landscapes to conserve biodiversity at the species level? And if a species needs conflict, how can they be rationalized within landscape level planning?

CAS theory may shorten the road to conservation effectiveness by integrating parallel probes of the processes, structures, and species interacting in a landscape. All three show fundamental clustering patterns and hierarchical structure. Lumpiness is evident in the temporal distribution of the structuring processes, the space and time distributions of landscape patterns, and the size distributions of the animals living in the landscape. The task remains to test whether these pattern correspondences translate into functional linkages that can guide conservation research and management practice. The association between the location of a species in the lumpy body size pattern and species attributes such as invasiveness or vulnerability to extinction suggests that such functional links do exist. If so, the daunting diversity of dozens of natural histories in a landscape may reduce to a small number of species groups (lumps), within which species share affinities for scale ranges of landscape pattern and structuring processes. For example, in an analysis of animal assemblages with species numbers ranging from 25 to 73 (Sendzimir 1998), the number of lumps ranged from 3 to 13, a reduction in numerical complexity ranging from a factor of 5 to 24.

The analysis of body mass patterns and their links with scales of structure in the landscape has many potential applications in wildlife management. For landscapes it may be possible to analyze the distribution of function within and across scales and estimate the relative ability of different ecosystems to cope with perturbations. We predict that systems with more lumps, greater functional group representation, and more even distribution of functional groups across lumps (Peterson et al. 1998) will be more resilient to human development or other large disturbances. Systems with fewer lumps, less functional group representation, and less even distribution of functional groups across lumps are less likely to tolerate development and more likely to need intensive management intervention after landscape change.

Even in a world in transition, it should be easier to study and manage species within groups rather than dozens of species individually. We can more easily identify critical landscape patterns if lump analysis identifies groups of animals likely to exploit such patterns. Conversely, identifying key landscape patterns simplifies monitoring the dynamics of critical or endangered populations of species related to those landscape structures. Also, it should be possible to predict species most at risk of decline, and thus most in need of monitoring, after perturbations. Species whose body masses place them at the edge of body mass aggregations are twice as likely to be endangered, threatened, or of special concern as species whose body masses place them solidly within lumps (Allen et al. 1999). Longer-term research might identify vulnerable clusters of species whose habitat use relies on landscape structure that has begun to change or is expected to change. Management interventions could address endangered species and structuring processes in parallel by protecting vulnerable species clusters while changing the degree of perturbation at critical scales. This might be done by diminishing other impacts on vulnerable species (e.g., hunting or competition for resources) while shaping resource spatial patterns through control of grazing, hydrology, or planting.

Two examples of predisturbance and postdisturbance research and management illustrate how integrating analyses of lumps and landscape spatial patterns of structure and function help to assess and manage the effects of perturbations at various scales on wildlife. Efforts to anticipate or respond to perturbation effects on native fauna could use lump analysis to identify species size clusters and compare the spatial scales of movement and habitat use critical to survival of species within each cluster with those of perturbation (such as patch size and interpatch distances). One postdisturbance opportunity to study and perhaps manage change was created when European colonization of Australia introduced new species of grazing herbivores that transformed vegetation patterns at regional scales. Introduction of cattle and rabbit drastically altered plant species composition in rare, fertile pockets of the arid landscape. These perturbations to the Australian landscape increased interpatch distances, making resources at mesoscales inaccessible to indigenous middle-sized mammals and hastening their disappearance (Morton 1990). Lump analysis might predict species or species groups in the size range that could profit from reestablishment of precolonial vegetation patterns or that could better exploit existing vegetation patterns.

We anticipate the use of a similar approach before a planned introduction of a new disturbance regime intended to support avian biodiversity conservation efforts in the Narew River valley in northeast Poland. This experiment tests ideas (Vera 2000) that proper management of disturbance regimes can sustain and promote biodiversity. Pollen stratigraphic analysis in lake bottoms revealed that land cover in many parts of prehistoric Europe was not closed forest but more open and savanna-like, perhaps in response to megafaunal foraging and browsing processes (Vera 2000). This suggests that habitat management might restore biodiversity to historic levels by reestablishing the full suite of processes, including browsing, that formerly structured the landscape. The impacts on the biodiversity of reintroduction of browsing or traditional forms of mowing are being tested in forests, heathlands, and grasslands (Bokdam and Wallis de Vries 1992; Bokdam 1995; Kampf 2001). We plan to assess the biodiversity impacts of browsing in the river floodplain of the Narew by monitoring avian populations and changes in vegetation patterns related to changes in hydrology or herbivory by local or ancient breeds of horses or cattle. Lump analysis of the avian species assemblage will be used to identify as candidates for monitoring individual species and species clusters that might be influenced by change in vegetation spatial distributions.

Conclusions

Ecosystems function and are organized as complex adaptive systems (Levin 1998). There is compelling evidence from time series and spatial data that the world is organized by a small set of structuring processes into a hierarchy of a limited number of spatial scales (a "lumpy" world). Measures of clustering in the time behavior of ecological processes, the spatial distributions of landscape structures, and the size distributions of resident animals can identify which groups of processes and landscape patterns might be associated with which groups of species over which time horizons. These process–landscape–species clusters may prove more practical to detect and manage than efforts to marshal data on dozens of species and landscape characteristics. They may also provide a more informed context for asking specific questions about the habitat needs of individual species. The most striking example to date of the conservation implications is the capacity of lump pattern analysis to predict species characteristics, such as nomadism, invasiveness, and vulnerability (Allen et al. 1999; Allen and Saunders 2002). We can test the larger potential of lump analysis by using it to predict the full range of vulnerabilities across a species assemblage by linking their body size–related resource use to scales of disturbance. Wildlife managers can then incorporate changes in resource distribution associated with slower and subtler perturbations such as climate change or shifts in land use and land cover in addition to other known threats such as hunting, catastrophic disturbances, and pollution.

Summary

Landscape patterns that are different at different scales, which change abruptly at scale breaks, entrain morphologic and behavioral characteristics of species (Holling 1992). That entrainment is reflected in discontinuous animal body mass patterns (lumps and gaps in body mass distributions). Clustering patterns evident in the time and space distributions of processes and structures and the body masses of species interacting in a landscape offer opportunities to study and manage wildlife based on functional links between animals and the scales of ecological structure they use. The potential for lump analysis to link clusters of animal body masses with ecological processes is demonstrated in its power to predict species characteristics, such as nomadism, invasiveness, and vulnerability. For managing wildlife where perturbations are shifting the landscape mosaic, this potential can be extended by linking predictions of species vulnerability and scales of habitat exploitation with analysis of the spatial scales of landscape structure changed by disturbance.

Acknowledgments

Earlier drafts of this manuscript were improved by comments from J. Fragoso and an anonymous reviewer. The ideas presented matured as a result of discussions with members of the Arthur McArthur Ecology Laboratory at the University of Florida and participants of lump analysis workshops supported by the Resilience Network, the National Center for Ecological Analysis and Synthesis, and the Santa Fe Institute. The South Carolina Cooperative Fish and Wildlife Research Unit is jointly supported by a cooperative agreement between the U.S. Geological Survey/Biological Resources Division, the South Carolina Department of Natural Resources, Clemson University, and the Wildlife Management Institute.

LITERATURE CITED

Agnew, W, D., W. Uresk, and R. M. Hansen. 1986. Flora and fauna associated with prairie dog colonies and adjacent ungrazed mixed-grass prairie in western South Dakota. Journal of Range Management 39:135–139.

Allen, C. R., and D. A. Saunders. 2002. Predictors of nomadism in birds of an Australian Mediterranean–climate ecosystem. Ecosystems 5:348–359.

Allen, C. R., E. A. Forys, and C. S. Holling. 1999. Body mass patterns predict invasions and extinctions in transforming landscapes. Ecosystems 2:114–121.

Allen, T. F. H., and T. W. Hoekstra. 1992. Toward a unified ecology. Columbia University Press, New York.

Allen, T. F. H., and T. B. Starr. 1982. Hierarchy: perspectives for ecological complexity. University of Chicago Press, Chicago.

Arnold, G. W. 1995. Incorporating landscape pattern into conservation programs. Pages 309–337 in L. F. L. Hansson and G. Merriam (eds.), Mosaic landscapes and ecological processes. Chapman & Hall, London.

Bokdam, J. 1995. Cyclic succession and shifting mosaics in a cattle grazed heathland in the Netherlands. Proceedings of the Fifth International Rangeland Conference: rangelands in a sustainable biosphere. Society for Range Management, Salt Lake City, UT.

Bokdam, J., and M. F. Wallis de Vries. 1992. Forage quality as a limiting factor for cattle grazing in isolated Dutch nature reserves. Conservation Biology 6:399–408.

Bowyer R. T., V. Van Ballenberghe, and J. G. Kie. 1997. The role of moose in landscape processes: effects of biogeography, population dynamics, and predation. Pages 265–287 in Bissonette, J. A. (ed.), Wildlife and landscape ecology. Springer-Verlag, NY.

Bratton, S. P. 1975. The effect of the European wild boar (*Sus scrofa*) on gray beech forest in the Great Smoky Mountain National Park. Ecology 56:1356–1366.

Brown, J. H. 1995. Macroecology. University of Chicago Press, Chicago.

Budd, J. W., T. D. Drummer, T. F. Nalepa, and G. L. Fahnenstiel. 2001. Remote sensing of biotic effects: zebra mussel (*Dreissena polymorpha*) influence on water clarity in Saginaw Bay, Lake Huron. Limnology and Oceanography 46:213–223.

Case, T. J. 1990. Invasion resistance arises in strongly interacting species-rich model competition communities. Proceedings of the National Academy of Science, USA 87:9610–9614.

Casti, J. 1982. Catastrophes, control and the inevitability of spruce budworm outbreaks. Ecological Modeling 14:293–300.

Clark, J. S. 1990. Fire and climate change during the last 750 years in northwestern Minnesota. Ecological Monographs 60:135–159.

Clark, W. C., D. D. Jones, and C. S. Holling. 1979. Lessons for ecological policy design: a case study of ecosystem management. Ecological Modeling 7:1–53.

Colborn, T., D. Dumanoski, and J. P. Myers. 1996. Our stolen future: are we threatening our fertility, intelligence and survival? Dutton, NY.

Drake, J. A., G. R. Huxel, and C. L. Hewitt. 1996. Microcosms as models for generating and testing community theory. Ecology 77:670–677.

Dubost, G. 1979. The size of African forest artiodactyls as determined by vegetation structure. African Journal of Ecology 17:1–17.

Fahrig, L., and G. Merriam. 1985. Habitat patch connectivity and population survival. Ecology 66:1762–1768.

Fahrig, L., and G. Merriam. 1994. Conservation of fragmented populations. Conservation Biology 8:50–59.

Fragoso, J. M. V. 1998. Home range and movement patterns of white-lipped peccary (*Tayassu pecari*) herds in the northern Brazilian Amazon. Biotropica 30:458–469.

Fragoso, J. M. V. 1999. Scale perception and resource partitioning by peccaries: behavioral causes and ecological implications. Journal of Mammalogy 80:993–1003.

Fragoso J. M. V. and J. Huffman. 2000. Seed-dispersal and seedling recruitment patterns by the last Neotropical megafaunal element in Amazonia, the tapir. Journal of Tropical Ecology 16:369–385.

Grebogi, C., E. Ott, and J. A. Yorke. 1987. Chaos, strange attractors, and fractal basin boundaries in nonlinear dynamics. Science 238:632–638.

Gunderson, L. 1992. Spatial and temporal hierarchies in the Everglades ecosystem. Ph.D. dissertation, University of Florida, Gainesville.

Hargis, C. D., J. A. Bissonette, and J. L. David. 1997. Understanding measures of landscape pattern. Pages 231–261 in J. A. Bissonette (ed.), Wildlife and landscape ecology: effects of pattern and scale. Springer-Verlag, New York.

Holland, J. 1995. Hidden order: how adaptation builds complexity. Addison-Wesley, Reading, MA.

Holling, C. S. 1973. Resilience and stability of ecological systems. Annual Review of Ecology and Systematics 4:1–23.

Holling, C. S. 1986. The resilience of terrestrial ecosystems: local surprise and global change. Pages 292–317 in W. C. Clark and R. E. Munn (eds.), Sustainable development of the biosphere. Cambridge University Press, Cambridge, UK.

Holling, C. S. 1988. Temperate forest insect outbreaks: tropical deforestation and migratory birds. Memoirs of the Entomological Society of Canada 146:21–32.

Holling, C. S. 1992. Cross-scale morphology, geometry and dynamics of ecosystems. Ecological Monographs 62:447–502.

Hostetler, M. E. 1997. Avian body-size clumps and the response of birds to scale-dependent landscape structure in suburban habitats. Ph.D. dissertation, University of Florida, Gainesville.

Houghton, J. T., Y. Ding, D. J. Griggs, M. Noguer, P. J. van der Linden, and D. Xiaosu (eds.). 2001. Climate change 2001: the scientific basis. Cambridge University Press, Cambridge, UK.

Huntley, N., and R. Inouye, R. 1988. Pocket gophers in ecosystems: patterns and mechanisms. Bioscience. 38:786–793.

Ims, R. A. 1995. Movement patterns related to spatial structures. Pages 85–109 in L. F. L. Hansson and G. Merriam (eds.), Mosaic landscapes and ecological processes. Chapman & Hall, New York.

Julliot, C. 1997. Impact of seed dispersal by red howler monkeys *Alouatta seniculus* on the seedling population in the understorey of tropical rain forest. Journal of Ecology 85:431–440.

Kampf, H. 2001. Grazing in nature reserves, an introduction. (Online at http://www.hans.kampf.org).

Kauffman, S. A. 1993. The origins of order: self-organization and selection in evolution. Oxford University Press, Oxford, UK.

Kay, J. 2000. Ecosystems as self-organizing holarchic open systems: narratives and the second law of thermodynamics. Pages 135–160 in S. Muller (ed.), Handbook of ecosystem theories and management. CRC Press–Lewis Publishers, Boca Raton, FL.

Kotliar, N. B., and J. A. Wiens. 1990. Multiple scales of patchiness and patch structure: a hierarchical framework for the study of heterogeneity. Oikos 59:253–260.

LaBarbera, M. 1989. Analyzing body size as a factor in ecology and evolution. Annual Review of Ecology and Systematics 20:97–117.

Lambert, W. D., and C. S. Holling. 1998. Causes of ecosystem transformation at the end of the Pleistocene: evidence from mammalian body mass distributions. Ecosystems 1:157–175.

Laws, R. M. 1970. Elephants as agents of habitat and landscape change in East Africa. Oikos 21:1–15.

Lawton, J. 1999. Are there general laws in ecology? Oikos 84:177–192.

Levin, S. A. 1992. The problem of pattern and scale in ecology. Ecology 73:1943–1967.

Levin, S. A. 1998. Ecosystems and the biosphere as complex adaptive systems. Ecosystems 1:431–436.

Lindstedt, M., and M. Boyce. 1984. Seasonality, fasting endurance and body size in mammals. American Naturalist 125:873–878.

Ludwig, D., D. D. Jones, and C. S. Holling. 1978. Qualitative analysis of insect outbreak systems: the spruce budworm and the forest. Journal of Animal Ecology 44:315–332.

MacIsaac, H. J. 1996. Potential abiotic and biotic impacts of zebra mussels on the inland waters of North America. American Zoologist 36:287–299.

Mandelbrot, B. B. 1982. The fractal geometry of nature. W.H. Freeman, New York.

Manly, B. F. J. 1994. Multivariate statistical methods: a primer. Chapman & Hall, London.

Maurer, B. A. 1999. Untangling ecological complexity: the macroscopic perspective. University of Chicago Press, Chicago.

McNamee, P. J., P. M. McLeod, and C. S. Holling. 1981. The structure and behavior of defoliating insect–forest systems. Research on Population Ecology 23:280–298.

Milne, B. 1997. Applications of fractal geometry in wildlife biology. Pages 32–69 in J. A. Bissonette (ed.), Wildlife and landscape ecology: effects of pattern and scale. Springer-Verlag, New York.

Morrison, P., and P. Morrison. 1994. Powers of ten: about the relative sizes of things in the universe. W.H. Freeman, San Francisco.

Morse, D. R., J. H. Lawton, M. M. Dodson, and M. H. Williamson. 1985. Fractal dimension of vegetation and the distribution of arthropod body lengths. Nature 314:731–733.

Morse, D. R., N. E. Stork, and J. H. Lawton. 1988. Species number, species abundance and body length relationship of arboreal beetles in Bornean lowland rainforest trees. Ecological Entomology 13:25–37.

Morton, S. R. 1990. The impact of European settlement on the vertebrate animals of arid Australia: a conceptual model. Proceedings of the Ecological Society 16:201–213.

Nittmann, J., G. Daccord, and H. E. Stanley. 1985. Fractal growth of viscous fingers: quantitative characterization of a fluid instability phenomenon. Nature 314:141–144.

Noss, R. F., and A. Y. Cooperrider. 1994. Saving nature's legacy: protecting and restoring biodiversity. Island Press, Washington, DC.

Odum, H. T. 1982. Systems ecology. Wiley, New York.

O'Neill, R. V., D. L. DeAngelis, J. B. Waide, and T. F. H. Allen. 1986. A hierarchical concept of ecosystems. Princeton University Press, Princeton, NJ.

Pastor, J., and W. M. Post. 1988. Response of northern forests to CO^2-induced climate change. Nature 334:55–58.

Peterson, G. 2000. Scaling ecological dynamics: self-organization, hierarchical structure and ecological resilience. Climate Change 44:291–309.

Peterson, G., C. R. Allen, and C. S. Holling. 1998. Ecological resilience, biodiversity and scale. Ecosystems 1:6–18.

Restrepo, C., L. M. Renjifo, and P. Marples. 1997. Frugivorous birds in fragmented neotropical montane forests: landscape pattern and body mass distribution. Pages 171–189 in W. F. Laurance and R. O. Bierregaard (eds.), Tropical forest remnants: ecology, management and conservation of fragmented communities. University of Chicago Press, Chicago.

Rogers, P. B., and M. B. Fiering. 1986. Use of systems-analysis in water management. Water Resources Research 22:146–158.

Ritchie, M. E. 1997. Populations in a landscape context: sources, sinks, and metapopulations. Pages 160–184 in J. A. Bissonette (ed.), Landscape and wildlife ecology: effects of pattern and scale. Springer-Verlag, NY.

Sendzimir, J. 1998. Patterns of animal size and landscape complexity: correspondence within and across scales. Ph.D. dissertation, University of Florida, Gainesville.

Senft, R. L., M. B. Coughenour, and D. W. Bailey. 1987. Large scale herbivore foraging and ecological hierarchies. BioScience 37:789–799.

Shorrocks, B., J. Marsters, I. Ward, and P. J. Evernett. 1991. The fractal dimension of lichens and the distribution of arthropod body lengths. Functional Ecology 5:457–460.

Siemann, E., and J. H. Brown. 1999. Gaps in mammalian body size distributions reexamined. Ecology 71:2788–2792.

Silvius, K. M. 1999. Interactions among attalea palms, bruchid beetles, and neotropical terrestrial fruit-eating mammals: implications for the evolution of frugivory. Ph.D. dissertation, University of Florida, Gainesville. 290pp.

Simon, H. A. 1962. The architecture of complexity. Proceedings of the American Philosophical Society 106:467–482.

Smith, T. B., R. K. Wayne, D. J. Girman, and M. W. Bruford. 1997. A role for ecotones in generating rainforest biodiversity. Science 276:1855–1857.

Turner, M. G. 1989. Landscape ecology: the effect of pattern on process. Annual Review of Ecology and Systematics 20:171–197.

Turner, M. G., and R. H. Gardner (eds.). 1991. Quantitative methods in landscape ecology. Springer-Verlag, New York.

Vera, F. W. M. 2000. Grazing ecology and forest history. CABI International, Oxon, UK.

von Bertalanffy, K. L. 1968. General systems theory. Braziller, New York.

Walters, C. J. 1986. Adaptive management of renewable resources. McGraw-Hill, New York.

Wiens, J. A. 1989. Spatial scaling in ecology. Functional Ecology 3:385–397.

CHAPTER SEVEN

Modeling Multiple Ecological Scales to Link Landscape Theory to Wildlife Conservation

THOMAS C. EDWARDS, JR., GRETCHEN G. MOISEN,
TRACEY S. FRESCINO, AND JOSHUA J. LAWLER

A successful understanding of linkages between different ecological scales is central to the transition of landscape theory to application (Wiens 1989; O'Neill et al. 1991). Yet as a general rule, ecologists have been unable to combine data collected at multiple scales to explore landscape theory, let alone make the transition from theory to practice. Often landscape data have scale-specific resolutions and extents as well as thematic content resulting from methods of observation, making it difficult to scale measured responses of ecological systems up or down. For example, use of satellite-derived data such as the National Oceanic and Atmospheric Administration's 1.1-km resolution advanced very high resolution radiometer (AVHRR) for mapping animal habitat automatically limits the scale of animal study to a 1.1-km resolution. Any gains in the ability to systematically map habitat over large spatial extents are offset by a loss of resolution relating back to the animals of interest. Similarly, the kinds of ecological characteristics that plants and animals are often associated with (e.g., microclimates, forest structure attributes) are of such fine resolution that they cannot be systematically mapped or modeled over large spatial extents. As before, gains in understanding the ecological processes that may determine species distributions are offset by an inability to map these distributions over large spatial extents.

These types of limitations unfortunately limit research aimed at understanding how landscape process and pattern affect the distribution of plants and animals, and they tend to force research efforts to focus at a single scale. For example, birds have been found to be associated with landscape patterns over large areas (Rosenberg and Raphael 1986; Dunning et al. 1992; Hansen and Urban 1992; Freemark et al. 1995), the composition and structure of vegetation in smaller areas (Cody 1968; James 1971; Wiens and Rotenberry 1981), and localized habitat features such as microclimate and nest substrate (Calder 1973; Walsberg 1981; Rodrigues 1994). Yet each of these studies necessarily focused on the relationship of birds to scale-specific variables (landscape, home range, nest substrate) and therefore was of limited utility for understanding how linkages between the scales affect landscape-level patterns and distributions.

Vegetation modeling suffers similarly, often integrating information having different thematic and spatial resolutions to depict plant and plant community distributions. Numerous studies have demonstrated the ability to integrate environmental data with a variety of remote sensing platforms for vegetation classification (Loveland et al. 1991; Homer et al. 1997), stratification (Franklin 1986), and predictive modeling (Frank 1988; Davis and Goetz 1990; Moisen and Edwards 1999). The underlying satellite data for these analyses had resolutions ranging from the 1.1-km resolution AVHRR to the 30-m, multispectral Landsat thematic mapper (TM) imagery and occurred at a variety of spatial extents. In some cases, satellite information was used to model fine-scaled attributes such as understory components (Stenback and Congalton 1990), basal area and leaf biomass (Franklin 1986), and stand density and height (Horler and Ahern 1986), but results and potential for application to landscape studies seem mixed. However, these studies were focused at single scales and were highly detailed depictions at small spatial extents or coarse depictions at large spatial extents. In particular, those focusing on fine-scaled attributes of vegetation communities (e.g., basal area, leaf biomass, stand density) had limited spatial extrapolation, making it difficult to apply the results to landscape extents.

Differences in variables, explored at different spatial extents and resolutions, limit any systematic exploration of possible linkages between ecological scales for most of these studies. This limitation places serious constraints on the application of landscape theory to conservation issues, such as wildlife habitat modeling, use and associations, or spatially explicit predictive models for resource management. Only recently have wildlife ecologists begun to investigate habitat associations at multiple spatial scales within a single study (Gutzwiller and Anderson 1987; Morris 1987; Schaefer and Messier 1995; Saab 1999). In part, the impetus for a multiscale approach can be largely attributed to the introduction of hierarchy theory to ecology (Allen and Starr 1982; O'Neill 1989; Lawler 1999).

The full exploration of landscape relationships entails spatially explicit depictions of habitat and other variables at fine resolutions over large spatial extents. Such depictions would allow simultaneous exploration of relationships of variables at small spatial extents (e.g., canopy closure at nest sites) and over large landscapes (e.g., pattern of canopy closure within the home range). Although it is possible to model structural attributes of habitats and vegetation on small regions using satellite imagery, the regional-scale focus of many cover-mapping efforts makes it difficult to build vegetation structure into cover maps. Current efforts provide good maps of broad cover classes at landscape levels (Homer et al. 1997) but typically provide no information on the structure of the cover type or the spatial distribution of structure within the cover type. Recently, emphasis has been placed on linking forest data with satellite-based information not only to improve the efficiency of estimates of forest population totals but also to produce regional maps of forest class and structure and to explore ecological relationships (Moisen and Edwards 1999; Moisen 2000; Frescino et al. 2001; Moisen and Frescino 2002). Accuracy of these types of map products is reasonably high (Edwards et al. 1998; Frescino et al. 2001).

Here we describe our collective efforts to develop and apply methods for linking different scales of landscapes for wildlife conservation modeling. Our process includes two steps. The first focuses on methods for modeling habitat that provide fine-grained estimations of habitat type and structure over large spatial extents. The second step is to use these representations of landscapes for modeling habitat use by terrestrial vertebrates at multiple scales. We illustrate how flexible regression techniques, such as generalized additive models (GAMs), can be linked with spatially explicit environmental information to map habitat structure. In this chapter we focus on forested systems. We demonstrate how these techniques can be used to develop spatially explicit probability maps for presence of forest, presence of lodgepole pine, basal area of forest trees, percentage cover of shrubs, and density of snags. We next illustrate how the spatially explicit maps of forest structure can be used to model wildlife habitat, focusing on the prediction of suitable habitat for cavity-nesting birds in forest systems at landscape scales. We close with discussion of future directions necessary to link multiple scales in landscape ecology.

Modeling Vegetation Pattern and Structure

If a major objective of landscape modeling is to enhance understanding of relationships at multiple scales as a precursor for regional conservation planning, then methods for modeling scale-related ecological parameters are paramount. From a vegetation perspective, the principal question is how to accurately and efficiently model vegetation structure and patterns at multiple scales. Recent advances in statistical modeling techniques (McCullagh and Nelder 1989; Hastie and Tibshirani 1990; Hastie et al. 2001) and geographic tools, such as remote sensing and geographic information systems (GISs), have increased the opportunities for delineating and analyzing vegetation structure and pattern. Numerous studies have demonstrated the use of statistical models to understand and display how plant species are distributed throughout the environment (e.g., Austin and Austin 1980; Davis and Goetz 1990; Austin et al. 1984), yet the unpredictability of natural ecosystems, along with the dramatic influence of human disturbance, has made it difficult to draw conclusions about landscape-level vegetation distribution patterns and relationships to environmental conditions. These limitations result, in part, from past reliance on statistical tools that incorporate classic assumptions of normality (e.g., ordination methods; Austin and Noy-Meir 1971; Austin 1985) rather than other distributions more closely related to underlying ecological processes. Other statistical models, such as GAMs (Hastie and Tibshirani 1990) and so-called data-mining techniques (Hastie et al. 2001), are more flexible and better suited to handle nonlinear relationships of vegetation and environmental gradients (Yee and Mitchell 1991).

In addition to advances in statistical modeling techniques, remote sensing technology has made it possible to identify, analyze, and classify extensive tracts of vegetation using satellite spectral information (e.g., 30-m resolution, multispectral, Landsat TM imagery). Satellite data have been used mainly for constructing vegetation cover type maps (e.g., Loveland et al. 1991; Congalton et al. 1993; Homer et al. 1997), but current studies are also using satellite data to explore ecological factors influencing vegetation patterns (e.g., Horler and Ahern 1986; Franklin 1986; Frank 1988; Congalton et al. 1993). One limitation of classified cover maps is that vegetation typically is classified into discrete units, thus adding a measure of subjectivity and bias. Recent studies have found that integrating ancillary data, such as elevation, aspect, and slope, with spectral information can enhance the precision of delineation of forest attributes (Strahler and Logan 1978; Woodcock et al. 1980; Frank 1988; Frescino et al. 2001) and reduce the subjectivity of classification procedures. When linked with flexible modeling tools such as GAMs, such spatially explicit ancillary data provide a powerful context for generating fine-resolution depictions of vegetation across landscapes (Fig. 7.1).

Although new analytical tools have increased our ability to model vegetation over large spatial extents, most research still focuses on modeling dominant vegetation features distinguishable from satellites or climax or seral types strongly associated with environmental factors. But how do we analyze the understory and composition of habitats that are not directly visible from satellites? For example, most assumptions are that stand composition in forested habitats is directly associated with the overstory canopy, yet the density of down, dead material may be a function of slope rather than of canopy cover type. The few studies that have attempted to link reflectance values measured by satellites with understory components (Stenback and Congalton 1990) or stand density and volume (Franklin 1986) have generally been unsuccessful.

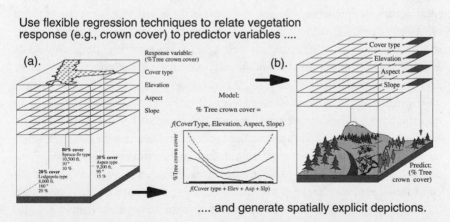

Figure 7.1 Conceptualized process for linking field data and remotely sensed information *(A)* with flexible statistical tools *(B)* for creating fine-resolution, large-spatial-extent maps of vegetation attributes.

The Context: Modeling Wildlife Pattern and Distribution

Wildlife habitat relations models (WHR; Salwasser 1982) are one common approach for modeling animal distribution patterns. These models are essentially databases consisting of lists of habitat types, suitability rankings for the different habitat types, range maps, and species notes (Chapter 13, this volume; Verner and Boss 1980). WHR models are often linked with coarse cover maps of general habitat classes to build spatial predictions. They have general application for regional perspectives, but lack local specificity (e.g., gap analysis; Scott et al. 1993). Therefore, they may be accurate for addressing questions of species richness at coarse spatial scales (Raphael and Marcot 1986; Edwards et al. 1996) but are by nature less accurate for addressing questions involving individual species occurrences at fine spatial scales. This is not a failure of this type of model but rather a realized limitation of its applicability.

At finer scales habitat modeling often involves defining relationships between species occurrences or abundances and a set of factors related to vegetation structure and composition. Often called habitat suitability indices (HSIs), these models typically use statistical tools (e.g., regression) to assess the strength and shape of a relationship between species presence or abundance and a suite of ecological predictor variables (Chapter 13, this volume). Data for these models are gleaned primarily from previously published studies (U.S. Fish and Wildlife Service 1981). The fine-scaled nature of HSI-type models may make them more accurate in specific environments at the expense of generality; therefore, different models may be needed for the same species in different habitats (Stauffer and Best 1986). Despite this limitation, HSIs are likely to be more accurate and appropriate for the management of parks and reserves than the coarser-scale WHR models.

Unfortunately, HSI models have no spatial component, representing instead quantitative relationships between species presence or abundance and the predictor variables. Although the variables modeled in HSIs usually have relevance to underlying ecological processes that influence the animal's presence or abundance, the lack of spatially explicit depictions of these variables makes it difficult to evaluate how they might be constrained by, or in turn affect, higher-order landscape processes. To the extent that fine-grained predictor variables could themselves be modeled in spatially explicit fashion, opportunity would exist to evaluate links between different landscape scales (Chapter 1, this volume). Spatially explicit depictions of vegetation-based habitat variables (e.g., canopy closure, stem density, species type) linked to wildlife models using the same variables can yield more accurate spatially explicit wildlife models (Fig. 7.2).

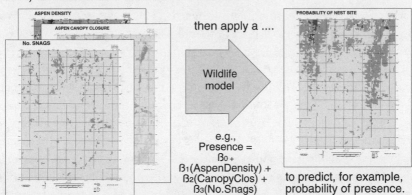

Use modern regression techniques (e.g., GAM) to model structure of wildlife variables ....

then apply a ....

Wildlife model

e.g.,
Presence =
β_0 +
β_1(AspenDensity) +
β_2(CanopyClos) +
β_3(No.Snags)

to predict, for example, probability of presence.

Figure 7.2 Conceptual process linking spatially explicit representations of vegetation type and structure with a wildlife habitat model.

The Context: Our Study Areas

Our work in this arena has focused on forest systems in the intermountain West, principally in the northern Utah mountain ecoregion (hereafter the Uinta Mountains) in the United States. The Uintas have an east–west orientation, an approximate length of 241 km, and a width of 48 to 64 km. Elevation ranges from about 1,700 m to about 4,000 m. The area contains conspicuously deep, V-shaped canyons on the south side of the range and less pronounced canyons on the north side of the range. The climate consists of long winters and high summer precipitation that is mainly a function of elevation, latitude, and storm patterns from the west and the Gulf of Mexico, with local effects from slope exposure or aspect (Mauk and Henderson 1984).

The distribution of vegetation in the Uinta Mountains is highly influenced by topographic position and geographic location. Lodgepole pine (*Pinus contorta*) is the dominant vegetation type, ranging from 1,700 to 3,000 m elevation. At elevations between 2,400 and 3,000 m, lodgepole is mixed with aspen (*Populus tremuloides*), with a few homogeneous aspen stands at lower elevations. As elevation increases, lodgepole forests are gradually replaced by spruce–fir (*Picea engelmannii–Abies lasiocarpa*) forest types and are often interspersed with large patches of wet and dry meadows. Other forest types include pinyon–juniper (*Pinus edulis–Juniperus osteosperma*) at lower elevations on the northeastern slope, Douglas fir (*Pseudotsuga menziesii*) on steep, protected slopes, and ponderosa pine (*Pinus ponderosa*) forests on exposed slopes on the south side of the range (Cronquist et al. 1972).

Example Application

Readers are referred to Moisen and Edwards (1999), Moisen (2000), Frescino et al. (2001), and Moisen and Frescino (in press) for details about the complexities of generating spatially explicit forest structure models. The process is necessarily complex, and only a short overview is presented here. As noted earlier, the GAMs we used for modeling purposes are nonparametric extensions of the more commonly used generalized linear models (GLMs). The GAM, like the GLM, uses a link function to establish a relationship between the mean of the response variables (Table 7.1) and a smoothed function of the explanatory variables (Table 7.2). The main attraction of GAMs for vegetation modeling is their ability to handle nonnormal features in the data such as bimodality or asymmetry. GAMs are best described as data driven rather than model driven, such that the data determine the shape of the response curves rather than fitting a known function to the data. A scatter plot smoother is fit to each predictor variable and then fitted simultaneously in an additive model. The major weakness of GAMs is the danger of overfitting the data (Austin and Meyers 1996).

Table 7.1 Summary of response variables for modeling forest attributes in the Uinta Mountains, Utah, USA.

Forest Attribute	Type	Description	Distribution
Forest presence	Binomial	≥10% tree cover	$P = .77$
Lodgepole pine presence	Binomial	Majority of forest cover	$P = .31$
Basal area (m²/ha)	Continuous	Area of trees at 1.37 m basal height (trees >2.5 cm DBH*)	Range: 0–70 Median: 16
Shrubs (%)	Continuous	Sum of total cover from upper, middle, and lower layers	Range: 0–92 Median: 15
Snag density	Continuous	Total salvable and nonsalvable (snags >10.2 cm DBH)	Range: 0–248 Median: 5

* Diameter breast height (DBH)
P = proportion of model-building points defined as forest and lodgepole pine, respectively. See Frescino et al. (2001) for additional details.

Table 7.2 Summary of explanatory variables used to model forest attributes in the Uinta Mountains, Utah, USA.

Variable	Type	Resolution	Source
Elevation (m)	Continuous	90 m	DMA[a]
Aspect (°)			Derived from DMA
	Continuous	90 m	Relative annual solar radiation (Swift 1976)
	Discrete	90 m	Nine categories (see text for descriptions)
	Continuous	90 m	Radiation/wetness index (Roberts and Cooper 1989)
Slope (%)	Continuous	90 m	Derived from DMA
Precipitation (mm)	Continuous	90 m	Downscaled from PRISM[b]; yearly precipitation climate maps (N. Zimmerman, unpublished data)
Geology			Hintze (1980)
	Discrete	1:500,000	Time frame (1, Precambrian; 2, Mississippian to Eocene; 3, Alluvium)
	Discrete	1:500,000	Nutrients (1, sandstone and limestone; 2, sedimentary; 3, alluvial)
	Discrete	1:500,000	Rock type (1, sedimentary; 2, alluvial)
Easting	Continuous	—	UTM[c] easting coordinates
Northing	Continuous	—	UTM northing coordinates
District	Discrete	—	National Forest Ranger Districts (1, Evanston; 2, Mountain View; 3, Flaming Gorge; 4, Vernal; 5, Roosevelt; 6, Kamas; 7, Duchesne)
TM-classified	Discrete	90 m	Gap analysis (Homer et al. 1997)
AVHRR[d]	Continuous	1,000 m	NOAA[e] (June 1990)
TM			Landsat TM (June 1990 and August 1991)
	Continuous	30 m	TM band 3 (red)
	Continuous	30 m	TM band 4 (near-infrared)
	Continuous	30 m	TM band 5 (mid-infrared)

[a] Defense Mapping Agency (DMA)

[b] Puget Sound Regional Synthesis Model (PRISM); for more information, see www.prism.washington.edu/

[c] Universal Transverse Mercator Map Coordinate System (UTM)

[d] Advanced very high resolution radiometer

[e] National Oceanic and Atmospheric Administration (NOAA)
See Frescino et al. (2001) for additional details.

Forest Structure Modeling: The First Link

For forest and lodgepole presence (nominal responses), a logit link was used to transform the mean of the response to a binomial scale (Hastie and Tibshirani 1990). For the continuous variables (basal area, percentage shrubs, snag density), a Poisson link was used to transform the data to the scale of the response (Hastie and Tibshirani 1990). A loess smoothing function (see Venables and Ripley 1997 for description) was chosen to summarize the relationship between the predictors and the response. The loess smoother fits a robust weighted linear function to a specified window of data (Venables and Ripley 1997). One limitation of smoothed functions obtained from GAMs is their inability to extrapolate outside the range of the data used to build the model. To handle this problem, values of the validation data set that were outside the range of the model-building data set were assigned the maximum or minimum value of the respective variable in the data set.

The functional relationships between each explanatory variable and the respective response variables were analyzed for potential parametric fits following guidelines in Hastie and Tibshirani (1990) and Yee and Mitchell (1991). If a potential parametric fit existed, piecewise and second- and third-order polynomial functions were fit to the data and assessed based on the relative degree of change to the residual deviance (Cressie 1991). All explanatory variables, including all potential parametric fits, were run through a stepwise procedure to determine the best-fit model for prediction (see Chambers and Hastie 1992) using Akaike's information criterion. A percentage deviance reduction (D^2) was also calculated for each model, representing the percentage of deviance explained by the respective model (Yee and Mitchell 1991). Once the model fits were derived (see Frescino et al. 2001, Tables 3 and 4), the model was applied to all the explanatory digital layers (Table 7.2) and predictive map surfaces generated. The result was a series of predictive maps of forest attributes having fine resolution (about 0.8 ha) and covering large spatial extents (more than 1 million ha; Fig. 7.3).

Accuracy of the models predicting forest and lodgepole presence was high (86 and 80 percent, respectively). Sixty-seven percent of the basal area validation points fell within ±15 percent (11.5 m^2/ha) of the true value, 75 percent of the shrub density validation points fell within ±15 percent of the true cover, but only 54 percent of the points fell within ±15 percent of the true snag count.

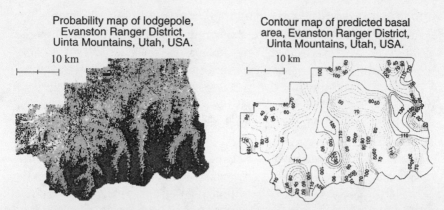

Figure 7.3 **Example maps of nominal (lodgepole presence) and continuous (basal area) responses generated for an ~100,000-ha region of the Uinta Mountains, Utah (from Frescino 1998).**

Cavity Bird Nesting Habitat: The Second Link

Once the maps of forest attributes were generated, the next step was to generate models of bird presence based partly on the spatially explicit forest maps. We modeled habitat associations, based on landscape patterns, for four species of cavity-nesting birds nesting in aspen stands in the Uinta Mountains in northeastern Utah. Cavity-nesting birds make up a large part of the avian community in aspen forests in the western United States (Winternitz 1980; Dobkin et al. 1995). We modeled habitat of red-naped sapsuckers (*Sphyrapicus nuchalis*), northern flickers (*Colaptes auratus*), tree swallows (*Tachycineta bicolor*), and mountain chickadees (*Parus gambeli*), four common species in the study area. We concentrated on these species because all four species are likely to be associated with landscape patterns. Tree swallows and northern flickers nest on forest–meadow edges (Conner and Adkisson 1977; Rendell and Robertson 1990). Mountain chickadees are arboreal feeders (Ehrlich and Daily 1988) and tend to be associated with forested areas (Wilcove 1985; Yahner 1988). Because they exploit a number of different food resources, including willow bark, tree sap, and insects (Ehrlich and Daily 1988), red-naped sapsuckers may select nest sites in landscapes that provide access to this diverse set of resources.

We built habitat models for each of the four species using classification trees (Breiman et al. 1984; Venables and Ripley 1997). Classification trees are a flexible and simple tool for modeling complex ecological relationships (De'ath and Fabricius 2000). Trees explain the variation in a single response variable with respect to one or more explanatory variables and offer a non-parametric alternative to generalized linear models. Classification trees work by recursive partitioning of the data into smaller and more homogeneous groups with respect to the response variable. Each split is made by the explanatory variable and the point along the distribution of that variable that best divides the data.

Tree models have several advantages for analyzing ecological data. First, decision trees are nonparametric and assume no underlying distribution in the data. Consequently the exact form of the relationship between the response variable and the explanatory variables (e.g., normal, logit) does not have to be known. Second, tree-based models readily capture nonadditive behavior and complex interactions. This ability to deal with complex interaction better mirrors ecological reality and can lead to superior models of ecological systems. Third, tree models are capable of modeling a large number and mixture of categorical and continuous explanatory variables. These types of data are very common in ecological studies, and the application of traditional linear statistical models can lead to erroneous conclusions. Finally, because their structure is easy to conceptualize and graphically represent, they are usually somewhat easy to interpret and explain. This latter point in particular is a critical aspect of building useful habitat models. See De'ath and Fabricius (2000) and Lawler and Edwards (2002) for a more thorough discussion of the use of classification trees in ecological modeling.

The four species models included a number of variables pertaining to the amount and configuration of aspen forest and open area (Fig. 7.4) (see Lawler 1999, and Lawler and Edwards 2002, for model specifics). We used these models to produce maps of predicted nesting habitat for each of the four species (Fig. 7.5). The spatial configuration of predicted suitable habitat differed between the four species. Red-naped sapsucker nesting habitat was often spread throughout the sites but tended to be concentrated at meadow edges. Tree swallow and northern flicker nesting habitat was even more closely associated with meadow edges and riparian areas, whereas mountain chickadee nesting habitat was patchily distributed and not necessarily associated with aspen–meadow edges.

We tested these models by searching new field sites for nests. We then mapped the nests on the prediction maps and assessed the accuracy of the maps for predicting the nests (Lawler and Edwards 2002). The northern flicker model was the most accurate (84 percent of nests correctly classified).

CART model
Red-naped sapsucker

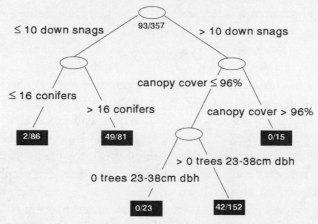

Figure 7.4 Classification and regression tree (CART) model predicting nesting habitat for red-naped sapsuckers. Models for the other species were similar in structure, varying only in the predictor variables and tree complexity (see Lawler and Edwards 2002).

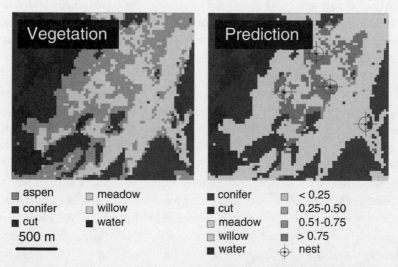

Figure 7.5 Vegetation and spatially explicit prediction maps for northern flicker nesting habitat. Medium gray in the vegetation map represents suitable nesting habitat and is based on classic WHR approaches (see text). Note how the amount and distribution of gray is reduced under the refined vegetation models, which then are incorporated in the wildlife models as described in the text. Nests are represented as circles with crosshairs.

The red-naped sapsucker and tree swallow models were also accurate (80 percent and 75 percent of the nests correctly classified, respectively). The mountain chickadee model was far less accurate, correctly predicting only 50 percent of the nests at the test sites.

Discussion

The ability to create spatially explicit depictions of vegetation type and structure depends, in part, on the flexibility and capability of the analytical procedures used to model vegetation. GAMs, in contrast to some analytical procedures (e.g., ordination and linear regression models), do not make a priori assumptions about underlying relationships, thus allowing the data to drive the fit of the model instead of the model driving the data. The graphic nature of GAMs also allows a visualization of the additive contribution of each variable to the respective response using smoothed functions. Smoothed functions are capable of fitting unusual variance patterns such as skewness and bimodality that are often overlooked with standard linear models (Austin and Noy-Meir 1971). One limitation of GAMs is the uncertainty associated with extrapolation of the smoothed functions, particularly at the tails of the distribution. As suggested by Hastie and Tibshirani (1990) and Yee and Mitchell (1991), we fitted parametric functions to the model whenever statistically allowable, thus constraining the behavior of the functions in the extreme ranges of the data. Often this involved a subjective interpretation based on visual inspection of the data.

Once the vegetation type and structure are modeled, the resultant maps can be linked with wildlife models and used to create predictive maps. We have demonstrated the potential for a linkage between habitat models and models of vegetation at large spatial extents. Although predictive models based on landscape patterns may prove to be accurate, models built solely at coarse spatial scales will be less accurate when fine-scale associations with structural attributes are strong. Cavity-nesting birds have been shown to respond to patterns of vegetation at several spatial scales finer than those modeled in our study. For example, nest tree size and condition (Dobkin et al. 1995; Schepps et al. 1999), snag and tree density (Flack 1976; Raphael and White 1984), and cavity availability (Brawn and Balda 1988) may all influence nest site selection decisions. To improve the predictive capability of coarser-scale habitat models, they must be linked with models of finer-scale habitat associations. Until now, making predictions with finer-scale models has been limited by the availability of fine-scale data over large spatial extents. Our vegetation modeling approach, which includes techniques capable of predicting fine-scale attributes (e.g., canopy closure, stem density) at fine resolutions, overcomes this problem and generally increases model predictive capabilities.

Summary

In general, ecologists have been unsuccessful in attempts to link information collected at multiple scales to explore landscape theory. Often these data have different resolutions and thematic content, making it difficult to scale measured responses of ecological systems up or down. This chapter explores our collective efforts to develop and apply methods for linking different scales of landscapes. Research focus has been at two levels. The first is approaches to modeling habitat that provide fine-grained estimations of landscape patterns at large spatial extents. The second is using these representations of landscapes to explore habitat use by terrestrial vertebrates at multiple scales. Current vegetation modeling efforts provide good maps of broad cover classes at landscape levels but typically provide no information on the structure of the cover type or the spatial distribution of structure within the cover type. Our work demonstrates how flexible regression techniques, such as generalized additive models, can be linked with spatially explicit environmental information for mapping forest structure. We demonstrated how these techniques can be used to develop spatially explicit probability maps for presence of forest, presence of lodgepole pine, basal area of forest trees, percentage cover of shrubs, and density of snags. We illustrated how these spatially explicit maps of forest structure can be used to model wildlife habitat, focusing on the prediction of suitable habitat for cavity-nesting birds in forest systems. We closed with discussion of future directions necessary to link multiple scales in landscape ecology.

Acknowledgments

Funding for this research was provided by the USDA Forest Service, Rocky Mountain Research Station, Ogden, Utah, in cooperation with the U.S. Geological Survey (USGS) Biological Resources Division, Utah Cooperative Fish and Wildlife Research Unit, Utah State University, and the USGS Biological Resources Division Gap Analysis Program. The USGS Utah Cooperative Fish and Wildlife Research Unit is jointly supported by the USGS, the Utah Division of Wildlife Resources, Utah State University, and the Wildlife Management Institute.

LITERATURE CITED

Allen, T. F. H., and T. B. Starr. 1982. Hierarchy, perspectives for ecological complexity. University of Chicago Press, Chicago.

Austin, M. P. 1985. Continuum concept, ordination methods and niche theory. Annual Review of Ecology and Systematics 16:39–61.

Austin, M. P., and B. O. Austin. 1980. Behaviour of experimental plant communities along a nutrient gradient. Journal of Ecology 68:891–918.

Austin, M. P., and J. A. Meyers. 1996. Current approaches to modelling the environmental niche of eucalypts: implication for management of forest biodiversity. Forest Ecology and Management 85:95–106.

Austin, M. P., and I. Noy-Meir. 1971. The problem of non-linearity in ordination: experiments with two gradient models. Journal of Ecology 59:762–773.

Austin, M. P., R. B. Cunningham, and P. M. Fleming. 1984. New approaches to direct gradient analysis using environmental scalars and statistical curve-fitting procedures. Vegetatio 55:11–27.

Brawn, J. D., and R. P. Balda. 1988. Population biology of cavity nesters in northern Arizona: do nest sites limit breeding densities? Condor 90:61–71.

Breiman, L., J. H. Friedman, R. A. Olshen, and C. J. Stone. 1984. Classification and regression trees. Wadsworth and Brooks/Cole, Monterey, CA.

Calder, W. A. 1973. Microhabitat selection during nesting of hummingbirds in the Rocky Mountains. Ecology 54:127–134.

Chambers, J. M., and T. J. Hastie (eds.). 1992. Statistical models in S. Wadsworth and Brooks/Cole, Pacific Grove, CA.

Cody, M. L. 1968. On the methods of resource division in grassland bird communities. American Naturalist 102:107–147.

Congalton, R. G., K. Green, and J. Teply. 1993. Mapping old growth forests on national forest and park lands in the Pacific Northwest from remotely sensed data. Photogrammetric Engineering and Remote Sensing 59:529–535.

Conner, R. N., and C. S. Adkisson. 1977. Principal component analysis of woodpecker habitat. Wilson Bulletin 89:122–129.

Cressie, N. A. C. 1991. Statistics for spatial data. Wiley, New York.

Cronquist, A., A. H. Holmgren, N. H. Holmgren, and J. L. Reveal. 1972. Intermountain flora volume 1: vascular plants of the intermountain West, U.S.A. Hafner Publishing Company, New York.

Davis, F. W., and S. Goetz. 1990. Modelling vegetation pattern using digital terrain data. Landscape Ecology 4:69–80.

De'ath, G., and K. E. Fabricius. 2000. Classification and regression trees: a powerful yet simple technique for ecological data analysis. Ecology 81:3178–3192.

Dobkin, D. S., A. C. Rich, J. A. Pretare, and W. H. Pyle. 1995. Nest-site relationships among cavity-nesting birds of riparian and snowpocket aspen woodlands in the northwestern Great Basin. Condor 97:694–707.

Dunning, J. B., B. J. Danielson, and H. R. Pulliam. 1992. Ecological processes that affect populations in complex habitats. Oikos 65:169–175.

Edwards, T. C., Jr., E. T. Deshler, D. Foster, and G. G. Moisen. 1996. Adequacy of wildlife habitat relation models for estimating spatial distributions of terrestrial vertebrates. Conservation Biology 10:263–270.

Edwards, T. C., Jr., G. G. Moisen, and D. R. Cutler. 1998. Assessing map uncertainty in remotely-sensed, ecoregion-scale cover-maps. Remote Sensing of Environment 63:73–83.

Ehrlich, P. R., and G. C. Daily. 1988. Red-naped sapsuckers feeding at willows: possible keystone herbivores. American Birds 42:357–365.

Flack, J. A. D. 1976. Bird populations of aspen forests in western North America. Ornithological Monographs 19. American Ornithologists' Union, Washington, DC.

Frank, T. 1988. Mapping dominant vegetation communities in the Colorado Rocky Mountain front range with Landsat thematic mapper and digital terrain data. Photogrammetric Engineering and Remote Sensing 54:1727–1734.

Franklin, J. 1986. Thematic mapper analysis of coniferous forest structure and composition. International Journal of Remote Sensing 7:1287–1301.

Freemark, K. E., J. B. Dunning, S. J. Hejl, and J. R. Probst. 1995. A landscape ecology perspective for research, conservation, and management. Pages 381–421 in T. E. Martin and D. M. Finch (eds.), Ecology and management of Neotropical migrant birds. Oxford University Press, New York.

Frescino, T. S. 1998. Development and validation of forest habitat models in the Uinta Mountains, Utah. Unpublished M.S. thesis, Utah State University, Logan.

Frescino, T. S., T. C. Edwards, Jr., and G. G. Moisen. 2001. Modelling spatially explicit forest structural variables using generalized additive models. Journal of Vegetation Science 12:15–26.

Gutzwiller, K. J., and S. H. Anderson. 1987. Multiscale associations between cavity-nesting birds and features of Wyoming streamside woodlands. Condor 89:534–548.

Hansen, A. J., and D. L. Urban. 1992. Avian responses to landscape pattern: the role of species life histories. Landscape Ecology 7:163–180.

Hastie, T. J., and R. J. Tibshirani. 1990. Generalized additive models. Chapman & Hall, London.

Hastie, T. J., R. J. Tibshirani, and J. Freidman. 2001. The elements of statistical learning: data mining, inference, and prediction. Springer-Verlag, New York.

Hintze, L. F. 1980. Geologic map index of Utah. Utah Geological and Mineralogical Survey, Salt Lake City, Utah.

Homer, C. G., R. D. Ramsey, T. C. Edwards, Jr., and A. Falconer. 1997. Landscape cover-type modelling using a multi-scene thematic mapper mosaic. Photogrammetric Engineering and Remote Sensing 63:59–67.

Horler, D. N. H., and F. J. Ahern. 1986. Forestry information content of thematic mapper data. International Journal of Remote Sensing 7:405–428.

James, F. C. 1971. Ordinations of habitat relationships among breeding birds. Wilson Bulletin 83:215–236.

Lawler, J. J. 1999. Modelling habitat attributes of cavity-nesting birds in the Uinta Mountains, Utah: a hierarchical approach. Ph.D. dissertation, Utah State University, Logan.

Lawler, J. J., and T. C. Edwards, Jr. 2002. Landscape patterns as predictors of nesting habitat: a test using four species of cavity-nesting birds. Landscape Ecology 17:233–245.

Loveland, T. R., J. W. Merchant, D. O. Ohlen, and J. F. Brown. 1991. Development of a land-cover characteristics database for the conterminous U.S. Photogrammetric Engineering and Remote Sensing 57:1453–1463.

Mauk, R. L., and J. A. Henderson. 1984. Coniferous forest habitat types of northern Utah. General Technical Report INT-170. USDA Forest Service, Intermountain Forest and Range Experiment Station, Ogden, UT.

McCullagh, P., and J. A. Nelder. 1989. Generalized linear models. Chapman & Hall, London.

Moisen, G. G. 2000. Comparing nonlinear and nonparametric modelling techniques for mapping and stratification in forest inventories of the interior western USA. Ph.D. dissertation, Utah State University, Logan.

Moisen, G. G., and T. C. Edwards, Jr. 1999. Use of generalized linear models and digital data in a forest inventory of northern Utah. Journal of Agricultural, Biological and Environmental Statistics 4:164–182.

Moisen, G. G., and T. S. Frescino. 2002. Comparing five modelling techniques for predicting forest characteristics. Ecological Modelling 156.

Morris, D. W. 1987. Ecological scale and habitat use. Ecology 68:362–369.

O'Neill, R. V. 1989. Perspectives in hierarchy and scale. Pages 140–156 in J. Roughgarden, R. M. May, and S. A. Levin (eds.), Perspectives in ecological theory. Princeton University Press, Princeton, NJ.

O'Neill, R. V., S. J. Turner, V. I. Cullinan, D. P. Coffin, T. Cook, W. Conley, J. Brunt, J. M. Thomas, M. R. Conley, and J. Gosz. 1991. Multiple landscape scales: an intersite comparison. Landscape Ecology 5:137–144.

Raphael, M. G., and B. G. Marcot. 1986. Validation of a wildlife habitat-relationships model: vertebrates in a Douglas-fir sere. Pages 129–144 in J. W. Hagan, III and D. W. Johnson (eds.), Ecology and conservation of Neotropical migrant birds. Smithsonian Institute Press, Washington, DC.

Raphael, M. G., and M. White. 1984. Use of snags by cavity-nesting birds in the Sierra Nevada. Wildlife Monographs 86:1–66.

Rendell, W. B., and R. J. Robertson. 1990. Influence of forest edge on nest-site selection by tree swallows. Wilson Bulletin 102:634–644.

Roberts, D. W. and S. V. Cooper. 1989. Concepts and techniques of vegetation mapping. In Ferguson, D., P. Morgan, and F. D. Johnson (eds.). Land classifications based on vegetation: applications for resource management. 90–96. USDA Forest Service General Technical Report INT-257, Ogden, UT.

Rodrigues, R. 1994. Microhabitat variables influencing nest-site selection by tundra birds. Ecological Applications 4:110–116.

Rosenberg, K. V., and M. G. Raphael. 1986. Effects of forest fragmentation on vertebrates in Douglas-fir forests. Pages 263–272 in J. Verner, M. L. Morrison, and C. J. Ralph (eds.), Wildlife 2000: modeling habitat relationships of terrestrial vertebrates. University of Wisconsin Press, Madison.

Saab, V. 1999. Importance of spatial scale to habitat use by breeding birds in riparian forests: a hierarchical analysis. Ecological Applications 9:135–151.

Salwasser, H. 1982. California's wildlife information system and its application to resource decisions. California–Nevada Wildlife Transactions 1982:34–39.

Schaefer, J. A., and F. Messier. 1995. Habitat selection as a hierarchy: the spatial scales of winter foraging by muskoxen. Ecography 18:333–344.

Schepps, J., S. Lohr, and T. E. Martin. 1999. Does tree hardness influence nest-tree selection by primary cavity nesters? Auk 116:658–665.

Scott, M. J., F. Davis, B. Csuti, R. Noss, B. Butterfield, C. Groves, H. Anderson, S. Caicco, F. D'Erchia, T. C. Edwards, Jr., J. Ulliman, and R. J. Wright. 1993. Gap analysis: a geographic approach to protection of biological diversity. Wildlife Monographs 123. Wildlife Society, Bethesda, MD.

Stauffer, D. F., and L. B. Best. 1986. Effects of habitat type and sample size on habitat suitability index models. Pages 71–91 in J. Verner, M. L. Morrison, and C. J. Ralph (eds.), Wildlife 2000: modeling habitat relationships of terrestrial vertebrates. University of Wisconsin Press, Madison.

Stenback, J. M., and R. G. Congalton. 1990. Using thematic mapper imagery to examine forest understory. Photogrammetric Engineering and Remote Sensing 56:1285–1290.

Strahler, A. H., and T. L. Logan. 1978. Improving forest cover classification accuracy from Landsat by incorporating topographic information. Pages 927–942 in Proceedings of the Twelfth International Symposium on Remote Sensing of Environment, Ann Arbor, Michigan. Environmental Research Institute of Michigan, Ann Arbor.

Swift, L. W., Jr. 1976. Algorithm for solar radiation on mountain slopes. Water Resources Research 12:108–112.

U.S. Fish and Wildlife Service. 1981. Standards for the development of suitability index models. Ecological Services Manual 103. United States Department of Interior, Fish and Wildlife Service, Division of Ecological Services. Government Printing Office, Washington, DC.

Venables, W. N., and B. D. Ripley. 1997. Modern applied statistics with S-plus. Springer-Verlag, New York.

Verner, J., and A. S. Boss. 1980. California wildlife and their habitats: western Sierra Nevada. U.S. Department of Agriculture, Forest Service, General Technical Report PSW-37. Pacific Southwest Forest and Range Experimental Station, Berkeley, CA.

Walsberg, G. E. 1981. Nest-site selection and the radiative environment of the warbling vireo. Condor 83:86–88.

Wiens, J. A. 1989. Spatial scaling in ecology. Functional Ecology 3:385–397.

Wiens, J. A., and J. T. Rotenberry. 1981. Habitat associations and community structure of birds in shrubsteppe environments. Ecological Monographs 5:21–41.

Wilcove, D. S. 1985. Nest predation in forest tracts and the decline of migratory songbirds. Ecology 66:1211–1214.

Winternitz, B. L. 1980. Birds in aspen. Pages 247–257 in Management of western forests and grasslands for nongame birds. USDA Forest Service General Technical Report INT-86. Intermountain Forest and Range Station, Ogden, UT.

Woodcock, C. E., A. H. Strahler, and T. L. Logan. 1980. Stratification of forest vegetation for timber inventory using Landsat and collateral data. Pages 1769–1787 in Fourteenth International Symposium on Remote Sensing of Environment, San Jose, Costa Rica.

Yahner, R. H. 1988. Changes in wildlife communities near edges. Conservation Biology 2:333–339.

Yee, T. W., and N. D. Mitchell. 1991. Generalized additive models in plant ecology. Journal of Vegetation Science 2:587–602.

PART TWO

LINKING PEOPLE, LAND USE, AND LANDSCAPE VALUES

L andscape ecology developed in Europe as a discipline focused primarily on planning for human values on changing landscapes. Although the discipline as practiced in North America and other places (e.g., Australia) is primarily geobiophysical in nature, increasingly it has developed a social and human focus. Using a landscape context to solve pressing ecological and natural resource problems is the only effective way to address problems and processes that affect society. Chapters 8–12 focus on linking people to the landscape and address societal values as integral to healthy ecosystem function.

In the recent past a major effort of environmental conservationists has been to preserve large areas of intact nature isolated from human intrusion. Today, given new knowledge about the status and the dynamics of the real world, the role of humans as long-term environmental modifiers is increasingly recognized by ecologists and is being considered more carefully. In Chapter 8, Almo Farina addresses the idea of linking humans with ecological processes by considering human and natural dynamics in terms of reciprocal integration as well as from the more common and familiar approach of conflicting relationships. He argues for a full-world paradigm to understand change in heavily modified landscapes.

Replicating natural change in landscapes that have been heavily modified is a way to reestablish a fuller complement of animal species that may have been lost. Understanding the extent to which land managers can re-create habitats that are sufficiently similar to those in which native species evolved is increasingly important in conservation biology and landscape management. In Chapter 9, Per Angelstam makes the case that maintaining forest biodiversity, for example, requires that both the range of natural disturbance regimes and the resulting forest and woodland environments to which species have adapted be understood and that a correspondingly wide range of different land management regimes can be applied. Natural disturbance regimes can be emulated by management both in forestry and in some ancient cultural landscapes, but conservation areas with both laissez-faire and active management strategies are usually a necessary part of a complete approach to maintaining biodiversity in diverse landscapes.

Even in areas that have suffered little structural modification (e.g., northern Australia), it would be wrong to conclude that the biota is similarly intact. In Chapter 10, Peter Whitehead, John Woinarski, Donald Franklin, and Owen Price suggest that although recent extinctions in Australia's tropical environments have been few, many species have declined in range and abundance, some severely and rapidly. In the absence of acute structural change, well-developed theory regarding the effects of habitat fragmentation on the dynamics of metapopulations have provided few clues about the causes of these apparently ongoing declines. These authors argue that empirical studies have been too few and too limited in scope to suggest coherent patterns. Despite deficiencies in understanding, the extent of change demands that we seek solutions actively. Principles and practice in landscape ecology can be used to design modified landscapes to optimize biodiversity conservation. Here, context is important. Implementation of such a framework must accommodate the prevailing political and administrative structures.

Similarly, context is important when planning management activities in landscapes with high levels of anthropogenic disturbance. Here, modeling and simulation methods can help us clarify the problem and gain a comprehensive picture of potential impacts of landscape interventions. In Chapter 11, Alfred Schultz, Reinhard Klenke, Gerd Lutze, Marion Voss, Ralf Wieland, and Bettina Wilkening suggest that it is crucial to distinguish between habitat models for different spatial and organizational landscape levels; indeed, it may be necessary to develop a set of habitat models for all relevant spatial planning levels. The ability to link landscape-related research results in evaluation, planning, and decision making is undoubtedly an important current and future challenge of applied landscape research. The lessons learned from models can give valuable hints and lead to practical planning tools.

Practical planning that links the intricate network of ecological and socioeconomic relationships is much more likely to succeed. It may be especially important in countries where the economies are more directly linked to the land. One of the most interesting and challenging conservation issues is the management of parks and reserves in developing countries. For example, Lake Mburo National Park in Uganda is small (260 km^2), its wildlife community is incomplete, and the surrounding landscape is heavily used for farming and herding by a growing human population. Illegal hunting and herding add to the difficulty of effective park management. In Chapter 12, Christiane Averbeck argues that for ecological as well as socioeconomic reasons, the park's existence and potential to sustain wildlife depend heavily on its surroundings. Integrating rural community development and wildlife conservation is a prerequisite for longer-term survival of the park. This situation pertains in many places around the world. The size of parks and reserve areas, as well as the wide spatial extent of ecological interactions between park and surroundings, means that effective management must increase its domain of interest to much larger spatial extents. Only by taking a landscape approach can managers hope to capture and successfully address the relevant threats to protected areas. At the same time, healthy ecosystems will benefit the local population with abundant resources. Establishing the links between people, land use, and landscape values is the subject of the chapters in Part 2.

CHAPTER EIGHT

Human Stewardship in Ecological Mosaics

Linking People to Landscape Dynamics

ALMO FARINA

In the recent past a major effort of environmental conservation has been to preserve large areas of intact nature isolated from human intrusion. Today, given new knowledge about the status and the dynamics of the real world, the role of humans as long-term environmental modifiers is increasingly recognized by ecologists and is being reconsidered more carefully (Lubchenko et al. 1991; Thompson et al. 2001). This chapter is an attempt to include human processes with other ecological processes by using new models in which human and natural dynamics are considered in terms of reciprocal integration as well as the more common and familiar approach of conflicting relationships (see also Lawton 2001). I have organized this contribution into five parts: the description of the general idea, the environmental problems posed by human intrusion, the modification of landscapes by human use, the discussion of some empirical evidence of human–nature integration, and the real possibilities and opportunities for applying new technologies to address these matters.

General Ideas and Principles

In this section I approach the role of human activity on the landscape from a new point of view, searching for an ecological integration between human

177

use of natural resources (stewardship) and normal environmental processes. Despite the general assumption that human use of natural resources has always had a negative effect on the environment, new cultural models are available to better understand the effective role of humans in shaping natural processes. To counter the conflicting attitudes of most current thinking, I describe new symbiotic relationships and use the paradigm of cultural landscapes as an example of such integration.

Most of the terrestrial parts of the earth are under the influence of human disturbance regimes. This influence varies in intensity, effects, and driving processes according to the heterogeneous distribution of human culture, political organizations, and economics. Human influences on ecological processes have been dramatic and of growing importance in the past two centuries, especially in more developed countries, visibly changing many ecological processes and aborting others.

Many human-occupied areas are used as agroecosystems. The recent expansion of such systems in the tropics and the equatorial regions of the world has reduced dramatically both pristine and old-growth ecosystems (Laurence et al. 2001) with unprecedented impacts on biodiversity. However, many areas used by humans for long periods (e.g., the Mediterranean basin) are still conserving, although under threat, a high number of species (Myers et al. 2000). Consequently, every action taken to preserve biodiversity must take into consideration that humans are part of and not apart from most terrestrial and aquatic ecosystems (Balmford et al. 2001; Odum 2001).

The Paradigm of the Cultural Landscape

Many agroecosystems around the world that have survived the industrial revolution of past two centuries have been called "cultural landscapes" by the United Nations Educational, Scientific and Cultural Organization (UNESCO; van Droste et al. 1995) and their preservation recognized to be of primary importance from a historical as well as environmental perspective (Bruns and Green 2001). According to Farina (2000b), cultural landscapes are examples of the highest integration between human activities and environmental dynamics, in which the additional neg-entropy introduced by human stewardship is increasing ecological complexity (Odum 1983; Naveh 1994, 1995). Neg-entropy is free energy that can be introduced into an open system from different sources. The cultural landscape is considered a broad area in which natural and human patterns and processes are mixed to produce properties that we perceive such as amenities, scenic importance, wilderness, and spiritual inspiration. These landscapes are complex entities in which feedback between human and natural processes, dating back thousands of years (Naveh and Vernet 1991), allow dynamic adaptive mechanisms (Prins 1998) and in which the natural and cultural capital are connected with the economical capital (Costanza et al. 1997b; Farina 2000a). Cultural landscapes could be usefully visualized as containers in which different ecological layers, created mainly by human historical events, have been stratified and through the legacy of time, from past to present, have created new opportunities for future ecological scenarios. For instance, in many environments human activities have created morphologic and ecological mosaics, overlapping hydrologic, geomorphologic, and biotic (*sensu latu*) processes with anthropogenic processes, thereby becoming a key element in generating and maintaining biodiversity (Austad and Hauge 2001; Green and Vos 2001).

The study of these landscapes and their protection is a priority if we are to save the cultural legacy and the stock of knowledge accumulated through the thousands of relationships between human and natural processes (Nassauer 1995; Ihse 1996; Olsson et al. 2000; Bruns and Green 2001).

The Empty World and Full World Paradigms

The history of human dynamics is rich with catastrophic events produced by mass emigration, forced invasion, and ethnic mixing. All have had consequences for ecological systems. In many countries across Europe and Asia, human influence on the environment has been controlled for a long time by feedback mechanisms that have compensated at least in part for the effects of human disturbance regimes.

Recently, environmental economists have considered the human impact on the ecosphere according to two different perspectives: the full world paradigm and the empty world paradigm (di Castri 2001b; Sorman 2001). The empty world perspective posits a world in which humans are not an integral part of the system and wilderness is an important part of the world that must be preserved as it is, far from human contact. The full world perspective posits world in which human beings are strictly connected with the natural entities (species, ecosystems, landscapes) and in which the reciprocal influences that are created are responsible for a large part of the observed ecological diversity, as seen in the Mediterranean basin, for example (Naveh 1994). These two different worldviews of the role of humans and their place and function on the earth are driven by different cultural models. It appears that the empty world vision comes from a society that moved from Europe to North America and that the coalescence of different people into an environmental context, characterized by large, wide-open spaces and the availability of abundant resources, a condition quite different from their original homeland, has contributed to the ascendancy of such a vision.

In Europe, especially around the Mediterranean basin, human presence and the subsequent influences on the environment have been interacting for thousands of years, forcing and changing the dynamics of natural processes. The Mediterranean cultural landscape can be used as one of the models to better understand the role of humans on the planet (*sensu* di Castri 2001a). Human influence especially in the Mediterranean, as described by Greek historian Erodoto from Alicarnasso (484–28 B.C.E.) and later by Latin agronomist Lucio Giunio Columella (first century C.E.), is largely responsible for heterogeneity of landscapes in the area at multiple spatial and temporal scales. At the end of the last glacial era, humans and ecosystems were under a reorganization phase, and natural and human processes contributed to create a mosaic of habitats or a mosaic of functional units (ecotopes, *sensu* Zonneveld 1995). There has never been a time during the postglacial period in which the Mediterranean basin has not experienced human occupation (di Castri 1981; Blondel and Aronson 1999). The low mobility in most human populations has allowed locally accelerated evolutionary processes that have resulted in differences in local cultures and land uses and thereby resulted in the distinctiveness of local attributes (e.g., language), local varieties or cultivars of plants and breeds of animals, and the typology of the land mosaic, particularly the local spatial arrangement of ecotopes. The disturbance regimes introduced by seasonal fires, grazing, forestry, and land reclamation have transformed and modified plant and animal communities in new ecological systems characterized by high resilience (Rundel 1998). Continued human stewardship today seems indispensable to the maintenance and dynamics of most of these landscapes.

The Environmental Problems Posed by Human Intrusion

Biodiversity in many cases is maintained and not quickly reduced by human stewardship, although in such cases the level of potential (presettlement) native biodiversity can be imagined to have been much higher. A coevolutionary process may explain the permanence of high levels of biodiversity in many regions that have been populated for long periods of time.

We often ignore the mechanisms directly involved in these kinds of coevolutionary processes, although they may be explained from a thermodynamic perspective (e.g., as the additional neg-entropy introduced by human activities). Field cultivation, livestock husbandry, and prescribed fires add new opportunities for autoregulating mechanisms to operate. In particular, in the Mediterranean basin, the high diversity of land uses and organisms coupled with high resiliency has resulted in species-rich biological systems (Naveh and Lieberman 1994).

There is empirical evidence that in these areas, in which climatic stresses are the rule more than the exception and in which climatic unpredictability has created resource uncertainty for human populations, alternative mechanisms that minimize the negative effects have arisen. The exchange of products and resources in an open market has influenced the cultural evolution of populations and resulted in the appearance of different waves of globalization in these systems. It is probable that new markets appeared at the end of a florid historical era as a consequence of social and environmental decline.

At present, we have only a rudimentary understanding of the mechanisms by which human intrusion across the world has affected so differently the diversity of living organisms and associated ecological processes. For instance, Balmford et al. (2001) found that many overpopulated regions across the African continent still contained rare species. Long-term studies, especially historical analysis of data from different sources, are needed (Rackham 1998). Recently, Jackson et al. (2001) discussed the role of overfishing on Caribbean coastal ecosystems and the role of historical data. These authors emphasized the dramatic role of overfishing as the first step in the chain of other pervasive human disturbances. The fish stock can be reduced for many centuries before the effects become visible. As recently stressed by Sugden and Stone (2001), the collection of long-term data, especially in human-influenced ecosystems, seems extremely important if we are to increase our knowledge of how ecosystems react to disturbance processes.

It is common wisdom among ecologists that complexity is the emergent attribute of every living system. Such complexity is responsible for what I have called centripetal (self-organized) and centrifugal (dispersing) mechanisms (Farina 2000b). To better understand the role of humans on the planet, it is necessary to develop a deep knowledge of the mechanisms that drive biodiversity. Large parts of modern ecological theory have been influenced by niche theory (Grinnell 1917; Hutchinson 1957) and by the mechanisms of ecological succession (Clements 1936), in which the coexistence of species and the dynamism of communities are regulated mainly by "deterministic mechanisms."

Human understanding of real-world complexity has strong limitations because of the inherent scale at which we can observe the environmental context. Recently, Farina (2000b) introduced the concept of eco-field as the dimension in which each functional trait of the organism interacts with the real world. This idea stems from the ideas of Laszlo (1996) and his concept of bio-field. I suggest that this is a useful concept because it combines the Hutchinsonian model of the ecological niche with the cognitive capacities of organisms. Every species changes its scale of external perception according to the different functions in which the species is engaged. In this way a species navigates through a multilayer dominion of scaled perceptions of reality, depending on its current activities. The eco-field concept allows a better understanding of the autopoietic (self-maintaining) properties of the species (Maturana and Varela 1980). I argue that the eco-field paradigm is a dissected vision of autopoiesis and functions as a bridge between human-perceived environmental properties and relational species-specific components. The eco-field helps us understand why there are so many species in apparent overlapping ecological layers. By using the eco-field paradigm, it is possible to reconsider the habitat of a species not just as a fixed space in which a species lives but as multiple layers of perceived contexts with associated functions and environmental constraints. In this way we can explain why a bird such as the European robin (*Erithacus rubecula*), in response to changing air temperature in winter, moves from woodlands to gardens and backyards, where climatic conditions are more favorable. The exploration of species-specific eco-fields allows one to view ecological complexity in a new way, allowing a new scaled vision of complexity of the real world.

The Modification of Landscapes by Human Use

In this section, relevant key arguments of landscape ecology (e.g., ecotones, corridors, and shifting mosaics) are revisited. I argue that human-modified environments show emerging patterns in ecotones and in corridors with which the diversity of life can be associated. But before such structures can be considered important for maintaining biodiversity, a new vision of species-specific subsystems must be considered if we are to approach environmental complexity in a realistic and effective way.

Human use of natural resources is responsible for dramatic changes in ecological systems. Such changes depend on the strategy used; for example, fishing and hunting can change the ratio between hunted organisms (prey or predator) and other organisms not directly influenced by human activity, producing dramatic changes in the communities when overfished or over-hunted. Harvesting fruits and seeds probably has a lower impact on community composition, although change can occur in this case also. Fire used for vegetation clearing or to chase animals results in a generalized disturbance to burned sites and has more impact on the system than does harvesting. But the most profound changes can occur when sedentary agriculture with its associated practices of livestock rearing and range grazing are maintained for a long time in a site. Clearing, terracing, fertilizing, changing the hydrologic regime with aqueducts, and adding cultivated trees and rotated crops change the structure and functions of the systems for a long period of time even if the land use ceases.

Over the short term, the disturbance produced by the human activity may be of very different levels of impact, but the final product is almost always a mosaic of differently disturbed patches. The creation of patch mosaics at different levels of disturbance is a rule in human-dominated systems, and the dimension of the resulting mosaics may depend largely on the level of technology used. In developed countries, the use of machines to plow, irrigate, seed, and harvest has enlarged the dimension of fields from less than a hectare in the Roman "centuriazione" (Caravello and Giacomin 1993; Caravello and Michieletto 1999) to hundreds of hectares in the present-day Canadian–U.S. wheat belt landscape. When focus is changed from the past to the present or from undeveloped to developed countries in human-dominated landscapes, the land mosaic changes shape and size according to the technology and the amount of additional neg-entropy introduced into the system. Such a comparison is extremely useful in investigating and understanding the level of modifications that have occurred in a system (Fig. 8.1).

The appearance of a distinct and different mosaic in an area occupied permanently by human populations is the result of a different use of the same natural resource. For instance, across the Mediterranean basin, along a hilly slope with the same soil and aspect, it is possible to find vineyards and olive groves associated with several early successional edge plants. Under non-tilled natural conditions, the same slope would be covered almost entirely by an oak woodland. The human-induced mosaic is characterized also by a strong contrast between patches and by the appearance of long edges. Edges or ecotones are considered tension zones between two or more areas with different structure and dynamics and through which energy and nutrients are moving (Risser 1995). The role of ecotones in attracting wildlife has been recognized for a long time (Leopold 1933). As a consequence, such

Figure 8.1   An agricultural landscape along the Tago River in Western Spain show-ing both a high-technology irrigation system *(big circles)* and a traditional agricul-tural landscape characterized by small fields and hedgerows on the other side of the river *(upper right corner)*.

structures have been conserved and used to increase the abundance of game species. Recently the importance of ecotones has been stressed by ecologists from different continents, ecoregions, and ecosystems, confirming their role in preserving local biodiversity and in acting as filters of surplus input of fer-tilizers into agricultural soils, especially in areas that have experienced great human impact (di Castri et al. 1988; Naiman and Decamps 1990; Holland et al. 1991; Hansen and di Castri 1992; Jorg 1994).

Some Empirical Evidence of Human–Nature Integration

In this section I present examples of models used in the recent past by human populations to intercept in a sustainable way scanty resources from the moun-tainous areas of the Mediterranean. The cultural landscapes of the upland Mediterranean area are an example of the integrated use of natural and human-made resources that have survived for centuries, as evidenced by a sustainable tenure of human population settlement. I describe the complexity and dynamics of cultural landscapes and present evidence of the strategies used by human populations based on a hierarchy of feedback between human and natural processes.

Across the Mediterranean, from Portugal to Greece, there are good examples of integration between human and natural processes inside the cultural landscapes (Farina and Naveh 1993). Although the environmental heterogeneity of this region is very high, and it is inhabited by different societies and characterized by different historical dynamics, the inhabitants have in common similar land use strategies. Common features include a fine-grained mosaic of land tenure, terracing on the slopes, agro-sylvo-pastoral systems, highly differentiated use of the land base, high number of (folk) cultivars and livestock breeds, resilience of the system to disturbance regimes such as fires, and a deep knowledge of the natural processes by people. All of these ingredients have generated and contributed to the maintenance of a land mosaic across the Mediterranean and preservation of resources and biodiversity, despite the challenge posed by recent land abandonment and by the impact of tourism along the coasts (Naveh and Lieberman 1994).

The capacity of the Mediterranean cultural landscape to preserve a broad spectrum of ecological processes and biological entities results largely from the ecological plasticity of such ecosystems (*sensu* Perevolotsky and Seligman 1998), where changes in human and natural stressors can be incorporated into the system without loss of ecological function. Ecological plasticity is the capacity of the system to adapt internal processes to external events and to cope with uncertainty. According to Thompson et al. (2001), ecological plasticity as defined here can be considered a hypothesis at a new frontier of ecology that can be tested in the context of the main ecological paradigms, such as general system theory (von Bertalanffy 1969) and the ecological complexity paradigm (Lewin 1999; Bossomaier and Green 2000). Ecological plasticity couples the time of evolution with the time of the ecological processes and integrates the adaptive processes of individual organisms with emergent properties of the ecological systems (Wu and Loucks 1995).

To explain the extraordinary capacity of the Mediterranean system to cope with complexity, it is necessary to evaluate the role of human stewardship in such a system. Human use of land has been so intensive for such a long time that coevolutionary mechanisms between human and natural processes can be considered (di Castri 1981). It seems reasonable to suggest that human intrusion has been so continuous in time and acting at so many spatial and temporal scales that the environment has had extraordinary input for driving evolutionary change. Every part of the Mediterranean has experienced different levels of human pressure linked to social and economical processes over millennia.

After the Pleistocene macrofaunal decline from overhunting, the sedentary nature of human populations has probably allowed the differentiation of local uses, dialects, cultivars, and livestock varieties, following enrichment with the introduction of new species into the disturbed ecosystems. The establishment of differentiated ecological mosaics across different spatial scales appears to have been the main process for the coalescence of biodiversity into patchily specific communities. In this scenario, grazing and forestry have played a fundamental role. Grazing has been a powerful tool in maintaining secondary succession at young stages, maximizing productivity of open space species (Papanastasis 1998). Most montane prairies along the Mediterranean uplands can be considered human-made ecotones created by deforestation or by transformation of forest in parklands (e.g., the Spanish *dehesa* or the Portuguese *montado*). In these ecotones, ranging from 600 to 1,200 m in altitude, many bird species (Farina 1995a) and some of the richest mesomammal fauna can be found. The recent abandonment of most of the upland across the Mediterranean (Farina 1995b) and central northern Europe has posed several problems in terms of biodiversity conservation (Aalen 2001). Despite a general assumption that human emigration and landscape depopulation would have positive effects on biodiversity, after a few years of abandonment, the systems have experienced a decline of the biodiversity, disappearance of species and communities, and rapid recovery of woodlands (Vos 2001). This effect is so common everywhere in Europe and is so well documented (Farina 1989, 1991; Farina and Naveh 1993; Ehrendorfer et al. 1999) that it is today used as the paradigmatic basis for adaptive dynamic ecosystem management.

When I try to understand the link between human and natural processes, it appears that there is an extraordinary relationship between the two, but when I compare the relationships of the past with the present, fundamental differences emerge. In the present, technology tends to erase most of the feedback between humans and nature, reducing the cybernetic characteristics of these complex systems. If, as I hope, the information gap is temporary, internal dynamics in the system will result in specific self-organizing functions. But if internal stabilizing dynamics do not develop, there is the risk of an environmental collapse with unpredictable consequences. We are learning lessons from large-scale processes linked to CO_2 doubling, global temperature rise, ozone depletion, and a spread of new and old human diseases, as well as from local-scale events such as watershed flooding and alien species invasion.

We are living in a mosaic of healthy and unhealthy patches (Rapport et al. 1998), yet we still receive ecosystem services (Costanza et al. 1997a, 1997b) that include availability of clean water and air, forest cover, scenic visions, wildlife observation, fishing, hiking trails, ski facilities, and other amenities. These services are strongly demanded by society, and the land mosaic is modified as a consequence (Green 1996). It seems that throughout recent human history, the landscape has been the product of the social paradigms on which the entire society is based. When the paradigm is changed by internal or external political and economic constraints, the landscape is shaped as a consequence. This story could have a happy ending, but ecologists have the duty to inform society that the time lag of reactions of ecological systems usually exceeds the time constants of economic and social processes. There exists a real risk of increasing our ecological debt (*sensu* Tilman et al. 1994) when we proceed so quickly so as to lose the feedback of natural processes.

New Technologies for Surveying and Evaluating Human Intrusion

Today, the sophisticated technologies of remote sensing and spatial data processing are available, and many are in the public domain (Maguire et al. 1991). They are used for resource inventory and evaluation in both international agencies and local governments. For instance, agriculture routinely uses information from satellites to evaluate threshold effects of ranch grazing pressure or crop irrigation.

These technologies are useful in building scenarios, but a survey of past processes remains largely outside the investigative capacity of these recent technologies. To investigate past processes, only traditional techniques, such as historical documentation deposited during property transition, appear useful. In many countries, cadastral maps document land use in the area. Recently, Rackham (1998) discussed the importance of historical ecology for conservation. This author described the importance of documents that showed individual estates, or woodland and marshland position, as reported in the example of Chalkney Wood in Earl's Colne (Essex, England). This wood has been maintained since 1520 as a park for a semidomestic wild boar population. Today this woodland can be observed with approximately the same shape and extension. The cadastral maps record the boundaries of ownership and the typology of land use and are relevant sources of information to evaluate the changes produced in a landscape by changes in land use or by natural processes (e.g., river meandering). Historical ecology is an important tool for investigating the past to interpret the present and for trying to predict the future (Pickrell 2001). There have recently been some notable advances in long-term ecological research (LTER). Previously, most LTER areas were selected in natural or seminatural ecosystems (Christian et al. 1999); however, two recent urban LTERs (Phoenix, Arizona, and Baltimore, Maryland) have been added in recognition of the importance of including human-modified systems. Undoubtedly more work is needed to include agricultural landscapes. Our society is an "information society" that is losing its memory (di Castri 2001a), and this can jeopardize our future because it means that we are losing our cultural roots. LTER systems based on human-modified systems will couple ecological information with social, economic, and cultural data. There is a need to locate such special observatories and laboratories along the biodiversity hot spots across the Mediterranean and to forge a new generation of scientific ecologists.

Summary

Human intrusion on ecosystems has dramatically increased during the last two centuries, negatively affecting biodiversity and the availability of non-renewable resources and transforming many terrestrial environments into agroecosystems.

Many agroecosystems that have undergone recent industrialization may be considered cultural landscapes in which anthropogenic and natural processes exhibit feedback relationships.

Human interactions with the natural world can be considered from a full world or empty world perspective. The full world perspective considers a world in which humans are strictly connected with ecosystems by feedback mechanisms. The empty world perspective considers humans as intruders in natural systems.

The Mediterranean basin is a good example of a full world system. The addition of neg-entropy by humans in agricultural practices has contributed to high and persistent ecological diversity in this overpopulated region.

Agricultural practices across the Mediterranean are characterized by a sequence of disturbance regimes that have been incorporated by the natural system and have shaped soil structure and dynamics (e.g., terracing) and influenced the resulting land mosaics.

The richness of ecological mosaics across the Mediterranean is largely human-dependent; land abandonment in recent times is a significant cause of declines in ecological diversity.

Historical ecology and remote sensing techniques are necessary tools to understand the links between land use practices and natural processes.

LITERATURE CITED

Aalen, F. H. A. 2001. Landscape development and change. Pages 3–20 in B. Green and W. Vos (eds.), Threatened landscapes, conserving cultural environments. Spon Press, London.

Austad, I., and L. Hauge. 2001. Sognefjord, Norway. Pages 57–64 in B. Green and W. Vos (eds.), Threatened landscapes, conserving cultural environments. Spon Press, London.

Balmford, A., J. L. Moore, T. Brooks, N. Burgess, L. A. Hansen, P. Williams, and C. Rahbek. 2001. Conservation conflicts across Africa. Science 291:2616–2619.

Blondel, J., and J. Aronson. 1999. Biology and wildlife of the Mediterranean region. Oxford University Press, Oxford, UK.

Bossomaier, T. R. J., and D. G. Green (eds.). 2000. Complex systems. Cambridge University Press, Cambridge, UK.

Bruns, D., and B. H. Green. 2001. Identifying threatened, valued landscapes. Pages 119–127 in B. Green and W. Vos (eds.), Threatened landscapes, conserving cultural environments. Spon Press, London.

Caravello, G., and F. Giacomin. 1993. Landscape ecology aspects in a territory centuriated in Roman times. Landscape and Urban Planning 24:77–85.

Caravello, G., and P. Michieletto. 1999. Cultural landscape: trace yesterday, presence today, perspective tomorrow for "Roman centuriation" in rural Venetian territory. Human Ecology Review 6:45–50.

Christian, R. R., C. French, J. Gosz, and R. Waide. 1999. Perspective on international long term ecological research. Pages 99–105 in A. Farina (ed.), Perspectives in ecology. Bachkuys Publishers, Leiden, the Netherlands.

Clements, F. E. 1936. Nature and structure of the climax. Journal of Ecology 24:252–284.

Costanza, R., J. Cumberland, H. Daly, R. Goodland, and R. Norgaard. 1997a. An introduction to ecological economics. St. Lucie Press, Boca Raton, FL.

Costanza, R., R. d'Arge, R. de Groot, S. Farber, M. Grasso, B. Hannon, K. Limburg, S. Naeem, R. V. O'Neill, J. Paruelo, R. G. Raskin, P. Sutton, and M. van den Belt. 1997b. The value of the world's ecosystem services and natural capital. Nature 387:253–260.

di Castri, F. 1981. Mediterranean-type shrublands of the world. Pages 1–52 in F. di Castri, D. W. Goodall, and R. L. Specht. Collection ecosystems of the world, Vol. 11. Elsevier, Amsterdam.

di Castri, F. 2001a. Impatto scientifico, culturale e sociale dell'ecologia mediterranea. Atti XXV anniversario Società Italiana di Ecologia (S.Lt.E), Rome.

di Castri, F. 2001b. Rural values and the European view of agriculture. Pages 483–513 in O. Solbrig, R. Paarlberg, and F. di Castri (eds.), Globalization and the rural environment. Harvard University Press, Cambridge, MA.

di Castri, F., A. J. Hansen, and M. M. Holland. 1988. A new look at ecotones. Emerging International Projects on Landscape Boundaries. Biology International, special issue 17. International Union of Biological Sciences (IUBS), Paris.

Ehrendorfer, F., H. Palme, and G. Schrammel. 1999. Changing agriculture and landscape: ecology, management and biodiversity decline in anthropogenous mountain grassland. EUROMAB Symposium, Proceedings. Federal Research Institute for Agriculture in Alpine Regions (BAL), Gumpenstein, Irdning, Austria.

Farina, A. 1989. Effects of changes of human disturbance regime on the structure and dynamics of bird communities in a Mediterranean landscape. Pages 332–340 in O. Ravera (ed.), Terrestrial and aquatic ecosystems. Ellis Horwood Series in Environmental Management, Science and Technology, Chichester, UK. Ellis Horwood, Chichester, UK.

Farina, A. 1991. Recent changes of the mosaic patterns in a montane landscape (north Italy) and consequences on vertebrate fauna. Option Méditerranéennes, Série Seminaires 15:121–134.

Farina, A. 1995a. Distribution and dynamics of birds in a rural sub-Mediterranean landscape. Landscape and Urban Planning 31:269–280.

Farina, A. 1995b. Upland farming systems of northern Apennines and the conservation of the biological diversity. Pages 123–135 in P. Halladay and D. A. Gilmour (eds.), Conserving biodiversity outside protected areas: the role of traditional agro-ecosystems. IUCN, Gland, Switzerland.

Farina, A. 2000a. The cultural landscape as an example of integration of ecology and economics. BioScience 50:313–320.

Farina, A. 2000b. Landscape ecology in action. Kluwer, Dordrecht, The Netherlands.

Farina, A., and Z. Naveh. 1993. Landscape approach to regional planning: the future of the Mediterranean landscapes. Landscape and Urban Planning 24:1–295.

Green, B. 1996. Countryside conservation: landscape ecology, planning and management. Spon Press, London.

Green, B., and W. Vos. 2001. Preface. Pages xi–xii in B. Green and W. Vos (eds.), Threatened landscapes: conserving cultural environments. Spon Press, London.

Grinnell, J. 1917. The niche-relationships of the California thrasher. Auk 34:427–433.

Hansen, A. J., and F. di Castri (eds.). 1992. Landscape boundaries: consequences for biotic diversity and ecological flows. Springer-Verlag, New York.

Holland, M. M., P. G. Risser, and R. J. Naiman. 1991. Ecotones: the role of landscape boundaries in the management and restoration of changing environments. Chapman & Hall, London.

Hutchinson, G. E. 1957. Concluding remarks: population studies: animal ecology and demography. Cold Spring Harbor Symposia on Quantitative Biology 22:415–427.

Ihse, M. (ed.). 1996. Landscape analysis in the Nordic countries. Swedish Council for Planning and Coordination of Research, Report 96:1. Swedish Council for Planning and Coordination of Research. Stockholm, Sweden.

Jackson, J. B. C., M. X. Kirby, W. H. Berger, K. A. Bjorndal, L. W. Botsford, B. J. Bourque, R. H. Bradbury, R. Cooke, J. Erlandson, J. A. Estes, T. P. Hughes, S. Kidwell, C. B. Lange, H. S. Lenihan, J. M. Pandolfi, C. H. Peterson, R. S. Steneck, M. J. Tegner, and R. R. Warner. 2001. Historical overfishing and the recent collapse of coastal ecosystems. Science 293:629–638.

Jorg, E. (ed.). 1994. Field margin-strip programmes. Proceedings of a technical seminar held at Mainz, Germany. Pretty Print, Mainz.

Laszlo, E. 1996. The whispering pond. Element Books, Rockport, MA.

Laurence, W. F., M. A. Cochrane, S. Bergen, P. M. Fearnside, P. Delamonica, C. Barber, S. D'Angelo, and T. Fernandes. 2001. The future of the Brazilian Amazon. Science 291:438–439.

Lawton, J. 2001. Earth system science. Science 292:1965.

Leopold, A. 1933. Game management. Charles Scribner's Sons, New York.

Lewin, R. 1999. Complexity: life at the edge of chaos, 2nd ed. University of Chicago Press, Chicago.

Lubchenko, J., A. M. Olson, L. B. Brudbaker, S. R. Carpenter, M. M. Holland, S. P. Hubbell, S. A. Levin, J. A. MacMahon, P. A. Matson, J. M. Melillo, H. A. Mooney, C. H. Peterson, H. R. Pulliam, L. A. Real, P. J. Regal, and P. G. Risser. 1991. The sustainable biosphere initiative: an ecological research agenda. Ecology 72:371–412.

Maguire, D. J., M. F. Goodchild, and D. W. Rhind (eds.). 1991. Geographical information systems. Longman Scientific and Technical, Harlow, UK.

Maturana, H. R., and F. J. Varela. 1980. Autopoiesis and cognition: the realization of the living. Reidel Publishing Company, Dordrecht, the Netherlands.

Myers, N., R. A. Mittermeier, C. G. Mittermeier, G. A. B. de Fonseca, and J. Kent. 2000. Biodiversity hotspots for conservation priorities. Nature 403:853–858.

Naiman, R. J., and H. Decamps (eds.). 1990. The ecology and management of aquatic–terrestrial ecotones. Parthenon Publishing Group, Paris.

Nassauer, J. I. 1995. Culture and changing landscape structure. Landscape Ecology 10:229–237.

Naveh, Z. 1994. From biodiversity to ecodiversity: a landscape-ecology approach to conservation and restoration. Restoration Ecology 2:180–189.

Naveh, Z. 1995. From biodiversity to ecodiversity: new tools for holistic landscape conservation. International Journal of Ecology and Environmental Sciences 21:1–16.

Naveh, Z., and A. Lieberman. 1994. Landscape ecology, 2nd ed. Springer-Verlag, New York.

Naveh, Z., and J. L. Vernet. 1991. The paleohistory of the Mediterranean biota. Pages 19–32 in R. H. Groves and F. di Castri (eds.), Biogeography of Mediterranean invasions. Cambridge University Press, Cambridge, UK.

Odum, E. P. 2001. The techno-ecosystem. Bulletin of Ecological Society of America 82:137–138.

Odum, H. T. 1983. Systems ecology: an introduction. Wiley, New York.

Olsson, E. G. A., G. Austrheim, and S. N. Grenne. 2000. Landscape change patterns in mountains, land use and environmental diversity, mid-Norway, 1960–1993. Landscape Ecology 15:155–170.

Papanastasis, V. 1998. Plant responses to grazing: a comparative evaluation of annual and perennial grasses. Pages 5–9 in V. Papanastasis and D. Peter (eds.), Ecological basis of livestock grazing in Mediterranean ecosystems. Office for Official Publications of the European Communities, Luxembourg.

Perevolotsky, A., and N. G. Seligman. 1998. Role of grazing in Mediterranean rangeland ecosystems. BioScience 48:1007–1017.

Pickrell, J. 2001. Where the grass never stops growing. Science 293:625.

Prins, H. H. T. 1998. Origin and development of grassland communities in northwestern Europe. Pages 55–97 in M. F. Wallis DeVries, J. P. Bakker, and S. E. Van Wieren (eds.), Grazing and conservation management. Kluwer Academic Publishers, Dordrecht, the Netherlands.

Rackham, O. 1998. Implication of historical ecology for conservation. Pages 152–175 in W. J. Sutherland (ed.), Conservation, science and action. Blackwell, Oxford, UK.

Rapport, D., R. Costanza, P. R. Epstein, C. Gaudet, and R. Levins. 1998. Ecosystem health. Blackwell Science, Oxford, UK.

Risser, P. G. 1995. The status of the science examining ecotones. BioScience 45:318–325.

Rundel, P. W. 1998. Landscape disturbance in Mediterranean-type ecosystems: an overview. Pages 3–22 in P. W. Rundel, G. Montenegro, and F. M. Jaksic (eds.), Landscape disturbance and biodiversity in Mediterranean-type ecosystems. Ecological Studies, Vol. 136. Springer-Verlag, Berlin.

Sorman, G. 2001. Prologue: A Europe without peasants. Pages xiii–xv in O. T. Solbrig, R. Paarlberg, and F. di Castri (eds.), Globalization and the rural environment. Harvard University Press, Cambridge, MA.

Sugden, A., and R. Stone. 2001. Filling generation gaps. Science 293:623.

Thompson, J. N., O. J. Reichman, P. J. Morin, G. A. Polis, M. E. Power, R. W. Sterner, C. A. Couch, L. Gough, R. Holt, D. U. Hooper, F. Keesing, C. R. Lovell, B. T. Milne, M. C. Molles, D. W. Roberts, and S. Y. Strauss. 2001. Frontiers of ecology. BioScience 51:15–24.

Tilman, D., R. M. May, C. L. Lehman, M. A. Nowak. 1994. Habitat destruction and the extinction debt. Nature 371:65–66.

van Droste, B., H. Plachter, and M. Rossler (eds.). 1995. Cultural landscapes of universal value. Gustav Fischer Publishers, Jena, Germany.

von Bertalanffy, L. 1969. General system theory. George Braziller, New York.

Vos, W. 2001. *Coltura promiscua* (mixed cropping). The Solano Basin, Italy. Pages 89–99 in B. Green and W. Vos (eds.), Threatened landscapes, conserving cultural environments. Spon Press, London.

Wu, J., and O. L. Loucks. 1995. From balance of nature to hierarchical patch dynamics: a paradigm shift in ecology. Quarterly Review of Biology 70:439–466.

Zonneveld, I. S. 1995. Land ecology. SPB Academic Publishing, Amsterdam.

CHAPTER NINE

Reconciling the Linkages of Land Management with Natural Disturbance Regimes to Maintain Forest Biodiversity in Europe

PER ANGELSTAM

In most economically well-developed parts of the world, an extensive loss and alteration of different forest environments predates the establishment of effective conservation area networks to secure the long-term survival or recovery of the associated species (Nilsson and Götmark 1992; Noss 1993; Pressey et al. 1996; Margules and Pressey 2000; Smith and Gillet 2000; Angelstam and Andersson 2001). Therefore, the long-term survival of forest-dependent species usually relies on the maintenance and development of land management systems that can integrate conservation needs with human land use interests. Ideally, the outcome should secure well-connected networks of habitats, greenways, or simply "green infrastructures" (Little 1990; Noss 1995; Scott et al. 2001), sufficiently similar in composition, structure, and function to the environments to which the species are adapted. This approach is considered a prerequisite for maintaining representative biodiversity in forest landscapes.

To maintain and restore forest biodiversity at landscape spatial extents, it is important to understand the extent to which existing land use practices harmonize with historical natural dynamics of different forest environments. This means that the range of natural disturbance regimes, the resulting forest and woodland environments to which species have adapted (the ecological dimension), and the range of different land management regimes that can be applied (the management dimension) must be reasonably well known. It also means that the management regime chosen for a given forest environment must harmonize closely with historical disturbance regimes. Forest biodiversity is usually associated with forests (Hunter 1999) but is also associated with managed woodland pastures and other habitat types in the old agricultural landscape once very common in most parts of Europe (Rackham 1988, 1990; Peterken 1996; Kirby and Watkins 1998). Forest management involves the consumptive use of forests to meet the objectives of both land owners and society (Davis and Johnson 1987). After a long history focused on wood production, a strong international trend toward multi objective management developed in the 1990s (Kennedy et al. 2001). One of the new challenges is to maintain forest biodiversity. As a consequence, there is interest and investment in retaining large volumes of timber at different spatial scales, as well as set-asides of forests in reserves (Angelstam and Pettersson 1997; Bergeron and Harvey 1997; Fries et al. 1997; Niemelä 1999; Bergeron et al. 2002), to enhance biodiversity.

Simultaneously, rapid transitions between different agricultural land use systems are taking place because of socioeconomic changes and are a major threat to existing forest biodiversity in regions with forest and different types of woodland (Tucker and Evans 1997; Mikusinski and Angelstam 1998). This has resulted in an ongoing change of the land base in Europe (Nilsson et al. 1992a, 1992b). In the postcommunist countries of eastern Europe, the collapse of collective and state-owned farms with the subsequent privatization of land is gradually altering the landscape by changes in management intensity, field size, and forest management regimes (Balciauskas and Angelstam 1993; Palang 1998). The disappearance of old cultural landscapes in western and central Europe, once characterized by orchards, wooded pastures, and meadows taken out of agricultural production, is another example of change in the landscape (Weitnauer and Bruderer 1987).

In this chapter, I give an overview of different natural disturbance regimes characteristic of temperate and boreal forests and of the associated forest and agricultural woodland management systems of Europe. I then discuss how to achieve long-term maintenance of species that have evolved under different disturbance regimes. I address how to achieve communication of biodiversity management issues between stakeholders. Finally, I propose that specialized species with large area needs that are well known to managers should be used as pedagogic umbrella species (Caro and O'Doherty 1999).

Ecosystem Management and the Natural Disturbance Paradigm

Society's concern about the world's forests in the 1980s and 1990s has drawn considerable attention to deforestation, loss of species, and the need for sustainable management (Kennedy et al. 2001). Consequently there has been an increased focus on trying to understand the ecology of forests (Leibundgut 1993; Attiwill 1994; Kimmins 1997; Barnes et al. 1998; Hunter 1990, 1999) in order to provide knowledge about the ecosystem, devise ways to describe it, and develop systems for predicting system responses to both natural and anthropogenic disturbance (Kimmins 1997). The idea is not new (cf. Leopold 1949).

In North America, the concepts of new forestry (Franklin 1989), forest ecosystem management (Salwasser 1994; Kohm and Franklin 1997), natural disturbance ecology (Coates and Burton 1997; Burton et al. 1999), and ecological forestry (Hunter 1999) have been advocated as tools for sustaining ecological integrity, including maintaining and restoring biodiversity. In practice, "manipulation of a forest ecosystem should work within the limits established by natural disturbance patterns prior to extensive human alteration of the landscape" (Hunter 1999, p. 29).

The key assumption behind the natural disturbance paradigm is that native species have evolved under natural disturbance conditions. Therefore, maintaining sufficiently similar conditions is the best way to maintain the species of those ecosystems. This has also been expressed as a coarse filter approach by which the characteristic ecosystems and landscapes are maintained (Hunter et al. 1988).

Similar ideas have been put forward in Europe. In both western (Peterken's 1996 "natural approach") and central Europe (Remmert's 1991 "mosaic cycle concept"), the natural dynamics of forests have been proposed as sources of inspiration for woodland and forest conservation. In Scotland, Quine et al. (1999) discussed the extent to which wind disturbance should be mimicked in forest plantations. Scherzinger (1996) argued that the dynamic nature of natural forest development should be used as a guide for nature conservation rather than the static view implied by protecting small conservation areas. In Scandinavia, biodiversity maintenance as a management objective began in the 1970s, primarily as a response to clear-cutting (Jordbruksdepartementet 1974). In the 1990s, the disturbance regime concept became an accepted argument for applying a wider range of silvicultural methods (Angelstam et al. 1993; Bradshaw et al. 1994; Angelstam and Pettersson 1997; Fries et al. 1997; Angelstam 1998; Niemelä 1999; Kellomäki 2000). There are other approaches to forest design that do maintain biodiversity explicitly but rather focus on cultural and aesthetic values that may appear natural to the untrained observer (Lucas 1991).

To describe the idea that biodiversity can be maintained by landscape management that builds on natural forest disturbance regimes, words such as *emulate, imitate,* and *mimic* have been used. In most cases, however, landscapes should harbor a wide range of goods and services in addition to biodiversity. Often, implementation of the full range of the natural disturbance regime would seriously conflict with the human commodity interests. Striking a balance implies that the idea of maintaining the full range of variability is not feasible. Rather, maintaining biodiversity in managed landscapes is a matter of letting management be sufficiently similar to the natural disturbance regimes but dampened so disturbances fall well within the range of natural variability. If this is not the case, part of the landscape must be set aside as reserves or managed with the explicit objective of maintaining forest biodiversity. This suggests an urgent need to develop quantitative targets regarding "how much is enough?" of different components, structures, and processes of forests across spatial and temporal scales (Angelstam 1997; Bachmann et al. 1998; Angelstam and Andersson 2001; Fahrig 2001). Measurement of the components of biodiversity (Noss 1990; Angelstam 1998; Kneshaw et al. 2000; Larsson et al. 2001) and efficient communication between science and practice (Raivio et al. 2001) are needed. The performance standards of various certification systems are one mechanism for specifying how intensively forest environments may be managed (Elliott 1999; Higman et al. 1999).

Natural Disturbance Regimes

Following Pickett and White (1985), I interpret disturbance as any discrete event in time that disrupts ecosystem, community, or population structure and changes resources, substrate availability, or the physical environment. I argue that a prerequisite for biodiversity maintenance in managed landscapes is to understand and emulate closely the natural disturbance regimes to which different species have adapted (Kohm and Franklin 1997; Hunter 1999). The diversity of forest types in a landscape is determined by the interaction between abiotic and biotic factors. Soils, topography, climate, and access to nutrients and water are landscape characteristics that largely determine the range of possible compositions of tree species (Arnborg 1964, 1990; Ellenberg 1996). Forest composition and structure are modified by different kinds of interactions and disturbances, ranging from abiotic (fire, wind, water) to biotic (grazing, browsing, predation), and include anthropogenic causes (forest clearing, livestock grazing; Pickett and White 1985; Ellenberg 1996; Peterken 1996; Esseen et al. 1997; Angelstam 1996, 1998; Kirby and Watkins 1998; Engelmark 1999; Engelmark and Hytteborn 1999). As a consequence, different combinations of landscape traits (abiotic, biotic, and anthropogenic; Angelstam 1997) create characteristic disturbance regimes (Pyne 1984; Pickett and White 1985). Disturbance regimes vary along a continuum from large-scale disturbances, such as fire, wind, floods, and insect outbreaks, to small-scale or localized disturbances such as gap formation caused by fungi, insects, and single treefall. Differences between disturbances are described by the parameters of the disturbance regime (Pickett and White 1985; White and Harrod 1997).

Here I attempt to merge different approaches in natural vegetation dynamics studies to summarize in a simple way how trees interact with abiotic and biotic disturbances. First I describe forest formation processes, including identifying and classifying different types of dynamic and successional stages or pathways. As a synthesis, I use a system with three groups of disturbance regimes in an attempt to simplify while acknowledging the enormous variation of interacting biotic and abiotic forces in boreal and temperate vegetation. I follow the logic presented by Dyrenkov (1984), who distinguished the following main types of stand age structures: even-aged, uneven-aged, and all-aged (Fig. 9.1). The same division was proposed independently by Angelstam (1998) and Angelstam et al. (1993). To stress the dynamic characteristics of each group, I use the words *successional, cohort,* and *gap dynamics* to describe the three types of forest dynamics.

Successional Dynamics

A given set of trees of a single age class, or cohort, proceeds through a series of developmental stages (Oliver and Larson 1996). Large-scale disturbances such as fire or wind initiate succession and allow forests to regenerate over large areas simultaneously. In the boreal forest, recent burns, young stands of

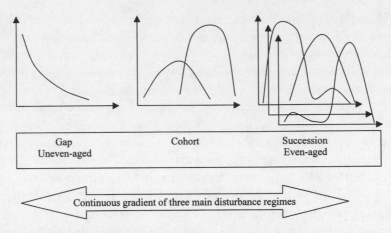

Figure 9.1 Generalized illustration of the age distribution of trees in stands of the three main groups of forest disturbance regimes (see Table 9.1).

mixed coniferous or deciduous trees, and old-growth forest stands are examples of different successional stages (Furyaev and Kireev 1979; Angelstam and Arnold 1993; Furyaev 1996; Angelstam 1998; Yaroshenko et al. 2001). Because of the spatial and temporal heterogeneity of disturbances, the structural complexity of age classes within a landscape increases with age (Johnson 1992). However, if viewed over longer time spans, successional stages are ephemeral at a particular site. To persist in the landscape, species characteristic of a particular stage must be able to disperse to colonize new sites.

Empirical data from boreal and temperate forests show that the maximum possible range of the different steps in succession usually exceeds 250 years (Jahn 1991; Johnson 1992). In a detailed study of boreal forest in Sweden, Niklasson and Granström (2000) showed that the range of age classes on mesic sites spanned 300 years. Similarly, in the last large remnant of the lowland temperate deciduous forest in Bialowieza in Poland, most tree species have maximum stand ages of much more than 200 years (Falinski 1986).

The development of a single cohort of trees after a disturbance event can be divided into several distinct stages. Oliver and Larson (1996) describe four stages of stand development. In the stand initiation stage, new species and individuals continue to appear. In the stem exclusion stage, no new individuals appear, but some die. Later, in the understory reinitiation stage, new herbs, shrubs, or trees start to regenerate but grow very slowly. Finally, much later, in the old-growth stage, overstory trees die and understory trees take over. Vertical vegetation structure develops from simple, with most of the cover in the tops of trees, to complex, with several vegetation layers. However, from a silvicultural and wildlife (*sensu* Hunter 1990) point of view, more than these four stages are needed to capture the relevant structural and compositional variation between different successional stages. In managed forests, the terms *harvested, young, thinning,* and *final felling* are useful because they link the development of the stand to the silvicultural operations (Smith et al. 1997). However, this division does not include later developmental stages of particular importance for forest biodiversity. Thomas (1979) and Angelstam (1999) distinguished six stages that provide a compromise between simplicity and detail, and these are adopted here.

The Six Developmental Stages

The first stage is *stand initiation.* After extensive disturbances such as fire, windthrow, large-scale insect outbreaks, or clear-cutting, environmental conditions are often unique. For example, many insect species have adapted to early postfire landscapes by using the burned dead wood as a substrate (Wikars 1992). Similarly, some plants need heat to germinate (Granström 1993). For other species, the cause of the disturbance is less important as long as the necessary substrates are available (Angelstam and Mikusinski 1994). The specific conditions of the site and the surrounding matrix that determine forest forming processes are created at this stage.

During the *young* phase, the typical herb, shrub, and tree layer vegetation has recovered, often after a phase of herb-rich pioneer ground vegetation. There are often still living trees and large amounts of coarse woody debris left from the previous stand. Remnants of the previous stand that died start to decay. Even a severe stand-replacing fire usually does not consume more than about 20 percent of the standing biomass of the burned stand (Furyaev and Kireev 1979; Johnson 1992), and large proportions of the disturbed area are often left intact as groups or stands of trees (Pyne 1984; Eberhart and Woodard 1987; Johnson 1992).

During the *middle-aged* phase, self-thinning and gradual replacement of light-demanding species (*Betula* and *Populus*) with shade-tolerant species (*Picea, Abies,* and *Fagus*) takes place. Toward the end of this stage, trees start to compete, and some die from lack of light or soil moisture, a process called suppression, which leads to stem exclusion (Smith et al. 1997).

In the *harvestable* phase, the light-demanding deciduous broad-leafed trees begin to die and shade-tolerant *Picea* and *Abies* in boreal and mountain forests and *Fagus* in western temperate and mountain forests become established. The forest gradually acquires a multistory vegetation structure, and the herb layer vegetation changes to more shade-tolerant species. Unless a new disturbance occurs, an aging stand will gradually enter the understory reinitiation stage (Oliver and Larson 1996). In this stage, scattered trees that were previously successful begin to become damaged and die because of insects, fungi, snowbreak, wind, falling trees, or other factors. The small gaps created in the canopy allow more light and moisture to reach the forest floor. As a consequence, there is an advance regeneration of shade-tolerant species.

These first four developmental stages in succession have equivalents in most managed forests. However, given specific silvicultural practices, tree species composition, vertical and horizontal vegetation structure, and the amount and type of dead wood will be manipulated for desired forest components.

In the *aging* phase, shade-tolerant species become older and start to develop diameters large enough for primary nest excavators (e.g., black woodpecker [*Dryocopus martius*]). Bark texture suitable for different specialized lichens (Uliczka and Angelstam 1999) and canopies that can carry the nests of large raptors develop. Dead wood accumulates, and the vertical and horizontal vegetation structure becomes more complex. This stage is usually not allowed to develop in a managed forest.

After a century or two without a stand-replacing disturbance, the stand gradually opens up with the formation of gaps in the canopy as large trees or groups of trees fall in the *old-growth* stage. Coarse woody debris is abundant, and vegetation structure is complex. As in a young forest, tree age distribution is usually bimodal (Oliver and Larson 1996), dominated by old trees but with young cohorts appearing both in gaps and as an additional vegetation layer. The relationship between the size and the age of the trees becomes less and less obvious.

Successional development is highly variable. Although the full range of successional stages often takes more than 200 years in boreal and temperate forests in Europe (Falinski 1986; Leibundgut 1993), the time varies according to site. In the Pacific Northwest of North America, some types of old-growth stands may take several hundred years to develop (Kohm and Franklin 1997). By contrast, succession in riparian forest with willows (*Salix* sp.) and other deciduous trees may enter an old-growth phase in only 60 years (Oliver and Larson 1996). Boreal broad-leafed deciduous tree species such as *Populus* and *Betula* may develop old-growth characteristics within similar time frames (Carlson and Stenberg 1995; Carlson 2000).

Multiple Successional Lengths and Pathways

It is rare that successional development after a stand-replacing disturbance is a linear sequence, passing through each step in the successional development described here. Instead, there are several pathways through which successions may proceed. In principle, disturbance can occur at any stage, albeit with different probabilities. For example, in mesic boreal forests, a new fire is unlikely to occur before a stand reaches 20 years of age because of low fuel loads. In the first three to five decades after a disturbance episode, fire risk increases because of fuel accumulation (Schimmel 1993; Niklasson and Granström 2000). Similarly, a stand's susceptibility to wind varies with age (Gardiner and Quine 2000).

Cohort Dynamics

Several tree species show clear adaptations to low-intensity disturbances. Scotch pine (*Pinus sylvestris*) and fire are a good example. In the boreal zone, natural Scotch pine forests on dry sites are characterized by frequent low-intensity fires that produce stands with several age cohorts of trees (Sannikov and Goldammer 1996; Angelstam 1998). Because of its thick bark and the long distance between the ground and canopy, a Scotch pine tree becomes less sensitive to fire damage with increasing time. As a consequence, a typical natural dry site Scotch pine forest has several distinct age cohorts of living trees and standing snags, both of which eventually produce a continuous supply of dead wood on the ground in different stages of decay (Sannikov and Goldammer 1996). Such a forest has a parklike appearance. Burned and grazed oak forests in old cultural landscapes can show similar dynamics (Ellenberg 1996). When grazing animals are at low densities, the regeneration of trees is possible, and a new cohort of trees is formed. According to Leibundgut (1982), Dyrenkov (1984), and Fedorchuk et al. (1998), this type of disturbance regime also occurs in Norway spruce forests on mesic well-drained sites in association with windthrow events that remove a portion of the canopy.

Dyrenkov (1984) distinguished three different types of uneven-aged cohort dynamics ranging from a dominance of young trees (regeneration) to dominance of old cohorts (digression). Following Dyrenkov (1984), I use the terms *regeneration, intermediate,* and *digression.*

Regeneration: Stands are dominated by younger trees but with an overstory of old and very old trees, as well as snags and coarse woody debris.

Intermediate: The different age cohorts are evenly distributed within the stand. In Scotch pine forests, there are typically three to five distinct cohorts that range over at least 200 years (Sannikov and Goldammer 1996).

Digression: Cohorts of old and very old trees dominate. Sometimes, because of the absence of fire for longer periods of time and an associated accumulation of nutrients, the site type may become more productive.

The three types are related to the relative frequency of occurrence of disturbances with different intensities and return intervals. For example, in Scotch pine forest on dry soils the first type should prevail after intensive disturbance such as crown fires or after frequent fire disturbance not allowing recruitment of trees into older, less fire damage–prone age cohorts. If fire disturbances are of lower intensity, the second type should prevail. Finally, with infrequent fire disturbance the third type would prevail.

Gap Dynamics

In the absence of large disturbances, the death of a single tree or groups of trees maintains the formation of gaps in the forest where shade-tolerant trees can regenerate. An even regeneration process determines the stand dynamics. The age and diameter distribution of trees within a stand is of the inverse J-type (Kuuluvainen 1994), and a simple mean age conveys no information about age structure. The internal age distribution can be all-aged or consist of multiple cohorts. The relationship between the size and age of trees is often poor because small trees can be very old (Oliver and Larson 1996). In naturally dynamic landscapes, these stands often form corridors, networks, or clusters in the moist parts of the landscape. Typically, these forests have a moist and stable microclimate and a continuous supply of dead, decaying wood. Such dynamics also occur in large areas where the climate is moist and fires are uncommon (Angelstam 1998; Ohlson and Tryterud 1999). The tree species involved include Norway spruce and *Abies* spp. in boreal and montane forests and beech and several broadleaf tree species in lowland temperate forests and in riparian forests (Mayer 1984; Giorgievskij 1992; Angelstam 1996; Drobyshev 2001). I follow Dyrenkov (1984) and distinguish two gap subtypes:

Even: This type is characterized by an even distribution of different tree ages in the stand and is associated with smaller gap sizes including one or a few trees.

Uneven: This type is characterized by a patchy distribution of different tree ages in the stand and is associated with larger gap sizes.

Silviculture and Other Tree Management Systems

Trees directly and indirectly influence the distribution and abundance of other forest species, but agriculture and other forms of land use that include trees as components also contribute to biodiversity.

Silvicultural Systems

Throughout the world, foresters divide different silvicultural systems using the gradient between even-aged and uneven-aged systems (Matthews 1989). There are three general types of age class structures that are managed: even-aged, stands with two age classes, and uneven-aged. Even-aged systems include clear-cutting or seed tree systems, the intermediate double-cohort systems include shelterwood systems, and uneven-aged systems include single-tree and group selection (Table 9.1; Wahlgren 1914; Amilon 1923; Morosov 1930; Børset 1986; Matthews 1989; Dengler 1944, 1990; Mayer 1992; Nyland 1996; Smith et al. 1997). The different systems can be understood better if envisioned as located on a continuum of the proportion of trees removed and the size of treatment unit (Fig. 9.2).

Table 9.1 Summary of the different management and utilization systems in forests and old cultural landscapes in Europe (if applicable, German names are also given).

Even-aged management
with clear-cutting systems

Clear-cutting or coppice (*Kahlschlag* or *Niederwald*)	In the most common silvicultural regime, the entire stand is removed in one cutting. Coppice systems depend on vegetative regeneration of sprouting broadleaf species such as *Populus, Corylis, Carpinus,* and *Fraxinus* after clear-cutting (Jahn 1991).
Seed tree method (*Kahlhieb mit Samenbäumen*)	Old stand is removed in one cutting, except for some seed trees that are left until a new tree generation has been secured. Seed trees often achieve valuable additional diameter growth (Smith et al. 1997).
Variable retention (with or without extended rotations)	Developed in response to criticisms of clear-cutting. Trees are retained during harvest for aesthetic reasons (e.g., to avoid the visual impression of almost complete harvesting [Lucas 1991]) or for biodiversity (e.g., to maintain components typical of old-growth stands such as large or old trees, snags, and coarse woody debris).

continued

Table 9.1 *continued*

Double-cohort management with shelterwood systems	
Shelterwood cutting (*Schirmschlag*)	The best trees (large crowns, strong boles) are preserved during cutting as shelter against wind and for seed production (Smith et al. 1997); shade-tolerant species regenerate under this remaining canopy.
Coppice with standards (*Mittelwald*)	Coppice growth with scattered older trees (standards). Coppice is harvested after a few decades, standards after a century or more. A common combination in central Europe is *Fraxinus, Carpinus,* and *Corylus* as coppice and *Quercus* as standards (Kirby and Watkins 1998).
Uneven-aged management with selection systems	
Single-tree selection (*Plenterung*)	Classically, every even-aged cohort of the uneven-aged stand occupies a space equal to that created by the removal of a single old tree. Characterized by scattered patches with small even-aged groups of shade-tolerant trees (e.g., *Fagus, Abies,* and *Picea*), which are thinned as they grow.
Group selection system (*Femelschlag and Saumschlag*)	Openings are made larger to satisfy needs of a range of tree species. In strip selection (*Saumschlag*), openings are created in slowly advancing strips rather than gaps. There is no clear distinction between group selection with large gaps and even-aged systems with small stands. On Vancouver Island, Canada, 1-ha openings in old growth are classified as group selection (G. Dunnsworth, Weyerhaeuser Co., personal communication 2001), whereas the same size of treatment unit is called an even-aged system in Austria (H. Malin and B. Maier, Stand Montafon, personal communication 2001).
Old cultural landscape	Woodland pasture, wooded meadow, pollarding, lopping.
Exploitation	High-grading.

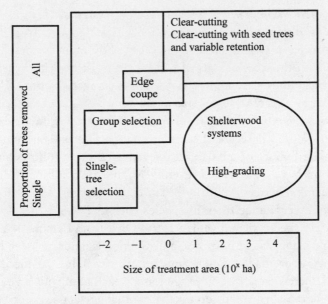

Figure 9.2 The different silvicultural methods can be characterized by the proportion of trees removed at harvest and the size of the treated area.

Even-Aged Management with Clear-Cutting Systems

In even-aged stands, all trees germinate, sprout, or are planted at about the same time. Although tree size varies increasingly with stand age, the calendar age of the trees is about the same when it is time to regenerate the stand. It is often easy to characterize stands just by stand age, which can be used to guide decisions about treatment and harvesting. It is also easy to manipulate the genetic makeup by planting or seeding. A wide range of terms are applied, and three methods are commonly used (Table 9.1). The smallest recommended stand size ranges from 0.5 ha (Børset 1986) to tens of hectares, but clear-cutting may also cover thousands of hectares (Devall 1993).

Double-Cohort Management with Shelterwood Systems

In this system, the removal of the old stand takes place in a series of cuttings that extend over a short part of the successional development. The establishment of the next cohort takes place under the partial shelter of the seed trees or under trees of other species (Table 9.1). Double-cohorts are an intermediate category in which the presence of both cohort stands can be temporary or continuous (Smith et al. 1997).

Uneven-Aged Management with Selection Systems

In uneven-aged stands there is no definite beginning cohort. Trees in a given area vary by age as well as size and are often of different species. Throughout their lives, the trees compete for light or moisture with nearby trees. Uneven-aged stands are composed of small even-aged cohorts of different ages located in gaps of different size in the stand. As each even-aged group becomes older, competition reduces the number of trees, first rapidly and later more slowly. Therefore, if each age class occupies the same area, the diameter distribution for a balanced uneven-aged stand follows an asymptotic relationship usually called reverse *J*-shaped distribution. Controlling the genetic origin of trees is difficult because new trees regenerate from seeds. The system favors shade-tolerant species such as *Picea, Abies,* and many broadleaf tree species (Kuuluvainen 1994; Oliver and Larson 1996).

For some management purposes, a distinction is made between balanced and irregular uneven-aged stands (Smith et al., 1997). In a balanced uneven-aged stand, there are three or more age classes, each occupying an equal area. Irregular uneven-aged stands do not contain all age classes, so trees arrive at uncertain times and at different rates. Here the distribution looks like a series of humps on the diameter distribution curve. The contemporary central European and old Scandinavian literature and terminology on uneven-aged silvicultural systems are very diverse. Following Mayer (1992), Børset (1986), and Smith et al. (1997) I include only two types: the single-tree and group selection systems (see Table 9.1).

High-Grading

Although not a silvicultural system, harvesting of the most valuable trees has usually been part of only the first phases of forest use. As a consequence, the mean diameter of the remaining trees is gradually being reduced. There is usually a need to restore sustainable wood production by introducing forest management of some kind.

Old Cultural Landscape Management Regimes

Clearing and cultivation of forested land has had a major impact on forests for millennia and has resulted in a dramatic reduction and fragmentation of the once naturally dynamic and more contiguous primeval forests (Mayer 1984; Mantel 1990). Hannah et al. (1995) estimated that the remaining proportions of largely intact forests in Europe in different biogeographic zones were 20 percent for the boreal coniferous forests, 2 percent for hemiboreal mixed deciduous and coniferous forests, and 0.2 percent for the broadleaf deciduous forests.

Nevertheless, in some regions forest biodiversity has been rescued by management methods that were practiced in old cultural landscapes (Mantel 1990; Tucker and Evans 1997). To maintain summer and winter fodder for cows, sheep, and other domestic animals, land was managed using fire, mowing, clearing, and tree and water management (Kirby and Watkins 1998). The range of cultural disturbances often resulted in the maintenance of forest biodiversity because of the presence of large, special trees in landscapes dominated by grazing and agriculture (Tucker and Evans 1997; Kirby and Watkins 1998). Today, such habitats usually remain as small isolated patches in a managed matrix. However, old management regimes are still in use in parts of Europe, usually in remote valleys in mountainous areas, as well as in regions that the agricultural revolution with intensive management has not yet reached. The ancient practice of pollarding and lopping, whereby branches of wild trees are cut but the tree is not, does maintain large trees that grow slowly. Coarse woody debris on the ground was often limited, but dead wood in the crowns of large trees was left to shade the ground. As a consequence, suitable substrate on tree trunks and in cavities provided habitat for many forest species, including shade-intolerant vascular plants, lichens, insects, and birds (Mikusinski and Angelstam 1998; Nilsson et al. 2001). Similar trends in the development of the composition and structure of domesticated trees (e.g., olive and fruit trees) have occurred in both central Europe and the Mediterranean (Ispikoudis et al. 1993; Tucker and Evans 1997). These areas may also include area-demanding raptors needing large trees for breeding as well as large carnivores in areas where shepherds protect livestock.

Do Management and Natural Disturbance Regimes Harmonize?

For foresters involved with managing trees to maintain biodiversity, it is important to develop forest management techniques that maintain and restore the composition, structure, and processes found in naturally dynamic forests (Bergeron and Harvey 1997; Angelstam 1998; Hunter 1999; Angelstam and Andersson 2001; Axelsson 2001; Axelsson and Östlund 2001). To succeed requires knowledge of the links between edaphic, geographic factors, and tree species as well as knowledge of the spatial and temporal distribution of different disturbance regimes and the needs of appropriate umbrella species (*sensu* Lambeck 1997; Martikainen et al. 1998; Simberloff 1998; Caro and O'Doherty 1999) in naturally dynamic reference forest landscapes.

The development of different management systems has been inspired by natural disturbance regimes (Mayer 1992), and as shown in the reviews of natural disturbance and management regimes earlier in this chapter, there is a basic similarity between the two. But there are also major differences. In this section I discuss the extent to which the two dimensions differ (Table 9.2). For the combinations forest and land management system of interest (Table 9.1), I analyze similarities and differences by comparing different natural disturbance regimes and their subtypes. The reasoning rests on the underlying assumption that maintaining biodiversity entails maintaining different developmental stages in succession and their characteristic habitat features at both stand and landscape scales.

Even-Aged Management versus Natural Disturbance Regimes

Because silviculture aims at maintaining a high yield, stands are usually harvested at a point when increase in volume growth starts to diminish. Consequently, old-growth stand age declines with increasing time of application of even-aged forest management under the sustained yield paradigm. Moreover, in the absence of stand-replacing disturbances such as fire and wind blowdown, very early successional stages with bare soil are missing. This inhibits the presence of species needing burned wood (Wikars 1992), bare soil (Esseen et al. 1997), and heat (Granström 1993) to allow germination. Tree age variation in natural systems is wide, and stands often include a high proportion of both younger and older age classes. In addition, large areas within a patch of recently disturbed forest contain undisturbed patches that gradually merge with the developing stand. To favor biodiversity, different systems of variable retention cutting have been developed (Oliver and Larson 1996). Although this certainly improves the quality of the future stands, logging of old and aging stands continues and reduces both the total amount and individual patch size of such forests.

Cohort Dynamics

Clear-cutting with residual seed trees is superficially similar to cohort dynamics in which the stand is dominated by younger cohorts. The obvious difference is the lack of dead wood of both snags and coarse woody debris in different dimensions and decay stages. However, with consistent retention of trees at every harvest event, a certain amount of dead wood in different stages of decay and several cohorts of different living trees could be restored over the long term.

Table 9.2 Matrix of the natural forest disturbance regimes (ecological dimension) and forest and tree management systems (the management dimension). The degree of relative match between the two dimensions is indicated by the signs – and +, used with or without parentheses.*

Disturbance Regime	Forest and Tree Management System	Succession						Cohort			Gap	
		1	2	3	4	5	6	1	2	3	1	2
Even-aged management with clear-cutting systems	Clear-cutting	(+)	(+)	(+)	(+)	–	–	–	–	–	–	–
	Coppice	(+)	(+)	(+)	–	–	–	–	–	–	–	–
	Seed tree method	(+)	+	(+)	(+)	–	–	–	–	–	–	–
	Clear-cutting with retention for biodiversity	+	+	+	+	–	–	+	–	–	–	–
	Clear-cutting with retention for biodiversity, and extended rotation	+	+	+	+	+	(+)	+	+	(+)	–	–
Double-cohort management with shelterwood systems	Shelterwood	(+)	(+)	(+)	(+)	–	–	(+)	–	–	–	–
	Coppice with standards	(+)	(+)	(+)	(+)	–	–	–	–	–	–	–
Uneven-aged	Selection cutting	–	–	–	–	–	–	–	–	–	+	(+)
	Group-system	–	–	–	(+)	(+)	(+)	–	(+)	–	(+)	(+)
	Edge coupe	–	–	–	(+)	(+)	(+)	–	(+)	–	(+)	(+)
Old cultural landscape	Woodland pasture	(+)	–	–	–	–	–	(+)	–	–	–	–
	Wooded meadow	(+)	–	–	–	(+)	(+)	(+)	(+)	–	–	–
	Pollarding, lopping	(+)	–	–	–	(+)	(+)	(+)	(+)	–	–	–
Exploitation	High-grading	–	–	(+)	(+)	(+)	–	(+)	–	–	–	–

* The + signs indicate the direction of agreement between the ecological and management dimensions, and (+) with the parentheses indicate that the relative strength of the agreement is less than + without the parentheses.

Double-Cohort Management versus Natural Disturbance Regimes

After large-scale disturbances, the establishment of the new stand can lead to a structure similar to that of a shelterwood system. For example, this could be a combination of oak with a turnover time of more than 100 years and coppice (i.e., the typical central European *Mittelwald*).

Cohort Dynamics

This kind of dynamics can be emulated with forest management character-ized by repeated retention of trees and dead wood and the use of fire (Fries et al. 1997). A dry pine forest where clear-cutting with seed tree regenera-tion is used can be restored using the following steps. Instead of harvesting the seed trees, after the regeneration of a new stand has been secured, a pro-portion of seed trees would be left to develop into a cohort of old trees. Dur-ing the next rotation, the procedure should be repeated. The dead wood could be restored actively by leaving high stumps or passively by leaving some of the windblown trees.

Uneven-Aged Management Systems versus Natural Disturbance Regimes

Opening gaps to allow regeneration of new trees is in principle the begin-ning of succession. However, this approach would not ensure a sufficiently wide distribution of patch sizes to satisfy the area needs of many of the species. Gap formation is often too weak a disturbance and not large enough in extent, so many species cannot reestablish. Uneven-aged management sys-tems could help to maintain the composition and structure of the final old-growth phase in succession. To succeed, the restoration and maintenance of dead wood would also be needed.

Cohort Dynamics

Uneven-aged group selection management systems could potentially be use-ful for stands, which naturally have a range of age classes. One example is *Pinus ponderosa* forests that naturally experience repeated low-intensity fires (Smith et al. 1997).

Gap Dynamics

The continuous application of single and group selection harvesting in forests with shade-tolerant tree species such as *Fagus sylvatica, Abies alba,* and *Picea abies* on fertile soils leads to a multilayered vegetation structure. Typically, an inverse *J*-shaped diameter distribution is the long-term result. Near-to-nature forestry (*Naturnahe Waldwirtschaft;* Bode and von Hohnhurst 1995) was developed in Germany and Switzerland with the aim of maintaining this forest structure. Despite the apparent good match between silvicultural systems and natural disturbance regimes, traditional uneven-aged near-to-nature silviculture does not emulate all components of the natural gap phase dynamics. The absence of dead wood is the most striking difference, but the absence of large old trees is also evident (see Leibundgut 1993).

Old Cultural Landscape versus Natural Disturbance Regimes

A characteristic feature of agriculture in Europe is land abandonment of various spatial extents. Small fields or whole land holdings may be abandoned because of individual preferences, family events, and disputes. Villages and whole regions may be deserted as a consequence of famine, disease, and changed economic conditions. As a result, despite active management, certain successional stages in the development from abandoned pastures, meadows, and fields may be present in the landscape (Chirot 1989; Vera 2000).

Cohort Dynamics

The maintenance of wooded meadows and pastures can allow the long-term presence of large old trees in a landscape for a very long time (Kirby and Watkins 1998). For maintaining forest biodiversity, these landscapes can provide a crucial rescue effect for a number of species. A large-scale example of this can be found in the Extremadura region in Spain. In combination with sheep, pig, and cork production, the area hosts both large raptors and mammalian carnivores (Tucker and Evans 1997). Similarly, old-fashioned apple orchards with large old trees can maintain a rich bird fauna (Weitnauer and Bruderer 1987; Weggler and Widmer 2000).

Exploitation

Often, the early phases of the use of forest resources can be described as tree mining (Yaroshenko et al. 2001). Only certain species or specific tree sizes are harvested per unit area, and the timber resource is viewed as infinite. From a biodiversity point of view this is not necessarily a problem.

Discussion

This chapter demonstrates that there is large variation both between different natural disturbance regimes and between the management systems used in forestry and old-fashioned agriculture. When considering the maintenance of forest biodiversity, some combinations provide an acceptable match between the ecological dimension and the management dimension. The most common paradigm, to practice only one form of forest and tree management, is clearly insufficient.

The Ecological and Management Dimensions

The comparisons between management systems and natural forest disturbance regimes show that no single near-to-nature land management or silvicultural system is universally suitable. Instead, many methods can be adopted in different combinations and contexts, depending on forest ecology, local land use history, and the management goal for the landscape (Mayer 1992; Seymour and Hunter 1999). However, even if there is a principal match between a given management system and a natural disturbance regime, there are usually several differences that must be mitigated. Special considerations may include variable retention of living and dead trees and tree groups or not using parts of the landscape at all.

To maintain forest biodiversity by even-aged management systems, it is insufficient to maintain only the commercially valuable tree species. Moreover, the traditional inclusion of age classes only up to final harvesting must be complemented by a continued and dynamic presence of both recently disturbed and aging and old-growth phases on the landscape. In even-aged, multiple-aged, and uneven-aged management systems, it is essential that different forest components and structures be maintained at a range of spatial scale extents (Larsson et al. 2001).

The maintenance of viable populations of forest specialists is a challenge not only for sustainable forestry but also to some extent for several ancient forms of agriculture and agroforestry management (Chapter 8, this volume). The reason is that many of the components of forest biodiversity have been rescued or introduced and maintained locally by ancient traditional management methods that were practiced in the old cultural landscape (Kirby and Watkins 1998). Europe, with its wide range of environments and management traditions, provides a good example of this. At present, the forest cover in Europe is expanding (Nilsson et al. 1992a, 1992b). If the expansion takes place on low productive agricultural land with a traditional land use, this may threaten many highly valued native species and landscapes.

Despite the good match between the ecological and management dimensions, conservation areas with both laissez-faire and active management strategies are usually a necessary part of a comprehensive approach to maintaining forest biodiversity (Hunter 1999; Angelstam and Andersson 2001). Although an appropriate silvicultural system may create the relevant habitat structures and dynamics, this will not automatically provide for the spatial needs of viable populations and metapopulations at landscape or even regional scale extents (Hunter 1999; Kouki and Väänänen 2000). Similarly, it may be necessary to balance both natural (browsing; Angelstam et al. 2000) and anthropogenic processes (airborne pollution; Bengtsson et al. 2000).

Ecology or Tradition?

Silvicultural systems, as well as the circumstances under which they are applied, differ between countries and regions and change over time (Smith et al. 1997; Lähde et al. 1999; Kenk and Guehne 2001; Malcolm et al. 2001). In many regions and countries, there have been clear changes in the use of different management methods. One example is the Swedish forest. Despite a wide range of disturbance regimes (Angelstam and Andersson 2001), silvicultural regimes have shown little spatial variation but have changed greatly over time (Ekelund and Hamilton 2001).

After a long period of overexploitation (Wieslander 1936; Östlund et al. 1997), Swedish silviculture started in the early 1800s with a strong influence from the German school of a strictly regulated even-aged management system (Wahlgren 1914; Amilon 1923). Different methods have since been advocated and applied in different time periods. Even-aged management was strongly criticized by Wallmo (1897), after which the silvicultural system developed into different forms of uneven management systems. Later, especially in northern Sweden, successful examples of regeneration after clear-cutting and prescribed burning in the boreal forest inspired a return to even-aged management. Only in the 1990s were site-adapted silvicultural regimes proposed (Angelstam et al. 1993; Hagner 1995; Fries et al. 1997) and later applied. Similar changes are occurring in Britain and central Europe. Since 1900, about 1.5 million ha of coniferous forest has been established by even-aged plantations of nonnative species. To enhance aesthetic, conservation, and environmental benefits, recent policies require managers to introduce alternative silvicultural systems to clear-cutting (Malcolm et al. 2001). In central Europe, past forest management has reduced the natural proportion of broadleaf forests from 66 to 33 percent of the forest area since the nineteenth century (Kenk and Guehne 2001). At present, there are proposals to restore the deciduous forests by transforming pure stands of planted *Picea abies* and *Pinus sylvestris*. These examples indicate that culture, history, policies, and institutional and economic limitations have determined the use of different management practices much more than consideration of the composition, structure, and function of the ecosystem.

Monitoring Progress

Silvicultural systems and their application can be viewed as a continuously revised working hypothesis based on a mixture of fact and opinion (Smith et al. 1997). Learning by mistakes is an important tool for improving future action. If rigorously applied, this implies adaptive management whereby objective monitoring of the outcomes is crucial. However, it is difficult to create operational goals and demonstrate progress. There are several challenges (Bunnell and Johnson 1998).

Visions

The first challenge is to have a clear definition of the goal. Because the biodiversity concept originated from the concern about the loss of species, the obvious short-term goal is to reverse negative population trends among native species. The long-term goal is to achieve population viability. However, conditions vary widely between stands, landscapes, and regions. The amount and distribution of naturally occurring, characteristic disturbance regimes provides a guide to management. In Europe and other parts of the world, both a natural and an old cultural landscape vision must be considered (Angelstam et al. 1997).

Tools

The second challenge is to define the tools that allow us to reach both the short- and long-term goals for biodiversity. They range from creating awareness and ensuring continuous capacity building to actual monitoring and management techniques. But the fundamental context is the way in which we manage forests. Both natural forest and old cultural disturbance regimes can provide the management context to reach a wide range of goals. Determining the degree of harmony between the vision and the management tools is a fundamental starting point.

Monitoring and Targets

The third challenge is to know when the goal has been reached. This includes documenting both short-term and long-term quantitative targets and then monitoring success. Ideally, efforts to emulate natural disturbance regimes in forest management should be linked across all spatial scales from trees to landscapes (Angelstam et al. 2001). This means that management steps (Table 9.3) must be tailored for each main forest type separately (Larsson et al. 2001). With sufficient knowledge about critical amounts of different forest structures in different forest types, it would be possible to determine whether the aggregated conservation efforts will successfully address the maintenance of viable populations and ecosystem function (Jansson and Angelstam 1999; Fahrig 2001).

Communication

Results of the monitoring and expected benchmarks must be communicated and understood by the different stakeholders in forest management. Ranking the relative importance of different methods (Table 9.2) for both production and biodiversity is a useful approach. Here, umbrella species (Thompson and Angelstam 1999; Uliczka and Angelstam 2000; Table 9.4) and positive examples are important. The relative fit between different disturbance regimes and the resulting forest environments to which species have adapted (ecological dimension) and the different forest management regimes (management dimension) provide a logic for monitoring progress in biodiversity management.

Table 9.3 To understand the total consequences of management for forest biodiversity, the efforts of all actors (private owners, forest companies, public owners, and regional planners) across spatial scales must be aggregated for each forest type (see Table 9.1) by providing quantitative answers to the questions in this table. For biodiversity assessment, the aggregated result could then be compared with a threshold value based on the most demanding species in each main forest ecosystem.

Trees in Stands	Stands in Landscapes	Landscapes in Regions
How much of natural stand-scale tree components are left during different silvicultural treatments (e.g., snags, downed wood, living trees)?	How natural are the remaining forests (e.g., the degree of fit between the ecological and management dimensions)?	How much former forested land remains uncleared for other kinds of land use?
		How representative and connected is the system of conservation areas within and outside reserves?

Table 9.4 Simplified systematics of disturbance regimes and habitat specialist bird species listed in the directive on the conservation of wild birds (European Commission 1979). The specialist species were selected by excluding from the 175 species listed those of habitats other than forest and cultural landscape and those that use forests mainly for nesting (Cramp and Parrins 1977–1994).

Disturbance Regimes	Subtypes	Species
Succession (even-aged stands)	Recently disturbed	Short-eared owl (*Asio flammeus*)
		Red-backed shrike (*Lanius collurio*)
		Hen harrier (*Circus cyaneus*)
	Young	Black grouse (*Tetrao tetrix*)
	Middle-aged	Hazel grouse (*Bonasa bonasia*)
	Harvestable	Capercaillie (*Tetrao urogallus*)
		Black woodpecker (*Dryocopus martius*)
	Ageing	White-backed woodpecker (*Dendrocopus leucotos*)
		Grey-headed woodpecker (*Picus canus*)
		Pygmy owl (*Glaucidium passerinum*)
		Tengmalm's owl (*Aegolius funereus*)
	Old-growth	Three-toed woodpecker (*Picoides tridactylus*)
Cohort dynamics (multiple-aged stands)	Dominated by younger cohort	Black grouse (*Tetrao tetrix*)
		Wood lark (*Lullula arborea*)
		Nightjar (*Caprimulgus europeus*)
		Roller (*Coracias garrulus*)
	Dominated by older cohorts	Capercaillie (*Tetrao urogallus*)
Gap dynamics (uneven-aged stands)	Boreal	Three-toed woodpecker (*Picoides tridactylus*)
	Temperate deciduous	Red-breasted flycatcher (*Ficudela parva*)
		Collared flycatcher (*Ficedula albicollis*)
Old cultural landscape	Woodland pastures and meadows	Roller (*Coracias garrulus*)
		Corncrake (*Crex crex*)
		Syrian woodpecker (*Dendrocopus syriacus*)
		Chough (*Pyrrhocorax pyrrhocorax*)

Conclusions

In addition to producing wood, forest managers also need to provide other resources, including biological diversity, environmental protection, and social benefits (Kohm and Franklin 1997; Liaison Unit in Lisbon 1998). As a consequence, since the 1990s there has been an increasing focus on developing management tools for combining wood production with other goods and services. Maintaining forest biodiversity means ensuring the long-term survival of naturally occurring forest species in viable populations and maintaining important processes. This, in turn, influences the composition and structure of the different forest environments. Forest biodiversity is affected by what happens in the forest itself and in the surrounding matrix.

Where land use has had a long history, healthy ecosystem function depends on both securing the existing natural remnants and restoring natural attributes that have been lost (Angelstam and Andersson 2001). Restoration involves re-creating lost habitats in sufficient amounts, including components at different spatial scales, ranging from green and dead tree retention on harvested areas to a continuous flow of successional stages from recently disturbed areas to old-growth stands (Fries et al. 1997; Kohm and Franklin 1997; Angelstam 1998). It also includes reintroducing and controlling some natural disturbances such as fire (Niklasson and Granström 2000) and herbivory (Angelstam et al. 2000; Vera 2000). Moreover, species and successful practical case studies are vital tools for advancing and applying management systems that allow us to maintain forest biodiversity.

Summary

Understanding the extent to which land management methods can produce habitats that are sufficiently similar to those in which native wild species evolved is a central issue in conservation biology and ecosystem management. Maintaining forest biodiversity means that both the range of natural disturbance regimes and the resulting forest and woodland environments to which species have adapted (the ecological dimension) must be understood and that a sufficiently wide range of different land management regimes must be applied (the management dimension). It also means that the management regime chosen for a given forest environment must harmonize with its ecological past. In this chapter I addressed natural boreal and temperate forest disturbance regimes to which populations have adapted and the range of management methods that have been applied both to forests and to trees in old agricultural landscapes of

Europe. I classed both natural disturbance and management regimes into three main groups: succession after large-scale natural disturbance, cohort dynamics after repeated low-intensity disturbance, and gap dynamics caused by mortality of trees in small patches followed by regeneration. I divided the tree management systems into three groups: even-aged, multi-aged, and uneven-aged. In addition, I considered methods used in ancient cultural landscape management. Using a matrix of the ecological and management dimensions, I reviewed the extent to which different combinations will result in the long-term maintenance of species that have evolved under different disturbance regimes. In general there is good potential for emulating natural disturbance regimes by management in both forestry and ancient cultural landscapes. However for even-aged management, a wider range of successional stages and tree species combinations, both recently disturbed and aging and old-growth forest, must be maintained than for situations in which wood production is the only objective. However, most traditional management practices are poor at maintaining coarse woody debris, decay classes, very large and old trees, and other components of naturally dynamic forests. Consequently, conservation areas with both laissez-faire and active management strategies are usually a necessary part of a complete approach to maintaining forest biodiversity. Finally, I addressed the problem of assessing and communicating the status of forest biodiversity to different stakeholder groups. Two solutions were proposed. First, the aggregated conservation efforts across spatial scales should be measured and then compared with threshold values for habitat loss. Second, specialized species with large area needs that are well known to managers and the public can be used as pedagogic tools to explain why land use management should harmonize closely with the original disturbance regimes.

Acknowledgments

This chapter was developed from a report written for the World Wildlife Fund project "Visions and Evaluation Tools for Forest Biodiversity." Ekaterina Shorohova assisted with the Russian literature. John A. Bissonette, Stefan Bleckert, Graham Forbes, Per Johan Pelle Gemmel, John Innes, Jean-Michel Roberge, Erik Sollander, and Ilse Storch provided useful comments.

LITERATURE CITED
Amilon, J. A. 1923. Skogsskötsel. Albert Bonniers förlag, Stockholm.
Angelstam, P. 1996. Ghost of forest past: natural disturbance regimes as a basis for reconstruction of biologically diverse forests in Europe. Pages 287–337

in R. DeGraaf and R. I. Miller (eds.), Conservation of faunal diversity in forested landscapes. Chapman & Hall, London.

Angelstam, P. 1997. Landscape analysis as a tool for the scientific management of biodiversity. Ecological Bulletins 46:140–170.

Angelstam, P. 1998. Maintaining and restoring biodiversity by simulating natural disturbance regimes in European boreal forest. Journal of Vegetation Science 9:593–602.

Angelstam, P. 1999. Reference areas as a tool for sustaining forest biodiversity in managed landscapes. Naturschutz Report 16:96–121. Landesanstalt für Umweltschutz, Thuringia, Germany.

Angelstam, P., and L. Andersson. 2001. Estimates of the needs for nature reserves in Sweden. Scandinavian Journal of Forestry Supplement 3:38–51.

Angelstam, P., and G. Arnold. 1993. Contrasting roles of remnants in old and newly cleared landscapes: lessons from Scandinavia and Australia for restoration ecologists. Pages 109–125 in D. A. Saunders, R. J. Hobbs, and P. Ehrlich (eds.), Reconstruction of fragmented ecosystems: global and regional perspectives. Surrey Beatty & Sons, Chipping Norton, New South Wales, Australia.

Angelstam, P., and G. Mikusinski. 1994. Woodpecker assemblages in natural and managed boreal and hemiboreal forest: a review. Annales Zoologici Fennici 31:157–172.

Angelstam, P., and B. Pettersson. 1997. Principles of present Swedish forest biodiversity management. Ecological Bulletins 46:191–203.

Angelstam, P., P. Rosenberg, and C. Rülcker. 1993. Aldrig, sällan, ibland, ofta. Skog och forskning 93:34–41.

Angelstam, P., V. Anufriev, L. Balciauskas, A. Blagovidov, S-O. Borgegård, S. Hodge, P. Majewski, E. Shvarts, A. Tishkov, L. Tomialojc, and L. Wesolowski. 1997. Biodiversity and sustainable forestry in European forests: how West and East can learn from each other. Wildlife Society Bulletin 25:38–48.

Angelstam, P., P. E. Wikberg, P. Danilov, W. E. Faber, and K. Nygrén. 2000. Effects of moose density on timber quality and biodiversity restoration in Sweden, Finland and Russian Karelia. Alces 36:133–145.

Angelstam, P., M. Breuss, and G. Mikusinski. 2001. Toward the assessment of forest biodiversity at the scale of forest management units: a European landscape perspective. In A. Franc, O. Laroussinie, and T. Karjalainen (eds.), Criteria and indicators for sustainable forest management at the forest management unit level. European Institute Proceedings 38:59–74. Gummerus Printing, Saarijärvi, Finland.

Arnborg, T. 1964. Det nordsvenska skogstypsschemat. Sveriges Skogsvårdsförbund, Stockholm.

Arnborg, T. 1990. Forest types of northern Sweden. Vegetatio 90:1–13.

Attiwill, P. M. 1994. The disturbance of forest ecosystems: the ecological basis for conservation management. Forest Ecology and Management 63:247–300.

Axelsson, A. L. 2001. Forest landscape change in boreal Sweden 1850–2000: a multi-scale approach. Acta Universitatis Agriculturae Sueciae, Silvestria 183, Umeå, Sweden.

Axelsson, A. L., and L. Östlund. 2001. Retrospective gap analysis in a Swedish boreal forest landscape using historical data. Journal of Forest Ecology and Management 147:109–122.

Bachmann, P., M. Köhl, and R. Päivinen (eds.). 1998. Assessment of biodiversity for improved forest planning. Kluwer Academic Publishers, Dordrecht, the Netherlands.

Balciauskas, L., and P. Angelstam. 1993. Ecological diversity: to manage it or restore it. Acta Ornitologica Lithuanica 7–8:3–15.

Barnes, B. V., D. R. Zak, S. R. Denton, and S. H. Spurr. 1998. Forest ecology. Wiley, New York.

Bengtsson J., S. G. Nilsson, A. Franc, and P. Menozzi. 2000. Biodiversity, disturbances, ecosystem function and management of European forests. Forest Ecology and Management 132:39–50.

Bergeron, Y., and B. Harvey. 1997. Basing silviculture on natural ecosystem dynamics: an approach applied to the southern boreal mixed woods of Québec. Forest Ecology and Management 92:235–242.

Bergeron, Y., A. Leduc, B. Harvey, and S. Gauthier. 2002. Natural fire regime: a guide for sustainable management of the Canadian boreal forest. Silva Fennica 36: 81–95.

Bode, W., and M. von Hohnhurst. 1995. Waldwende: vom Försterwald zum Naturwald. Verlag C. H. Beck, München, Germany.

Børset, O. 1986. Skogskjøtsel II. Skogskjøtselens teknikk. Landbruksvorlaget, Oslo.

Bradshaw, R., P. Gemmel, and L. Björkman. 1994. Development of nature-based silvicultural models in southern Sweden: the scientific background. Forest and Landscape Research 1:95–110.

Bunnell, F. L., and J. F. Johnson. 1998. Policy and practices for biodiversity in managed forests: the living dance. University of British Columbia Press, Vancouver.

Burton P. J., D. D. Kneshaw, and K. D. Coates. 1999. Managing forest harvesting to maintain old-growth in boreal and sub-boreal forests. Forestry Chronicle 75:623–629.

Carlson, A. 2000. The effect of habitat loss on a deciduous forest specialist species: the white-backed woodpecker (*Dendrocopos leucotos*). Forest Ecology and Management 131:215–221.

Carlson, A., and I. Stenberg. 1995. Vitryggig hackspett (*Dendrocopos leucotos*): biotopval och sårbarhetsanalys. Department of Wildlife Ecology, Report 27. Swedish University of Agricultural Sciences, Uppsala.

Caro, T. M., and G. O'Doherty. 1999. On the use of surrogate species in conservation biology. Conservation Biology 13:805–814.

Chirot, D. (ed.) 1989. The origins of backwardness in eastern Europe: economics and politics from the Middle Ages to the early twentieth century. University of California Press, Berkeley.

Coates, K. D., and P. L. Burton. 1997. A gap-based approach for development of silvicultural systems to address ecosystem management objectives. Forest Ecology and Management 99:337–354.

Cramp, S., and Perrins, C. M. 1977–1994. Handbook of the birds of Europe the Middle East and North Africa. Volumes 1–9. Oxford University Press, Oxford, UK.

Davis, L. S., and K. N. Johnson. 1987. Forest management. McGraw-Hill, New York.

Dengler, A. 1944. Waldbau. Springer-Verlag, Berlin.

Dengler, A. 1990. Waldbau auf ökologischer Grundlage. II Baumartenwahl, Bestandsgründung und Bestandspflege, 6th ed. revised by E. Röhrig and H. A. Gussone. Verlag Paul Parey, Hamburg, Germany.

Devall, B. 1993. Clearcut: the tragedy of industrial forestry. Sierra Club Books and Earth Island Press, San Francisco.

Drobyshev, I. V. 2001. Effect of natural disturbances on the abundance of Norway spruce (*Picea abies* (L.) Karst) regeneration in nemoral forests of the southern boreal zone. Forest Ecology and Management 140:151–161.

Dyrenkov, S. A. 1984. Structure and dynamics of taiga spruce forest. Nauka, Leningrad.

Eberhart, K. E., and P. M. Woodard. 1987. Distribution of residual vegetation associated with large fires in Alberta. Canadian Journal of Forest Research 17:1207–1212.

Ekelund, H., and G. Hamilton. 2001. Skogspolitisk historia. Skogsvårdsorganisationens utvärdering av skogspolitikens effecter. Rapport 8a. Skogsstyrelsen, Jönköping. 237 pp.

Ellenberg, H. 1996. Vegetation Mitteleuropas mit den Alpen. 5. Auflage. Verlag Eugen Ulmer, Stuttgart, Germany.

Elliott, C. 1999. Forest certification: analysis from a policy network perspective. Ph.D. thesis 1965, Ecole Polytechnique Fédérale de Lausanne, Switzerland.

Engelmark, O. 1999. Boreal forest disturbances. Pages 161–186 in L. R. Walker (ed.), Ecosystems of disturbed ground. Ecosystems of the World 16. Elsevier, Amsterdam.

Engelmark, O., and H. Hytteborn. 1999. Coniferous forests. Acta Phytogeographica Suecica 84:55–74.

Esseen, P. A., B. Ehnström, L. Ericson, and K. Sjöberg. 1997. Boreal forests. Ecological Bulletins 46:16–47.

European Commission. 1979. Council directive 79/409/EEC of April 2, 1979, on the conservation of wild birds.

Fahrig, L. 2001. How much is enough? Biological Conservation 100:65–74.

Falinski, J. B. 1986. Vegetation dynamics in temperate lowland primeval forests. Dr. W. Junk Publishers, Dordrecht, the Netherlands.

Fedorchuk, V. N., M. L. Kuznetsova, A. A. Andreyeva, and D. V. Moiseev. 1998. Forest reserve "Vepssky Les." Forestry research. Report, Saint Petersburg Forestry Research Institute, Saint Petersburg.

Franklin, J. F. 1989. Toward a new forestry. American Forests (Nov–Dec):37–44.

Fries, C., O. Johansson, B. Pettersson, and P. Simonsson. 1997. Silvicultural models to maintain and restore natural stand structures in Swedish boreal forests. Forest Ecology and Management 94:89–103.

Furyaev, V. V. 1996. Pyrological regimes and dynamic of the southern taiga forests in Siberia. Pages 168–185 in J. Goldammer and V. V. Furyaev (eds.), Fire in ecosystems of boreal Eurasia. Kluwer Academic Publishers, Dordrecht, the Netherlands.

Furyaev, V. V., and D. M. Kireev. 1979. A landscape approach in the study of post-fire forest dynamics. Nauka, Novosibirsk, Russia.

Gardiner, B. A., and C. P. Quine. 2000. Management of forests to reduce the risk of abiotic damage: a review with particular reference to the effects of strong winds. Forest Ecology and Management 135:261–277.

Giorgievskij, A. B. 1992. Gap-phase in pristine spruce forests of southern taiga. Botanicheskij Journal 72:52–62.

Granström, A. 1993. Spatial and temporal variation in lightning ignitions in Sweden. Journal of Vegetation Science 4:737–744.

Hagner, S. 1995. Silviculture in boreal forest. Unasylva 46:18–25.

Hannah, L., J. L. Carr, and A. Lankerani. 1995. Human disturbance and natural habitat: a biome level analysis of a global data set. Biodiversity and Conservation 4:128–155.

Higman, S., S. Bass, N. Judd, J. Mayers, and R. Nussbaum. 1999. The sustainable forestry handbook. Earthscan Publications, London.

Hunter, M. L. 1990. Wildlife, forests and forestry: principles of managing forests for biological diversity. Prentice Hall, Englewood Cliffs, NJ.

Hunter, M. L. (ed.). 1999. Maintaining biodiversity in forest ecosystems. Cambridge University Press, Cambridge, UK.

Hunter, M. L., G. L. Jacobson, and T. Webb. 1988. Paleoecology and coarse-filter approach to maintaining biological diversity. Conservation Biology 2:375–385.

Ispikoudis, I., G. Lyrintzis, and S. Kyriakakis. 1993. Impact of human activities on Mediterranean landscapes in western Crete. Landscape and Urban Planning 24:259–271.

Jahn, G. 1991. Temperate deciduous forests of Europe. Pages 377–402 in E. Röhrig and B. Ulrich (eds.), Temperate deciduous forests. Elsevier, Amsterdam.

Jansson, G., and P. Angelstam. 1999. Thresholds of landscape composition for the presence of the long-tailed tit in a boreal landscape. Landscape Ecology 14:283–290.

Johnson, E. A. 1992. Fire and vegetation dynamics: studies from the North American boreal forest. Cambridge University Press, Cambridge, UK.

Jordbruksdepartementet. 1974. Kalhyggen. Ds Jo 1974:2. Jordbruksdepartementet, Stockholm.

Kellomäki, S. 2000. Forests of the boreal region: gaps in knowledge and research needs. Forest Ecology and Management 132:63–71.

Kenk, G., and S. Guehne. 2001. Management of transformation in central Europe. Forest Ecology and Management 151:107–119.

Kennedy, J. J., J. W. Thomas, and P. Glueck. 2001. Evolving forestry and rural development beliefs at midpoint and close to the 20th century. Forest Policy and Economics 3:81–95.

Kimmins, J. P. 1997. Forest ecology: a foundation for sustainable management. Prentice Hall, Englewood Cliffs, NJ.

Kirby, K. J., and C. Watkins. 1998. The ecological history of European forests. CAB International, Wallingford, UK.

Kneshaw D. D., A. Leduc, P. Drapalon, S. Gauthier, D. Pare, R. Carignon, R. Doucet, L. Bouthillier, and C. Messier. 2000. Development of integrated ecological standards of sustainable forest management at an operational scale. Forestry Chronicle 76:481–493.

Kohm, K. A., and J. F. Franklin. 1997. Creating a forestry for the 21st century: the science of ecosystem management. Island Press, Washington, DC.

Kouki, J., and A. Väänänen. 2000. Impoverishment of resident old-growth forest bird assemblages along an isolation gradient of protected areas in eastern Finland. Ornis Fennica 77:145–154.

Kuuluvainen, T. 1994. Gap disturbance, ground microtopography, and the regeneration dynamics of boreal coniferous forests in Finland: a review. Annales Zoologici Fennici 31:35–51.

Lähde E., O. Laiho, and Y. Norokorpi. 1999. Diversity oriented silviculture in the boreal zone of Europe. Forest Ecology and Management 118:223–243.

Lambeck, R. J. 1997. Focal species: a multi-species umbrella for nature conservation. Conservation Biology 11:849–856.

Larsson, T.-B., P. Angelstam, G. Balent, A. Barbati, R.-J. Bijlsma, A. Boncina, R. Bradshaw, W. Bücking, O. Ciancio, P. Corona, J. Diaci, S. Dias, H. Ellenberg, F. Manuel Fernandes, F. Fernandez-Gonzalez, R. Ferris, G. Frank, P. Friis Møller, P. S. Giller, L. Gustafsson, K. Halbritter, S. Hall, L. Hansson, J. Innes, H. Jactel, M. Keannel Dobbertin, M. Klein, M. Marchetti, F. Mohren, P. Niemelä, J. O'Halloran, E. Rametsteiner, F. Rego, C. Scheidegger, R. Scotti, K. Sjöberg, I. Spanos, K. Spanos, T. Standovar, L. Svensson, B. Å. Tømmerås, D. Trakolis, J. Uuttera, D. Van Den Meerschaut, K. Vanderkerkhove, P. M. Walsh, and A. D. Watt. 2001. Biodiversity evaluation tools for European forest. Ecological Bulletins 50, Wallin & Dalholm, Lund, Sweden.

Leibundgut, H. 1982. Europäische Urwälder der Bergstufe. Verlag Paul Haupt, Bern, Switzerland.

Leibundgut, H. 1993. Europäische Urwälder: Wegweiser zur naturnahen Waldwirtschaft. Verlag Paul Haupt, Bern, Switzerland.

Leopold, A. 1949. A Sand County almanac. Oxford University Press, New York.

Liaison Unit in Lisbon. 1998. Third ministerial conference on the protection of forests in Europe. General declarations and resolutions adopted. Ministry of Agriculture, Lisbon.

Little, C. E. 1990. Greenways for America. John Hopkins University Press, Baltimore, MD.

Lucas, O. W. 1991. The design of forest landscapes. Oxford University Press, New York.

Malcolm, D. C., W. L. Mason, and G. C. Clarke. 2001. The transformation of conifer forests in Britain: regeneration, gap size and silvicultural systems. Forest Ecology and Management 151:7–23.

Mantel, K. 1990. Wald und Forst in der Geschichte. Verlag M. & H. Schaper, Alfeld and Hannover, Germany.

Margules, C. R., and R. L. Pressey. 2000. Systematic conservation planning. Nature 405:243–253.

Martikainen, P., L. Kaila, and Y. Haila. 1998. Threatened beetles in white-backed woodpecker habitats. Conservation Biology 12:293–301.

Matthews, J. D. 1989. Silvicultural systems. Oxford University Press, Oxford, UK.

Mayer, H. 1984. Die Wälder Europas. Gustav Fischer Verlag, Stuttgart, Germany.

Mayer, H. 1992. Waldbau auf soziologisch-ökologischer Grundlage. Gustav Fischer Verlag, Stuttgart, Germany.

Mikusinski, G., and P. Angelstam. 1998. Economic geography, forest distribution, and woodpecker diversity in central Europe. Conservation Biology 12:200–208.

Morosov, G. F. 1930. Forest doctrine, 5th ed. Nauka, Moscow.

Niemelä, J. 1999. Management in relation to disturbance in the boreal forest. Forest Ecology and Management 115:127–134.

Niklasson, M., and A. Granström. 2000. Numbers and sizes of fires: long-term spatially explicit fire history in a Swedish boreal landscape. Ecology 81:1484–1499.

Nilsson, C., and F. Götmark. 1992. Protected areas in Sweden: is natural variety adequately represented? Conservation Biology 6:232–242.

Nilsson, S., O. Sallnäs, and P. Duinker. 1992a. Future forest resources of western and eastern Europe. The Parthenon Publishing Group, Carnforth, UK.

Nilsson, S., O. Sallnäs, M. Hugosson, and A. Shvidenko. 1992b. The forest resources of the former European USSR. Parthenon Publishing Group, Carnforth, UK.

Nilsson, S., M. Niklasson, J. Hedin, G. Aronsson, J. M. Gutowski, P. Linder, H. Ljungberg, G. Mikusinski, and T. Ranius. 2001. Densities of large living and dead trees in old-growth temperate and boreal forests. Forest Ecology and Management 5544:1–16.

Noss, R. F. 1990. Indicators for monitoring biodiversity: a hierarchical approach. Conservation Biology 4:355–364.

Noss, R. F. 1993. Sustainable forestry or sustainable forests. Pages 17–43 in G. H. Aplet, N. Johnson, J. T. Olson, and V. A. Sample (eds.), Defining sustainable forestry. Island Press, Washington, DC.

Noss, R. F. 1995. Maintaining ecological integrity in representative reserve networks. World Wide Fund for Nature, Toronto, ON.

Nyland, R. D. 1996. Silviculture: concepts and applications. McGraw-Hill, Boston.

Ohlson, M., and E. Tryterud. 1999. Long-term spruce forest continuity: a challenge for sustainable Scandinavian forestry. Forest Ecology and Management 124:27–34.

Oliver, C. D., and B. C. Larson. 1996. Forest stand dynamics. McGraw-Hill, New York.

Östlund, L., O. Zackrisson, and A. L. Axelsson. 1997. The history and transformation of a Scandinavian boreal forest landscape since the 19th century. Canadian Journal of Forest Research 27:1198–1206.

Palang, H. 1998. Landscape changes in Estonia: the past and the future. Dissertationes geographicae universitatis Tartuensis 6. Tartu University, Tartu, Estonia.

Peterken, G. 1996. Natural woodland: ecology and conservation in northern temperate regions. Cambridge University Press, Cambridge, UK.

Pickett, S. T. A., and P. S. White. 1985. The ecology of natural disturbance and patch dynamics. Academic Press, New York.

Pressey, R. L., S. Ferrier, T. C. Hager, C. A. Woods, S. L. Tully, and K. M. Weinman. 1996. How well protected are the forests of north-eastern New South Wales? Analyses of forest environments in relation to formal protection measurements, land tenure, and vulnerability to clearing. Forest Ecology and Management 85:311–333.

Pyne, S. J. 1984. Introduction to wildland fire. Wiley, New York.

Quine, C. P., J. W. Humphrey, and R. Ferris. 1999. Should the wind disturbance patterns observed in natural forests be mimicked in planted forests in the British uplands? Forestry 72:337–358.

Rackham, O. 1988. Trees and woodland in a crowded landscape: the cultural landscape of the British Isles. Pages 53–77 in H. H. Birks, H. J. B. Birks, P. E. Kaland, and D. Moe (eds.), The cultural landscape: past, present and future. Cambridge University Press, Cambridge, UK.

Rackham, O. 1990. Trees and woodland in the British landscape. J. M. Dent, London.

Raivio, S., E. Normark, B. Pettersson, and P. Salpakivi-Salomaa. 2001. Science and the management of boreal forest biodiversity: forest industries' view. Scandinavian Forest Research Supplement 3:99–104.

Remmert, H. (ed.). 1991. The mosaic cycle concept of ecosystems. Ecological Studies V. 85. Springer-Verlag, Heidelberg, Germany.

Salwasser, H. 1994. Ecosystem management: can it sustain diversity and productivity? Journal of Forestry 92:6–10.

Sannikov, S. N., and J. G. Goldammer. 1996. Fire ecology of pine forests of northern Eurasia. Pages 151–167 in J. Goldammer and V. V. Furyaev (eds.), Fire in ecosystems of boreal Eurasia. Kluwer Academic Publishers, Dordrecht, the Netherlands.

Scherzinger, W. 1996. Naturschutz im Wald: Qualitätsziele einer dynamischen Waldentwicklung. Verlag Eugen Ulmer, Stuttgart, Germany.

Schimmel, J. 1993. Fire behavior, fuel succession and vegetation response to fire in Swedish boreal forest. Dissertations in forest vegetation ecology 5. Swedish University of Agricultural Sciences, Umeå.

Scott, J. M., P. J. Heglund, M. Morrison, M. Raphael, J. Haufler, and B. Wall (eds.). 2001. Predicting species occurrences: issues of scale and accuracy. Island Press, Covelo, CA.

Seymour, R. S., and M. L. Hunter. 1999. Principles of ecological forestry. Pages 22–64 in M. L. Hunter (ed.), Maintaining biodiversity in forest ecosystems. Cambridge University Press, Cambridge, UK.

Simberloff, D. 1998. Flagships, umbrellas, and keystones: is single-species management passé in the landscape era? Biological Conservation 83:247–257.

Smith, D. M., B. C. Larson, M. J. Kelty, and P. M. S. Ashton. 1997. The practice of silviculture: applied forest ecology. Wiley, New York.

Smith, G., and H. Gillet. 2000. European forests and protected areas: gap analysis. World Conservation Monitoring Centre, Cambridge, UK.

Thomas, J. W. 1979. Wildlife habitats in managed forests: the Blue Mountains of Oregon and Washington. Handbook 553, U.S. Department of Agriculture, Washington, DC.

Thompson, I. D., and P. Angelstam. 1999. Special species. Pages 434–459 in M. L. Hunter (ed.), Maintaining biodiversity in forest ecosystems. Cambridge University Press, Cambridge, UK.

Tucker, G. M., and M. I. Evans. 1997. Habitats for birds in Europe. BirdLife International, Cambridge, UK.

Uliczka, H., and P. Angelstam. 1999. Occurrence of epiphytic lichens in relation to tree species and age in managed boreal forest. Ecography 22:396–405.

Uliczka, H., and P. Angelstam. 2000. Assessing conservation values of forest stands based on specialised lichens and birds. Biological Conservation 95:343–351.

Vera, F. W. M. 2000. Grazing ecology and forest history. CABI Publishing, Wallingford, UK.

Wahlgren, A. 1914. Skogsskötsel. P. A. Norstedt & Söners Förlag, Stockholm.

Wallmo, U. 1897. Rationell skogsafverkning. Länstidningens tryckeri, Örebro, Sweden.

Weggler, M., and M. Widmer. 2000. Vergleich der Brutvogelbestände im Kanton Zürich 1986–1988 und 1999. I. Was has der ökologische Ausgleich in der Kulturlandschaft bewirkt? Der Ornithologische Beobachter 97:123–146.

Weitnauer, E., and B. Bruderer. 1987. Veränderungen der Brutvogel-Fauna der Gemeinde Oltingen in den Jahren 1935–85. Der Ornithologische Beobachter 84:1–9.

White, P. S., and J. Harrod. 1997. Disturbance and diversity in a landscape context. Pages 128–159 in J. A. Bissonette (ed.), Wildlife and landscape ecology: effects of pattern and scale. Springer-Verlag, New York.

Wieslander, G. 1936. The shortage of forest in Sweden during the 17th and 18th centuries. Sveriges Skogsvårdsförbunds Tidskrift 34:593–633.

Wikars, L. O. 1992. Forest fires and insects. Entomolgisk Tidskrift 13:1–12.

Yaroshenko, A. Yu, P. V. Potapov, and S. A. Turubanova. 2001. The intact forest landscapes of northern European Russia. Greenpeace Russia and the Global Forest Watch, Moscow.

CHAPTER TEN

Landscape Ecology, Wildlife Management, and Conservation in Northern Australia

Linking Policy, Practice, and Capability in Regional Planning

PETER J. WHITEHEAD, JOHN C. Z. WOINARSKI, DONALD
FRANKLIN, AND OWEN PRICE

Human impacts on wildlife caused by resource monopolization reach into all parts of the globe (Vitousek et al. 1997). But in tropical northern Australia those effects have seemed less threatening. Conservationists have often celebrated opportunities for well-informed and well-motivated resource managers to map a different path, leading to a future free of the worst excesses and mistakes of other times and places (e.g., Whitehead et al. 1993). This argument has been attractive because in much of the extensive eucalypt forests and woodlands of the north Australian tropical savannas (1.9 million km^2) the primary land use has been extensive pastoralism. Until recently, there has been little land clearing (Graetz et al. 1995), intensive agriculture occupies a small proportion of the land surface, and human populations are sparse (around 0.1 people per km^2). Most parts of the region appear structurally and, by some measures, ecologically intact. For example, the north maintains species that have disappeared elsewhere in Australia (Woinarski and Braithwaite 1990).

Optimism for sensible land use has been maintained despite recent acceleration in rates of infrastructure development, agriculture intensification, and associated increases in human populations because these changes are occurring in a social and political milieu that is ostensibly sensitive to demands for high standards of environmental management. Public interest in conservation is reinforced by dependence of the north Australian economy on tourism revenues.

Although the north has supported an active ecological research community for some decades, the knowledge base and a capacity to apply it have been improved by the recent (1989) creation of Northern Territory University in Darwin. This development has stimulated support from the Australian government to establish new or expanded research centers with a focus on tropical Australia and some emphasis on management at landscape scales. Government agencies with responsibilities for land allocation and management are active partners in these centers. Moreover, northern Australia has the opportunity to learn from the land management practices of Aboriginal people, which have developed over tens of thousands of years (Yibarbuk et al. 2001).

All seems well primed to identify new approaches to wildlife conservation at large spatial scales and, in particular, to set achievable goals before major developments take place. Northern Australians have an extraordinary opportunity to actively connect ecological theory with systems of land and resource management policy and practice; however, wildlife conservation interests are not alone in seeing northern Australia as a land of special opportunity.

The various political jurisdictions in northern Australia have long subscribed to the myth of the north as a cornucopia (Lacey 1979; Woinarski and Dawson 2002). Though eager to consider other forms of more intensive agriculture to supplant or supplement extensive pastoralism, they have tenaciously refused to accept that lands marginal for pastoralism could or should be used for nonagricultural purposes (Holmes 1990, 1991). Woinarski and Dawson (2002) describe some of the consequences of a determination to clumsily challenge biophysical constraints on conventional agricultural production. The frequent abject failure of agricultural schemes and the loss of public and private monies are the most obvious. However, huge areas of pastoral leasehold and Aboriginal freehold land continue to be seen as a blank canvas on which vivid development scenarios should be splashed, with little apparent concern for the integrity of the larger picture.

Only over the last decade or so has there been a sufficiently public awareness of land management issues to question naively optimistic views of production potential and to encourage a more considered approach to regional development and conservation. However, there remain a number of barriers to improved performance. In this chapter, we explore those barriers and propose ways to surmount them. Specifically, we review the performance of the northern Australian states and Northern Territory in planning for wildlife conservation, explore principles and practice in landscape ecology and connected ecological theory that may be applied to design modified landscapes to optimize biodiversity conservation in north Australia, illustrate the challenges and the potential for applying the framework to wildlife using examples including granivorous birds and nectivorous and frugivorous birds and mammals, and propose a science-based planning framework consistent with the letter and intent of relevant federal legislation. We also consider the prospects for implementing such a framework under prevailing political and administrative strictures and the role of wildlife managers in promoting its application.

The Wildlife Management Discipline in Australia

A reasonable characterization of wildlife management in Australia would identify two distinct emphases. The first is a preoccupation with pest control, left as a legacy of the assiduous efforts of early colonists and their successors to render Australia a warmer imitation of the familiar landscapes of Britain (Dunlap 1993). In this they succeeded remarkably, establishing huge populations of rabbits and foxes while simultaneously persecuting native herbivores and predators as threats to agricultural production. At the other extreme, the conservation of rare and endangered native species has been less than spectacular. Problems have been tackled species by species, but few efforts have improved the status of endangered species under formal recovery plans. Some species (e.g., the mala [*Lagorchestes hirsutus*]) have declined to extinction on the Australian mainland, without serious steps being taken to improve habitat management. The major response to the appalling record of extinction of small mammals in the arid zone has been to establish captive breeding populations (Serena 1995) rather than confront and deal with habitat-related issues that led to the losses (Morton 1990).

Nonindigenous Australians have rarely considered native animals as renewable resources that could legitimately be exploited to meet a range of social goals, including recreational hunting and commercial harvest.

Australia has no equivalent of the strong game management ethos that obliged U.S. and European biologists to develop understanding of the population dynamics and habitat needs of many fauna. The contemporary situation is nicely summarized by the decision of a number of tertiary institutions in southern Australia when proposing new university curricula in wildlife management. They titled their initiative "Wildlife Management: Beyond Preservation and Pest Control."

Perhaps as a result, most Australians remain strongly attached to the notions that wildlife is best managed by excluding humans and that maintaining healthy populations depends on the balance of nature. Regulatory processes limit access to wildlife in sites managed to preserve an arbitrary, mostly ill-defined but apparently static natural condition. Conservation institutions have therefore been poorly equipped to integrate management of multiple values. Failures have been spectacular and include the loss of the Western Australian wheat belt biota (Saunders 1989, 1990), the destruction of wetland habitats in eastern Australia, and severe degradation of the Murray-Darling River systems (Kingsford 2000). Although these experiences are by no means unique, Australia has been perhaps unusually slow among developed nations to respond to the obvious and pressing need to improve performance. What are the implications of continuing the prevailing practice for northern Australia?

Wildlife Management Issues in Northern Australia

Although the most spectacular wildlife management failures have occurred in southern and central Australia, a need for action in tropical Australia is clear. Woinarski et al. (2001a) summarized the conservation status of wildlife in the Australian rangelands, a huge area incorporating most of the north Australian mainland. The climate is influenced by the northwest monsoon, characterized by predominantly summer rainfalls and an extended dry season drought when very little or no rain falls. There is a steep rainfall gradient from the coast inland. For example, the average annual rainfall near Darwin is about 1,600 mm but declines to less than 600 mm at the southern inland margin of the area shown in Fig. 10.1. Space does not permit a full explanation as it relates to the tropics. We provide here a very brief synopsis.

Since European settlement, declines among mammals have been most significant in the drier interior, where extinction rates have been catastrophic (Woinarski and Braithwaite 1990). Although losses have been fewer in northerly, wetter coastal areas, there is a controversial suggestion that

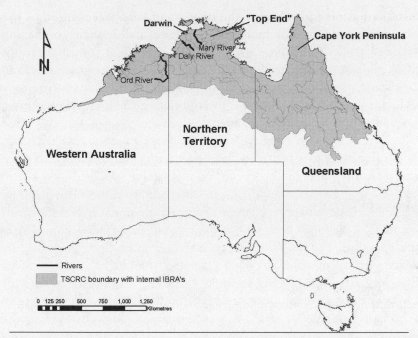

Figure 10.1 The shaded area is that adopted by the Tropical Savannas Cooperative Research Centre (TSCRC) to describe its area of interest and is the area considered in this chapter. The internal divisions are recognized biogeographic regions.

adverse change affecting a similar range of species, especially larger rodents, smaller macropods, larger dasyurids, and bandicoots is now extending into many parts of northern Australia, including major conservation reserves. However, localized observations of decline are difficult to interpret because populations of some species fluctuate markedly and the causes of change are imperfectly understood (Braithwaite and Griffiths 1996; Braithwaite and Muller 1997; Woinarski et al. 2001b).

Birds have fared better than mammals, but evidence of adverse change is accumulating. For example, Franklin (1999) found that many granivorous birds had declined in range and abundance over the last few decades. More localized studies covering a wider range of taxa suggest that habitat change associated with grazing has decimated many other functional groups (J. Woinarski and C. Caterall, unpublished data). Declines often appear to have preceded major structural change associated with land clearing. Some argue that the better condition of the avifauna reflects a time lag between changes associated with European settlement and loss of native species and that the status of birds will ultimately be similar to the fate of mammals (Recher 1999).

There is little evidence of persistent change in the status of north Australian herpetofauna (Recher and Lim 1990), perhaps because the historical record is so sparse. Contemporary local variation in the status of a number of species can be attributed to grazing and fire (Braithwaite 1987; Trainor and Woinarski 1994; Griffiths and Christian 1996; Fisher 1999; Woinarski et al. 1999; Woinarski and Ash 2002). The areas over which these influences may have displaced poorly known taxa entirely will perhaps never be reliably determined.

Sources of Change

Influences on wildlife and their habitats likely to be implicated in these adverse changes include the following.

Grazing by Domestic Herbivores

Pastoralism is the dominant land use in northern Australia (Fig. 10.2). Nonetheless, the impacts of grazing on wildlife are little studied. Evidence of grazing effects has been built mostly on observations of the rapid disappearance of once-common mammals and birds of the arid zone after the arrival of Europeans and cattle (Burbidge et al. 1988; Burbidge and McKenzie 1989) and extreme habitat change in heavily grazed areas (Barnard 1925). Conjecture about the importance of less obvious grazing-related change in availability of resources, such as densities of seeds of perennial grasses, has been a persistent theme (Barnard 1925, 1934; Woinarski 1993; Franklin 1999). Morton (1990) formalized these ideas in a model of decline of arid zone mammals, positing strong prepastoral dependence of fauna on resource-rich landscape elements that were resilient to prolonged drought. After pastoral settlement, concentration of exotic herbivores and predators in these sites, especially during drought, placed the native fauna at great risk through competition for food, loss of shelter, and increased vulnerability to predation. Emphasis on readily identifiable, semipermanent refugia is less likely to be useful for understanding grazing-related change in the northern tropics because resource availability cannot be readily ascribed to persistent or clearly delineated patches (Woinarski 1999). In the semihumid tropics, recent studies of faunal assemblages along gradients of cattle grazing intensity have identified "increaser" and "decreaser" species. Their status appears more readily related to continuous variation in condition of homogeneous vegetation types rather than discrete patches of especially favorable habitat (Fisher 1999).

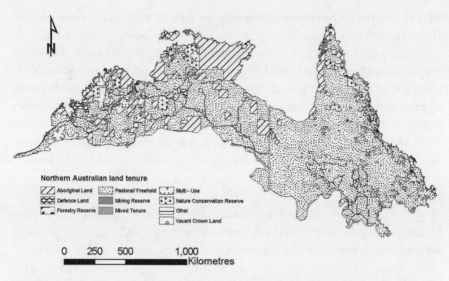

Figure 10.2 Generalized land tenures in northern Australia. Land use is dominated by extensive pastoralism, mostly on leasehold land. Some Aboriginal land is also used for pastoralism and often grazed by large populations of feral ungulates.

Feral Herbivores

Feral exotic herbivores are extraordinarily abundant in northern Australia (Bayliss and Yeomans 1989; Freeland 1990), sometimes exceeding densities of managed domestic herds and causing damage on all tenures (Russell-Smith and Bowman 1992). If grazing impacts are to be ameliorated, large feral populations of Asian water buffalo (*Bubalus bubalis*), cattle (*Bos taurus* and *Bos indicus*), horses (*Equus caballus*), donkeys (*Equus asinus*), and pigs (*Sus scrofa*) must be managed. Unfortunately, low human densities in many areas result in a reduced capacity to assert effective control.

Inappropriate Fire Regimes

Frequent and widespread fires are conspicuous features of north Australian landscapes (Fig. 10.3). Fire return times for individual sites are often annual to biennial. Management is problematic, given the high flammability of the environment for much of the year (Williams et al. 1999), frequent uncoordinated anthropogenic ignitions, and constraints of access, equipment, and human resources for controlling wildfire (often lightning-ignited) at remote, inaccessible sites. The impacts of prevailing fire regimes are imperfectly known, but some ecosystem types are particularly threatened. Sandstone heaths, supporting many endemic plants with life history strategies that make them highly sensitive to fire frequency (obligate seeders *sensu* Gill 1981) and their populations of endemic fauna, are particularly vulnerable (Russell-Smith et al. 1998, 2002). Unfavorably frequent or intense fire patterns are now common over large areas because regimes that were previously imposed by Aboriginal people have collapsed (Price and Bowman 1994; Bowman et al. 2001). In pastoral and other heavily grazed landscapes, too little fire may also be a problem, contributing to woody species invasions of grasslands (Dyer et al. 1997).

Exotic Predators

Feral cats are widespread. It has been suggested that they arrived on the Australian mainland well before European settlement, perhaps through shipwrecks or accompanying Macassan traders from Indonesia. Cats consume native fauna. However, no studies of cat densities or predation rates relative to natural mortalities have been done to permit robust conclusions about

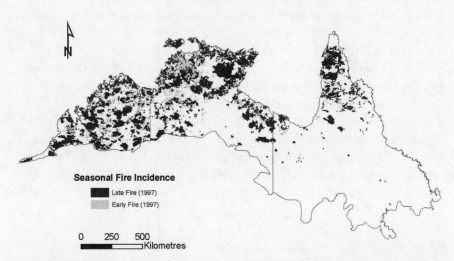

Seasonal Fire Incidence

■ Late Fire (1997)

Early Fire (1997)

0   250   500
Kilometres

Figure 10.3   Patterns of early and late dry season fires in northern Australia in 1997 derived from NOAA satellite imagery. The dry season extends from April to November in most years, with little rainfall during this period, contrasting with wet season rainfall exceeding 1,600 mm along parts of the coast. Annual cycles of reliably wet growing seasons with consistent high temperatures with extended dry seasons make for a highly fire-prone environment. Many individual fires are very large, often affecting areas exceeding 100,000 ha. Late dry season fires (after July) are usually more intense, so large, late dry season fires pose greater threats to wildlife and their habitats.

the individual or additive impact of cats on wildlife populations. Pigs prey on many small vertebrates. Foxes, which have a substantial impact on the population status of many temperate and arid zone mammals in Australia (Smith and Quin 1996; Kinnear et al. 1998), are largely confined to non-tropical zones. There are no significant exotic avian or reptilian predators on native vertebrates in northern Australia.

Land Clearing

In the Northern Territory and northern Western Australia, land clearing has been minor (Fig. 10.4). In stark contrast, savannas have been severely damaged along their southeastern edge in Queensland. In the 1960s and 1970s, huge areas of Brigalow (forest and woodland dominated by *Acacia harpophylla* on clay soils) were cleared, and in the 1990s eucalypt woodlands in central Queensland were cut. Contemporary woody vegetation clearing rates are now among the world's highest (Brock 2001). The Brigalow Belts of Queensland provide extreme examples of effectively uncontrolled clearing, where all but a small proportion of 6 million ha has been ravaged (Fensham et al. 1998). There is a risk that similar scenes will be repeated across much of northern Australia. In the past, most clearing was done to reduce

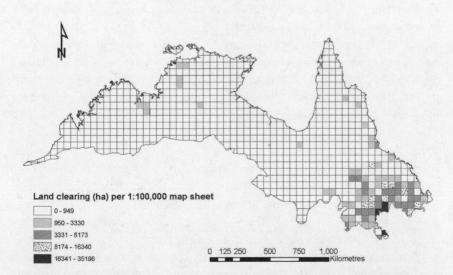

Land clearing (ha) per 1:100,000 map sheet

▫ 0 - 949
▨ 950 - 3330
▨ 3331 - 8173
▨ 8174 - 16340
■ 16341 - 35196

0 125 250   500   750   1,000
Kilometres

Figure 10.4   Land clearing in northern Australia. The limited total clearing effort in northern Australia is readily apparent. Most of the area comprises woodlands, open woodlands, or grasslands. However, in some regions (the southeastern margin of the area of interest), denser woody vegetation has been removed to improve pasture.

competition of woody vegetation with grasses to improve grazing production; however, large schemes have begun for mixed farming and for cropping and plantation forestry (Woinarski 1999; Woinarski et al. 2000a).

Weeds

Exotic plants, including environmental and agricultural weeds, make up a small proportion of the flora across much of the north Australian landscape (Taylor and Dunlop 1985; Yibarbuk et al. 2001). However, over the last few decades pasture agronomists have introduced and established many new weeds (Lonsdale 1994). Their trade is viewed increasingly as a bizarre anachronism, but change in practice may come too late to avoid severe damage to both conservation and production values (Whitehead and Dawson 2000). Many exotic plants have yet to realize their full potential and are spreading rapidly. Some species influence other processes (e.g., wildfire) to put wildlife habitat at additional jeopardy. For example, the introduced Gamba grass (*Andropogon gayanus*) generates almost twice the fuel loads of the densest native grass, producing much more intense and damaging fires.

Water Use for Production

Few north Australian rivers have been regulated by significant impoundments or other watercourse modification. Water for irrigation is mostly sourced from minor impoundments or groundwater. Understanding of groundwater dynamics is rudimentary, yet contemporary plans for water use may involve extracting a large proportion of estimated total annual recharge. Such developments may place at risk flows to springs and their dependent habitats (Jolly and Yin Foo 1988) and flows to watercourses that depend for their dry season discharges on subterranean water (e.g., the Daly River).

Wildlife Harvest

Native wildlife provides a large proportion of dietary protein and energy for many of north Australia's indigenous peoples (Altman 1987). Recreational hunting is not a major pastime among the region's nonindigenous population (Whitehead et al. 1988). There is no unequivocal evidence that either recreational or subsistence hunting has caused substantial decline in any wildlife species in northern Australia. However, some Aboriginal people are expressing concern at the breakdown of traditional constraints on overhunting and have sought assistance to examine trends.

The north Australian situation can be summarized as a background of often diffuse but cumulatively substantial degradation of habitats, probably related to grazing and fire use, that has compromised the status of many species of wildlife; a rapidly increasing intensity of land use, including land clearing, especially of more fertile, often moister sites that play important roles in maintaining regional biota; and an array of effectively unmanaged processes, chiefly involving exotic organisms and wildfire. In contrast to many other regions, human population pressures are not a major factor; conservation problems are sometimes most severe in areas that are least inhabited (Bowman et al. 2001).

Special Challenges in Wildlife Conservation and Management

A number of ecologists, planners, and managers in tropical Australia are developing tools for improved conservation planning to mitigate these existing problems and provide greater capacity to avoid mistakes. We illustrate that work and the principles on which it is based with the following examples.

Granivorous Birds

The specialist granivorous bird assemblage of northern Australia is made up of 49 endemic or widespread species from six families (Franklin 1999). The assemblage is dominated by obligate terrestrial foragers but also includes several obligate arboreal foragers and a suite of facultative arboreal foragers (Franklin et al. 2000).

Changes in the abundance of granivorous birds during the era of pastoral settlement have been geographically widespread, with at least 15 species affected (Franklin 1999). A large number of decliners are complemented by a small number of widespread increasers, indicating an assemblage undergoing simplification and adjustment to a new set of environmental circumstances. Decliners include both widespread and restricted species and are taxonomically and ecologically diverse. The sole common denominator appears to be an obligate reliance on seed collected on the ground or from standing herbage. Current management regimes are clearly inconsistent with the maintenance of characteristic grassland fauna over vast areas of apparently intact savanna landscapes.

Recent studies of these changes have emphasized the spatial and seasonal availability of grass seed and the impacts of fire and grazing on these resources (Crowley and Garnett 1999; Fraser 2000; Dostine et al. 2001). Dry season soil seed banks are depleted by germination after wet season rains. Grasses that produce seed during the wet season do not have a persistent seed bank. Birds respond to the resultant decline in resources by either switching diet (to other seed or food types) or by searching for patches in the landscape that provide alternative seed resources. The mobile or strictly granivorous species appear to be less able to cope with contemporary conditions, presumably because the suite of resources that previously moderated periods of low seed availability have been suppressed or displaced. The pattern of seed availability within savanna landscapes appears likely to occur at scales as small as a few meters but to be expressed in impacts on suites of granivorous birds at much larger scales, ranging from a few hectares to the regional scale and larger. Consequently, dealing with this acute conservation problem poses extraordinary challenges. At a technical level, we currently lack the means to readily describe such structurally subtle patterning and relate it to the status of individual species or assemblages over the huge areas affected. Favorable configurations of grassland patterning are unknown. Furthermore, we have management regime options that might restore or maintain favorable patterns. Finally, our capacity to assert favorable management practice over much of the landscape remains an open question, especially with regard to fire. A great deal of work remains to be done to link understanding of grassland dynamics at scales ranging from individual patches to the regional and beyond to a capability to influence those dynamics for wildlife conservation.

Frugivorous Birds and Mammals

Monsoon rainforest ecosystems in northern Australia are naturally highly fragmented within an extensive matrix of eucalypt forests and woodlands. Fruit resources are mostly confined to rainforests, and they exhibit strong seasonal and spatial variation in abundance. The typically small (less than 5 ha) individual patches are unlikely to fully support resident frugivore populations, and production is so variable that frugivores are often forced to move among patches or to eat nonfruit resources.

Pied imperial pigeons (*Ducula bicolor*) and figbirds (*Sphecotheres viridis*) move between patches at about three-day intervals, with flight distance averaging about 4 km (Price 1998). Black flying foxes (*Pteropus alecto*) move up to 25 km every night from their roost sites and also move as far as 60 km from month to month as patterns of resource distribution vary (Palmer and Woinarski 1999). The presence of several bird species in 149 surveyed patches also showed a strong relationship with the area of rainforests in the surrounding savanna matrix within a 50-km radius (Price et al. 1999). These observations suggested that loss or degradation of a small proportion of existing patches may affect frugivore populations over large areas. This notion was supported by a spatially realistic simulation model that described the movements of pied imperial pigeons between 69 patches (Price 1998). Fruit production in each patch varied according to the pattern of seasonal and interpatch variation measured in a subset of the patches by Bach (1998). Pigeons consumed available fruit and moved when resources became low. Movement was eight times more costly than remaining stationary, when cost was expressed as increased fruit consumption. Simulations indicated that under normal conditions, movement was a very small proportion of the total energy budget of the birds because movements were rare and very quickly accomplished. However, when fruit was scarce, costs increased rapidly as birds left patches frequently and searched many patches before finding a suitable one. During periods of fruit shortage, the elimination of patches from the network increased demands on the birds by a proportion much larger than the relative reduction in total patch area. This effect was detectable even when removal of a single patch was simulated. This situation poses a particular challenge to regional conservation planning because the commonly used criterion of representing each ecosystem by protected areas is insufficient to maintain frugivore populations and, ultimately, the plants whose seeds they disperse. Rather, it is important to maintain the area and spatial arrangement of rainforest patches at or very close to their existing level. Given that rainforest ecosystems are so limited in the tropical savannas (0.5 percent of the area) and have a distinctive flora (13 percent of the Northern Territory flora; Dunlop et al. 1994), the protection of all existing rainforest patches from development is a reasonable and achievable objective. However, patches are threatened by fire, weed invasion, and feral animal damage. Russell-Smith and Bowman (1992) showed that levels of damage were similar and substantial across pastoral, Aboriginal, and conservation tenures, indicating that active management is needed to maintain ecological function over the long term. Refinement of models may be needed to incorporate variation in habitat quality and connect it with management practice in different regional settings.

Radio-tracking studies of birds and flying foxes revealed that they also access nonrainforest habitat during periods of low fruit abundance (Price 1998; Palmer and Woinarski 1999). Flying foxes and figbirds feed on nectar that may be many kilometers distant from rainforests, and yellow orioles (*Oriolus flavocinctus*) feed on insects in woodlands within 500 m of the rainforest boundary. Protection of all rainforest patches will not be sufficient to maintain all species. Major flowering resources in neighboring savannas must also be maintained, with priority given to areas within 500 m of each patch.

Nectivorous Birds and Mammals

Nix (1993) argued that many nectivorous birds of the east coast of Australia have been adversely affected by clearing over huge areas in central Queensland, hundreds to thousands of kilometers to the north. Flying foxes consume nectar, pollen, and fruit of woody plants and have enormous ranges in northern and eastern Australia (Sinclair et al. 1996; Webb and Tidemann 1996). Decline in populations of the gray-headed flying fox (*Pteropus poliocephalus*) has been attributed to loss of wooded habitat (Tidemann 1999). These observations imply that effects of changes in the landscape may extend great distances from the sites directly affected to damage wildlife values at a subcontinental scale. A number of lines of evidence support the hypothesis that many nectivore populations in northern Australia depend on a capacity to track the flowering schedules of different dominant woody plants through often widely dispersed landscapes.

First, observations of seasonal movements of nectivorous birds show broad-scale, long-distance movements (Blakers et al. 1984). Birds such as the varied lorikeet (*Psitteuteles versicolor*) may appear in huge numbers in landscapes in which they have not been sighted for months to take advantage of synchronous flowering in the dominant eucalypts (Woinarski and Tidemann 1991; Franklin 1996). Second, Woinarski et al. (2000b) and Franklin and Noske (2000) have documented the acute spatial and temporal variation in nectar availability that might drive such wide-ranging foraging strategies in northern Australia. Third, more localized studies of foraging by flying foxes (*Pteropus* spp.) confirm the diversity of resources exploited in different elements of the landscape mosaic at different times (Palmer and Woinarski 1999; Palmer et al. 2000). Impacts of habitat loss through land clearing are likely. If randomly or haphazardly distributed through a region, reduced cover of woody vegetation will reduce the total amount of resources available so that regional populations are smaller and hence more vulnerable. For example, clearing for horticulture or pasture improvement may selectively remove components of the resource mosaic that are critical for particular species (Woinarski et al. 2000b). Fourth, extensive clearing may so fragment resource distribution that the costs of using the modified landscape and moving between remaining patches may seriously affect population viability.

In addition, short-term effects of fire include changes in the phenology of flowering of many woody plants, potentially including total suppression of annual flowering over substantial areas (Setterfield and Williams 1996). Unfavorable fire regimes cause long-term changes in both the floristics and the structure of woodlands and forests (Lonsdale and Braithwaite 1991; Russell-Smith et al. 1998). The impact of these effects is likely to be greater in fragmented landscapes than in unaltered ones.

We suggest that sufficient information is available to derive foraging models, based on energetic costs of maintenance and flight, and climate-driven variation in resource distribution and density under a variety of potential land use scenarios. Subject to the availability of thematic (e.g., vegetation) mapping at appropriate spatial scales, spatially explicit (incorporating measures of landscape pattern in model parameters) or even spatially realistic models (based on real, actively managed landscapes) can be used to examine the effects of variation in habitat configuration. Ideally, a number of competing models would be produced, covering a number of the better-known taxa and including species with contrasting foraging strategies. Predictions would initially be tested against measures of nectivore status in a range of environments subject to various degrees of modification.

The greatest impediment to predicting the impact of land use change and management practice at large spatial scales is the unavailability of environmental mapping at scales and resolution necessary to identify patterns of resource (nectar) availability. The fine-scale mapping of rainforest patches used by Price et al. (1999) to derive spatially realistic models for frugivorous birds is unique. For most of northern Australia, vegetation or other thematic mapping is available only at scales to 1:250,000 or cruder, and often for classifications that do not give weight to the relative distribution and abundance of important flowering plants. Therefore, the most likely modeling outcomes for nectar-dependent wildlife will be crude models that identify highly and uniformly destructive practices rather than a refined capacity to ensure protection of all or most species.

An array of entrenched problems in the north Australian savannas demand timely intervention. The scientific understanding necessary to address these issues is most robust in respect to taxa occupying distinct and easily described subsets of the environment (e.g., rainforest patches and wetlands). With wildlife in the savannas, there is an urgent need to develop methods to arrest the decline of small mammals and birds, especially granivorous birds. But our ability to predict long-term outcomes of existing land allocations and management practice in the savannas is weak, and the probability of effective management interventions is low.

Under ideal circumstances, these changes in wildlife status would be investigated in some detail, beginning with the most severe, preferably by replicated experiment, and management responses based on interpretation of experiments. However, the acute adverse changes affecting diverse taxa over a large proportion of the Australian continent demand responses more immediate and more profound than are likely to be offered by a measured program of taxon-by-taxon and site-by-site studies and derived local palliatives. Urgency is increased by the intrusion of broad-scale clearing of woody vegetation into new areas and the prospect that this source of change will exacerbate pressures on already fragile wildlife populations.

In considering the significance of the range of potential responses to this situation, we find the analysis of Fagan et al. (2001) germane. Using time series analysis of trends in well-studied wildlife populations to estimate extinction risk, they show that 46 to 90 percent of taxa fluctuate so dramatically that dispersal or some other refuge mechanism is likely to be key to their persistence. Their argument regarding the significance of dynamic refugia is consistent with our view of many north Australian taxa; that is, it is extraordinarily prone to fluctuation in distribution and abundance over a range of time and spatial scales (Woinarski et al. 1992). Suppression of seed production by unfavorable grazing or fire regimes, wider average separation of productive monsoon rainforest patches caused by loss or degradation, loss of wetlands or suppression of food plants by invasive exotic pastures, and creation of gaps in the temporal sequencing and spatial configuration of nectar availability by land clearing are among the changes that may render such refugia ecologically dysfunctional.

Management implications are profound. Dependence on a fixed suite of sites occupying a small proportion of the landscape, as offered by a traditional conservation reserve system, is a recipe for failure because different sites assume critical importance at different times (Whitehead et al. 1990, 1992). Adverse change among the vertebrate fauna suggests that the quality, availability, or spatial and temporal links between these ephemeral, seasonal, and semipermanent refugia are already compromised. If wildlife losses are to be arrested or reversed, then a creative and integrated application of theory and practice for management of landscapes and wildlife populations is needed on all land tenures and over large spatial scales. What does our contemporary performance suggest will be achievable in a sparsely populated, logistically challenging landscape, with limited technical capacity?

Regional Planning Initiatives: Linking with Landscape Ecology

Examples of regional conservation plans are few in Australia. Here we consider a small number spanning the north Australian jurisdictions.

Queensland

North Australia's most ambitious attempt to plan conservation at a large spatial scale is centered on Cape York Peninsula (see Fig. 10.1). Initiated in 1991, the Cape York Peninsula Land Use Study (CYPLUS) grew from different perceptions of the value of Cape York. On one hand, it is considered one of Australia's most significant conservation and wilderness areas (Abrahams et al. 1995), and on the other hand, it is viewed as a suitable site for low-intensity production for commerce (pastoralism) or subsistence (through restoration of traditional Aboriginal use of wild resources). By Australian standards, CYPLUS involved an unusually large commitment of public funds. However, progress has been halting, the engagement of different stakeholders uneven, and processes for conceiving, debating, and implementing various visions of an appropriate future clumsy. The fundamental problem appears to be a project conceived without a clear view of how implementation might be achieved.

Since the inception of CYPLUS, the Queensland Parliament has enacted the Integrated Planning Act of 1997 for coordinating and integrating planning at local, regional, and state levels. Attempts to achieve this goal include guidelines for regional strategies on natural resource management and biodiversity conservation (Anonymous 1999), and a partnership framework (Beattie n.d.) to recognize the interests of indigenous people and other land users. Although potentially useful, these instruments have yet to help the protagonists of various positions reach consensus about the primary goal: Cape York as a wilderness free of the pernicious influence of people or as a site capable of meeting other social goals as well.

Northern Territory

In the Northern Territory, legislation with the potential to facilitate wildlife management at large spatial scales is not directed explicitly at that option. The Planning Act of 1999 primarily guides urban planning. However, it does provide for description and public review of land use objectives (policy) and development provisions (regulation), which may cover any area of land. Some developments may be prohibited or constrained. Potentially, the act could provide a useful statutory vehicle for planning to allocate lands and specify development intensities and configurations that meet wildlife conservation objectives.

Other legislation (Territory Parks and Wildlife Conservation Act 2000) provides options for addressing subsets of regionally comprehensive conservation plans, especially to select and manage wildlife reserves. Provisions are made for making conservation agreements with individual land owners and declaring essential habitat. They are likely to be most useful in respect to relict species or populations with narrow distributions and far more effective within a framework that specifies regional wildlife management objectives. There have been two notable attempts to derive large-scale land use and management plans integrating wildlife conservation with development objectives and land management practice.

The Mary River Catchment

Wetlands of the Mary River sustain a recreational barramundi (*Lates calcarifer*) fishery, productive native pasture, and high densities of regionally significant wildlife (Whitehead et al. 1990). Tourism based on wildlife and other natural values is growing in importance. All values are threatened by intrusion of the sea into previously freshwater wetlands through breaches of low-lying barriers (Woodroffe and Mulrennan 1993). Given large tidal ranges, the extent of new and expanded channels formed before intervention, and the absence of secure points to anchor constructions, restoring the barriers at the site of the original breaches has proved difficult. Land managers have responded by building new barriers further inland, where tidal volumes and velocities are lower. Even these modest interventions have caused concern. Recreational anglers are worried about the disruption of pathways for fish movement. Wildlife interests are worried about the homogenization of floodplains caused by pooling of water behind the barriers and the use of exotic semiaquatic grasses to provide favorable grazing areas (Jonauskas 1996). Public concern has stimulated a number of government actions culminating in a catchment management plan, drafted mostly by a landholder group. The plan was somewhat disappointing from a wildlife conservation perspective (Whitehead 1999) but did set some ambitious goals, including preventing the loss of any species from the catchment and maintaining large populations of fauna strongly associated with the region.

Ways of achieving these goals were to be set down in a comprehensive nature conservation plan. However, a subsequent draft land use plan developed under the Planning Act of 1999 potentially disabled many recommendations. For example, the plan specified that conservation goals would be met predominantly through the existing system of parks and reserves, even though they were known to be unrepresentative of the region's ecosystems and poorly located in regard to wildlife hotspots or major wildlife aggregations, including breeding colonies of waterbirds.

Douglas and Daly River Agricultural Development

Large parts of the Daly River catchment are scheduled for conversion from pastoral use by subdivision of leases into freehold farms. Here the specified conservation goal is to secure viable populations of all vertebrate wildlife in the bioregion. This is to be accomplished by a system of reserves selected to meet criteria of comprehensiveness, adequacy, and representativeness. Comprehensiveness and representativeness are determined using minimum-set computer algorithms (Bedward et al. 1992) and adequacy by checking configurations against arbitrary targets for the area of each ecosystem under protection and the prospects of capturing viable populations of all vertebrate wildlife. Minimum viable population sizes and area needs are unknown for most species and were inferred from empirical relationships for better-known taxa.

The process of proposing configurations of protected lands has been exhaustive, within the constraints of a poor knowledge base. But the extent to which the favored configurations will influence land allocation has yet to be seen, and the way in which the Planning Act of 1999 might be used to determine patterns of land use and management is problematic given the Mary River precedent.

Western Australia

Western Australian statutes do not include provisions directed explicitly at integrated planning to achieve conservation and development goals over large areas. Systematic biological surveys of the Kimberley region were used as a base for planning major expansions of the conservation reserve system (Burbidge et al. 1991). Implementation of this system has been difficult, partly because of problems with consultation with affected parties and competing land use bids. The Ord River Scheme, which has impacts over at least the regional scale, involved constructing two impoundments, one of which formed the huge Lake Argyle. Water availability was more than sufficient to provide for the initially modest area devoted to irrigated crops. Accordingly, the Stage 2 development seeks to increase areas under irrigation by 32,000 ha (Kinhill Pty. Ltd. 2000).

An area of approximately 40,000 ha is proposed for conservation management, mostly on less favorable soil types. Most of the distinctive black soil plains in the region will be used for farming. The adequacy of the reserved areas of black soil to retain viable populations of their characteristic fauna was unresolved during the environmental impact assessment process, and final configurations are yet to be negotiated by the proponents and government. Moreover, the ecological information needed to comprehensively inform such negotiations is unavailable.

This small sample indicates some moves on the part of conservation and land use planners to apply elements of landscape science to wildlife conservation in northern Australia. However, the science is often crude and the legislative underpinning weak and uncertainly applied.

An Improved Approach to Regional Conservation Planning

We have identified a number of important barriers to improved performance in wildlife conservation and management in northern Australia. Proposals for change must address all of them in some way if performance is to be significantly enhanced.

First, there is evidence that many taxa are already at substantial risk under prevailing management regimes. Many declines have occurred rapidly, over the last few decades (Franklin 1999), and appear to be continuing. Declining taxa are often quintessential savanna animals. Grassland fauna are in trouble in huge areas of apparently little-modified grassland, suggesting that the causal factors are altering fundamental ecological processes and probably damaging other, less conspicuous fauna. In our opinion, a complacent, business-as-usual approach would number among the most risky and ultimately costly strategies.

Second, our knowledge base is limited, so levels of uncertainty are high. Uncertainty confronts all decisions in natural resource management. Notwithstanding increases in the number of workers in resource management in northern Australia, accrual of relevant information of a quality to substantially reduce uncertainty is unlikely to keep pace with land use change. We therefore see no alternative to an adaptive management approach of the sort that Walters and Holling (1990) have refined and promoted for more than two decades.

Third, projected changes in land use patterns will increase risk without necessarily ameliorating existing sources of damage. Land use intensification may be accompanied by increased human populations, access to improved infrastructure, and enhanced capacity to actively manage elements of the landscape. For example, ongoing studies suggest that the fragmentation of wooded landscapes in semirural settings in the Top End of the Northern Territory is associated with increased densities of a few species of small mammals, perhaps because the incidence of fire is lower and habitat quality higher. However, the long-term value of fire-protected sites depends on their size and relative isolation, neither of which is specified under current land allocation arrangements. Moreover, the impact of land use intensification will most often homogenize management treatment and weaken the habitat condition rather than increase diversity and enhance quality. A case in point is the more uniform grazing impacts and loss of fauna that follow supplementation of watering points (Landsberg et al. 1997).

Fourth, legislation to underpin regional conservation plans is mostly weak in a regulatory sense and provides few or no positive incentives for landholder conservation activity. There is no culture of community engagement in development of regional conservation plans. Efforts have been limited in scope and government commitment. In the absence of leadership and other incentives, participants have tended to use the few opportunities presented as platforms from which to restate well-known sectoral positions rather than to resolve conflict (Whitehead 1999).

Finally, physical infrastructure is sparse and human population densities are low, with limited technical and professional support in wildlife management. Human capital, built infrastructure, equipment, and financial resources for implementing regional conservation and resource use plans must be stretched extremely thin (Fig. 10.5). This has at least two important implications. First, the intensity of management proposed cannot be too ambitious. Second, the active involvement of a large proportion of the human population is needed to improve performance. Community involvement will be indispensable and must incorporate all relevant interests, including the region's indigenous people. Participants will need technical support, including training.

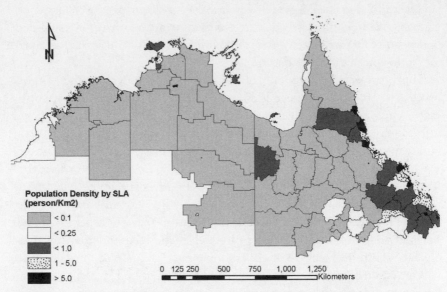

Figure 10.5   Human population density in northern Australia by Statistical Local Area (SLA). Over most of the region, human population densities average less than 0.1 persons per square kilometer. Higher average densities occur in the small proportion of SLAs that contain substantial settlements or towns. An SLA is the whole or part of a Local Government Area or, where there is no local government, an unincorporated area. They are used to standardize the collection, analysis, and presentation of human census data. They can vary greatly in size with population density. Given the sparse population of northern Australia, many in this region are very large. Local government is the third tier of government in the hierarchy: federal—›state—›local.

Therefore, strategy for effective wildlife management at a regional scale in northern Australia must include the following:

A statutory obligation to develop regional conservation plans in areas subject to significant change in types or intensity of land use, including extension of existing land uses to areas previously free of those influences.

Equivalent obligations in regions where no immediate change is proposed but existing land uses cause substantial detriment or where change is needed to complement actions in other regions. There must be a capacity to relate and integrate regional goals with supraregional issues, especially regarding movement of migratory native fauna and widespread wildlife declines.

Incentives for landholders to enter into conservation arrangements, perhaps including increased access to government funding, covering infrastructure and training to improve capability in conservation management.

Facilitation of efforts of land managers, planners, and community members to clearly state conservation and wildlife management goals for the region in terms that can be rendered operational (unambiguous and measurable). Assistance from researchers and other scientists will be needed, including specification of spatial and temporal scales at which outcomes can reasonably be sought and measured.

Recognition of the special situation of indigenous landholders as strongly tied to individual sites, well informed and highly experienced with a suite of faunal and floral management techniques, and having well-established expectations and goals regarding the desired state and management of wild plants and animals.

Financial and other incentives for local people to occupy or reoccupy vacant lands as stewards to manage broad-scale threats, especially fire, weeds, and feral animals.

Reserve systems that are comprehensive, adequate, and representative at regional and larger scales.

Genuine application of an adaptive management approach (Walters 1997) to derive and implement regional plans, including development of competing quantitative models of wildlife outcomes expected under a range of experimental treatments of land use and landscape configuration within regions; integration of design and implementation of regional plans so that adaptive management experiments cross regions, taking regions as experimental units for combinations of dominant land use type and ecosystem types, with subregional variants of land allocation patterns as treatments; and design of wildlife monitoring systems as integral, funded elements of all development plans.

Institutional arrangements for ongoing analysis and refinement of experiments and for additional study to progressively derive mechanistic explanations for observed responses to land allocation and management treatments.

Legislative and financial support to implement the changes in land management practice necessary to arrest declines.

Challenges for Implementation

The proposals summarized here present many challenges and could be dismissed as utopian. We see no reasonable alternative to an approach incorporating these key features, but it may be stretching credulity too far to suppose that the northern Australian states and territory will spontaneously come together to develop such a collective approach to regional development and conservation.

It is also important to acknowledge that special opportunities to design landscapes in unmodified systems also have a darker side. The limited built infrastructure and largely intact natural structures that permit this option also complicate adaptive management. Government and private developers face scale-related threshold issues. Infrastructures such as roads, bridges, electrical power, and urban facilities are often entirely lacking, necessitating large initial investments of public funds to support development. These investments in turn demand that economic returns be large and maintained over long periods. In these circumstances, how is it possible to entertain the notion that lies at the heart of adaptive management: that access to resources will be curtailed, perhaps severely, if early experience indicates adverse outcomes for biodiversity? If the initial overinvestment problem cannot be overcome, experience is too consistently bleak to warrant any optimism that local regulators, who are often simultaneously the promoters of development, will find the will to correct errors (Ludwig et al. 1993).

We suggest that if broader national perspectives are brought to bear, then regional development initiatives and associated conservation plans are more likely to be assessed on their merits. If local communities, including those with strong views of the value of native wildlife, take larger roles in setting goals and making decisions, inflated economic expectations can also be reduced and greater weight given to wildlife outcomes. The federal government, through Australia's ratification of the Convention on Biological Diversity, has the power, the legal instruments, and the obligation to realize special opportunities in northern Australia and, in particular, to pursue genuine adaptive management within frameworks that avoid the promoter–regulator syndrome. The federal government recently consolidated much national environmental legislation in a compendium statute, the Environmental Protection and Biodiversity Conservation Act of 1999 (EPBCA).The EPBCA provides that bioregional plans may set objectives for components of biodiversity and important economic and social values, develop mechanisms to achieve the objectives, promote community involvement in implementing plans, and adopt measures for monitoring and review. These make up most of the necessary components of an adaptive management experiment. The largest missing piece is the political will to narrow the gap between rhetoric and performance.

Narrowing that gap will take strong incentives for state and territory governments to collaborate with the national government and to engage with local communities, which in remote northern Australia are often numerically dominated by indigenous people with limited capital and income. An effective glue to build and maintain such alliances is access to federal funds, which could be used to consolidate and reward the substantial contribution already made by Aboriginal people to meeting Australia's obligations and objectives in biodiversity conservation (Whitehead 2000; Altman 2001). Most federal funding is distributed through the Natural Heritage Trust, delivered in fragments and in ways that highlight its political dimensions. Correcting entrenched problems over small areas in places with large human populations has been emphasized at the expense of avoiding the emergence of severe broad-scale problems in newly developing sites. Independent reviews of the program have highlighted its strategic inadequacies and led to proposals to emphasize regional plans (NHT Ministerial Board 2000). Such reorientation could provide the necessary funds for regional conservation planning.

But even with substantial funding support, north Australian society is unlikely to embrace a highly prescriptive approach. Solutions are likely to differ from region to region and recognize the different social aspirations of people with traditional commitments to individual sites. Specifying core principles and providing an operational template will be a major and arguably sufficient achievement.

Wildlife managers can make a critical contribution to building the social and political will to enhance performance. The task is to promote regionally and nationally a credible view of the way well-managed northern Australian landscapes might make a major contribution to the national well-being without trading real wildlife for the illusion of the free lunch that lurks behind many of the wilder fantasies about the future of northern Australia. As well as celebrating the intrinsic value of wildlife, this will take collaboration with resource economists to offer much more comprehensive balance sheets for development costs and benefits than are usually considered by decision makers.

Regional politicians have appropriated the special lifestyle of north Australians for the smorgasbord they offer electors, and nationally the remote north has entered the public imagination as one of the few places where the true Australia lives on. The wildlife of Australia's tropics is part of both images but is too loosely linked to be seen as indispensable to the maintenance of national well-being. Wildlife managers number among those who exploit their relationships with wildlife to earn mostly comfortable livings. The obligation to wildlife extends beyond competent science to include responsible advocacy to strengthen those links.

Summary

Little of the northern Australian landscape has suffered significant structural modification: Land clearing for agriculture or other development has been limited. However, it would be wrong to conclude that the biota is similarly intact. Recent extinctions in Australia's tropical environments have been few, but many species have declined in range and abundance, some severely and rapidly. In the absence of acute structural change, well-developed theory in regard to effects of habitat fragmentation and dynamics of metapopulations provide few clues to the causes of these apparently continuing declines. Empirical studies so far have been too few and too limited in scope to suggest coherent patterns. Despite deficiencies in understanding, the extent of change demands that solutions be sought actively. Now that the north is adding rapid structural change from accelerating rates of land clearing to poorly understood, chronic impacts, to delay effective responses is to invite repetition of Australia's appalling record of wildlife extinction in arid lands.

Under the Australian Constitution, states and territories are responsible for land and resource management. Historically, the federal government has therefore intervened on the limited estate of areas owned by the Commonwealth or in respect to species listed under international treaties. Recently, the Australian federal government comprehensively recast Australia's environmental and biodiversity management legislation but largely maintained this position. Nonetheless, the EPBCA of 1999 does offer a potentially significant advance in providing a federal role in bioregional plans for conservation. The developing discipline of landscape ecology offers some of the tools needed to design developments to minimize loss of biological diversity, especially if used in combination with adaptive management of natural resources.

In this chapter we reviewed the performance of the northern Australian states and Northern Territory in bioregional planning, examined some principles and practices in landscape ecology to design modified landscapes to optimize biodiversity conservation in a north Australian context, and proposed a science-based planning framework consistent with the letter and apparent intent of federal legislation. We illustrated the challenges and potential for application of the framework using examples including waterfowl; nectivorous, granivorous, and frugivorous birds; and flying foxes. We also considered the prospects for implementing such a framework under prevailing political and administrative strictures and suggested a role for wildlife managers in promoting its application.

Acknowledgments

Phillip McMahon prepared the figures. David Bowman provided valuable comment on an earlier draft of the manuscript. The Australian Bureau of Statistics provided population data and the Bureau of Rural Sciences information on land clearing. The Bushfires Council of the Northern Territory provided the fire map.

LITERATURE CITED

Abrahams, H., M. Mulvane, D. Glasco, and A. Bugg. 1995. Areas of conservation significance on Cape York Peninsula. Australian Heritage Commission and Environmental Resources Information Network and Cape York Peninsula Land Use Strategy, Canberra.

Altman, J. C. 1987. Hunter–gatherers today. Australian Institute of Aboriginal Studies, Canberra.

Altman, J. C. 2001. Sustainable development options on Aboriginal land: the hybrid economy in the twenty-first century. CAEPR Discussion Paper 226, Centre for Aboriginal Economic Policy Research, The Australian National University, Canberra.

Anonymous. 1999. Guidelines for developing regional strategies on natural resources management and biodiversity conservation. Department of Natural Resources, Brisbane, Queensland.

Bach, C. S. 1998. Resource patchiness in time and space: phenology and reproductive traits of monsoon rainforests in the Northern Territory, Australia. Ph.D. thesis, Faculty of Science, Northern Territory University, Darwin.

Barnard, C. A. 1925. A review of the bird life on Coomooboolaroo Station, Duaringa district, Queensland, during the past fifty years. Emu 24:252–265.

Barnard, H. G. 1934. Observations on the disappearance and probable cause of many of our native birds in central Queensland. Queensland Naturalist 9:3–7.

Bayliss, P., and K. M. Yeomans. 1989. The distribution and abundance of feral livestock in the Top End of the Northern Territory (1985–1986) and their relation to population control. Australian Wildlife Research 16:651–676.

Beattie, P. n.d. Cape York partnerships: some practical ideas. Queensland Government, Brisbane. (Online at http://www.premiers.qld.gov.au/about/pcd/cape.pdf).

Bedward, M., R. L. Pressey, and D. A. Keith. 1992. A new approach for selecting fully representative reserve networks: addressing efficiency, reserve design and land suitability with an iterative analysis. Biological Conservation 62:115–125.

Blakers, M., S. J. J. F. Davies, and P. N. Reilly. 1984. The atlas of Australian birds. Melbourne University Press, Melbourne.

Bowman, D. M. J. S., O. Price, P. J. Whitehead, and A. Walsh. 2001. The "wilderness effect" and the decline of *Callitris intratropica* on the Arnhem Land Plateau, northern Australia. Australian Journal of Botany 49:1–8.

Braithwaite, R. W. 1987. Effects of fire regimes on lizards in the wet–dry tropics of Australia. Journal of Tropical Ecology 3:265–275.

Braithwaite, R. W., and A. D. Griffiths. 1996. The paradox of *Rattus tunneyi*: endangerment of a native pest. Wildlife Research 23:1–21.

Braithwaite, R. W., and W. J. Muller. 1997. Rainfall, groundwater and refuges: predicting extinctions of Australian tropical mammal species. Australian Journal of Ecology 22:57–67.

Brock, J. 2001. Clearing moves north: a review of land clearing in the Northern Territory. Environment Centre of the Northern Territory, Darwin.

Burbidge, A. A., and N. L. McKenzie. 1989. Patterns in the modern decline of Western Australia's vertebrate fauna: causes and conservation implications. Biological Conservation 50:143–198.

Burbidge, A. A., K. A. Johnson, and R. I. Southgate. 1988. Aboriginal knowledge of the mammals of the central deserts of Australia. Australian Wildlife Research 15:9–39.

Burbidge, A. A., N. L. McKenzie, and K. F. Kenneally. 1991. Nature conservation reserves in the Kimberley, Western Australia. Department of Conservation and Land Management, Perth.

Crowley, G., and S. Garnett. 1999. Seeds of the annual grasses *Schizachyrium* spp. as a food resource for tropical granivorous birds. Australian Journal of Ecology 24:208–220.

Dostine, P. L., G. C. Johnson, D. C. Franklin, Y. Zhang, and C. Hempel. 2001. Seasonal use of landscapes by the Gouldian finch *Erythrura gouldiae* in the Yinberrie Hills area, Northern Territory. Wildlife Research 28:445–458.

Dunlap, T. R. 1993. Australian nature, European culture: Anglo settler in Australia. Environmental History Review 17:25–48.

Dunlop, C. R., G. J. Leach, P. K. Latz, M. J. Barrit, I. D. Cowie, and D. E. Albrecht. 1994. Checklist of the vascular plants of the Northern Territory, Australia. Conservation Commission of the Northern Territory, Darwin.

Dyer, R., A. Craig, and A. C. Grice. 1997. Fire in northern pastoral lands. Pages 24–40 in T. C. Grice and S. M. Slatter (eds.), Fire in the management of northern Australian pastoral lands. Occasional Publication No. 8. Tropical Grassland Society of Australia, St. Lucia, Queensland.

Fagan, W. F., E. Meir, J. Prendergast, A. Folarin, and P. Karieva. 2001. Characterising population vulnerability for 758 species. Ecology Letters 4:132–138.

Fensham, R. J., J. C. McCosker, and M. J. Cox. 1998. Estimating clearance of *Acacia*-dominated ecosystems in central Queensland using land-system mapping data. Australian Journal of Botany 46:305–319.

Fisher, A. 1999. Conservation assessment of Mitchell grasslands in northern Australia. Final report to National Reserves System Program, Parks and Wildlife Commission of the Northern Territory, Darwin.

Franklin, D. 1996. A massive aggregation of the varied lorikeet. Eclectus 1:6–7.

Franklin, D. C. 1999. Evidence of disarray among granivorous bird assemblages in the savannas of northern Australia, a region of sparse human settlement. Biological Conservation 90:53–68.

Franklin, D. C., and R. A. Noske. 2000. Nectar sources used by birds in monsoonal north-western Australia: a regional survey. Australian Journal of Botany 48:461–474.

Franklin, D. C., J. C. Z. Woinarski, and R. A. Noske. 2000. Geographic patterning of species richness among granivorous birds in Australia. Journal of Biogeography 27:829–842.

Fraser, F. J. 2000. The impact of fire and grazing on the partridge pigeon: the ecological requirements of a declining tropical granivore. Ph.D. thesis, Australian National University, Canberra.

Freeland, W. J. 1990. Large herbivorous mammals: exotic species in northern Australia. Journal of Biogeography 17:445–449.

Gill, A. M. 1981. Adaptive responses of Australian vascular plant species to fires. Pages 243–271 in A. M. Gill, R. H. Groves, and I. R. Noble (eds.), Fire and the Australian biota. Australian Academy of Science, Canberra.

Graetz, R. D., M. A. Wilson, and S. K. Campbell. 1995. Landcover disturbance over the Australian continent: a contemporary assessment. Biodiversity Series Paper No. 7. Department of Environment, Sport and Territories, Canberra.

Griffiths, A. D., and K. A. Christian. 1996. The effects of fire on the frillneck lizard (*Chlamydosaurus kingii*) in northern Australia. Australian Journal of Ecology 21:386–398.

Holmes, J. H. 1990. Ricardo revisited: submarginal land and non-viable cattle enterprises in the Northern Territory Gulf District. Journal of Rural Studies 6:45–65.

Holmes, J. 1991. Land tenures in the Australian pastoral zone: a critical appraisal. Australian National University, NARU, Darwin.

Jolly, P., and D. Yin Foo. 1988. Lambells lagoon groundwater resource investigations. Water Resources Division, Power and Water Authority of the Northern Territory, Australia.

Jonauskas, P. 1996. Making multiple use work. Proceedings of the Wetland Workshop, 6–7 December 1994, Darwin. Department of Lands, Planning and Environment, Darwin.

Kingsford, R. T. 2000. Ecological impacts of dams, water diversions and river management on floodplain wetlands in Australia. Austral Ecology 25:109–127.

Kinhill Pty. Ltd. 2000. Ord River irrigation area Stage 2 proposed development of the M2 area: environmental review and management programme (ERMP)/

environmental impact statement (EIS). Report for Wesfarmers Sugar Company Pty. Ltd., Marubeni Corporation and the Water Corporation of Western Australia, Kinhill Pty. Ltd., Perth.

Kinnear, J. E., M. L. Onus, and N. R. Sumner. 1998. Fox control and rock-wallaby population dynamics. II: An update. Wildlife Research 25:81–88.

Lacey, C. J. 1979. Forestry in the Top End of the Northern Territory. Search 10:174–180.

Landsberg, J., C. D. James, S. R. Morton, T. J. Hobbs, J. Stol, A. Drew, and H. Tongway. 1997. The effects of artificial sources of water on rangeland biodiversity. Final Report to the Biodiversity Group, Environment Australia. CSIRO Wildlife and Ecology, Canberra.

Lonsdale, W. M. 1994. Inviting trouble: introduced pasture species in northern Australia. Australian Journal of Ecology 19:345–354.

Lonsdale, W. M., and R. W. Braithwaite. 1991. Assessing the effects of fire on vegetation in tropical savannas. Australian Journal of Ecology 16:363–374.

Ludwig, D., R. Hilborn, and C. Walters. 1993. Uncertainty, resource exploitation, and conservation: lessons from history. Science 260:17–36.

Morton, S. R. 1990. The impact of European settlement on the vertebrate animals of arid Australia: a conceptual model. Proceedings of the Ecological Society of Australia 16:201–213.

NHT Ministerial Board. 2000. Mid-term review of the Natural Heritage Trust: the response. Department of Agriculture, Fisheries and Forestry Australia and Environment Australia, Canberra.

Nix, H. A. 1993. Bird distributions in relation to imperatives for habitat conservation in Queensland. Pages 12–21 in C. P. Catterall, P. Driscoll, K. Hulsman, and A. Taplin (eds.), Birds and their habitats: current knowledge and conservation priorities in Queensland. Queensland Ornithological Society, Brisbane.

Palmer, C., and J. C. Z. Woinarski. 1999. Seasonal roosts and foraging movements of the black flying fox (Pteropus alecto) in the Northern Territory: resource tracking in a landscape mosaic. Wildlife Research 26:823–838.

Palmer, C., O. Price, and C. Bach. 2000. Foraging ecology of the black flying fox (Pteropus alecto) in the seasonal tropics of the Northern Territory, Australia. Wildlife Research 27:169–178.

Price, O. F. 1998. Frugivorous bird movement and the conservation of monsoon rainforests in the Northern Territory, Australia. Ph.D. thesis, Centre for Resource and Environmental Studies, Australian National University, Canberra.

Price, O. F., and D. M. J. S. Bowman. 1994. Fire-stick forestry: a matrix model in support of skillful fire management of Callitris intratropica R. T. Baker by north Australian Aborigines. Journal of Biogeography 21:573–580.

Price, O. F., J. C. Z. Woinarski, and D. Robinson. 1999. Very large area requirements for frugivorous birds in monsoon rainforests of the Northern Territory, Australia. Biological Conservation 91:169–180.

Recher, H. F. 1999. The state of Australia's avifauna: a personal opinion and prediction for the new millennium. Australian Zoologist 31:11–27.

Recher, H. F., and L. Lim. 1990. A review of current ideas of the extinction, conservation and management of Australia's terrestrial vertebrate fauna. Proceedings of the Ecological Society of Australia 16:287–301.

Russell-Smith, J., and D. M. J. S. Bowman. 1992. Conservation of monsoon rainforest isolates in the Northern Territory, Australia. Biological Conservation 59:51–63.

Russell-Smith, J., P. G. Ryan, D. Klessa, G. Waight, and R. Harwood. 1998. Fire regimes, fire-sensitive vegetation and fire management of the sandstone Arnhem Plateau, monsoonal northern Australia. Journal of Applied Ecology 35:829–846.

Russell-Smith, J., P. G. Ryan, and D. Cheal. 2002. Fire regimes and the conservation of sandstone heath in monsoonal northern Australia: frequency, interval, patchiness. Biological Conservation 104:91–106.

Saunders, D. A. 1989. Changes in the avifauna of a region, district and remnant as a result of fragmentation of native vegetation: the wheatbelt of Western Australia: a case study. Biological Conservation 50:99–135.

Saunders, D. A. 1990. Problems of survival in an extensively cultivated landscape: the case of Carnaby's cockatoo *Calyptorhynchus funereus latirostris*. Biological Conservation 54:277–290.

Serena, M. (ed.). 1995. Reintroduction biology of Australian and New Zealand fauna. Surrey Beatty & Sons, Chipping Norton, Sydney.

Setterfield, S. A., and R. J. Williams. 1996. Patterns of flowering and seed production in *Eucalyptus miniata* and *E. tetrodonta* in a tropical savanna woodland, northern Australia. Australian Journal of Botany 44:107–122.

Sinclair, E. A., N. J. Webb, A. D. Marchant, and C. R. Tidemann. 1996. Genetic variation in the little red flying-fox *Pteropus scapulatus* (Chiroptera, Pteropodidae): implications for management. Biological Conservation 76:45–50.

Smith, A. P., and D. G. Quin. 1996. Patterns of extinction and decline in Australian conilurine rodents. Biological Conservation 77:243–267.

Taylor, J. A., and C. R. Dunlop. 1985. Plant communities of the wet–dry tropics of Australia: the Alligator Rivers region, Northern Territory. Proceeding of the Ecological Society of Australia 13:83–121.

Tidemann, C. R. 1999. Biology and management of the grey-headed flying-fox, *Pteropus poliocephalus*. Acta Chiropterologica 1:151–164.

Trainor, C. R., and J. C. Z. Woinarski. 1994. Responses of lizards to three experimental fires in the savanna forests of Kakadu National Park. Wildlife Research 21:131–148.

Vitousek, P. M., H. A. Mooney, J. Lubchenco, and J. M. Melillo. 1997. Human domination of Earth's ecosystems. Science 277:494–499.

Walters, C. 1997. Adaptive policy design: thinking at large spatial scales. Pages 386–394 in J. A. Bissonette (ed.), Wildlife and landscape ecology: effects of pattern and scale. Springer-Verlag, New York.

Walters, C. J., and C. S. Holling. 1990. Large-scale management experiments and learning by doing. Ecology 71:2060–2068.

Webb, N. J., and C. R. Tidemann. 1996. Mobility of Australian flying-foxes, *Pteropus* spp. (Megachiroptera): evidence from genetic variation. Proceedings of the Royal Society of London Series B: Biological Sciences 263:497–502.

Whitehead, P. J. 1999. Promoting conservation in landscapes subject to change: lessons from the Mary River. Australian Biologist 12:50–62.

Whitehead, P. J. 2000. The clever country: where cows manage wildlife. Pages 155–168 in R. Dixon (ed.), Business as usual: local conflicts and global challenges. North Australian Research Unit, Australian National University, Darwin.

Whitehead, P. J., and T. J. Dawson. 2000. Let them eat grass. Nature Australia Summer 2000:46–55.

Whitehead, P. J., P. G. Bayliss, and R. E. Fox. 1988. Recreational hunting activity and harvests in the Northern Territory, Australia. Australian Wildlife Research 15:625–631.

Whitehead, P. J., B. A. Wilson, and D. M. J. S. Bowman. 1990. Conservation of coastal wetlands of the Northern Territory of Australia: the Mary River floodplain. Biological Conservation 52:85–111.

Whitehead, P. J., B. A. Wilson, and K. Saalfeld. 1992. Managing the magpie goose in the Northern Territory: approaches to conservation of mobile fauna in a patchy environment. Pages 90–104 in I. Moffatt and A. Webb (eds.), Conservation and development issues in northern Australia. North Australian Research Unit, Australian National University, Darwin.

Whitehead, P. J., J. C. Z. Woinarski, and O. Price. 1993. Planning for conservation of natural resources in the Northern Territory: keeping a little in reserve. Pages 78–87 in Anonymous (ed.), Ancient lands: new perspectives. Regional Seminar of the Australian Institute of Landscape Architects. Australian Institute of Architects, Darwin.

Williams, R. J., A. M. Gill, and P. H. R. Moore. 1999. Seasonal changes in fire behaviour in a tropical savanna in northern Australia. International Journal of Wildland Fire 8:227–239.

Woinarski, J. C. Z. 1993. Australian tropical savannas, their avifauna, conservation status and threats. Pages 45–63 in C. Catterall, P. Driscoll, K. Hulsman, and A. Taplin (eds.), Birds and their habitats: current knowledge and conservation priorities in Queensland. Queensland Ornithological Society, Brisbane.

Woinarski, J. C. Z. 1999. Prognosis and framework for the conservation of biodiversity in rangelands: building on the north Australian experience. Pages 639–645 in D. Eldridge and D. Freudenberger (eds.), People and rangelands: building the future. Proceedings of the VIth International Rangelands Congress. VI International Rangelands Congress, Inc., Aitkenvale, Queensland.

Woinarski, J. C. Z., and A. J. Ash. 2002. Responses of vertebrates to pastoralism, military land use and landscape position in a tropical savanna near Townsville, northern Australia. Austral Ecology 27:311–323.

Woinarski, J. C. Z., and R. W. Braithwaite. 1990. Conservation foci for Australian birds and mammals. Search 21:65–68.

Woinarski, J. C. Z., and F. Dawson. 2002. Limitless lands and limited knowledge: coping with uncertainty and ignorance in northern Australia. Pages 83–115 in J. W. Handmer, T. W. Norton, and S. R. Dovers (eds.), Ecology, uncertainty and policy: managing ecosystems for sustainability. Prentice-Hall, Upper Saddle River, NJ.

Woinarski, J. C. Z., and S. C. Tidemann. 1991. The bird fauna of a deciduous woodland in the wet–dry tropics of northern Australia. Wildlife Research 18:479–500.

Woinarski, J. C. Z., P. J. Whitehead, D. M. J. S. Bowman, and J. Russell-Smith. 1992. Conservation of mobile species in a variable environment: the problem of reserve design in the Northern Territory, Australia. Global Ecology and Biogeography Letters 2:1–10.

Woinarski, J. C. Z., C. Brock, A. Fisher, D. Milne, and B. Oliver. 1999. Response of birds and reptiles to fire regimes on pastoral land in the Victoria River District, Northern Territory. Rangelands Journal 21:24–38.

Woinarski, J. C. Z., K. Brennan, C. Hempel, R. Firth, and F. Watt. 2000a. Biodiversity conservation on the Tiwi Islands: plants, vegetation types and terrestrial vertebrates on Melville Island. Report to the Tiwi Land Council. Parks and Wildlife Commission of the Northern Territory, Darwin.

Woinarski, J. C. Z., G. Connors, and D. C. Franklin. 2000b. Thinking honeyeater: nectar maps for the Northern Territory, Australia. Pacific Conservation Biology 6:61–80.

Woinarski, J. C. Z., R. Fensham, P. J. Whitehead, and A. Fisher. 2001a. Developing an analytical framework for monitoring biodiversity in Australia's rangelands: Background Paper 1—A review of status and threatening processes. Report to the National Land and Water Audit. Tropical Savannas Cooperative Research Centre, Darwin.

Woinarski, J. C. Z., D. J. Milne, and G. Wanganeen. 2001b. Changes in mammal populations in relatively intact landscapes of Kakadu National Park, Northern Territory, Australia. Austral Ecology 26:360–370.

Woodroffe, C., and M. E. Mulrennan. 1993. Geomorphology of the lower Mary River plains, Northern Territory. Australian National University and Conservation Commission of the Northern Territory, Darwin.

Yibarbuk, D. M., P. J. Whitehead, J. Russell-Smith, D. Jackson, C. Godjuwa, A. Fisher, P. Cooke, D. Choquenot, and D. M. J. S. Bowman. 2001. Fire ecology and Aboriginal land management in central Arnhem Land, northern Australia: a tradition of ecosystem management. Journal of Biogeography 28:325–344.

CHAPTER ELEVEN

Habitat Models to Link Situation Evaluation and Planning Support in Agricultural Landscapes

ALFRED SCHULTZ, REINHARD KLENKE, GERD LUTZE,
MARION VOSS, RALF WIELAND,
AND BETTINA WILKENING

Agricultural landscapes are complex systems, structured in space and time, that change naturally but are also subject to induced change. Reliable forecasting is desirable to assess sustainability of anthropogenic interventions, to evaluate and compare management options, and to effectively support planning activities. Interactions between human interventions and landscape elements occur over a wide range of scales in space, time, and organizational complexity. To get a comprehensive understanding of the effects of induced changes, all the scales and phenomena should be covered with appropriate empirical information. This obviously is not possible for experimental, fiscal, and epistemological reasons. For example, experimental investigations are only conditionally suited because they can usually be carried out only at shorter time intervals and in smaller spatial units than those that are actually of interest. The inherent problem is making the match between the limited understanding achieved by experimentation and the complexity of the problem in question. On one hand, it is necessary to find a limited number of dynamic landscape elements that allow one to deduce and predict the dynamics of the entire landscape. On the other hand, it is necessary to know how indicator values and land use are quantitatively linked. Here we define an indicator set as a selected set of different variables in which quantitative and qualitative characteristics describe the state of another object or one feature therein (e.g., variables to describe the habitat suitability of landscapes for different animals). This provides the opportunity to compare model outcomes with a certain standard.

Thus, the challenge to explain long-term land use effects is twofold: to find appropriate empirical landscape state indicators and to find formal approaches (models) describing their relationships to land use effects. In the past various kinds of mathematical-cybernetic models have turned out to be suitable for describing these dependencies formally. A mathematical-cybernetic model is a simplified formal representation of essential structures and functions of a real phenomenon using mathematical or cybernetic means (e.g., equations or algorithms). Models are built to facilitate the investigation and understanding of the considered phenomenon. Habitat models are one special class of models that formalize the relationships between the occurrence of plant or animal species and certain environmental conditions including those arising from human activities. However, there is no unique or best approach for habitat modeling (Kleyer et al. 2000). Different approaches can coexist well.

The first part of this chapter discusses some fundamentals for developing habitat models and some specific criteria for their application in situation evaluation and planning support. In the second part we outline one special habitat modeling approach and discuss its application for the common crane (*Grus grus* L.). We chose the common crane because of its special habitat needs concerning natural landscape elements and land use in the northeast German lowland. We close the chapter with general conclusions concerning the development and application of habitat models.

Concept of Habitat Model

Mathematical habitat modeling began in the 1970s in the United States with habitat suitability index (HSI) models (U.S. Fish and Wildlife Service 1981; Pearsall et al. 1986). The original idea of conservation biologists was to find a fast and reliable method to predict the occurrence of species from remote sensing data or vegetation maps. The first models were essentially algebraic calculations combining these data. With the development of software, new data sources, and computational methods, the spectrum and character of habitat models have changed since then.

Like many terms in ecology, *habitat, habitat quality,* and *habitat suitability* are used ambiguously in the literature and in practice. When these terms are used in an applied sense in connection with modeling, it is important to clarify their use. Thus, to avoid possible misunderstanding, we begin with explaining how *habitat, habitat suitability,* and *habitat model* are used in this chapter.

In a general sense habitat is described as the place where a microorganism, plant, or animal lives (Begon et al. 1996). This very general definition is certainly unsuited for formal descriptions because it hardly leads to cause–effect hypotheses concerning the occurrence of a species. According to Morrison et al. (1998, p. 10), a "habitat is an area with the combination of resources (e.g., food, cover, water) and environmental conditions (e.g., temperature, precipitation, presence or absence of predators and competitors) that promotes occupancy by individuals of a given species (or population) and allows those individuals to survive and to reproduce." This definition is better suited because it offers a natural pathway to describe habitats. But it should be added that for many species habitat is not a unique area but can be split into different parts with different functions on different spatiotemporal scales. Survival and reproduction must not be guaranteed continuously in the same area. Thus developing habitat models may mean developing models only for selected aspects of survival and reproduction. The habitat definition of Morrison et al. (1998) implicitly suggests a decomposition of habitat influence factors into different logical levels and branches that may follow the different spatial and temporal habitat components. In certain circumstances it is impossible or may not be not useful to integrate these components. To consider only one spatial or temporal part of a species habitat must not be a disadvantage if this particular one is influenced by management activities.

The basic purpose of mathematical habitat models is to establish formal links between resource conditions and a measure of habitat quality or habitat suitability. Habitat models evaluate the abiotic and biotic attributes of a habitat of a certain species. They result in ordinal classifications from unsuitable to optimal, or from 0 to 1. Because we deal with models and because of demographic and synecological factors, it is obvious that the actual occurrence of a species cannot be explained completely with the help of abiotic and biotic attributes (Schamberger and O'Neill 1986). With this in mind, habitat models classify areas in terms of their potential to be habitat.

It is impossible to completely elucidate the habitat relationships of a certain species or the dependencies between influencing factors. The reason for this is that the presence of a species in a certain environment does not necessarily imply conditions that ensure long-term survival and reproduction. Additionally, as pointed out by Pulliam (1996), suitable habitats are often unoccupied; density is not always an indicator of habitat quality. This suggests that a certain habitat suitability represents a necessary but not sufficient condition for the occurrence of species or communities. Clearly, it is always easier to formulate habitat needs than to predict sufficient habitat conditions. However large and sophisticated a habitat model may be, it remains an incomplete human reflection of reality. Therefore, although numeric values or indices are calculated, habitat models produce qualitative results.

The idea of habitat suitability based on mathematically derived indices avoids sharp separations between habitat patches and nonhabitat patches and comes closer to reality. We have continuous transitions between different habitat suitabilities. This corresponds with practical observations. Not only areas with optimal values in all resources and environmental conditions can be occupied. Under certain circumstances deficiencies in one condition can be compensated for by improvements in other conditions. Occasionally species change their reported behavior. Actually, a species' habitat usually consists not of a contiguous optimal area but of a patchwork of suboptimal areas considering the single habitat influence factors. In this way, habitat suitability is a matter of definition.

Types of Habitat Models and Application Areas

The development of habitat suitability models; that is, the description of the formal relationships between habitat suitability and environmental conditions, usually takes place in two principal ways. The first one is data guided; that is, on the basis of empirical observations of the occurrence of a species or communities and geographic or other space-related information in the vicinity of the observation points, algebraic algorithms or other empirical models are derived. This group chiefly includes univariate or multivariate statistical approaches such as discriminant analysis, logistic regression, and multidimensional scaling (Brennan et al. 1986). In recent years geostatistical approaches have also become popular (Rossi et al. 1992). The other way is guided by knowledge or theory and is based on biological information on the species. Here we find knowledge-based and artificial intelligence (AI) approaches such as expert systems, fuzzy systems, and cellular automata (Wieland et al. 1996). Artificial intelligence is a branch of computer science concerned with making computers behave like humans. Depending on the modeling goal, knowledge, and data availability, one or the other of the different ways is favored. With the increasing use of geographic information systems (GISs) in the early 1990s, habitat modeling became more common as a basis for environmental planning. With the coupling of habitat models with GIS, it became possible to ascertain and display spatially explicit habitat changes for larger regions, enabling the immediate visualization of changes within a landscape. Currently, the use of habitat models is widespread. It includes purely statistical approaches such as regression to sophisticated algorithms coupled with GIS. State-of-the-art habitat modeling is addressed in a recent article by Kleyer et al. (1999/2000).

Habitat models can be applied for theoretical or scientific purposes as well as for practical goals. With theoretical questions, habitat models offer a good opportunity to systematize and integrate different pieces of biological–ecological information. It is possible to investigate existing hypotheses and to formulate new ones concerning species–environment dependencies and processes. If one considers questions in practical situation evaluation and decision support, habitat models can provide a valuable support in investigating and forecasting the environmental effects of human interventions or conservation measures. Practical applications usually use simpler habitat models. For practical applications habitat models must provide sufficient predictive power.

Demands on Habitat Models for Practical Applications

As always in modeling there is a connection between model goal, modeling approach, and available data. For this chapter we use an approach that serves land use impact analysis and planning purposes. For these goals, the following model design criteria and contents should be kept in mind:

> The available biological–ecological knowledge and data bases for modeling species–habitat relationships come from very different sources and may be vague sometimes; observations can be subjectively influenced; accuracy statements such as significance levels are often missing; measures of dispersion are not always reliable because the statistical parent populations are not exactly differentiated; and therefore species–habitat relationships are more often qualitative than exact numeric relationships.

Habitat suitability is a relative property of landscape sections; it should be defined so that it can be displayed at an ordinal scale allowing comparisons between variants or to a standard reference.

The resulting habitat model should be transparent and easily applicable. Decision makers are interested in clear rules, so the final habitat model should evaluate different habitat conditions in an integrative fashion, and the application should lead to specific management proposals.

Model calculations should rely on measurable or reasonable exact inputs; land use changes and other possible planning impacts should be capable of representation through the variation of these model input factors.

Methodological approaches for developing habitat models must take into consideration these requirements and restrictions. Especially in situations where available data amounts are limited, there are consequences for the mathematical apparatus used. Only for a few species do we have long-run and reliable observation series.

Testing of Habitat Models and Spatiotemporal Correspondence

A general requirement for the application of a model is to evaluate its suitability for the specific purpose. The activities necessary for this are summed up under the concept of "validation," whereby the extent of the tasks to be performed should be strongly determined by the application goal. The literature on the validation of ecological models is extensive but in no way unambiguous. An overview of validation procedures is found in Rykiel (1996). Models for practical applications need not be universally valid, but their application goal should be. For example, if one considers the model only as a help to summarize the biological–ecological knowledge of a biological object exclusively for theoretical formulation, one can get by very well without practical comparisons. If, as is the case here, one considers the model primarily as a prognosis tool and planning support instrument, a practical examination is recommended before application. But one should always bear in mind that absolute validation is impossible because formerly unknown situations are derived from a limited set of existing situations.

A particular requirement for developing and applying habitat models is the necessary correspondence of the spatial and temporal reference (i.e., the spatiotemporal scale). This correspondence is twofold. If we develop a habitat model, we have to identify that spatiotemporal scale that provides the most information for the considered species and to derive appropriate variables that describe the habitat. To find this most appropriate scale means to get a maximum of output information from a minimum of input data. If we use habitat models to investigate changes in species habitats caused by alternative land use, we have to choose species whose habitats are in correspondence with the spatial dimension of the land use changes. That is, the land use, or the problem to be examined, and the indicator object chosen must correspond in terms of their spatial relation. For instance, the common crane, because of its demands with regard to space, roosts, and food, is well suited for investigating consequences of land use changes starting from the regional scale (regional planning tasks), and the fire-bellied toad (*Bombina bombina*) can more readily be used as an indicator for local, small-area effects. Ultimately, the practical application of habitat models in large areas necessitates a thematically coordinated and complete GIS database, which in many cases is a limiting criterion.

Development of Hierarchical Habitat Models with Neuro-Fuzzy Techniques

In the following sections aspects of the favored modeling approach are outlined. A more detailed description of the modeling process can be found in Schultz et al. (2000) and Lutze et al. (2002). In the model development process we emphasize the hierarchical nature of Morrison et al.'s (1998) habitat definition. We define *habitat hierarchy* as different branches and logical levels of dependencies between habitat influence factors. The branches can be understood as temporary habitats or habitat parts different in content. A higher, more aggregated influence factor is decomposed into a set of lower, more detailed influence factors. From that definition it can be derived that habitat can be defined as the hierarchically organized totality of ecological environmental factors affecting species or a community, including factors caused by the species or the community itself. The modeling approach can be briefly characterized as hierarchical, based on biological and ecological knowledge, using neuro-fuzzy techniques. The models are called neuro-fuzzy habitat models. When coupling the abstract habitat model with spatial data, spatially explicit habitat suitability values can be calculated.

Neuro-fuzzy habitat models emerge in a multistage, iterative process. Neuro-fuzzy habitat models are hybrid models that connect the concept of fuzzy models and neural networks and describe the suitability of landscapes as habitats for plants or animals. First, an initial number of influence factors is identified.

The factors are based on biological, ecological, and agricultural information and are presumed to determine the habitat. That is, changes in these factors will probably cause changes in the habitat suitability. Next, a top-down splitting of these factors into logical branches and hierarchical levels is carried out. This is followed by a preliminary quantitative description of the individual factors and their reciprocal interdependence. The resulting structure represents available knowledge and should be limited to a practical degree of detail. Using the initial model, we then investigate which factors dominate, how their interconnections affect the overall result (sensitivities), and which synergistic and compensatory effects appear. The goal is a set of results arrived at through the model approach that agrees as closely as possible with the biological knowledge of the experts and behaves as closely as possible to the actual dynamics of the system. For these investigations, fuzzy and neuro-fuzzy approaches are particularly well suited (Zadeh 1965). They allow insignificant influences to be identified and discarded. The model approach is modified step by step with the cooperation of model designers and experts from other disciplines and brought into agreement with biological–ecological scientific knowledge. The hierarchical structure should be designed so that at the lowest levels of the hierarchic branches such factors appear, which can be measured or estimated. These model inputs serve as interface variables to transform the landscape use information into relevant model variables. Figure 11.1 gives a schematic overview of the hierarchical decomposition and model input processing.

Considering the subsequent application in planning practices, the model structure should be kept as simple as possible to handle data-poor situations. The initial number of influence factors should be small, with more and more detail added as needed. More variables may have to be added, or constants turned into variables, before the model suits its objective. More complexity is no assurance of smaller errors and better reality match. Figure 11.2 gives an overview of the main steps of habitat model development and application. Model verification and validation are achieved by iterative runs through the steps of the model development stage.

Selected Modeling Steps

Given the heterogeneous nature of biological–ecological knowledge (different sources, degree of uncertainty, subjective influence) mathematical-cybernetic approaches that can deal with this are needed. Neuro, fuzzy, and combined techniques have proven to be very suitable for this. For the preliminary quantification of the qualitative model, feedforward neural networks using

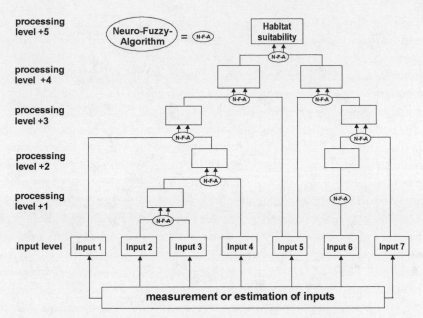

Figure 11.1 Principle of factor decomposition and input processing in neuro-fuzzy habitat models.

the backpropagation learning algorithm are applied (Freeman 1994). A neural network is a computational algorithm composed of mathematically defined elements that are thought to approximate the working of biological neurons. Neural networks contain a series of nodes connected with directed edges that are organized in three classes of layers (input, hidden, and output layers). Neural networks can be trained to provide the right output if enough empirical input–output patterns are available and if these patterns effectively describe the system to be modeled. A feedforward network is a mode of input processing often used in neural networks. Calculation takes place in one direction successively from inputs to outputs. A backpropagation algorithm is used to train complex, multilayer neural networks. Input vectors and the corresponding target vectors are used to train a network until it can approximate a function, associate input vectors with specific output vectors, or classify input vectors in an appropriate way as defined by the user. Properly trained backpropagation networks tend to give reasonable answers when presented with new inputs, making them useful for prediction.

According to the presumed habitat structure, it is in principle possible to construct a hierarchy of neural networks where the influence factors of a lower hierarchical level serve as inputs for an influence factor of the next

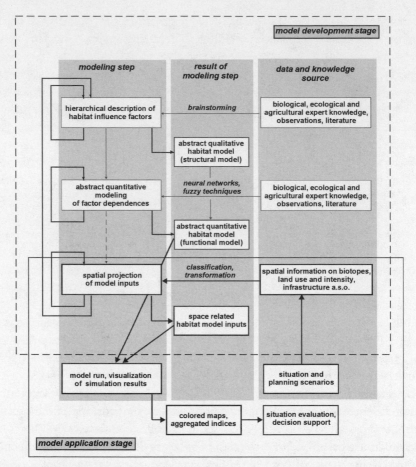

Figure 11.2 Conceptual framework of habitat model development and application.

upper level (see Fig. 11.1). On the uppermost hierarchical level, an overall value of habitat suitability is calculated. To train the algorithms in the different processing levels it is necessary to transform biological knowledge into numerical values. These numerical values serve as network inputs together with firm biological–ecological measurements. An advantage of using neural networks in this stage of model development is the ability to be retrained if new knowledge becomes available.

But combining a too large series of backpropagation networks for a multilevel hierarchy of influence factors can cover up desired different reaction patterns. This is especially true for the representation of so-called elementary processes; that is, for the designation of habitat relationships at the lower hierarchical levels (e.g., the connection between area size and the food supply of birds). Here it is effective to use fuzzy technology instead of backpropagation networks. With fuzzy components it is easier to consider known biological–ecological experience, such as typical threshold value behavior. At a certain threshold value or at class boundaries, a very sensitive reaction is observable (i.e., slight changes in a key influence factor or in the key variable of a complex of influences can cause a dramatic change in different key condition variable, whereas otherwise a less precipitous behavior is observed).

The disadvantage of fuzzy models compared with neural networks is their inability to "learn." New data cannot be included as easily as in neural networks. But this drawback can be weakened if the fuzzy model is converted into a network representation. One possibility is shown by Schultz and Wieland (1997). A fuzzy model is a mathematical model based on fuzzy set theory. Fuzzy set theory (fuzzy sets and fuzzy logic) implements classes or groupings of data with boundaries that are not sharply defined (i.e., fuzzy). In fuzzy models, general linguistic terms such as *large, medium,* and *small* can be used to capture a range of numerical values. Fuzzy set theory provides a simple way to draw definite conclusions from vague, ambiguous, or imprecise information. In a sense, fuzzy set theory resembles human decision making with its ability to work from approximate data and find precise solutions. Fuzzy models are useful in ecological modeling because ecological problems inevitably entail some degree of imprecision and noise in the variables and parameters measured and processed for the application.

The desired behavior improvement of the pure network model is finally reached by combining fuzzy and neuro techniques in a single model approach. At higher levels of the factor hierarchy, where complex influences are combined, neural networks are used. These show a more continuous and equalizing behavior. Influences can mutually compensate in parts. At lower hierarchical levels fuzzy models are favored. These show a more differentiated response to thresholds. Here compensation is not important because one resource or environmental condition may predominate the whole process. All in all, the combination approach is characterized by both desired qualities of ecological system models: compensation capability and steplike behavior.

Model Examples

Several habitat or population models exist for northeast German animals. These models were developed within several collaborative research projects.

Within an integrated nature conservation research project for the Biosphere Reserve Schorfheide-Chorin in the Federal State of Brandenburg (Germany), habitat models for the barn owl (*Tyto alba*), the common crane, and the fire-bellied toad were developed according to the neuro-fuzzy approach. The habitat models were developed to present conflict situations between land use and nature conservation and to develop management strategies to avoid or at least to mitigate negative impacts of land use. The goals of the whole project and the biological–ecological background of the habitat models are presented by Flade (2002).

Within an integrated research project to investigate the impact of land-scape fragmentation on animal populations, habitat models for the common crane, the white-tailed eagle (*Haliaeetus albicilla*), and the European badger (*Meles meles*) were developed according to the well-known HSI approach (U.S. Fish and Wildlife Service 1981; Baier et al. 2002). Moreover, population models were developed for the European badger and the Eurasian otter (*Lutra lutra*). In this project the impact of roads and other human activities on vertebrate animals with large spatial needs was the focus of interest. The aim of the study was to develop a new strategy of nature conservation as an alternative to the traditional strategy of habitat connection.

Model Applications

In the following sections three typical application examples are discussed, illustrating the use of the habitat models. Using habitat models in different contexts can help answer quite different questions. Depending on the species of concern and the spatial scale of causes and effects, special conservation goals, general infrastructure impact assessments, or local integrity effects can be addressed. The first example, which is presented in the most detail, shows how a habitat model can be used to determine the changes in habitat suitability resulting from local influences. The second example hints at the potentials of habitat models to display conflicting conservation goals and help in decision making. The third example deals with local effects of large-scale changes.

Habitat Models for Analyzing Single-Species Conservation Goals

In ecology it is necessary to consider interspecies relationships as well as landscape processes when management measures are planned. But in conservation often the practice is to consider only one favorite target species.

We used the common crane, which is a protected bird species in Germany. The common crane model was developed and validated in the integrated nature conservation research project for the Biosphere Reserve Schorfheide-Chorin (Flade 2002). In the case of common cranes we distinguish between reproduction and resting habitats. Essential habitat-influencing factors for breeding cranes are the landscape water regime (which is closely coupled to the amount of small water bodies), a sufficient supply of cover (preferably woods or wood lots), a good foraging situation, and the availability of areas without disturbance by agricultural or human leisure activities. For cranes migrating from Scandinavia to Spain, suitable sleeping locations and foraging areas are the decisive influence factors. The biological and ecological bases for the common crane habitat model are described in depth by Wilkening (2002). Under German and European law, identification and protection of special protected areas for breeding and migrating common cranes are required. For a landscape in northeast Germany we investigate how two different uses of arable land would influence the habitat suitability for breeding and resting common cranes.

Initial Situation

Fig. 11.3A shows the landscape south of Neubrandenburg that we evaluated. It is part of the young Pleistocene landscape of northeast Germany and shows large, mostly unfragmented areas and a comparatively low intensity of anthropogenic use and therefore is different from most regions in western Germany. The population density is very low compared with the German average (20 people/km^2 versus 230 people/km^2). Because of its diversity and agricultural use patterns, the landscape offers habitats for a great variety of plants and animals, including several threatened animals such as the common crane. The prevailing agricultural crops are winter and spring cereals, oilseed rape, grassland, and legume and root crops. Because of current agricultural policy, up to 10 percent of the agricultural area is set aside for market relief.

Areas where common cranes occur in this landscape are shown in Fig. 11.3B. A tremendous part of potential habitat is occupied by breeding cranes. Current agricultural policies suggest that land use patterns will be changing in the near future. One example is the decline of root crop cultivation. This area will be used for other crops, set aside, or used for human leisure purposes. The resulting foraging and disturbance situations will certainly influence the potential breeding and resting habitats. The question is whether the economically motivated land use change is compatible with

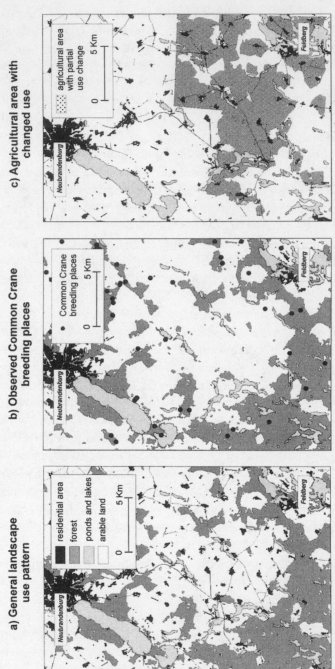

a) General landscape use pattern

residential area
forest
ponds and lakes
arable land

0   5 Km

Neubrandenburg

Feldberg

b) Observed Common Crane breeding places

● Common Crane breeding places

0   5 Km

Neubrandenburg

Feldberg

c) Agricultural area with changed use

agricultural area with partial use change

0   5 Km

Neubrandenburg

Feldberg

Figure 11.3   Use pattern, observed common crane breeding places, and agricultural area with potential for changes in use.

habitat preservation. Using the common crane habitat model we investigate how the decline and the total cessation of root crop cultivation might influence potential habitat suitability. From the whole landscape we selected a smaller agricultural part (Fig. 11.3C) and assumed a distribution of crops from the early 1990s. Root crops (potatoes and sugar beets) are grown on about 4.5 percent of the area. We then applied two scenarios to this agricultural area.

Scenario 1: Increasing the Cereal and Grassland Share

In this scenario the percentage of winter cereals and of grassland was increased. On two thirds of the area winter cereals were simulated, and on one third of the substitution area grassland was grown. The former root crop areas were randomly occupied with cereals or grassland. From the habitat model, continuous suitability values in the interval from 0 to 1 were calculated. To give a better interpretable visual impression of the distribution of habitat suitability values, the continuous values were classified. On the basis of expert experience, four classes were derived (unsuitable, bad, acceptable, very good). The two upper classes include areas where potentially favorable conditions are present.

Scenario 2: No Cultivation of Root Crops, Grassland Favored

In this scenario the growing of root crops is stopped completely in favor of grassland. Fig. 11.4 summarizes the changes in breeding habitats resulting from both the scenarios compared with the initial situation. The region where the changes are recognizable is marked. The share of potentially favorable habitats decreases from about 4 percent to 2.7 percent for scenario 1 and 2.4 percent for scenario 2. This is caused primarily by a decrease in the area of the acceptable habitats.

Fig. 11.5 summarizes the changes in resting habitats. The region where the changes are recognizable is marked again. Here the share of better resting habitats decreases from 4.6 to 3.4 percent for scenario 1 and to 3.1 percent for scenario 2. The class of acceptable habitats is again most influenced. Although different factor dependencies are influenced, both the breeding and the resting habitat suitability deteriorate. But the proportion of area where habitat suitability is influenced is less than the proportion of area where crop growth is changed. This suggests that part of the changes resulting from potential foraging is compensated by other factors independent of the mode of agricultural production. To some extent it is possible to identify compensatory effects. We further conclude that improvements of overall habitat suitability can be reached by changes in agricultural production (improved foraging, less disturbance) or by changes in factors outside the real agricultural areas (small water bodies, wood lots). As far as common crane habitat suitability is concerned, fundamentally no insoluble conflicts exist between the habitat needs of common cranes and agricultural needs. Temporary and local conflicts that have occurred in practice are largely controllable through intelligent agrarian land management.

Habitat Suitability and Improvement of Landscape and Infield Structures

The switch to industrial agricultural production methods in the former East Germany until 1989 was accompanied by the enlargement of fields under cultivation and by a tremendous reduction of woodlots and other structural elements. This caused a reduction of biodiversity (Flade 2002). Now conservationists are demanding an increase of such structural elements within open agricultural areas to help increase biodiversity.

Using the common crane habitat model, we investigated the impact of an increase of structural elements on common crane populations. A moderate extension of structural elements had practically   ,nificant influence on the habitat properties. We observed a deteriorating effect on the breeding and resting habitats of cranes as field size was decreased by hedgerows and other elements that obstructed visibility.

It is true that the increase of hedgerows leads to a striking increase of habitats for potential hedgerow-dwelling species including birds. But this narrowing of visibility results in avoidance by common cranes (Wilkening 2002). This example shows the potential conflicting habitat demands of infield animals and suggests that well-meant management activities for one species may lead to unintended negative consequences for other species. In such cases habitat models can help to identify otherwise difficult to determine but contradictory consequences and provides a mechanism for balancing them.

Effects of Large-Scale Changes on Local Habitats

Anthropogenic landscapes in northeast Germany are currently experiencing an increasing water shortage, primarily in spring. On the whole, it is the result of far-reaching water-related activities over a period of more than 300 years with heavy activities in the eighteenth and twentieth centuries. To

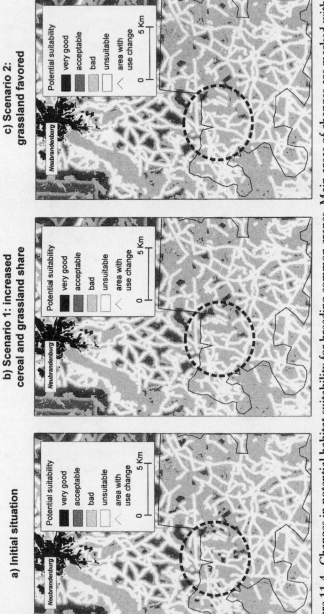

Figure 11.4 Changes in potential habitat suitability for breeding common cranes. Main areas of changes are marked with a dashed circle.

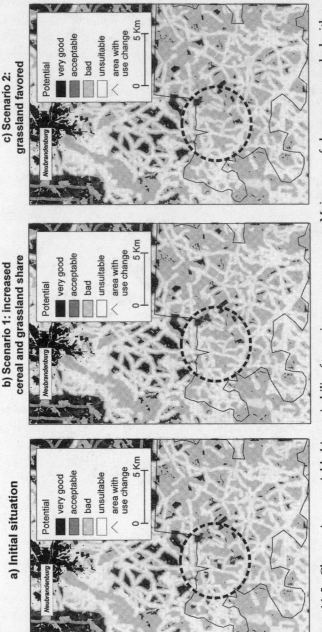

Figure 11.5   Changes in potential habitat suitability for resting common cranes. Main areas of changes are marked with a dashed circle.

increase the proportion of arable land, the water discharge in wetlands was regulated and numerous small water bodies were drained. Now there are plans to reverse these measures to revive more natural landscape hydrodynamics. The question is what effects these large-scale dynamics in water levels have on the local species.

Model calculations showed that a longer retention of precipitation water in the landscape especially influences the water level of temporary small water bodies. This is a very sensitive aspect of common crane reproduction habitat. The duration of water in the widespread, infield potholes decisively influences the suitability of these places as breeding sites. A longer-lasting and sufficiently high water table offers a high degree of security against predators in the vicinity of breeding places.

Altogether, prolonging the persistence of water in infield potholes, which formerly had water only temporarily, contributes to making these places suitable habitats for common cranes. Area analyses show that the area of suitable reproduction habitats could increase by about 15 percent and lead to a sustainable improvement of habitat conditions.

Conclusions

To demonstrate better pathways to use landscape-related research results in practical situation evaluation, planning and decision support is undoubtedly an important current and future challenge of applied landscape research. The lessons learned from models can give valuable hints and can lead to practical planning tools. With the help of these tools it is possible to better visualize planning variants and detect critical points for intervention.

To investigate impacts on biotic landscape elements habitat models seem to provide the elements of a promising toolkit:

Habitat models can be valuable tools to sort out and systematize species-related biological and ecological knowledge; with their help habitat properties can be explicitly located spatially, quantified, and clearly displayed.

From the methodological point of view, neuro-fuzzy techniques in connection with GIS have turned out to be suitable quantitative approaches in habitat modeling, although there is no unique or best approach; different approaches can coexist.

Habitat models open new possibilities for model-based complex landscape analysis in both research and practical application; in landscape planning it becomes possible to ascertain risk potentials with regard to habitat suitability arising from human interventions in landscapes and to avoid recommendations whose outcomes are vague or unclear.

Experience shows that habitat models may contribute to a better understanding of species–environment relationships and to a more objective analysis of habitat demands of one or conflicting habitat demands of different animal species.

The well-founded application of habitat models makes high demands on spatial data provision and quality; for practically used habitat models it is therefore advisable to limit the data demand to a manageable extent or to use data that are available in the planning process. To ensure the reliability of later model predictions, it is necessary to choose appropriate methodological modeling approaches.

To get a comprehensive picture of potential impacts of landscape interventions, it is crucial to distinguish between habitat models for different spatial and organizational landscape levels. It may be a goal to develop a set of habitat models for all relevant spatial planning levels (landscape planning scale 1:10,000–1:25,000; regional planning scale 1:50,000–1:200,000; state development planning scale 1:300,000–1:600,000).

Although it may be necessary to develop new habitat models to address a wider scale of impacts, the full application of existing habitat models has by no means been explored completely; we need also to provide these models to educate landscape planners and other specialists.

From the viewpoint of science, habitat models help to formalize the qualitative concept of biological integrity and to disseminate biological–ecological research results.

Summary

Habitat models are promising tools to investigate impacts on biotic landscape elements. This chapter discusses some fundamentals for developing habitat models and some specific criteria for applying them to situation evaluation and planning support. A special modeling approach that uses neuro-fuzzy techniques is briefly outlined. Three applications of the common crane habitat model exemplify different application aspects of habitat models.

Acknowledgments

This work was supported by the German Federal Ministry of Consumer Protection, Food and Agriculture (BMVEL), the German Federal Ministry of Education and Research (BMBF) project number 0339541, and the Ministry of Agriculture, Environmental Protection and Regional Planning of the Federal State of Brandenburg (MLUR).

LITERATURE CITED

Baier, H., R. Holz, A. Waterstraat, K. Billwitz, F. Erdmann, M. Roth, J. Ulbricht, and R. Klenke. 2002. Freiraum und Naturschutz: die Wirkungen von Störungen und Zerschneidungen in der Landschaft (Open space and nature conservation: the impact of disturbations and dissections in landscape). Springer-Verlag, Berlin.

Begon, M., J. L. Harper, and C. R. Townsend. 1996. Ecology: individuals, populations and communities. Blackwell Science, London.

Brennan, L. A., W. M. Block, and R. J. Guttiérrez. 1986. The use of multivariate statistics for developing habitat suitability index models. Pages 177–182 in J. Verner, M. L. Morrison, and C. J. Ralph (eds.), Wildlife 2000: modeling habitat relationships of terrestrial vertebrates. University of Wisconsin Press, Madison.

Flade, M. (ed.). 2002. Nature conservation in agricultural ecosystems. Quelle & Meyer, Wiebelsheim, Germany.

Freeman, J. A. 1994. Simulating neural networks with Mathematica. Addison-Wesley, Reading, MA.

Kleyer, M., R. Kratz, G. Lutze, and B. Schröder. 1999/2000. Habitatmodelle für Tierarten: Entwicklung, Methoden und Perspektiven für die Anwendung (Habitat models for animal species: development, methods and perspectives for application). Zeitschrift für Ökologie und Naturschutz 8:177–194.

Lutze, G., R. Wieland, and A. Schultz. 2002. Habitat models: instruments for the integrative representation and analysis of habitat demands directly related to landscape structure and land use. In M. Flade (ed.), Nature conservation in agricultural ecosystems. Quelle & Meyer, Wiebelsheim, Germany.

Morrison, M. L., B. G. Marcot, and R. W. Mannan. 1998. Wildlife–habitat relationships: concepts and applications. University of Wisconsin Press, Madison.

Pearsall, S. H., D. Durham, and D. C. Eagar. 1986. Evaluation methods in the United States. Pages 111–133 in M. B. Usher (ed.), Wildlife conservation evaluation. Chapman & Hall, London.

Pulliam, H. R. 1996. Sources and sinks: empirical evidence and population consequences. Pages 45–69 in O. E. Rhodes, R. K. Chesser, and M. H. Smith (eds.), Population dynamics in ecological space and time. University of Chicago Press, Chicago.

Rossi, R. E., D. J. Mulla, A. G. Journel, and E. H. Franz. 1992. Geostatistical tools for modeling and interpreting ecological spatial dependence. Ecological Monographs 62:277–314.

Rykiel, E. J., Jr. 1996. Testing ecological models: the meaning of validation. Ecological Modelling 90:229–240.

Schamberger, M. L., and L. J. O'Neill. 1986. Concepts and constraints of habitat-model testing. Pages 5–10 in J. Verner, M. L. Morrison, and C. J. Ralph (eds.), Wildlife 2000: modeling habitat relationships of terrestrial vertebrates. University of Wisconsin Press, Madison.

Schultz, A., and R. Wieland. 1997. The use of neural networks in agroecological modelling. Computers and Electronics in Agriculture 18:73–90.

Schultz, A., R. Wieland, and G. Lutze. 2000. Neural networks in agroecological modelling: stylish application or helpful tool? Computers and Electronics in Agriculture 29:73–97.

U.S. Fish and Wildlife Service. 1981. Standards for the development of habitat suitability index models. U.S. Fish and Wildlife Services, Washington, DC.

Wieland, R., G. Lutze, and J. Hoffmann. 1996. Fuzzy-Methoden und Neuronale Netze in der Landschaftsmodellierung. Pages 50–59 in H. B. Keller, R. Grützner, and R. Hohmann (eds.), Werkzeuge für Simulation und Modellbildung in Umweltwissenschaften. Forschungszentrum, Karlsruhe, Germany.

Wilkening, B. 2002. Common crane (Grus grus Linnaeus, 1758). In M. Flade (ed.), Nature conservation in agricultural ecosystems. Quelle & Meyer, Wiebelsheim, Germany.

Zadeh, L. A. 1965. Fuzzy sets. Information and Control 8:338–353.

CHAPTER TWELVE

A Park Is Not an Island

Linking Different Wildlife Management Strategies in the Area of Lake Mburo National Park, Uganda

CHRISTIANE AVERBECK

Terborgh (1999, p. 59) stated that national parks are the last bastions of nature, but "few are large enough to maintain healthy populations of top predators. A majority of parks exist only on paper, having no staff whatsoever. Most are poorly designed, the boundaries having been drawn in such a way as to make them indefensible against encroachment. A great many have people living within them. A significant number are already seriously degraded by illegal activity. Some no longer exist in a biological sense." Lake Mburo National Park (LMNP) in Uganda (Fig. 12.1) is a good case in point: At 260 km^2, the park is not large enough to maintain viable populations of top predators such as lions (*Panthera leo*), leopards (*Panthera pardus*), and hyenas (*Crocuta crocuta*); staffing is insufficient; the park is arbitrarily drawn; fishers are living in the park; pastoralists graze illegally in the park; and hunters poach wild animals. But the processes of habitat degradation, encroachment, poaching, and poor management of LMNP and environs did not begin recently; they started decades ago.

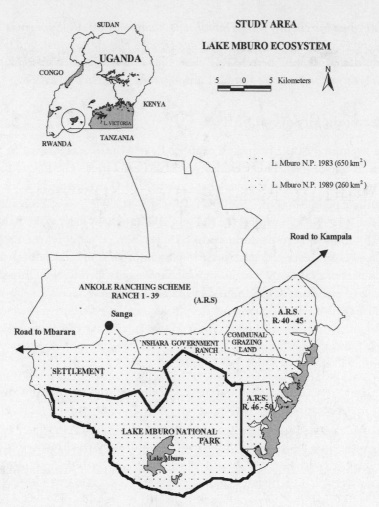

Figure 12.1 Lake Mburo area in Uganda.

Lake Mburo National Park

LMNP is situated in southwestern Uganda, in Mbarara District, Nyabua-hozi County, near the Equator. LMNP is a biologically diverse area that is part of the Akagera ecosystem, which covers parts of northern Rwanda and Tanzania and southwestern Uganda and is characterized by thickets, *Combretum* and *Acacia* woodlands, and wetlands. Various parts of the ecosystem are protected: Akagera National Park in Rwanda, Ibanda Game Reserve in Tanzania, and LMNP in Uganda. At LMNP, large mammal species include zebra (*Equus burchelii*), topi (*Damaliscus lunatus*), buffalo (*Syncercus caffer*), eland (*Taurotragus oryx*), waterbuck (*Kobus ellipsiprymnus*), and hippo (*Hippopotamus amphibius*). LMNP is the only area of Uganda where impala (*Aepyceros melampus*) are found (Lamprey and Michelmore 1996).

Conservation History of LMNP

At the beginning of the twentieth century, Lake Mburo was known to naturalists as one of the premier wildlife areas in East Africa. The Lake Mburo ecosystem included large areas that constituted the grazing land of the Banyankole people and their Ankole cattle. The ethnic group of Banyankole is divided into two subgroups, the Bahima and Bawiru. Whereas the Bahima by tradition have been pastoralists have never hunted wildlife, the Bawiru have been cultivators and have occasionally hunted. The Lake Mburo area formed part of the Nkore Kingdom, which was controlled by the Omugabe, the king of the Banyankole. The Omugabe controlled access to the land around Lake Mburo, allowing his people to graze their cattle only in times of drought. By tradition he had to be a Muhima (singular for Bahima), and because hunting has not been part of the tradition of the Bahima, there was no hunting in the Lake Mburo area. In the first decades of the twentieth century, an outbreak of the cattle disease rinderpest decimated the Bahima's herds. Livestock numbers took 20 years to recover, and competition between wildlife and cattle was low during this time (Snelson and Wilson 1994).

In 1935, the area around Lake Mburo was declared a Controlled Hunting Area by the British colonial government. The British colonial government permitted both regulated big-game hunting and traditional human activities. As professional hunter B. Herne (1979, p. 81) put it, "Lake Mburo is a most interesting beautiful place with a wide variety of terrain from the short grass plains, lightly wooded hills and in the east the long narrow Lake Kachira. . . . Lake Mburo is a natural game paradise for one reason only: the dreaded tsetse fly (*Glossina* sp.) The tsetse fly is a carrier of trypanosome that causes sleeping sickness. The tsetse fly which occurred at Lake Mburo was fatal to all domestic stock but inflicted painful bites on humans without proving fatal. . . . The natural barrier against man's exploitation of Lake Mburo accounted for the vast stocks of game found there, wild animals having developed immunity to trypanosomiasis."

In the 1940s, a severe outbreak of sleeping sickness and nagana (a form of sleeping sickness found in cattle) carried by tsetse fly forced pastoralists out of the area. However, many of the farmers and fishers remained. Tsetse flies need two basic resources to persist in an area: shade and blood. It was assumed that if all shade and wild animals were removed, then the tsetse fly would be eradicated. The United States funded a drastic tsetse eradication program of spraying, bush burning and cutting, and shooting, which severely reduced game populations. Entire herds of eland, topi, and buffalo were slaughtered. Only a few animals survived.

By the early 1960s, tsetse had been eradicated, once again opening up the area to pastoralists. To protect the remaining wildlife, the newly independent Ugandan government gazetted the Lake Mburo Game Reserve. All forms of use except controlled hunting were banned, although resident farmers were permitted to remain. The government of Uganda decided that ranching was the best use for this dry and sparsely populated land. Plans were made and activities initiated with the main objective of ensuring "rapid and radical" development through livestock husbandry on commercially productive and economically viable beef cattle ranches (Kamugisha and Ståhl 1993). Establishment of the Ankole Ranching Scheme to the north pushed more pastoralists into the game reserve, and large blocks of land were excised from the reserve to form more government and private ranches (Snelson and Wilson 1994).

In 1983, the Obote government established the LMNP within the boundaries of the original game reserve. The park comprised an area of 650 km^2 (see Fig. 12.1). LMNP was established without the consent of local people and involved their forced removal. This was perceived as a major injustice and turned many people against the park, and when the Obote government weakened, former settlers in the area returned and destroyed the park facilities. By 1986, the entire park was again occupied by settlers. To resolve the conflict, a government task force was established and decided that the park should remain but be reduced in area by 60 percent to 260 km^2 (Snelson and Wilson 1994).

LMNP Today

The LMNP today is directly bordered by farm and ranch land; the park has no buffer zone. Pastoralists and cultivators live on its periphery. Between 1980 and 2000, human population growth of 2.7 percent per year in the region adjacent to LMNP reduced the area to a remnant of what was formerly a much more extensive wildlife area. The pastoral Bahima and their cattle have roamed throughout the region for centuries. However, the reduction in size and availability of former communal rangelands outside the park caused by privatization and cultivation of land has confined pastoralists to an area that is too small to support the numbers of cattle needed to sustain their lifestyle. The result has been overstocking and range deterioration. The pressure on people to develop new and sustainable forms of land use is intense (Averbeck 2001).

Historically the prevailing approach of conservation authorities toward local communities was simply to keep them out of the protected areas. Emphasis was on strict protection, and as a result hunting was banned even outside the park. In the late 1980s and early 1990s this policy changed. With the support of foreign donors, community conservation programs in the form of protected area outreach programs were established in parts of Uganda. Wildlife managers realized that relationships between rural resource users and conservation agencies were a prerequisite for building sustainable community systems (Barrow et al. 1995). Established community conservation units, which worked in areas adjacent to protected reserves, instituted a process of dialogue and problem solving. However, this approach was not as successful as hoped (Hulme and Infield 2001; Infield and Namara 2001). Formal environmental education, capacity building, and support for community development have not stopped the local communities from using wildlife in an unsustainable manner inside and outside the park.

Wildlife Conservation Policy in Uganda

Political instability in Uganda has resulted in decades of uncontrolled wildlife exploitation in the Lake Mburo area, leading to the depletion of what were once significant resources. Uganda National Parks and the Game Department were the two agencies nominally responsible for managing wildlife in the country. With the passing of the new Uganda Wildlife Statute in 1996, the management of the protected area network became the responsibility of a single organization, the Uganda Wildlife Authority (UWA). UWA is responsible for conserving and managing all wildlife within and outside protected areas. Because of a lack of funding and staff, UWA lacks the capacity to manage wildlife outside protected areas.

Under the Uganda Wildlife Statute of 1996, new mechanisms were established to enable local communities to manage their wildlife rather than having wildlife management imposed from outside. The statute created a new entity: wildlife management areas. Wildlife management areas may be occupied by people but are areas where wildlife conservation are promoted. One category of wildlife management area is called a community wildlife area (CWA). With permission from the UWA, communities benefit directly from wildlife conservation and use activities. The effective management of CWAs, coupled with community wildlife use and other management strategies, can help protect resources in the park and also in a larger area around LMNP.

The Lake Mburo Wildlife Use Study

Within the framework of this new policy, sustainable wildlife use was discussed as an option of integrating rural communities and wildlife conservation by UWA. With financial support from the Gesellschaft für Technische Zusammenarbeit (GTZ), I obtained information on wildlife populations and the attitudes of the communities. I then developed recommendations for a community-based wildlife use scheme. My goal was to assess whether sustainable use of wildlife was a viable solution for integrating rural communities and wildlife conservation. I assumed that if indigenous Ugandan land owners living around LMNP were able to derive tangible and legitimate benefits from the wildlife on their land, they would have an incentive to protect wildlife from poachers and might be more efficient than government agencies.

Wildlife Populations

To obtain information on population dynamics, density, distribution, and movements of the large mammal population, I conducted three aerial surveys, systematic reconnaissance flights, and monthly ground counts along 150 km of tracks in the area during 1997 to 1999 (Norton-Griffiths 1978). These data were needed to develop recommendations for a wildlife use scheme. The aerial surveys and ground counts indicated that populations of large mammals in the Lake Mburo area were on the decline. The most common species were impala and zebra. The number of impalas decreased from around 7,000 to 3,000 individuals in the period from 1995 to 1999 (Lamprey and Michelmore 1996). The zebra population has remained roughly stable for several years at about 3,000 animals. The local people were very reluctant to hunt zebra, and very few animals were taken by poachers. The population estimates for other large mammals ranged between 150 and 1,000 for the whole area (Table 12.1). According to Lamprey and Michelmore (1996), aerial survey population estimates of less common species in 1995 are not reliable. Therefore, I will not elucidate population trends.

Table 12.1 Population estimates for 1995 and 1999, estimated quotas, and prices of a trophy hunting scheme in the Lake Mburo area, Uganda.

Species	Population 1995[a]	Population 1999[b]	% Off-Take	Quota	Price ($US)	($US) Total
Buffalo (*Syncerus caffer*)	25	500	3	13	600	7,800
Bushbuck (*Tragelaphus scriptus*)	152	500	3	15	500	7,500
Duiker (*Sylvicapra grimmia*)	44	150	0			
Eland (*Taurotragus oryx*)	273	500	3	15	850	12,750
Impala (*Aecyperos melampus*)	6,599	3,000	2	45	275	12,375
Leopard (*Panthera pardus*)	?	?	?	2	2,500	5,000
Oribi (*Ourebia ourebia*)	?	250	0			
Reedbuck (*Redunca redunca wardi*)	140	150	0			
Topi (*Damaliscus lunatus*)	57	400	2	8	500	4,000
Warthog (*Pachochoerus aethiopicus*)	571	1,000	3	30	300	9,000
Waterbuck (*Kob ellipsiprymnus*)	241	500	3	15	500	7,500
Zebra (*Equus burchelli*)	2,430	3,000	2	45	600	27,000
Total						92,925

[a]Lamprey and Michelmore, 1996 (aerial surveys).
[b]Averbeck unpublished data (aerial surveys and ground counts).

Leopards were seen regularly outside and inside the park, but their numbers remained unknown. Spotted hyenas, black-backed jackals (*Canis mesomelas*), and common jackals (*Canis aureus*) occurred in small numbers. Elephants (*Loxodonta africana*), wild dogs (*Lycaon pictus*), and lions were extirpated from LMNP some two to three decades ago (Guard 1991).

Indigenous Communities

To obtain information and evaluate attitudes on wildlife use from the indigenous Ugandan communities owning land around LMNP, I conducted 28 interviews with 340 people in focus groups. Focus group interviews showed that communities did not appreciate wildlife (Averbeck 2001). Although they did not object to the existence of wild animals in the protected area, everybody (100 percent) interviewed disliked wild animals on their land. Depending on the economic activities of the various groups interviewed, they complained about wildlife-related problems such as competition with domestic animals for salt, water, and pasture; disease transmission; broken fences; and raided crops. For cultural reasons most land owners living adjacent to the park neither hunted nor were interested in hunting (62 percent). However, 73 percent did not object to people from other ethnic groups, including non-Ugandans, harvesting wildlife. Some (20 percent) welcomed poachers from other areas on their land because they reduced the numbers of animals, 33 percent resented the sense of insecurity they introduced, and 47 percent had mixed feelings toward poachers. In general, land owners were willing to organize themselves to obtain permission to use wildlife on their property for their own benefit. However nobody was aware of or understood the opportunities presented by sustainable wildlife use. At the same time, poachers realized that the numbers of wild animals were decreasing. They were concerned about opportunities to hunt in the future and stated that they would welcome a wildlife use scheme if they could be involved.

Raising Interest: The Kenya Study Tour

In June 2000 I traveled to Kenya with eight land owners of the Ankole Ranching Scheme (ARS), five staff members of the UWA, an environmental journalist, two meat-processing experts from the Uganda Meat Technology Centre, and one veterinarian from the Wildlife and Animal Resource Management (WARM) Department, Makerere University, Kampala. We visited existing wildlife use and conservation projects, a research center, a lodge, and a cultural village run by communities in Kenya, Laikipia District. The visit and discussions with Kenyan community members and staff of Kenya Wildlife Service involved in community wildlife projects exposed the participants to the real problems and opportunities of wildlife use and conservation projects.

At the end of the study tour land owners from Nyabushozi formed an interim steering committee. They chose one participant as chairperson. Other land owners, the Community Conservation Unit of LMNP, and participants of the study tour became members of the steering committee. The committee will organize follow-up meetings in Nyabushozi with other community members to share their experiences. After the ideas have been presented and the communities have responded, the steering committee will decide, together with other community members, whether community wildlife use is a viable option for Nyabushozi. They then will discuss how to proceed.

Testing the Market

In 1998, 100 impalas were cropped for research purposes to generate information on the health status of the animals, methods and techniques of culling, and potential returns from wildlife cropping in the LMNP area. The exercise was carried out in collaboration with Uganda Meat Technology Centre, Kampala, and the WARM Department of Makerere University, Kampala. The UWA granted permission to market the wildlife products under strict conditions for a limited time (Averbeck 2001).

The returns from the cropping of 100 impalas produced about US$100 per carcass. This income was 10 times higher than from illegally sold impalas when wildlife products were properly processed and marketed. However, the resource base in the Lake Mburo area is limited. An investment estimated at US$100,000 and requiring the culling of 200 impala (10 percent of the impala population outside the park) might generate a net income of less than US$8,000; clearly this is not viable. Even if moderate numbers of other species such as zebra were cropped in addition to impala, the income generated probably would not justify the investment. However, trophy hunting can generate much more income while removing fewer animals (see Table 12.1). As a rough estimate, US$90,000 could be collected for trophy fees and an additional US$80,000 could be realized from hunting packages that included accommodation, guides, transportation, and trophy fees.

Wildlife Management Strategies in the Lake Mburo Area

An assessment of the impact of anthropogenic threats on 93 protected areas in 22 tropical countries including LMNP by Bruner et al. (2001) showed that parks are more effective at mitigating some impacts than others. Parks are in a far better condition than their surroundings with respect to land clearing, with the majority of parks being intact or only slightly cleared. Habitat loss by land alteration and clearing is arguably the most serious threat to biodiversity. Tropical parks have been surprisingly effective at protecting the ecosystems and species within their borders despite chronic underfunding and significant land use pressure. Even in the Lake Mburo area, the park is in better condition than the surrounding farmland and ranchland. Although LMNP is small, conservation works. Populations of topi, eland, and warthog increased recently, especially inside the park.

However, if we accept a minimum population size of 50 individuals to preserve demographic viability and 500 to maintain genetic variation and genetic adaptability in mammals (Frankel 1983), the populations of most species in LMNP (buffalo, bushbuck, duiker, eland, oribi, topi, and waterbuck) are already threatened (see Table 12.1). The large mammal populations of LMNP are all well below 500 individuals. Most of the species' populations are found in the park and the ranches. It is clear that protecting the park without regard for the surrounding landscape is insufficient to serve the well-being of the wildlife species and their habitats in LMNP.

Conservation and Use

One approach UWA might consider is to conserve wildlife in the Lake Mburo area. First, law enforcement work is the central feature of Ugandan conservation practice and has been moderately successful. But the present number of rangers involved in law enforcement activities is too small to cover the area inside and outside LMNP. Only UWA has the means and resources to conduct an effective antipoaching program inside the park. Tourism is the main source of income for the parks, but the number of tourists traveling to Uganda in general and LMNP specifically is low. In the last years LMNP has had less than 10,000 visitors per year. The income generated from the park entrance fees is hardly sufficient to pay staff salaries and operating costs. Therefore, UWA probably will not be able to employ more staff in the near future to ensure the protection of the wildlife outside the protected area.

Second, despite significant policy changes and practical actions, the UWA retains a protectionist culture, and ideas about a more proactive approach to the communities that neighbor protected areas have only recently begun to filter through to the majority of rangers and wardens. Moreover, the U.S. Agency for International Development (USAID)-funded community conservation program in the communities living adjacent to the park has not helped to stop illegal hunting inside or outside the park because illegal hunters originate primarily from outside the program area. The community conservation program has not altered significantly the cost–benefit equation for communities around the park. Most projects supported have been to construct social infrastructure. Because of their communal nature, individuals may not necessarily perceive them as direct benefits (Infield and Namara 2001). The ultimate achievement of community conservation at LMNP, from a conservation perspective, are the ways in which it has changed the ideas local communities hold about conservation. The initial contribution of community conservation has been positive in helping to reduce the antiwildlife values so strongly held by local people in the late 1980s (Hulme and Infield 2001).

Third, communal wildlife management projects in other parts of Africa have shown that the sustainable use of wildlife can complement the income derived from agriculture. These projects lead to an improvement of the household situation and therefore offer an incentive for the protection of flora and fauna of the communal area (Nuding 1996). Wildlife use that is not financially viable, such as the first attempts at wildlife use for meat in Zimbabwe (Child 1988) and Kenya (Elliott and Mwangi 1997), ultimately will fail. Trophy hunting can generate much more income than wildlife cropping.

Trophy hunting is currently under attack from antiuse activists. However, different arguments favor trophy hunting over tourism or cropping. Experiences from Zimbabwe and Tanzania show that trophy hunting can be a valuable source of income even while wildlife populations are low and recovering. The off-takes are limited (see Table 12.1), and the negative impact on local environments is minimal. With the focus on high-quality trophies, economically sustainable harvests are small and include a high proportion of males, which are surplus in ungulate populations with polygynous breeding systems. The argument in favor of shooting males should not be taken to extremes, however. Certain male:female sex ratios are desirable for healthy populations. Impacts of removal on social behavior are unknown. Trophy hunting is a labor-intensive service industry that is beneficial to people in areas unsuited to general tourism (Baldus 1991; Child 1995). Trophy hunting in Uganda could easily become an attraction. Uganda was once one of the prime hunting areas in Africa (Herne 1979).

Possible Institutional Setup of a Wildlife Use Scheme

The World Conservation Union in Gland, Switzerland (IUCN) maintains that sustainable use requires an institutional structure of management and control, both incentives and negative sanctions, good governance, and implementation at an appropriate scale. Such structure should include participation of relevant stakeholders and take account of land tenure, access rights, regulatory systems, traditional knowledge, and customary law.

Considering the size of the wildlife population, the values of the communities, the outcome of the study tour to Kenya, and the results of the cropping exercise, I suggest the following steps as an appropriate wildlife use project in the Lake Mburo area (Fig. 12.2):

Step 1: Land owners living adjacent to the park together with a representative of the UWA, the Mbarara District, and local leaders should form an organization. The organization might be called the Lake Mburo Wildlife Forum (LMWF).

Step 2: Land owners might then sign a contract with UWA to create a community wildlife area and to receive the user rights of wildlife on their land. UWA will be responsible for monitoring the wildlife populations and fixing a hunting quota. The land owners are responsible for controlling illegal hunting.

Step 3: LMWF would then auction the quota to a private operator. The private operator could sell the wildlife products (the trophy, meat, hides) to the consumer. The consumer pays the operator, and the operator pays LMWF.

Step 4: Throughout the process, LMWF would receive advice from different institutions, such as the WARM Unit, Makerere University, the Uganda Meat Technology Center, and UWA.

In 2001 as a result of the study tour to Kenya, the land owners of Rurambira, east of LMNP, with assistance of the Community Conservation Unit of LMNP, founded an organization called the Rurambira Wildlife Utilization Association (RWUA). The senior management of UWA, on the basis of the findings of this study, agreed to a pilot wildlife use project in Nyabushozi. UWA signed a contract with RWUA and a private Ugandan operator for a period of 1 year, from June 2001 to June 2002. The first clients for sport hunting arrived in Nyabushozi in September 2001.

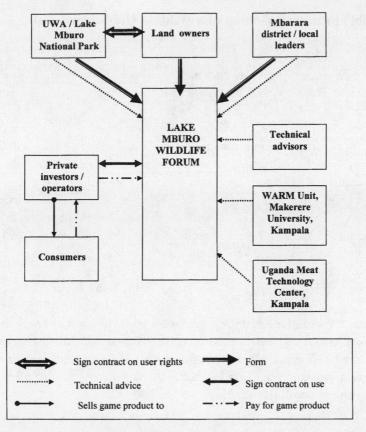

Figure 12.2 Possible institutional setup of a wildlife use project in the Lake Mburo area, Uganda.

UWA decided to allow active management by the communities of the area adjacent to LMNP for 1 year. After a trial phase of 1 year UWA will decide whether to continue with community-based wildlife conservation in the Lake Mburo area.

Conclusion

In an unpredictable world that is complex, diverse, and contingent, with goals that are constantly refined and redefined, the idea that a single right policy can be identified and then indefinitely pursued is unrealistic. What is needed are broad-based enabling policies that promote the creation and strengthening of networks of institutions and organizations that have the flexibility to deal with contingency and complexity. The question is not whether state action or community action is better: Both are essential. So too is private sector support. The challenge is how to develop effective mixes of state, community, and private action in specific contexts (Adams and Hulme 1998). Management should be an iterative process that is adaptable and flexible to suit local conditions. Law enforcement, community conservation in the form of environmental education, and community wildlife use projects, with a combination of data-based management strategies, are all needed and can help ensure the persistence of the wildlife resource (Ostrom 1990). I argue that park authorities and managers should acknowledge that the park is not an island and cannot be managed without reference to the surrounding landscape and the people who inhabit it. Parks such as LMNP in Uganda are threatened because they have not served the needs of the local communities. This must change.

J. Terborgh (1999, p. 208) concluded in his book *Requiem for Nature* that the "person who leads the way to ending the tragedy of the commons (Hardin 1968) will truly be the person who saves the world." One might not save the world by starting a community-based wildlife use project in Nyabushozi, but such a project could provide an exit strategy from the tragedy of the commons that has occurred in the Lake Mburo area and in many other parts of the world.

Summary

Like many other protected areas in Africa, LMNP in Uganda is small (260 km^2), its wildlife community is incomplete (e.g., lions and elephants have been extirpated), and the surrounding landscape is used heavily for farming and herding by a growing human population. Illegal hunting and herding within the park are additional problems. For ecological as well as socioeconomic reasons, the park's existence and potential to sustain wildlife depend heavily on its surroundings. At present, LMNP is in danger of becoming a paper park.

In this chapter I illustrate the intricate network of ecological and socioeconomic relationships between the park and its surroundings and point to problems that affect wildlife conservation. I argue for integrating rural community development and wildlife conservation around LMNP as a vital prerequisite for longer-term persistence of the Lake Mburo ecosystem. To the extent that land owners living around LMNP are able to derive tangible and legitimate benefits from the wildlife on their land, they would have an incentive to protect wildlife from illegal hunting. As residents on the land, land owners may be more efficient than government in protecting the wildlife populations. Legalization, coupled with effective control of hunting, may be the only viable option to stabilize the wildlife population in the Lake Mburo area.

Acknowledgments

For their cooperation and support I would like to thank the people of Nyabushozi, Mbarara District, and the Uganda Wildlife Authority. This study was funded by the Gesellschaft für Technische Zusammenarbeit (GTZ), Tropical Ecology Support Program. Thanks to I. Storch, J. Bissonette, and an anonymous reviewer for their comments on this chapter.

LITERATURE CITED

Adams, W. M., and D. Hulme. 1998. Conservation and communities: changing narratives, policies, and practices in African conservation. Pages 24–37 in D. Hulme and M. Murphree (eds.), African wildlife and livelihoods: the promise and performance of community conservation. James Carrey, Oxford, UK.

Averbeck, C. 2001. Integrating local communities and wildlife conservation in Nyabushozi, Uganda: sustainable use as a viable solution. TZ-Verlagsgesellschaft mbH, Rossdorf, Germany.

Baldus, R. D. 1991. Community wildlife management and the Selous Game Reserve. Wildlife Division and SCP Discussion Paper No. 12. Dar es Salaam, Tanzania.

Barrow, E., P. Bergin, M. Infield, and P. Lembuya. 1995. The people's voice: partnership and community conservation. Pages 255–259 in J. A. Bissonette and P. R. Krausman (eds.), Integrating people and wildlife for a sustainable future. Proceedings of the 1st International Wildlife Management Congress. The Wildlife Society, Bethesda, Maryland, USA.

Bruner, A. G., R. E. Gullison, R. E. Rice, and G. A. B da Fonseca. 2001. Effectiveness of parks in protecting tropical biodiversity. Science 291:125.

Child, B. 1988. The role of wildlife in the sustainable economic development of semiarid rangelands in Zimbabwe. Ph.D. Dissertation, Oxford University, Oxford, U.K.

Child, G. 1995. Wildlife and people: the Zimbabwean success. Wisdom Foundation, Harare, Zimbabwe, and New York, N.Y., USA.

Elliott, J., and M. M. Mwangi. 1997. Increasing landowner earnings from wildlife cropping in Laikipia, Kenya. African Wildlife Foundation (AWF), Conservation, Economics and Commerce Programme, Laikipia Wildlife Economics Study, Discussion Paper CEC-DP-2.

Frankel, O. H. 1983. The place of management in conservation. Pages 1–14 in C. M. Schonewald-Cox (ed.), Genetics and conservation. Benjamin/Cummings, Menlo Park, CA.

Guard, M. 1991. The interactions between domestic animals and wild ungulates in Lake Mburo National Park, Uganda: a question of competition or complementarities. M.S. thesis, Makerere University, Kampala, Uganda.

Hardin, G. 1968. The tragedy of the commons. Science 162:1243–1248.

Herne, B. 1979. Uganda safaris. Winchester Press, 1421 South Sheridan, Tulsa, Oklahoma, USA.

Hulme, D., and M. Infield. 2001. Community conservation, reciprocity and park-people relationships. Lake Mburo National Park, Uganda. Pages 106–130 in D. Hulme and M. Murphree (eds.), African wildlife and livelihoods: the promise and performance of community conservation. James Carrey, Oxford, UK.

Infield, M., and A. Namara. 2001. Community attitudes and behaviour towards conservation: an assessment of a community conservation programme around Lake Mburo National Park, Uganda. Oryx 35:48–60.

Kamugisha, J. R., and M. Ståhl. 1993. Parks and people: pastoralists and wildlife. Proceedings from a seminar on environmental degradation in and around Lake Mburo National Park, Uganda. SIDA's Regional Soil Conservation Unit, RSCU, Nairobi, Kenya.

Lamprey, R., and F. Michelmore. 1996. A survey of the wildlife protected areas of Uganda. Phase I: September 1995–January 1996. Ministry of Tourism Wildlife and Antiquities, Kampala, Uganda, unpublished report.

Norton-Griffiths, M. 1978. Counting animals. Handbook No. 1. African Wildlife Foundation, Nairobi, Kenya.

Nuding, M. 1996. The potential of wildlife management for development cooperation. Tropical Ecology Support Program, TÖB P/1E. German Technical Cooperation (GTZ), Germany.

Ostrom, E 1990. Governing the commons. Cambridge University Press, Cambridge, UK.

Snelson, D., and A. Wilson. 1994. Lake Mburo National Park Guide Book. African Wildlife Foundation, Kampala, Uganda.

Terborgh, J. 1999. Requiem for Nature. Island Press/Shearwater Books, Washington, DC.

The Uganda Wildlife Statute, 1996. Uganda Gazette 32:1–77.

PART THREE

LINKING THEORY AND APPLICATION
Case Studies

N atural environments are patchy, so species have evolved a number of adaptations to cope with patchiness. However, human land use activities alter and intensify the natural patchiness in space and time, and this often happens at extents and rates that exceed a species' ability to adapt. Consequently, habitat fragmentation is a central issue in conservation biology. As conservation aims to minimize the adverse effects of human-caused loss and fragmentation of wildlife habitats on species, ecological concepts that allow predictions about the dynamics and survival chances of populations in patchy environments offer valuable guidance to practitioners.

In this situation, case studies that explicitly apply theory for finding concrete management solutions are important in two ways. First, case studies test the usefulness of an ecological concept for conservation tasks. They bring a theory from the ivory towers of basic research into the real world, and the outcome is often that a number of unrealistic assumptions on which the theory originally was based are unveiled. Thus case studies may lead to necessary adjustments of a concept before it is adopted by practitioners. Second, case studies test the relevance of theoretical frameworks to practice and provide concrete examples of how theory can be applied in wildlife management and conservation practice. When successful, case studies can stimulate others to adopt landscape ecological thinking in their own research and management efforts. This is the intention of Chapters 13–17.

In Chapter 13, Ilse Storch argues that in conservation practice, despite the advances in landscape ecological thinking among scientists, habitat is commonly still described exclusively through the vegetation types a species inhabits, and the spatial dimensions of the habitat are neglected. She uses the capercaillie (*Tetrao urogallus*) in central Europe as an example to show that species–habitat relationships are characterized by multiple spatial scales and concludes that a multiscale habitat concept is needed that is widely adopted by land managers and conservationists. In Chapter 14, David Maehr, John Cox, and Jeffery Larkin further illustrate the significance of a landscape perspective to conservation programs using wide-ranging large mammals in the United States. Despite contrasting life history strategies, the elk (*Cervus elaphus*) in eastern Kentucky, the Florida panther (*Puma concolor coryi*), and the black bear (*Ursus americanus floridanus*) in Florida are all examples of species whose current status is a product of autecology and varying degrees of landscape denaturement. The authors suggest that extensive habitat needs and broad public appeal make these species ideal conservation flagships for combining landscape restoration with species recovery. They conclude that strategic promotion of flagship species and the adoption of an ecosystem philosophy by natural resource agencies will benefit conservation programs.

In Chapter 15, Christof Schenck, Jessica Groenendijk, Frank Hajek, Elke Staib, and Karin Frank also apply the flagship species concept. The giant otter (*Pteronura brasiliensis*) was once common in the rivers, lakes, and swamps throughout the South American lowland rainforests. The population has been significantly reduced by poaching and is now under threat from deforestation, river pollution, overfishing, and tourism. Because the giant otter is a major ecotourist attraction in the Manu National Park of Peru, it has become a symbol for the park and is an important flagship for the conservation of the ecosystem at very large spatial extents. Schenck et al. used their field studies on otters in Peru to develop an individual-based simulation model. The model shows that small-scale events that reduce the numbers of dispersing otters may result in a large-scale decline of the entire population. The results indicate that the giant otter population of Manu National Park, one of the largest protected areas worldwide, is not large enough to be considered viable in the long term. Connectivity with other populations seems to be a prerequisite for long-term viability. Another example for the need for landscape-scale approaches to species conservation is provided in Chapter 16. David Sample, Christine Ribic, and Rosalind Renfrew argue that protected lands, such as public wildlife areas enhanced through prairie restoration, are not sufficient for grassland bird preservation in the midwestern United States. For successful management of these species, landscape management must be linked with conservation goals at the landscape scale (i.e., throughout the human-dominated agricultural system). To deduce management guidelines for grassland birds at the landscape scale, the authors assess the effects of within-patch and landscape-level characteristics on grassland bird abundance and productivity based on their studies on secondary grasslands in southwestern Wisconsin over a period of 15 years.

This volume ends with a plea not to forget individual variation and adaptation within populations despite the need for large-scale approaches to ecology and conservation. In Chapter 17, Frederick Provenza, Juan Villalba, and John Bryant argue that ecosystem function and stability are integral components of biological diversity, although little is known about how biochemical links between herbivores and plant diversity influence the sustainability of ecosystems. They discuss how plant biochemical diversity influences herbivores and plants and links upward to landscapes. They argue that associational effects involving plant chemistry and herbivore learning may influence species coexistence and plant species diversity and either enhance or counteract the evolution of plant defenses. Grazing management can encourage the use of all plants by herbivores, thereby maintaining plant diversity.

CHAPTER THIRTEEN

Linking a Multiscale Habitat Concept to Species Conservation

ILSE STORCH

Habitat is the most basic necessity for the survival of any individual, population, or species. However, the habitat of many species is rapidly disappearing. In fact, habitat deterioration is the leading threat to biodiversity worldwide (Hilton-Taylor 2000). More than 80 percent of all globally Red List mammal, bird, and plant species are threatened with extinction because of habitat loss and fragmentation (Hilton-Taylor 2000). Consequently, habitat preservation, mitigation, and restoration are the central focus of many species conservation programs. The hope is that improving habitat will result in increased carrying capacity for the species of interest and thus will lead to an upward population trend.

In practice, however, populations don't always respond to habitat mitigation measures. These measures may fail to address the key factors limiting a population, and the improvement in habitat quality may only marginally improve the situation. From my experience with habitat-centered species conservation projects in central Europe and elsewhere, it seems that a significant part of this problem is a common misconception among conservation practitioners and their scientific advisors about what *habitat* means. In this chapter, I argue the need for a multiscale habitat concept that can be easily applied by land managers and conservationists. Such a concept will help to link practical conservation approaches to current landscape ecological understanding of species–habitat relationships. As an example, I use the capercaillie (*Tetrao urogallus*) in central Europe to illustrate that species–habitat relationships involve various spatial scales from patches to landscapes, all of which must be considered in conservation planning to maximize the chances of success.

A Multiscale Habitat Concept

According to classic definitions, habitat is the environment in which an animal of a certain species can survive and reproduce or, more simply, any place where the species occurs (Odum 1971). Most commonly (e.g., in field guides and in conservation practice), a species' habitat is simply described as one or more vegetation types. Check your guidebooks: according to *Birds of Europe* (Jonsson 1992), the chukar (*Alectoris chukar*), for example, occurs "on dry rocky mountain slopes with or without scrub vegetation," and the nuthatch (*Sitta europaea*) is "common in open deciduous or mixed woods, parks and gardens."

These and similar popular descriptions of habitat imply an aspatial habitat concept. These descriptors reduce habitat to a simple description of the vegetation a species inhabits. This is not wrong. We do often find a species associated with these habitat features. However, these simple descriptions are incomplete. What the guidebooks do not mention is that nuthatches are unlikely to be found if the woodlot is small and far from other such woodlots (Verboom et al. 1991). The spatial dimensions of the habitat are completely missing in most descriptions and thus also in the public perception of what habitat is. Does the species need contiguous habitat, or can it cope with a certain degree of fragmentation? How must the different vegetation types used by the species be interspersed in the landscape? And how much habitat is needed to ensure the survival of a certain population?

Species–habitat relationships often exist at several hierarchically structured spatial scales, ranging from a species' geographic range, to the spatial structure of populations, to the home ranges of individuals and the distribution of specific resources therein (Johnson 1980; Hamel et al. 1986; Morrison et al. 1992; Hall et al. 1997). At each scale, different sets of habitat relationships are likely to exist. The components of these relationships often must be described with different extents and resolutions. Larger scales (contrary to the cartographic usage) imply larger extents and coarser resolutions. Furthermore, spatial scale is correlated with temporal scale in the sense that at larger scales, ecological processes are slower than at smaller scales (Holling 1992): Globally, the distribution of forest changes at a rate of tens of thousands of years (unless humans get involved); regionally, forest disturbances such as fire occur at intervals of tens to a few hundreds of years;

and locally, vegetation changes within annual cycles. This correlation may explain why humans are intuitively less aware of the role played by large spatial scales in species–habitat relationships; because processes at these scales are slow we tend to perceive patterns as being constant.

Spatial Scale in Capercaillie Habitat

Here, I use the capercaillie as an example to illustrate a multiscale habitat concept. Capercaillie habitat is made up of boreal and montane forest. However, a minimum of three scales are necessary to describe the habitat relevant to this species: vegetation in forest stands, stands in the forest, and forests within the landscape (Fig. 13.1; Storch 1997a). At the level of forest stands, small-scale features of the vegetation influence daily habitat use of individuals (Storch 1993a, 1993b, 1994). Capercaillie prefer conifer-dominated forest with a well-developed ground vegetation that offers food and cover. Cover and height of the ground vegetation are limited by the closure of the canopy; therefore, dense stands are rarely used by capercaillie. Forest stands are the scale of the classic descriptions of capercaillie habitat.

At the next larger scale, the mosaic of stands within the forest affects the size of capercaillie home ranges. In the course of a year, each capercaillie uses an area of several hundred hectares (Storch 1995), so a home

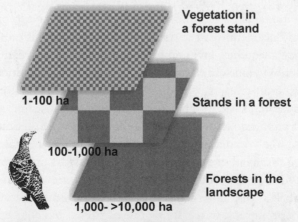

Figure 13.1 A multiscale view of capercaillie habitat. Vegetation in forest stands (fine resolution; extent 1–100 ha) influences individual habitat use. Stands within the forest mosaic (intermediate resolution; extent 100–1,000 ha) affect the size and spacing of home ranges, and the distribution of forest within the landscape (coarse resolution; extent 1,000–>10,000 ha) plays an important role in the dynamics and persistence of populations.

range is composed of stands of different successional stages or cutting classes. The birds select ranges with a great amount of older forest that offers the preferred vegetation structures (Wegge and Rolstad 1986; Storch 1995). The more area is covered by old stands, the smaller the home range and, most importantly, the lower the predation risk (Gjerde and Wegge 1989; Wegge et al. 1990; Storch 1997b).

Finally, at the landscape scale, the interspersion of forests and open land determines the size, spatial structure, and dynamics of populations. In the boreal forest, variation in local capercaillie breeding success is best explained by the proportion of farmland within areas of 100 km^2 (Kurki and Lindén 1995; Kurki et al. 2000), and capercaillie populations are assumed to disappear as forest fragmentation exceeds a critical threshold (Rolstad and Wegge 1987). In central Europe, the mosaic of capercaillie forests distributed as islands within a matrix of farmland and settlements results in a metapopulation pattern with spatially distinct subpopulations (Storch and Segelbacher 2000).

In summary, there is good evidence that capercaillie populations may be influenced by habitat factors at spatial scales that range from forest stands to landscapes of 100 km^2 and beyond. For a capercaillie population to persist, its habitat needs must be met at all scales. The extent of a forest is as relevant as its stand mosaic and vegetation structure.

Habitat Factors Influencing Capercaillie Populations

Every animal has a number of certain basic needs to survive and reproduce. These include adequate water and food, appropriate climate, mates and nest sites, protection from weather and predators, and the ability to cope with competitors and parasites. These factors, and many others, play a role in an animal's habitat selection. For each factor, there exists an optimum condition, but rarely are factors optimal at the same place and time. Therefore, habitat selection is an optimization problem, and the habitat an animal uses is simply the best available compromise. Species with narrow ranges of suitable values for each controlling factor have little room for compromise and are often labeled habitat specialists.

Habitat Suitability within Forest Stands

The capercaillie is a good example of a habitat specialist. It is closely associated with late successional stages of conifer-dominated forests (Storch 2001a).

Its habitat preferences can be described by a small set of variables: successional stage, tree species composition, canopy cover, height and composition of the ground vegetation, and steepness of slope. Based on these variables, different sites can be compared in their suitability for capercaillie with the help of a habitat suitability index (HSI) model (Storch 2001b). The HSI model provides scores between 1 for optimal suitability and 0 for conditions unsuitable for capercaillie. The higher the HSI score at a site, the greater the chances of finding signs of capercaillie such as droppings, molted feathers, dust baths, or tracks (Fig. 13.2). This relationship has proven to be general enough to apply in different areas of the Alps (Storch 2001b) as well as over the years (Storch, unpublished data). The guidebook-style description of capercaillie habitat as old conifer forests with a well-developed ground cover rich in bilberry (*Vaccinium myrtillus*) agrees with these results (Fig. 13.2); this is where one should go to maximize one's chances of finding the bird.

Small-scale habitat variables, as described through HSI scores, are an excellent predictor of capercaillie habitat use in the Alps (Storch 2001b).

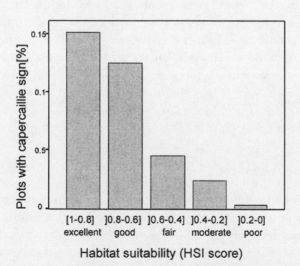

Figure 13.2 A habitat suitability index (HSI) model exclusively built with small-scale habitat features such as canopy cover and ground vegetation height is well suited to predict the chances of finding evidence of capercaillie use. The figure shows the relationship between habitat suitability as measured by HSI scores and capercaillie habitat use, represented by the proportion of 5-m sample plots with capercaillie sign such as feces and moulted feathers, based on 2,901 plots in six 2,000-ha study areas in the Bavarian Alps, Germany, summer 1997. Data from Storch (2001b).

Habitat structures preferred by capercaillie support greater numbers of birds. Consequently, a forest manager in charge of capercaillie conservation would try to improve habitat suitability by working toward increasing HSI scores. He or she would thin dense stands to reduce the canopy cover and favor the growth of ground vegetation, would support coniferous trees, and would introduce longer rotation periods to have more stands in late successional stages (Storch 1999). After some years the manager would remap the area and calculate HSI scores once again and would be proud of having increased the average HSI from, say, 0.3 to 0.4. To achieve such an improvement in a forest managed primarily for timber production would not be easy. In the Alps, major deviations from production-oriented forest management plans are rarely acceptable economically and politically,

At first glance, it does appear that increasing HSI scores in a stand would lead to increases in capercaillie populations. According to data from nine mountain ranges in the Alps, an increase in the frequency of finding capercaillie sign, and thus in population density, was positively correlated with HSI scores ($R^2 = 0.55$, $p = 0.023$; Fig. 13.3). However, this relationship is not a tight one. Although there is an obvious trend for greater population density in areas with greater HSI scores, there can be enormous differences in capercaillie abundance in areas with similar HSI scores, indicating that abundance cannot be explained solely by the habitat variables considered. Furthermore, the variance in estimated population density is not constant but increases with HSI scores. Thus, although capercaillie show strong preferences for the fine-scale habitat features described by high HSI scores, population trends are clearly affected by other factors as well (Storch 2001b).

Stands within the Forest

Several factors other than small-scale vegetation features as considered by the HSI model may significantly influence a population. In addition to stochastic events, areas may differ in climate, predation pressure, human disturbance, and other abiotic and biotic factors that may affect capercaillie populations (Storch 2001a). Also, the spatial distribution of habitat may affect populations in various ways. Telemetry results showed that capercaillie prefer larger old forest stands over smaller ones (Storch 1997a). Preliminary results from the Bavarian Alps suggest that the distribution of patches with high HSI scores within the forest may influence a mountain range's carrying capacity. Capercaillie seem to fare better where good habitat is clumped rather than evenly dispersed as small patches (Storch 2001b).

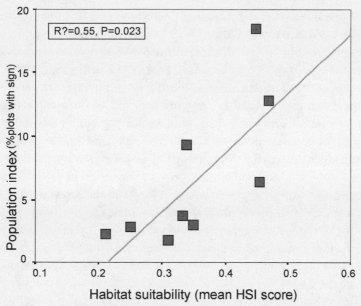

Figure 13.3 The relationship between mean habitat suitability index (HSI) scores and an index of capercaillie abundance (the proportion of 5-m sample plots with capercaillie sign) for nine 2,000-ha study areas in the Alps. Despite the good representation of capercaillie habitat use by the HSI model (see Fig. 13.2), there are great differences in capercaillie abundance between study areas with similar HSI scores. The small-scale habitat features represented by the model cannot explain these differences. Data from Storch (2001b) (six areas); I. Storch, unpublished data (two areas); and H. Moser and H. Zeiler, unpublished data (1 area). Line according to least-square linear regression.

Forests within the Landscape

In most parts of Europe, forests inhabited by capercaillie are more or less fragmented by farmland and settlements. The major central European ranges of the species, such as the Alps, the Bohemian Forest, the Black Forest, the Vosges, and the Pyrenees, are separated by 50 to 100 kilometers of open land. Within these ranges, the landscape may be dominated by forest, but nevertheless is interspersed by pastures, fields, and villages.

Landscape-Scale Edge Effects

In a fragmented forest, however, processes involved with forest–farmland edges may significantly affect the demography of forest species (Laurance

2000). Work in Finland indicates that local breeding success of grouse is negatively correlated with habitat fragmentation over an extent of 100 km^2, as measured by the proportion of farmland and young forest resulting from clearcutting (Kurki and Lindén 1995; Kurki et al. 2000). The explanation is that farmland and young forest support great densities of generalist predators that also prey on capercaillie and their eggs. In Bavaria, southern Germany, a study with artificial ground nests in forested mountain ranges revealed that nest predation risk decreased as the distance to the forest edge increased (Storch 2001b). Most probably, as in Finland, red foxes (*Vulpes vulpes*) and carrion crows (*Corvus corone*) living around the farming communities moved some distance into the forest to feed. Thus there is a gradient in predation risk in the landscape declining from the forest edge to the forest interior. This may explain why capercaillie in the Alps are rarely found in forest directly bordering farmland and settlements, and are most common in the forest interior (I. Storch and A. Zeitler, unpublished data).

Landscape-scale edge effects may help to explain why capercaillie populations show local declines, or even disappear, without any noticeable change in forest structure. A significant increase in predator densities in the surrounding farmland matrix may result in greater predation pressure in the forest. This increased pressure has likely been felt in fragmented forests throughout central Europe during the second half of the twentieth century. Increases in the amount of favorable habitat in suburbanized landscapes (Reynolds 1990) and the availability of anthropogenic food sources along with the relaxation of the formerly intensive persecution of predators have likely increased capercaillie predator populations (e.g., Klaus et al. 1989; Reynolds 1990; Klaus and Bergmann 1994; Storch 2001a). I speculate that the limited size of many of the ranges (Fig. 13.4) and an overall increase in landscape-scale edge effects during the second half of the twentieth century are major causes of the decline and local extinction of the capercaillie in central Europe.

If the hypothesis of landscape-scale edge effects is correct, small capercaillie distribution ranges should be more affected than large ones. In small ranges, the entire forest area may be influenced by the surroundings, whereas in large forests, an unaffected core may remain. How large a forest needs to be to have a core unaffected by increased predator densities in the surrounding farmland matrix will depend on the accessibility of the forest and the mobility of the predators involved.

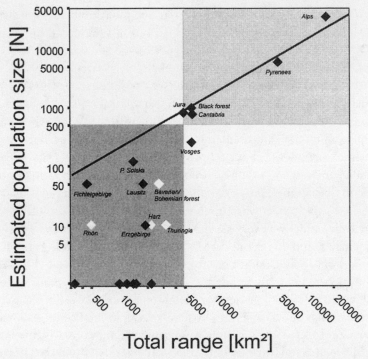

Figure 13.4   Total area of capercaillie distribution ranges (including all land cover types) in western and central Europe plotted against the estimated sizes of their capercaillie populations. Note the logarithmic scales. White symbols indicate populations restocked with released birds. Populations of size 0 indicate that extinctions occurred after 1970. Data from IUCN/SSC Grouse Specialist Group.

Spatial Habitat Requirements and Minimum Viable Population

All else being equal, large populations should have a higher probability of surviving than small ones. Small populations are more susceptible to chance environmental or demographic events. In this context, the concept of minimum viable population size is important. A minimum viable population (MVP) is defined as the minimum number of individuals required for a population to have high probability (e.g., 95%) for long-term (e.g., 100 years) survival (Shaffer 1987). For conservation planning, the question of how much habitat is needed, or how large an area must be set aside for a population to survive, is even more important. Among conservation practitioners, however, the concept of the MVP is often misunderstood.

The first common misunderstanding is that a population below the size of an MVP has no chance of survival. The second misunderstanding is that the size of the MVP is something like a species-specific natural law. Additional misconceptions include the idea that MVP calculations and the future they predict are close to accurate (see Belovsky et al. 1994).

It is helpful to go through the modeling exercises necessary to calculate MVP size. We have done this for capercaillie in the Bavarian Alps, based on demographic data collected during a telemetry study of habitat use (Grimm and Storch 2000). For some key processes, such as density-dependent mortality and dispersal, data were completely lacking both from our own study and in the literature, and even our conceptual understanding was poor. Thus, a very simple model was built based on best available knowledge. We found that the model was very sensitive to key parameters such as survival of adult females, and that resulting MVP sizes strongly depended on the initial assumptions. Any changes in factors such as weather and climate, or predation, that regulate these key parameters, may lead to major changes in calculated MVP sizes. For capercaillie in the Bavarian Alps in the 1990s, we concluded that an MVP should probably have about 500 birds (Grimm and Storch 2000). Capercaillie populations may fluctuate greatly in relation to annual weather conditions and other environmental factors (Storch 2001a). A series of years with poor reproductive success due to unsuitable weather or the loss of a few females to a predator can be enough to extirpate a small population, whereas a large population can buffer such stochastic losses.

To a practitioner, it may not seem wise to uncritically trust in an MVP figure based on educated guesswork. Furthermore, for most species, MVP estimates will not be available at all. As an alternative approach, it may be helpful to look at the biogeographic patterns of the species of interest, to compare the sizes of those populations and their ranges that appear to be stable to ranges where populations decline or have become extinct (Shaffer 1981). In Fig. 13.4, the total extent of capercaillie distribution ranges (including all land cover types, not just forests inhabited by capercaillie) in western and central Europe is plotted against the estimated sizes of their capercaillie populations. For the larger ranges, such as the Alps, the Pyrenees, and the Black Forest, there is a close correlation between area and population size (Fig. 13.4; light gray, upper right). In ranges below about 5000 km² in size, this correlation seems to disappear, many populations are small, rapidly declining, and some went extinct during the past few decades (Fig. 13.4, dark gray, lower left). According to this very simple exercise, it appears that capercaillie populations below about 500 birds are more vulnerable than populations with more than 500 birds. This supports the modeling result. For a capercaillie population under the present-day ecological conditions of central Europe to be on the safe side, 500 birds and a range large enough to support them are required.

Metapopulation Patterns

It appears that the larger capercaillie populations in western and central Europe are still relatively safe. In the Alps, for example, an estimated 30,000–40,000 capercaillie are distributed over a range of 200,000 km^2. These figures are several orders of magnitude beyond the estimates for a minimum viable population and its spatial requirements. A closer look at a map of the Alps reveals, however, that this is not likely to be one contiguous population of capercaillie. The birds inhabit mountain forests that are separated by farmland valleys and interspersed by areas with alpine vegetation and rocks above tree line. Thus, capercaillie populations are spatially structured; their distribution resembles a metapopulation pattern with distinct subpopulations (see Fig. 13.5). In the Bavarian Alps, Germany, for example, patches of contiguous forest inhabited by capercaillie vary between 0.1 and 100 km^2 in size (median 2 km^2) (based on forest and alpine habitats >1000 m altitude; Storch unpublished data). Clearly, such patches are far too small for a minimum viable capercaillie population of several hundred birds (see above). Therefore, contact and exchange between neighboring populations are vital for their survival. From telemetry studies we know that capercaillie occasionally do cross open valleys 5 to 10 km wide (see Storch and Segelbacher 2000). Also, genetic studies indicate that capercaillie readily disperse between mountain ranges, as there is little genetic differentiation among birds from various parts of the Alps (Segelbacher and Storch 2000).

The genetic and demographic connectivity within a metapopulation depends on the frequency of dispersal events. Unfortunately, very little is known about the ethological and ecological circumstances of dispersal in grouse. It is reasonable to assume that the more juveniles a population produces, the more will disperse. Any factor that leads to a reduction in reproductive success may thus threaten the connectivity within a metapopulation system. A locally induced population decline on one mountain range may thus have regional effects, because fewer dispersers will reach neighboring populations.

Metapopulation dynamics may also offer one possible explanation why, in capercaillie, populations in the center of a distribution range tend to fare

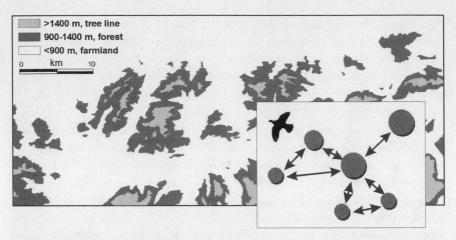

Figure 13.5   Distribution of forest patches in the Bavarian Alps, Germany. Caper-caillie predominantly inhabit forests in altitudes between 1,000 and 1,400 m, sepa-rated by farmland valleys and interspersed by alpine meadows and rocks above tree-line. The resulting distribution indicates a metapopulation system with local populations on distinct mountain ranges connected by dispersal.

better than those along the edges. In the Alps and other regions of Europe where capercaillie show negative population trends, major range contrac-tions have been observed, and the outermost populations have declined and disappeared first (e.g., Klaus and Bergmann 1994). This observation is in accordance with predictions from metapopulation theory: the better a sub-population is connected to others by dispersing individuals, the better its chances to survive (see Wiens 1996 for a review). At the edge of a distribu-tion range, dispersers can be expected only from one side, whereas a (sub)population in the center of the range is surrounded by other (sub)pop-ulations. Therefore, achieving a population increase through habitat miti-gation measures at the edge of the distribution range may be more difficult than in an area surrounded by other capercaillie forests.

Toward a Multiscale Conservation Approach

In the previous sections, I have proposed a multiscale habitat concept based on an example, the capercaillie. Although the details are species-specific, the overall idea of multiple-scale species–habitat relationships is not. Hierar-chical scales can and should be distinguished in the habitat of any species.

The definition of these depends on the species of interest and the ecological processes of importance for the dynamics of its habitat. The home ranges of vertebrates range in extent from square meters to thousands of square kilometers. Accordingly, different species perceive the environment at different resolutions. A clear-cut a few hectares in size may be the world to a field vole (*Microtus agrestis*), but it may be just another patch for a brown bear (*Ursus arctos*). Therefore, wildlife biologists must choose different scales to describe the habitat of different species.

Once a species' habitat relationships have been described at the appropriate scales, scale-specific conservation guidelines must be set. In other words, we must make the connection between research results and management prescriptions. For the capercaillie, the key habitat features are vegetation in forest stands, stands in forests, and forests in the landscape (see Fig. 13.1). Based on these features, components of high habitat quality can be identified at each scale and can then be used to formulate goals for habitat management (Table 13.1). The final challenge lies in implementing the management prescriptions by forest managers and conservation agencies.

The basic concepts in this chapter are not new. In the past 20 years, many authors have pointed out that species–habitat relationships are scale dependent and have recommended that research biologists place their studies in the proper spatial and temporal scales (Johnson 1980; Wiens 1989; Morrison et al. 1992; Bissonette 1997). Nonetheless, multiscale habitat concepts have only started to become a standard in conservation biology (Hall et al. 1997). In conservation practice, there is still a long way to go before scale dependency of species–habitat relationships is widely perceived by land managers and conservationists.

I hope that the background and examples provided in this chapter will help land use managers in charge of species conservation programs to ask the right questions. At what spatial scales are habitat relationships relevant? What ecological processes operate at each of the scales to define the relationships? What information can be used to describe and analyze species–habitat relationships at the levels from individual habitat use and home ranges over population and metapopulation to the species' range? And how can scale-specific species–habitat relationships be translated into guidelines and goals for conservation? The answers to these questions will obviously be different for different species, but the general rationale, I believe, should be broadly applicable.

Table 13.1 Three spatial scales can be distinguished in capercaillie habitat, based on the ecology of the species and the patterns and processes in the forests it inhabits (see Fig. 13.1).

Forest Stand Level

Spatial scale	1–100 ha
Key habitat feature	Vegetation structure
Components of high habitat quality	Forest conifer-dominated; deciduous trees <30%
	Preferred winter food tree species occur (pine or fir)
	Moderate canopy cover (50–60%)
	Complete ground vegetation cover; 30–50 cm high
	Ericaceous shrubs, especially bilberry
In charge	Local forester, forest owner

Forest District Level

Spatial scale	100–1,000 ha
Key habitat feature	Mosaic of stands (succession stages or cutting classes)
Components of high habitat quality	Suitable stands (see above) ≥50 ha
	Suitable stands (see above) cover ≥2/3 of forest area
	Distances between suitable stands (see above) <500 m
	Clear-cuts and regenerating patches small (<5 ha)
In charge	District forest office, forest owner

Landscape Level

Spatial scale	1,000–>10,000 ha
Key habitat feature	Mosaic of forest and nonforest
Components of high habitat quality	Extended contiguous forests ≥10,000 ha
	Forest cover ≥85%
	Minimal fragmentation through roads and tracks
	5–10 km maximum distance between neighboring ranges
In charge	State forest authorities, district forest office

Translated from Storch (1999).

Summary

In this chapter, I stress the importance of a multiscale habitat concept for making the connection between ecological understanding and practical conservation approaches. Species–habitat relationships are characterized by multiple hierarchical spatial scales; nevertheless, habitat is commonly described exclusively through the vegetation types a species inhabits, and the spatial dimensions of the habitat are neglected.

I use the capercaillie (*Tetrao urogallus*) the largest Eurasian grouse, as an example to illustrate a multiscale view of habitat. Three spatial scales are relevant to the habitat associations of capercaillie. At each scale, different key habitat variables operate. Vegetation in forest stands influences individual habitat use, stands within the forest affect the size and spacing of home ranges, and the distribution of forest within the landscape plays an important role for the dynamics and persistence of populations.

Small-scale habitat variables have proven to be an excellent predictor of capercaillie habitat use at the forest stand level in the Alps. However, there are great differences in capercaillie abundance between areas with similar small-scale habitat suitability. Obviously, factors other than small-scale habitat variables may influence a population. One of these factors is the spatial distribution of habitats: Capercaillie abundance seems to be greater in areas where good habitat is clumped; populations in the middle of a distribution range tend to fare better than those along the edges; and gradients in predation risk exist from farmland to the forest interior. Empirical and modeling results indicate that an isolated capercaillie population in the fragmented landscape of central Europe may need about 500 birds to persist. Because capercaillie populations appear to be spatially structured in metapopulations, dispersal between neighboring populations is vital for their survival. For a multiscale approach to conservation, based on the species–habitat relationships analyzed at the various scales, key habitat features and components of high habitat quality can be identified and translated into conservation guidelines.

Acknowledgments

This chapter builds on results from 15 years of research on capercaillie–habitat relationships and experience with grouse habitat conservation in the Alps and elsewhere in central Europe. My studies have received major financial support from the Bavarian State Ministry of Agriculture and Forestry and from the Deutsche Forschungsgemeinschaft (DFG). Comments by John Bissonette and Joshua Lawler helped to improve the manuscript.

LITERATURE CITED

Belovsky, G. E., J. A. Bissonette, R. D. Dueser, T. C. Edwards, C. M. Luecke, M. E. Ritchie, J. B. Slade, and F. H. Wagner. 1994. Management of small populations:

concepts affecting the recovery of endangered species. Wildlife Society Bulletin 22:307–316.

Bissonette, J. A. 1997. Scale-sensitive ecological properties: historical context, current meaning. Pages 3–31 in J. A. Bissonette (ed.), Wildlife and landscape ecology: effects of pattern and scale. Springer-Verlag, New York.

Gjerde, I., and P. Wegge. 1989. Spacing pattern, habitat use and survival of capercaillie in a fragmented winter habitat. Ornis Scandinavica 20:219–225.

Grimm, V., and I. Storch. 2000. Minimum viable population size of capercaillie *Tetrao urogallus:* results from a stochastic model. Wildlife Biology 6:219–225.

Hall, L. S., P. R. Krausman, and M. L. Morrison. 1997. The habitat concept and a plea for standard terminology. Wildlife Society Bulletin 25:173–182.

Hamel, P. A., N. D. Cost, and R. M. Sheffield. 1986. The consistent characteristics of habitats: a question of scale. Pages 121–128 in J. Verner, M. L. Morrison, and C. J. Ralph (eds.), Wildlife 2000: modeling habitat relationships of terrestrial vertebrates. University of Wisconsin Press, Madison.

Hilton-Taylor, C. 2000. 2000 IUCN red list of threatened species. IUCN, Gland, Switzerland.

Holling, C. S. 1992. Cross-scale morphology, geometry, and dynamics of ecosystems. Ecological Monographs 62:447–502.

Johnson, D. H. 1980. The comparison of usage and availability measurements for evaluating resource preference. Ecology 61:65–71.

Jonsson, L. 1992. Birds of Europe with north Africa and the Middle East. Christopher Helm Publishers Ltd., A&C Black, London.

Klaus, S., and H.-H. Bergmann. 1994. Distribution, status and limiting factors of capercaillie in central Europe, particularly in Germany, including an evaluation of reintroductions. Gibier Faune Sauvage 11:57–80.

Klaus, S., A. V. Andreev, H.-H. Bergmann, F. Müller, J. Porkert, and J. Wiesner. 1989. Die Auerhühner. Die Neue Brehm-Bücherei, Band 86. Westarp Wissenschaften, Magdeburg, Germany.

Kurki, S., and H. Lindén 1995. Forest fragmentation due to agriculture affects the reproductive success of ground-nesting black grouse *Tetrao tetrix.* Ecography 18:109–113.

Kurki, S., A. Nikula, P. Helle, and H. Lindén. 2000. Landscape fragmentation and forest composition effects on grouse breeding success in boreal forests. Ecology 81:1985–1997.

Laurance, W. F. 2000. Do edge effects occur over large spatial scales? Trends in Ecology and Evolution 15:134–135.

Morrison, M. L., B. G. Marcot, and R. W. Mannan. 1992. Wildlife–habitat relationships. University of Wisconsin Press, Madison.

Odum, E. P. 1971. Fundamentals of ecology. Saunders, Philadelphia.

Reynolds, J. C. 1990. The impact of generalist predators on gamebird populations. Pages 172–184 in J. T. Lumeij and Y. R. Hoogeveen (eds.), The future of wild galliformes in the Netherlands. Organisatiecommissie Nederlandse Wilde Hoenders, Amersfoort, the Netherlands.

Rolstad, J., and P. Wegge. 1987. Distribution and size of capercaillie leks in relation to old forest fragmentation. Oecologia 72:389–394.

Segelbacher, G. and I. Storch. 2002. Capercaillie in the Alps: genetic evidence of metapopulation structures and population decline. Molecular Ecology 11:1669–1677.

Shaffer, M. L. 1981. Minimum population sizes for species conservation. BioScience 31:131–134.

Shaffer, M. 1987. Minimum viable populations: coping with uncertainty. Pages 69–86 in M. E. Soulé (ed.), Viable populations for conservation. Cambridge University Press, New York.

Storch, I. 1993a. Habitat selection of capercaillie in summer and autumn: is bilberry important? Oecologia 95:257–265.

Storch, I. 1993b. Patterns and strategies of winter habitat selection in alpine capercaillie. Ecography 16:351–359.

Storch, I. 1994. Habitat and survival of capercaillie nests and broods in the Bavarian Alps. Biological Conservation 70:237–243.

Storch, I. 1995. Annual home ranges and spacing patterns of capercaillie in central Europe. Journal of Wildlife Management 59:392–400.

Storch, I. 1997a. The importance of scale in habitat conservation for an endangered species: the capercaillie in central Europe. Pages 310–330 in J. A. Bissonette (ed.), Wildlife and landscape ecology: effects of pattern and scale. Springer-Verlag, New York.

Storch, I. 1997b. Male territoriality, female range use, and spatial organization of capercaillie leks. Wildlife Biology 3:149–161.

Storch, I. 1999. Auerhuhn-Schutz: Aber wie? Ein Leitfaden, 3rd ed. Brochure, Wildbiologische Gesellschaft München. Ettal, Germany.

Storch, I. 2001a. Capercaillie. BWP Update. Journal of Birds of the Western Palearctic (Oxford University Press, Oxford, UK) 3:1–24.

Storch, I. 2001b. Prädatoren im Bergwald. Report for the Bavarian State Ministry of Agriculture and Forestry. Wildbiologische Gesellschaft München. Ettal, Germany.

Storch I. 2002. On spatial resolution in habitat models: Can small-scale forest structure explain Capercaillie numbers? Conservation Ecology 6: 6. (Online: http://www.consecol.org/vol16/iss1/art6).

Storch, I., and G. Segelbacher. 2000. Genetic correlates of spatial population structure in central European capercaillie and black grouse: a project in progress. Wildlife Biology 6:239–243.

Verboom, J., A. Schotman, P. Opdam, and A. J. Metz. 1991. European nuthatch metapopulations in a fragmented agricultural landscape. Oikos 61:149–156.

Wegge, P., and J. Rolstad. 1986. Size and spacing of capercaillie leks in relation to social behavior and habitat. Behavioural Ecology and Sociobiology 19:401–408.

Wegge, P., I. Gjerde, L. Kastdalen, J. Rolstad, and T. Storaas. 1990. Does forest fragmentation increase the mortality rate of capercaillie? Pages 448–453 in S. Myrberget (ed.), Transactions of the XIXth Congress of the International Union of
Game Biologists. Norwegian Institute for Nature Research, Trondheim.

Wiens, J. A. 1989. Spatial scaling in ecology. Functional Ecology 3:385–397.

Wiens, J. A. 1996. Wildlife in patchy environments: metapopulations, mosaics, and
management. Pages 53–84 in D. R. McCullough (ed.), Metapopulations and
wildlife conservation. Island Press, Covelo, CA.

CHAPTER FOURTEEN

Landscape History

Linking Conservation Approaches for Large Mammals

DAVID S. MAEHR, JOHN J. COX, AND JEFFERY L. LARKIN

An airplane ride across most of the eastern United States reveals a sobering glimpse of denatured landscapes and fragmented ecosystems. In such altered regions, the potential for returning lost components of the large mammal fauna seems limited at best. Although it is generally agreed that restoring biotic communities and processes in native ecosystems and landscapes is our most important conservation challenge (Grumbine 1994; Simberloff 1998; Harris et al. 2001), large mammals have been increasingly turned to as conservation flagships (Western 1987; McNeely 2000; Zhi et al. 2000; Maehr et al. 2001). Large mammal restoration can facilitate large-scale conservation efforts and offers several advantages over the more holistic view of ecosystem management (adapted from McNeely 2000):

- Individual species are a more objective currency for designing biotic reserves.
- Large mammals are often environmental quality indicators.
- Emotional connections with the public and subsequent popular support are more likely with large mammals than with abstract ecosystems.
- Large mammals are often ecological keystones.

However, restoring large mammals can be problematic, especially if they are carnivorous. Despite a decade-long process to plan for grizzly bear expansion in the western United States (Roy et al. 2001), political interests appear to have short-circuited a regional consensus for their return in at least one area (National Wildlife Federation 2001). In the East, wolf (*Canis lupus*) restoration is jeopardized by long-standing prejudice and fragmented habitat (Maehr 2001; Paquet et al. 2001). Large herbivores provide fewer onerous restoration challenges because they are more popular among the hunting public, are less controversial among livestock owners, and are generally more amenable to reintroduction (Griffith et al. 1989). Therefore, elk (*Cervus elaphus*) reintroduction projects have become common in the eastern United States and have occurred with little controversy and increasing frequency (Larkin et al. 2001). In this chapter, we examine the contribution of historical land uses and settlement patterns in dictating the efficacy of large mammal conservation and the degree of community restoration that can be expected in eastern Kentucky and Florida, states with very similar pre-Columbian large terrestrial mammal fauna but very different postcolonial settlement.

Condominiums versus Conservation: Florida's Land Endgame

Although Florida was colonized by Europeans in the sixteenth century and is home to the oldest permanent European settlement in North America (Patton 1996), the pattern of landscape change after human colonization is very different than in Kentucky, where the landscape was more rapidly denatured by settlers (Carter 1974; Raitz et al. 1998). Whereas parts of Florida's coast were settled quickly, some Atlantic beaches continued to be frequented by black bears (*Ursus americanus floridanus*) hunting for sea turtle eggs as late as the 1960s, and the state continues to support the only known cougar (*Puma concolor coryi*) population east of the Mississippi River. Extensive interior forests and prairies avoided widespread fragmentation and reduction well into the twentieth century. As a result, the only large terrestrial carnivore to have disappeared since the end of the Pleistocene is the red wolf (*Canis rufus*). Overharvest and persecution by humans probably caused the extinction of this southeastern canid (Robson 1992).

Unlike Kentucky, Florida was not immediately a Mecca for agriculture and urbanization until two centuries after biotic explorations began. The rich accounts of naturalists, ranging from Bartram (1791) to Carr (1940), preceded the mosquito control, wetland drainage, and air conditioning that made widespread, permanent human occupation in this subtropical state possible. Although surface mining, highway construction, and a twentieth-century human population explosion have dramatically altered the distribution and abundance of Florida's biodiversity, its large mammal fauna remains remarkably intact (Table 14.1). Kentucky has not been as fortunate. With the exception of the white-tailed deer (*Odocoileus virginianus;* Gassett 2001), all of its large terrestrial mammals larger than 20 kg were gone by the early 1900s. Even eradication efforts to rid Florida of a potential source of cattle-infecting diseases were insufficient to eliminate local deer populations in the mid-twentieth century (Harlow 1965). This was largely because of the existence of large, remote wilderness lands such as the Big Cypress Swamp and the Fakahatchee Strand, subtropical forest systems that hindered

Table 14.1 Conservation status of large, terrestrial mammal faunas in Kentucky and Florida.

Species	Region	
	Kentucky	Florida
Elk		
Recent status	Extirpated mid-1800s	Unknown in fossil record[a]
Cause for decline	Habitat loss; overharvest	—
Current population trend	Up	—
Black bear		
Recent status	Extirpated mid-1800s	Widespread
Cause for decline	Habitat loss; overharvest	Habitat loss; hunting
Current population trend	Undetermined	Up
Puma		
Recent status	Extirpated mid-1800s	Remnant population
Cause for decline	Overharvest; prey decline	Habitat loss; overharvest
Current population trend	None	Up
Wolf		
Recent status	Extirpated mid-1800s	Extirpated early 1900s
Cause for decline	Overharvest; prey decline	Overharvest
Current population trend	None	None
White-tailed deer		
Recent status	Nearly extirpated 1900	Widespread, abundant
Cause for decline	Overharvest	Local habitat loss
Current population trend	Up	Up or stable

[a]A small herd was introduced in the 1960s, but its status is currently unknown (Layne 1993).

human exploration and eventually became cornerstones of Florida's system of conservation lands (Hoctor et al. 2000).

Florida's biotic communities, unlike those of Kentucky, have been spared the diversity- and keystone-decimating influences of pathogen-driven extinctions (e.g., chestnut blight) but have suffered a galaxy of exotic introductions and subsequent alien invasions. South Florida, in particular, has become a magnet for new tropical plant species (more than 300 million plants were brought to Florida through the Miami International Airport in 1990; U.S. Congress 1993). Melaleuca (*Melaleuca quinquenervia*), Brazilian pepper (*Schinus terebinthefolius*), Australian pine (*Casurina* spp.), and Japanese climbing fern (*Lygodium japonicum*) are just a few of the more than 900 introduced plant species that make up 27 percent of Florida's modern flora (Ward 1989). Among Florida's vertebrates, introduced species account for 20 percent of the fish (Courtenay 1997), 20 percent of the reptiles and amphibians (Butterfield et al. 1997), 5 percent of the birds (Stevenson and Anderson 1994), and 22 percent of the mammals (Layne 1997). Despite these significant invasions and the competitive interactions that have resulted, large mammals in Florida have been largely unaffected by such changes. It is even likely that the introduced nine-banded armadillo (*Dasypus novemcinctus*) and wild boar (*Sus scrofa*) were instrumental to the persistence of the Florida panther as alternative prey during the years of deer eradication (Maehr 1997b). Thus, not only has Florida been resistant to widespread vertebrate extinctions (the only extinct large mammals in Florida include the red wolf, plains bison [*Bison bison bison*], and West Indian monk seal [*Monachus tropicalis*]), it has also absorbed many species without catastrophic results. This is not to say that exotic species are benign in Florida (Simberloff et al. 1997) but rather that the state has been remarkably successful in avoiding the impoverishment that has occurred elsewhere in eastern North America.

Large Mammals in Florida

Maehr (1997b) has suggested that the continued existence of the Florida panther has more to do with the subspecies' inherent hardiness than the recovery actions enacted on its behalf. It is likely that landscape pattern and the distribution of forest explain the existence of the Florida panther today (Maehr and Cox 1995). Despite burgeoning development, increasing human numbers, and an inelastic habitat base, the panther appears to be holding its own and exhibits a reproductive performance that could lead to population growth (Maehr and Caddick 1995). Perhaps the most controversial aspect of recovery is the potential for genetic swamping caused by the 1995 introduction of individuals from another subspecies. This interagency effort intends to enhance genetic variability in the panther by replacing long-impossible interchange with the introduction of individuals from the nearest extant population (Land and Lacy 2000). In this case, cougars from rugged and arid western Texas have been released into flat, wet, and subtropical southern Florida. The panther inhabits one of the most remote and inhospitable regions of North America, probably a key in reducing human disturbance and persecution (Belden 1983). Because of its extensive spatial needs, however, the panther has not fared nearly as well as the state's largest terrestrial vertebrate. This southernmost population of the widespread black bear has been fragmented into several units throughout the state (Maehr 1992) that are centered on large federal land-holdings (Fig. 14.1). The arrangement of these distribution centers appears to represent a statewide metapopulation that is connected by occasional dispersal from adjacent subpopulations (Maehr et al. 1988; Smith 2001). Thus,

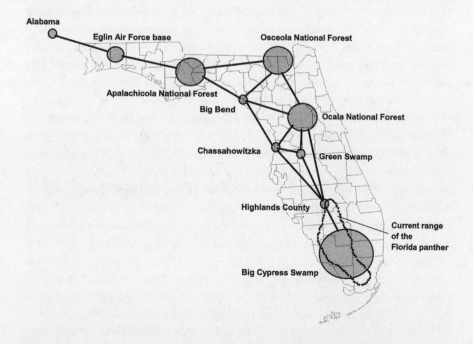

Figure 14.1 Potential metapopulation structure of the black bear and current range of the panther in Florida. Solid lines represent actual or hypothetical links between adjacent bear subpopulations. Circle sizes represent estimated relative sizes of local bear populations. Panther range is demarcated by the dashed line in south Florida.

even if a small population, such as the one inhabiting the Greater Chassahowitzka ecosystem in west-central Florida, becomes extinct, there is some chance that it will be recolonized by dispersing bears. This is not the case with the area currently occupied by the Florida panther, an isolated forest that exists at a distributional extreme. Extinction of this single population would eliminate the only known breeding population of *Puma concolor* in the East.

Management strategies differ markedly between Florida's largest members of the order Carnivora. Whereas official agency policy has turned to seemingly last-ditch methods to save the Florida panther (genetic introgression; Maehr and Caddick 1995), the same state agency has targeted only bear populations that are reasonably capable of sustaining long-term population viability (Cox et al. 1994). The suggestion here is that current management philosophies disdain the adoption of a landscape approach to large carnivore conservation in Florida: The panther currently occurs only in extreme south Florida as a highly managed genetic mish-mash, whereas a potential metapopulation approach is disregarded in favor of managing five separate, disjunct bear populations. These unimaginative choices have been made despite the potential not only to manage a regional carnivore metapopulation (black bear) but to expand the panther to parts of the state that have been without its top-down influence for more than a century. Individuals within both bear and panther populations have the ability to move far enough to connect existing populations or to establish new ones (Maehr et al. 1988; Maehr 1997a), and both species have the reproductive capability to grow quickly (Maehr and Caddick 1995; Maehr 1997a). Therefore, both species have the potential to be active participants in their own management and recovery in the large areas that were spared intensive human settlement and in others that might be targeted for restoration. The long-distance movement of several bears demonstrates the potential for a metapopulation dynamic, whereas movements of panthers as far as 200 km away from the south Florida habitat core hint at the possibility of population expansion (Maehr et al. 2001). The encouragement of additional long-distance dispersal in both species would go far in securing viable populations and preventing long-term population management that has the potential to reduce at least the panther to a seminatural zoolike existence.

Nonetheless, the natural physiographic features of Florida and late-blooming settlement patterns have created numerous conservation opportunities that are unparalleled in other eastern states. The recent development boom in Florida has allowed the bear and panther to persist in swamps and other habitats that were not easily converted to agriculture. This late start in the denaturing of Florida delayed the losses of large mammal species that were so characteristic in most of the eastern United States until a more enlightened populace could moderate the smothering spread of humanity. Although Floridians have exhibited great abilities in turning otherwise "useless" lands into productive agriculture (e.g., the Everglades Agricultural Area), they have also been persistent land conservationists. That 20 percent of the state has been set aside in some form of government-managed conservation use (Hoctor et al. 2000) is remarkable by world standards. Even more encouraging is a recent conservation blueprint that seeks to link all public lands into an ecological network (Hoctor et al. 2000). This effort, encouraged by the governor-appointed Florida Greenways Commission and led by the University of Florida, is a state-scale version of the continental vision of the Wildlands Project (Foreman et al. 1992). Had conditions in Florida been as amenable to human colonial settlement as were those in Kentucky, current and future conservation opportunities for large mammals and biodiversity in general would have been equally difficult.

The Kentucky Landscape: Revisiting the Dark and Bloody Ground

Kentucky's landscape has experienced more modifications during the last two centuries than since the last glaciation. As in Florida, settlement and subsequent development were dictated largely by topography, soil fertility, and water availability. The oak savannas of the western two thirds of the state have been replaced largely by farms and cities, and eastern mountain forests have been perforated with grasslands created by coal mining and small family farms. In the western and central regions of the state, oak savannas, interspersed with grasses and cane (*Arundinaria gigantia*), once supported herds of elk and bison and were an important hunting ground for both large carnivores and Native Americans (Wharton and Barbour 1991). Natural and incendiary fires (Hodge 1907) and keystone species such as beaver (*Castor canadensis*) and bison (Knapp et al. 1999) were principal habitat modifiers that maintained a patchwork of forest and grass that was quickly consumed by settlers' livestock. Market hunting and the conversion of habitat to row crops and pasture led to the extirpation of characteristic faunal and floral components such as bison and cane by the early 1800s. The gray wolf, red wolf, black bear, and mountain lion were largely gone before the Civil War (Young and Goldman 1946, 1964). Today, the western and central portions of Kentucky remain agriculturally based and are subject to expanding urban development. Intensive land uses, high road densities, and rising property values are now barriers to effective large-scale wildlife management and restoration.

In contrast, the eastern Cumberland Plateau was composed of unbroken deciduous forests that supported the most diverse temperate deciduous forest in the Northern Hemisphere (Barbour and Davis 1973). Openings in the forest canopy were rare, typically occurred along floodplains, and were created by flood, fire, wind, and megaherbivore disturbance (Owen-Smith 1988). Inevitably, settlement spread upstream from more fertile lowlands along the floodplains and into the "hollers" of rivers and creeks (Eller 1982). The rugged topography and scarcity of tillable land limited agriculture to narrow, shaded bottomlands. This dendritic pattern of land settlement and ownership that evolved in the mountains in the nineteenth century "minimize[d] the establishment of organized communities and formal social institutions" (Eller 1982, p. 9) and created America's largest continuous subculture (Shackleford and Weinberg 1977) that even today often is considered isolated from modern society (Caudill 1962). Limited settlement and low-intensity land uses probably facilitated the continued existence of all but the largest species. Although early settlers in the mountains formed a self-reliant agrarian society, the socioeconomic community of Appalachia in the twentieth century was transformed by industrialization, predominantly coal mining and logging (Eller 1982). The result was an exploited human population and the disruption of ecosystem processes. More recently, costly incentive-laden industrial recruitment and infrastructure development (Hazard Herald Leader 2000) have been touted as solutions to regional poverty that is both pervasive and persistent and threatens to maintain a cycle of environmental and social degradation that has persisted for more than a century (Caudill 1962). Like many other global regions containing high biodiversity, Appalachia is yet another example of the ironic dichotomy often found between biological richness and human poverty.

Eastern Kentucky's mixed mesophytic forest is the geographic center of the deciduous forests of eastern North America (Braun 1950). The canopy composition of mature forests is complex, highly evolved, and dominated by nearly 30 tree species (Barbour and Davis 1973). The loss of the American chestnut (*Castanea dentata*) and a century of intense logging have altered the abundance and availability of mast (Martin et al. 1951), created more xeric forest soils (Kalisz 1986), and resulted in the loss of primary habitat for many forest species (Harris 1984). In Kentucky alone, 48 species of plants and animals have been extirpated, 538 (17 percent) are considered rare, and 34 (1 percent) are currently listed as federally endangered or threatened (Kentucky Biodiversity Task Force 1995). Approximately 9 percent of the land in Kentucky is managed for nature conservation, but only 0.4 percent is considered protected (Kentucky Biodiversity Task Force 1995).

Although a number of successful wildlife reintroductions have occurred in the past century, the Appalachian region (Fig. 14.2) still contains 8 of the top 15 states with species most vulnerable to extinction (Kentucky Environmental Quality Commission 1997). Overharvest initially reduced the numbers of many species, but habitat fragmentation and loss caused by rapid settlement, pollution, and exotic species now are the major threats to regional biodiversity (Kentucky Environmental Quality Commission 1997).

Figure 14.2 Appalachia *(unshaded)* as defined by the Appalachian Regional Commission, Washington, DC.

Traditional management and conservation programs remain important, but it has become increasingly clear that regional reserve networks are needed to preserve existing biotic components and the integrity of their evolutionary processes (Soulé and Terborgh 1999). Despite new conservation initiatives, landscape fragmentation and species loss continue to threaten the integrity of existing ecosystems and the unique biological and cultural landscape of Appalachia.

Elk Restoration in Kentucky: An Exception to the Rule?

The presettlement distribution of North American elk encompassed southern Canada and much of the contiguous United States (Murie 1951). Two subspecies, the eastern elk (*Cervus elaphus canadensis*), which occurred in Kentucky, and the Merriam elk (*Cervus elaphus merriami*), were eliminated by habitat loss and overharvest (Bryant and Maser 1982). Because elk remain a popular recreational resource, numerous reintroduction attempts have been made in North America in the past century (Schmidt 1978). Many early reintroductions failed because of insufficient habitat; removals caused by crop depredation, disease, and poaching; and lack of sufficient funding for adequate management (Witmer 1990). Currently, seven reintroduced elk herds exist east of the Mississippi River (Layne 1993), including the growing herd in eastern Kentucky.

In 1997, the Kentucky Department of Fish and Wildlife Resources (KDFWR), in conjunction with the Rocky Mountain Elk Foundation, established an elk reintroduction program aimed at translocating approximately 1,800 elk to Kentucky by 2006. KDFWR selected a 1 million-ha, 14-county area in the southeastern portion of the state with low road and row crop density for elk release and establishment (Phillips 1997; Fig. 14.3). The population objective for elk is targeted at 7,500, or 2.6 per square km^2 within the release zone (Phillips 1997). To date, more than 1,000 elk have been released at five sites, four on active or reclaimed strip mines and one in the Daniel Boone National Forest.

Because of the domination of forest, forage availability probably determined the original distribution and movements of elk in Appalachia. Large generalist herbivores such as elk and white-tailed deer evolved in disturbed ecotonal landscapes where edge provided both food and cover (Geist 1982, 1998). Therefore, components of Appalachian elk habitat consisted primarily of river floodplains, natural forest openings (glades), herbaceous understories, and forest mast. Elk in the Cumberland Plateau

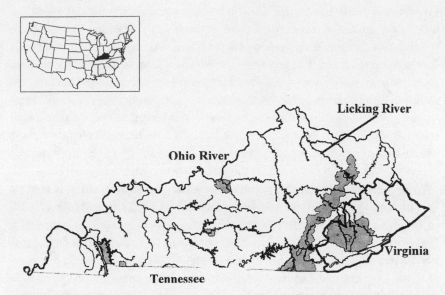

Figure 14.3 Major river drainages and federal lands *(shaded)* that could serve as the backbone of a regional conservation network in Kentucky. The thick outline in the southeastern portion of the state represents the 14-county elk reintroduction zone.

of Kentucky probably used more energy during daily foraging routines that often traversed the steep topographic gradients from ridgetop to streambank than did their Bluegrass counterpart, which did not need to migrate in response to seasonal forage availability. Elk of the Cumberland Plateau may have migrated primarily along the tributaries of the Kentucky and Licking Rivers to the Bluegrass region of Kentucky in winter and remained there through early spring green-up, then returned to the mountains before calving when grasses matured and forbs and browse became more readily available. Several reintroduced elk in Kentucky have dispersed out of the elk zone along these corridors, using openings and cropland during downstream travels toward the Bluegrass (J. J. Cox, unpublished data).

Coal mining and subsequent reclamation have changed both the topography and associated biotic communities in eastern Kentucky by replacing forest with grasslands. These vast areas of reclaimed land with reduced topographic gradients allow elk to maximize forage intake, minimize energy expenditure, and remain close to forest edges and thermal cover (Coop 1973; Grace and Easterbee 1979). Reintroduced elk in Kentucky prefer grassy openings

(Wichrowski 2001) and avoid the interior of large contiguous blocks of forest (Secrist 2000). However, 92 percent of the elk release zone is composed of second- and third-growth hardwood forest. Towns, agriculture, and roads have replaced historically important bottomlands, conditions that promote elk–human conflict (Lyon and Ward 1982). Although elk will continue to gravitate toward clearings on private lands, conflicts can be alleviated by maintaining existing wildlife clearings, food plots, and early successional stages of forest. In particular, replacing Fescue 31 (*Festuca arundinacea*, an exotic hybrid grass) with native warm season grasses on public lands will be important for increasing the nutritional value and palatability of available elk forage.

Although the contemporary eastern Kentucky landscape probably is more conducive to elk than were pre-Columbian conditions, increased access on minelands can promote disturbance that increases elk mortality (Lyon 1979; Unsworth et al. 1993). In addition, elk may affect forest succession by dispersing exotic plants, transporting nutrients, browsing, trampling, and tree-rubbing in fragmented minescapes. Another disadvantage of minelands as primary elk habitat is the insecurity of short-term lease agreements between wildlife agencies and private landowners. Fluctuating commodity prices and the evolution of cost-effective mining technologies can lead to further extraction of coal and timber (Power 1996) on lands leased as wildlife management areas. Such looming landscape threats often prevent wildlife agencies from investing in habitat improvements. An example of this problem is the forthcoming construction of a coal-burning power plant and industrial park at the first elk release site in Kentucky. The development of Elk Run Industrial Park will involve paving over 360 ha of habitat used by nearly 300 reintroduced elk and their offspring. Although mine owners originally were enthusiastic supporters of elk restoration with offers of reclaimed habitat, the same land is now destined for another round of mineral extraction.

Land acquisition within the restoration zone will be critical to maintaining key landscape components and reducing the reliance of the herd on uncertain land management practices on unstable private land holdings. Despite these disadvantages, it will be important to maintain some reclaimed areas for the purpose of providing open habitat that may enhance release site fidelity of reintroduced elk and alleviate future crop depredation from a growing population (Moran 1973). In addition, such lands will be important in providing recreational opportunities for viewing and hunting elk. Conversion of exotic cover species (e.g., *Lespedeza cuneata*) to native warm season grasses and integration of this technique within reclamation methods should be strongly encouraged for the benefit of elk and other wildlife.

Creating Blueprints for Conservation in Florida and Kentucky

Florida's ecological network proposes to link conservation lands along paths of least resistance that include riparian zones, proposed conservation land acquisition projects, and strategically located agricultural lands (Hoctor et al. 2000). Some amount of landscape restoration will be necessary to implement a vision of about 50 percent of the state in some form of biodiversity protection, but significant headway has already been made, and the public is generally supportive of land conservation initiatives. The Kentucky landscape is more dominated by agriculture than Florida, and human settlement is more widespread and diffuse. Thus, the challenges to large carnivore restoration are more daunting in Kentucky. Nonetheless, Kentucky still has physiographic features that could serve as the sites for future landscape-scale conservation. The two most notable of these are the mountains of the Cumberland Plateau and its rivers. The former occupy approximately 25 percent of the state in Appalachia, support much of the region's original plant communities (Ulack et al. 1998), and contain the state's largest collection of "conservation" lands (Daniel Boone National Forest; see Fig. 14.3). Kentucky rivers are more numerous than in any other state in the contiguous United States (more than 144,000 km; Ulack et al. 1998) and largely occupy their original, meandering channels. Rivers could serve as a regional corridor system that emanates from the eastern Kentucky Highlands, which are already connected to an extensive conservation network in the Appalachian Mountains. This, in turn, could link isolated preserves in the state and throughout the region. The Wildlands Project is the continental vision of an ecological network that proposes to integrate carnivore restoration with corridor and reserve design (Soulé and Noss 1998). Although it has not yet been implemented throughout North America, the idea is driving conservation initiatives at the regional scale (Hoctor et al. 2000; Dugelby et al. 2001) and is gaining momentum in Florida.

The relative integrity of many of Florida's ecosystems results from the congruency of late settlement with the rise of environmentalism. Living in close proximity to wildlands and large charismatic species has resulted in a proconservation attitude that has been accompanied by biological awareness and tolerance for wildlife. In addition, popular literature from well-known writers such as Marjorie Stoneman Douglas and Carl Hiassen has further sensitized the public to environmental issues. The persistence of all but one species (red wolf) of large fauna has obviated potentially controversial reintroductions to restore top-down influences. Instead, these species have served as important regional flagships for state and national conservation agencies and agendas. Although economic growth is in part responsible for financing the bold conservation initiatives currently under way in Florida, it will further fragment the state's unique ecosystems and subdivide its wildlife populations unless additional protective measures are applied. We believe that financial and political resources in Florida are capable of taking on this challenge.

In stark contrast, the socioeconomic, political, cultural, and educational challenges that confront humanity and biological conservation in Kentucky remain as diverse and imposing as in many undeveloped countries. In a state suffering from the decline of the tobacco and coal industries and with a lagging educational system, conservation is not a priority. However, opportunity exists to use species such as the charismatic elk as a flagship to spearhead regional conservation and promote environmental awareness and education in Appalachia. An elk reintroduction that spawns recreational and, perhaps more importantly, economic and educational opportunities could generate public support that paves the way for restoring keystone components and processes of Kentucky's ecosystems.

Perhaps after centuries of natural resource exploitation (Caudill 1962), both the eastern Kentucky landscape and public attitudes are poised for a shift toward a future that places biodiversity before short-term economic gain. Shifts in public perceptions can be cultivated if Kentucky and federal natural resource agencies promote regional biotic restoration that transcends the introduction of a charismatic large herbivore. Such work should begin now, before the exhaustion of regional fossil fuel supplies and the economic downturn that will follow. For Kentucky elk restoration to be an ecological success, it must also include the reestablishment of predators that maintain behavioral and ecological tensions (Maehr 2001). Although there are several carnivores that prey on elk in the western United States (Taber et al. 1982), the bobcat (*Lynx rufus*), naturalized coyote (*Canis latrans*), and black bear are the only predators in Kentucky known to occasionally prey on ungulates (Young and Jackson 1951; Barbour and Davis 1974; Major and Sherburne 1987; Parker 1995). Although it is unlikely that these species will use elk as a major food source, elk may cause these predators to alter their food habits indirectly through competition with and subsequent reduction of white-tailed deer. However, they are unlikely to have substantial impacts on elk survival and demography.

With elk restoration still a qualified success, Kentucky is not yet ready to promote the return of native carnivores that will return ecological tensions that have been absent from the commonwealth for nearly two centuries (Maehr 2001). And yet black bear sightings have increased steadily in the eastern highlands since the mid-1980s (Plaxico 1997), and there is increasing grassroots interest in restoring the cougar to the central Appalachians (Bolgiano 2001). Whether the landscape has recovered some of the vegetational diversity needed to support bears or whether local human residents have become more tolerant of them is unknown. However, it appears that like the black bear in the Trans Pecos (Onorato and Hellgren 2001) and the panther in Florida (Maehr et al. 2001), the species is expanding its range without intentional human encouragement. Are the limits to large fauna restoration in Kentucky as dismal as Caudill's (1962) account? Evidence from elsewhere suggests that such limits have yet to be realized.

A remarkable case study is unfolding in one of Europe's most technologically advanced regions. It suggests that large predators can return even where humans dominate the landscape. In the last few decades the gray wolf, lynx (*Lynx lynx*), and brown bear (*Ursus arctos*) have all expanded their ranges into industrial forestland in the populated heartland of Sweden and Norway (Gustafsson and Ahlen 1996). The most diurnal of these species, the gray wolf, apparently recolonized Fennoscandia along a narrow coastal corridor from extreme northwestern Russia in the late 1970s (Wabakken et al. 2001) and continues to increase at a 25 percent annual rate. Despite potential conflicts with domestic dogs (*Canis familiaris*) and livestock, "a great majority of Swedes and Norwegians do not want the species to be exterminated" (Wabakken et al. 2001, p. 13). Were such an attitude prevalent in eastern Kentucky, wildlife agencies would be engaged in restoring not only elk but also wolves and mountain lions, all components of the natural biota. Managers of eastern North American wildlife need look no farther than local landscape history to understand modern patterns of large mammal distributions. To change the trend of increased impoverishment in perpetually depressed areas such as eastern Kentucky will first require the realization that change is possible.

LITERATURE CITED

Barbour, R. W., and W. H. Davis. 1973. Trees and shrubs of Kentucky. University Press of Kentucky, Lexington.

Barbour, R. W., and W. H. Davis. 1974. Mammals of Kentucky. University Press of Kentucky, Lexington.

Bartram, W. 1791. Travels through North and South Carolina, Georgia, east and west Florida. James & Johnson, Philadelphia.

Belden, R. C. 1983. Florida panther recovery plan implementation: a 1983 progress report. Pages 159–172 in S. D. Miller and D. D. Everett (eds.), Cats of the world: biology, conservation and management. National Wildlife Federation, Washington, DC.

Bolgiano, C. 2001. Confirming eastern cougar presence. Wild Earth 11:54–56.

Braun, E. L. 1950. Deciduous forests of eastern North America. Macmillan, New York.

Bryant, L. D., and C. Maser. 1982. Classification and distribution. Pages 1–59 in J. W. Thomas and D. Toweill (eds.), Elk of North America: ecology and management. Stackpole Books, Harrisburg, PA.

Butterfield, B. P., W. E. Meshaka, Jr., and C. Guyer. 1997. Nonindigenous amphibians and reptiles. Pages 123–139 in D. Simberloff, D. C. Schmitz, and T. C. Brown (eds.), Strangers in paradise: impact and management of nonindigenous species in Florida. Island Press, Washington, DC.

Carr, A. F. 1940. A contribution to the herpetology of Florida. Biological Sciences Series III(1). University of Florida, Gainesville.

Carter, L. J. 1974. The Florida experience: land and water policy in a growth state. Johns Hopkins University Press, Baltimore, MD.

Caudill, H. M. 1962. Night comes to the Cumberlands: a biography of a depressed area. Little, Brown, Boston.

Coop, K. J. 1973. Habitat use, distribution, movement, and associated behavior of elk. Pages 97–100 in Western States Elk Workshop Proceedings, Bozeman, Montana.

Courtenay, W. R., Jr. 1997. Nonindigenous fishes. Pages 109–122 in D. Simberloff, D. C. Schmitz, and T. C. Brown (eds.), Strangers in paradise: impact and management of nonindigenous species in Florida. Island Press, Washington, DC.

Cox, J. A., R. Kautz, M. MacLaughlin, and T. Gilbert. 1994. Closing the gaps in Florida's wildlife habitat conservation system. Florida Game and Fresh Water Fish Commission, Tallahassee.

Dugelby, B., D. Foreman, R. List, B. Miller, J. Humphrey, M. Seidman, and R. Howard. 2001. Rewilding the Sky Islands region of the Southwest. Pages 65–81 in D. S. Maehr, R. F. Noss, and J. L. Larkin (eds.), Large mammal restoration: ecological and sociological challenges in the 21st century. Island Press, Washington, DC.

Eller, R. D. 1982. Miners, millhands, and mountaineers: industrialization of the Appalachian South, 1880–1930. University of Tennessee Press, Knoxville.

Foreman, D., J. Davis, D. Johns, R. Noss, and M. Soulé. 1992. The Wildlands Project mission statement. Wild Earth (special issue):2–3.

Gassett, J. W. 2001. Restoration of white-tailed deer in Kentucky. Pages 119–123 in D. S. Maehr, R. F. Noss, and J. L. Larkin (eds.), Large mammal restoration: ecological and sociological challenges in the 21st century. Island Press, Washington, DC.

Geist, V. 1982. Adaptive behavioral strategies. Pages 181–218 in J. W. Thomas and D. Toweill (eds.), Elk of North America: ecology and management. Stackpole Books, Harrisburg, PA.

Geist, V. 1998. Deer of the world. Stackpole Books, Mechanicsburg, PA.

Grace, J., and N. Easterbee. 1979. The natural shelter for red deer (*Cervus elaphus*) in a Scotland glen. Journal of Applied Ecology 16:37–48.

Griffith, B., J. M. Scott, J. W. Carpenter, and C. Reid. 1989. Translocation as a species conservation tool: status and strategy. Science 245:477–480.

Grumbine, R. E. 1994. What is ecosystem management? Conservation Biology 8:27–38.

Gustafsson, L., and I. Ahlen. 1996. National atlas of Sweden: geography of plants and animals. Royal Swedish Academy of Sciences, Stockholm.

Harlow, R. F. 1965. Diseases and parasites. Pages 125–139 in R. F. Harlow and F. K. Jones (eds.), The white-tailed deer in Florida. Technical Bulletin No. 9. Florida Game and Fresh Water Fish Commission, Tallahassee.

Harris, L. D. 1984. The fragmented forest. University of Chicago Press, Chicago.

Harris, L. D., L. C. Duever, R. P. Meegan, T. S. Hoctor, J. L. Schortemeyer, and D. S. Maehr. 2001. The biotic province as the minimum critical unit for biodiversity conservation. Pages 321–343 in D. S. Maehr, R. F. Noss, and J. L. Larkin (eds.), Large mammal restoration: ecological and sociological challenges in the 21st century. Island Press, Washington, DC.

Hazard Herald Leader. 2000. Plans for 886-acre industrial park, power plant raise hopes, fears. 90(18):A1.

Hoctor, T. S., M. H. Carr, and P. D. Zwick. 2000. Identifying a linked reserve system using a regional landscape approach: the Florida ecological network. Conservation Biology 14:984–1000.

Hodge, F. W. 1907. Handbook of North American Indians north of Mexico. Smithsonian Institution, Bureau of American Ethnology, Bulletin 30. Part 1, Government Printing Office, Washington, DC.

Kalisz, P. J. 1986. Soil properties of steep Appalachian old fields. Ecology 67:1011–1023.

Kentucky Biodiversity Task Force. 1995. Kentucky alive. Kentucky Department for Natural Resources, Frankfort.

Kentucky Environmental Quality Commission. 1997. State of Kentucky's environment: natural resources. Kentucky Environmental Quality Commission, Frankfort.

Knapp, A. K., J. M. Blaer, J. M. Briggs, S. L. Collins, D. C. Hartnelt, L. C. Johnson, and E. G. Townsend. 1999. The keystone role of bison in the North American tallgrass prairie. BioScience 49:39–50.

Land, E. D., and R. C. Lacy. 2000. Introgression level achieved through Florida panther genetic restoration. Endangered Species Update 17:100–105.

Larkin, J. L., R. Grimes, L. Cornicelli, J. Cox, and D. S. Maehr. 2001. Returning elk to Appalachia: foiling Murphy's law. Pages 101–117 in D. S. Maehr, R. F. Noss, and J. L. Larkin (eds.), Large mammal restoration: ecological and sociological challenges in the 21st century. Island Press, Washington, DC.

Layne, J. N. 1993. History of an introduction of elk in Florida. Florida Field Naturalist 21:77–80.

Layne, J. N. 1997. Nonindigenous mammals. Pages 157–186 in D. Simberloff, D. C. Schmitz, and T. C. Brown (eds.), Strangers in paradise: impact and management of nonindigenous species in Florida. Island Press, Washington, DC.

Lyon, L. J. 1979. Habitat effectiveness for elk as influenced by roads and cover. Journal of Forestry 77:658–660.

Lyon, L. J., and A. L. Ward. 1982. Elk and land management. Pages 443–447 in J. W. Thomas and D. Toweill (eds.), Elk of North America: ecology and management. Stackpole Books, Harrisburg, PA.

Maehr, D. S. 1992. Florida black bear. Pages 265–275 in S. R. Humphrey (ed.), Rare and endangered biota of Florida. Vol. 1. Mammals. University Press of Florida, Gainesville.

Maehr, D. S. 1997a. The comparative ecology of bobcat, black bear, and Florida panther in south Florida. Bulletin of the Florida Museum of Natural History 40:1–176.

Maehr, D. S. 1997b. The Florida panther: life and death of a vanishing carnivore. Island Press, Washington, DC.

Maehr, D. S. 2001. Restoring the large mammal fauna of the East: what follows the elk? Wild Earth 11:50–53.

Maehr, D. S., and G. B. Caddick. 1995. Demographics and genetic introgression in the Florida panther. Conservation Biology 9:1295–1298.

Maehr, D. S., and J. A. Cox. 1995. Landscape features and panthers in Florida. Conservation Biology 9:1008–1019.

Maehr, D. S., J. N. Layne, E. D. Land, J. W. McCown, and J. C. Roof. 1988. Long distance movement of a Florida black bear. Florida Field Naturalist 16:1–6.

Maehr, D. S., T. S. Hoctor, and L. D. Harris. 2001. The Florida panther: a flagship for regional restoration. Pages 291–312 in D. S. Maehr, R. F. Noss, and J. L. Larkin (eds.), Large mammal restoration: ecological and sociological challenges in the 21st century. Island Press, Washington, DC.

Major, J. T., and J. A. Sherburne. 1987. Interspecific relationships of coyotes, bobcats, and red foxes in western Maine. Journal of Wildlife Management 51:606–616.

Martin, A. C., H. S. Zim, and A. L. Nelson. 1951. American wildlife and plants: a guide to wildlife food habits. Dover, New York.

McNeely, J. A. 2000. Practical approaches for including mammals in biodiversity conservation. Pages 355–367 in A. Entwistle and N. Dunstone (eds.), Priorities for the conservation of mammalian diversity. Cambridge University Press, Cambridge, UK.

Moran, R. J. 1973. The Rocky Mountain elk in Michigan. Michigan Department of Natural Resources, Wildlife Division Research and Development Report 267. East Lansing, MI.

Murie, O. J. 1951. The elk of North America. Teton Bookshop, Jackson, WY.

National Wildlife Federation. 2001. Bush administration may reject citizen management approach to grizzly recovery. (Online at http://www.nwf.org/grizzly/bushrejectplan.html).

Onorato, D. P., and E. C. Hellgren. 2001. Black bear at the border: natural recolonization of the Trans Pecos. Pages 245–259 in D. S. Maehr, R. F. Noss, and J. L. Larkin (eds.), Large mammal restoration: ecological and sociological challenges in the 21st century. Island Press, Washington, DC.

Owen-Smith, R. N. 1988. Megaherbivores. The influence of very large body size in ecology. Cambridge University Press, Cambridge, UK.

Paquet, P. C., J. R. Strittholt, and N. L. Staus. 2001. Feasibility of timber wolf reintroduction in Adirondack Park. Pages 47–64 in D. S. Maehr, R. F. Noss, and J. L. Larkin (eds.), Large mammal restoration: ecological and sociological challenges in the 21st century. Island Press, Washington, DC.

Parker, G. R. 1995. The eastern coyote. Nimbus Publishing, Halifax, NS.

Patton, D. J. 1996. History and culture. Pages 78–125 in E. A. Fernald and E. D. Purdum (eds.), Atlas of Florida, revised ed. University Press of Florida, Gainesville.

Phillips, J. 1997. Technical proposal for free-ranging elk in Kentucky. Kentucky Department of Fish and Wildlife Resources, Frankfort.

Plaxico, J. 1997. Kentucky. Eastern Black Bear Workshop on Management and Research 14:4–5.

Power, T. M. 1996. Lost landscapes and failed economies: the search for a value of place. Island Press, Washington, DC.

Raitz, K., R. Schein, B. Clay, and N. O'Malley. 1998. Historical and cultural landscapes. Pages 47–77 in R. Ulack, K. Raitz, and G. Pauer (eds.), Atlas of Kentucky. University Press of Kentucky, Lexington.

Robson, M. S. 1992. Red wolf. Pages 29–34 in S. R. Humphrey (ed.), Rare and endangered biota of Florida. Vol. 1. Mammals. University Press of Florida, Gainesville.

Roy, J., C. Servheen, W. Kasworm, and J. Waller. 2001. Restoration of grizzly bears to the Bitterroot Wilderness: the EIS approach. Pages 205–224 in D. S. Maehr, R. F. Noss, and J. L. Larkin (eds.), Large mammal restoration: ecological and sociological challenges in the 21st century. Island Press, Washington, DC.

Schmidt, J. L. 1978. Early management: intentional and otherwise. Pages 257–270 in J. L. Schmidt and D. L. Gilbert (eds.), Big game of North America. Stackpole Books, Harrisburg, PA.

Secrist, D. E. 2000. Impacts of introduced elk on amphibian distribution and abundance in an eastern Kentucky forest. M.S. thesis, University of Kentucky, Lexington.

Shackleford, L., and B. Weinberg. 1977. Our Appalachia. Hill & Wang, New York.

Simberloff, D. 1998. Flagships, umbrellas, and keystones: is single-species management passé in the landscape era? Biological Conservation 83:247–257.

Simberloff, D., D. C. Schmitz, and T. C. Brown. 1997. Why we should care and what we should do. Pages 359–367 in D. Simberloff, D. C. Schmitz, and T. C. Brown (eds.), Strangers in paradise: impact and management of nonindigenous species in Florida. Island Press, Washington, DC.

Smith, J. S. 2001. Ecology and conservation of the black bear in west central Florida. M.S. thesis, University of Kentucky, Lexington.

Soulé, M., and R. Noss. 1998. Rewildling and biodiversity: complementary goals for continental conservation. Wild Earth 8(3):18–28.

Soulé, M. E., and J. Terborgh. 1999. Continental conservation: scientific foundations of regional reserve networks. Island Press, Washington, DC.

Stevenson, H. M., and B. H. Anderson. 1994. The birdlife of Florida. University Press of Florida, Gainesville.

Taber, R. D., K. Raedeke, and D. A. McCaughran. 1982. Population characteristics. Pages 279–298 in J. W. Thomas and D. E. Toweill (eds.), Elk of North America: ecology and management. Stackpole Books, Harrisburg, PA.

Ulack, R., K. Raitz, and G. Pauer (eds.). 1998. Atlas of Kentucky. University Press of Kentucky, Lexington.

Unsworth, J. W., L. Kuck, M. D. Scott, and E. O. Garton. 1993. Elk mortality in the clearwater drainage of north-central Idaho. Journal of Wildlife Management 57:495–502.

U.S. Congress. 1993. Harmful non-indigenous species in the United States. OTA-F-565, Office of Technology Assessment, U.S. Congress, Washington, DC.

Wabakken, P., H. Sand, O. Liberg, and A. Bjarvall. 2001. The recovery, distribution, and population dynamics of wolves on the Scandinavian peninsula, 1978–1998. Canadian Journal of Zoology 79:1–16.

Ward, D. B. 1989. How many plant species are native to Florida? Palmetto 9(4):3–5.

Western, D. 1987. Africa's elephants and rhinos: flagships in crisis. Trends in Ecology and Evolution (TREE) 2:343–345.

Wharton, M. E., and R. W. Barbour. 1991. Bluegrass land and life. University Press of Kentucky, Lexington.

Wichrowski, M. W. 2001. Activity, movement, and habitat use of a reintroduced elk population in Appalachia. M.S. thesis, University of Kentucky, Lexington.

Witmer, G. 1990. Re-introduction of elk in the United States. Journal of the Pennsylvania Academy of Science 64:131–135.

Young, S. P., and E. A. Goldman. 1946. The puma: mysterious American cat. American Wildlife Institute, Washington, DC.

Young, S. P., and E. A. Goldman. 1964. The wolves of North America. Dover Publications, New York.

Young, S. P., and H. H. T. Jackson. 1951. The clever coyote. University of Nebraska Press, Lincoln.

Zhi, L., P. Wenshi, Z. Xiaojian, W. Dajun, and W. Hao. 2000. What has the panda taught us? Pages 325–334 in A. Entwistle and N. Dunstone (eds.), Priorities for the conservation of mammalian diversity. Cambridge University Press, Cambridge, UK.

CHAPTER FIFTEEN

Giant Otters in the Peruvian Rainforest

Linking Protected Area Conditions to Species Needs

CHRISTOF SCHENCK, JESSICA GROENENDIJK,
FRANK HAJEK, ELKE STAIB, AND KARIN FRANK

The giant otter (*Pteronura brasiliensis*) is the largest of the world's 13 otter species and is endemic to the rainforests and wetlands of South America (Duplaix 1980; Forster-Turley et al. 1990). In 2000, it was classified as endangered by the International Union for Conservation of Nature and Natural Resources (IUCN), and it has been listed since 1973 under Appendix 1 of the Convention on International Trade of Endangered Species (CITES; Hilton-Taylor 2000). In the past, pelt hunting greatly depleted giant otter numbers in South America. Currently the species is threatened by multiple anthropogenic influences arising from increased colonization and tourism in lowland tropical forests.

In 1990, the long-term project Status, Habitat, Behaviour and Conservation of Giant Otters in Peru was initiated by the Frankfurt Zoological Society (FZS) under the Help for Threatened Wildlife program (Staib and Schenck 1994; Schenck and Staib 1992, 1995a, 1995b, 1996; Schenk et al. 1997a, 1997b, 1999; Groenendijk et al. 2000;). The key objectives were to determine giant otter habitat needs and behavioral ecology, to identify the distribution of remaining populations throughout Peru to establish the status of the species, to identify principal threats, and to develop a comprehensive plan for conservation. A full-time fieldwork period between July 1990 and October 1992 was followed by shorter periods of up to 2 months of monitoring undertaken annually until 1996. Since 1999, the fieldwork has been intensified and is operating on a full-time basis. Data collected during the period 1990–1996 form the basis for a mathematical model that explores the dynamics of giant otter populations and allows minimum conditions for long-term persistence to be determined. Use of this information will facilitate development of guidelines for a giant otter conservation management plan.

Monitoring Giant Otters

One of the key focus areas of the project is the 18,800-km^2 Manu Biosphere Reserve (including the 15,300-km^2 National Park) in Madre de Dios in southeastern Peru (Fig. 15.1). The entire watershed of the Manu River lies within the Manu Biosphere Reserve and forms the heart of this protected area. It is a lowland, meandering river, slow-flowing during the dry season but experiencing strong floods during the wet season. Erosion rates are rapid during this time of the year, occasionally resulting in the creation of oxbow lakes that are the favored habitats of giant otters. No other river in the Manu Biosphere Reserve gives rise to oxbow lakes that are sufficiently large to be attractive as otter habitat, and only a small proportion of the population inhabits the smaller tributaries of the Manu (see Fig. 15.1).

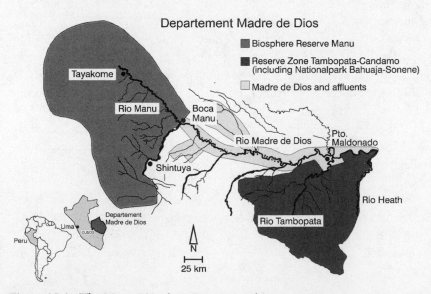

Figure 15.1   The Manu Biosphere Reserve study area.

Since 1990, we have conducted annual surveys of the giant otter population along the Manu River (Fig. 15.2) and its 28 oxbow lakes (Schenck
1997; Staib 2002). The surveys are usually carried out toward the end of the
dry season, when cubs are old enough to participate fully in group activities.
Each giant otter has a characteristic cream-colored throat pattern that provides the most reliable means of identification and prevents an individual
from being counted more than once. By filming the throat patterns with a
handheld video camera, we identified and recognized individuals over suc-
cessive years and obtained accurate figures of the total number of different
individuals seen per census (Schenck and Staib 1998; see Fig. 15.2). By these
means, we assembled a throat marking catalog, including information on
group members such as date and place of birth, sex, date and location of
sightings, number of cubs born within each group per year per female, season when an individual was first seen as a solitary or floater, and date when
an individual was last seen.

Long-term monitoring in the Manu Biosphere Reserve has provided
insights into giant otter population structure and dynamics and the species'
behavioral and reproductive ecology (Staib 2002). Briefly, a typical giant
otter population comprises highly social family groups averaging five or six

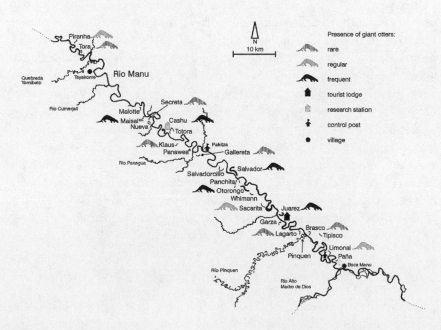

Figure 15.2   Giant otter presence in the Manu National Park.

individuals with well-established territories, and sexually mature, solitary individuals known as floaters. As a rule, only a single reproductive pair in each family produces up to four cubs once a year during the dry season. Juvenile mortality is high, despite the fact that the parents are assisted in rearing the cubs by remaining group members (i.e., offspring from previous years). Each year, several otter families fail to raise a litter of cubs. After reaching sexual maturity at 2 to 3 years of age, individuals gradually leave the parent group and become floaters temporarily, adopting a more nomadic way of life in their search for a mate and their own territories. They may travel large distances (more than 100 river km), and we suspect that floaters suffer a high mortality rate.

Giant otter family group territories do not overlap. A typical family territory includes two or three oxbow lakes as well as areas of surrounding swamps, creeks, and rivers. Our research in Manu has shown that both group size and average group reproductive success are correlated with the total surface area of the oxbow lakes available to a group (Schenck 1997). Therefore, the larger the lake, the more important its role in supporting large family groups with high reproductive output. The larger oxbow lakes in the study area are critical to maintaining the otter population. In any given year, about 70 percent of the giant otter population is found in five key territories that have a single large lake as their core area. Each year, at least 80 percent of cub births recorded occurred in these same five territories. Although these key territories have been occupied continually by giant otter families over the last 10 years, a certain number of lakes are always uninhabited. The absence of otters varied between lakes and periods of time. Investigation of prey availability and other habitat factors did not lead to any clear explanation for giant otter absence (Schenck 1997).

Although otters may attain an age of more than 10 years in the wild, a typical population generally has a young age structure, with approximately 75 percent of otters dying or disappearing before they are 4 years old. Mortality factors in well-protected natural areas are little known, but human disturbance (resulting in part from tourism) is considered to be a cause of stress and, on occasion, death, particularly for juveniles still dependent on their mother's milk (Wünnemann 1992; Schenck 1997; Schenck and Staib 1998).

Analyzing the Viability of the Giant Otter Population

The most important result of the monitoring has been that the giant otter population in the Manu National Park shows a metagroup structure with

the risk of local extinction of single family groups and the chance of recolonization of free suitable oxbow lakes by dispersing individuals (the
floaters). Therefore, the dynamics of the otter population are qualitatively
similar to the dynamics of a metapopulation (Levins 1969); that is, a network of local populations where local extinction can be compensated by
recolonization. It is well known from classic metapopulation theory that a
metapopulation can persist in the long term only if the average colonization
rate of empty habitats is higher than the extinction rate of a local population.

This condition for long-term metapopulation persistence provides a good
basis for analyzing giant otter population viability. A detailed understanding of the colonization process is needed to identify both the key causes of
extinction and the minimum conditions for long-term persistence. Therefore,
the following questions are of particular importance in this context:

- What variables influence the rate of successful colonization?
- What conditions must be met to ensure that a vacant territory can be colonized sufficiently rapidly?

To support decision making for conservation management in the park, tools
for assessing the current viability status of the otter population are needed.
Finally, to advise management, it is important to understand how population viability can best be sustained.

Empirical studies of the giant otter in the Manu Biosphere Reserve
(Schenck 1997; Staib 2002) have revealed that filling vacant reproductive
positions in existing family groups occurs quite fast (within a few weeks),
but colonization of a free oxbow lake takes much longer (1 year or longer).
This suggests that finding a suitable oxbow lake and obtaining information
about the occupancy status of the lake (e.g., free, occupied by a complete
group, or vacant reproductive position) is not a serious problem for a floater.
It seems reasonable to suppose that the bottleneck for a successful colonization is whether a floater meets a potential mate at the right time and
place.

To test this hypothesis and to analyze the consequences, we developed a
model to simulate the probability of a male and female otter being present
at the same time. We purposefully kept the model as simple as possible.
Rather than simulate detailed paths of individual floaters through the landscape, we focused on the essential effect: their visits to specific unoccupied
oxbow lakes. The simulation model is based on the following assumptions:

the population contains a total number of N_F floaters per year; each floater visits the oxbow lake f_V times a year, where the specific timing is random; a visiting floater waits T_W days (7 to 14 days) for a partner and leaves the oxbow lake in case of failure; and the sex ratio among the floaters is assumed to be 1:1 because there is no empirical evidence for a different value. By taking these rules as a basis for the model, the daily number of visiting females and males at a certain oxbow lake can be simulated. We ran this simulation over the expected lifetime of the family groups (T_G) and determined the probability of at least one successful otter meeting during this time (an otter meeting is said to be successful if both sexes are present at the oxbow lake at the same time). We conducted 100 runs and determined the probability of an otter meeting (p_{meet}) given by the percentage of successful runs.

The model revealed that there is a threshold condition for long-term population persistence. Fig. 15.3A shows how the probability of an otter meeting (p_{meet}) is influenced by the annual number of floaters (N_F). As indicated by the arrow, there is a critical number of floaters, N_F^{crit}, above which an otter meeting within the expected lifetime of a family group is almost certain ($p_{meet} \approx 1$). Below this threshold value, however, the value of p_{meet} decreases rapidly, suggesting that finding a mate and establishing a new family group becomes more and more of a problem (i.e., it takes too much time). This means that the yearly total number of floaters (N_F) available in the system determines whether the entire otter population can use an empty suitable habitat quickly enough. Therefore, N_F can be interpreted as an indicator of the colonization potential of the population. To fully understand the colonization process, we need to look at the factors that determine the annual total number of floaters (N_F). Moreover, we need to analyze the preconditions that must be met to ensure that the critical number of floaters (N_F^{crit}) is met or exceeded.

Undoubtedly, the annual total number of floaters (N_F) in the system depends on the family groups and their ability to recruit young into the floater pool. N_F can be expressed in terms of the number of family groups (N_G), the number of subadults recruited per family group per year (N_S), and the annual floater mortality (μ). The reciprocal value ($1/\mu$) of the annual floater mortality (μ) determines the mean number of years a floater survives. Therefore, $1/\mu$ also gives the mean number of age classes of floaters in the system (the class of floaters from this year, from one year before, from two years before and so on). In consequence, the total number of floaters (N_F) in the system is given as $N_F = 1/\mu \times N_S \times N_G$. Fig. 15.3B shows the threshold number of family groups (N_G^{crit}, indicated by the arrow) needed to exceed the critical threshold number of floaters (N_F^{crit}, dashed line)

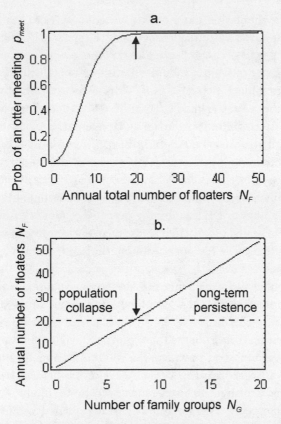

Figure 15.3   *(A)* Probability of an otter meeting (p_{meet}) versus annual total number of floaters (N_F). The arrow indicates the existence of a threshold value below which p_{meet} decreases rapidly. *(B)* Total number of floaters in relation to the number of family groups (N_G). The dashed line indicates the critical number of floaters (N_F^{crit}), and the arrow refers to the resulting critical number of family groups (N_G^{crit}), both needed for sustaining a viable otter population.

Above this threshold value, the resulting total amount of floaters (N_F) is above the critical value (N_F^{crit}). As a result, otter meetings on average take place quickly enough to ensure that an empty oxbow lake can be colonized before the next extinction of a family group occurs (see Fig. 15.3A). Therefore, the number of family groups (N_G) and hence the number of floaters in the system increases further. Such a population obviously has a good chance to persist over a longer period of time. Moreover, the population is highly resilient to moderate accidental extinction of family groups because of a rapid recolonization. Because there is an accompanying increase in the numbers of floaters, the population has a higher potential to serve as a source for expansion; that is, for the colonization of new habitats. Therefore, as long as the critical number of N_G^{crit} family groups is exceeded, the population is secure.

A totally different picture occurs if the number of family groups (N_G) falls below the threshold value (N_G^{crit}). In this case, the total number of floaters (N_F) is below the critical value (N_F^{crit}, see Fig 15.3B), resulting in an increasing risk that otter meetings do not occur frequently enough and that an extinction occurs before an empty oxbow lake is colonized. As a result, the number of family groups decreases further. This means that a strong downward trend in both N_F and N_G is induced, each amplifying the negative effect of the other. Therefore, the population is in imminent danger of collapsing and cannot persist over the long term. Such a population has a low probability of expansion. Even if suitable habitats are available for expansion, the colonization potential of the population is too low to occupy them quickly enough.

Our model analysis reveals that the qualitative dynamic behavior of the entire otter population changes completely if the number of family groups (N_G) falls short of the threshold value N_G^{crit}. The population can persist in the long term or serve as a source for expansion only if a minimum number of N_G^{crit} family groups or, equivalently, a minimum annual number of N_F^{crit} floaters is established. This threshold behavior has serious consequences. Populations that are already close to threshold values are in a critical situation: Any further decrease in the number of family groups and the number of floaters from whatever source can induce a collapse of the population. This is also the case if the corresponding threshold value increases so that a formerly safe population becomes vulnerable to extinction because of the risk that the heightened threshold condition (e.g., $N_G > N_G^{crit}$) can no longer be met. For conservation practice, it is critical to know where the threshold values lie and what may influence them.

Assessing Threshold Values and Identifying Threats

In the following, we present equations that allow threshold values for the number of floaters (N_F^{crit}) and the number of family groups (N_G^{crit}) to be predicted and the major threats to populations to be identified. The model contains only four parameters: the annual total number of floaters (N_F), the per floater and year frequency of visiting a certain oxbow lake (f_V), the waiting time at the oxbow lake (T_W), and the expected lifetime of a family group (T_G). Because of this simplicity, the functional relationship between the probability of an otter meeting (p_{meet}) given by the model and the model parameters can be calculated as follows. One can easily check that

$$p_{meet} = 1 - \exp[-T_W/365\ (T_G) \times (f_V \times N_F/2)^2] \qquad \text{(Equation 15.1)}$$

By taking this relation as a basis, an equation for the critical number of floaters (N_F^{crit}) can be developed. We define the threshold value N_F^{crit} to be the number of floaters at which the probability of meeting (p_{meet}) becomes larger than $1 - e^{-4}$. By algebraic manipulation, we get

$$N_F^{crit} = 4/f_V \times \sqrt{365/(T_W \times T_G)} \qquad \text{(Equation 15.2)}$$

Once the threshold value (N_F^{crit}) for the total number of floaters is known, the critical value N_G^{crit} for the number of family groups can be determined by taking into account that N_F and N_G are related to each other in a linear manner ($N_F = 1/\mu \times N_S \times N_G$). Therefore, $N_G^{crit} = \mu/N_S \times N_F^{crit}$. By replacing N_F^{crit} with the term given in Equation 15.2, we come up with

$$N_G^{crit} = 4/(f_V/\mu)\ (1/N_S)\ (\sqrt{365/(T_W \times T_G)}) \qquad \text{(Equation 15.3)}$$

Equations 15.2 and 15.3 allow the threshold values N_F^{crit} and N_G^{crit} to be calculated and used as yardsticks for assessing the viability status of the population under consideration ("Is the number of family groups above or below N_G^{crit}?"). Certainly, the precision of the predicted threshold values N_F^{crit} and N_G^{crit} can be only as high as the precision of the model parameters (e.g., the frequency [f_V] of visiting a certain oxbow lake) used in the calculation. Much more important for conservation practice, however, is the fact that the functional structure of the equations we present also provides understanding of the major threats to populations that are close to the threshold values.

Equation 15.3 reveals that the critical number of family groups, N_G^{crit}, depends on the ratio f_V/μ, that is, the total number of visits at a certain oxbow lake by a single floater during its lifespan ($1/\mu$) on average. Fig. 15.4A shows that as long as f_V/μ is above a certain threshold value, N_G^{crit} is nearly constant and 5 to 10 family groups are found to be sufficient for sustaining a viable population. But whenever f_V/μ falls short of this threshold value (about 0.1 if the maximum possible number of four subadults recruited per year per family group is assumed), N_G^{crit} rapidly increases to 50 or more family groups needed. This means that whenever less than a tenth of the floaters are visiting the oxbow lake under consideration once in their life, N_G^{crit} is sensitive to any further decrease in f_V/μ. In this case, increasing floater mortality and thinning of the habitat distribution (larger distances between the patches) become important threats to the population because both diminish the total number of visits (f_V/μ) a single floater can perform in its life (Fig. 15.4).

The functional structure of Equation 15.3 also indicates that the critical value N_G^{crit} depends on certain characteristics of the family groups themselves, such as their expected lifetime (T_G) and the number of subadults (N_S) a family group recruits per year on average. Fig. 15.4B shows that the value of N_G^{crit} grows rapidly if N_S falls short of a threshold value of about two subadults recruited per year. This means that whenever the production of subadults is in the critical region, N_G^{crit} is very sensitive to any further reduction in N_S. In this situation, any destabilization on the local level (i.e., within the individual family groups) may induce a collapse of the entire population. The different curves in Fig. 15.4 indicate that the threshold values found for f_V/μ and N_S are independent of both the floaters' waiting time (T_W) at the oxbow lake under consideration and the expected lifespan of the family groups (T_G). Although both parameters have been varied within a biologically reasonable range of values, the corresponding curves are close to each other.

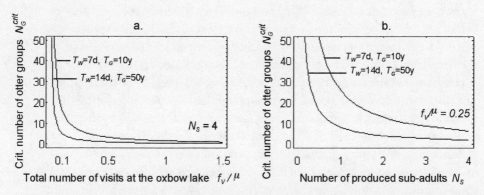

Figure 15.4   (A) The critical number of family groups (N_G^{crit}) needed to sustain a viable otter population versus the total number of visits at a certain oxbow lake (f_V/μ) performed by each floater during its life on average for $N_S = 4$. (B) N_G^{crit} versus the number of subadults (N_S) recruited by each family group per year on average for $f_V/\mu = 0.25$. In (A) and (B), the floaters' waiting time (T_W) and the expected lifespan of the family groups (T_G) are varied in a range that is relevant for the Manu population (T_W: 7 to 14 days; T_G: 10 to 50 years).

These model results show that populations near the threshold level are more susceptible to threats such as increasing isolation and local destabilization than populations well above the critical number of otter groups (N_G^{crit}). However, these threats are nonlinear and are important only if isolation exceeds a certain level or if family groups recruit less than two subadults per year on average. Therefore, for conservation practice, it is important to know whether the population is near threshold levels.

What Do These Findings Mean for Otter Population Viability?

The otter population along the Manu River is valued as one of the largest and most natural populations for these highly endangered top predators in Peru and South America (Forster-Turley et al. 1990; Schenck 1997). Monitoring and modeling data have shown that even this population, located in a natural area largely protected by national park legislation, is far from being safe. The reasons for this precarious situation are as follows.

Low Population Density

Despite the fact that Manu National Park and the Biosphere Reserve are among the largest protected areas on Earth (18,800 km², equivalent to half the size of Switzerland), they support under natural conditions a giant otter population of fewer than 100 animals. Compared with other carnivores, giant otters occupy astonishingly small territories (e.g., less than 110 ha for an otter group of five to seven animals [Schenck 1997]; the average territory size for jaguars [*Panthera onca*] is more than 3,000 ha [Rabinowitz 1986]). Overall otter density nevertheless remains low because they concentrate on wetland habitats, covering less than 1 percent of the total area. Additionally, giant otters are tied to large oxbow lakes, which themselves are limited in numbers and are distributed along a linear riverine corridor. Terrestrial predators such as jaguars and pumas (*Felis concolor*) might patrol territories 150 times the size of an otter territory but populate the Manu area with more than 400 individuals (Schenck 1997).

Few Reproducing Animals and High Risk of Group Extinction

Given an intermediate group size of about five animals (Staib 2002) and a maximum number of about 100 animals, fewer than 20 groups (reproductive pairs) colonize the huge Manu area. The model shows that with one subadult recruited from each family group per year on average, the population is already in the critical region (see Fig. 15.4B) where it suffers from threats of local destabilization. Any additional mortality can lead to a reduced meeting possibility among floaters, a low recolonization rate of adequate habitat, and a strong, self-perpetuating downward trend.

Human Influences Concentrating on the Otters' Habitat

Despite the extraordinary size of Manu National Park and its status as one of the most natural areas of South American rainforest (Terborgh 1983, 1992, 1999), there is significant human impact on the otters. Natives of the Machiguenga tribes live along the river in the core area of the park. Their domestic dogs carry distemper and parvovirus, both of which are lethal for otters (Schenck et al. 1997b). Tourism, with its fast motorboats on the river, canoe tours on the lakes, and trails along the shoreline, can reduce reproduction success and force otters to abandon a lake. In some cases, scientific research and filming have added to the disturbance level (Schenck 1997; Schenck and Staib 1998). Fish tissue analyses have shown that mercury contamination, resulting from gold-mining areas and incorporated into the flesh of migrating fish, is present in the area (Gutleb et al. 1997). The effects on otters are still unknown, but these threats represent potential forces for destabilization of family groups.

Near Isolation from Other Populations

Manu National Park and other areas where giant otters exist today may not always have been the best habitats. Before human occupation, areas with big rivers and many oxbow lakes, such as the lower Madre de Dios, may have supported higher giant otter densities with higher group and population stability than are found in Manu today. Otters have largely disappeared from these habitats as human settlement occurred. Otters have survived only in the remote headwaters of rivers such as Manu. The remaining populations are far from each other and probably have little exchange (Schenck 1997). These findings strongly suggest that the giant otter population in Manu National Park is already close to the critical number of family groups needed for long-term persistence. Moreover, the population is vulnerable to both increasing isolation and local destabilization, as evidenced by the empirical finding that there are suitable but empty habitats.

By combining population monitoring with population modeling we gain insight into both the qualitative behavior of giant otter population dynamics and the long-term consequences for population viability. Important key factors leading to extinction can be identified and minimum conditions for long-term persistence for the entire otter population formulated. Model-based tools for assessing the viability status of the population are then easy to derive (see also Hanski and Ovaskainen 2000; Vos et al. 2001; Frank and Wissel 1998, 2002).

Discussion: Consequences for Managing the Manu Biosphere Reserve

The results of the combined monitoring and modeling analysis of the giant otter population in the Manu Biosphere Reserve offer valuable information for conservation management. They have provided a better understanding of the dynamics (e.g., threshold behavior) and the viability status of the population. Moreover, potential sources of further endangerment have been identified. This information provides an indispensable basis for setting sound management priorities.

First Consequence: Stabilizing the Core Population Is Essential for Any Expansion

The Manu population may provide a source for colonizing surrounding habitats outside the biosphere reserve. The Madre de Dios River downriver from the confluence with the Manu River provides an ideal habitat for giant otters with high numbers of large oxbow lakes (Schenck 1997). Because of high hunting pressure during the period of international fur trade (1940–1970), otters are absent from most of the oxbow lakes in the Madre de Dios area, even though there is still adequate habitat outside gold-mining and agriculture areas. However, the Manu population must be stabilized before focusing on connecting populations and recolonizing the Madre de Dios.

Second Consequence: Guidelines for Stabilizing the Manu Population

To stabilize the Manu otter population, the oxbow lakes must be protected. Given human impacts along the river and on oxbow lakes, it is important to know which lakes are of particular importance for contributing to the maintenance of a viable population. Local stability is strongly related to group size. Therefore, large family groups are of central importance for the viability of the entire otter population. For effective protection, it is important to know what characteristics of oxbow lakes allow large otter groups to be sustained. We (Schenck 1997) found that large otter groups occur only in large and undisturbed oxbow lakes. The larger the lake, the more fish are available and the more otters can be sustained. Additionally, single large lakes are more easily scent-marked and controlled by the group. Migration to neighboring lakes with young cubs, who are vulnerable to predators, can be minimized. There is evidence from observations in the field (Schenck 1997; Staib 2002) and from captivity (Wünnemann 1992) that reproducing otter females are very sensitive to any kind of human disturbance. The resulting stress seems to affect the condition of the female, causing immediate termination of lactation. Juveniles, depending fully on their mother's milk in the first two months and partly until the age of six months, risk starvation.

These findings give rise to the following conclusion: In the case of Manu Biosphere Reserve and National Park, conservation management should concentrate on the few large lakes. Most of these lakes should be set aside as no-enter zones. Because visitor tours to the lakes form an important part of Manu tourism, it is difficult or impossible to close all lake access. Tourism should concentrate on smaller lakes. Long-term observation has shown that the disturbance level depends largely on the management of the area. Trails more than 100 m from the shoreline, safety zones on the lake with no canoe traffic, a limited number of one to two boats at the same time, and well-trained guides form the basis of low-impact tourism. Additionally, otter observation is easier and more successful. Continuous monitoring is essential.

Conclusion

A rethinking of conservation strategies for the park is needed. Although the Manu Biosphere Reserve is one of the largest protected areas worldwide, long-term persistence of the giant otter population is not guaranteed. This means that a large protected area alone is not yet a guarantee for sustaining a viable population. The question of whether to invest in the conservation of giant otters is not an academic one. For the Manu Biosphere Reserve, the giant otter is just one of 190 mammal species (Pacheco et al. 1993). However, giant otters are top predators of complex aquatic systems, and they play an important role in ecosystem dynamics (Terborgh 1992). Additionally, giant otters are charismatic flagship species (see Chapter 4, this volume) with extraordinary importance for ecotourism, one of the very few economic activities for the region, which can be carried out in a sustainable way if managed properly. Giant otters are excellent bioindicators of the health of tropical lowland in southeastern Peru.

The naturally low number of otters, the increased isolation, and the loss of neighboring otter populations because of hunting and colonization by settlers and gold miners along the Madre de Dios River are the main reasons for the current situation in the Manu Biosphere Reserve. Manu's giant otters show that even the largest protected areas can be too small to safeguard their biodiversity (Terborgh 1999). For the biggest of all otters, we have to think big.

Summary

Giant otters (*Pteronura brasiliensis*) were once common in the rivers, lakes, and swamps throughout the South American lowland rainforests from Columbia to Argentina. Poaching for the international fur trade has reduced the population and the range of the species significantly. Today, the giant otter is threatened, and any trade is prohibited. Ever-increasing deforestation, rivers polluted with mercury used for gold mining, overfishing, uncontrolled tourism, and possibly diseases transmitted by domestic animals are the major threats. Protected areas play a critical role in the giant otter's survival. However, the question of whether existing preserves are large enough to sustain viable populations of giant otters is a reasonable one. Our long-term studies in Manu National Park in southeast Peru have shown that, compared with other carnivores, family groups of giant otters use exceptionally small territories. Still, the population density remains surprisingly low (approximately 75 animals in the 15,300-km^2 National Park).

Based on our behavioral studies, we developed an individual-based simulation model. The model indicated that the number of family groups and the number of dispersing, sexually mature subadults are the two factors most critical for the long-term persistence of the Manu population. In the model, we calculated the probability that two potential partners will meet in a vacant territory. The greater the number of animals in the population, the sooner a vacant territory became occupied. Below a critical population size, however, the probability of colonization dropped significantly. The modeling results demonstrated that small-scale events that reduced the numbers of dispersing otters may result in a large-scale decline of the entire population. The results also indicate that the giant otter population in Manu National Park, one of the largest protected areas worldwide, is isolated and not large enough itself to be considered viable in the long term.

Acknowledgments

The project was financed by the Frankfurt Zoological Society, Help for Threatened Wildlife. The Gottfried Daimler and Karl Benz Foundation supported the project with two fellowships. The UFZ Center for Environmental Research Leipzig-Halle made it possible to analyze data and construct the model. We would like to thank the Peruvian authorities Instituto Nacional de Recoursos Naturales (INRENA) for all their support, the administration of the national parks for the opportunity to do the fieldwork, and the Peruvian nongovernment organization ProNaturaleza for its cooperation. Special thanks are due to Jesus Huaman, our most important collaborator in the field.

LITERATURE CITED

Duplaix, N. 1980. Observation on the ecology and behavior of the giant river otter (*Pteronura brasiliensis*) in Suriname. Revue DíEcologie (Terre et Vie) 34:496–620.

Forster-Turley, P., S. Macdonald, and C. Mason. 1990. Otters: an action plan for their conservation. IUCN, Gland, Switzerland.

Frank, K., and C. Wissel. 1998. Spatial aspects of metapopulation survival: from model results to rules of thumb for landscape management. Landscape Ecology 13:363–379.

Frank, K., and C. Wissel. 2002. A formula for the mean lifetime of metapopulations in heterogeneous landscapes. American Naturalist 159:530–552.

Groenendijk, J., F. Hajek, S. Isola, and C. Schenck. 2000. Giant Otter Project in Peru: field trip and activity report, 1999. IUCN Otter Specialist Group Bulletin 17(1):34–45.

Gutleb, A., C. Schenck, and E. Staib. 1997. Giant otter (*Pteronura brasiliensis*) at risk? Total mercury and methylmercury levels in fish and otter scats, Peru. Ambio 8:511–514.

Hanski, I., and O. Ovaskainen. 2000. The metapopulation capacity of a fragmented landscape. Nature 404:755–758.

Hilton-Taylor, C. (comp.). 2000. 2000 IUCN Red List of threatened species. IUCN, Gland, Switzerland.

Levins, R. 1969. Some demographic and genetic consequences of environmental heterogeneity for biological control. Bulletin of the Entomological Society of America 15:237–240.

Pacheco, V., B. D. Patterson, J. L. Patton, L. H. Emmons, S. Solari, and C. F. Ascorra. 1993. List of mammal species known to occur in Manu Biosphere Reserve, Peru. Publication Museum of Natural History USMSM, Lima, Peru (A) 44:1–12.

Rabinowitz, A. R. 1986. Ecology and behaviour of the jaguar (*Panthera onca*) in Belize, Central America. Journal of Zoology 210:149–159.

Schenck, C. 1997. Vorkommen, Habitatnutzung und Schutz des Riesenotters (*Pteronura brasiliensis*) in Peru. Berichte aus der Biologie, Shaker Verlag, Aachen, Germany.

Schenck, C., and E. Staib. 1992. Giant otters in Peru. IUCN Otter Specialist Group Bulletin 7:24–26.

Schenck, C., and E. Staib. 1995a. The Giant Otter Project in Peru 1995. IUCN Otter Specialist Group Bulletin 12:25–30.

Schenck, C., and E. Staib. 1995b. News from the Giant Otter Project in Peru. IUCN Otter Specialist Group Bulletin 11:5–8.

Schenck, C., and E. Staib. 1996. The Giant Otter Project in Peru 1995. IUCN Otter Specialist Group Bulletin 12:25–30.

Schenck, C., and E. Staib. 1998. Status, habitat use and conservation of giant otters in Peru. Pages 359–370 in N. Dunstone and M. Gorman (eds.), Behaviour and ecology of riparian mammals. Cambridge University Press, Cambridge, UK.

Schenck, C., E. Staib, and I. Storch. 1997a. 1996 news from the Giant Otter Project in Peru. IUCN Otter Specialist Group Bulletin 14(1):13–19.

Schenck, C., E. Staib, and I. Storch. 1997b. Domestic animal disease risks for Peruvian giant otters (*Pteronura brasiliensis*). IUCN Veterinary Specialist Group Newsletter 14:7–8.

Schenck, C., J. Groenendijk, and F. Hajek. 1999. Giant Otter Project in Peru: field trip and activity report 1998. IUCN Otter Specialist Group Bulletin 16(1):33–42.

Staib, E. 2002. Öko-Ethologie von Riesenottern (*Pteronura brasiliensis*) in Peru. Ph.D. dissertation, Ludwig-Maximillians-Universität, Munich.

Staib, E., and C. Schenck. 1994. Giant otters and ecotourism in Peru. IUCN Otter Specialist Group Bulletin 9:7–8.

Terborgh, J. 1983. Five new world primates: a study in comparative ecology. Monographs in behavior ecology. Princeton University Press, Princeton, NJ.

Terborgh, J. 1992. Diversity and the tropical rainforest. Scientific American Library, New York.

Terborgh, J. 1999. Requiem for nature. Island Press, Washington, DC.

Vos, C., J. Verboom, P. F. M. Opdam, and C. J. F. ter Braak. 2001. Towards ecologically scaled landscape indices. American Naturalist 157:24–41.

Wünnemann, K. 1992. Das Verhalten von Landraubtieren mit überdurchschnittlicher Cephalisation. Ph.D. dissertation, Tierärztliche Hochschule, Hannover, Germany.

CHAPTER SIXTEEN

Linking Landscape Management with the Conservation of Grassland Birds in Wisconsin

DAVID W. SAMPLE, CHRISTINE A. RIBIC,
AND ROSALIND B. RENFREW

In the last three decades, grassland birds have had a greater percentage of species exhibiting population declines than all other avian guilds in North America (Vickery and Herkert 2001). Major causes include land use changes that have resulted in habitat loss, fragmentation, and simplification (reduction in the number and complexity of relationships between species and their environments; Addis et al. 1995) and changes in agricultural practices on breeding and wintering grounds. Concern over the status of these species in Wisconsin began in the 1970s (Hine 1973) and early 1980s (Robbins 1982). Grassland birds have recently become a high conservation priority in Wisconsin and throughout the hemisphere (Sample and Mossman 1997; Vickery et al. 1999).

Although we seldom have complete knowledge of the causal factors limiting grassland bird populations, management activities promoting the establishment and improvement of habitat are some of the primary tools for advancing the conservation of these communities (Herkert et al. 1996). There are many questions about how best to manage grassland habitats and at what scale. The diversity of habitat needs among grassland birds makes management complex (Sample and Mossman 1997). In addition, studies suggest that many grassland bird species are area-sensitive and therefore need fields above a certain size; however, these results have been highly variable from region to region (Herkert 1994; Vickery et al. 1994; McCoy 1996; Winter and Faaborg 1999; Johnson and Igl 2001). Regional differences in landscape composition and structure may change how birds use habitat patches, accounting for some of this variability. Lingering questions related to area sensitivity have led to studies that address landscape-level effects in grassland birds (Ryan et al. 1998; Winter 1998; Niemuth 2000; see also reviews in Rodenhouse et al. 1995 and Freemark et al. 1995). Proposals for landscape-scale management areas for grassland birds (Sample and Mossman 1997; Fitzgerald et al. 1998) also reflect recognition of potential landscape effects. However, a better understanding of landscape-level influences on grassland bird populations in agricultural landscapes is needed (Herkert et al. 1996; Best et al. 1997).

The purpose of this chapter is to investigate how the concept of landscape-scale management of grassland birds has developed in Wisconsin and how it has begun to be implemented on the ground. We first provide background on the history and status of grasslands and grassland birds in Wisconsin. We then address the basic management philosophy of the Wisconsin Department of Natural Resources (DNR) and the development of a landscape-scale management model for grassland birds. We review the evidence for landscape-level effects in Wisconsin, including some new analyses of extant data. Finally, we provide examples of landscape-scale management projects in Wisconsin and management recommendations for the conservation of grassland birds. Throughout, our emphasis is on linking concepts with implementation of large-scale management.

History of Grasslands in Wisconsin

Wisconsin lies at the northeastern edge of North America's extensive midcontinental grassland biome (Fig. 16.1A). Before European American settlement in the mid-1800s, Wisconsin had an estimated 1.26 million ha of native prairie and sedge meadow in the southern, central, and western portions of the state, as well as about 4 million ha of the related communities of oak savanna and oak and pine barrens (Fig. 16.1B; Ventura 1990). Presettlement land cover in this prairie–forest border region was a continuous mosaic of prairie, savanna, barrens, woodland, and wetland communities, including large, unbroken expanses of upland and lowland grassland. After settlement, native grasslands in Wisconsin were quickly degraded by conversion to agriculture, overgrazing, or the rapid invasion by shrubs and trees caused by lack of fire or grazing. Along with the conversion of native prairie to agriculture came the swift fragmentation of the landscape. Today, Wisconsin has only 0.5 percent of its original native grasslands remaining. Much of what remains is fragmented into small patches and has been degraded by some degree of grazing or woody invasion (Henderson and Sample 1995).

Almost all of the grasslands currently in the state are surrogate grasslands (Fig. 16.1C). Surrogate grasslands consist of plant species of European

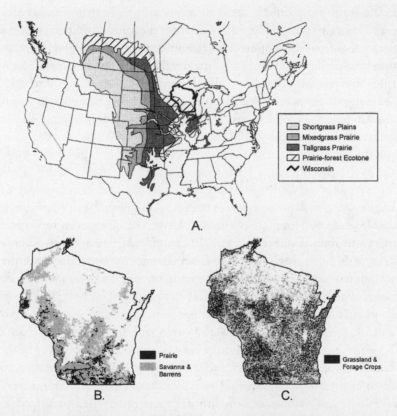

Figure 16.1 *(A)* The location of Wisconsin in the United States with respect to the historical distribution of prairie types; *(B)* presettlement distribution of prairie, oak savanna, and oak and pine barrens in Wisconsin; and *(C)* contemporary distribution of grasslands (i.e., noncultivated herbaceous vegetation, including pastures, old fields, fallow fields, Conservation Reserve Program fields, and remnant prairies) and forage crops (alfalfa hay, grass hay, and mixed grass–legume hay) in Wisconsin (Wisconsin Department of Natural Resources 1998b).

origin that are similar to and have replaced the native species that historically occurred in Wisconsin. These grasslands are primarily current or former agricultural fields and are arranged in a fragmented, geometric pattern
on the landscape very different from the more continuous distribution of the
original native grasslands. Although the distribution of surrogate grasslands
covers more of the state because agriculture occupies former forested
regions, the acreage equals roughly one half the original amount of original
native prairie, savanna, barrens, and sedge meadows. The majority of surrogate grasslands are hayfields, but also included are pastures and other idle
grassland habitats such as fallow fields, old fields, grassland planted for
wildlife habitat on public lands, and fields enrolled in the Conservation
Reserve Program (CRP). The CRP is a federal program that pays farmers
to remove highly erodible or other environmentally sensitive lands from agricultural production and plant with approved ground cover (e.g., grass–forb
mixtures that provide cover for wildlife; Farm Service Agency Online 2000).
The term *grassland* as it is used in this chapter includes all native grasslands
(e.g., sedge meadows, open bogs, prairies, savannas, and barrens) and surrogate grasslands (Sample and Mossman 1997).

Grassland Birds in Wisconsin

Populations of grassland birds were changed during European American settlement (Henderson and Sample 1995). However, changes in bird species
numbers and abundance resulted not only from replacement of native prairie
plants by European species but also from changes in the quality and quantity of habitat structure (e.g., presence of trees, vegetation height and density, and cover and depth of the litter layer). Because of current land use patterns, grassland birds in Wisconsin are now largely associated with
agriculture. Conservation of grassland birds will depend heavily on management practices implemented on privately owned lands within the agricultural landscape. The very survival of many populations is directly attributable to agricultural habitats that provide suitable structure. However, in
the last 35 years, changes in agricultural practices have led to a decline in
habitat quality and quantity. Habitat quality has declined because of a loss
of structural diversity, disturbance from increased tillage, early and more frequent hay cutting, or increased pesticide use. Habitat quantity has decreased
because of replacement of grass hay and pasture by row crops and alfalfa
hay. Accompanying these changes has been an increase in size of row crop
fields (Herkert et al. 1996). In the last 15 years, some of these declines may

have been counteracted by federal farm programs, most importantly the CRP (Johnson 2000).

We consider grassland birds to be the species that use grassland habitats during the breeding season for courtship, nesting, foraging, rearing young, and resting. Specifically for this chapter, we concentrate on 17 Wisconsin grassland obligates; these are species that need grasslands for most or all parts of their breeding cycles and do not need nongrassland features such as trees or open water. Of the 17 grassland obligates, 16 are of management concern in the state (Table 16.1). All are dependent on grasslands, and most have unique habitat structure needs (Sample and Mossman 1997).

Table 16.1   Obligate grassland bird species in Wisconsin and their breeding habitat needs (based on information in Sample and Mossman 1997).

Species	Species of Management Concern	Breeding Habitat	Vegetation Structure	Grazing Tolerance
Northern harrier (*Circus cyaneus*)	Yes	A, I, S	Tallgrass[a]	Light
Greater prairie chicken (*Tympanuchus cupido*)	Yes	I	Short- to tallgrass[a]	Very light
Yellow rail (*Coturnicops noveboracensis*)	Yes	S	Tallgrass	None
Upland sandpiper[b] (*Bartramia longicauda*)	Yes	A, I, S	Short- to midgrass	Light to moderate
Short-eared owl (*Asio flammeus*)	Yes	I, S	Tallgrass[a]	Very light
Horned lark (*Eremophila alpestris*)	No	A	Shortgrass	Heavy
Sedge wren[b] (*Cistothorus platensis*)	Yes	A, I, S	Tallgrass	Very light
Dickcissel[b] (*Spiza americana*)	Yes	A, I	Midgrass	Very light
Vesper sparrow (*Pooecetes gramineus*)	Yes	A, I	Shortgrass	Heavy

continued

Table 16.1 *continued*

Species	Species of Management Concern	Breeding Habitat	Vegetation Structure	Grazing Tolerance
Savannah sparrow[b,c] *(Passerculus sandwichensis)*	Yes	A, I, S	Midgrass	Light to moderate
Grasshopper sparrow[b,c] *(Ammodramus savannarum)*	Yes	A, I	Shortgrass	Light to moderate
Henslow's sparrow[b] *(Ammodramus henslowii)*	Yes	A, I, S	Tallgrass	Very light
Le Conte's sparrow *(Ammodramus leconteii)*	Yes	A, I, S	Tallgrass	Very light
Nelson's sharp-tailed sparrow *(Ammodramus nelsoni)*	Yes	S	Tallgrass	None
Bobolink[b,c] *(Dolichonyx oryzivorus)*	Yes	A, I, S	Midgrass	Light to moderate
Eastern meadowlark[b,c] *(Sturnella magna)*	Yes	A, I, S	Midgrass	Light to moderate
Western meadowlark[b,c] *(Sturnella neglecta)*	Yes	A, I	Shortgrass	Light to moderate

A = agricultural habitats including fallow fields, pastures, hay, small grains, and (for horned lark and vesper sparrow) row crops; I = idle cool and warm season grasslands; S = sedge meadow or sedge marsh.

[a]Species needs large areas (area sensitive) for breeding; overall amounts, types, and distribution of grassland habitats are more important than individual field sizes.

[b]Species contributing to species richness in the 1985 data set (see "Grassland Species Richness: Study Area and Methods" for details).

[c]Species contributing to species richness in the 1997–1998 data set (see "Grassland Species Richness: Study Area and Methods" for details).

Evolution of the Wisconsin DNR Management Strategy

In 1995, with the publication of the report *Wisconsin's Biodiversity as a Management Issue* (Addis et al. 1995), the Wisconsin DNR formally committed to a change from a traditional paradigm of natural resource management to a more community-based ecosystem approach to managing resources. Concepts included in this approach were management at a landscape scale and socioeconomic considerations (e.g., the inclusion of stakeholders in management decisions). Management at a landscape scale includes determining which spatial and temporal scales are appropriate for a project and how decisions at one scale affect the scales above and below (i.e., an overt recognition of the hierarchical nature of natural resource problems). For example, a decision to maximize grassland bird diversity at a large (statewide) scale may mean that management decisions made at local levels will emphasize managing for unique local features that contribute to statewide diversity but may not maximize local diversity (Sample and Mossman 1997). This view also contends that for effective conservation, restoration plans should consider the placement and configuration of conservation areas to be just as important as the total area managed. In other words, it recognizes that pattern is important (see Chapter 1, this volume).

Development of a Heuristic Model for Landscape-Scale Management of Grassland Birds

The idea of landscape-scale management for grassland birds in Wisconsin initially emerged from the Wisconsin Grassland Bird Study, carried out in the late 1980s. This study led to a collection of observations about how grassland birds used landscapes in the state. Some grassland bird species were restricted to or were most abundant in either large blocks of grassland habitat or landscapes that had few trees and a high percentage of idle or lightly disturbed grassland habitats. The study also observed that the amount and distribution of habitats in the landscape around a field appeared to influence the bird community in that field (Sample and Mossman 1997).

Based on these observations, the concept of landscape-scale management for grassland birds in Wisconsin was formally developed by Henderson and Sample (1995) and refined by Sample and Mossman (1997). This concept was expressed as a model for the conservation of grassland bird diversity that addressed landscape-scale management of habitat. The model was developed for Wisconsin, where grassland landscapes tend to be highly fragmented and composed of a patchwork of land uses, including agricultural fields, wetlands, woodlots, hedgerows, and farmsteads. Because the Wisconsin landscape is highly fragmented, habitat patch area is a critical element for grassland birds and a management issue we needed to consider.

To address the issues of fragmentation and habitat size in a region dominated by agricultural land uses, Sample and Mossman (1997) proposed that grassland bird habitat should be managed at three different landscape scales: large landscapes of more than 4,000 ha, intermediate landscapes of 400 to 2,000 ha, and small blocks of 16 to 400 ha. An increase in the extent of a landscape (i.e., larger habitat blocks) often incorporates greater spatial heterogeneity (Wiens 1989; Bissonette et al. 1994). In this case, large landscapes are more likely than small habitat blocks to harbor suitable habitat for diverse bird species because of the natural variation in vegetation structure resulting from variability in soils, topography, and moisture regimes.

A key concept for large-scale management areas is the establishment of a core area consisting of permanent grassland at least 800 ha in size, established through both acquisition and conservation easements. Most of the land outside the core but within the management area may be in private ownership with compatible agricultural land uses; however, at least 35 percent of the area outside the core should be in scattered blocks of permanent or long-term grass cover, including both native prairie and surrogate grasslands such as CRP fields, conservation easements, and pastures (see sections on "Core Area of Permanent Grassland" and "Surrogate Grassland Outside the Core Grassland" later in this chapter for justification; Sample and Mossman 1997). Desirable landscape values are best achieved if woody cover, especially upland woodlots, major linear woody features (e.g., hedgerows), and large amounts of developed land (e.g., farmsteads and homes) in the selected area are minimized. Intermediate-scale management follows the same pattern as large-scale management. In this case, the core area is smaller (100–400 ha in permanent grassland), but the recommendations for areas outside the core remain the same. This level of management is for areas where large-scale management is not feasible or where the extent of suitable landscape is limited. Small-scale management of grasslands does not explicitly incorporate a core area concept. Rather, the minimum area to be considered is 16 ha, with blocks of habitat clustered in the landscape to mimic a core area. The large-scale management model has been adopted by Partners in Flight for managing grassland birds throughout their physiographic regions that encompass prairies; Partners in Flight is a voluntary international coalition of government agencies, conservation groups, academic institutions, private businesses, and citizens formed to promote the conservation of landbirds (Fitzgerald et al. 1998; Pashley et al. 2000).

Evidence of Landscape Effects in Wisconsin

The first evidence of landscape effects on grassland birds in Wisconsin was found in research on the greater prairie chicken (*Tympanuchus cupido*) in central Wisconsin. Hamerstrom et al. (1957, p. 11) studied these birds in the Buena Vista Marsh, a roughly 20,000-ha former tamarack swamp and marsh that had been drained for agriculture. By the 1950s land use in the area was predominantly bluegrass seed farming, pasture, and tame grass hay for dairy farming. Hamerstrom et al. (1957) recognized that prairie chickens "do not like to be hemmed in" and needed "large sweeps of open country." Based on their research, they recommended that management for prairie chickens occur on areas at least 4,600 ha in size (one half township) or larger if the population was hunted. They proposed a system of "ecological patterning" whereby reserves of permanent grass cover were scattered throughout the prairie chicken management area while the predominant land uses remained bluegrass seed production, dairy farming, and cattle ranching. These private land uses were largely compatible with prairie chicken management. They also recognized that the number and distribution of publicly owned grass reserves depended on the type and pattern of land use on privately owned parcels in the landscape.

Currently, the Buena Vista prairie chicken management area includes approximately 4,400 ha of managed grassland in scattered blocks, including two large blocks of permanent grass more than 800 ha in size and several other blocks of more than 400 ha. Average block size for scattered managed grasslands is far greater than what Hamerstrom et al. originally prescribed; this has proved critical as habitat quality in the surrounding agricultural landscape matrix has declined. During the Wisconsin Grassland Bird Study, the Buena Vista prairie chicken management area harbored diverse populations of grassland birds, including area-sensitive species (Sample, unpublished data). It ultimately served as the inspiration for the concept of landscape-scale management for grassland birds in Wisconsin.

Until recently, research in Wisconsin did not focus on the effect of landscape configuration on grassland species of management concern. Niemuth (2000) found evidence of effects of landscape configuration on greater prairie chicken populations in Wisconsin; other studies have confirmed this elsewhere in its range (Ryan et al. 1998; Merrill et al. 1999). Temple (1992) estimated that at least 4,000 ha of suitable habitat were needed to maintain an isolated population of the related sharp-tailed grouse (*Tympanuchus phasianellus*) in Wisconsin. Recent work (Ribic and Sample 2001) found that the densities of different grassland bird species were affected by the land cover types surrounding the study patch. In some cases, landscape factors were more important than within-patch habitat composition. For example, woodlots were negatively associated with densities of some grassland bird species, whereas linear shrubby features such as hedgerows were positively associated with densities of other species. Renfrew and Ribic (2002) found that local topography affected densities of some grassland bird species. For example, densities of savannah sparrows (*Passerculus sandwichensis*) and bobolinks (*Dolichonyx oryzivorus*) were higher in upland pastures than in lowland pastures and were higher in larger pastures, regardless of topography. Grasshopper sparrow (*Ammodramus savannarum*), eastern meadowlark (*Sturnella magna*), western meadowlark (*Sturnella neglecta*), and sedge wren (*Cistothorus platensis*) densities did not differ between uplands and lowlands. These studies focused on individual species. In the next section we present additional analyses focusing on grassland species richness.

Grassland Species Richness: Study Area and Methods

We analyzed richness of nine Wisconsin grassland bird species of management concern (see Table 16.1) in relation to habitat and landscape metrics for 23 fields surveyed in 1985. We also analyzed richness of five of these species in relation to topography, patch size, and local vegetation for 52 pastures surveyed in 1997 and 1998 (see Table 16.1).

The 1985 data are a subset of data analyzed by Ribic and Sample (2001). We summarize the field and analysis methods here; details are in Ribic and Sample (2001). Four habitat types were included in this study: alfalfa hay (seven fields), dry pasture (four fields), cool season grass (nine fields), and dry prairie (three fields). We defined habitats based on the classification scheme of Sample (1989). Fields averaged 22.3 ha in size (*SD*, 19.8 ha; range, 3.9–76 ha) and averaged 4.6 km from the next nearest sampled field (*SD*, 10 km; range, 0.4–38 km). A single 2-ha strip transect was placed at least 20 m from the field edge in visually homogeneous vegetation. We surveyed each transect three times during the breeding season. Total numbers of species were tabulated by transect. Land use in the surrounding landscape out to 800 m from the perimeter of the transects was mapped using aerial photos. We used 200-, 400-, and 800-m distances from the transect perimeter as buffers; areas of these three buffers were 26 ha, 75 ha, and 246 ha, respectively. A variety of characteristics of linear and nonlinear woody and grassy cover and nonvegetative features (e.g., sand blows, or nonvegetated areas of exposed sand) were measured within the buffers.

We considered five models for their ability to predict grassland bird species richness in our analysis. These models were developed based on the literature and our previous experience and knowledge of grassland bird ecology (Ribic and Sample 2001). The models were species richness as a function of field habitat, species richness as a function of mean patch size in the buffers, species richness as a function of linear cover types, species richness as a function of distance to woody vegetation features, and species richness as a function of field characteristics and landscape variables.

All variables used in the models had correlations less than .70, with a majority having correlations less than .50; this is one recommendation for adjusting for possible multicollinearity issues (Weisberg 1985). To choose the models with the best support of the data, we used the small sample version of Akaike's information criterion (AIC; Burnham and Anderson 1998). We used a stepwise procedure based on AIC to pick final models.

The 1997–1998 data are a subset of data analyzed by Renfrew and Ribic (2002). We summarize the methods here; details can be found in Renfrew and Ribic (2002). Pastures were located in southwestern Wisconsin, which is considered part of the Driftless Area. The Driftless Area is a region characterized by rolling hills. Historically it was dominated by oak savanna and tallgrass prairie, but agriculture is now the predominant land use. Pasture management was characterized by continuous grazing or management-intensive rotational grazing systems (Undersander et al. 1991). Stocking rates varied between pastures and often within pastures within a season. We used a subset of pastures with a range of sizes: 28 upland (mean, 23.3 ha; *SD*, 15.3; minimum, 3.6 ha; maximum, 57.8 ha) and 24 lowland (mean, 20.4 ha; *SD*, 14.2; minimum, 3.1 ha; maximum, 55.8 ha). Lowland pastures were located in valley bottoms with permanent streams. Upland pastures did not include streams or valley bottoms and were well drained. Pasture size included all contiguous grazed grassland. Birds were surveyed twice during the breeding season using 100-m-radius 5-minute point counts. When multiple point counts were conducted on a pasture, a single randomly chosen point count was used for analysis of species richness. Three uncorrelated ($r < 0.40$) vegetation variables were used in the analysis: percentage bare ground, litter depth (in centimeters), and vegetation height density (in centimeters). We used a repeated-measures analysis to assess the relationships between richness of grassland bird species and the following variables: year, upland or lowland pastures, pasture area, and vegetation. Similar to the analysis of the 1985 data, we used AIC to determine which combination of variables and their interactions were associated with bird species richness.

In the analyses of both data sets, the modeling techniques assume an underlying Gaussian or normal error structure (Keppel 1991; Cressie 1993), and response variables were square root transformed to meet this assumption. The linear regression modeling and spatial analyses were done in S+ (MathSoft 1996, 1997). The generalized least-squares and repeated-measures analyses were run in SAS PROC MIXED (Littell et al. 1996). Significance was assessed at $p < 0.05$ and tendencies at $p < 0.10$.

Results

Richness of Wisconsin grassland species was associated only with landscape variables in the 1985 data set. An index of cover type diversity, mean size of sand blows, and mean size of patches within the 800-m buffer were the significant variables in the minimum AIC model ($p < 0.001$, adjusted $R^2 = 0.60$). Specifically, higher richness (five to six species) was associated with landscapes with lower cover type diversity and larger patches of cover types in general and of sand in particular. Overall, lower cover type diversity at 800 m from the transect resulted from domination by both hay and grassland. Cover type diversity was negatively correlated ($r = -0.68$) with area of hay and grassland combined in the 800-m buffer. A competing model found an association between species richness and area of shrub swamp, residential areas, and woodlots within 200 m of the transect ($p < 0.001$, adjusted $R^2 = 0.57$). Specifically, after adjustment for spatial correlation (correlation in the residuals occurred over a range of 12 km), higher richness of species of management concern was associated with fewer residential areas and lesser amounts of shrub swamp within 200 m of the transect. There was a tendency for higher richness to be associated with less area in woodlots within 200 m of the transects.

From the 1997–1998 data set we determined that richness of grassland bird species was associated with upland or lowland status of the pasture, the size of the pasture, and their interaction. Vegetation variables did not appear in the minimum AIC model, and there were no competing models. Overall, species richness was higher in upland pastures (mean, 2.3 and 2.5 in 1997 and 1998, respectively) than in lowland pastures (mean, 1.3 and 1.7 in 1997 and 1998, respectively). The positive relationship between richness and log area depended on whether the pasture was in the lowlands or in the uplands (interaction term, $p < 0.05$). Specifically, the slope of the relationship between richness and log area in the lowlands was 4 times (in 1997) and 2 times (in 1998) as great as that found for upland pastures. In the lowlands, larger pastures had 2.7 (in 1997, $p < 0.001$) and 1.7 (in 1998, $p = 0.02$) times as many species as smaller pastures. In the uplands, larger pastures had the same number of (in 1997, $p = 0.11$) or 1.4 times as many (in 1998, $p = 0.05$) species as smaller pastures.

The results of these two studies show that landscape and patch size factors are important determinants of grassland bird species richness. In neither of the studies did local vegetation variables enter into the models that had the greatest explanatory power. In the 1985 data set, the structure and composition of the landscape, including patch sizes and the diversity and amount of different cover types, were shown to influence grassland bird species richness. In the 1997–1998 study, upland sites had greater species richness than lowland, and the relationship of area to species richness was influenced by topography, with area being more important in lowland than in upland pastures. The implication of these results is that management for grassland birds must include consideration of landscape features and patch size.

Discussion: Landscape Impacts on Grassland Birds

In Wisconsin, density and richness of the grassland bird community are associated with landscape features. Studies elsewhere have found that the context in which the patch is situated affects the density of birds found in the patch. Bakker (2000) found that the composition of the landscape surrounding a patch (e.g., proportion of wooded or grassland habitat) influenced the probability of occurrence of some grassland passerines in South Dakota. Horn (2000) found that the abundance of some grassland passerines in CRP fields was positively correlated with the proportion of grassland in the surrounding landscape in North Dakota (the same study did not find this relationship in Iowa, however, citing differences in the configuration of the landscapes as one possible reason). In Kansas, dickcissel (*Spiza americana*) abundance in a field was lower with increasing percentage of woody edge and amounts of forested cover within 800 m of the field edge (Hughes et al. 1999). In Missouri, McCoy (1996) observed that landscape variables such as percentage of field interiors in the buffer composed of hay and grassland influenced abundance of some grassland bird species and species richness. Grassland bird density was affected by landscape variables at the 1-, 3-, and 5-km scales in Winter's (1998) study. For example, the abundance of dickcissels and Henslow's sparrows (*Ammodramus henslowii*) increased as the total area of grass in the landscape within 5 km of the study field increased.

What Is the Landscape Effect?

The question then becomes, What is this landscape effect? It may simply be a question of definition and scale. One problem faced by grassland bird researchers is defining a habitat patch. In common with all other researchers, we have defined a patch as being a delineated area of a specific land use or habitat type under the same management (e.g., a hayfield or CRP field). But how we define patches affects our conclusions about bird habitat size needs (Sample and Mossman 1997). We suggest that the landscape effect we are measuring for the passerines we have studied is, at least in part, what Sample and Mossman (1997) called "effective habitat size." Sample and Mossman (1997) discuss the idea that birds may perceive or interpret habitat size not as we define a patch but rather as the amount of suitable grassland habitat contiguous with or very near the patch they occupy. For example, we may draw a distinction between a hayfield, an adjacent pasture, and a CRP field, but a bird might perceive these three fields as one contiguous patch of grassland habitat with variable vegetation structure. Some species such as upland sandpipers (*Bartramia longicauda*) may use all of these fields (e.g., one for nesting and another for chick rearing). For larger-bodied birds (greater prairie chicken, northern harrier [*Circus cyaneus*], short-eared owl [*Asio flammeus*]), the patch that the bird perceives may be a landscape that encompasses multiple continuous grassland patches imbedded in an extensive matrix of open land, including cropland, wetlands, and some woody cover (Herkert et al. 1999). How effective habitat size is defined in a given landscape thus depends on the target bird species or community. We are uncertain about the scale at which different grassland birds perceive effective habitat size and about the interaction between landscape structure and perceived habitat size. This may depend on the scale and juxtaposition of grassland and agricultural habitats, on the amount and distribution of woody cover, and on topography in a landscape. In a wooded landscape, effective habitat size may be limited to areas of contiguous grass cover, whereas in open, treeless landscapes dominated by grassland habitats but including some cropland, the entire landscape may be regarded as one large habitat patch.

Productivity Issues

All of the research reported so far deals with the association of landscape features and grassland bird abundance and species richness. However, from a conservation perspective, productivity is a key parameter as well. Investigations into the association of grassland bird productivity and landscape features have been initiated recently (Hughes et al. 1999; Winter and Faaborg 1999; Winter et al. 2000b). Most studies have focused on a patch scale, evaluating whether grassland birds are experiencing edge effects (e.g., higher predation rates near grassland edges than in grassland interiors). If edge effects exist, nests in smaller patches with higher edge-to-interior-area ratios probably will have lower overall survival rates than nests in large patches. Studies evaluating edge effects have had conflicting results (see Andren 1995 for a review). Hughes et al. (1999) found that only patch level variables were associated with dickcissel productivity. Winter and Faaborg (1999) found that dickcissel productivity was affected by patch size but Henslow's sparrow productivity was not. Much more work is needed in this area. Gathering adequate sample sizes for a landscape-scale approach has proven to be challenging, and meta-analyses of several databases may be necessary to evaluate these relationships.

Predation can be a dominant mechanism by which fragmentation affects bird populations because it strongly influences nest survival (Martin 1988b) and nest site preference (Martin 1988a). Review of the studies evaluating both predators and nest predation rates in forest fragments reveals that patterns in predation rates, particularly the presence and extent of edge and landscape effects, are highly dependent on the local predator community (Cotterill 1996; Tewksbury et al. 1998; Heske et al. 2001).

Studies of predators in relation to nest success of grassland passerines are needed (Robinson 1995). Winter et al. (2000b), using track stations and artificial nests with clay eggs, found edge effects for dickcissels and Henslow's sparrows and attributed them to midsized mammalian predators. Research on waterfowl has been conducted in grasslands (Sovada et al. 2000; Phillips 2001), but potential differences in the predator community affecting waterfowl and passerines may limit the ability to extrapolate results. However, the studies on waterfowl illustrate that predator movements and activity are influenced by landscape composition, subsequently influencing nest success (Phillips 2001).

Sample and Mossman (1997) stated that management should be concerned with trying to achieve both high abundance and high productivity of grassland birds. Currently, we know much more about grassland bird abundance in different habitats than about productivity. The age and relative fitness (via productivity) of individuals provide the best measure of relative habitat quality. However, gathering such data is expensive and time consuming, and managers must use whatever information is available. The assumption that greater bird density equals better habitat quality has been demonstrated to be valid (Bollinger and Gavin 1989) but can also be erroneous (Van Horne 1983; Vickery et al. 1992). We suggest that even though abundance is not always correlated with productivity, we may be able to assume, when productivity data are lacking, that management recommendations based on abundance will not often result in a detrimental effect on productivity (Ribic and Sample 2001). However, we need to verify this assumption; Winter (1998) reported that landscape variables associated with the density of dickcissels in Missouri were different from those associated with productivity. By using an adaptive management framework, we can build in monitoring protocols to determine whether management for increased abundance also results in increased productivity.

Summary and Recommendations for Implementing Landscape-Scale Management

One of the issues facing landscape ecology is how to play an active role in biodiversity conservation (With 1999). Biodiversity management in agricultural landscapes is an area where landscape ecology principles are being applied. Sample and Mossman (1997) made several recommendations for landscape-scale management of grassland bird biodiversity. We will now review and discuss these based on our results and those of other studies.

Importance of Local Habitat: Choose the Right Landscape

Before establishing a landscape-scale management strategy, appropriate local breeding habitat for the targeted grassland bird community must be in place or feasible to establish and maintain. The most important step is to make sure that the management opportunities and potentials of the landscape match the habitat needs of the targeted bird species and community. Sample and Mossman (1997) recommend that grassland bird management maximize grassland bird diversity at a large (in their case, statewide) scale by taking advantage of regional differences through careful location of landscape-scale management areas. Some landscapes may present unique opportunities for management of specific habitats that will be complemented by different opportunities in landscapes in other regions. One of the key concepts here is to let both the current and potential vegetation structure of the site drive the management goals for both birds and habitats. An example of this would be to select a landscape that was historically open dry prairie and is currently dominated by surrogate grasslands and low-intensity agriculture and then manage the area for shortgrass grassland birds rather than trying to create shortgrass habitat in a landscape that was formerly either forested or mesic grassland and is currently dominated by row crops. Local management for structure can increase the richness of bird community in a landscape if increasing local bird diversity is a goal. Given adequate landscape area, the existence of appropriate breeding habitat, and good potential for expanding and restoring suitable habitat, a landscape-scale approach can be considered.

Core Area of Permanent Grassland

The core area concept is based on the premise that bigger patches are better than smaller patches. Evidence that large compact patches are better than elongated irregular patches for grassland birds (Helzer and Jelinski 1999) supports the idea of a core area. The core area is an attempt to protect area-sensitive species such as greater prairie chickens that need large undisturbed grasslands to be successful breeders; by an umbrella effect, this would benefit the other grassland species as well. What size the core grass area should be is not certain. Factors to consider are the targeted bird community, current landscape composition, management options, and restoration potential of the landscape. Sample and Mossman (1997) based their recommendation of an 800-ha core on their experience of the benefits to prairie chickens and other grassland birds of blocks of that size in the Buena Vista prairie chicken management area. About 27 percent of the management area is under conservation management, almost all of which is permanent grassland, and an 800-ha core grass area equals 20 percent of a 4,000-ha large-scale management area. Twenty percent was seen as a reasonable compromise between what is biologically beneficial to grassland birds and socioeconomically acceptable in an active agricultural landscape. However, recent papers have demonstrated the need to reexamine area size recommendations for grassland birds. Horn et al. (2000) demonstrated that faulty analyses could lead to an erroneous conclusion of area sensitivity. Johnson and Igl (2001) demonstrated regional variation in area sensitivity; species could be area-sensitive in one county but not in an adjacent county.

Surrogate Grassland Outside the Core Grassland

Embedding patches of managed grassland in a landscape of compatible grass-land land use has some support from our investigations. Higher richness of bird species and increased densities of individual species can occur in land-scapes with higher amounts of surrogate grasslands surrounding habitat blocks. In addition, when working in rolling terrain, upland areas could be a primary focus, with large, open lowland areas also considered. We based our recommendation of at least 35 percent grass cover outside the core on the Buena Vista prairie chicken management area. In combination with an 800-ha core, an additional 35 percent grass cover brings the total amount of long-term and permanent grass cover in a 4,000-ha area up to 48 percent. That is close to the more than 55 percent of grass cover that the Buena Vista management area had in the early 1950s, not all of which was high-quality nesting cover (Hamerstrom et al. 1957). To go much above the 35 percent figure did not seem feasible in an area with a background matrix of active agriculture.

Pasture is a common secondary grassland in the state of Wisconsin and is one of the surrogate grasslands Sample and Mossman (1997) consider appropriate as part of a landscape management area. We know that grass-land bird species of management concern use grazed pastures for breeding (Sample 1989; Temple et al. 1999; Renfrew and Ribic 2001), but it is unclear how to balance grassland bird productivity and grazing production. Cor-rectly timed light to moderate grazing, typically associated with beef cattle or dairy heifer ranching in Wisconsin, is an effective management strategy (Herkert et al. 1996). Recently, Temple et al. (1999) designed a bird-friendly grazing system that in essence sets aside one of several paddocks on an indi-vidual farm from a rotational grazing system until mid-July, thus providing a refuge for breeding birds while still allowing use of the remaining paddocks by the farmer. Details of implementation can be found in Undersander et al. (2000). However, an owner may not be willing to allow the paddock to lie fallow until mid-July, thus accepting lowered nutritional quality of pas-ture forage (Paine et al. 1997). This system would benefit from further appli-cations and refinements in an adaptive management framework.

The timing and amount of disturbance associated with pastures and other agricultural land uses are important considerations for landscape-scale man-agement because sufficient undisturbed grass is needed during the breeding season to allow successful nesting of grassland birds. Grass-dominated hay may be harvested later than most alfalfa hay and therefore be beneficial to nesting birds. Small grains, though receiving low use by grassland birds, are harvested after most of the nesting season has passed and therefore may be considered a beneficial habitat type.

Minimize or Restrict Woody Vegetation and Developed Areas

Certain types of woody vegetation such as woodlots should be minimized in a grassland conservation area for grassland birds through careful site selection or through management. Exceptions include areas with topographic relief where wooded habitats are limited to lowland riparian zones or steep-sided draws, or where savanna or shrub grassland birds are among the targeted groups (Sample and Mossman 1997). The assumption has been that many predators are associated with woods, travel into grasslands, and depredate nests incidentally. Therefore, removing features allowing them access to grasslands would increase nest success. Winter et al. (2000b) suggest that removing woody features in the landscape would help slow the decline in grassland bird species. However, our work (Renfrew and Ribic, unpublished data) and that of others (Pietz and Granfors 2000) has revealed a wide variety of predators, some of which are resident in grassland patches and might increase if hedgerows or woody areas were removed. Examining the response of predator communities in the landscape using adaptive management is an important objective for future grassland bird research.

Our Wisconsin data show that large patches of residential land use near local habitat patches are associated with both decreased species richness and density of grassland birds (Ribic and Sample 2001). Siting areas in landscapes with less residential development, as suggested by Sample and Mossman (1997), is a good management objective.

Implementing Landscape-Scale Management in Wisconsin

Once we have an idea of landscape-scale effects on grassland birds, we can begin to make the match between knowledge and management implementation. The implementation of landscape-scale management for grassland birds in Wisconsin is in its early stages. One project is the DNR's Western Prairie Habitat Restoration Area, a management area of nearly 142,000 ha in the former prairie pothole region of western Wisconsin. The goal is to restore viable grassland and wetland communities (Wisconsin Department of Natural Resources 1998a, 1998b). A specific objective is to restore 10 percent (8,000 ha) of the original prairie and wetland acreage in this agricultural area with the help of a wide variety of partner agencies and organizations. For grassland birds, the plan calls for establishing large-, intermediate-, and small-scale management areas. As of December 2001, 330 ha of habitat have been protected through easement, acquisition, and donation (Kris Belling, Wisconsin DNR, personal communication 2001).

Another major landscape-scale (17,000-ha) project, called the Military Ridge Prairie Heritage Area (MRPHA), has been initiated recently by the Wisconsin chapter of the Nature Conservancy (TNC) in conjunction with the U.S. Fish and Wildlife Service, U.S. Natural Resources Conservation Service, Wisconsin DNR, and private groups such as Pheasants Forever and the Prairie Enthusiasts (Wisconsin Chapter, The Nature Conservancy 2001). Conservation strategies for the project include protecting land through a variety of tools including land acquisition and easements, purchase of development rights to keep land in agriculture, prairie restoration and management, and working with diverse conservation partners to encourage landowners to enroll their lands in agricultural set-aside and incentive programs.

The MRPHA is in a hilly region of southwest Wisconsin where agriculture is of low intensity and prairie remnants are abundant. TNC envisions the MRPHA as

> a site where the natural processes and systems that support the biodiversity of grasslands are protected, restored, and maintained in a manner that provides suitable conditions for the long-term survival of conservation targets; a site where TNC works with multiple conservation partners to maintain a landscape-scale grassland area that is large enough to accommodate area-dependent species while maintaining land in private agricultural ownership whenever possible; a site that is healthy and sustainable for both humans and natural systems; and a site that exists within a community of citizens who understand the value of the area historically, biologically and culturally. (Wisconsin Chapter, the Nature Conservancy 2001, p. 6)

The conservation target for the MRPHA is the prairie community mosaic, including the red-tailed prairie leafhopper (*Aflexia rubranura*), regal fritillary butterfly (*Speyera idalia*), prairie bush clover (*Lespedeza leptostachya*), and grassland birds such as Henslow's sparrow.

A unique feature of the MRPHA, one that makes it adaptable to an agricultural landscape, is the division of lands into four zones of protection: the

Core Areas Zone (2,200 ha), consisting of three large areas of contiguous grassland; the Prairie Remnant Zone (200 ha), where high-quality prairie remnants and prairie pastures are protected; the Priority Grassland Landscape Zone (9,300 ha), where the best examples of open grassland landscapes, especially on open ridgetops and wide valleys, will be maintained in scattered blocks of idle grass cover and compatible agricultural uses; and the Agricultural/Limited Development Zone (5,700 ha), where efforts will be made to encourage compatible farming practices, limit home development to woods and valleys, and limit tree planting.

Challenges to the successful implementation of the MRPHA project include mitigating the major threats to the conservation targets. For grassland birds, these threats include home development, tree planting, conversion of CRP land to agriculture, and incompatible crop production practices. Securing permanent grass cover in the core areas through easement and acquisition will be important for the success of the project.

Applying the Heuristic Model to Other Areas

There is no reason to expect that a model developed for one landscape will hold when applied to a different landscape. Although the heuristic model of Sample and Mossman (1997) was developed in Wisconsin, the model, particularly the idea of the core area underlying the Partners in Flight Conservation Plan for the Northern Tallgrass Prairie physiographic area, is currently being tested in Minnesota and the Dakotas (Winter et al. 2000a). In this case, the landscape where the model is being tested is inherently different from the one in which the model was developed. For example, Winter et al. (2000a) describe their landscapes dominated by grassy-like habitats as "neutral" habitats. In Wisconsin, these habitats would be considered beneficial, given the other potential land uses that could occur in the Wisconsin landscape. We believe that any landscape model must be tested to define its limits of application and to improve understanding of landscape-scale management in general.

An appreciation of the importance of landscape has been a part of grassland bird management in Wisconsin since the 1950s. Integrating research and management needs in an adaptive management framework that uses landscape ecological principles as a basis gives us an opportunity to test and refine our understanding of the system, ultimately improving strategies to help conserve grassland birds.

Summary

In the last three decades, grassland birds have had a larger percentage of species exhibiting population declines than any other avian guild in North America. Major causes of these declines include land use changes that have resulted in habitat loss, fragmentation, and simplification. In Wisconsin, grassland landscapes are highly fragmented and composed of a patchwork of land uses, including agricultural fields, wetlands, woodlots, hedgerows, and farmsteads. An appreciation of the importance of landscape has been part of grassland bird management in Wisconsin since the 1950s, but the concept of landscape-scale management of habitat for grassland birds in Wisconsin was not formally developed until the late 1980s. Recent research demonstrates that the density and richness of Wisconsin grassland bird communities are associated with landscape features. One important recommendation for landscape-scale management of grassland birds in Wisconsin is to make sure that the management opportunities and potentials of landscapes to be managed match the habitat needs of the targeted bird species. Other recommendations include designing landscape-scale management areas around large core patches of suitable grassland habitat, embedding patches of managed grassland in the landscape surrounding the core patches, and minimizing or restricting woody vegetation and developed areas in the landscape. The implementation of landscape-scale management for grassland birds in Wisconsin is in its early stages. Challenges to the successful implementation of landscape management projects include mitigating major threats such as home development, tree planting, conversion of CRP land to agriculture, and incompatible crop production practices. Integrating research and management needs in an adaptive management framework based on landscape ecological principles gives us an opportunity to test and refine our understanding of the system, ultimately improving strategies to help conserve grassland birds.

Acknowledgments

We would like to acknowledge Amanda Schwoegler and Sonya Knetter for their help in preparing the figure and Lisa Dlutkowski for help with fieldwork and digitizing cover maps. This work was supported in part by funds from the Federal Aid to Wildlife Restoration Act under Pittman-Robertson Project W-160-P. Data analysis was supported by the U.S. Geological Survey Biological Resources Division (BRD) Wisconsin Cooperative Wildlife Research Unit. The USGS Wisconsin Cooperative Wildlife Research Unit is jointly sponsored by the U.S. Geological Survey, the Wisconsin Department of Natural Resources, the University of Wisconsin, the Wildlife Management Institute, and the U.S. Fish and Wildlife Service.

LITERATURE CITED

Addis, J., R. G. Eckstein, A. Forbes, D. Gebken, R. A. Henderson, J. Kotar, B. L. Les, P. Matthiae, W. M. McCown, S. W. Miller, B. A. Moss, D. W. Sample, M. D. Staggs, and K. Visser. 1995. Wisconsin's biodiversity as a management issue: a report to Department of Natural Resources managers. Wisconsin Department of Natural Resources, Madison.

Andren, H. 1995. Effects of landscape composition on predation rates at habitat edges. Pages 225–255 in L. Hansson, L. Fahrig, and G. Merriam (eds.), Mosaic landscapes and ecological processes. Chapman & Hall, London.

Bakker, K. K. 2000. Avian occurrence in woodlands and grasslands on public areas throughout eastern South Dakota. Ph.D. dissertation, South Dakota State University, Brookings.

Best, L. B., H. Campa III, K. E. Kemp, R. J. Robel, M. R. Ryan, J. A. Savidge, H. P. Weeks, Jr., and S. R. Winterstein. 1997. Bird abundance and nesting in CRP fields and cropland in the Midwest: a regional approach. Wildlife Society Bulletin 25:864–877.

Bissonette, J. A., S. S. Sherburne, and R. D. Ramsey. 1994. Analyzing telemetry data with a GIS-based vector structure. International Journal of Geographic Information Systems 8:533–543.

Bollinger, E. K., and T. A. Gavin. 1989. The effects of site quality on breeding-site fidelity in bobolinks. Auk 106:584–594.

Burnham, K. P., and D. R. Anderson. 1998. Model selection and inference, a practical information-theoretic approach. Springer-Verlag, New York.

Cotterill, S. E. 1996. Effects of clearcutting on artificial egg predation in boreal mixed wood forests in north-central Alberta. M.S. thesis, University of Alberta, Edmonton.

Cressie, N. A.C. 1993. Statistics for spatial data, rev. ed. Wiley, New York.

Farm Service Agency Online. 2000. Conservation programs. (Online at www.fsa.usda.gov/dafp/cepd/conserva.htm).

Fitzgerald, J. A., D. N. Pashley, S. J. Lewis, and B. Pardo. 1998. Partners in Flight bird conservation plan for the Northern Tallgrass Prairie (physiographic area 40). American Bird Conservancy, The Plains, VA.

Freemark, K. E., J. B. Dunning, S. J. Hejl, and J. R. Probst. 1995. A landscape ecology perspective for research, conservation, and management. Pages 381–427 in T. E. Martin and D. M. Finch (eds.), Ecology and management of neotropical migratory birds. Oxford University Press, New York.

Hamerstrom, F. N., Jr., O. H. Mattson, and F. Hamerstrom. 1957. A guide to prairie chicken management. Technical Bulletin 15. Wisconsin Conservation Department, Madison.

Helzer, C. J., and D. E. Jelinski. 1999. The relative importance of patch area and perimeter–area ratio to grassland breeding birds. Ecological Applications 9:1448–1458.

Henderson, R. A., and D. W. Sample. 1995. Grassland communities. Pages 116–129 in J. Addis, R. G. Eckstein, A. Forbes, D. Gebken, R. A. Henderson, J. Kotar, B. L. Les, P. Matthiae, W. M. McCown, S. W. Miller, B. A. Moss, D. W. Sample, M. D. Staggs, and K. Visser (eds.), Wisconsin's biodiversity as a management issue: a report to managers. Wisconsin Department of Natural Resources, Madison.

Herkert, J. R. 1994. The effects of habitat fragmentation on midwestern grassland bird communities. Ecological Applications 4:461–471.

Herkert, J. R., D. W. Sample, and R. E. Warner. 1996. Management of midwestern grassland landscapes for the conservation of migratory birds. Pages 89–116 in F. R. Thompson, III (ed.), Management of midwestern landscapes for the conservation of neotropical migratory birds. USDA Forest Service North Central Forest Experiment Station General Technical Report NC-187, St. Paul, MN.

Herkert, J. R., S. A. Simpson, R. L. Westmeier, T. L. Esker, and J. W. Walk. 1999. Response of northern harriers and short-eared owls to grassland management in Illinois. Journal of Wildlife Management 63:517–523.

Heske, E. J., S. K. Robinson, and J. D. Brawn. 2001. Nest predation and neotropical migrant songbirds: piecing together the fragments. Wildlife Society Bulletin 29:52–61.

Hine, R. L. 1973. Endangered birds. Passenger Pigeon 35:155–158.

Horn, D. J. 2000. The influence of habitat features on grassland birds nesting in the prairie pothole region of North Dakota. Ph.D. dissertation, Iowa State University, Ames.

Horn, D. J., R. J. Fletcher, Jr., and R. R. Koford. 2000. Detecting area sensitivity: a comment on previous studies. American Midland Naturalist 144:28–35.

Hughes, J. P., R. J. Robel, K. E. Kemp, and J. L. Zimmerman. 1999. Effects of habitat on dickcissel abundance and nest success in Conservation Reserve Program fields in Kansas. Journal of Wildlife Management 63:523–529.

Johnson, D. H. 2000. Conservation Reserve Program (CRP). Pages 19–33 in W. L. Hohman and D. J. Halloum-Findham (eds.), A comprehensive review of farm bill contributions to wildlife conservation, 1985–2000. U.S. Department of Agriculture, Natural Resource Conservation Service, Wildlife Habitat Management Institute, Technical Report USDA/NRCS/WHMI-2000, Ames, IA.

Johnson, D. H., and L. D. Igl. 2001. Area requirements of grassland birds: a regional perspective. Auk 118:24–34.

Johnson, R. G., and S. A. Temple. 1990. Nest predation and brood parasitism of tallgrass prairie birds. Journal of Wildlife Management 54:106–111.

Keppel, G. 1991. Design and analysis, a researcher's handbook, 3rd ed. Prentice Hall, Englewood Cliffs, NJ.

Littell, R. C., G. A. Milliken, W. W. Stroup, and R. D. Wolfinger. 1996. SAS system for mixed models. SAS Institute Inc., Cary, NC.

Martin, T. E. 1988a. Habitat and area effects on forest bird assemblages: is nest predation an influence? Ecology 69:74–84.

Martin, T. E. 1988b. Processes organizing open-nesting bird assemblages: competition or nest predation? Evolutionary Ecology 2:37–50.

MathSoft. 1996. S+SPATIALSTATS user's manual, Version 1.0. MathSoft, Inc., Seattle, WA.

MathSoft. 1997. S-PLUS 4 guide to statistics. MathSoft, Inc., Seattle, WA.

McCoy, T. D. 1996. Avian abundance, composition, and reproductive success on Conservation Reserve Program fields in northern Missouri. M.S. thesis, University of Missouri, Columbia.

Merrill, M. D., K. A. Chapman, K. A. Poiani, and B. Winter. 1999. Land-use patterns surrounding greater prairie-chicken leks in northwestern Minnesota. Journal of Wildlife Management 63:189–198.

Niemuth, N. D. 2000. Land use and vegetation associated with greater prairie-chicken leks in an agricultural landscape. Journal of Wildlife Management 64:278–286.

Paine, L. K., D. J. Undersander, S. A. Temple, and D. W. Sample. 1997. Managing rotationally grazed pastures for forage production and grassland birds. Pages 54–58 in M. J. Willrany (ed.), Proceedings of the 1997 Forage and Grassland Conference. American Forage and Grassland Council, Georgetown, TX.

Pashley, D. N., C. J. Beardmore, J. A. Fitzgerald, R. P. Ford, W. C. Hunter, M. S. Morrison, and K. V. Rosenberg. 2000. Partners in Flight: conservation of the land birds of the United States. American Bird Conservancy, The Plains, VA.

Phillips, M. L. 2001. Landscape ecology of mammalian predators and its relationship to waterfowl nest success in the Prairie Pothole Region of North Dakota. Ph.D. dissertation, Iowa State University, Ames, Iowa.

Pietz, P. J., and D. A. Granfors. 2000. Identifying predators and fates of grassland passerine nests using miniature video cameras. Journal of Wildlife Management 64:71–87.

Renfrew, R. B., and C. A. Ribic. 2001. Grassland birds associated with agricultural riparian practices in southwestern Wisconsin. Journal of Range Management 54:546–552.

Renfrew, R. B., and C. A. Ribic. 2002. Influence of topography on density of grassland passerines in pastures. American Midland Naturalist 147: 315–325.

Ribic, C. A., and D. W. Sample. 2001. Associations of grassland birds with landscape factors in southern Wisconsin. American Midland Naturalist 146:105–121.

Robbins, S. D. 1982. Wisconsin's Breeding Bird Survey results: 1966–1980. Passenger Pigeon 44:97–121.

Robinson, S. K. 1995. Threats to breeding neotropical migratory birds in the Midwest. Pages 1–21 in F. R. Thompson, III (ed.), Management of midwestern landscapes for the conservation of neotropical migratory birds. USDA Forest Service North Central Forest Experiment Station General Technical Report NC-187, St. Paul, MN.

Rodenhouse, N. L., L. B. Best, R. J. O'Connor, and E. K. Bollinger. 1995. Effects of agricultural practices and farmland structures. Pages 269–293 in T. E. Martin and D. M. Finch (eds.), Ecology and management of neotropical migratory birds. Oxford University Press, New York.

Ryan, M. R., L. W. Burger, Jr., D. P. Jones, and A. P. Wywialowski. 1998. Breeding ecology of greater prairie-chickens (*Tympanuchus cupido*) in relation to prairie landscape configuration. American Midland Naturalist 140:111–121.

Sample, D. W. 1989. Grassland birds in southern Wisconsin: habitat preference, population trends, and response to land use changes. M.S. thesis, University of Wisconsin, Madison.

Sample, D. W., and M. J. Mossman. 1997. Managing habitat for grassland birds, a guide for Wisconsin. Publication SS-925-97. Wisconsin Department of Natural Resources, Madison.

Sovada, M. A., M. C. Zicus, R. J. Greenwood, D. P. Rave, W. E. Newton, R. O. Woodward, and J. A. Beiser. 2000. Relationships of habitat patch size to predator community and survival of duck nests. Journal of Wildlife Management 64:820–831.

Temple, S. A. 1992. Population viability analysis of a sharp-tailed grouse metapopulation in Wisconsin. Pages 750–758 in D. R. McCullough and R. H. Barrett (eds.), Wildlife 2001: populations. Elsevier Applied Science, London.

Temple, S. A., B. M. Fevold, L. K. Paine, D. J. Undersander, and D. W. Sample. 1999. Nesting birds and grazing cattle: accommodating both on midwestern pastures. Pages 196–202 in P. D. Vickery and J. R. Herkert (eds.), Ecology and conservation of grassland birds of the Western Hemisphere. Studies in Avian Biology 19. Cooper Ornithological Society: Camarillo, CA.

Tewksbury, J. J., S. J. Hejl, and T. E. Martin. 1998. Breeding productivity does not decline with increasing fragmentation in a western landscape. Ecology 79:2890–2903.

Undersander, D. J., B. Albert, P. Porter, and A. Crossley. 1991. Wisconsin pastures for profit: a hands-on guide to rotational grazing. Publication A32529, University of Wisconsin Cooperative Extension Publishing, Madison.

Undersander, D. J., S. A. Temple, J. A. Bartelt, D. W. Sample, and L. K. Paine. 2000. Grassland birds: fostering habitats using rotational grazing. Publication A3715, University of Wisconsin Cooperative Extension Publishing, Madison.

Van Horne, B. 1983. Density as a misleading indicator of habitat quality. Journal of Wildlife Management 47:893–901.

Ventura, S. 1990. Digital database of the map of the original vegetation cover of Wisconsin. (Map originally prepared by R. W. Finley, University of Wisconsin Extension, 1976; modified by Scott Sauer. Scale 1:500,000). University of Wisconsin Institute for Environmental Studies and Soil Science, Madison.

Vickery, P. D., and J. R. Herkert. 2001. Recent advances in grassland bird research: where do we go from here? Auk 118:11–15.

Vickery, P. D., M. L. Hunter, Jr., and J. V. Wells. 1992. Is density an indicator of breeding success? Auk 109:706–710.

Vickery, P. D., M. L. Hunter, Jr., and S. M. Melvin. 1994. Effects of habitat area on the distribution of grassland birds in Maine. Conservation Biology 8:1087–1097.

Vickery, P. D., P. L. Tubaro, J. M. Cardoso Da Silva, B. G. Peterjohn, J. R. Herkert, and R. B. Cavalcanti. 1999. Conservation of grassland birds in the Western Hemisphere. Pages 2–26 in P. D. Vickery and J. R. Herkert (eds.), Ecology and conservation of grassland birds of the Western Hemisphere. Studies in Avian Biology 19. Cooper Ornithological Society: Camarillo, CA.

Weisberg, S. 1985. Applied linear regression, 2nd ed. Wiley, New York.

Wiens, J. A. 1989. Spatial scaling in ecology. Functional Ecology 3:385–397.

Winter, M. 1998. Effect of habitat fragmentation on grassland-nesting birds in southwestern Missouri. Ph.D. dissertation, University of Missouri, Columbia.

Winter, M., and J. Faaborg. 1999. Patterns of area-sensitivity in grassland-nesting birds. Conservation Biology 13:1424–1436.

Winter, M., D. H. Johnson, T. M. Donovan, and W. D. Svedarsky. 2000a. Evaluation of the bird conservation area concept in the northern tallgrass prairie, annual report: 2000. USGS Northern Prairie Wildlife Research Center, Jamestown, ND.

Winter, M., D. H. Johnson, and J. Faaborg. 2000b. Evidence for edge effects on multiple levels in tallgrass prairie. Condor 102:256–266.

Wisconsin Chapter, The Nature Conservancy. 2001. Military Ridge Prairie Heritage Area site conservation plan. Unpublished report, Wisconsin Chapter of the Nature Conservancy, Madison.

Wisconsin Department of Natural Resources. 1998a. Western Prairie Habitat Restoration Area: feasibility study and environmental impact statement. Unpublished report, Wisconsin Department of Natural Resources, Madison.

Wisconsin Department of Natural Resources. 1998b. WISCLAND land cover database of Wisconsin. Wisconsin Department of Natural Resources, Madison.

With, K. A. 1999. Landscape conservation: a new paradigm for the conservation of biodiversity. Pages 78–82 in J. A. Wiens and M. R. Moss (eds.), Issues in landscape ecology. International Association for Landscape Ecology, Guelph, Ontario.

CHAPTER SEVENTEEN

Foraging by Herbivores

Linking the Biochemical Diversity of Plants to Herbivore Culture and Landscape Diversity

FREDERICK D. PROVENZA, JUAN J. VILLALBA,
AND JOHN P. BRYANT

The importance of biological diversity in ecosystem function and stability has been known for more than a century, but the topic is still controversial (Kaiser 2000). Despite the importance of diversity in ecological theory, little is known about the biochemical links between herbivores and plant diversity. These relationships are critical for natural and managed ecosystems, land reclamation, ecosystem restoration, and conservation biology. Basic ecological processes and ecosystem management are governed by the interactions between plant biochemical diversity and herbivory.

The influence of herbivores on plant diversity has attracted more attention than have the biochemical interactions between plants and herbivores (Landsberg et al. 1999). The biotic–abiotic interactions by which herbivores affect plant diversity include the time of grazing, the kinds and abundances of plants and herbivores, and the availability of moisture, nutrients, and light (Milchunas et al. 1988). These interactions have been studied in grasslands (Olff and Ritchie 1998) and woodlands (Bryant et al. 1983a, 1991b, 1992). Understanding relationships between plant biochemical diversity and herbivores can help conceptualize basic ecological processes and management options.

Traditionally, herbivores have been viewed merely as consumers of plants, and animal populations have been portrayed as outputs of plant communities. However, herbivores regulate ecosystem processes, and their influences vary across time and space (reviewed by Hobbs 1996). The outcome of foraging processes is affected by an animal's evolutionary and cultural histories and its current experiences (Provenza 1995a, 1995b; Provenza et al. 1998, 1999). How herbivores learn to mix their diets from an array of plant chemotypes can influence plant biochemical diversity (Villalba, Provenza, and Bryant unpublished data).

In this chapter, we discuss the reciprocal relationships between plants and herbivores (Fig. 17.1). We show how the diversity of plant biochemicals influences plants and herbivores. We focus on the sagebrush steppe ecosystem to illustrate the influence of grazing on plant biochemical diversity.

Satiety Hypothesis

Models of diet selection are based on the assumption that body size and digestive capacity influence food selection such that larger species tolerate low-quality forages better than do smaller species (Hanley 1982; Demment and Van Soest 1985). Thus, herbivore morphology and plant physical characteristics are wed to how herbivory influences vegetation diversity (Olff and Ritchie 1998; Illius et al. 1999). However, such an approach fails to consider that the nutrition and physiology of herbivores also influence diet selection, which in turn affects the biochemical diversity of vegetation.

Behavioral Bases of Varied Diets

Optimal foraging theory assumes that herbivores forage to maximize energy intake per unit effort (Stephens and Krebs 1986). According to optimality models, a herbivore should either eat or ignore a type of food (the zero–one rule). In other words, a high-quality food is always better than a low-quality food. Accordingly, herbivores should not exhibit partial preferences for poorer-quality foods, which is contrary to the partial preferences that have been documented (Stephens and Krebs 1986; Belovsky and Schmitz 1991; Wilmshurst et al. 1995; Belovsky et al. 1999). Partial preferences have been attributed to the inability of herbivores to discriminate between different plant species (Illius et al. 1999), to attempts to meet nutritional needs (Westoby 1978), or to toxin avoidance (Freeland and Janzen 1974). Others contend that partial preferences result from interactions between flavors, nutrients, and toxins (Provenza 1995a, 1996; Provenza et al. 1998).

In support of the latter hypothesis, consider the flavor feedback interac-

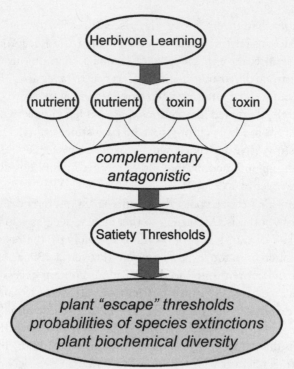

Figure 17.1 Herbivores satiate on nutrients and toxins, and nutrient–toxin interactions limit the intake of a food. Most plants, even common vegetables, contain toxins, so herbivores cannot avoid ingesting plants with toxins. Rather, they must regulate their intake. The consumption of toxic plants depends on the quantity and quality of nutrients and the classes of toxins. A herbivore's experience influences nutrient–nutrient, nutrient–toxin, and toxin–toxin interactions. This then influences diet mixing and vegetation dynamics. Satiety thresholds affect plant escape thresholds, probabilities of local extinction of plant species, and the biochemical diversity of plants. These interactions define relationships between plants and herbivores. Functional analyses suggest that use of a specific plant chemotype disproportionately increases when these species are rare components of the vegetation complex. A threshold of abundance occurs when chemical defenses satiate the detoxification capabilities of herbivores. Above this threshold, herbivory favors the dominant plant chemotype. Below this threshold, herbivory may result in local extinction of the chemotype.

tions that influence palatability, thereby forming the basis for what is known as "nutritional wisdom" (Provenza 1995a, 1996; Provenza et al. 1998). Flavor is a complex sensation that integrates odor, taste, and texture with the postingestive effects of nutrients and toxins. Flavor results when sensory receptors in the mouth and nose respond to gustatory (sweet, salt, sour, bitter), olfactory (an array of odors), and tactile (astringency, pain) stimuli.

These receptors then interact with the visceral receptors that respond to nutrients and toxins (chemoreceptors), osmolality (osmoreceptors), and distension (mechanoreceptors). Thus flavor feedback interactions occur along complex continua that range from preference to aversion. An animal's response depends on the intensity and frequency of stimulation. Collectively, these are neurally mediated interactions that enable animals to discriminate between different foods, each of which has a distinct utility. The ability to integrate postingestive feedback with sensory experiences results in flavor–nutrient–toxin interactions that ultimately are manifest as differences in palatability (Provenza 1995a, 1996).

The relationship between palatability and partial preferences is explained by the satiety hypothesis. According to this theory, decreases in palatability occur as a result of transient food aversions, which are the result of eating any food too often or in too large an amount (Provenza 1995a, 1996). These aversions become more pronounced when foods contain excessive levels of either nutrients or toxins, cause nutrient imbalances, or cause nutrient deficits. These aversions can occur even when a diet is nutritionally adequate because satiety (adequate) and surfeit (excess) are matters of degree. Transient aversions that temporarily decrease the palatability of any food encourage animals to eat a variety of foods and to forage in a variety of locations (Pfister et al. 1997; Early and Provenza 1998; Villalba and Provenza 1999b; Scott and Provenza 1998; 2000; Atwood et al. 2001a, 2001b).

Influence of Nutrients on Food Intake

Preferences for foods high in protein or energy are governed by the nutritional state of insects (Simpson and Raubenheimer 1993, 1999), rodents (Gibson and Booth 1986, 1989; Perez et al. 1996; Ramirez 1997; Gietzen 2000; Sclafani 2000), and ruminants (Cooper et al. 1993; Kyriazakis and Oldham 1993; Kyriazakis et al. 1994; Berteaux et al. 1998; Villalba and Provenza 1999b). Animals prefer a food high in energy after a meal high in protein and vice versa (Perez et al. 1996; Villalba and Provenza 1999b). Elk optimize macronutrient intake by selecting appropriate patches of grass, although there is debate over whether energy (Wilmshurst et al. 1995) or protein (Langvatn and Hanley 1993) is more important. Results of modeling efforts and experiments show that both energy and protein are important and that the preferred ratio of protein to energy depends on needs for growth, gestation, and lactation (Wilmshurst and Fryxell 1995; Fisher 1997; Villalba and Provenza 1999b).

Animals learn to discriminate between foods based on feedback from nutrients. Sheep learn to prefer poorly nutritious foods such as straw when their intake is accompanied by intraruminal infusions of energy (Villalba and Provenza 1996, 1997a, 1997c) or protein (Villalba and Provenza 1997b). They maintain suitable ratios of energy to protein (Egan 1980; Provenza et al. 1996; Wang and Provenza 1996) by discerning feedback after ingesting energy and protein (Villalba and Provenza 1999b). Sheep also respond to synchrony in the rates of nutrient fermentation. Palatability increases with a balanced supply of energy and protein and decreases when there is an excess of either (Kyriazakis and Oldham 1993; Villalba and Provenza 1997b; Early and Provenza 1998).

Micronutrients also influence preferences. Mineral imbalances—deficits or excesses—cause food aversions (Provenza 1995a). A phosphorus deficiency in cattle, sheep, and goats depresses intake by 10 to 50 percent (Ternouth 1991). The rapidity and strength of the aversion depend on the rapidity and severity of the deficiency. Sheep rectify deficits of minerals such as phosphorus, sulfur, and selenium by ingesting mineral supplements (White et al. 1992), and the pica exhibited by cattle foraging on heathlands evidently is a response to a phosphorus deficit (Wallis de Vries 1994). Excess minerals also cause food aversions. As mineral concentrations increase or as electrolyte balance improves, intake increases up to a point and then declines as concentrations increase beyond needs or as balance changes (Ross et al. 1994). For example, sheep strongly prefer flavored straw paired with oral gavage of water to oral gavage of a sodium chloride solution when their needs for sodium are met (Villalba and Provenza 1996). The same is true for sulfur (Hills et al. 1999).

Influence of Toxins on Food Intake

Because most plants, including garden vegetables, contain toxins (Osweiler et al. 1985; Palo and Robbins 1991; Cheeke 1998), foraging is not a matter of avoidance but of regulation (Provenza 1996; Foley et al. 1999). Herbivores seldom consume enough toxins to result in poisoning and death, but they regulate their toxin intake (Provenza 1995a). Oral gavage of toxins causes dose-dependent decreases in intake of toxin-containing foods (Wang and Provenza 1997). Toxins satiate herbivores, and the more quickly plants satiate foragers, the more likely these plants are to survive (Garcia 1989). The rate at which toxin-containing foods can be ingested is probably a function of how quickly toxic compounds can be detoxified and eliminated (Foley and McArthur 1994).

An assessment of the nutritional costs of detoxification is not possible until these processes have been elucidated for different toxins (Foley et al. 1999). Where it has been possible to make this assessment, the costs have been substantial (Thomas et al. 1988; Foley 1992; Guglielmo et al. 1996). Most toxins are lipophilic compounds that must be transformed into hydrophilic substances before excretion in the urine (Cheeke and Shull 1985; Cheeke, 1998). These transformations use substantial amounts of energy and protein (Illius and Jessop 1995, 1996). Many toxins are excreted as conjugated amino acids, glucuronic acid, or sulfate; the creation of these compounds promotes formation of organic acids that disrupt acid–base balance and deplete amino acids and glucose (Foley et al. 1995; Illius and Jessop 1995, 1996). Detoxification and elimination reduce the energy and protein that would otherwise be available for maintenance and production (Freeland and Janzen 1974; Illius and Jessop 1995). Compounds such as tannins also inhibit nutrient use, further increasing the costs associated with ingesting toxins (Robbins et al. 1987a, 1987b, 1991).

Nutrient–Toxin Interactions

To minimize these nutritional costs, it appears that herbivores modify their feeding behavior (Freeland and Janzen 1974; Foley et al. 1999). For example, tannins deplete protein relative to energy, and a herbivore probably experiences a high-tannin diet as a low-protein diet (Robbins et al. 1987a, 1987b, 1991). This is consistent with the fact that sheep and goats select foods with a higher ratio of protein to energy after they consume a high-tannin food (Villalba et al. 2002b, 2002c).

The degree to which toxins constrain intake is influenced by kinds and amounts of nutrients herbivores ingest. When tannic acid was added to foods containing various levels of protein and energy, food intake and growth of locusts both declined when the ratio of protein to energy was not balanced; the decline was more pronounced when levels of protein were suboptimal. When the ratio of macronutrients was near-optimal, there were no adverse effects on food intake or growth (Raubenheimer 1992; Simpson and Raubenheimer 2000). Sheep and goats fed concentrates high in protein or allowed to select concentrates high in either energy or protein ate much more of the terpene-containing shrub sagebrush (Villalba et al. 2002a) and of a high-tannin diet (Villalba et al. 2002b) than when they received only concentrates high in energy. When lambs were infused with terpenes, nitrate, tannins, or lithium chloride, they preferred foods with high protein to energy ratios; after infusions with cyanide, lambs preferred foods with low protein to energy ratios (Villalba et al. 2002c). Thus, toxins influence intake of nutrients, and nutrients influence intake of toxins.

If the ability to tolerate toxins depends on nutrient intake (Illius and Jessop 1995), then providing appropriate nutrients should increase the threshold of toxic satiation, thus making animals more willing to increase their intake of toxin-containing foods. Providing supplemental macronutrients increased the intake of foods that contain toxins as diverse as lithium chloride (Wang and Provenza 1996), terpenes (Banner et al. 2000; Villalba et al. 2002a), menthol (Illius and Jessop 1996), and tannins (Villalba et al. 2002b). Conversely, the sodium-depleting effects of many toxins may deter herbivores from eating plants low in sodium (Freeland et al. 1985; Freeland and Choquenot 1990).

Herbivores also avoid foods containing nutrients that exacerbate the effects of toxins. For instance, terpenes in sagebrush inhibit the cellulolytic activity of rumen microbes (Nagy and Tengerdy 1968). Foods high in soluble carbohydrates, which inhibit cellulolytic activity and lower rumen pH, can exacerbate the effects of terpenes and inhibit detoxification. Lambs eat little sagebrush when supplemented with energy but increase their intake when supplemented with protein or allowed to select from energy and protein concentrates (Villalba et al. 2002a).

Conversely, mature ewes at maintenance selected a high-energy food (50 percent corn, 50 percent beet pulp) over a high-protein food (85 percent alfalfa, 15 percent soybean meal) when offered a choice while foraging on sagebrush (Villalba, Provenza, and Bryant unpublished data). The lower protein needs of ewes compared with lambs, the needs of ewes for energy while foraging on sagebrush during cool fall days, and the protein supplied by the high-energy supplement plus the sagebrush can explain the contrasting supplement selection by ewes during fall relative to lambs and during summer. These relationships illustrate that preference for macronutrients depends on needs for growth, gestation, and lactation; environmental conditions; and the kind and amount of toxin ingested (Villalba et al. 2002c).

Toxin–Toxin Interactions

To obtain energy and protein, herbivores must ingest mixtures of plants that contain nutrients and toxins that are biochemically complementary (Freeland and Janzen 1974). To date, however, little is known about how different toxins interact to influence the intake of plants.

Interactions are complementary when intake of plant species with different toxins increases relative to intake of one plant species. Lambs that could choose between foods containing either amygdalin or lithium chloride (or nitrate and oxalate) ate more than lambs offered food with only one of these toxins (Burritt and Provenza 2000). Mule deer also ate more when offered both sagebrush and juniper (12.3 g/kg body weight), which contain different terpenes, than when offered only sagebrush (4.2 g/kg body weight) or juniper (7.8 g/kg body weight) (Smith 1959). Possums ate more of two diets containing phenolics and terpenes than of diets with only one of these toxins (Dearing and Cork 1999), and squirrels behaved likewise with diets containing oxalates and tannins (Schmidt et al. 1998).

Toxin–toxin interactions can also be antagonistic. For example, lambs offered foods containing either sparteine and saponin (or tannin and saponin) ate no more of both foods than lambs offered one of these foods (Burritt and Provenza 2000).

Summary and Implications

The satiety hypothesis helps to explain why the growth of insects, fish, birds, and mammals improves with varied diets (Rapport 1971; Krebs and Avery 1984; Freeland et al. 1985; Pennings et al. 1993; Bernays et al. 1994). Because satiation varies with the kinds and amounts of nutrients and toxins and the physiological state of the animal, animals that eat a variety of foods can ingest diets that are biochemically complementary. Variety also enables different individuals, each with unique needs for nutrients and abilities to cope with toxins, to express their individuality (Provenza et al. 1990, 1992; Scott and Provenza 1998, 1999, 2000; Atwood et al. 2001a, 2001b).

These interactions also help to explain why the efficacy of plant defenses varies with the mixture of plants and why the chemical attributes of a single plant chemotype must be considered within the context of the entire plant community. The deterrent effect of toxins is probably greatest in habitats low in nutrients (e.g., tannic acid–protein; Raubenheimer 1992), high in nutrients that interact negatively with toxins (e.g., terpenes–soluble carbohydrates; Villalba et al. 2002a), or low in complementary toxins (e.g., saponin–sparteine; Burritt and Provenza 2000). An animal's preference for a mix of plants and habitats may range from strongly aversive to strongly positive depending on complementarity of nutrients and toxins (Belovsky and Schmitz 1991, 1994; Provenza 1996).

Learning how toxins and nutrients interact will clarify how biochemical diversity influences herbivores and plant diversity. The lack of biochemical diversity and complementarity appear to be linked with the decline in plant diversity in natural and managed systems. Selective grazing, often encouraged in managed systems, is inimical to the maintenance of mixtures. Only recently have managers recognized the importance of biochemical complementarity in pastures (Emmick 2000). Identifying the complementary mixtures of nutrients and toxins, whether in managed pastures or in natural systems, also could aid the reestablishment and maintenance of plant diversity (Plummer et al. 1968; West 1993). It is necessary to study nutrient–toxin interactions in grasses, forbs, and shrubs to elucidate complementarities between nutrients and toxins.

Satiety and Vegetation Dynamics

Herbivores satiate on nutrients and toxins, and that limits food intake. Thus, flavor–nutrient–toxin interactions set the asymptote of functional response curves that define relationships between plants and herbivores. These dynamics are influenced by plant abundance because the chemical defenses of a species will satiate the detoxification capabilities of herbivores at a critical threshold of plant abundance. Above this threshold, herbivory will favor domination by a plant chemotype. Below it, local extinction is more likely as a species becomes less abundant.

Assumptions for Functional Response Set by Nutrient–Toxin Satiation

Herbivores must consume enough biomass to meet their nutritional needs and avoid poisoning. This herbivory also affects the dynamics of vegetation. We advance four generalizations about these relationships: Nutrient and toxin satiation limit biomass intake, the mass of a plant chemotype that an animal can consume daily is usually insufficient to meet daily energy and protein needs, a mixed diet is essential to meet nutritional needs and avoid poisoning, and the biomass consumed of a particular chemotype varies with the plant's total available biomass.

Notion of Proportional Browsing and Importance to Vegetation Dynamics

The proportionate consumption of individual plants is important in indices of browsing or grazing intensity, and most palatability indices are based on biomass consumption on a percentage basis (Stoddart and Smith 1955; Edwards et al. 1994). When predation is analyzed as a function of predator to prey density, the relative consumption of prey declines as the density of prey increases (Holling 1959). When vertebrate herbivory is analyzed within the framework of functional response theory (Holling 1959), an increase in biomass is associated with an increase in the rate of food intake (Renecker and Hudson 1986; Spalinger et al. 1988; Astrom et al. 1990; Lundberg and Astrom 1990). These findings associated with functional response theory are relevant to the spatial and temporal dynamics of vegetation. Herbivores remove a disproportionately large percentage of biomass from a plant species when it is a rare component of the vegetation. Conversely, when a plant becomes abundant it faces a much lower risk of herbivore-induced mortality (Lundberg 1988; Lundberg and Astrom 1990; Lundberg and Danell 1990; Bryant et al. 1991a, 1991b; Bryant et al. 2002).

Most studies of functional response have considered only mechanical limitations to grazing, such as travel time between feeding patches and time needed to ingest plants (Lundberg 1988; Lundberg and Astrom 1990; Lundberg and Danell 1990). Nevertheless, toxin and nutrient satiation also influence the upper limit of biomass intake (Bryant et al. 1991a, 1991b; Villalba and Provenza 1999a, 2000). Within the limits imposed by mechanical constraints (Spalinger et al. 1988; Astrom et al. 1990; Lundberg and Astrom 1990; Illius et al. 1999), the relative consumption of a plant chemotype declines as the available biomass of that chemotype increases.

For a given plane of nutrition, the asymptote of the function depends on flavor–nutrient–toxin interactions (Fig. 17.2). According to the satiety hypothesis, herbivory should increase as a plant becomes rare (Bryant et al. 1991a, 1991b; Pennings et al. 1993; Bryant et al. 2002). In a mix of plant species, herbivory destabilizes vegetation dynamics (Abrams 1987; Abrams and Shen 1989) and increases the mortality of rare chemotypes. Herbivory also reduces the biochemical diversity of vegetation when several species are rare (Bryant et al. 1991a, 1991b; Pennings et al. 1993).

Evidence of Proportional Browsing from Field Studies

Support for the hypothesis that proportionate consumption of individual plants declines as the biomass of the plant increases is found in the fact that livestock use unpalatable plant species such as sagebrush more when these species are sporadically distributed throughout a better forage; livestock use declines in dense stands (Heady 1964). Deer, moose, and snowshoe hares also exhibit disproportionately intense browsing of rare woody species. For

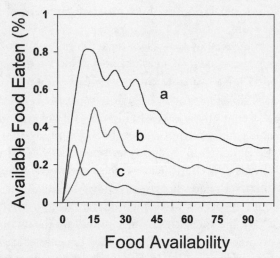

Figure 17.2   Hypothetical plant consumption curves. *(A)* One extreme represents a plant or plant combinations high in complementary nutrients and low in toxins. *(C)* The other extreme represents plants or plant combinations low in nutrients and high in toxins or high in noncomplementary toxins. *(B)* The middle region represents plants or plant combinations whose toxin concentrations are similar to those in C but whose levels of complementary nutrients are higher than in C but lower than in A. When plants or plant mixtures provide the appropriate combinations of nutrients, the threshold of toxin satiation increases (from curve C to B). With nutrient imbalances, the threshold of toxic satiation decreases (from curve A to B to C). Cyclic patterns reflect interactions between flavor, nutrients, and toxins.

example, Douglas fir (*Pseudotsuga mensiesii*) and eastern white cedar (*Thuja occidentalis*), moderately palatable evergreens, are staple foods of Columbian black-tailed deer (Cowen 1945), eastern white-tailed deer (Bookhout 1965), and snowshoe hare (Bookhout 1965). Browsing of these trees is inversely proportional to the density of each of these species (Cowen 1945; Bookhout 1965). Field measurements in Alaska in winter show that browsing of saplings of woody species by snowshoe hares is most severe when the species are rare (Bryant et al. 2002). A similar type of severe browsing by snowshoe hares and other mammals occurred on woody species whose palatability was high (Alaska feltleaf willow [*Salix alaxensis*]), moderate (Alaska paper birch [*Betula resinifera*]), or very low (green alder [*Alnus crispa*]; (Bryant and Kuropat 1980).

Evidence of Toxin Satiation as the Cause of Functional Response

Daily intake is influenced by toxin satiation. Terpenes limit intake of sage-brush, Douglas fir, and cedar by livestock, deer, and hares (Longhurst et al. 1968; Dimock 1974; Radwan and Crouch 1978; Bryant and Kuropat 1980; Personius et al. 1987; Bray et al. 1991; Ngugi et al. 1995; Vourc'h et al. 2001). Toxins also limit the intake of alder, birch, and willow. Green alder contains the highly toxic phenols pinosylvin and pinosylvin methyl ether (Frykholm 1945; Bryant et al. 1983b; Clausen et al. 1986). Juvenile Alaska paper birch contains papyriferic acid, which is aversive to hares (Reichardt et al. 1984). Conversely, hares browse juvenile Alaska feltleaf willow, which contains low concentrations of condensed tannin and phenol glycosides (Bryant et al. 1985). In winter, these compounds limit the intake of snowshoe hares to 16 g dry mass/hare/day for alder, 33 g dry mass/hare/day for birch, and less than 150 g dry mass/hare/day for willow (Bryant et al. 2002).

Habitat Deterioration in Woodlands and Forests

Toxin satiation appears to be the primary cause of varied diets in ecosystems dominated by woody vegetation and mammals (Bryant and Kuropat 1980; Palo and Robbins 1991; Bryant et al. 1991a, 1991b, 1992). If so, the functional response theory predicts that browsing will reduce vegetation diversity and habitat quality, and chemically monotonous assemblages of unpalatable plants will become dominant. The "threshold of escape biomass" is lower for unpalatable than for palatable species (Bryant et al. 1991a, 1991b). For example, on the floodplains of interior Alaska, palatable willow is usually replaced by unpalatable alder after browsing by snowshoe hare and moose (Wolff and Zasada 1979; Walker et al. 1986; MacAvinchey 1992; Kielland and Bryant 1998), apparently because the escape threshold of green alder is much lower than that of Alaska feltleaf willow.

Nevertheless, plants with high levels of chemical defense do not always dominate the landscape. If a heavily defended species is below the "escape threshold" of abundance, it is likely to be eliminated by herbivores. Nutrients in alternative forages can increase the use of toxin-containing plants, thus exacerbating the decline of rare species (see Fig. 17.2). On Alaskan floodplains, alder invades during the willow stage of succession because mast crops of alder seedlings "chemically swamp" snowshoe hares (Walker et al. 1986; Bryant et al. 2002). Without a mast crop of alder, willow becomes dominant (MacAvinchey 1992). In willow-dominated vegetation, alder is browsed more heavily than when alder is abundant, and alder may go extinct locally (Walker et al. 1986; Bryant et al. 2002).

Summary and Implications

Interactions between nutrients and toxins influence biomass intake by herbivores. These interactions, in concert with mechanical constraints, mean that herbivory can be analyzed as a functional response of a predator to the density of its prey (Holling 1959). In many cases, flavor–nutrient–toxin interactions probably set the asymptote of the functional response (Bryant et al. 1991a, 1991b, 2002), thereby affecting the biochemical diversity of vegetation and population dynamics of plants and herbivores.

These dynamics are influenced by plant abundance. The chemical defenses of a species, in accord with nutrient availability, satiate the detoxification capabilities of herbivores at a critical threshold of plant abundance. Above this threshold, herbivory favors domination by a species. Below it, local extinction is more likely as a species becomes less abundant. In most cases, unpalatable species with effective chemical defenses become dominant (Harper 1969; Crawley 1983; Bryant et al. 1991a, 1991b). However, species most defended chemically do not always dominate the vegetation. Where seedling establishment is limited for reasons such as seed rain (Walker et al. 1986), species with less effective chemical defenses can reach a "threshold of escape," and species with more effective defenses can be reduced or eliminated because they do not satiate herbivores.

According to the satiety hypothesis, toxic plants should be best defended when neighboring plants have low levels of nutrients needed to mitigate toxicosis or high levels of nutrients that interact adversely with toxins (see Fig. 17.2). If a plant community supplies appropriate nutrients, the threshold of toxin satiation increases, which is consistent with the high levels of herbivory experienced by toxic species that constitute a minor proportion of the diet (Bryant et al. 1991a, 1991b; Augustine and McNaughton 1998). As a toxic plant becomes more abundant and the availability of nutrients declines, toxin satiation thresholds and use both decline. Thus use of a toxic plant may increase or decrease without any change in the toxin content of the plant.

Some believe palatable plants benefit by association with toxic plants (associational refuge theory; Atsatt and O'Dowd 1976; Pfister and Hay 1988), thereby maintaining plant species richness (Hay 1986). Others believe herbivory of unpalatable plants increases by association with palatable plants (associational susceptibility; White and Whitham 2000). However, we postulate that the complementary and antagonistic relationships between flavors, nutrients, and toxins determine susceptibility and resistance of toxic plants. Preferences for some combinations of plants may differ from that predicted by the nutrient or toxin content of any one species. The use of plant species associated with toxic neighbors is likely to increase if they supply appropriate nutrients. Negative nutrient–toxin interactions may benefit plants, thereby offsetting the costs of competition, and positive nutrient–toxin interactions may aid the survival of less competitive nutritious plants. Integrating nutrient–toxin interactions with plant refuge theory will clarify these relationships.

Enhancing and Maintaining Plant Diversity: Sagebrush Steppe as a Case Study

As described earlier in this chapter, nutrient–toxin interactions describe the relationship between plants and herbivores, thereby influencing vegetation dynamics. Herbivore culture and experience can also influence the outcome of these interactions, and managed herbivory can enhance and maintain plant diversity.

Enhancing Plant Biochemical Diversity

Even though grazing can enhance plant diversity in sagebrush steppe ecosystems (Bork et al. 1998), diversity declined in the past century when toxin-containing woody plants such as sagebrush (*Artemisia* spp.) and juniper (*Juniperus* spp.) came to dominate more than 39 million hectares of land in the western United States (West 1993). Domination by sagebrush resulted from at least four factors. First, it reflects the dearth of herbivores and the changes in grazing patterns as grazers such as cattle and elk replaced mixed feeders and browsers such as sheep, goats, deer, and antelope (Hofmann 1988). Second, livestock were often confined and grazed the same herbs repeatedly, particularly in spring (Burkhardt 1996). Under low- to moderate-intensity grazing, palatable grasses and herbs were dominated by toxin-containing plants such as sagebrush. Third, sagebrush biomass eventually exceeded the escape threshold, and rare species were grazed more severely than sagebrush. The decrease in herbs reduced fine fuels for fires and created conditions that favored severe firestorms which also reduced biodiversity (Burkhardt 1996; West 1999; West and Young 2000).

The decline in diversity in sagebrush steppe landscapes meant less water was available for other plant species because sagebrush transpires year-round (Link 1994). Nutrient cycling, plant production, and herbivore nutrition declined because sagebrush contains high concentrations of terpenoids, which are toxic to soil and rumen microbes (Oh et al. 1968) and to ruminants (Johnson et al. 1976). To reverse these trends, management must enhance diversity by decreasing the abundance of sagebrush and maintaining a mixture of plant species.

Grazing can enhance plant diversity. Intensive grazing by sheep for short periods during the fall, when herbs are dormant, increases plant diversity in sagebrush steppe (Bilbrough and Richards 1993; Bork et al. 1998). Providing herbivores with supplemental macronutrients facilitates detoxification, which markedly increases the use of sagebrush. Sheep and goats receiving supplemental energy and protein consumed nearly twice as much sagebrush as unsupplemented animals (Banner et al. 2000; Villalba et al. 2002a). When large herbivores browse sagebrush, the reduction in sagebrush increases soil moisture. The feces and urine from supplemented herbivores add organic matter and nutrients to soils, further increasing herb production and nutrient content.

Finally, grazing management that encourages the use of all plants trains herbivores to mix diets to use all species, thereby maintaining plant diversity, as has occurred with grazing by large herds of herbivores (Savory 1988; Burkhardt 1996). With grazing practices that encourage preferential consumption, herbivores are unlikely to learn how to mix nutritious and toxic foods. In contrast, animals repeatedly forced to eat all plants in an area are encouraged to mix nutritious and toxic plants to mitigate toxicity if the appropriate biochemical choices are available.

Maintaining Diversity: Theoretical Considerations Concerning Experience and Diet Mixing

Prevailing theories of food (optimal foraging theory) and habitat (ideal free distribution) selection assume that foods and environments vary with respect to their intrinsic quality (called "optimal diet" in Stephens and Krebs 1986 and "basic suitability" in Fretwell and Lucas 1970). Intrinsic quality is the fitness associated with selection of the diet or habitat. More importantly, these theories assume that the intrinsic value of different diets and habitats is the same for every individual in the species.

There are several reasons why it is time to reevaluate this assumption. Reproductive success improves if postdispersal foods and habitats are similar to predispersal foods and habitats (Stamps 2001). Animals learn from social and environmental experiences, and experiences early in life can even influence gene expression (McCormick et al. 2000). Experience improves performance by inducing neurologic, morphologic, and physiologic changes in animals (Provenza and Balph 1990; Provenza 1995b, 1996; Piersma and Lindstrom 1997; Schlichting and Pigliucci 1998; Provenza et al. 1998). These interactions enable animals to adapt to changing conditions and imply that a high-quality diet and habitat differs for individuals reared under different conditions.

One example of how experiences early in life influence foraging occurred during a three-year study involving 32 cows (five years of age) that were fed straw as a major part of their diet from December to May (Wiedmeier et al. 2002). Half of the cows had been exposed to straw during their first three months of life. Throughout the three-year study, experienced cows lost less weight, maintained a better body condition, produced more milk, and bred back sooner than cows not exposed to straw. Goats reared on blackbrush (*Coleogyne ramosissima*)-dominated land from one to four months of age consumed more than 2.5 times more blackbrush than did goats naive to blackbrush; experienced goats consumed 30 percent more blackbrush than inexperienced goats when allowed to choose between the poorly nutritious blackbrush and alfalfa pellets (Distel and Provenza 1991). Lambs exposed to wheat early in life (one hour/day for five days at six weeks of age) consumed notably more wheat 3 years later as adults than did animals that never consumed wheat (Green et al. 1984). Experiences early in life result in neurologic, morphologic, and physiologic changes that help goats and sheep use poor-quality forages (Distel and Provenza 1991; Distel et al. 1994, 1996). In the process, young herbivores learn forage harvesting techniques (Flores et al. 1989a, 1989b; Ortega-Reyes and Provenza 1993) and preferences for foods (sheep, Nolte et al. 1990; goats, Biquand and Biquand-Guyot 1992) and habitats (sheep, Key and MacIver 1980; cattle, Howery et al. 1996, 1998; moose, Andersen 1991).

Herbivores learn to select appropriate diets (Provenza 1995a, 1995b). They also learn to use medicines to attenuate the aversive effects of acidosis (Phy and Provenza 1998) and tannin toxicosis (Provenza et al. 2000; Villalba and Provenza 2001). Nevertheless, little is known about how herbivores learn to mix their diets given a variety of alternatives. Humans learn which combinations of foods will meet macronutrient needs and mitigate toxicosis (Rozin 1988, 1996). Cattle also appear to learn to mix palatable and unpalatable foods in their diets (R. Banister, personal communication 2000).

The variety of plant species on western landscapes may make it difficult for herbivores to determine which combinations of foods meet nutritional needs, minimize toxin intake, and optimize interactions between nutrients and toxins. Although much more must be learned about this behavior (Belovsky and Schmitz 1991, 1994; Provenza 1996), it is known that sheep can select diets that provide necessary amounts of energy and protein, synchronize the supply of energy and protein, and balance supplies of macronutrients and toxins. For example, sheep prefer high-protein foods after consuming a meal high in energy, and they prefer high-energy foods after consuming a meal high in protein (Villalba and Provenza 1999b). Protein intake also increases during growth (Kyriazakis and Oldham 1993), pregnancy (Cooper et al. 1993), and parasite infections (Kyriazakis et al. 1994). Intake of macronutrients also changes with toxin intake (Villalba et al. 2002c), and toxin intake changes with nutrient availability (Banner et al. 2000; Villalba et al. 2002a, 2002b). Herbivores also increase their consumption of combinations of foods with complementary toxins (Schmidt et al. 1998; Dearing and Cork 1999; Burritt and Provenza 2000). All of these examples show that herbivores can learn about associations between nutrients and toxins.

Maintaining Diversity: Empirical Evidence Concerning Experience and Diet Mixing

Ray Banister, who manages 7,200 acres of land in eastern Montana, has modified his grazing management from reliance on rotational grazing to boom–bust grazing involving intense periods of grazing followed by two years of rest. Such intense grazing ensures that unpalatable plants do not acquire a competitive advantage over more palatable species. The ranch has some of the highest vegetation cover and diversity in eastern Montana.

Changing from rotational to boom–bust grazing meant cattle could no longer select only the most preferred plants. Based on cow and calf performance, it took three years to adapt to the new grazing regime. Weaning weights of calves dropped from more than 500 pounds to 350 pounds before rebounding. During that time, cows learned to eat shrubs such as snowberry and sagebrush, which are usually considered highly unpalatable because of their levels of toxins. Cattle evidently learned to eat unpalatable and palatable species simultaneously to mitigate the aversive effects of toxins. Such learned patterns are likely to be transmitted from mothers to their offspring (Thorhallsdottir et al. 1990; Mirza and Provenza 1990, 1992; Biquand and Biquand-Guyot 1992; Provenza 1994, 1995b).

We hypothesize that herbivores can optimize intakes of nutrients and toxins in a manner consistent with their previous experiences with the mix of foods offered. If animals are familiar with only some of the foods, and those foods provide adequate nutrition, herbivores are unlikely to eat other foods and are less likely to learn about the possible benefits of mixing different foods. Instead, they will probably eat all of the familiar foods before they accept unfamiliar foods and will mix the foods so as to balance nutrients and toxins (Fig. 17.3). If so, herbivores repeatedly forced to eat all plants should learn to eat mixtures that mitigate toxicity if appropriate choices are available to them.

In pen trials, lambs that learned to eat foods that contained either tannins, terpenes, or oxalates ate more when they could select two of the foods offered simultaneously (tannins–terpenes, tannins–oxalates, or terpenes–oxalates) than lambs offered only one food. Lambs offered foods containing all three toxins ate more than lambs offered two of the toxins, and their intake was comparable to that of lambs offered the food that contained no toxins (Villalba et al., unpublished data).

We then compared food intake of lambs with 3 months' experience mixing foods with intake of lambs naive to the toxin-containing foods (Villalba et al., unpublished data). All lambs were offered five foods, two of them familiar to all of the lambs (ground alfalfa and a 50:50 mix of ground alfalfa and ground barley) and three foods familiar only to experienced lambs (a ground ration containing either tannins, terpenes, or oxalates). Half the lambs were offered the familiar foods ad libitum, and half the lambs were offered only 200 g of each familiar food daily.

Experience and the availability of nutritious alternatives both influenced food choice. Naive lambs ate much less of the foods with toxins if they had ad libitum access, as opposed to restricted access, to the nutritious alternatives (66 versus 549 g/day). Experienced lambs also ate less of the foods with toxins if they had ad libitum access, as opposed to restricted access, to the nutritious alternatives (809 versus 1,497 g/day). In both cases, however, lambs with experience ate more of the foods containing the toxins than naive lambs, whether access to the alfalfa–barley alternatives was ad libitum (811 versus 71 g/day) or restricted (1,509 versus 607 g/day). When access to familiar foods was restricted, experience also affected the pattern of diet mixing. Experienced animals ate large amounts of all three foods containing toxins, whereas naive lambs ate only the foods with tannins and oxalates.

These findings suggest that different management systems may change how animals forage. Light stocking encourages selective foraging, whereas

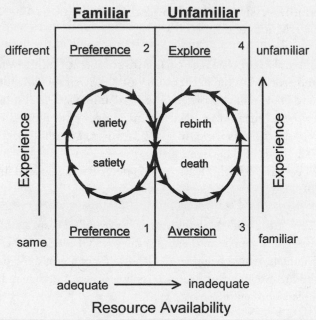

Resource Availability

Figure 17.3 Experiences early in life affect preferences for foods and habitats (quadrant 1) and explain why animals are reluctant to ingest unfamiliar foods and explore unfamiliar habitats (Provenza 1995b, 1998). Satiating on the same foods encourages animals to eat a variety of familiar foods and to forage in various familiar locations (satiety–variety quadrants 1 and 2). If familiar foods and haunts are not adequate (aversion, quadrant 3), animals are more likely to investigate new options (explore, quadrant 4) and acquire new habits. If they encounter suitable foods and habitats, they acquire new preferences (quadrants 1 and 2). This dynamic, nonlinear view is consistent with mythological notions (Campbell and Moyers 1988) and emerging views of human development and organizational performance (Senge 1994), economics (Bernstein 1998), history (McNeill 1979), behavior (Provenza et al. 1998, 1999), ecology (Gunderson et al. 1995), evolutionary biology (Kauffman 1995), climatology (Lorenz 1963), thermodynamics, and physics (Prigogine and Stengers 1984).

heavy stocking for short periods encourages diet mixing. What was traditionally considered proper grazing management—rotational grazing at low stock densities—may have trained generations of livestock parents and offspring to eat the best and leave the rest, thus inadvertently accelerating a decline in biodiversity and an increase in the abundance of less desirable plant species.

Maintaining Diversity: Culture, Social Organization, and Grazing Management

Bob Jackson and Sharon Magee own a bison operation in Iowa. Bob also has lived and worked in the backcountry of Yellowstone Park for 30 years. Both Bob and Sharon have worked with herd animals. They understand the relationships between culture, social organization, and grazing management. Intact family units—offspring, mothers, fathers, grandmothers, grandfathers—are the basis of their operation.

Frank Mayer and Charles Roth (1995) describe these social units in *The Buffalo Harvest*:

> Do you remember reading about buffalo herds millions strong, moving in a solid mass, and stopping trains and wagons? . . . Of course the herd, this vast mass of animals, would be under the leadership of a grand old buffalo bull, who would trot serenely at its head, issuing orders and demanding instant and complete obedience.

But as they point out, these are misconceptions:

> Most of the herds would run from three to sixty animals, with an average of around fifteen. In these small herds the buffalo traveled and fed, scattered over the plains, but each one separate and apart from the other herds. Whenever they stampeded they did come together and charged as one vast, solid herd. But when the fight passed they'd separate into their peculiar small herd formation . . . [whose] leader wasn't a bull at all. . . . It was a cow, a sagacious old cow who by the power of her intellect had made herself a leader. Buffalo society, you see, was a matriarchy, and the cow was queen.

Bob and Sharon manage bison and land on the basis of these "peculiar small herds" under the leadership of matriarchs. They contend that bison and cattle family units are necessary for proper management. Young animals benefit from the social behavior and food and habitat selection of older generations. Bison culture, as with other social species such as goats, sheep, cattle, deer, elk, and elephants, transmits knowledge about social and physical environments (Provenza 1995b).

Members of family groups learn how to mix diets and achieve uniform use of different plant species, which enhances biodiversity. Management that considers family groups can achieve the same outcome as management-intensive grazing: more uniform use of all plant species within the area where the family group is foraging. Competition between family groups promotes rotational grazing, without the need for fencing, as family groups displace one another while grazing across landscapes.

Bob and Sharon contend that social interactions also discourage the over-use of riparian areas. Matriarchs maintain identity of family groups by moving from riparian areas when other families enter the area, ensuring that groups do not linger along watering points. Historical accounts in Yellowstone and elsewhere indicate that riparian areas were heavily used primarily during the winter, when families tolerated more contact as they foraged along riparian areas.

Knowledge of environments depends on the maintenance of family order. This is not possible when family units are dismantled or when domestic or wild animals are moved from familiar to unfamiliar environments. Animals rely on their culture to learn the locations of food, water, and shelter. They also learn how to mix their diets to eat a variety of nutritious and toxic foods. The destruction of culture explains why animals introduced into unfamiliar environments suffer from malnutrition, overingestion of poisonous plants, and predation (Provenza and Balph 1990).

Summary and Implications

The unfamiliarity of animals with new environments explains why captive-reared birds and mammals often fail to thrive when they are released into habitats formerly occupied by their species (Provenza and Balph 1990; Beck et al. 1994; Shepherdson 1994). Animals trained to select mixed diets would be more successful when transplanted to new areas (Provenza et al. 1992; Provenza 1994, 1995b; Stamps 2001). Conservation biologists advocate food and habitat training before introducing animals to unfamiliar habitats. This is consistent with the hypothesis that animals acquire a variety of skills in their natal habitat (Beck et al. 1994; Shepherdson 1994; Stamps 2001). By creating and maintaining well-mixed vegetation landscapes, it may be possible to encourage herbivores to use a more diverse array of plants. It also may be possible to train groups of animals to better use forages and habitats. Such knowledge would be passed from generation to generation, thus setting in motion a method of maintaining landscape diversity.

Populations of sage grouse and mule deer have declined markedly in the West during the past decades, in part because of the lack of diverse forages (Plummer et al. 1968; Wallestad 1971; Braun et al. 1977; Austin 2000). Sagebrush in excess of 30 percent in the diet is detrimental to mule deer (Carpenter et al. 1979). Of course, sagebrush steppe can be fertilized to increase the production of grasses, forbs, and shrubs, aiding mule deer and elk (Bayoumi and Smith 1976). With fertilizers and herbicides, the nutritional quality of mule deer winter ranges can be improved, but the cost of these practices is prohibitive (Bayoumi and Smith 1976; Carpenter 1976). On the other hand, managed grazing by livestock can convert sagebrush into a source of forage, thereby enhancing and maintaining biodiversity of sagebrush steppe ecosystems, with substantial long-term economic benefits (Atwood, unpublished economic analysis).

Ecological systems, even monocultures of sagebrush, are not unchanging (Holling 1995). Disturbances such as grazing can enhance and maintain the biochemical richness of sagebrush steppe without the use of herbicides or fertilizers. Light, season-long grazing helped create monocultures of sagebrush. Replacing it with short-duration grazing and supplements can result in a diverse mix of plants. That diversity can be maintained by animals that learn to select mixed diets that include a wider variety of plants. By understanding how herbivore culture is related to biochemical interactions between plants and herbivores, managers can address phenomena such as the decreasing intake of abundant species such as sagebrush and the increasing intake of rare species.

Summary

Ecosystem function and stability are integral components of biological diversity, although little is known about how the biochemical links between herbivores and plant diversity influence the sustainability of ecosystems. In this chapter, we discussed how plant biochemical diversity influences herbivores and plants. Biochemical diversity increases the resiliency, adaptability, and productivity of ecosystems by increasing the diversity of options for plants, herbivores, and people.

Herbivores satiate on nutrients and toxins, and that limits food intake. Most plants, even common vegetables, contain toxins, so complete avoidance is not feasible. Rather, herbivores must regulate toxin intake. Intake of toxic plants depends on both the quantity and quality of nutrients and the kinds of toxins. Some interactions increase intake; others do not. The kinds and amounts of nutrients and toxins in a plant or its neighbors determine the effectiveness of a toxin and influence the probability of extinction of plant chemotypes. How herbivores learn to mix their diets from an array of chemotypes also influences plant diversity. Collectively, such associational effects involving plant chemistry and herbivore learning may influence species coexistence and hence plant species diversity and either enhance or counteract the evolution of plant defenses.

Flavor–nutrient–toxin interactions set the asymptote of functional response curves that define relationships between plants and herbivores. These dynamics are influenced by plant abundance because the chemical defenses of a species satiate the detoxification capabilities of herbivores at a critical threshold of plant abundance. Above this threshold, herbivory favors domination by a plant chemotype. Below it, local extinction is more likely as a species becomes less abundant. In most cases, unpalatable species with effective chemical defenses become dominant. However, species most defended chemically do not always dominate the vegetation. Where seedling establishment is limited for reasons such as seed rain, species with less effective chemical defenses can reach a "threshold of escape," and species with more effective defenses can be reduced or eliminated.

The sagebrush steppe illustrates how grazing by herbivores can enhance plant biochemical diversity. Terpenes in sagebrush (*Artemisia tridentata* spp.) limit intake of sagebrush. Season-long spring grazing enables sagebrush to cross the "escape threshold" where rare species are grazed more severely than sagebrush, thereby decreasing plant diversity. Conversely, grazing during fall, when grasses and forbs are dormant, can decrease the abundance of sagebrush relative to herbs, thereby enhancing plant diversity. Sagebrush use during fall can be further increased by providing supplemental macronutrients to facilitate detoxification. Reducing the prevalence of sagebrush increases soil moisture available for herbs. In addition, herbivores add organic matter and nutrients to soils, which also enhances herb production and nutrient content.

Finally, grazing management can encourage the use of all plants by herbivores, thereby maintaining plant diversity. Herbivores learn to optimize their intake of nutrients and toxins. If herbivores are allowed to eat only the most preferred plants, they probably will not learn to mix foods high in nutrients with foods high in toxins. Conversely, herbivores trained to eat all plants in an area can learn to eat mixtures of plants that mitigate toxicity. Experienced animals eat large amounts of foods with toxins, even when nutritious alternatives are available, whereas naive animals eat limited amounts of foods with toxins, especially when they have access to preferred alternatives.

LITERATURE CITED

Abrams, P. 1987. The functional response of adaptive consumers of two resources. Theoretical Population Biology 32:262–288.

Abrams, P. A., and L. Shen. 1989. Population dynamics of systems with consumers that maintain a constant ratio of intake rates of two resources. Theoretical Population Biology 35:51–89.

Andersen, R. 1991. Habitat deterioration and the migratory behaviour of moose (*Alces alces* L.) in Norway. Journal of Applied Ecology 28:102–108.

Astrom, M., P. Lundberg, and K. Danell. 1990. Partial prey consumption by browsers: trees as patches. Journal of Animal Ecology 59:287–300.

Atsatt, P. R., and D. J. O'Dowd. 1976. Plant defense guilds. Science 193:24–29.

Atwood, S. B., F. D. Provenza, R. D. Wiedmeier, and R. E. Banner. 2001a. Changes in preferences of gestating heifers fed untreated or ammoniated straw in different flavors. Journal of Animal Science 79:3027–3033.

Atwood, S. B., F. D. Provenza, R. D. Wiedmeier, and R. E. Banner. 2001b. Influence of free-choice versus mixed-ration diets on food intake and performance of fattening calves. Journal of Animal Science 79:3034–3040.

Augustine, D. J., and S. J. McNaughton. 1998. Ungulate effects on the functional species composition of plant communities: herbivore selectivity and plant tolerance. Journal of Wildlife Management 62:1165–1183.

Austin, D. D. 2000. Managing livestock grazing for mule deer (*Odocoileus hemionus*) on winter range in the Great Basin. Western North American Naturalist 60:198–203.

Banner, R. E., J. Rogosic, E. A. Burritt, and F. D. Provenza. 2000. Supplemental barley and activated charcoal increase intake of sagebrush by lambs. Journal of Range Management 53:415–420.

Bayoumi, M. A., and A. D. Smith. 1976. Response of big game winter range to fertilization. Journal of Range Management 29:44–48.

Beck, B. B., L. G. Rapaport, S. Price, M. R. Wilson, and A. C. Wilson. 1994. Reintroduction of captive-born animals. Pages 265–286 in P. J. Olney, G. M. Mace, and A. T. Feistner (eds.), Creative conservation: interactive management of wild and captive animals. Chapman & Hall, London.

Belovsky, G. E., and O. J. Schmitz. 1991. Mammalian herbivore foraging and the role of plant defenses. Pages 1–28 in R. T. Palo and C. T. Robbins (eds.), Plant defenses against mammalian herbivory. CRC Press, Boca Raton, FL.

Belovsky, G. E., and O. J. Schmitz. 1994. Plant defenses and optimal foraging by mammalian herbivores. Journal of Mammalogy 75:816–832.

Belovsky, G. E., J. Fryxell, and O. J. Schmitz. 1999. Natural selection and herbivore nutrition: optimal foraging theory and what it tells us about the structure of ecological communities. Pages 1–70 in H. G. Jung and G. C. Fahey, Jr. (eds.), Nutritional ecology of herbivores: proceedings of the Vth International Symposium on the Nutrition of Herbivores. American Society of Animal Science, Savoy, IL.

Bernays, E. A., K. L. Bright, L. Gonzalez, and J. Angel. 1994. Dietary mixing in a generalist herbivore: tests of two hypotheses. Ecology 75:1997–2006.

Bernstein, P. L. 1998. Against the gods: the remarkable story of risk. Wiley, New York.

Berteaux, D., M. Crete, J. Huot, J. Maltais, and J.-P. Ouellet. 1998. Food choice by white-tailed deer in relation to protein and energy content of the diet: a field experiment. Oecologia 115:84–92.

Bilbrough, C. J., and J. H. Richards. 1993. Growth of sagebrush and bitterbrush following simulated winter browsing: mechanisms and tolerance. Ecology 74:481–492.

Biquand, S., and V. Biquand-Guyot. 1992. The influence of peers, lineage and environment on food selection of the criollo goat (*Capra hircus*). Applied Animal Behavior Science 34:231–245.

Bookhout, T. A. 1965. The snowshoe hare in Upper Michigan and its biology and feeding coactions with white-tailed deer. Michigan Department of Conservation Research Development Report No. 38.

Bork, E. W., N. E. West, and J. W. Walker. 1998. Cover components on long-term seasonal sheep grazing treatments in three-tip sagebrush steppe. Journal of Range Management 51:293–300.

Braun, C. E., T. Britt, and R. O. Wallestad. 1977. Guidelines for maintenance of sage grouse habitats. Wildlife Society Bulletin 5:99–106.

Bray, R. O., C. L. Wambolt, and R. G. Kelsey. 1991. Influence of sagebrush terpenoids on mule deer preference. Journal of Chemical Ecology 17:2053–2062.

Bryant, J. P., and P. Kuropat. 1980. Subarctic browsing vertebrate winter forage selection: the role of plant chemistry. Annual Review of Ecology and Systematics 11:261–285.

Bryant, J. P., F. S. Chapin, III, and D. R. Kline. 1983a. Carbon/nutrient balance of boreal plants in relation to vertebrate herbivory. Oikos 40:357–368.

Bryant, J. P., G. D. Wieland, P. B. Reichardt, V. E. Lewis, and M. C. McCarthy. 1983b. Pinosylvin methyl ether, a snowshoe hare antifeedant isolated from green alder (*Alnus crispa*) resin. Science 222:1023–1025.

Bryant, J. P., G. D. Wieland, T. P. Clausen, and P. Kuropat. 1985. Interactions of snowshoe hares and feltleaf willow (*Salix alaxensis*) in Alaska. Ecology 66:1564–1573.

Bryant, J. P., P. J. Kuropat, P. B. Reichardt, and T. P. Clausen. 1991a. Controls over the allocation of resources by woody plants to antiherbivore defense. Pages 83–102 in R. T. Palo and C. T. Robbins (eds.), Plant chemical defenses against mammalian herbivory. CRC Press, Boca Raton, FL.

Bryant, J. P., F. D. Provenza, J. Pastor, P. B. Reichardt, T. P. Clausen, and J. T. DuToit. 1991b. Interactions between woody plants and browsing mammals mediated by secondary metabolites. Annual Review of Ecology and Systematics 22:431–446.

Bryant, J. P., F. D. Provenza, P. B. Reichardt, and T. P. Clausen. 1992. Mammal–woody plant interactions. Pages 343–370 in G. A. Rosenthal and M. Berenbaum (eds.), Herbivores: their interaction with plant secondary metabolites. Vol. 2. Academic Press, New York.

Bryant, J. P., F. D. Provenza, and J. J. Villalba. 2002. A functional response analysis of toxin satiation in interactions between plants and mammals: implications for plant biochemical diversity. Oikos submitted.

Burkhardt, J. W. 1996. Herbivory in the intermountain West. Idaho Forest, Wildlife and Range Experiment Station Bulletin 58. Moscow, ID.

Burritt, E. A., and F. D. Provenza. 2000. Role of toxins in intake of varied diets by sheep. Journal of Chemical Ecology 26:1991–2005.

Campbell, J., and B. Moyers. 1988. The power of myth. Doubleday, New York.

Carpenter, L. H. 1976. Nitrogen-herbicide effects on sagebrush deer range. Ph.D. thesis, Colorado State University, Ft. Collins.

Carpenter, L. H., O. C. Wallmo, and B. B. Gill. 1979. Forage diversity and dietary selection by mule deer. Journal of Range Management 32:226–229.

Cheeke, P. 1998. Natural toxicants in feeds, forages and poisonous plants. Interstate Publications, Danville, IL.

Cheeke, P., and L. R. Shull. 1985. Natural toxicants in feeds and poisonous plants. Avi Publishing, Westport, CT.

Clausen, T. P., J. P. Bryant, and P. B. Reichardt. 1986. Defense of winter-dormant green alder against snowshoe hares. Journal of Chemical Ecology 12:2117–2131.

Cooper, S. D. B., I. Kyriazakis, D. H. Anderson, and J. D. Oldham. 1993. The effect of physiological state (late pregnancy) on the diet selection of ewes. Animal Production 56:469A.

Cowen, I. M. 1945. The ecological relationships of the food of the Columbian black-tailed deer, *Odocoileus hemionus columbianus* (Richardson), in the coast forest region of southern Vancouver Island, British Columbia. Ecological Monographs 15:110–139.

Crawley, M. J. 1983. Herbivory: the dynamics of animal–plant interactions. Blackwell Scientific Publications, Oxford, UK.

Dearing, M. D., and S. Cork. 1999. Role of detoxification of plant secondary compounds on diet breadth in a mammalian herbivore, *Trichosurus vulpecula*. Journal of Chemical Ecology 25:1205–1219.

Demment, M. W., and P. J. Van Soest. 1985. A nutritional explanation for body-size patterns of ruminant and nonruminant herbivores. American Naturalist 125:641–672.

Dimock, E. J., II. 1974. Animal resistant Douglas-fir: how likely and how soon? Pages 95–101 in H. C. Black (ed.), Wildlife and forest management in the Pacific Northwest. Forest Research Laboratory School of Forestry, Oregon State University, Corvallis.

Distel, R. A., and F. D. Provenza. 1991. Experience early in life affects voluntary intake of blackbrush by goats. Journal of Chemical Ecology 17:431–450.

Distel, R. A., J. J. Villalba, and H. E. Laborde. 1994. Effects of early experience on voluntary intake of low-quality roughage by sheep. Journal of Animal Science 72:1191–1195.

Distel, R. A., J. J. Villalba, H. E. Laborde, and M. A. Burgos. 1996. Persistence of the effects of early experience on consumption of low-quality roughage by sheep. Journal of Animal Science 74:965–968.

Early, D., and F. D. Provenza. 1998. Food flavor and nutritional characteristics alter dynamics of food preference in lambs. Journal of Animal Science 76:728–734.

Edwards, G. R., J. A. Newman, A. J. Parsons, and J. R. Krebs. 1994. Effects of the scale and spatial distribution on the food resource and animal state on diet selection: an example with sheep. Journal of Animal Ecology 63:816–826.

Egan, A. R. 1980. Host animal–rumen relationships. Proceedings of the Nutrition Society 39:79–87.

Emmick, D. (ed.). 2000. Prescribed grazing and feeding management for lactating dairy cows. New York State Grazing Lands Conservation Initiative in Cooperation with the USDA Natural Resources Conservation Service, Syracuse, New York.

Fisher, D. S. 1997. Modeling ruminant feed intake with protein, chemostatic, and distention feedbacks. Journal of Animal Science 74:3076–3081.

Flores, E. R., F. D. Provenza, and D. F. Balph. 1989a. The effect of experience on the foraging skill of lambs: importance of plant form. Applied Animal Behavior Science 23:285–291.

Flores, E. R., F. D. Provenza, and D. F. Balph. 1989b. Role of experience in the development of foraging skills of lambs browsing the shrub serviceberry. Applied Animal Behavior Science 23:271–278.

Foley, W. J. 1992. Nitrogen and energy retention and acid–base status in the common ringtail possum (*Pseudocheirus peregrinus*): evidence of the effects of absorbed allelochemicals. Physiological Zoology 65:403–421.

Foley, W. J., and C. McArthur. 1994. The effects and costs of allelochemicals for mammalian herbivores: an ecological perspective. Pages 370–391 in D. J. Chivers and P. Langer (eds.), The digestive system in mammals: food, form and function. Cambridge University Press, Cambridge, UK.

Foley, W. J., S. McLean, and S. J. Cork. 1995. Consequences of biotransformation of plant secondary metabolites on acid–base metabolism in mammals: a final common pathway? Journal of Chemical Ecology 21:721–743.

Foley, W. J., G. R. Iason, and C. McArthur. 1999. Role of plant secondary metabolites in the nutritional ecology of mammalian herbivores: how far have we come in 25 years? Pages 130–209 in H. G. Jung and G. C. Fahey, Jr. (eds.), Nutritional ecology of herbivores. Proceedings of the Vth International Symposium on the Nutrition of Herbivores, Savoy, IL.

Freeland, W. J., and D. Choquenot. 1990. Determinants of herbivore carrying capacity: plants, nutrients, and *Equus asinus* in northern Australia. Ecology 71:589–597.

Freeland, W. J., and D. H. Janzen. 1974. Strategies in herbivory by mammals: the role of plant secondary compounds. American Naturalist 108:269–287.

Freeland, W. J., P. H. Calcott, and L. R. Anderson. 1985. Tannins and saponin: interaction in herbivore diets. Biochemical Systematics and Ecology 13:189–193.

Fretwell, S. D., and H. L. Lucas. 1970. On territorial behavior and other factors influencing habitat distribution in birds. I. Theoretical development. Acta Biotheoretica 19:16–36.

Frykholm, K. D. 1945. Bacteriological studies of pinosylvin and its monomethyl ether and dimethyl ethers and toxicologic studies of pinosylvin. Nature 155:454–455.

Garcia, J. 1989. Food for Tolman: cognition and cathexis in concert. Pages 45–85 in T. Archer and L. Nilsson (eds.), Aversion, avoidance and anxiety. Erlbaum, Hillside, NJ.

Gibson, E. L., and D. A. Booth. 1986. Acquired protein appetite in rats: dependence on a protein-specific need state. Experientia 42:1003–1004.

Gibson, E. L., and D. A. Booth. 1989. Dependence of carbohydrate-conditioned flavor preference on internal state in rats. Learning and Motivation 20:36–47.

Gietzen, D. W. 2000. Amino acid recognition in the central nervous system. Pages 339–357 in H. R. Berthoud and R. J. Seeley (eds.), Neural and metabolic control of macronutrient intake. CRC Press, New York.

Green, G. C., R. L. Elwin, B. E. Mottershead, and J. J. Lynch. 1984. Long-term effects of early experience to supplementary feeding in sheep. Proceedings of the Australian Society of Animal Production 15:373–375.

Guglielmo, C. G., W. H. Karasov, and W. J. Jakubas. 1996. Nutritional costs of a plant secondary metabolite explain selective foraging by ruffed grouse. Ecology 77:1103–1115.

Gunderson, L. H., C. S. Holling, and S. S. Light (eds.). 1995. Barriers and bridges to the renewal of ecosystems and institutions. Columbia University Press, New York.

Hanley, T. A. 1982. The nutritional basis for food selection by ungulates. Journal of Range Management 35:146–151.

Harper, J. L. 1969. The role of predation in vegetational diversity. Brookhaven Symposium in Biology 22:48–62.

Hay, M. E. 1986. Associational plant defenses and the maintenance of species diversity: turning competitors into accomplices. American Naturalist 128:617–641.

Heady, H. F. 1964. Palatability of herbage and animal preference. Journal of Range Management 17:76–82.

Hills, J., I. Kyriazakis, J. V. Nolan, G. N. Hinch, and J. J. Lynch. 1999. Conditioned feeding responses in sheep to flavoured foods associated with sulphur doses. Animal Science 69:313–325.

Hobbs, N. T. 1996. Modification of ecosystems by ungulates. Journal of Wildlife Management 60:695–713.

Hofmann, R. R. 1988. Anatomy of the gastrointestinal tract. Pages 14–43 in D. C. Church (ed.), The ruminant animal. Prentice Hall, Englewood Cliffs, NJ.

Holling, C. S. 1959. The components of predation as revealed by a study of small-mammal predation of the European pine sawfly. Canadian Entomologist 91:293–320.

Holling, C. S. 1995. What barriers? What bridges? Pages 3–34 in L. H. Gunderson, C. S. Holling, S. S. Light (eds.), Barriers and bridges to the renewal of ecosystems and institutions. Columbia University Press, New York.

Howery, L. D., F. D. Provenza, R. E. Banner, and C. B. Scott. 1996. Differences in distribution patterns among individuals in a cattle herd. Applied Animal Behavior Science 49:305–320.

Howery, L. D., F. D. Provenza, R. E. Banner, and C. B. Scott. 1998. Social and environmental factors influence cattle distribution on rangeland. Applied Animal Behavior Science 55:231–244.

Illius, A. W., and N. S. Jessop. 1995. Modeling metabolic costs of allelochemical ingestion by foraging herbivores. Journal of Chemical Ecology 21:693–719.

Illius, A. W., and N. S. Jessop. 1996. Metabolic constraints on voluntary intake in ruminants. Journal of Animal Science 74:3052–3062.

Illius, A. W., I. J. Gordon, D. A. Elston, and J. D. Milne. 1999. Diet selection in goats: a test of intake-rate maximization. Ecology 80:1008–1018.

Johnson, A. E., L. F. James, and J. Spillet. 1976. The abortifacient and toxic effects of big sagebrush (*Artemisia tridentata*) and juniper (*Juniperus osteosperma*) on domestic sheep. Journal of Range Management 29:278–280.

Kaiser, J. 2000. Rift over biodiversity divides ecologists. Science 289:1282–1283.

Kauffman, S. 1995. At home in the universe. Oxford University Press, New York.

Key, C., and R. M. MacIver. 1980. The effects of maternal influences on sheep: breed differences in grazing, resting and courtship behavior. Applied Animal Ethology 6:33–48.

Kielland, K., and J. P. Bryant. 1998. Moose herbivory in taiga: effects on biogeochemistry and vegetation dynamics in primary succession. Oikos 82:377–383.

Krebs, J. R., and M. L. Avery. 1984. Chick growth and prey quality in the European bee-eater (*Merops apiaster*). Oecologia 64:363–368.

Kyriazakis, I., and J. D. Oldham. 1993. Diet selection in sheep: the ability of growing lambs to select a diet that meets their crude protein (nitrogen x 6.25) requirements. British Journal of Nutrition 69:617–629.

Kyriazakis, I., J. D. Oldham, R. L. Coop, and F. Jackson. 1994. The effect of subclinical intestinal nematode infection on the diet selection of growing sheep. British Journal of Nutrition 72:665–677.

Landsberg, J., T. O'Conner, and D. Freudenberger. 1999. The impacts of livestock grazing on biodiversity in natural systems. Pages 752–777 in H. G. Jung and G. C. Fahey, Jr. (eds.), Nutritional ecology of herbivores. Proceedings of the Vth International Symposium on the Nutrition of Herbivores. American Society of Animal Science, Savoy, IL.

Langvatn, R., and T. A. Hanley. 1993. Feeding-patch choice by red deer in relation to foraging efficiency. Oecologia 95:164–170.

Link, S. O. 1994. Effects of coppice dune topography and vegetation on soil water dynamics in a cold-desert ecosystem. Journal of Arid Environments 27:265–278.

Longhurst, W. M., H. K. Oh, M. B. Jones, and R. E. Kepner. 1968. A basis for the palatability of deer forage plants. Transactions of the North American Wildlife and Natural Resources Conference 33:181–189.

Lorenz, J. 1963. Deterministic non-periodic flow. Journal of Atmospheric Science 20:130.

Lundberg, P. 1988. Functional response of a small mammalian herbivore: the disc equation revisited. Journal of Animal Ecology 57:999–1006.

Lundberg, P., and M. Astrom. 1990. Functional response of optimally foraging herbivores. Journal of Theoretical Biology 144:367–377.

Lundberg, P., and K. Danell. 1990. Functional response of browsers: tree exploitation by moose. Oikos 58:378–384.

MacAvinchey, R. J. P. 1992. Winter herbivory by snowshoe hares and moose as a process affecting primary succession on an Alaskan floodplain. M.S. thesis, University of Alaska, Fairbanks.

Mayer, F. H., and C. B. Roth. 1995. The buffalo harvest. Pioneer Press, St. Paul, MN.

McCormick, J. A., V. Lyons, M. D. Jacobson, J. Noble, J. Diorio, M. Nyirenda, S. Weaver, W. Ester, J. L. Yau, M. J. Meaney, J. R. Seckl, and K. E. Chapman. 2000. 5´-heterogeneity of glucocorticoid receptor messenger RNA is tissue specific: differential regulation of variant transcripts by early-life events. Molecular Endocrinology 14:506–517.

McNeill, W. H. 1979. The human condition: an ecological and historical view. Princeton University Press, Princeton, NJ.

Milchunas, D. G., O. Sala, and W. K. Lauenroth. 1988. A generalized model on the effects of grazing by large herbivores on grassland community structure. American Naturalist 132:87–106.

Mirza, S. N., and F. D. Provenza. 1990. Preference of the mother affects selection and avoidance of foods by lambs differing in age. Applied Animal Behavior Science 28:255–263.

Mirza, S. N., and F. D. Provenza. 1992. Effects of age and conditions of exposure on maternally mediated food selection in lambs. Applied Animal Behavior Science 33:35–42.

Nagy, J. G., and R. P. Tengerdy. 1968. Antibacterial action of essential oils of *Artemisia* as an ecological factor. II. Antibacterial action of the volatile oils of *Artemisia tridentata* (big sagebrush) on bacteria from the rumen of mule deer. Applied Microbiology 16:441–444.

Ngugi, R. K., F. C. Hinds, and J. Powell. 1995. Mountain big sagebrush browse decreases dry matter intake, digestibility and nutritive quality of sheep diets. Journal of Range Management 48:487–492.

Nolte, D. L., F. D. Provenza, and D. F. Balph. 1990. The establishment and persistence of food preferences in lambs exposed to selected foods. Journal of Animal Science 68:998–1002.

Oh, H. K., M. B. Jones, and W. M. Longhurst. 1968. Comparison of rumen microbial inhibition resulting from various essential oils isolated from relatively unpalatable plants. Applied Microbiology 16:39–44.

Olff, H., and M. E. Ritchie. 1998. Effects of herbivores on grassland plant diversity. Trends in Ecology and Evolution (TREE) 13:261–265.

Ortega-Reyes, L., and F. D. Provenza. 1993. Amount of experience and age affect the development of foraging skills of goats browsing blackbrush (*Coleogyne ramosissima*). Applied Animal Behavior Science 36:169–183.

Osweiler, G. D., T. L. Carson, W. B. Buck, and G. A. Van Gelder. 1985. Clinical and diagnostic veterinary toxicology. Kendall/Hunt, Dubuque, IA.

Palo, R. T., and C. T. Robbins. 1991. Plant defenses against mammalian herbivory. CRC Press, Boca Raton, FL.

Pennings, S. C., T. Masatomo, T. Nadeau, and V. J. Paul. 1993. Selectivity and growth of the generalist herbivore *Dolabella auricularia* feeding upon complementary resources. Ecology 74:879–890.

Perez, C., K. Ackroff, and A. Sclafani. 1996. Carbohydrate- and protein-conditioned flavor preferences: effects of nutrient preloads. Physiology Behavior 59:467–474.

Personius, T. L., C. L. Wambolt, J. R. Stephens, and R. G. Kelsey. 1987. Crude terpenoid influence on mule deer preference for sagebrush. Journal of Range Management 40:84–88.

Pfister, C. A., and M. E. Hay. 1988. Associational plant refuges: convergent patterns in marine and terrestrial communities result from differing mechanisms. Oecologia 77:118–129.

Pfister, J. A., F. D. Provenza, G. D. Manners, D. R. Gardner, and M. H. Ralphs. 1997. Tall larkspur ingestion: can cattle regulate intake below toxic levels? Journal of Chemical Ecology 23:759–777.

Phy, T. S., and F. D. Provenza. 1998. Sheep fed grain prefer foods and solutions that attenuate acidosis. Journal of Animal Science 76:954–960.

Piersma, T., and A. Lindstrom. 1997. Rapid reversible changes in organ size as a component of adaptive behaviour. Trends in Ecology and Evolution (TREE) 12:134–138.

Plummer, A. P., D. R. Christensen, and S. B. Monsen. 1968. Restoring big-game range in Utah. Utah Division of Fish and Game Publications No. 68-3:183.

Prigogine, I., and I. Stengers. 1984. Order out of chaos: man's new dialogue with nature. Bantam Books, New York.

Provenza, F. D. 1994. Ontogeny and social transmission of food selection in domesticated ruminants. Pages 147–164 in B. G. Galef, M. Mainardi, and P. Valsecchi (eds.), Behavioral aspects of feeding: basic and applied research in mammals. Harwood Academic Publishers, Singapore.

Provenza, F. D. 1995a. Postingestive feedback as an elementary determinant of food preference and intake in ruminants. Journal of Range Management 48:2–17.

Provenza, F. D. 1995b. Tracking variable environments: there is more than one kind of memory. Journal of Chemical Ecology 21:911–923.

Provenza, F. D. 1996. Acquired aversions as the basis for varied diets of ruminants foraging on rangelands. Journal of Animal Science 74:2010–2020.

Provenza, F. D., and D. F. Balph. 1990. Applicability of five diet-selection models to various foraging challenges ruminants encounters. Pages 423–459 in R. N. Hughes (ed.), Behavioural mechanisms of food selection. NATO ASI Series G: Ecological Sciences, Vol. 20. Springer-Verlag, Berlin.

Provenza, F. D., E. A. Burritt, T. P. Clausen, J. P. Bryant, P. B. Reichardt, and R. A. Distel. 1990. Conditioned flavor aversion: a mechanism for goats to avoid condensed tannins in blackbrush. American Naturalist 136:810–828.

Provenza, F. D., J. A. Pfister, and C. D. Cheney. 1992. Mechanisms of learning in diet selection with reference to phytotoxicosis in herbivores. Journal of Range Management 45:36–45.

Provenza, F. D., C. B. Scott, T. S. Phy, and J. J. Lynch. 1996. Preference of sheep for foods varying in flavors and nutrients. Journal of Animal Science 74:2355:2361.

Provenza, F. D., J. J. Villalba, C. D. Cheney, and S. J. Werner. 1998. Self-organization of foraging behavior: from simplicity to complexity without goals. Nutrition Research Reviews 11:199–222.

Provenza, F. D., J. J. Villalba, and M. Augner. 1999. The physics of foraging. Volume III, pages 99–107 in J. G. Buchanan-Smith, L. D Bailey, and P. McCaughey (eds.), Proc. XVIII International Grassland Congress. Saskatchewan Agriculture & Food, Saskatoon.

Provenza, F. D., E. A. Burritt, A. Perevolotsky, and N. Silanikove. 2000. Self-regulation of intake of polyethylene glycol by sheep fed diets varying in tannin concentrations. Journal of Animal Science 78:1206–1212.

Radwan, M. A., and G. L. Crouch. 1978. Selected chemical constituents and deer browsing preference of Douglas-fir. Journal of Chemical Ecology 4:675–687.

Ramirez, I. 1997. Intragastric carbohydrate exerts both intake-stimulating and intake-suppressing effects. Behavioral Neuroscience 111:612–622.

Rapport, D. J. 1971. An optimization model of food selection. American Naturalist 105:575–587.

Raubenheimer, D. 1992. Tannic acid, protein and digestible carbohydrates: dietary imbalances and nutritional compensation in locusts. Ecology 73:1012–1027.

Reichardt, P. B., J. P. Bryant, T. P. Clausen, and G. D. Wieland. 1984. Defense of winter-dormant Alaska paper birch against snowshoe hares. Oecologia 65:58–69.

Renecker, L. A., and R. J. Hudson. 1986. Seasonal foraging rates of free-ranging moose. Journal of Wildlife Management 50:143–147.

Robbins, C. T., T. A. Hanley, A. E. Hagerman, O. Hjeljord, D. L. Baker, C. C. Schwartz, and W. W. Mautz. 1987a. Role of tannins in defending plants against ruminants: reduction in protein availability. Ecology 68:98–107.

Robbins, C. T., S. Mole, A. E. Hagerman, and T. A. Hanley. 1987b. Role of tannins in defending plants against ruminants: reduction in dry matter digestion. Ecology 68:1606–1615.

Robbins, C. T., A. E. Hegerman, P. J. Austin, C. McArthur, and T. A. Hanley. 1991. Variation in mammalian physiological responses to a condensed tannin and its ecological implications. Journal of Mammalogy 72:480–486.

Ross, J. G., J. W. Spears, and J. D. Garlich. 1994. Dietary electrolyte balance effects on performance and metabolic characteristics in finishing steers. Journal of Animal Science 72:1600–1607.

Rozin, P. 1988. Social learning about food by humans. Pages 165–187 in T. R. Zentall and B. G. Galef, Jr. (eds.), Social learning: psychological and biological perspectives. Lawrence Erlbaum Associates, Hillsdale, NJ.

Rozin, P. 1996. Sociocultural influences on human food selection. Pages 233–263 in E. D. Capaldi (ed.), Why we eat what we eat: the psychology of eating. American Psychological Association, Washington, DC.

Savory, A. 1988. Holistic resource management. Island Press, Washington, DC.

Schlichting, C. D., and M. Pigliucci. 1998. Phenotypic evolution: a reaction norm perspective. Sinauer Publications, Sinauer, MA.

Schmidt, K. S., J. S. Brown, and R. A. Morgan. 1998. Plant defense as complementary resources: a test with squirrels. Oikos 81:130–142.

Sclafani, A. 2000. Macronutrient-conditioned flavor preferences. Pages 93–106 in H.-R. Berthoud and R. J. Seeley (eds.), Neural and metabolic control of macronutrient intake. CRC Press, New York.

Scott, L. L., and F. D. Provenza. 1998. Variety of foods and flavors affects selection of foraging locations by sheep. Applied Animal Behavior Science 61:113–122.

Scott, L. L., and F. D. Provenza. 1999. Variation in food selection among lambs: effects of basal diet and foods offered in a meal. Journal of Animal Science 77:2391–2397.

Scott, L. L., and F. D. Provenza. 2000. Lambs fed protein or energy imbalanced diets forage in locations and on foods that rectify imbalances. Applied Animal Behavior Science 68:293–305.

Senge, P. M. 1994. The fifth discipline: the art and practice of the learning organization. Currency Doubleday, New York.

Shepherdson, D. 1994. The role of environmental enrichment in the captive breeding and reintroduction of endangered species. Pages 167–177 in P. J. Olney, G. M. Mace, and A. T. Feistner (eds.), Creative conservation: interactive management of wild and captive animals. Chapman & Hall, London.

Simpson, S. J., and D. Raubenheimer. 1993. A multi-level analysis of feeding behavior: the geometry of nutritional decisions. Philosophical Transactions of the Royal Society London B 342:381–402.

Simpson, S. J., and D. Raubenheimer. 1999. Assuaging nutritional complexity: a geometrical approach. Proceedings of the Nutrition Society 58:779–789.

Simpson, S. J., and D. Raubenheimer. 2000. The hungry locust. Advances in the Study of Behaviour 29:1–43.

Smith, A. D. 1959. Adequacy of some important browse species in overwintering mule deer. Journal of Range Management 12:9–13.

Spalinger, D. E., T. A. Hanley, and C. T. Robbins. 1988. Analysis of the functional response in foraging in the Sitka black-tailed deer. Ecology 69:1166–1175.

Stamps, J. 2001. Habitat selection by dispersers: proximate and ultimate approaches. Pages 230–242 in J. Clobert, E. Danchin, A. Dhondt, and J. Nichols (eds.), Dispersal. Oxford University Press, Oxford, UK.

Stephens, D. W., and J. R. Krebs. 1986. Foraging theory. Princeton University Press, Princeton, NJ.

Stoddart, L. A., and A. D. Smith. 1955. Range management. McGraw-Hill, New York.

Ternouth, J. H. 1991. The kinetics and requirements of phosphorus in ruminants. Pages 143–151 in Y. W. Ho, H. K. Wong, N. Abdullah, and Z. A. Tajuddin (eds.), Recent advances on the nutrition of herbivores. Malaysian Society of Animal Production, Vinlin Press, Kuala Lumpur.

Thomas, D. W., C. Samson, and J. M. Bergeron. 1988. Metabolic costs associated with the ingestion of plant phenolics by *Microtus pennsylvanicus*. Journal of Mammalogy 69:512–515.

Thorhallsdottir, A. G., F. D. Provenza, and D. F. Balph. 1990. Ability of lambs to learn about novel foods while observing or participating with social models. Applied Animal Behavior Science 25:25–33.

Villalba, J. J., and F. D. Provenza. 1996. Preference for flavored wheat straw by lambs conditioned with intraruminal administrations of sodium propionate. Journal of Animal Science 74:2362–2368.

Villalba, J. J., and F. D. Provenza. 1997a. Preference for flavored wheat straw by lambs conditioned with intraruminal infusions of acetate and propionate. Journal of Animal Science 75:2905–2914.

Villalba, J. J., and F. D. Provenza. 1997b. Preference for flavoured foods by lambs conditioned with intraruminal administration of nitrogen. British Journal of Nutrition 78:545–561.

Villalba, J. J., and F. D. Provenza. 1997c. Preference for wheat straw by lambs conditioned with intraruminal infusions of starch. British Journal of Nutrition 77:287–297.

Villalba, J. J., and F. D. Provenza. 1999a. Effects of food structure and nutritional quality and animal nutritional state on intake behaviour and food preferences of sheep. Applied Animal Behavior Science 63:145–163.

Villalba, J. J., and F. D. Provenza. 1999b. Nutrient-specific preferences by lambs conditioned with intraruminal infusions of starch, casein, and water. Journal of Animal Science 77:378–387.

Villalba, J. J., and F. D. Provenza. 2000. Postingestive feedback from starch influences the ingestive behavior of sheep consuming wheat straw. Applied Animal Behavior Science 66:49–63.

Villalba, J. J., and F. D. Provenza. 2001. Preference for polyethylene glycol by sheep fed quebracho tannin. Journal of Animal Science 79:2066–2074.

Villalba, J. J., F. D. Provenza, and R. E. Banner. 2002a. Influence of macronutrients and activated charcoal on utilization of sagebrush by sheep and goats. Journal of Animal Science (in press).

Villalba, J. J., F. D. Provenza, and R. E. Banner. 2002b. Influence of macronutrients and polyethylene glycol on utilization of quebracho-tannin containing diet by sheep and goats. Journal of Animal Science (in press).

Villalba, J. J., F. D. Provenza, and J. P. Bryant. 2002c. Consequences of nutrient–toxin interactions for herbivore selectivity: benefits or detriments for plants? Oikos 97: 282–292.

Vourc'h, G., J. L. Martin, P. Duncan, J. Escarre, and T. P. Clausen. 2001. Defensive adaptations of *Thuja plicata* to ungulate browsing: a comparative study between mainland and island populations. Oecologia 126:84–93.

Walker, L. R., J. C. Zasada, and F. S. Chapin, III. 1986. The role of life history processes in primary succession on an Alaskan River Floodplain. Ecology 67:1243–1253.

Wallestad, R. O. 1971. Summer movements and habitat use by sage grouse broods in central Montana. Journal of Wildlife Management 35:129–136.

Wallis de Vries, M. F. 1994. Foraging in a landscape mosaic: diet selection an performance of free-ranging cattle in heathland and riverine grassland. Ph.D. thesis, University of Wageningen, the Netherlands.

Wang, J., and F. D. Provenza. 1996. Food deprivation affects preference of sheep for foods varying in nutrients and a toxin. Journal of Chemical Ecology 22:2011–2021.

Wang, J., and F. D. Provenza. 1997. Dynamics of preference by sheep offered foods varying in flavors, nutrients, and a toxin. Journal of Chemical Ecology 23:275–288.

West, N. E. 1993. Biodiversity of rangelands. Journal of Range Management 46:2–13.

West, N. E. 1999. Juniper–pinon savannas and woodlands of western North America. Pages 288–308 in R. C. Anderson, J. S. Fralish, and J. M. Baskin (eds.), Savannas, barrens, and rock outcrop plant communities of North America. Cambridge University Press, New York.

West, N. E., and J. A. Young. 2000. Intermountain valleys and lower mountain slopes. Pages 256–284 in M. G. Barbour and W. D. Billings (eds.), North American terrestrial vegetation, 2nd ed. Cambridge University Press, New York.

Westoby, M. 1978. What are the biological bases of varied diets? American Naturalist 112:627–631.

White, C. L., D. G. Masters, D. W. Peter, D. B. Purser, S. P. Roe, and M. J. Barnes. 1992. A multi element supplement for grazing sheep. I. Intake, mineral status and production responses. Australian Journal of Agricultural Research 43:795–808.

White, J. A, and T. G. Whitham. 2000. Associational susceptibility of cottonwood to a box elder herbivore. Ecology 81:1795–1803.

Wiedmeier, R. D., F. D. Provenza, and E. A. Burritt. 2002. Performance of mature beef cows wintered on low-quality forages is affected by short-term exposure to the forages as suckling heifer calves. Journal of Animal Science (in press).

Wilmshurst, J. F., and J. M. Fryxell. 1995. Patch selection by red deer in relation to energy and protein intake: a re-evaluation of Langvatn and Hanley's (1993) results. Oecologia 104:297–300.

Wilmshurst, J. F., J. M Fryxell, and R. J. Hudson. 1995. Forage quality and patch choice by wapiti (*Cervus elaphus*). Behavioral Ecology 6:209–217.

Wolff, J. O., and J. Zasada. 1979. Moose habitat and forest succession on the Tanana River floodplain and Yukon–Tanana upland. Proceedings of the North American Moose Conference 15:213–244.

Conclusion

The essence of science is that it is always willing to abandon a given idea, however fundamental it may seem to be, for a better one.

Minority Report no. 232, H. L. Mencken, 1956

Abandoning given ideas for better ones adroitly describes the business of science and is one of the reasons for the development of this book. Our explicit purpose was threefold. First, we wanted to demonstrate that much exciting work is providing new ways to think about how one can understand the pervasive effects of landscape fragmentation. Second, we wanted to provide some examples of how ecologists around the world have tried to link theory with its application in different landscapes. Third, it was our explicit purpose to assemble chapters that would be heuristic and would encourage landscape ecologists to think about application, wildlife biologists to think about larger-scale approaches, and resource managers to think about the benefits of using landscape approaches in policy, planning, and management exercises. Although the 17 chapters included in this book cover diverse approaches and topics, they were not intended to provide exhaustive coverage of ongoing research activities in landscape ecology or large-scale research in wildlife biology. That is probably not possible in any single book. With few exceptions, we have purposefully limited our coverage to the topics wherein we have some expertise, namely biophysical ecological approaches to fragmentation and its impacts on wild organisms. There is still much to be done. In this concluding chapter, we briefly examine the tenuous assumption of a direct correspondence between observation (data) and ecological reality, review a report that has assessed the efficacy of fragmentation experiments and assess its implications for ecologists, suggest two analytical procedures that appear to have high potential for understanding complex ecological issues, and briefly discuss four interesting avenues for future research in landscape ecology.

Earlier, we argued that linking theory and data with practice, that is, providing a conceptually sound data set on which to base management decisions, was not an easy task, especially at larger spatial extents and temporal horizons. Ecologists tend to adhere to what has been called a realist philosophy; that is, a widespread belief that research data correspond on a one-to-one basis with ecological reality. Even a cursory examination of the results of studies reported in any ecology journal demonstrates that simple correspondence does not exist. The chapters in this book reinforce that same idea. There is seldom a one-to-one correspondence between any set of data and ecological reality. Ecological complexity at all scales tends to blur research results, with patterns that are more often than not equivocal, especially when results from several studies are compared (Debinski and Holt 2000). Therefore, one is left to interpret study results, if not from a "realist philosophy," in the light of what are assumed to be realistic theoretical and conceptual frameworks.

The origins of the realist philosophy may spring from the mostly successful attempts of mechanistic and experimental science to discover answers to smaller-scale ecological questions. However, all answers are circumscribed by what O'Neill et al. (1985) call an observation set. The questions one asks, the variables one measures, and the analyses one uses always constrain the domain of possible answers. Additionally, ecologists have tended to ask solvable questions. Messy, intractable problems have not been addressed until advances in technology or paradigmatic theory made them more tractable. For example, the development of landscape metrics software, the ability to gather and analyze digital landscape data, and the realization that scale matters have allowed ecologists to ask questions about the effects of landscape fragmentation that could not have been addressed earlier. However, even the most sophisticated technological tools are just tools, and new paradigms are always more complex than their initial use indicates. Given these tendencies, it is easy for ecologists to be insufficiently introspective when interpreting their results. We may think that a rigorous experimental approach would give reliable results that explain the effects of larger-scale fragmentation, but is a realist philosophy pervading our thinking? Many, perhaps most, ecologists would tend to agree that experimentation is a more rigorous and preferable approach to understanding. Would not an experimental approach to fragmentation problems provide more enlightenment than the more traditional observational, historical, and comparative approaches? Not necessarily, as Debinski and Holt's (2000) recent survey of habitat fragmentation experiments suggests.

Fragmentation Experiments: Is the Message Clear?

In an enlightening review of habitat fragmentation experiments, Debinski and Holt (2000) provide an excellent analysis of the few studies that have actually used experiments to refute or support a priori hypotheses about fragmentation effects, and their results speak volumes about the complexity of causal mechanisms attendant to habitat change. They report the results of 20 studies (21 if a notational account given in the acknowledgments is included) that tested six major groups of hypotheses related to (1) the relationship of species richness to area or (2) species abundance or density to area, (3) whether interspecific interactions are modified by fragmentation, (4) whether edge effects influence ecosystem services, (5) the relationship between corridors and movement between habitat fragments, and (6) whether connectivity increases species richness. The results are interesting and informative. Only 6 of 14 (43 percent) studies supported the expectation of hypotheses 1 and 6; that is, that species richness should increase with increasing area or connectivity. The expectation for hypothesis 2 is that specialist species' abundance and density should decrease with increasing area, although movement dynamics between different habitat elements (matrix versus patch) might result in increases. Debinski and Holt (2000) found that species abundance decreased with increasing fragmentation in only 6 of 13 studies (46.2 percent). The prediction for hypothesis 3 is that some modification is expected. This prediction was supported in the two studies that addressed the question. Both involved arthropod populations. An expectation from theory is that an increase in edge relative to core areas (hypothesis 4) can have profound effects on ecological processes (Saunders et al. 1991; Debinski and Holt 2000). Two of three (66.6 percent) studies supported the hypothesis on edge effects. The expectation for hypothesis 5 is that fragmentation inhibits movement and the presence of corridors, so connectivity should be positively correlated with increased movement. Debinski and Holt (2000) found that 4 of 5 (80 percent) of the studies they evaluated supported the hypothesis, at least for some species. They found mixed results for predictions involving species richness (Laurance and Bierregaard 1996; Collinge 1995 versus Schmiegelow et al. 1997; Margules 1996), density and abundance of species (Foster and Gaines 1991; Margules and Milkovits 1994 versus Barrett et al. 1995; Collins and Barrett 1997), edge effects (Bierregaard et al. 1992; Klenner and Huggard 1997 versus Robinson et al. 1992), and corridors and movements (Haddad 1997; Wolff et al.

1997 versus Andreassen et al. 1998). The results were "entirely mixed." Debinski and Holt (2000) credit time lags, scale inconsistencies, contingent social interactions between species, and habitat generalists as some of the reasons for the results.

The hypotheses examined are of fundamental interest to ecologists, who strive to understand the underlying conceptual framework governing fragmentation effects, and to managers charged with conducting ecosystem management (Walters 1986; Walters and Holling 1990; Forest Ecosystem Management Assessment Team 1993; Grumbine 1994, 1997) or conserving biodiversity (Noss and Cooperrider 1994; Noss et al. 1995; IUCN 2000). The message appears to be that clear and simple predictions often do not capture the multicausal nature of organism response to fragmentation. For example, generalist species can be expected to respond differently than specialists. Similarly, early successional species, transient (usually younger individuals) organisms, and edge- and core-sensitive species can be expected to respond differently to landscape fragmentation (Bissonette et al. 1997; Debinski and Holt 2000; Storch 2002). Time lags can be expected to be common and to have profound effects. Additionally, matching time and spatial domains remains a problem.

Delcourt et al. (1983), Wiens (1989), Holling (1992), and Bissonette (1997) all suggest that there is an approximate matching between spatial and temporal scales in ecological processes. For example, the global distribution of forested landscapes changes at a speed of tens of thousands of years; regionally, forest disturbances such as fire occur at intervals from a few to hundreds of years; and locally, vegetation changes within annual cycles. What this means is that one can expect time lags to be prevalent in landscape-scale interactions. The decline of sugar maple (*Acer saccharum*) forests in the northeastern United States over the past half century or more is an excellent example in which not only is the extent of the damage more difficult to quantify but its cause is exceedingly difficult to determine because of the time lags involved. Additionally, the pattern of decline extends over hundreds of miles but appears to be caused by local soil acidification effects. Airborne pollutants from the midwestern United States are carried by the prevailing west-to-east weather pattern, and acidified pollutants are deposited in the eastern United States. Several hypotheses have been suggested for the large-scale decline of sugar maple trees. Insect defoliation, drought, and historic land use practices have been proposed as causal (Driscoll et al. 2001) but have not been strongly supported (Swistock et al. 1999; Drohan 2000; Horsley et al. 2000). Rather, Sharpe and Sunderland

(1995) and Sharpe et al. (1999) argue persuasively that acid deposition on forest soils, coupled with very long lag times in soil response, accounts for the sugar maple decline. The mechanism appears to be soil acidification and apparently is referenced by critically low calcium-to-aluminum and calcium-to-magnesium ratios (Sharpe et al. 1999; Swistock et al. 1999). Time lags of many years and perhaps even decades appear to be operating, suggesting that critical thresholds of soil acidity must be reached before effects become apparent. This is but one example, but time lags and threshold effects may be more prevalent than we have supposed. Much longer multiscale studies are needed to understand the putative causes. Time lags also involve major ramifications for management. Land management or species conservation measures that are likely to take years to show the desired effects are difficult to defend and are not popular with decision makers, who work with annual budgets and may be elected for short periods of time. Additionally, the public and media appear to respond much more readily to more concrete and immediate results that appear to have a connection with causality closer to one-to-one.

In their study, Debinski and Holt (2000) have done landscape ecologists a remarkable service. Their results tell us something very important about the effects of fragmentation. The essence of the message is that the effects of fragmentation can be understood as multicausal, exhibiting thresholds where they are unexpected; are characterized by time lags that may be unpredictable; are heavily influenced by the structural differences between the matrix and the patches, especially if the patches are disturbance rather than remnant patches; and depend heavily on the temporal and spatial scales of observation, whose dynamics are contingent on system history and therefore subject to unpredictable stochastic events. What we have just described is a complex adaptive system (Levin 1999) that may be characterized by deterministic chaotic events (Peak 1997). Weather pattern dynamics are an excellent example of this kind of system. The question then becomes, Do we think that we, as landscape-oriented animal ecologists, can beat the meteorologist in prediction? Weather forecasts are notoriously poor once they exceed time frames of more than a few days, despite the enormous amounts of data and sophisticated analytical tools meteorologists have at their disposal. Sensitivity to initial conditions (i.e., system history) has an enormous effect. So what makes us believe that we should be able to do much better? Perhaps the message is that at some general level of explanation, we may have predictive power, but when we seek specifics, they may always be local and empirically based, making prediction difficult or impossible.

What follows is our view of some areas where work is needed to expand our understanding of fragmentation effects on biodiversity and its practical application to management. It is by no means exhaustive; rather, it is our reflection on some pressing needs that we think could benefit from study.

New Analytical Methods for Complex Science Problems

It is becoming increasingly clear that there is more than one analytical paradigm by which to gain ecological understanding. Hypothetico-deductive approaches are not the only approach to understanding landscape phenomena. In addition, null hypothesis testing has fallen from favor in recent years (Johnson 1999; Anderson et al. 2000), not because these traditional methods are wrong but because they are suitable only for a very limited range of ecological research problems and often are not very helpful.

Burnham and Anderson (2002) provide a synthesis of new statistical methods useful for addressing complex ecological problems. These methods are based on Kullback–Leibler (K-L) information (Kullback and Leibler 1951) and are therefore called information-theoretic. Strong emphasis is placed on a priori thinking regarding the science question and on developing multiple alternative hypotheses as well as mathematical models to carefully represent these hypotheses. The approach is to develop candidate models, each representing a plausible scientific hypothesis, based on ecological knowledge that can be brought to bear on the problem. The general form of K-L information is

$$I (f,g) = \int f(x) \, \log[f(x)/ g(x, \theta)] \, dx$$

where I is the information lost when full reality f is approximated by model g; θ represents variables that will be included as model parameters and d represents a change in variable x (see Burnham and Anderson 2001 for a clear explanation).

K-L information cannot be computed directly because neither full reality nor the parameter values in the approximating models are known. Akaike (1973) derived a simple way to estimate the relative, expected value of K-L information, and this leads to a simple criterion (Akaike's information criterion, AIC). AIC allows a formal relationship between K-L information and the maximum of the log-likelihood function (simple relationships often exist to map the estimated residual variance from regression models into the maximized log-likelihood function). AIC allows candidate models to be ranked from best to worst and is the basis for a rigorous and very broad analysis theory. Models can be scaled to reflect their relative support, and evidence ratios provide a strength of evidence for model i versus model j. Estimates of precision can incorporate model selection uncertainty. All these methods are simple to compute and understand (D. Anderson, personal communication 2002).

In the past, scientists have attempted to select the best model (e.g., using stepwise, step-forward, or step-backward methods; Mallows's Cp; or AIC) and then made inferences conditional on this estimated best model. If p regressors are selected from a set of k, Mallow's Cp is defined as:

$$S\ (y - yp)2\ /\ s2 - n \div 2p$$

Where yp is the predicted value of y from the p regressors; s2 is the residual mean square after regression on the complete set of k; n is the sample size. The current state of the science is to make formal statistical inference from all the models in the set, that is, multimodel inference. Burnham and Anderson (2002) discuss the advantages of doing so.

Another approach that shows great promise is described in detail in Chapter 7. The approach of Edwards et al. focuses on obtaining fine-grained estimations of habitat type and structure over large spatial extents and then using those representations to model habitat use at multiple scales. The use of generalized additive models (flexible regression techniques) allows a linkage of spatially explicit environmental information with habitat structure. Although it is computer intensive, we think this approach shows great promise in addressing one of the thorniest problems landscape ecologists encounter: that of integrating multiple scales of resolution in a manner that can be used to assess species response to fragmentation.

What Next? Future Research Focuses

In this last section we discuss four areas in which recent and current work suggests that we have just scratched the surface of important and interesting areas of research where learning more would be enlightening and important for both the development of theory and its application by resource managers.

Habitat Complementation

One of the growth areas in landscape ecology will almost certainly involve the idea of landscape complementation; that is, the compositional contribution by different habitat elements in the landscape to population persistence or to the expression of other processes (see Chapter 15, this volume). This is not a new idea (Pulliam 1988; Pulliam and Danielson 1991; Dunning et al. 1992), and there has been some progress in determining the contribution of individual habitats or elements in a landscape to population processes or animal movement dynamics. Sisk et al. (1997) addressed the effects of the surrounding matrix on species assemblages, and Wagner and Edwards (2001) have described the contribution of individual patches to species richness. Because each landscape is unique, the size and distribution of habitat patches are different and putatively express a landscape-specific constraint on species richness and abundance, recruitment, productivity, and levels of perceived risk and predation and should affect other important landscape processes. However, if the constraints of each landscape result in qualitatively different responses without apparent thresholds rather than in responses that are different in degree, then we may have no hope of making progress toward a predictive theory of fragmentation. It may be fruitful to look for domains of scale (Wiens 1989) or ecological neighborhoods (Addicott et al. 1987) in which over a range of patterns animal response is reasonably similar. Although it is certain that each landscape is unique, it seems reasonable to assume that there must be some similarity of response by organisms if we are to gain understanding of the effects of fragmentation. Scaling power laws (Schneider 1994, 2001) may be very useful in understanding habitat complementation. If one can discover scaling relationships that appear to be consistent, then one can ask about the biological reasons for their existence.

Trade-Offs between Landscape Attributes

A related area of interest for ecologists and managers is how to decide in fragmented landscapes where the trade-off is between size, isolation, and quality of remnant habitat patches. Metapopulation dynamics studies have emphasized patch size and isolation, but it is clear that with increasing fragmentation, habitat quality is diminished. Which of these patch attributes (size, isolation, or quality) is most important and under what circumstances? How do managers decide which attribute to optimize when setting land management policy? In a recent article, Thomas et al. (2001) attempted to reconcile this question. They presented evidence that for three butterfly species, both habitat isolation and quality were important and could not be considered separately. Furthermore, they suggested that habitat quality is the third parameter that must be incorporated into metapopulation dynamics. In Roslin's (2002) review of the Thomas et al. (2001) article, he suggested that the lesson is clear and important for managers. Some balance between conserving connectivity in the landscape and including high-quality habitat should be the goal. The devil is in the details, however. The concepts of isolation, size, and quality are imprecise and must be specified and scaled for the species or community in question. Roslin (2002) referenced what we have suggested earlier in this chapter: The observation set and, in particular, the metrics used to assess any of the three attributes, will undoubtedly influence any interpretation of the relative and proportional contribution of each attribute to understanding the relevant dynamics. This suggests that some redundancy in measurement, such as the use of several metrics, may help elucidate proportional causality. Some of the analytical approaches mentioned earlier should provide reasonable and useful answers to questions such as this. Of course, knowing the natural history of the species in question is a necessary first step.

Buffer Effects

A related subject of interest that is receiving some attention is the impact buffer areas can have on population dynamics across larger landscape extents. Buffer effects occur when there is a pronounced difference in quality between occupied sites, and when disproportionately high densities and rates of increase of organisms occur at seemingly poorer-quality sites and small increases occur at high-quality sites (Gill et al. 2001). If there are demographic costs of inhabiting the poorer sites, buffering can affect population regulation. Gill et al. (2001) have shown that the buffer effect had a large impact on godwits (*Limosa limosa islandica*) wintering in Great Britain. Buffer effects have been demonstrated in passerine birds (Krebs 1970; Murphy 2001), eagles (Ferrer and Donazar 1996), minnows (Fraser and Sise 1980), and mammals (Halama and Dueser 1994). If buffer effects are common at larger spatial scales, there may be important consequences for reproductive success that have been overlooked by studies conducted at smaller spatial extents, especially for species that migrate.

Hot Spots or Gradients

Finally, the issue of biodiversity hotspots has been contentious for some time (Kitching 2000; Myers et al. 2000). Hotspots are locations where exceptional concentrations of species exist. Meyers et al. (2000, p. 853) reported, "As many as 44% of all species of vascular plants and 35% of all species in four vertebrate groups . . . (mammals, birds, reptiles, and amphibians) . . . are confined to 25 hotspots comprising only 1.4% of the land surface of the earth." The four vertebrate groups number more than 27,000 species (Meyers et al. 2000; Glaw and Kohler 1998). The idea of conserving so many species easily (but see Kitching 2000) seems to be a readily acceptable idea. However, Smith et al. (2001, p. 431) suggest that, given putative impending climate shifts with their expected effects on local habitats, "the hotspots of today are unlikely to be the hotspots of tomorrow" and that taking a hotspot perspective is therefore risky. They suggest that risk can be more broadly distributed by conserving the adaptive diversity within a species. What this means is a focus on conserving the environmental gradients in which adaptive diversity is found. Indeed, Schluter (2000) and Schilthuizen (2000) have found that environmental gradients are closely linked to species diversification and speciation. However, Brooks et al. (2001) argue that, although transition areas are important, for practical reasons prioritization is necessary. Expanding the concept to include transition zones over the short term would critically damage any chance of conserving hotspots. No doubt the controversy will continue.

"Pay It Forward"

In a recent movie by the same name, the "pay it forward" idea illustrated how individual actions can sometimes have profound and widespread effects: Person 1 passes on a good turn to persons 2, 3, and 4, and so forth until the effort is very widespread. Likewise, in science we can "pay it forward." We do so by synthesis, explanation, and publication. To the extent that technical developments and individual contributions in landscape ecology result in usable theory and conceptual constructs that have generality, are readily understood, and can be applied easily, the ideas will ramify and spread. The heuristic value one can gain from clearly enunciated ideas that cross disciplines and have the potential to make an impact is immeasurable. This book is our modest attempt to pay it forward.

LITERATURE CITED

Addicott, J. F., J. M. Abo, M. F. Antolin, D. F. Padilla, J. S. Richardson, and D. A. Soluk. 1987. Ecological neighborhoods: scaling environmental patterns. Oikos 49:340–346.

Akaike, H. 1973. Information theory as an extension of the maximum likelihood principle. Pages 267–281 in B. N. Petrov and F. Csaki (eds.), Second International Symposium on Information Theory. Akadimiai Kiado, Budapest, Hungary.

Anderson, D. R., K. P. Burnham, and W. L. Thompson. 2000. Null hypothesis testing: problems, prevalence, and an alternative. Journal of Wildlife Management 64:912–923.

Andreassen, H. P., K. Hertzberg, and R. A. Ims. 1998. Space-use response to habitat fragmentation and connectivity in the root vole *Microtus oeconomus*. Ecology 79:1223–1235.

Barrett, G., J. D. Peles, and S. J. Harper. 1995. Reflection on the use of experimental landscapes in mammalian ecology. Pages 157–174 in W. Lidicker (ed.), Landscape approaches in mammalian ecology and conservation. University of Minnesota Press, Minneapolis.

Bierregaard, R. O., Jr., T. E. Lovejoy, V. Kapos, A. A. dos Santos, and R. W. Hutchings. 1992. The biological dynamics of tropical rainforest fragments: a prospective comparison of fragments and continuous forest. BioScience 42:859–866.

Bissonette, J. A. 1997. Scale-sensitive ecological properties: historical context, current meaning. Pages 3–15 in J. A. Bissonette (ed.), Wildlife and landscape ecology: effects of pattern and scale. Springer-Verlag, New York.

Bissonette, J. A., D. J. Harrison, C. D. Hargis, and T. G. Chapin. 1997. Scale-sensitive properties influence marten demographics. Page 368–385 in J. A. Bissonette (ed.), Wildlife and landscape ecology: effects of pattern and scale. Springer-Verlag, New York.

Brooks, T., L. Hannah, G. A. B. da Fonseka, and R. A. Mittermeier. 2001. Prioritizing hotspots, representing transitions. Trends in Ecology and Evolution 16:673.

Burnham, K. P., and D. R. Anderson. 2001. Kullback–Leibler information as a basis for strong inference in ecological studies. Wildlife Research 28:111–119.

Burnham, K. P., and D. R. Anderson. 2002. Model selection and multimodel inference: a practical information-theoretic approach. Springer-Verlag, New York.

Collinge, S. K. 1995. Spatial arrangement of patches and corridors in the landscape: consequences for biological diversity and implications for landscape architecture. Ph.D. dissertation, Harvard University, Cambridge, MA.

Collins, R. J., and G. W. Barrett. 1997. Effects of habitat fragmentation on meadow vole (*Microtus pennsylvanicus*) population dynamics in experimental landscape patches. Landscape Ecology 12:63–76.

Debinski, D. M., and R. D. Holt. 2000. A survey and overview of habitat fragmentation experiments. Conservation Biology 14:342–355.

Delcourt, H. R., P. A. Delcourt, and T. Webb, III. 1983. Dynamic plant ecology: the spectrum of vegetation change in time and space. Quaternary Science Reviews 1:153–175.

Driscoll, C. T., G. B. Lawrence, A. J. Bulger, T. J. Butler, C. S. Cronon, G. Eagar, K. F. Lambert, G. E. Likens, J. L. Stoddard, and K. C. Weathers. 2001. Acidic deposition in the northeastern United States: sources and inputs, ecosystem effects, and management strategies. BioScience 51:180–198.

Drohan, P. J. 2000. A study of sugar maple (*Acer saccharum* Marsh) decline during 1979–1989 in northern Pennsylvania. Ph.D. dissertation, Pennsylvania State University, University Park.

Dunning, J. B., B. J. Danielson, and H. R. Pulliam. 1992. Ecological processes that affect populations in complex landscapes. Oikos 65:169–175.

Ferrer, M., and J. A. Donazar. 1996. Density-dependent fecundity by habitat heterogeneity in an increasing population of Spanish imperial eagles. Ecology 77:69–74.

Forest Ecosystem Management Assessment Team. 1993. Forest ecosystem management: an ecological, economic, and social assessment. U.S. Government Printing Office, Washington, DC.

Foster, J., and M. S. Gaines. 1991. The effects of a successional habitat mosaic on a small mammal community. Ecology 72:1358–1373.

Fraser, D., and T. Sise. 1980. Observations on stream minnows in a patchy environment: a test of theory of habitat selection. Ecology 61:790–797.

Gill, J. A., K. Norris, P. M. Potts, T. G. Gunnarsson, P. W. Atkinson, and W. J. Sutherland. 2001. The buffer effect and large-scale population regulation in migratory birds. Nature 412:436–438.

Glaw, F., and J. Kohler. 1998. Amphibian species diversity exceeds that of mammals. Herpetological Review 29:11–12.

Grumbine, R. E. 1994. What is ecosystem management? Conservation Biology 8:27–38.

Grumbine, R. E. 1997. Reflections on "What is ecosystem management?" Conservation Biology 11:41–47.

Haddad, N. M. 1997. Do corridors influence butterfly dispersal and density? A landscape experiment. Ph.D. dissertation, University of Georgia, Athens.

Halama, K. J., and R. D. Dueser. 1994. Of mice and habitats: tests for density-dependent habitat selection. Oikos 69:107–114.

Holling, C. S. 1992. Cross-scale morphology, geometry, and dynamics of ecosystems. Ecological Monographs 62:447–502.

Horsley, S. B., R. P. Long, S. W. Bailey, R. A. Hallett, and T. J. Hall. 2000. Factors associated with the decline disease of sugar maple on the Allegheny Plateau. Canadian Journal of Forest Research 30:1365–1378.

IUCN. 2000. The 2000 IUCN Red List of threatened species. Gland, Switzerland. (Online at www.redlist.org).

Johnson, D. H. 1999. The insignificance of significance testing. Journal of Wildlife Management 63:763–772.

Kitching, R. 2000. Biodiversity, hotspots, and defiance. Trends in Ecology and Evolution 15:484–485.

Klenner, W., and D. Huggard. 1997. Faunal biodiversity studies at Sicamous Creek: background and rationale for the choice of species indicator groups. Pages 187–194 in C. Hollstedt and A. Vyse (eds.), Sicamous Creek Silvicultural Systems Project: workshop proceedings. British Columbia Ministry of Forests Research Publication 24/1997, Victoria.

Krebs, J. R. 1970. Regulation of numbers of the great tit (Aves: Passeriformes). Journal of Zoology 162:317–333.

Kullbach, S., and R. A. Leibler. 1951. On information and sufficiency. Annals of Mathematical Statistics 22:79–86.

Laurance, W. F., and R. O. Bierregaard. 1996. Fragmented tropical forests. Bulletin of the Ecological Society of America 77:34–36.

Levin, S. A. 1999. Fragile dominion: complexity and the commons. Helix Books, Perseus Publishing, Cambridge, MA.

Margules, C. R. 1996. Experimental fragmentation. Pages 128–137 in J. Settele, C. R. Margules, P. Poschlod, and K. Henle (eds.), Species survival in fragmented landscapes. Kluwer Academic Publishers, Dordrecht, the Netherlands.

Margules, C. R., and G. A. Milkovits. 1994. Contrasting effects of habitat fragmentation on the scorpion *Cercophonius squama* and an amphipod. Ecology 75:2033–2042.

Murphy, M. T. 2001. Source–sink dynamics of a declining eastern kingbird population and the value of sink habitats. Conservation Biology 15:737–748.

Myers, N., R. A. Mittermeier, C. G. Mittermeier, G. A. B. da Fonseca, and J. Kent. 2000. Biodiversity hotspots for conservation priorities. Nature 403:853–858.

Noss, R. F., and A. Y. Cooperrider. 1994. Saving nature's legacy: protecting and restoring biodiversity. Island Press, Washington, DC.

Noss, R. F., E. T. LaRoe, and J. M. Scott. 1995. Endangered ecosystems of the United States: a preliminary assessment of loss and degradation. U.S. Geological Survey, Washington, DC.

O'Neill, R. V., D. L. DeAngelis, J. B. Waide, and T. F. H. Allen. 1985. A hierarchical concept of ecosystems. Monographs in Population Biology, no. 23, Princeton University Press, Princeton, NJ.

Peak, D. 1977. Taming chaos in the wild: a model-free technique for wildlife population control. Pages 70–100 in J. A. Bissonette (ed.), Wildlife and landscape ecology: effects of pattern and scale. Springer-Verlag, New York.

Pulliam, H. R. 1988. Sources, sinks and population regulation. American Naturalist 132:652–661.

Pulliam, H. R., and B. J. Danielson. 1991. Sources, sinks, and habitat selection: a landscape perspective on population dynamics. American Naturalist 137:50–60.

Robinson, G. R., R. D. Holt, M. S. Gaines, S. P. Hamburg, M. L. Johnson, H. S. Fitch, and E. A. Martinko. 1992. Diverse and contrasting effects of habitat fragmentation. Science 257:524–526.

Roslin, T. 2002. Who said that size is all that matters? Trends in Ecology and Evolution 17:10–11.

Saunders, D. A., R. J. Hobbs, and C. R. Margules. 1991. Biological consequences of ecosystem fragmentation: a review. Conservation Biology 5:18–32.

Schilthuizen, M. 2000. Ecotone: speciation-prone. Trends in Ecology and Evolution 15:130–131.

Schluter, D. 2000. The ecology of adaptive radiation. Oxford University Press, Oxford, UK.

Schmiegelow, F. K. A., C. S. Machtans, and S. J. Hannon. 1997. Are boreal birds resistant to forest fragmentation: an experimental study of short-term community responses. Ecology 78:1914–1932.

Schneider, D. C. 1994. Quantitative ecology: spatial and temporal scaling. Academic Press, San Diego, CA.

Schneider, D. C. 2001. The rise of the concept of scale in ecology. BioScience 51:545–553.

Sharpe, W. E., and T. L. Sunderland. 1995. Acid–base status of upper rooting zone in declining and nondeclining sugar maple (*Acer saccharum* Marsh) stands in Pennsylvania. Pages 172–178 in K. W. Gottschal and S. L. C. Fosbroke (eds.), Proceedings of the Tenth Central Hardwood Forest Conference. U.S. Department of Agriculture, Forest Service General Technical Report NE-197.

Sharpe, W. E., B. R. Swistock, and T. L. Sunderland. 1999. Soil acidification and sugar maple decline in northern Pennsylvania. Pages 191–197 in W. E. Sharpe and J. R. Drohan (eds.), The effects of acid deposition on Pennsylvania's forests. Pennsylvania State University Environmental Resources Research Institute, University Park.

Sisk, T. D., N. M. Haddad, and P. R. Ehrlich. 1997. Bird assemblages in patchy woodlands: modeling the effects of edge and matrix habitats. Ecological Applications 7:1170–1179.

Smith, T. B., S. Kark, C. J. Schneider, R. K. Wayne, and C. Moritz. 2001. Biodiversity hotspots and beyond: the need for preserving environmental transitions. Trends in Ecology and Evolution 16:431.

Storch I. 2002. On spatial resolution in habitat models: can small-scale forest structure explain capercaillie numbers? Conservation Ecology 6(1): 6. (Online at http://www.consecol.org/vol6/iss1/art6).

Swistock, B. R., D. R. DeWalle, S. B. Horsley, R. P. Long, T. J. Hall, and S. Bailey. 1999. Pages 63–73 in W. E. Sharpe and J. R. Drohan (eds.), Soil water chemistry in declining and nondeclining sugar maple stands: the effects of acid deposition on Pennsylvania's forests. Pennsylvania State University Environmental Resources Research Institute, University Park.

Thomas, J. A., N. A. D. Bourn, R. T. Clarke, K. E. Steward, D. J. Simcox, G. S. Pearman, R. Curtis, and B. Goodger. 2001. The quality and isolation of habitat patches both determine where butterflies persist in fragmented landscapes. Proceedings of the Royal Society of London Series B, Biological Sciences 268(1478):1791–1796.

Wagner, H. H., and P. J. Edwards. 2001. Quantifying habitat specificity to assess the contribution of a patch to species richness at the landscape scale. Landscape Ecology 16:121–131.

Walters, C. J. 1986. Adaptive management of renewable resources. Macmillan, New York.

Walters, C. J., and C. S. Holling. 1990. Large-scale management experiments and learning by doing. Ecology 71:2060–2068.

Wiens, J. A. 1989. Spatial scaling in ecology. Functional Ecology 3:385–397.

Wolff, J. O., E. M. Schauber, and W. D. Edge. 1997. Effects of habitat loss and fragmentation on the behavior and demography of gray-tailed voles. Conservation Biology 11:945–956.

About the Contributors

CRAIG R. ALLEN is a research wildlife biologist with the South Carolina Cooperative Fish and Wildlife Research Unit, where his research focuses on landscape change and biological invasions. He is an assistant professor in the Department of Biological Sciences and the Department of Aquaculture, Fisheries and Wildlife at Clemson University. He serves on the board of directors of the Resilience Alliance and the editorial board of the journal *Conservation Ecology*. In 2001, Dr. Allen received a 21st Century Research Award: Studying Complex Systems from the James S. McDonnell Foundation. Contact information: SC Cooperative Fish & Wildlife Research Unit, G27 Lehotsky Hall, Clemson University, Clemson, SC 29634, allencr@CLEMSON.EDU.

PER ANGELSTAM is an applied ecologist who earned his B.Sc. from the University of Lund and his Ph.D. from Uppsala University. His research focuses on the composition, structure, and function of reference areas for forest biodiversity in boreal and temperate forests, biodiversity status assessment in managed landscapes, and the problem of communication between different actors to apply research results in practice. He is an assistant professor at the Swedish University of Agricultural Sciences and is also an adjunct professor in landscape ecology at the Department of Natural Sciences, Örebro University, Sweden, with funding from WWF Sweden/International. Contact information: Grimsö Wildlife Research Station, Department of Conservation Biology, Forest Faculty, Swedish University of Agricultural Sciences (SLU), SE-730 91, Riddarhyttan, Sweden, per.angelstam@nvb.slu.se.

CHRISTIANE AVERBECK earned a Ph.D. in wildlife management at the Technische Universität München in 2002. She worked as a zoologist for the Federal Environmental Agency in Germany on pollution of the North Sea and for seven years as a development worker for a German nongovernmental organization in Uganda and South Sudan. From 1997 to 2000 she conducted field research in and around a protected area in Uganda by looking at the opportunities and challenges of community-based natural resource management. Contact information: Wildlife Research and Management Unit, Center for Life Sciences Weihenstephan, Technische Universität München, Am Hochanger 13, 85354 Freising, Germany, christiane_averbeck@t-online.de.

JOHN A. BISSONETTE is a research scientist with the U.S Geological Survey. He leads the Utah Cooperative Fish and Wildlife Research Unit and is a professor in the College of Natural Resources at Utah State University. His research interests include landscape effects on wildlife species. He is interested in the conceptual foundation for landscape ecology and how it might be used in real-life applications. He has published two other volumes: *Integrating People and Wildlife for a Sustainable Future* (The Wildlife Society, 1995) and *Wildlife and Landscape Ecology: Effects of Pattern and Scale* (Springer, 1997) and is coauthor of *Road Ecology: Science and Solutions* (Island Press, 2002). He has been invited to present keynote addresses in Australia, Germany, and Portugal and was a Senior Fulbright Scholar at the Technic University of Munich in 2002. When not working or traveling, he rides his horse in the mountains of Utah. Contact information: USGS Utah Cooperative Fish and Wildlife Research Unit, College of Natural Resources, Utah State University, Logan, UT, 84322-5290, john.bissonette@cnr.usu.edu.

JOHN P. BRYANT is Emeritus Professor of Ecology at the University of Alaska, Fairbanks. His research in chemical ecology has resulted in three of the most cited articles in the study of plant–herbivore interactions. His current interests include the ontogeny of plant defense, effects of browsing by mammals on vegetation and ecosystem function, and biogeographic variation in plant chemical defenses. The University of Alaska acknowledged Dr. Bryant's pioneering research in ecology with the Emile Usibelli Distinguished Research Award. Contact information: Institute of Arctic Biology, University of Alaska, 311 Irving 1, P.O. Box 757000, Fairbanks, AK, 99775-7000, ffjpb@xpressweb.com. Mailing address: P.O. Box 306, Cora, WY, 82925.

JOHN J. COX earned his B.S. and M.S. at Morehead State University researching hybridization and taxonomy of coyotes. He is currently a Ph.D. student at the University of Kentucky, investigating the effects of reintroduced elk on white-tailed deer and coyotes. Recent publications include investigations of faunal place name biogeography and reintroduced elk demographics. His other interests include conservation issues in Appalachia, large carnivore ecology, photography, and spending time with his two children. Contact information: University of Kentucky, Department of Forestry, #7 T.P. Cooper Building, Lexington, KY, 40546-0073, Coyote1701@yahoo.com.

THERESE M. DONOVAN is the assistant unit leader for the USGS Vermont Cooperative Fish and Wildlife Research Unit. Her current research is directed toward migratory birds and mammals, with a focus on how habitat fragmentation affects wildlife population dynamics. She recently coauthored two books on modeling: *Spreadsheet Exercises in Ecology and Evolution* and *Spreadsheet Exercises in Conservation Biology and Landscape Ecology* (Sinauer Associates 2002). Contact information: USGS Vermont Cooperative Fish and Wildlife Research Unit, 311 Aiken Center, University of Vermont, Burlington, VT, 05405, tdonovan@nature.snr.uvm.edu.

THOMAS C. EDWARDS, JR., is a research ecologist with the USGS Utah Cooperative Research Unit and associate professor of wildlife ecology, Utah State University. His research interests include bioregional conservation planning and developing methods for assessing and monitoring biological diversity at large landscape scales. His current efforts include applying statistical tools to assess temporal and spatial patterns of rare ecological events affected by management, conservation, and open space place planning in the western United States and spatially explicit biodiversity modeling in central Europe. He was a recent corecipient of the Wildlife Society's 2001 Publications Award, Outstanding Book Category for *Conservation Corridor Planning at the Landscape Level: Managing for Wildlife Habitat*. Contact information: USGS Utah Cooperative Fish and Wildlife Research Unit, Utah State University, Logan, UT, 84322-5290, tce@nr.usu.edu.

ALMO FARINA is professor of ecology and nature conservation in the Faculty of Environmental Sciences at Urbino University, Italy. His main interest is landscape ecology, specifically integrating natural and human processes. He has published two books in this field: *Landscape Ecology, Principles and Methods* (Chapman & Hall 1998) and *Landscape Ecology in Action* (Kluwer 2000). In 1998 he organized the VII International Congress of Ecology (INTECOL) in Florence, editing the proceedings. Recently he was guest editor (with Gary Barrett) of a special issue of *Economics and Ecology of Bioscience*. He is serving as secretary general of INTECOL. Contact information: Faculty of Environmental Sciences, The University of Urbino, Campus Scientifico-Sogesta, 61029 Urbino, Italy, farina@uniurb.it.

KARIN FRANK studied mathematics and is working as an ecological modeler. Since 2000, she has been deputy head of the Department of Ecological Modelling at the UFZ-Centre for Environmental Research Leipzig-Halle, Germany. Her interests include metapopulation theory and modeling, population viability analysis, and the deduction of model-based tools for decision support for conservation management. Her recent publications can be found in *Landscape Ecology* and *The American Naturalist*. She and her colleagues have developed metapopulation software (META-X: Software for Metapopulation Viability Analysis, Springer-Verlag, 2002). Contact information: UFZ-Centre for Environmental Research Leipzig-Halle, Department of Ecological Modelling, P.O. Box 500136, D–04301, Leipzig, Germany, karf@oesa.ufz.de.

DONALD W. FRANKLIN is a research officer with the Key Centre for Tropical Wildlife Management at Northern Territory University. His research interests include avian life histories, plant ecology, and conservation biology. He is currently investigating the ecology and sustainable use of the Top End bamboo *Bambusa arnhemica,* a long-lived species that flowers gregariously and then dies. In a 1999 article in *Biological Conservation,* he provided an analysis of the historic records of granivorous birds for the extensive and sparsely populated savanna landscapes of northern Australia, identifying widespread declines among ground-foraging species. Contact information: Key Centre for Tropical Wildlife Management, Northern Territory University, Darwin NT, Australia, 0909, don.franklin@ntu.edu.au.

TRACEY S. FRESCINO is a forest analyst with the USDA Forest Service, Rocky Mountain Research Station, Interior West Resource Inventory, Monitoring and Evaluation Program. Her research interests include forest inventory applications and predictive modeling with current emphasis in geographic information systems, remote sensing techniques, and Web-based analysis tools. Contact information: USDA Forest Service, Rocky Mountain Research Station, 507 25th Street, Ogden, UT, 84401, tfrescino@fs.fed.us.

JESSICA GROENENDIJK has been project co-leader of the Frankfurt Zoological Society Giant Otter Conservation Project, Peru, since early 1999. She is species coordinator (*Pteronura brasiliensis*) for the IUCN/SSC Otter Specialist Group and edits the *Friends of the Giant Otter Bulletin*. Contact information: Giant Otter Project, Frankfurt Zoological Society, Aurelio Fernandez Concha 675, El Rosedal, Lima 18, Peru, fzsgop@terra.com.pe, fzsgop@hotmail.com, fzsgop@leafar.com.pe.

LANCE GUNDERSON attended the University of Florida, receiving degrees in botany and environmental engineering sciences. He has worked as a botanist with the U.S. National Park Service and as a research scientist in the Department of Zoology at the University of Florida and since 1999 has been chair of the Department of Environmental Studies at Emory University. His ongoing research seeks to understand how ecosystem processes and structures interact across space and time scales and how scientific understanding influences resource policy and management. His interests include the human and institutional dimensions to resource ecology; to that end, he has edited *Barriers and Bridges to the Renewal of Ecosystems and Institutions* (Columbia University Press 1995), *Panarchy: Understanding Transformations in Systems of Humans and Nature* (Island Press 2002), and *Resilience and the Behavior of Large Scale Systems* (Island Press 2002), all of which attempt to synthesize interdisciplinary concepts that underpin sustainable actions. Contact information: Associate Professor and Chairman, Department of Environmental Studies, Emory University, 400 Dowman Drive, Atlanta, GA, 30322, lgunder@emory.edu.

FRANK HAJEK is a chartered environmental engineer currently working as project co-leader of the Frankfurt Zoological Society Giant Otter Conservation Project in Peru. Frank has been involved with research and conservation in Manu Biosphere Reserve since 1993 and manages the Web site www.giantotters.com. Contact information: Giant Otter Project, Frankfurt Zoological Society, Aurelio Fernandez Concha 675, El Rosedal, Lima 18, Peru, fzsgop@terra.com.pe, fzsgop@hotmail.com, fzsgop@leafar.com.pe.

LARRY D. HARRIS is Professor Emeritus of Forest Biodiversity Conservation at the University of Florida, Gainesville. His research has grown from natural history and conservation in east Africa (1960s), to biometry and system analysis (1960s–1970s), to experimental approaches to forest biodiversity issues (1970s), and finally to the regional landscape level of sustainable development analysis. In 2000 he coauthored chapters in and coedited *Landscape Ecology, a Top-Down Approach* and received the Distinguished Landscape Ecology Practitioner Award from the International Association for Landscape Ecology, U.S. Regional Chapter. Contact information: Professor Emeritus, Department of Wildlife Ecology and Conservation, P.O. Box 110430, University of Florida, Gainesville, FL 32611-0430, ldh@ufl.edu. Mailing address: 14425 S.W. 79th Street, Archer, FL, 32618.

REINHARD KLENKE is a research fellow at the field station of the Society for Nature Conservation and Landscape Ecology at Kratzeburg, Germany. He studied biology at the University of Leipzig. His research interests are population ecology and landscape ecology. His current research work is related to the influence of habitat structure and composition in managed and unmanaged (seminatural and natural) forests on threatened hole-breeding birds and mammals (rodents and bats). Contact information: Society for Nature Conservation and Landscape Ecology (GNL), Dorfstrasse 31, D-17237 Kratzeburg, Germany, klenke.gnl@t-online.de.

JEFFERY L. LARKIN is a postdoctoral scholar in the Department of Forestry at the University of Kentucky. His current research focuses on Florida black bear conservation. He recently completed a five-month appointment as a visiting scholar at Yellowstone National Park, where he directed an effort to develop a science-based ungulate research plan. His research interests include large mammal restoration, songbird conservation, and wildlife genetics. He also coedited *Large Mammal Restoration: Ecological and Sociological Challenges for the 21st Century* (Island Press, 2001). Contact information: University of Kentucky, Department of Forestry, 205 T.P. Cooper Building, Lexington, KY, 40546-0073, Jllark0@uky.edu.

JOSHUA J. LAWLER is a National Research Council associate at the U.S. Environmental Protection Agency. His research interests include conservation biology and landscape ecology and revolve around the roles of scale and spatial variation in shaping species–habitat relationships and large-scale patterns of species diversity. His current projects involve investigating methods for prioritizing areas for biodiversity conservation in the mid-Atlantic and Pacific Northwest regions of the United States. Contact information: U.S. Environmental Protection Agency, 200 SW 35th Street, Corvallis, OR, 97333, lawler.joshua@epa.gov.

GERD LUTZE studied agricultural science at Karl-Marx-University in Leipzig and at Martin-Luther-University in Halle/Saale. He graduated in the field of applied entomology and investigated aspects of insect population dynamics in agroecosystems. Since 1993 he has been working at the ZALF Institute of Landscape Systems Analysis in Müncheberg, Germany. He is dealing with problems of landscape structure analysis and evaluation. Contact information: ZALF, Institute for Landscape Systems Analysis, Eberswalder Strasse 84, D-15374 Müncheberg, Germany, glutze@zalf.de.

DAVID S. MAEHR is assistant professor of conservation biology at the University of Kentucky. His research interests include large mammal ecology, conservation, and restoration and landscape-scale conservation planning. He is the author of *The Florida Panther: Life and Death of a Vanishing Carnivore*, lead editor of *Large Mammal Restoration: Ecological and Sociological Challenges in the 21st Century*, and coauthor of *Florida's Birds* (Pineapple Press, Sarasota, FL 1990). Contact information: University of Kentucky, Department of Forestry, 205 Cooper Building, Lexington, KY, 40546-0073, dmaehr@uky.edu.

MICHAEL S. MITCHELL is assistant unit leader at the USGS Alabama Cooperative Fish and Wildlife Research Unit at Auburn University. His research interests include the ecology and management of large carnivores, associating landscape patterns with the behavior and distribution of animals, and exploring the interface between forest and wildlife management. Contact information: USGS, Alabama Cooperative Fish and Wildlife Research Unit, School of Forestry and Wildlife Sciences, 108 M. White Smith Hall, Auburn University, Auburn, AL, 36849, mike_mitchell@auburn.edu.

GRETCHEN G. MOISEN is a research forester with the Forest Inventory and Analysis program of the U.S. Forest Service, Rocky Mountain Research Station. She earned a bachelor's degree in forestry from the University of New Hampshire and a master's degree in statistics and a Ph.D. in mathematical sciences from Utah State University. She is actively involved in developing national sampling, estimation, and modeling strategies for forest inventory and monitoring efforts in the United States. Her research interests include regional mapping of forest characteristics through nonlinear and nonparametric modeling with remotely sensed data, refining nonparametric model-assisted estimation procedures for improving forest population estimates, and developing data mining tools for analyzing broad-scale ecological data. Contact information: USDA Forest Service, Rocky Mountain Research Station, 507 25th Street, Ogden, UT, 84401, gmoisen@fs.fed.us.

ROGER A. POWELL is a professor of zoology at North Carolina State University. For more than three decades he has investigated how limiting resources affects animals, especially mammalian predators. His research has contributed significantly to understanding about the evolution of sexual dimorphism in body size and how and why resources and conspecifics affect how individuals use space. Contact information: North Carolina State University, Department of Zoology, Campus Box 7617, 218-J David Clark Labs, Raleigh, NC, 27695-7617, newf@ncsu.edu.

OWEN PRICE is a senior scientist with the Parks and Wildlife Commission of the Northern Territory, Australia. After completing his Ph.D. on the conservation of mobile frugivores in the Northern Territory in 1998, he worked on conservation planning issues related to landscape fragmentation. In particular, he was the principal author of two government initiatives attempting to plan for intensification of agriculture: "A Conservation Plan for the Daly Basin Bioregion" and "Guidelines for the Retention of Native Vegetation in Top-End Woodlands." Contact information: Biodiversity Unit, DIPE, P.O. Box 496, Palmerston NT, 0810, and Tropical Savannas Cooperative Research Centre, Northern Territory University, Darwin NT, 0909, Australia, owen.price@nt.gov.au.

FREDERICK D. PROVENZA is a professor in the College of Natural Resources at Utah State University. His research focuses on understanding behavioral processes and using that understanding to inform management. For the past two decades, his emphasis has been on the role of learning in food and habitat selection by herbivores. He has been senior author or coauthor of more than 120 peer-reviewed papers. He has been asked to write an additional 38 synthesis papers for peer-reviewed journals and books and has been invited to speak at national and international symposia. In 1999, he received the W. R. Chapman Research Award from the Society for Range Management. That same year, he also received the University Outstanding Graduate Mentor Award from Utah State University. Contact information: Range, Forestry and Wildlife Department, College of Natural Resources, Utah State University, Logan, UT, 84322-5230, stan@cc.usu.edu.

ROSALIND B. RENFREW graduated in 1989 with a bachelor's degree in wildlife biology from the University of Vermont. Before she went on to graduate school, Rosalind conducted bird research and worked on educational projects about issues affecting family farms. Her research projects ranged from winter ecology of hooded warblers to the status of common loon populations, from Mexico to Vermont. For her master's degree and Ph.D., Rosalind combined her passion for birds and concern about agricultural issues. She is currently a dissertator in the Department of Wildlife Ecology at the University of Wisconsin, and her research evaluates the influence of patch and landscape characteristics on nesting grassland birds and nest predators in pastures. In her free time, she enjoys backpacking, falconry, soccer, and birding. Contact information: Vermont Institute of Natural Science, Church Hill Road, Woodstock, VT, 05091, rrenfrew@.wisc.edu.

CHRISTINE A. RIBIC is the unit leader of the USGS BRD Wisconsin Cooperative Wildlife Research Unit, University of Wisconsin, Madison, where she is also an associate professor in the Department of Wildlife Ecology. Her main research interest is landscape-scale conservation and management. She is interested in understanding how the surrounding landscape influences processes within the patch and implications for management. Her current focus is on the conservation of grassland birds in active agricultural areas in Wisconsin. Contact information: USGS Wisconsin Cooperative Wildlife Research Unit, University of Wisconsin, Department of Wildlife Ecology, Room 204 Russell Laboratories, 1630 Linden Drive, Madison, WI, 53706-1598, caribic@facstaff.wisc.edu.

DAVID W. SAMPLE is the grassland community ecologist for the Wisconsin Department of Natural Resources Bureau of Integrated Science Services. He conducts research on grassland bird ecology, including examining the impacts of habitat and landscape management and agricultural land uses on grassland birds. He was the senior author of *Managing Habitat for Grassland Birds: A Guide for Wisconsin* (Wisconsin Department of Natural Resources, Madison, Wisconsin 1997), which was given the Wildlife Society's 1999 award for outstanding publication in wildlife ecology and management in the monograph category. Contact information: Bureau of Integrated Science Services, Wisconsin Department of Natural Resources, 1350 Femrite Drive, Monona, WI, 53716, sampld@dnr.state.wi.us.

JAMES G. SANDERSON works for the Center for Applied Biodiversity at Conservation International. He received his Ph.D. from the University of New Mexico in 1976. He is an avid traveler and has collected and synthesized wildlife issues from around the world. His interests include quantitative, community, and landscape ecology. He maintains an active research program on small wild cats in South America. Contact information: Center for Applied Biodiversity Science, Conservation International, 1919 M Street NW, Suite 500, Washington, DC, 20036-3521, gato_andino@yahoo.com.

CHRISTOF SCHENCK is executive director of the Frankfurt Zoological Society, a worldwide active nature conservation organization. He studied biology in Tübingen and Freiburg in Germany, with zoology as a main subject. His research activities focused on giant otters, and he was project coordinator for the Peruvian Giant Otter Research and Conservation Project with Elke Staib for 9 years. Together they produced a film and a popular scientific book on their Peruvian experience. Contact information: Frankfurt Zoological Society, Alfred-Brehm-Platz 16, D-60316, Frankfurt, Germany.

ALFRED SCHULTZ studied mathematics at Eötvös-Lorand-University, Budapest, and specialized in probability theory and mathematical statistics. His main research topics are ecological modeling and ecosystem theory. Today he works as scientist in the ZALF Institute of Landscape Systems Analysis in Müncheberg and develops habitat models. Contact information: ZALF, Institute for Landscape Systems Analysis, Eberswalder Strasse 84, D-15374, Müncheberg, Germany, aschultz@zalf.de.

JAN P. SENDZIMIR is a system ecologist who works as a research scholar at the International Institute for Applied Systems Analysis in Laxenburg, Austria, and as a senior fellow at the Institute for Agriculture and Trade Policy, Minneapolis. His research interests involve using methods (adaptive management) and theory (resilience, catastrophe, complex adaptive systems) on applications concerned with "wicked" problems, problems with complex combinations of ecological, economic, and sociopolitical factors that occur over large areas such as river basins, major watersheds, and mountain chains. He currently works on research and project development with a number of organizations (World Wide Fund for Nature, Environmental Partnership for Central Europe) on projects for sustainable development and biodiversity conservation of rural areas in central Europe. Contact information: International Institute for Applied Systems Analysis (IIASA), Schlossplatz 1, A-2361, Laxenburg, Austria, sendzim@iiasa.ac.at.

ELKE STAIB was project coordinator for the Peruvian Giant Otter Research and Conservation Project together with Christof Schenck for 9 years. She studied biology in Freiburg, Germany, with a focus on zoology. She completed her Ph.D. in 2002 on giant otter behavior ecology. She has worked part time in giant otter research since she left Peru in the end of 1993. Contact information: Frankfurt Zoological Society, Alfred-Brehm-Platz 16, D-60316, Frankfurt, Germany, fzshq@compuserve.com. Mailing address: Am Bornrain 12, 63589, Linsengricht, Germany.

ILSE STORCH is a research scientist and lecturer with the Weihenstephan Centre of Life Sciences at the Technische Universität München, where she leads a conservation biology working group. As a researcher and consultant, she has worked in Europe, North and South America, Africa, and Asia. Her research interests include wildlife–habitat relationships at various scales. The effects of habitat fragmentation on individuals, populations, and metapopulations and their implications for conservation are the major focus of her work. Since 1996, she has chaired the IUCN Grouse Specialist Group. Contact information: Wildlife Research and Management Unit, Technische Universität München, Linderhof Research Station, D-82488, Ettal, Germany, ilse.storch@t-online.de. Mailing address: Max Planck Research Center for Orinthology, Radzolfzell, Germany.

CRAIG STOW is a visiting assistant professor in the Duke University Nicholas School of the Environment and Earth Sciences. His interests include aquatic biogeochemical processes, watershed transport processes, and Bayesian inference for implementation of adaptive management. Contact information: Environmental Science and Policy Division, Nicholas School of the Environment and Earth Sciences, Duke University, Box 90328, Durham, NC, 27708 cstow@duke.edu.

ALLAN M. STRONG is a visiting assistant professor in the Wildlife and Fisheries Biology Program at the University of Vermont. His research seeks to understand the ecological processes that influence habitat quality for migratory birds, particularly food availability, predator dynamics, and habitat structure. His dissertation research won the George Henry Penn Memorial Award, an occasional award given for outstanding graduate research in the Ecology and Evolutionary Biology Department at Tulane University. Contact information: University of Vermont, School of Natural Resources, 341 Aiken Center, Burlington, VT, 05405, astrong@nature.snr.uvm.edu.

JUAN J. VILLALBA is a research assistant professor in the Department of Rangeland Resources at Utah State University. His research focuses on understanding the mechanisms that influence food selection and intake by herbivores, with the aim of creating efficient alternatives to manage animals and their environment. His research program has resulted in more than 30 peer-reviewed publications, several in the best journals in the field, including *The British Journal of Nutrition, The Journal of Animal Science, Nutrition Research Reviews, Oikos,* and *The Journal of Chemical Ecology and Animal Behaviour.* Contact information: Research Assistant Professor, Range, Forestry and Wildlife Department, College of Natural Resources, Utah State University, Logan, UT, 84322-5230, villalba@cc.usu.edu.

MARION VOSS studied at Friedrich-Schiller-University in Jena, Germany, and graduated as Diplom-Ingenieur (Dipl.-Ing). Since 1996 she has worked at the Institute of Landscape Modelling, ZALF. She has been working with landscape system analysis on several different projects. Contact information: ZALF, Institute for Landscape Systems Analysis, Eberswalder Strasse 84, D-15374, Müncheberg, Germany, mvoss@zalf.de.

PETER J. WHITEHEAD is director of the Key Centre for Tropical Wildlife Management at the Northern Territory University, a position he has held for 3 years. Before joining the university, Peter was employed as a wildlife manager and wildlife researcher with the Parks and Wildlife Commission of the Northern Territory, heading the wildlife research group at the time of his departure. His research interests center on wetlands and their fauna, especially crocodiles and waterfowl. Contact information: Key Centre for Tropical Wildlife Management, Northern Territory University, Darwin NT, 0909, peter.whitehead@ntu.edu.au.

RALF WIELAND studied technical cybernetics in Leipzig. His main research topics are system design and neural and fuzzy technologies. Today he works as scientist in the ZALF Institute of Landscape Systems Analysis in Müncheberg and develops simulation systems for ecosystems and landscapes. Contact information: ZALF, Institute for Landscape Systems Analysis, Eberswalder Strasse 84, D-15374, Müncheberg, Germany, rwieland@zalf.de.

BETTINA WILKENING studied biology at the university of Constance, Germany. In 1993 she graduated with a thesis on breeding behavior of peregrine falcons at the Humboldt-University, Berlin. Her specialty is eco-ethology, and she now works on behavior and habitat use of common cranes in northeastern Germany and concentrates on habitat models with fuzzy technologies. Contact information: Seestrasse 18, D-16278, Peetzig, Germany, kranich@blaue-wiese.de.

JOHN C. Z. WOINARSKI is principal research scientist with the Parks and Wildlife Commission of the Northern Territory and is also a project leader in the Tropical Savannas Cooperative Research Centre. He leads a group focusing on bioregional conservation planning in northern Australia, which works to promote conservation on Aboriginal and pastoral lands and to enhance the existing conservation reserve network. He has published widely on the biogeography and conservation management of plants, invertebrates, frogs, reptiles, birds, and mammals. In 2001 he was awarded the Eureka Prize for biodiversity research in Australia and the Serventy Medal for contributions to Australian ornithology. Contact information: Parks and Wildlife Commission of the Northern Territory, P.O. Box 496, Palmerston NT, 0831, and Tropical Savannas Cooperative Research Centre, Northern Territory University, Darwin NT, 0909, Australia, john.woirnarski@nt.gov.au.

Index